Hermia Lambie · Northfield · November 1994
Bibliophile · Birthday book-token from H. & W.

From a Uniform List

All clothes should be marked with Cash's numbers.
Coats, skirts and pullovers should have loops for hanging.

1 Blazer
1 Navy anorak
2 Navy skirts
3 Long-sleeved blous ... v,
the other two eit
2 Navy pullovers – V
3 Short sleeved blue b
3 White games shirts
1 Yellow games pullove
1 Games skirt
1 Regulation black swim suit
1 Tracksuit

ALL THE ABOVE ITEMS ARE UNIFORM AND MUST BE ORDERED THROUGH PETER JONES
(Girls are *not* allowed to wear alternative designs or makes)

Other requirements which may be purchased at any leading store:

4 Pairs navy knickers
6 Pairs pants
1 Full length, warm dressing gown
3 Nightdresses or Pyjamas
1 Leotard (Marden only)
1 Swim cap (white for those proficient at swimming – otherwise red)
2 Bath towels (not robes) maximum size 30″ × 48″ with loops for hanging
3 Hand towels
1 Continental quilt/duvet with 2 lightweight washable covers
1 Small night case
1 Large case (not trunk, please)
1 Lockable tuck box
1 Clothes brush

The Best Type of Girl

The Best Type of Girl

A History of Girls' Independent Schools

GILLIAN AVERY

ANDRE DEUTSCH

Books by the same author

NINETEENTH CENTURY CHILDREN
VICTORIAN PEOPLE
THE ECHOING GREEN:
MEMORIES OF VICTORIAN AND REGENCY YOUTH
CHILDHOOD'S PATTERN:
A STUDY OF THE HEROES AND HEROINES OF
CHILDREN'S FICTION 1770–1950

First published in 1991 by
André Deutsch Limited
105–106 Great Russell Street
London WC1B 3LJ

British Library Cataloguing in Publication Data
Avery, Gillian, *1926*–
The best type of girl: a history of girls' independent schools.
1. Great Britain. Independent girls' schools, history
I. Title
371.020941

ISBN 0 233 98642 1

Phototypeset by Setrite. Hong Kong
Printed in Great Britain by
Butler & Tanner Ltd Frome Somerset

Contents

	List of Illustrations	vii
	Preface	xi
1	Introduction	1
2	Little Eleemosynaries	18
	Charity Hospitals	18
	Endowed Secondary Schools	34
	Boarding Schools for the Middle Classes	40
3	The Day School Pioneers	54
	Early Difficulties	54
	The High School Movement	62
	The Twentieth Century	76
4	Public Schools: the Gridiron and the Book	83
	The System	83
	The Schools	90
	The Gridiron	111
5	'Individuals, even Eccentrics': Private Schools Before World War II	125
	Freedom	125
	Ladies in Distressed Circumstances	129
	Women of Vision	135
	Growing up Gracefully: Schools for the Upper Class	142
6	Religion and Religious Foundations	149
	Environment and Practice	149
	Non-conformist Establishments	159
	Nathaniel Woodard and his Schools	166

7 Convent Schools 172

The Tradition 172
Mary Ward and the 'English Ladies' 180
American and French Connections 184

8 Boarding School Life 197

9 Authority: Headmistresses and their Staff 214

Flaming Catherine Wheels 214
Custodians and Teachers 229

10 Work and Play 243

Curriculum 243
Extra-curricular 260
Physical Education 266

11 Discipline 277

12 Sex and Emotion 301

Febrile Friendships 301
Boys and Girls 310
'Keep the Girl a Child' 316

13 Crises 323

Finance 323
Natural Disasters 331
Hazards of War 338

14 Envoi 352

Glossary 359

Notes 361

Bibliography 384

Index 397

List of Illustrations

Frontispiece. On the way to church. Cheltenham Ladies' College, 1950s.

1. An early Georgian orphan.
2. The schoolroom at Red Maids School, Bristol (detail from painting).
3. A Victorian photograph of St Leonards.
4. Benenden: the school buildings.
5. Oxford High School, Girls' Public Day School Trust.
6. North London Collegiate School, Canons Park.
7. The Buss family with early pupils.
8. Lydia Rous, superintendent of The Mount School, York 1866–79.
9. Dorothea Beale, principal of Cheltenham Ladies' College 1858–1906.
10. The founders of Roedean: Dorothy, Penelope and Millicent Lawrence.
11. Jane Frances Dove, the founder of Wycombe Abbey.
12. Dr Sophie Bryant, successor to Miss Buss as headmistress of North London Collegiate School.
13. B.M. Baker, headmistress of Badminton 1911–46, with a Swiss guide, on a School Journey.
14. Dormitory cubicles at St Mary's Hall, 1920s.
15. A classroom at Cheltenham Ladies' College, 1950s.
16. The domestic staff at Benenden, 1930s.
17. Headmistress's room, St Mary's Hall, in the early years of the century.
18. Truman & Knightley advertisement, 1930.
19. The days before school uniform: Winchester High School (now St Swithun's) VI form, 1897.
20. St Mary's Hall tennis team, 1920s.
21. Middle school pupils at the Sacred Heart, Rochampton in the 1890s.
22. The cricket team at St Leonards, 1891.
23. The high noon of uniform: Moreton Hall juniors, 1950s.
24. The casual look of the 1980s. Three Oxford High School juniors.
25. Roedean pupils march to salute the flag on Empire Day.
26. Olive Willis in 1915 with Downe House seniors.
27. Heathfield Chapel Choir about the time of World War I.
28. School of S. Mary and S. Anne, Abbots Bromley. Commemoration service, 1958.

29. Red Cross cadets at Cheltenham Ladies' College, 1911.
30. Wycombe Abbey, Mission Day, 1904.
31. A 1920s dancing class at St James's, West Malvern.
32. Piano quartet, 1980s, North London Collegiate School.
33. A 1940s production of Maeterlinck's *The Blue Bird* at Tudor Hall.
34. Oxford High School and the Oxford University Experimental Theatre Club in *Living Creation*, 1985.
35. The gridiron: Wycombe Abbey pupils stretched on the gym ribstalls, *c*. 1902.
36. Informal hockey, 1890s, at Winchester High School.
37. Early Girl Guides at St James's, West Malvern.
38. As in the Army, bedmaking at girls' schools, in the days before duvets, was a solemn ritual with much attention paid to hospital corners. A dormitory at Moreton Hall, 1950s.
39. A changing cubicle in use as a study at Cheltenham Ladies' College in 1940.
40. A lacrosse house match on the sands when Benenden was evacuated to Newquay.
41. A wartime class at St Brandon's School.
42. Pupils at St James's, West Malvern.
43. By the pond at North London Collegiate School, Canons Park.
44. A group of friends at Walthamstow Hall.
45. Tudor Hall. Wartime bicycle trip in the Cotswolds.
46. The schoolgirl view. Record by Letitia Opie, aged 10, of school food.
47. Drawings from St James's, West Malvern, Junior House scrapbook.
48. Drawings from *The Book of Bedgebury*, Christmas, 1923.
49. Overseas pupils at the School of S. Mary and S. Anne, Abbots Bromley, 1973.
50. Roedean VI formers and their teachers with the electric car built at the school.

Acknowledgements

I am grateful to Cheltenham Ladies' College for permission to reproduce the frontispiece, 9, 15, 29, 39; to the Bodleian Library, Oxford, for 1, 46 (both in the Opie Collection of Historical Children's Books); to Red Maids School for 2; to St Leonards School for 3, 22; to Penelope Tweedie for 4; to Oxford High School for 5, 24, 34; to North London Collegiate School for 6, 7, 12, 32, 43; to The Mount School for 8; to Roedean School for 10, 25; to Wycombe Abbey School for 11, 30, 35; to Badminton School for 13; to St Mary's Hall for 14, 17, 20; to T.S.C. Busby for providing 16; to St Swithun's School for 19, 36; to the Society of the Sacred Heart for 21; to Moreton Hall for 23, 38; to Downe House for 26; to Heathfield School for

27; to the School of S. Mary and S. Anne for 28, 49; to St James's and the Abbey for 31, 37, 42, 47; to Benenden School for 40; to St Brandon's School for 41; to Walthamstow Hall for 44; to Belinda Morse for providing 33, 45; to Bedgebury School for 48; to the *Evening Argus*, Brighton, for 50.

Preface

This book is an attempt to piece together the history of schools in the Girls' Schools Association, the female equivalent of the Headmasters' Conference schools. Since the origins of these are very various and include charity hospitals, religious foundations, high schools, convents and small idiosyncratic private ventures as well as the schools that used to be known as 'public' until all were lumped together under the generic and less confusing term 'independent', the book has spread itself over a fairly large field while in no way attempting to be a history of women's education. I have tried to avoid educational technicalities; when this is unavoidable, I hope the brief glossary on page 359 will help.

Compared to boys' public schools, the past of girls' schools is short, but even so it makes fascinating social history and reveals much in the way of forgotten attitudes and ideologies. And, as far as I can make out, no one has set down their histories side by side and compared their ethics and what they were attempting to achieve. Individual schools are strikingly unaware of how they resemble or differ from others, and sometimes oddly casual about their own history. Records have irretrievably disappeared, and in one or two cases where there is a published history the school does not possess a copy (Downe House at one point even refused to have the excellent biography of its founder by an old pupil because it did not want to look back to the past). Convents are the most elusive of all; each individual school was seen as only one unit in a grand religious whole; besides, the way of life seemed so immutable that it was felt to be unnecessary to set it down. But now that so many have vanished or are under lay management, most of their traditions have disappeared overnight.

I have been largely dependent for my facts on published histories, and inevitably – though it was possible to do a certain amount of work in archives – it is the schools where these are available that have been covered most thoroughly. Although deliberately limiting my historical account of particular schools to those in the GSA, where there was a particularly lively assembly of recollections, as in the case of the City of Cardiff High School or the Mary Datchelor School, both now in the maintained sector, I have sometimes drawn on them for the more general chapters. I have also used memoirs and autobiographies, and have visited many schools. The kindness and the hospitality of headmistresses, librarians and teaching staff have made the whole exercise very pleasant, and I could only wish there had been time to take in more. Among those to whom I owe a special debt of gratitude for the trouble they have taken on my behalf are Mrs Jennifer Anderson (Francis Holland School, SW1), Miss L. Bristol (St Mary's Hall), Mrs A. Byatt (New Hall), Mrs Jacqueline Childs (St Paul's), Sister Clare Veronica (Assumption School), Miss Jane Claydon (St Leonards), Mrs Galloway (S. Helen and S. Katharine), Miss Helen Gichard (Haberdashers' Monmouth School), Mrs J. Jeffers (Christ's Hospital), Mrs Pamela Johnston (St Swithun's), Mrs Janet Johnstone (Cheltenham Ladies' College), Mrs Jacqueline Lang (Walthamstow Hall), Mrs Pauline Mathias (More House), Miss Elizabeth Mullenger (St James's and the Abbey), Mr A.S. Nipper (Bedgebury), Mrs Robin Townley (North London Collegiate), and Mrs Pat Wood (Riddlesworth Hall). Many schools have trusted me with unique historical material; in addition, Dr Donald Clarke very kindly allowed me to see in manuscript his history of the Princess Helena College; Miss Muriel Kilvert sent me pages from her history of Runton Hill, and Mrs Lavinia Cohn-Sherbok, though she had only recently arrived at West Heath, pieced together a short history of the school for me.

I am most grateful to all the people who have been willing to reminisce about their schools. These include Ursula Aylmer, Barbara Chalkley, Mary Clapinson, Dolly Clay, Jenny Dennis and fellow Felicians, Joanna Dodsworth, Jenny Geach, Jo Harries, Nesta Inglis, Caroline Knox, Freda Levson, Judith MacFarlane, Esther Mills, Philippa O'Mahoney, Virginia Pasley, Imogen Rose, Lady Salisbury-Jones, Mariette Saye and Sele, Mary Warnock and Marjorie Williams; while Anne Anderson, Rosemary Bellamy Law, Anne Buckley, Angela Bull, Cecily Don, Mary Don, Christine Flemington, Anne Halewood, Cordelia James, Charmian Knight, Frances Knight, Marjorie Morris, Isabel Morse, Jenny Paterson, Priscilla Quayle, Constance Roberts, Katherine Soulsby, Lady Jane Turnbull, Ayesha Venkataswaran and Laura Williams have all taken the trouble to write about schooldays past and present. Mary Keen has given me many leads and supplied me with valuable material; Diana Harker has throughout taken a great interest, and has put me in touch with friends who could help; Lorna Flint, in the midst of writing her own history of Wycombe Abbey, has spared the time to talk to me about the school; Belinda Morse one memorable August day took me to Burnt Norton, where Tudor Hall spent the war years; Sara Delamont allowed me to see the typescript of her *Knowledgeable Women*. I am specially indebted to Mary Habakkuk who has given immense help over the Girls' Public Day School Trust, to Janet Sondheimer who made many useful suggestions, to John Brierley who has read some of the chapters, and to Sister April O'Leary without whom the convents chapter could never have been written. Much of the work has been done in the Education

Library of Reading University, which possesses an extensive collection of school histories, and whose staff have been very kind. Nearer home, I have also had much help from Gillian Ledger, librarian at the Education Department of Oxford University. In the final stages, Michael Dudley of the Ashmolean Museum has done a superb job copying photographs, many of them old and faded, and Sue Phillpott in her copy-editing has saved me from infelicities and discrepancies. And finally I would like to thank Olivia Gordon of Oxford High School for her warm encouragement. All in all it has been a very enjoyable three years, and I am almost sorry that they have come to an end.

Oxford, 1990

1
Introduction

> Almost all private schools rest in some degree on social distinctions [pronounced the Schools Inquiry Commission in 1868]. The Grammar schools know nothing of such distinctions at all. Every boy who can pass the entrance examination ... and can pay the fees ... can demand admission. But social distinctions in the matter of education are exceedingly strong, and the private schools are powerless to ignore them. In fact the inferior private schools owe their very existence to the unwillingness of many of the tradesmen and others just above the manual labourers to send their sons to the National or the British School.

And, quoting the adjectives – 'exclusive', 'genteel', 'limited' – used in prospectuses, the commissioners went on to reinforce this: 'Social considerations outweigh educational considerations in the eyes of parents of all grades.'[1]

As has often been stressed, the findings of this Commission (known as the Taunton Commission, after its chairman) were supremely important for women's education. They showed how educational endowments of the past that could be used to give girls secondary education were being misapplied and mishandled; and it was the Commission's castigation of the total inadequacy of what was then provided for girls at the private schools, and their commendation of the work being done by the pioneer headmistresses, Miss Buss and Miss Beale, that led to the demand for solid secondary education for girls in the 1870s as a result of which so many new schools were founded. The point that they made about social considerations is also a very pertinent one, for though they were in this instance speaking about boys, the part that such motives have played in the history of women's education in England cannot be over-estimated. State education has traditionally been viewed by the middle and upper classes as a form of charity designed not for them but for the lower classes, and their children have been dispatched to schools where they would meet their own kind. More care had to be taken over the social environment of girls than was necessary with boys; boys could make their own way and to a great extent establish a position for themselves, but it is only in the last few decades that women have expected an independent professional career, the instinct of the upper and middle classes having been that their daughters would marry at the social level at which they had been educated. 'If you play with them you'll work with them,' a Lancashire schoolboy in a mining village was told by his father, the local primary school headmaster, eighty years ago, and the middle classes were guided for many years by this precept, feeling that it was better for a girl to be unhappy at a cheap boarding school or indifferently taught at a private day school than to mix with children from whom she might pick up the wrong accent, even though she might proceed from there to a university education.

> My parents had been well educated at local schools, but were great believers in self-sufficiency and 'getting on'. They did not like their children acquiring a strong local Lancashire accent, although they had a 'refined' Lancashire accent themselves. They were devoted parents and made an enormous sacrifice to send their three children to public schools, thinking of a broader education and 'nicer' friends.[2]

Here, forty years ago, the degree of northern accent is shown to be important, and the 'broader' education was in this case (as in so many) no more than the experience of being a boarder; the writer, the daughter of a Lancashire doctor, was miserably unhappy at one Yorkshire school, as her sister had been at another in Harrogate. She tried to run away, and only submitted to staying because she knew the sacrifices her parents had made. Among the upper classes there was an additional consideration: a strong-minded, 'brainy' daughter would probably have difficulty in finding a husband; a school, therefore, that encouraged her to go to university was not desirable, and she would be far better off, they reasoned, at a small, easy-going establishment where she would mingle with daughters of like-minded parents. 'It is doubtful whether even now the majority of English people really believe in education, either for boys or girls,' said a headmistress in 1911, and spoke about 'the dumb conviction that education is a necessary evil . . . a feeling not confined to the labouring class'.[3]

Parents, beginning with Victorian parents, forced a policy of class distinction upon many schools, as will be shown in later chapters. Even when pupils came supposedly from the same background, as at the Royal School where all fathers were army officers, there might be doubts about pedigree or rank; and, ironically, social segregation can be seen at its most marked in the religious foundations of the period. It was standard practice for convents to have 'upper' and 'middle' schools (the term referring to social standing rather than to age of pupils, as they would now); '[they] never meet or see each other, even in Church,' reported the Schools Inquiry commissioners in 1868. The Anglo-Catholic Woodard schools founded a little later in the century often included further stratifications – a 'lower-middle' school, and an 'industrial' school which catered for girls who were going to be servants, while the Congregational establishment, Milton Mount College, went in for the most elaborate subdivisions of all. The middle school would always be very much cheaper and its pupils left earlier. A few of the early high schools, recognizing the need for this type of school where pupils would acquire modest qualifications for earning a living, organized their own middle schools, such as the North London Collegiate's Camden School, and Bedford High School's middle school on the Harpur foundation.

While this sort of segregation gradually disappeared in the twentieth century (the two Woodard schools of S. Mary and S. Anne at Abbot's Bromley gave up separate identity in 1921), it was still implicit in much of the advertising. 'The Lawn is essentially a school for the daughters of gentlemen only', runs a typical 1930s announcement in the Truman and Knightley schools directory, while the School of S. Mary and S. Anne – perhaps feeling that since the amalgamation it might be accused of harbouring tradesmen's daughters – affirmed that it catered for 'the daughters of gentlefolk'. Other schools accepted only 'gentle people' or girls 'from a suitable background', and many small schools of the period made a point of asserting that they only took boarders – since it had always been felt that moral and social contagion was spread through day girls. Cheltenham Ladies' College at the turn of the century did not 'receive all comers, but is distinctly intended for the "daughters of gentlemen" and references in regard to social standing are required before admission'.[4] What was more, Miss Beale herself felt that the local examinations which women were allowed to take for the first time in the mid-Victorian period were not for her girls. She told the Taunton Commission in 1866:

> There seems to be some difficulty in applying them to the higher middle classes. I think of our own case. The brothers of our pupils go to the universities. Now, generally speaking, those who go in for the Local Examinations occupy a much lower place in the social scale, and our pupils would not like to be classed with them, but regarded as equal in rank to those who pass at university.[5]

In the early years Cheltenham therefore devised its own system of assessment, bringing in examiners from Oxford.

It was the high schools – pioneers in this as well as in providing girls with an academic education – which set out to try to override prejudice and to eliminate distinction of class, and sometimes of sect (though some of them, like the Alice Ottley School, Worcester, were emphatically Church of England foundations); Penzance High School, indeed, handed itself over to the Woodard Foundation in 1928 and became the School of St Clare. In 1870s and 1880s this attempt at class mix was an exceedingly bold move, and was deplored by many women who had themselves been educated at home and felt that it was the only place where a girl might be safely reared.

I doubt if we knew what all the parents did, but among them were

> certainly a parson, a baker, a doctor, a printer, a dentist, a stationer, a don, an estate agent, a lawyer, and the governor of H.M. Prison ... This democratic nature of the school did not command universal approval. Some parents, especially perhaps in the academic world, would not send their daughters to such a 'mixed' school where they might pick up that hypothetical infection known as 'High School manners'.[6]

And Nathaniel Woodard, who against his will was obliged to accept the presence of girls' schools in his foundation, had a particular horror of high schools, saying that 'the high school system and knowledge, without the grace of female gentleness and devotion, is another cloud in the gathering storm which is awaiting society'.[7]

Nevertheless, the high school venture made a good start; after the Taunton Commission's censure of the pitifully inadequate education provided by existing boarding schools, there was a surge of local interest in the sort of school that had been recommended. The assistant commissioner for Lancashire had traced out the lines, pressing for

> in every town, sufficiently large, the establishment of a day school for girls under public management; considerable changes in the course of instruction, with more stress on Arithmetic, the introduction of Mathematics everywhere, and Latin where it was possible to give time enough; and provision for institutions where women could receive the higher education given by the Universities to men.[8]

It became exciting and fashionable to send one's daughters to the new high schools, and local communities competed to found them. To forestall objections that might be raised about the dangers of class mix, authority ensured that opportunities for social contact would be very limited; all conversation on school premises was usually forbidden, and girls were not allowed to walk home together unless written parental permission had been received.

But when local authorities set up their own secondary schools in the early decades of the twentieth century, drawing their pupils mainly from the elementary schools, middle-class parents, who stood aloof on that account, instinctively drew back from the high schools as well, feeling they were tarred by the same brush. The housemistresses of Winchester High School, as will be seen, felt that a school with this name lost upper-class pupils, and that their own social standing was at stake.[9]* And one of the last wishes of Alice Ottley was that the school of which she had been the first headmistress should change its name from Worcester High School 'which now suggests a school controlled by the Board of Education, and obliged to take pupils from the elementary schools'.[10]

* The school dropped the offending 'High' and became Winchester School for Girls in 1914, and St Swithun's in 1927.

Though the Taunton commissioners called upon a handful of headmistresses (among them Miss Buss and Miss Beale) to give evidence about the education in their schools, they reported on few girls' establishments, and noted the implacable opposition of many headmistresses to any sort of investigation. But those that existed then, with about a dozen exceptions most of which were charitable foundations, were in the hands of private proprietors. And in this lies the great difference between the history of boys' and that of girls' independent schools. The former have evolved from mediaeval collegiate foundations like Eton and Winchester, ancient grammar schools, or have been set up later by public trusts; few if any have ever been in private ownership, whereas a majority of the latter, if the high schools are excluded, have grown out of private ventures which have later formed themselves into charitable trusts. They have nearly always been pinched for funds; they have patched and contrived, added here a little, there a little, sometimes taking what their advisers have considered appalling financial risks, mostly doing things in the cheapest possible way and rarely able to build on a large scale; few, as will be seen, have not experienced grave financial crises. Except for a handful of eighteenth-century charitable foundations, their history is very short. Even the senior ones only began in the mid-Victorian period, as a result of the renaissance of women's education; many arose through efforts made by women with the determination and vision to realize their own dream of what girls' education should be like; others were started as a means of providing a livelihood for widowed ladies or the daughters of large families of small means.

For this is a second strand in the history of girls' schools: the fecundity of the Victorian mother. Foreigners in the last century (especially the French, who were not so wedded to domestic life) marvelled at the size of the English family, and this did undoubtedly create great economic problems for poorer professional men who might be able to set their sons on the way to earning a living, but could do nothing for their daughters. Thus the charitable schools for daughters of the clergy and of serving officers came into existence, schools aiming higher than the charity hospitals founded in the previous century which, with the exception of the Godolphin School at Salisbury, designed for orphan gentlewomen, catered for the really poor and offered only elementary education. Unlike these, schools for the daughters of clergy and serving officers, all of which preceded the high schools and boys'-style public schools of the 1870s and 1880s, aimed to teach their pupils enough for them to earn a living as a governess in a private family, the traditional and only way that a gentleman's daughter could keep herself alive. The schools still survive, but beyond offering rather more scholarships they are in every respect the same as other independent schools.

But the teeming loins of Victorian parenthood resulted not only in charitable establishments to cope with the progeny; they produced some of the most influential of the private establishments. Nearly all the educational pioneers and the women who set out to found their own schools were daughters of huge middle-class families who had been sent to school for a few years so that they could help teach younger brothers and sisters. In a family crisis the only way they could support themselves was by teaching other people's children, and if there was to be any degree of independence, this meant starting one's own school. As will be seen in Chapter 3, the North London Collegiate School was initially a venture by the whole Buss family, the mother teaching the younger children, Mr Buss providing elocution, drawing and science lessons, and older brothers helping out with such subjects as arithmetic, Latin and divinity. The three Lawrence sisters, Penelope, Millicent and Dorothy, who founded Roedean, came from a family of thirteen children (eight daughters were at one time associated with the school). Their father's health failed in middle age and the oldest sisters took on the whole burden of supporting the family and educating their youngest siblings. Dame Frances Dove (1847–1942), founder of Wycombe Abbey, was the eldest of ten children of a Lincolnshire parson. Life in the vicarage was bleak in the extreme, and for the mother 'literal slavery'. The young Frances, spending an unhappy year at a wretched Chiswick boarding school, was fired with the resolve to try to provide for girls an education comparable to boys' public school education, a school 'at which lonely country girls could gain the same advantages of intellectual stimulus and the inspiration of noble ideals of life as their brothers did at their schools'.[11] St James's, West Malvern, was started by two sisters (there were five others who all at some stage were to be involved) whose father felt that the best thing he could give them was education, and after that was acquired his children must make their own way in life. Moreton Hall arose out of another family venture where mother and daughters all contributed their individual skills, and Talbot Heath grew out of the small school started by Mary Broad, eldest of twelve children and without any private resources, who fought to provide it with endowments and turn it into a high school.

It is these women of vision, shining courage and very slender means who have done most for girls' schools in the past. 'The spending of oneself utterly in a great cause was part of the struggle of women to secure their freedom,' said a past member of the North London Collegiate School. 'Fashioned within the family circle, tempered by a sense of strong family loyalty, this greatest of professional qualities became one of the distinctive features of girls' secondary schools.'[12]

The greatest pioneer of them all, and one who would have been able to do far more for women's education had she not met with such implacable hostility from the Catholic Church, was Mary Ward (1585–1645), a Yorkshire woman of invincible spirit and great beauty who never seems to have received due recognition either from church or from feminist historians. She had determined to enter the religious life when she was fifteen, refusing several suitors against the advice of her confessor, who urged her to marry and propagate children for the Catholic cause in the North. When she was twenty-one she set off for France, and after an initial period with the Poor Clares she was joined by a group of remarkable women whose ambition was to work in England among the persecuted Catholics. The first of these was Mary Poyntz. She too had dismissed an ardent suitor – giving him a portrait of herself (still preserved in Munich), one half showing her living likeness and the other her corrupting corpse. Profoundly shaken, he also had entered a religious order.

Mary Ward and her companions wanted the freedom to move about England, helping as and where they were needed, and teaching the Catholic girls for whom it was now forbidden to provide convent schools in England. But so far as women were concerned the Church then only recognized enclosed religious communities. The constitution of the Jesuits, the one rule that met Mary Ward's needs, forbade them to take care of an order of women. 'When all is done they are but women,' one Jesuit said of them contemptuously, to which she replied:

> There is no such difference between men and women that women may not do great things, as we have seen by the example of many saints who have done great things. And I hope in God it will be seen that women in time to come will do much . . . If women were made so inferior to men in all things, why were they not exempted in all things, as they are in some? . . . For what think you of this word 'but women', but as if we were in all things inferior to some other creature, which I suppose to be man? Which I dare to be bold to say is a lie; and with respect to the good Father may say it is an error.[13]

This challenging pronouncement came three centuries before its time, as did her aspirations for an unenclosed religious life where members of her order would be free to teach where they were most needed. Relentlessly opposed by the Church, she was imprisoned as a heretic, and she and her companions were described as 'galopping gurles', 'wandering gossips', 'gad-abouts', 'apostolical viragoes'; their critics sought to discredit them by censuring the way they allowed their pupils to act in plays and speak in public. Mary Ward herself in middle age tramped from Munich to Rome in shoes that did not fit her to plead her cause with the Pope, but so implacable was the hatred of the English clergy that he dared not intervene. Her order, known as the Institute of English Ladies, flourished in Austria and Bavaria, and did secret work in England, where Mary Ward herself spent the last six years of her life, teaching the daughters of Catholics and training young nuns as teachers. The curriculum, described in Chapter 7, was both solid and extensive, for 'she was a great enemy of ignorance and did not love to see people of little mean spirits'. Besides, 'she could not find out a reason why knowledge should be damageable, but many that it should be advantageous'. But these views were so little to the taste of the Church that for two centuries Mary Ward's order was obliged to suppress her name, and only after Vatican II were women religious free to move about and do the work they thought best.

'The destruction of the monasteries . . . found women quite unprepared,' wrote C.S. Bremner in 1897, 'and dealt their education such a severe blow that it is no exaggeration to say that it passed under a cloud for 300 years.'[14] Certainly the education given by Mary Ward's 'English Ladies' in the seventeenth century, described in Chapter 7, was admirable, and perhaps if the Institute had remained unenclosed as its foundress had wished it would have continued, wide-ranging and inquiring. But its English house, the Bar Convent in York, which somehow managed to keep its school going all through the penal days when the practice of the Roman Catholic religion was forbidden, by the early nineteenth century had had enclosure forced upon it by ecclesiastical authority. It became isolated from the outside world, and the education it offered suffered accordingly.

And this is what can be noticed about the history of convent education generally; up until Vatican II it tended to be inflexible, hampered by the deadweight of tradition, by over-zealous obedience to the founder's precepts (designed often for the society of a bygone age), by a timidity which was entirely foreign to Mary Ward, and by the tiresome officiousness of male ecclesiastical authority which all the orders had to consult and to which they had to submit. The editor of the memoirs of an eighteenth-century Polish noblewoman who had been educated at the most fashionable French convent of its day, discussed the advantages and disadvantages of the system. Here the pupils entered the convent when they were five or six and left it only to marry. They had beautiful manners, had learnt that 'consummate art of good taste and tone, that facility of conversation which enabled them to glance at the lightest subjects, or discuss the most serious topics with ease and grace', but they were wholly unprepared for the world and its temptations.[15] A Sacred Heart nun this century admitted the drawbacks: 'The danger of narrowness could . . . never be ignored in convent life. Too much concentration upon essentials, too perfect an organization, too much sacrifice of the individual to the general good, could and in many cases surely *did* result.'[16] And since there was rarely any higher education for the nuns, their teaching had to depend on the culture they had themselves absorbed at home or at school, often of a high order but not enough to take their pupils through public exams – though this was not the disadvantage it might seem, as it was not until the late 1920s that most convents concerned themselves with these matters.

The Bar Convent, as an early seventeenth-century foundation, goes back further than any existing girls' school in England, though as it is no longer independent it does not strictly come within the scope of this book. The charity hospitals have no claim to a long history of secondary education – though Christ's Hospital began as early as 1552 with a girl's name first on its register, and there are several of Queen Anne's period – since it was not until the late Victorian period that they attempted to give anything but elementary instruction. Their prime aim was to teach their inmates their duty to the Church of England and to their superiors, and after that to prepare them to be domestic servants. They learnt enough to be able to read their bibles and the catechism; anything above that was superfluous, and the Bishop of London in 1724 told charity school teachers that singing lessons, like fine writing and fine needlework, had no place in schools designed to make good Christians and good servants. Such accomplishments, said the bishop, tended to grow by degrees 'unto a more polite kind of education', and must be stopped.[17]

The charity schools record, as will be seen, is not edifying. Sometimes their governors, as in the case of Christ's Hospital, fought prolonged battles to resist spending more on girls' education; sometimes, like Red Maids' School in Bristol, they clung to the past and piously evoked the wishes of long-dead founders. Sometimes it must have been collective turpitude, as with the Grey Coat Hospital in Westminster that was so ill run that the children were spurred into violence so that they could draw attention to their wretchedness and suffering. The Merchant Maiden Hospital in Edinburgh, always better administered than any English equivalent, realized far sooner that the sort of education they were giving their children was not helping them to get on in life – but the Scots have never been so class-conscious as the English, who had settled that their charity children were to be servants and saw no reason to prepare them for anything else. As far as charity girls in England were concerned, they received their best treatment from the Freemasons, who, with children from rather higher strata than the London hospitals, had begun to adapt the curriculum at their Royal Masonic Institution some years before the Schools Inquiry Commission reported and who finally, this century, made amends for any deprivations its children might have suffered in the past by moving them out of London to some of the most splendid premises occupied by any girls' school.

But no charity school – the schools for clergy daughters and the like, far less the hospitals – was ever in the van of educational progress, and all were content with low academic achievement for far longer than they should have been; this was due in part to the innate conservatism of their administrators, who had a horror of educating girls above their station, and also to a fear of upsetting subscribers who might be presumed to be equally conservative. The religious foundation with an outstanding record is the Mount School at York. Quakers had from the first a profound concern with education, and since they held that women could minister equally with men there was the same necessity to provide schooling for them. Children of Friends had to be instructed by Friends and not sent to schools 'where they are taught the corrupt ways, manners, fashions and language of the world'. Usually these schools were co-educational, but since there was a boys' school, Bootham, in York, it was to be expected that there should be a parallel one for girls.

Since no fashionable accomplishments might be taught, the Quaker schools concentrated at first on a solid background of reading, writing, arithmetic, history and geography, though, as will be seen in a later chapter, by the middle of the century very much more was offered at the Mount. The insubstantial fripperies and frills of the standard girls' education then – the music, dancing and drawing that all had to learn, however untalented – were not for them. Thus when the assistant commissioner for Yorkshire visited the school in the course of the Schools Inquiry Commission he was greatly impressed by the girls' wide and thoughtful reading, the standard of their written work and the general level of culture, and by the professional way the teachers carried out their duties – all this in notable contrast to what he had found in the private boarding schools. The first was perhaps characteristic of any Quaker school, but the second was undoubtedly due to a most remarkable woman, Lydia Rous (superintendent 1866–79). To her the opening of Girton in 1864 was of great moment, and she set before the girls the prospect of college life as a practicable ambition. The spirit of her pupils was rather fainter. One wrote to a friend: 'The other Saturday evening Lydia Rous was reading us an account of Girton College. It seemed so grand for women to be able to go in for the same studies as men; and to gain the same degrees, but the drudgery sometimes disheartens me.'[18] It was not until the 1880s that the first Mount girl gained a degree, and came back to the school to teach, though many years before that Lydia Rous had started a training department where girls were introduced to the theory and practice of teaching.

In spite of the distinguished work of so many women like Lydia Rous, it was rare to find one on the governing body of a Victorian school, or named among the promoters of the high schools; the presence in 1873 of five lady governors on the board that was planning Bedford High School was unusual. The Endowed Schools Commissioners (see page 18) had insisted on the importance of appointing female governors: 'In every case where a girls' school is part of the scheme we require that a certain number of ladies should be governors.'[19] But the trustees of boys' schools with a girls' school attached to the foundation often reacted to this with alarm, and declined to implement it. Earlier, the Schools Inquiry Commission had affected to foresee no opposition to their own insistence that girls should at last be fairly treated: 'The exclusion of girls from the benefit of Educational Endowments would be in the highest degree inexpedient and unjust; and we cannot believe that in any comprehensive adjustment of these great questions, it will be defended or maintained.'[20] But though it might not be defended it was certainly maintained. Christ's Hospital fought the issue doggedly, not yielding until 1891. The Merchant Taylors' School in Crosby, Liverpool, where the same board of governors administered both the boys' and the girls' schools, rejected the needs of the girls at every turn, at one point threatening to close their school, and its existence was not assured until both schools came under the control of the Board of Education in 1910. At least one Victorian headmaster felt his school should be fully equipped with recreational amenities before any move to establish a girls' school on the foundation should be contemplated. Thus with the notable exception of Manchester High School (largely funded from the seventeenth-century William Hulme benefaction), the girls' schools that had to share endowments with boys lagged many years behind the new high schools which sprang up in the 1870s and 1880s. St Paul's, one of the richest and most influential of all the endowed boys' schools, did not have a sister school until 1904.

But though in the climate of the late twentieth century the injustice of this male reluctance to share their wealth strikes us so forcibly, it has to be remembered how doubtful a starter women's education must have seemed to many mid-Victorians, especially with a curriculum that was based on boys'. For what use was that going to be to them, many must have asked. And girls who might have enjoyed escaping from the confines of home for a few years found it even more of a prison when they came back. 'I don't think you know what it feels like to live at home, after being handicapped by a modern education,' mourned one girl in 1910. 'You see, the daughter has gone on and the home hasn't.'[21]

The more intellectual might seize the opportunity greedily and relish the chance to grapple with Greek and calculus, but these were a minority, and the pioneers like Emily Davies would have been saddened at the number (even of Paulinas, a notably intellectual breed) who complained of the lack of provision of subjects like domestic science on the curriculum – indeed, of the lack of any recognition that they were female and had special needs. It was a complaint that high school pupils were to continue to make in the twentieth century, oblivious, most of them, of the campaign Miss Davies and her kind had fought to prove that their girls could do as well as boys on the boys' ground, that they had the same aptitude for classics and that mathematics would not unhinge their nervous system, as was so often claimed. Edward Thring, who had himself introduced new subjects into the curriculum at Uppingham, had urged a headmistresses' conference in 1887 to dare to be innovatory: 'You are fresh and enthusiastic, and comparatively untrammelled, whilst we are weighed down by tradition, cast, like iron, into the rigid moulds of the past ... The hope of teaching lies with you.'[22] But the burning desire to turn out girls who could compete with boys on their own ground, which dominated many of the early pioneers, made the high school curriculum very arid.

The high schools did not suit all girls, of course. There would always be many who did not live within walking distance of one, and public transport was not something to which ordinary Victorian parents were willing to expose their daughters. Then there were others who wished only for boarding school. And there were those who thought there was more to education than books. The old-fashioned type of seminary, where a lady with no qualifications except genteel poverty presided over some twenty pupils whose ages might range from eight to eighteen, had been seriously discredited by the Schools Inquiry Commission, who had voiced grave doubts about the moral and intellectual atmosphere. But if boys had their characters beaten into shape on the anvil of a public school, why should not girls?

The two earliest girls' public schools, Cheltenham Ladies' College and St Leonards, were not in fact founded with this aim in mind. Both started off as day schools with boarding houses for those who lived too far away to attend daily, and gradually evolved into large highly regulated boarding organizations like their brothers' schools. It was Roedean, founded in 1885, that really established the mould, and with its highly competitive house system, its emphasis on games, its rule by prefects, set out to imitate boys. A reluctant pupil at Wycombe Abbey testified that in the 1950s the system still held sway: 'The school aped the traditions of the boys' public school, encouraging competitiveness and aggressiveness with a rigidly hierarchical structure which depended upon eccentric but unbreakable rules.'[23] But it was Roedean that introduced the gridiron element into the education of girls. The roe deer in its armorial bearings is fettered to a book and is charged on its shoulder with a gridiron (the emblem of the founders, the Misses Lawrence – St Lawrence having been martyred thus), but the book at those early public schools was of little account; the high schools could deal with that – their girls would be wage-earners. Indeed, one high school girl of the 1920s remembered how School Certificate had been the eternal cloud on the horizon: 'We were given to understand that no one would employ a School Certificate-less girl; she would be simply beyond the pale, cast into the outer darkness of serving in shops. Oh, the loss of face, a High School girl behind a counter!'[24]

Schools for the more privileged tended to distance themselves from this sort of academic plodding. Cheltenham, for instance, had started out with high intellectual ideals, but by the 1920s these had waned.

> I have heard [teachers] say 'College girls are delightful in one way, there's no trouble about discipline; but we prefer the little alert child in a London school who knows her future career depends altogether on what she learns.' She is hungry for knowledge; you are not, you don't realize how important it is.[25]

It was the gridiron that was far more important. After five or six years of being stretched upon it a girl should have acquired *esprit de corps*, the qualities of leadership, selflessness and self-discipline, and be ready to go out into the world to serve others. It was an inspiring ideal and a new one – the old-fashioned seminary was commonly run by a combination of fear and espionage, and few could have felt much loyalty to it – and for seventy years or more the gridiron ethic held sway. Few schools escaped some aspect of it, and it became the *raison d'être* of most of the larger ones. It was also to be found in the high schools, though few of the staunch advocates of the public school system appeared to recognize it.

> One of the many things I learnt at the Mary Datchelor, not in the curriculum, was that it was not necessarily what one achieved in life that mattered but what one had to give, and this spirit of service was inspired by the selfless giving of time and energy, often after a hard day's teaching, of [the headmistress] and the staff.[26]

At the larger boarding schools the prefect system, by which it was sought to develop responsibility and powers of leadership, became a tyranny, and the games which the Misses Lawrence introduced in protest against the unhealthy regime common to the schools of the past (where no exercise was taken except in crocodile) turned almost into a religion to which everyone who wished to be accepted had to bend the knee. 'You discuss games with never-ending delight,' Miss Faithfull told her Cheltonians, lamenting the lack of other conversation. The discomfort and rigours were extreme, since this also was character-forming, as was the inflexibly structured day (a traditional feature of girls' schools which the reformers did not discard).

But though most who have endured the system and still complain about it appear to have emerged unscarred, it is not one that commonly endears itself to girls, who prefer privacy and freedom and leisure, and small communities rather than large ones. Some men may regret they did not have a public school education (though far less now than in the past), mostly because it used to be difficult to rise in certain professions without it. But it is rare for women to feel anything but horrified pity for those of their own sex who have been through it. It is evident that the happiest memories come from people who were at one of the small, idiosyncratic private schools that flourished between the wars, when educational expectations were low and there was an abundance of dedicated, unmarried women who wanted employment as teachers. One or two of these, like Downe House and Benenden, though started by private individuals and with a very much more relaxed outlook than establishments like Cheltenham, Roedean, St Leonards, Wycombe Abbey and their imitators, rapidly became recognized as 'public' schools; others achieved this rank through virtue of turning themselves into trusts, though the fashion now is to style them all 'independent' schools. The small pre-war type of school is no longer economically viable, and could not have survived. But there is no doubt that the limited numbers and wide age range – Moreton Hall was typical in having in the 1930s fifty girls aged between eight and eighteen – made for a far more congenial atmosphere. As described in Chapter 5, the curriculum was necessarily narrow, limited in almost every case to arts subjects. But this was how parents wished it to be, there being a strong presumption that if one's daughters needed to earn a living afterwards they should be sent to a high school. Thus the main subjects taught were English, French and history, very often by unqualified teachers, who nevertheless might make a lasting impression on their pupils. Sometimes the proprietors had enthusiasms of their own which in those undemanding days could dominate the curriculum – eurhythmics and choral speaking at Moira House, music and ballet at Moreton Hall, music at Tudor Hall. But there are far fewer complaints about that than about the public school gridiron.

The life of the small privately owned school, unless the proprietor made the sacrifice of turning it into a non-profit-making trust, was necessarily short, and World War II brought a huge number of them to an end. Many were in south-coast resorts or in other potential danger areas, or found their numbers had dropped to a point where they could not carry on. Few had any savings to draw upon; even the larger public schools, as will be seen, were thankful if they could finish the term without an overdraft. Some were requisitioned, and the girls' public schools suffered far more over this than the boys'. Wycombe Abbey, indeed, was obliged to close down altogether and had the utmost difficulty wresting its property back from the Air Ministry at the end of the war, and in getting sufficient compensation. The courage with which headmistresses and staff, after six exhausting wartime years, returned to shattered premises and tried to build up a new life, is deeply impressive, as is their calm acceptance of the damage done by the occupiers, and the lack of adequate reparation.

Even in the late 1950s the independent schools seemed very much as they had been before the war. There were fewer of them but they existed in the same isolation, and many, like Roedean, whose ethos had temporarily relaxed under evacuation conditions, had reverted to the inflexibility of pre-war days. What was more, the smaller ones were then lagging behind the state schools both in equipment and in what they could afford to pay their staff. *How to be Topp* puts the 1954 point of view.

> The oiks have become v. well dressed certainly better than pauncefootes pater and their skools are quite remarkable with all those windows to let the sunshine in. You only hav to look to see what goes on in there. First the foyer then the palm court and swimming pool and lovely women ect . . . and you can pla as long as you like with the skool plutonium plant. Yet our paters and maters shell out to send us to st custards but that is the way we just have to put up with it.[27]

Nevertheless, the independent schools were thought to be so much more privileged that there had been brief experimentation in the wake of the Fleming Report with sending 'guinea-pig' children from less advantaged homes to boarding schools. The schools themselves were willing to co-operate, but the scheme was to be administered and paid for by the local education authorities rather than by the Ministry of Education or the Treasury, and few of the former had the money to take up places – and besides, they were apprehensive of ratepayers' reactions. For the children themselves the experiment was of doubtful value; girls, especially, could be very cruel – particularly in those class-conscious days – to contemporaries who had the wrong accent or social usages. 'Karen's getting on much better now that she's stopped saying things like "pardon" and "toilet"', as one fictional account of post-war Downe House put it, and the memoirs of a Wycombe Abbey guinea-pig give a bleak account of how she felt an alien both at school and latterly among her own family.[28] The influx of non-fee-paying pupils worked much better at the direct-grant high schools – there were of course far more of them at these schools – which from the start had tried to rise above class, and some thirty years of meritocracy were to ensue, during which children of all classes competed for the sort of academic education at which the high schools had always excelled, though in the past they had often had to take in children who were not best suited to it. All this was abolished by a Labour government in 1976, and one of the decisive factors may well have been the articulate middle-class pressure groups formed by parents whose children had not passed the 11+ exam and were barred from the sort of education that professional parents thought was the right of their class. Many direct-grant schools chose to become independent rather than be absorbed into the comprehensive system, and thus, to their deep regret, were obliged to charge fees that excluded many clever children.

Meanwhile, the boarding schools had vastly improved their academic standards. The larger public schools had hitherto, as has been seen, valued the gridiron rather than the book, and the smaller private schools had been easy-going, feeling little need to compete with the high schools. But the expansion of the universities in the mid-1960s, and the necessity of obtaining good A-level grades to get into them, put all independent schools, both boys' and girls', on their mettle. Few of the private schools had ever entered girls for A-levels, and the larger ones had only done so if their pupils were set on further education; most had spent their sixth-form years on general subjects. But now that university education was possible for all who could win a place, and professional qualifications were seen to be more and more desirable – if only to help pay the school fees of the next generation – parents were beginning to rate academic success rather more highly and schools were forced to adapt. In most cases it could only be an improvement.

The criticism that the schools were turning themselves into examination factories did not bear scrutiny; it assumed that before exam results mattered the independent schools offered a form of pure education for its own sake that encouraged pupils to develop intellectual gifts and cultural interests. But this was true, if at all, only of a handful of schools. In the majority the new academic emphasis replaced not intellectual stimulus and cultural freedom but a barren mixture of academic mediocrity and rampant athleticism.[29]

It was never as bad in the girls' schools as in the boys', and a leavening of gifted and humane women like Olive Willis of Downe House and the three founders of Benenden shaped highly individual schools where culture was important, and where the teaching, even if it did not necessarily lead to university, was long-remembered by the pupils. But undoubtedly there was an abundance of schools that were inadequate by any standard, and these were to feel the draught, with falling numbers, rising expectations from parents, and pupils in the new restlessness of the 1960s leaving to go to crammers and colleges of further education for their senior years, or if at boarding school to transfer to day schools.

There was another chill wind that affected all girls' schools, however prestigious: the admission, beginning with Marlborough in 1969, of girls into the boys' sixth forms, and indeed the change-over of a number of schools, pleased with the experiment, to co-education. The girls' schools in the past have experienced many setbacks and unfair treatment. They have been denied funds that were properly theirs, seen their premises requisitioned when boys' schools were untouched, but this poaching on their territory, and the wounding enthusiasm with which the girls have left, has angered them most of all. To them it seems the ultimate betrayal since they are well aware that they could tempt few boys to a girls' school, and had supposed that there would be mutual support between the Headmasters' Conference and Girls' Schools Association. Nor was there any element of altruism on the part of the headmasters: they did not make the change because they thought it would be good for the girls, but for economic reasons and because it was hoped that a female presence would have a civilizing effect on their boys. But the girls' schools have faced this act of treachery, as they see it, with the indomitable resourcefulness with which they have dealt with other crises. They have done their best to persuade sixth-formers to stay by finding money to equip them with their own premises, by raising the standard of their A-level teaching and giving them more freedom.

And in general, even the small schools are vastly more efficient than twenty years ago. Any amateurism has long since disappeared; they have bursars and proper financial advice, and hire professional fund-raisers when the next sports hall or craft design technology block is required. Though the quality of the teaching varies greatly, the subjects they cover are standard; every establishment expects to send girls to further education and proudly lists academic success. This has meant, though, that there is now less scope for individuality. All schools are now much more like each other than they were a generation ago; the religious foundations are more secular, the old-style public schools put less emphasis on the gridiron, the smaller ones have increased their numbers and broadened their curriculum. All of them lay stress on general culture, and encourage social service and involvement with the outside world. In general, they would appear to be better run than at any other time in their history. They are also far less insular. As numbers of the British school population fall they recruit pupils from the Middle and Far East and from Africa, whose wealthy parents are useful when the next appeal is launched, and who add lustre (particularly the Hong Kong Chinese) to the honours boards. Indeed, at one of the more recent public schools it was noticeable that all the names on the academic boards were Eastern, while the pupils had voted for English head girls and prefects.

All independent schools are aware that their future may well be precarious, that a future government that chose to deprive them of their charitable status could threaten their whole existence. In the late twentieth century they benefit from middle-class dissatisfaction with the comprehensive system, of which Richard Crossman warned when the Labour Party was proposing to abolish the grammar schools. But a vast improvement of the maintained system such as no government has yet attempted would do more to bring about their demise than any negative action against them could achieve. Whether the system as it stands is a fair one is another matter, and not within the scope of this historical account. One novelist imagined the issue debated by a liberal headmistress and her more conservative sixth-formers:

> 'Suppose such schools as these were to be abolished? Let's hypothetize,' Miss Bedford said.
>
> 'Abolished?' said Oenone. 'But they can't do that.'
>
> 'Why not? Suppose it were the case that only by dispersing schools like this – say like the dissolution of the monasteries, which you might consider not much different in a way' – they smiled – 'and the quality of teaching here went into the schools everywhere, and better brains were educated there and not exclusively in places of this kind?'
>
> 'It would be *fair*,' said Mousey.
>
> 'Should we make life fair by law?' Miss Bedford said. 'Indeed, we might well ask ourselves: *can* we make life fair by law?'[30]

2

Little Eleemosynaries

Charity Hospitals

> A girl is not expected to serve God in Church or State [wrote Joshua Fitch in 1873, in a biting denunciation of the charity schools of the time] and is therefore not invited to the University or the grammar-school; but she may, if poor, be wanted to contribute to the comfort of her betters, as an apprentice or servant, and the charity schools are therefore open to her.

He went on to speak of the joyless lives of the inmates:

> The children are dressed in a hideous costume; they are subject to many restraints of a humiliating kind which are presumed to be appropriate in a charity school, but which would not be tolerated in a free and open boarding school by parents who paid for their children's maintenance. The fact that all the scholars come from one class, and that a low one, causes the tone of thinking and of social life to become narrow and enervating, and the absence of stimulus, aid, or supervision from without renders the teachers satisfied with educational results of the most meagre kind.

Joshua Fitch (later to be knighted for his services to education) was at that time serving on the Endowed Schools Commission, set up in the wake of the Endowed Schools Act of 1869 which permitted ancient foundations, established to meet the educational needs of long ago, to adjust themselves to modern requirements. That this Act, which gave the commissioners such sweeping powers – they were attempting to overturn the past in an endeavour to adapt the endowed schools to the needs of the present – should have gone through Parliament with relatively little trouble is probably due more to the fact that the Irish Church Act was absorbing most members' energy and emotion at the time, than to eagerness for educational reform. But the Commission lasted only until 1874, when Disraeli became prime minister. It was regarded as very much a creation of the Liberals, and it greatly upset powerful Anglican and Tory interests, which saw the established Church's control over education vanishing. The Commission was disbanded, and the implementation of the Endowed Schools Act was handed over to the Charity Commissioners.

Fitch, who was an ardent campaigner for women's education (he helped establish Girton and the Girls' Public Day School Company), had a very different background from that of the public school, Oxford- or Cambridge-educated ruling classes. Self-educated, he had been a pupil teacher, later principal, at Borough Road Training College, and had managed to take a London University degree in his spare time. He was profoundly conscious that the boys' schools had absorbed nearly all the money left by pious benefactors for educational purposes, and that the charity schools gave girls little beyond the most meagre elementary education. Although schools which began as charitable foundations are the oldest in the present-day girls' public school system, educationally they never took the initiative. Until a hundred years ago or less, with the single exception, as will be seen, of the Edinburgh Merchant Maiden Hospital, they provided only the minimum. They reformed under protest, with their governors either dragging their heels in the wake of the campaigners for women's education, or, as in the extreme case of Christ's Hospital, even appealing to the Privy Council to be let off the hook.

Of the charity schools that Mr Fitch had in mind, some have vanished and others have become part of the state secondary system, like Burlington School and Grey Coat Hospital in London; the Merchant Maiden Hospital early became a fee-paying day school; some always were day schools and are now independent and fee-paying. In the case of those that are boarding schools still – like Queen Anne's, Caversham; the Godolphin in Salisbury; the two Howell's schools in Wales; Red Maids' at Bristol; the Royal Masonic Institution, now Rickmansworth Masonic School (all of which now take day-pupils as well, in spite of prolonged Victorian resistance to the idea), and the schools founded for daughters of the clergy or armed services – there are a few scholarships, but most of the income is derived from fees paid by wealthy parents, and the former charity schools are indistinguishable from the ordinary independent school. Christ's Hospital alone exists to provide public school boarding education for children whose parents have not the means to give it to them; only need, not money, can buy what the school provides.

Mr Fitch had exempted Christ's Hospital from his strictures, and the Schools Inquiry Commission had described it as 'a grand relic of the mediaeval spirit, a monument of the profuse munificence of that spirit, and of that constant stream of individual beneficence'.[2] It is surprising that he, who fought vigorously for women's education, should have been so enthusiastic about the hospital, for it was not until 1891 that the girls received the same grammar school education as the boys; perhaps because it was the first of its kind, it was trapped in its own traditions, which it regarded as sacrosanct and immutable. Christ's Hospital came into being after Nicholas

Ridley, Bishop of London, had preached an eloquent sermon at Westminster before the young king Edward VI about the plight of the London poor. The king himself wrote to the Mayor of London urging action; money was raised and probably in the autumn of 1552 380 children – boys, girls and infants – were brought to the monastery of Greyfriars in Newgate Street, dissolved in Henry VIII's time and now newly repaired. It is a curious fact that though the original thought seems to have been to rescue destitute children, and most of those first brought were very young – indeed, more than a quarter were babes in arms[3] – almost from the start it was a grammar school as well as a refuge, and within thirteen years the first Old Blue (as former members are termed) was being sent to Oxford. But despite the fact that the very first name on the register was a girl's, Ann Church, girls were in a minority, and have remained so. For 250 years or more the only secular subjects they were taught were reading and needlework, the Bible was their only book, and they stitched all the linen for themselves, the boys and the infants. By 1837 writing, history and geography had been added, and after 1852 they learned arithmetic.

From early times it was the Christ's Hospital practice to send children up to the age of ten or so into the country, especially Hertfordshire, where they were lodged in foster homes, and in the seventeenth century the younger girls – the older ones remaining in London – were taught in a schoolhouse in Hoddesdon. Then followed a period when they were accommodated in Hertford, after which they went back to Newgate Street and did not return to Hertford until 1778, to occupy buildings especially designed for them. Until 1902, when they took over the prep school premises in Hertford upon the removal of the whole boys' school to the huge new site at Horsham, they suffered from the impermanence of their surroundings, always likely to be ejected from their premises by an influx of boys. Their numbers steadily decreased, and from 1854 until the 1870s were kept permanently at eighteen. It was admitted that the standard of education was much lower than it was for the boys, the reason being that 'if you put [the standard of education] too high, you really did not benefit them'.[4]

This always has to be taken into account when one considers the wretched crumbs of learning offered to charity school girls in the pre-1870s period. They invariably learned less than the boys, who were taught to write a good hand and to cast accounts, so that they could become clerks. All reputable foundations wanted to ensure that their children were set on a suitable course when they left, and until there was an alternative to domestic service for girls, to be highly cultivated was a positive disadvantage. The Christ's Hospital girls might have become governesses, as was the destiny of the girls at the clergy daughters' schools, but for this they needed accomplishments like music and drawing which at that stage the hospital did not teach; and besides, the charity school taint would very likely have made it difficult to find such employment in a private family. (There was also the problem, which the inspectorate was finding as late as 1910, of what to do with the girls who were better with their hands than with their heads, and whose homes were so poor that it was essential they should earn at once without any period of training or apprenticeship.) The Schools Inquiry Commission had recommended in 1868 that because of 'the magnitude of the funds and the obvious circumstances' a part of the endowments should be appropriated for girls and, with a courageous and far-sighted board of governors, Christ's Hospital could have decided to expand their girls' school to make provision for the new generation of teachers who were going to be needed after the 1870 Education Act. But they resisted, fighting the Charity Commissioners' recommendations and appealing, as has been noted, to the Privy Council; and in the end they were to lag far behind the schools that had been founded by women.

The response of the charity schools to the mid-Victorian demands for girls' education is discussed later. But the first to remodel itself was the Merchant Maiden Hospital, now the Mary Erskine School, one of the Edinburgh Merchant Company schools and one which might be called the Scottish equivalent of Christ's Hospital, in that it provided a first-class secondary education, for the boys at least, within a hospital environment. (The first to be founded was Heriot's in 1659, followed by the Merchant Maiden in 1694, the Trades Maiden in 1704 – the only one still to remain as a hospital, the children being sent out to day schools – and George Watson's in 1734.) The sturdy northern independence, the self-reliance that was notably lacking in the southerner who accepted charity in the eighteenth century, meant that the Edinburgh merchant schools never took on that servile, lick-spittle character which the English patrons appeared to expect from their own beneficiaries. Though for the purposes of the Schools Inquiry Commission Scotland was as foreign a territory as the United States, an outline of the Scottish educational system was given in the report, and the assistant commissioner found there a far greater popular interest in education than existed in England; parents were ambitious that their boys should do well, and a child going home after school would be asked, 'What place in the class today?' Unlike England, there was a national system of burgh schools, or academies, giving secondary education, maintained and controlled by the municipal authorities, and here the social classes mixed to a degree that would have been impossible in England. Far more boys received secondary education and went to university, though this ascendancy over England was to engender a complacency which resulted in the Scottish system being overtaken by the English pioneers of education for women (see Chapter 3).

At the Merchant Maiden school, and indeed at the Edinburgh hospitals generally, the children were not 'all of one class, and that a low one', as Joshua Fitch had said of the English charity schools. But the wide variety of backgrounds from which the Merchant Maidens came in the early days does say something about national poverty at that time; trade had suffered greatly as a result of the Union of 1707, and there had been a series of bad harvests which had brought starvation to many parts of the country. Mary Erskine (her maiden name), the widow of a James Hair, 'druggist burgess', had in 1694 placed ten thousand Scots merks* 'to be imployed and expended for maintaining and educating at bed boord & Schools, & Clothing of young children of the female sex of Merchant burgesses of Edinburgh'.[5] (A generous woman, she also gave four thousand merks to the Trades Maiden Hospital.) 'Burgesses' indicated parents of more substance than the depressed classes who sought charity in England, and in the first decade of the new century those who applied for admission included daughters of knights, of ministers of the gospel and of Writers to the Signet,† as well as of artisans, some of whom represented themselves as completely destitute.

The provision for the children seems to have been on a fairly comfortable scale. The hospital was staffed by a governess and two schoolmistresses, as well as servants. At a time when fresh meat was expensive and in the winter rare, the hospital bought it in impressive quantities; much milk, butter, cream and sugar were ordered, and special items such as chicken, veal and whey for sick or convalescent children. An early entry in the account book of '2/- to the bairns at the faire' shows an unexpected humanity; most English charity children were kept locked up for fear of meeting unsuitable people. It is significant, too, that at both the Edinburgh girls' hospitals the communities always referred to themselves as 'families'. Though for the first hundred years the education was fairly limited, it included writing, arithmetic and vocal music in addition to reading, which was considerably more than English hospitals offered. Moreover, by the early years of the last century it was recognized that some girls might want to be governesses, and appropriate subjects like French, dancing and music were offered. Admittedly, the pupils were kept hard at their needle, but the prudent management saw that it brought in a profit (the English hospitals seem never to have managed this), and in addition they were taught such skills as mantua-making and millinery, and how to work black lace and spin thread for linen. Compared to their English contemporaries, far fewer went into domestic service. Of the 114 girls who left the Merchant Maiden Hospital between 1858 and 1867, for instance, eighty-one had gone into teaching, ten into dressmaking, twenty-two had married and none, it seemed, was in service. Throughout, the Edinburgh hospitals appear far better run and more ready to shed the deadweight of past tradition than their English contemporaries, and when the Royal Commission on Scottish Education, appointed in 1868, drew attention to their large funds and the improvements that might be made, they acted promptly; the hospitals were converted into day schools (with

* A merk was then worth a little more than thirteen English pence.

† A higher class of solicitors in Scotland.

provision for lodging those who had no homes), and by 1870 the Merchant Maiden was the Edinburgh Educational Institution for Young Ladies with twelve hundred pupils and eighty staff.

Joshua Fitch had said that the dress of a Bluecoat boy was 'the one charity dress in the whole country which has no dishonouring associations'. Just how degrading the charity school uniform was generally considered can be gauged from the fact that at a Bath boarding school at the beginning of the last century, the most dreaded punishment was to be stripped of one's clothes and dressed as a charity school girl, in the costume of the Red Maids of Bristol. 'Anything more unbecoming or more uncomfortable could scarcely be imagined, and there was hardly one of us that would not have preferred a flogging.'[6] This is not so surprising if one remembers what happened to Dickens' young Biler, the child of Paul Dombey's nurse, newly clad in the uniform of a Charitable Grinder – 'a nice, warm, blue baize tailed coat and cap, turned up with orange-coloured binding; red worsted stockings; and very strong leather small-clothes'. 'The youth of the neighbourhood could not endure [his appearance] ... His social existence had been more like that of an early Christian, than an innocent child of the nineteenth century.'[7] But though young Biler had to submit to the hostility and contempt of the local boys on his way to and from the Grinders' school, he was fortunate in that he was living at home; some charity children were incarcerated in hospitals for years on end.

The object of the philanthropists who founded hospitals and schools in the later seventeenth century and during the eighteenth was rescue, unlike the Tudor founders of schools who were primarily interested in providing education – rescue from possibly unsatisfactory parents and a certainly unsavoury background. From the late seventeenth century until the last quarter of the eighteenth, when there was a move to establish Sunday schools, the only education available to the poor was at charity schools, and thousands were set up to give children of the labouring poor a 'Christian and useful education'. It was a time when the serious-minded looked at the degeneration of public morals with dismay, and sought to bring about a reformation of manners. Indeed, a society was founded in 1691 to do just that and was followed in 1698 by the Society for Promoting Christian Knowledge. The problem of the poor and abandoned children who roamed the streets of a city such as London was acute; Defoe talked about the infant army of blackguard boys – wicked, idle, pilfering vagrants, thieves, robbers, gamblers, pickpockets, blasphemers and caterpillars.[8] Nor, even if day schools were set up by the charitably disposed, did this make much impact on children who were picked from amongst those of 'known evil habits and customs', who were 'the curse and trouble of all places where they live', and who returned to crowded slum cellars and attics where all the day's good would be undone.

It is hardly surprising, therefore, that some schools felt the only solution was to take over such children as boarders. Thus Grey Coat day school in Westminster became Grey Coat Hospital, though the very heavy additional expense precluded most schools from following suit. Once handed over to the hospital, children were locked away inside, sheltered against contact with their parents and former associates for fear of infection, moral and physical. Even church-going presented a problem, as relations would lie in wait for the little uniformed procession and try to waylay children and press money, unsuitable food, even quack medicine into their hands; or children might try to run away, showing the desperate straits they felt themselves to be in, because most of them were well aware of the value of sticking it out until the end, when the leaver was dispatched with a suit of clothes and a small sum of money and an apprenticeship. (At Christ's Hospital the punishments for boy absconders as described by Charles Lamb were horrifying.)

A pamphlet of 1716, *The Methods Used to Erecting Charity-Schools*, sets out the qualifications that benefactors should look for when appointing masters (and by inference, mistresses) to take charge of charity children. The primary concern should be that they were members of the Church of England over the age of twenty-three; were meek and humble, and 'of sober life and conversation'; understood well 'the Grounds and Principles of the Christian Religion'; exercised good government of themselves and their passions; and, finally, wrote a good hand and understood arithmetic. Their academic duties were to 'teach the children the true spelling of Words, make them mind their Stops, and bring them to read slowly and distinctly'. All the children were to be taught 'to write a fair legible hand, with the Grounds of Arithmetick', and the girls to knit their stockings and gloves and to mark, sew and mend their clothes.

No hospital inmate, in the early days, was allowed home for holidays. Christ's Hospital had found that such indulgence 'was not only contrary to what was anciently used but very prejudicial to the good order and Governm^{t} of this House'.[9] And when the rule was relaxed in 1785, it only applied to children who had been in the school for a full three years and who spent the vacation at least five miles from London. The Royal Masonic Institution finally gave way in 1853 to a doctor who urged that there should be regular summer and winter vacations.

Little allowance was made for recreation; it was clearly easier to control children while they were working, and in any case there was rarely adequate space for recreation within the confines of the hospital. But there was another consideration: charity children should not be seen to enjoy themselves. The French Assumption Sisters who ran an orphanage in Richmond, Yorkshire, found 'the English very serious-minded concerning the way orphans should be brought up, the general opinion being that recreation was no training for the life of laborious service that girls would have in future'. In deference to the views of Richmond worthies the nuns had to reduce the recreation of their orphans and see that they played out of sight of passers-by.[10]

Uniform was conspicuous and uncomfortable; the Grey Coat girls, for instance, were dressed in the female equivalent of young Biler's leather small-clothes – that is, coarse material with great powers of standing up to the rough-and-tumble of juvenile life, though not up to washing, which rarely entered into the governors' calculations. The black serge petticoats and the home-made stays were passed down from child to child, unwashed; when a Victorian laundress was told to wash them she said with indignation that she had been there for seven years and it had never been done. Nor were the counterpanes ever washed; the normal dirty ones were covered by the 'Governors'' counterpanes (as they were termed) on the days when the board met.[11] There was little attempt to adapt the uniform to changing times; most hospital children carried into the late Victorian period the mark of their Queen Anne origins. The Christ's Hospital governors decided in the 1870s to change the style of the girls' dress so that it should be 'more assimilated to that of the day'. However, they forgot to do anything for fifty years after that; a girl who entered the school in 1916 recorded the antediluvian outerwear and the even more amazing undergarments (see page 289), and the 1921 inspectors criticized the 'ugly white pinafores, heavy boots and uncomfortable straw hats'. The Royal Masonic Institution long kept its 'pinbefores', which had been an essential part of the uniform from the earliest days. A hundred years on, at the centenary celebrations in 1888, they were worn even during the traditional marching and drill display. They survived the move to Rickmansworth in 1934, much detested as a badge of charity, and were only abandoned in 1939 after vigorous representations by a new headmistress. Charity costume has lingered longest at Red Maids', finally to be worn with pride. In 1907 the outdoor summer dress was the traditional white linen tippet and apron, white gloves and straw bonnet, and these are still worn for ceremonial occasions.

Life was harsh at all charity hospitals. The children were worked long hours; the daily routine at Red Maids' in the eighteenth century is typical. The girls rose at six, the older pupils dressing the little ones and making the beds. At seven the Mistress read prayers and then the four 'servants' went to prepare breakfast. From eight till twelve everyone worked in the schoolroom. At one they ate dinner, and then worked from two till seven. They went to bed at nine, after supper and prayers. During the winter they rose an hour later. Until 1836 the Mistress of the school took the profit from their many hours of sewing and, as at other hospitals, she was given an allowance for the maintenance of each child – a system easily abused. They were allowed to play in the yard, but there was no other provision for exercise.[12]

Physical punishment seems to have stopped earlier at girls' schools. (The

Christ's Hospital boys endured terrifying flogging and solitary confinement, recorded by both Lamb and Coleridge.) Discipline latterly more often took the form of docking holidays or shaming the culprit; at Red Maids' the really recalcitrant were made to wear the Black Cap, as in the 1830s when there was particular trouble with a girl who had absented herself for a whole weekend. But sullenness and apathy seem to have been more characteristic of hospital girls than overt rebellion. The diet, while mostly adequate, was coarse and monotonous, consisting mainly of meat, potatoes and an unconscionable amount of bread; it is not surprising that occasional cases of scurvy are recorded, and anaemia was frequent. Fruit and vegetables (except root vegetables) never appear in the early diet sheets, and indeed do not play much part in institutional catering until late in the nineteenth century; it has taken a very long time for schools to shake off the carbohydrate habit. In all hospitals disease was a recurrent problem; the children lived at such close quarters, two to a bed, and there might well be no infirmary where infectious cases could be isolated. There was even an outbreak of typhus at the Casterton school for clergy daughters – a disease spread by lice and associated with gross and insanitary overcrowding – and there were many epidemics of diphtheria and scarlet fever, which always resulted in anxiety about the drains. Consumption, scrofula and itch are much in evidence in the accounts of funeral payments.

Against this it has to be remembered what ordinary boarding school life was like 150 years ago. Most girls slept two to a bed (it was warmer as well as economical of space). Washing conditions and sanitation were primitive, epidemics frequent. At the time of the 1864–7 Schools Inquiry Commission few schools of any sort were equipped, as Red Maids' was, with gas lighting, warm water, warm-air heating and a basement bathroom – though it has to be said that these were installed in premises that the inspectors considered to be in an unhealthy part of Bristol, with far too little space for play. (In 1837 it had been decided not to move the children to a new building erected for them, on the grounds that 'the very beauty and magnificence of the edifice' would unfit them for 'the closer and humbler dwellings it must necessarily be their lot in after life to inhabit'.) However, there was very little recreation generally for any girls until the late Victorian period; boarding school diet was often not much better than the charity hospitals' (though probably more appetizingly presented), and the pupils were watched with the same vigilance and kept constantly occupied. And as for the unreformed boys' public schools, you had to be very fit to survive: the squalor, dissipation and violence at Eton in the Georgian period were notorious; even worse were the atrocities that went on in Long Chamber at night. Here the 'Collegers' were locked up between 8.30 at night and seven next morning, and 'there were many things done, which one cannot but remember with horror and regret'.[13] At all boys' schools flogging was the rule, for errors in construing quite as much as for more serious lapses. In short, it is only comparatively recently that school could be said to be at all pleasurable, or even healthy.

The loss of liberty must have been a great affliction.

> How I used to pity those tender little lads [wrote an Edinburgh schoolmaster], taken suddenly from under a mother's care and dropped into these strange and uncomfortable establishments! ... There was no love in the moral atmosphere. Fear was the pervading feeling. A hospital a home! Why, it was a prison, and the teachers were jailers, and the pupils were culprits.[14]

And he remembered a dominie who was kind and genial in an ordinary classroom, but a monster of cruelty when he taught in a charity school. The supreme disadvantage that the hospital children suffered was bad management and lack of supervision. Out of sight, out of mind, and there is no doubt that the schools had a very unsavoury reputation. Between inspection visits the masters and mistresses were able to exploit the children, steal their food, and pocket the funds. Occasionally there was gross cruelty as well as neglect; girls as well as boys were so savagely flogged at the Grey Coat Hospital in 1788 that the matron was arrested. In 1789 the boys deliberately smashed windows to draw the governors' attention to their plight, and six years later the girls set fire to the woodwork with the same motive. The governors were told that the children were so 'utterly wretched' from hunger and constant flogging that they could bear it no longer.[15] In 1802 the girls at the Royal Masonic Institution rose up against an over-severe regime in what was recorded as 'General Rebellion'. Disaffection spread through the school of sixty children, and the member of the committee who tried to quell it was resisted; it was a month before the conduct of the girls was said to improve. Even in the Edinburgh hospitals, which were on the whole far better run than the English ones – with a regular rota of governors to see for themselves that all was well (it was suggested that a lady should be taken too, since she would have a keener eye for domestic detail) – the questions that the visitors were instructed to ask related to whether the children were receiving proper religious instruction and behaving themselves rather than to whether they were happy.

Grey Coat Hospital, Westminster, was founded in 1698, and girls were taken from 1701. The school's managers had hoped that the regime would be mild; the code of rules that they drew up for the guidance of the master they appointed urged him 'to study to endeavour to win the love and affection of the children, whereby to invite and encourage them, rather than by correction to force them to learne'. When it was still a day school and a new one at that, the trustees, full of zest, met every week to supervise the charity they had set up, devising schemes for testing the children's learning and taking great pride in their appearance. Interest waned when it changed from a day school into a hospital, and moved to the workhouse in Tothill Fields. Here the children subsisted in conditions that became more and more deplorable, and which remained unchanged for longer than at most such establishments. In the 1870s the girls were still wearing their Queen Anne costume of heavy grey dresses with white pique stomachers laced with blue cord; they were known by number, not name, and the food was so sparse and monotonous that they were reduced to stealing raw parsnips and bacon parings. Even then, when there was already a greater understanding of the needs of childhood, there was no provision for leisure – no playthings, no storybooks. (The Edinburgh Trades Maiden Hospital governors had provided a library as early as 1758, financing it partly by fines paid by deacons for non-attendance at meetings.[16]) When a new head was appointed in 1874, just before the hospital school gave way to an entirely day school, she was horrified to find how abject and cowed the pupils were. 'The surprise of the children at having ordinary consideration and kindness shown to them, came to the Head Mistress with a pathetic shock which she cannot forget.'[17]

At Burlington School, the oldest girls' school in London, founded in 1699 and now in Hammersmith, conditions eased sooner, and indeed probably always were more salubrious, since whereas the Grey Coat Hospital occupied a seventeenth-century workhouse, Burlington from 1725 had its own imposing purpose-built school designed by Colin Campbell. As at all hospital schools, children were not allowed outside, but had to take their exercise in the school yard. They spent much time in contract knitting and spinning, but humanity prevailed earlier here than at the Grey Coat, for in 1804 an official was concerned enough to report that the children were undersized and 'sit too long, being young and full of humours for want of air and exercise'. And in 1810 it was ordered that each child should be given a skipping rope and have one hour's exercise a day; and that they should all be taken outside for a walk in the evenings if it was fine.[18]

The life lived in these institutions seems bleak indeed, with very little to commend it. But the pious founders of asylums to shelter poor children were, it seems, often moved by genuine feelings of tenderness towards the young. The founders of the Grey Coat Hospital had aimed to rule with love, and the fact that fear replaced it a hundred years later was not their fault. Frequently childless themselves – like Charles and Elizabeth Godolphin who founded the Godolphin School in Salisbury, John Whitson who founded the Red Maids' School in 1634 and whose own daughters had died young, or Mary Erskine who founded the Edinburgh Merchant Maiden Hospital – they wanted to help the poor children of their cities. What better could they do than rescue them from lamentable surroundings, provide them with religion, food and clothing, and the means of earning a modest livelihood? Sometimes the motive may have been a wish to perpetuate their own memory, like Thomas Howell who in one of his wills made provision for orphans who were to be labelled with his name back and front and thus 'bear the name Howell ever more'. But this sort of self-advertisement was not the norm.

Nor was the original intention always that the children should be destined for the lowest sort of labour. The Royal Masonic Institution, founded in 1788 at the instigation of the Chevalier Bartholomew Ruspini, a distinguished dental surgeon, and known then as the Royal Cumberland Freemason School, announced that its purpose was 'to train young female minds destitute of parental care and attention to Industry, virtue and social and religious duties; to qualify the children to occupy a useful, though not a menial, station in life'.[19] However, five years later, when a committee reported on the future of their girls, who were to leave at fifteen, it seemed to be expected that they should go into domestic service – though this should not be with 'a Boys' Academy or Single Gentleman or any Person who Letts Furnished Lodgings either to Single Men or others' – with the proviso that if the child should be physically unfit for such work she should be apprenticed to 'any Trade or Business which they shall think prudent'. John Whitson of Bristol, providing in his will for the maintenance of 'Forty poore women Children' in the hospital that was to be known, from the children's dress, as Red Maids', had said they should be taught to 'read English and to sowe or to do some other laudable worke towards theire maintenance'. And since they were to be admitted at eight and ten to stay until they were eighteen, it would seem that he had something better in mind than invariable domestic service. But the benefaction never seems to have been properly considered by the administrators, and though there were trades the girls could have learned in those ten years in the hospital – such as lace-making, button-making and embroidery, as at the Merchant Maiden Hospital – in practice there was no choice. They had to accept what the mistress in charge could teach (since they were formally apprenticed to her). This was limited to housework, spinning and sewing, and sometimes reading (though only from the Church of England catechism and the Bible).

The finance of these institutions was often precarious, particularly at the clergy daughters' schools, as will be seen. Much depended on individual donations; subscribers might die or have a lean year, and it was often in the early days very difficult to know how to invest surplus funds. It was always easier in London, where the gifts and donations of the prosperous middle class meant that by the early nineteenth century many schools had a steady income from endowments. The sight of the children in their uniforms, though it might not appeal to their more fortunate peers, had a melting effect on their elders, and they were often paraded at fund-raising dinners. The Burlington trustees sold tickets for five shillings, and a hundred pounds might be raised thereby. Although the trustees found that these functions resulted in drunkenness, they were too profitable to give up. They came to an end, however, in 1819, when it was decided that the way the parents lay in wait for the children was unendurable. The sound of thousands of childish voices singing the Old Hundredth under the dome of St Paul's at the famous annual service for the London charity schools – Blake's 'Holy Thursday' – moved many to unloose their purse strings; it was also an opportunity for many a distinguished preacher to remind the 'little Eleemosynaries' to abjure vanity and pride.

Christ's Hospital was from the start in a class of its own. Edward VI's appeal to the Lord Mayor had resulted in massive London support; the City companies were canvassed; fund-raising sermons were preached in all the parishes; collecting boxes were distributed in which householders might 'gather of their ghests theire benevolence to that good worcke'.[20] The foundation thus started life on a firm financial footing and in a far more lavish way than any other similar charity, with a domestic entourage that included steward, butlers, cook, porters, tailor, barber and surgeons, as well as teaching staff. The City links, too, were very useful when it came to Old Blues finding profitable employment. Apart from the Edinburgh Merchant Company, the only other body that approached Christ's Hospital in resources were the Freemasons: though there was never a general levy, lodges as well as individuals gave support to the Royal Masonic Institution. An annual fund-raising festival brought in comfortable sums, which increased from £82 in 1789 to £1,129,544 in 1972. (Until 1856 the children used to be displayed at these, and there is a painting of the Chevalier Ruspini, a toddler at either hand, leading a little procession of girls into the presence of the Prince Regent and fellow masons.) When the girls' school finally moved to Rickmansworth in 1934 it was to premises uniquely luxurious and spacious, surrounded by their own land.

Joshua Fitch in 1873 commended the speed and energy with which the Edinburgh Merchant Company had remodelled their foundations, abandoning the hospital set-up and providing a completely reorganized system of secondary schools in its stead. In sharp contrast was the determined opposition the Endowed Schools Commissioners met with in their attempt to modernize the constitution of English hospital schools. Their governors, said Fitch, spoke with emotion of 'robbery of the poor' and 'violation of the sacred wishes of the dead', but the real truth was that their own patronage was liable to be interfered with.[21] Of these, Christ's Hospital would have been uppermost in his mind, for in 1872, with women's education in the air, newspapers had been asking on what authority the trustees had appropriated most of the benefits for the boys. And when the Endowed Schools Bill had been debated in the Lords, Lord Lyttelton said that the numerical disparity of the sexes educated on the foundation was most extraordinary, considering that girls had been expressly included in the constitution. But though after 1875 more girls were admitted, and French, music and drawing were added to the curriculum, it was not until 1891, as we noted earlier, that the governors, with much lamentation, finally bowed to the insistence of the Charity Commissioners, and the whole status of the girls' school was changed.

The leaving age was extended to seventeen with the possibility of extension to nineteen, and this became a rung on the ladder to university. When the school was inspected in 1910, the inspectors could report that of one hundred girls discharged between 1906 and 1910, fifteen were teaching in secondary schools (eight of them being university exhibitioners) and fifteen in elementary schools; one was a librarian, several were civil servants or engaged in clerical or commercial work, and several were receiving some sort of professional training.

That the Bluecoat girls did take a pride in their foundation is made clear by the recollections of Louie Angus, who went to the Hertford school in 1916 and stayed there for nine years.[22] The girls had by then taken over the splendid buildings vacated by the younger boys, and inherited the centuries-old traditions. They marched through the cloisters and up the oak staircase into the hall for meals (it had been the boys' Writing School and contained a handsome carved screen from Newgate Street). Food was served on blue-crested crockery which the girls so coveted that leavers often contrived to break a piece, since items that broke cleanly were allowed to be taken away and riveted. In 1916 there was still an awe-inspiring ceremony, a reminder of its foundling hospital origins, when a new child was handed over by a parent to the governors all sitting behind a huge horseshoe table in the council room, as well as a dismissal ceremony when leavers thanked the foundation for the many benefits they had received. (These particular rites were later discontinued.) By the end of one's time one was imbued with the hospital's customs and traditions, and had a sense of continuity with the past that few girls, because of the relative newness of their schools, can feel. A common experience bound them together: 'We were formed by the same traditions, trod the same paths, led much the same life,' said Louie Angus. Those who had shared this experience must inevitably have lamented the governors' decision to integrate the girls into the boys' school at Horsham in 1985 (leaving the Hertford premises to be divided up between an old people's home and a Tesco training centre), though the girls who moved (still in a minority – in 1988, 230 girls and 600 boys), perhaps initially doubtful about the loss of their identity, are now enthusiastic about the change and the vastly increased opportunities it offers.

Christ's Hospital had resisted change passionately. Other charity schools had adapted themselves to new demands with varying degrees of reluctance. Having turned itself into a day school in 1875, Grey Coat Hospital gradually moved to meet modern educational requirements, providing library, gymnasium and music rooms. It was in 1891 that the first girl achieved London University matriculation. The Endowed Schools Commissioners had stipulated that there should also be a fee-paying boarding school, where children who had spent at least three years in one of the Westminster elementary schools could also be supported. This, given the then attitudes to social mix, presented grave difficulties, but it was resolved that no elementary school child should board until she had gone to the day school first and been approved as suitable in work and conduct. The boarding school is the present Queen Anne's School at Caversham, where foundation scholarships and bursaries are still offered as a relic of its hospital past. The day school was enlarged in 1955 to take about six hundred pupils, new classrooms being built behind the old facade, and became a Church of England girls' comprehensive school in 1977 with nine hundred pupils.

The Royal Masonic Institution, with girls from a rather higher social stratum than the ordinary London hospital, was a little more liberal in the education it provided in the early days, though in 1846, when a member of the house committee proposed that French and music should be added to the curriculum so that the girls might rise above the servant level, the attitude of the majority was that the school had prospered in the past, so why change things now? It was 1856 that marked the beginning of a move away from the charity hospital concept. Spurred by an outside examiner's comments on the 'unnecessary and unnatural diffidence exhibited by the girls in the presence of strangers', the school's committee introduced sweeping changes. Needlework (which had hitherto brought in a profit) was to be reduced to the repair of one's own clothes; drawing was to be taught throughout the school, and French and music to the seniors until they should be fit to instruct the others. But it was not until 1888 that pupils took the Cambridge local examinations, which had been open to girls for over twenty years, and only in 1912 that the headmistress insisted teachers should be properly trained. The association of charity schools with domestic service died hard, for in that year the High Commissioner for New Zealand had asked the school – and it was appropriately outraged by the request – to send out girls as servants. It remained a wholly charitable institution until 1963 when fee-paying pupils were first taken, and day-girls followed in 1972, but, like the former, with masonic connections. When it was finally decided that the school would have to take daughters of non-masons, a new constitution was drawn up and the school renamed Rickmansworth Masonic School. The proportion of boarders to day-girls is now three to one, and masonic 'petitioners' (the children on foundation bursaries) form two fifths of the school.

Of all the hospitals, the governors of Red Maids' were most deeply entrenched in the past. In part their difficulty was to decide whether their duty was to shelter a comparatively few orphans, to use the funds to provide good day-school education for the non-disadvantaged, or to combine both and charge fees – but in that case, would the levels of achievement be compatible? And should candidates be chosen on intellectual merit or because they were deserving cases? The Edinburgh Merchant Company had had precisely the same problems, but by 1868 they had come to the conclusion that their money was not being spent in the most useful way, and that the hospital system was good neither for the children themselves nor for their education – and here they had been influenced by a frank report by Simon Laurie (later Professor of Education at the University of Edinburgh), who had also inspected their other schools. His suggestions had been revolutionary: he urged far greater liberty for the children, absence of restraint, abolition of the uniform and contact with the outside world, with as many residents as possible becoming day pupils. Fired with the Scottish belief in making the best possible use of resources, and an even stronger belief in education, the Merchant Company had acted at once and with decision, setting up large day schools in place of the hospitals, and sending their orphans to foster homes. In all this they had to face opposition, for some of those who had been enthusiastic about the policy at the start saw lesser schools, and with them perhaps their own livelihood, disappearing in the face of these new schools which, because of the endowments, were able to charge comparatively low fees. In contrast, the story of Red Maids' is the story of a foundation that until halfway through the present century was still determined to provide for orphans in the style of a past age, refusing to listen to any of the advice lavished by Charity Commissioners and school inspectors.

In 1870 Joshua Fitch had visited Bristol to discuss reform of the Red Maids' and the two other Bristol charity schools: the feeling of the Endowed School Commissioners was that these three schools, with a combined income of £14,000, should extend their benefits to more than 436 children (the number then educated there) out of a total of 160,000 in the city. But the trustees had no intention of co-operating, and by leaking Fitch's tentative proposals as though they were final they succeeded in rousing the citizens of Bristol into a fury of indignation. However, the *Western Daily Press* supported the commissioners, saying of Red Maids' that it was scandalous that £3,000 a year should be spent for 'teaching the three R's, saying the Catechism and bobbing a curtsey ... [and] for the sake of supplying Clifton people with servants (about fifteen per annum) warranted to have as little education as possible and to know how to "Keep their Place"'.[23] It was fair comment, for at this period the majority of girls still went into domestic service, though with an income of £2,850 Red Maids' was by far the richest of all the endowed girls' schools. The only one that approached it was the Clergy Orphan School at St John's Wood (now St Margaret's, Bushey) which with an income of £1,478 maintained and provided a secondary education for seventy-six girls. But though a Red Maid stayed until she was eighteen (a most unusual if not unique feature of the hospital, and one that naturally produced problems with discipline), an elementary education was all that was offered.

In 1875 there was some attempt at reorganization: numbers were reduced to eighty, the leaving age was fixed at fifteen, and the curriculum enlarged. An undertaking was also given that 'when Trust Funds shall suffice' the school should move to a healthier area, outside Bristol. This was something that was occasionally discussed over the next thirty years, but always shelved, and the school did not move out to Westbury until 1911. In the late Victorian period fewer girls went into domestic service; some became teachers, telegraph clerks or shop assistants, or went to learn a trade. But even in 1906 when the school advertised for a headmistress, no mention was made of educational qualifications, and the first graduate teacher was not appointed until 1911. The majority of the children were still orphans and were to remain so for many years to come. Up until twenty-five years ago the record seems to show a school making slow headway in spite of governors who resisted or ignored the advice of HM Inspectors of Schools about expansion and financial policy (all females, including the headmistress, were excluded from discussion of finance), and children and staff struggling against adverse conditions. But the inspectors' 1963 report seemed to turn the tide: 'You have able, delightful girls, a devoted Staff and an outstandingly capable Head Mistress. They are doing very good work, but they are doing it under really frustrating and austere conditions. I cannot believe it is wholesome or educative for girls to be brought up with quite so much pinching.' This time the governors listened, and by 1967 Red Maids' had emerged from its charity hospital chrysalis. The foundationers were allowed to be day-girls (they had long grumbled about having to be boarders); the majority of boarders were now fee-paying, and the school was redecorated and re-equipped so that it could compete with other schools. From direct-grant, it became independent in 1965, when it was decided that 75 per cent of its endowment income should be used for the remission of fees. The school still helps the needy, but in a manner adapted to modern conditions.

Endowed Secondary Schools

The report of the Schools Inquiry Commission of 1868 had shown how boys' schools had absorbed nearly all the money left by benefactors for educational purposes, and that whereas there were 36,874 boys receiving secondary education in 820 endowed schools – and this excluded Charterhouse, Eton, Harrow, Merchant Taylors', Rugby, St Paul's, Shrewsbury, Westminster and Winchester – there were only some twelve comparable schools that attempted to do this for girls (and, judging by the curriculum printed in the Commission's report, it would have been more correct to class at least a quarter as elementary).[24] A writer in the *Victoria Magazine* in 1876 estimated that out of a sum that could be calculated as £10,000,000 bequeathed over the centuries to provide education, £400,000 a year was being spent on forty thousand lads, and less than £3,000 went to their sisters, despite the fact that the endowers rarely excluded girls and commonly left the sex of the children or 'youngerlings' unspecified. Dorothea Beale more than ten years before had expanded on the same theme:

> There are a few endowed schools where girls are fed and clothed, and taught to read and write indifferently; and a few schools have been lately established and maintained by public subscription where orphan girls can obtain superior instruction; but the numerous foundations of ancient endowment for the religious and intellectual education of young females, scattered over the country in the middle ages, were all swept away at the dissolution of religious houses in the sixteenth century. The great ecclesiastical foundations for men were reformed and re-established on an improved system, but the endowments for the benefit of women were either seized by court favourites, or transferred to schools and colleges for men, and our sex to this day has not recovered from the fatal blow.[25]

But the ancient foundations were in no hurry to make reparation, and almost without exception they were to be overtaken by the new high schools which were set up from 1873 onwards. There was, however, one foundation which in fact anticipated the Endowed Schools Act – by almost twenty years. This was at Loughborough, where in 1495 Thomas Burton, a wool merchant, had left land for charitable purposes. The scheme for the administration of this charity property was reorganized in 1849 to include, as well as a grammar and commercial school for boys, an upper school for girls, and on 11 March 1850, some months before Miss Buss opened her school, thirty pupils began their education at the New Girls' School (or, as it was later to be called, Loughborough High School), the first girls' grammar school to open in England.

Manchester High School, which had opened in 1874, used commendable initiative when it boldly addressed itself to the Charity Commissioners the following year, pleading for help from the benefaction which William Hulme had left in 1691. There had been no mention of girls, or even the vague term 'children', in his will, so the school stressed the need for a girls' school in Manchester and the importance of a first-rate building, and made the point that the increase in the Hulme income was due 'directly to the development of the city, and doubtless indirectly to the labours and increase of the class from which the school draws its pupils'. They appealed again in 1877, and finally in 1884 a new scheme for the administration of the Hulme funds was drawn up, which gave the school not only a regular income but also a substantial lump sum with which they could pay off the mortgage on the new buildings.[26]

The Harpur Trust in Bedford also acted fairly swiftly. This exceedingly rich foundation had been offering free schooling on a scale unequalled anywhere in England – to the extent that the town attracted genteel immigrants such as widows and half-pay officers, who settled there in order to claim what the Taunton Commission described as 'a supposed birthright to educational alms', sending their sons either to Bedford School (which provided a classical education) or to the Modern School (which, charging lower fees, taught commercial subjects to boys who would leave comparatively early). In 1873 the Harpur Trust appointed some of its members to act as 'Governors of the Girls' School', and, unusually, five ladies were elected too. Five years later designs for a girls' high school and a modern school were commissioned. The estimates, for a combined sum of £20,564 (Manchester was to spend over £30,000 on a single school), caused local uproar, and 'Fair Play' wrote to the *Bedfordshire Times* that he hoped the people of Bedford would not submit quietly to such a gross waste of money.[27] However, the trust did not waver, and the schools were duly opened in 1882, the high school headmistress being Mrs McDowall, who as Ada Benson (formidable sister of the formidable archbishop) had been headmistress briefly of both Oxford and Norwich High Schools and aimed to run all her schools as her brother had run Wellington when he was headmaster. A unique example of a Victorian who combined career and motherhood, she was to die five months later, after the birth of her second child.

Many charitable trusts, however, doggedly resisted change. The schools provided by private benefactors, notably during Queen Anne's reign, were later to form the backbone of the secondary system, but until the mid-Victorian period all they did for girls, as Dorothea Beale said tartly, was to teach them 'to read and write indifferently'. Sir William Perkins's School in Chertsey, Surrey, was a typical example. Sir William was an eighteenth-century philanthropist who left provision for twenty-five boys to be taught 'reading, writing and arithmetic and the Catechism of the Church of England', but the twenty-five girls who were added in 1736 were only to be taught 'reading, the Catechism and plain work'. The girls were clothed in conspicuous yellow-bound blue serge dresses, hand-knitted yellow stockings and heavy nailed boots. Their aprons were checked blue and white and they wore an oval brass medal with their number on it. Children were taken from the very poorest families who would otherwise be receiving parish relief; a parent had to be desperate indeed to allow a child to be dressed in the uniform of charity. It was not until 1914 and after two decades of wrangling with the Board of Education and the local authority that the school was reorganized as a fee-paying girls' grammar school and the boys were incorporated into a nearby school at Egham. James Allen's Girls' School likewise began as an elementary school, founded by a Master of Dulwich College in 1741 for children, both boys and girls, of poor people of Dulwich and its neighbourhood; after reorganization of the whole foundation in 1857, the boys were moved elsewhere and the girls were finally provided with secondary education in 1886.

The early history of the Lady Eleanor Holles School is similar. Lady

Eleanor died in 1708, leaving her cousin, Anne Watson, to administer her estate, and directing that when all the bequests had been settled any 'overplus' should be invested and used for charitable purposes. Mistress Watson, having made prudent investments in land and property in London, decided to use the income to found a charity school for fifty poor girls, and in 1711 this opened in three rooms owned by the Cripplegate Boys' School in Redcross Street. The girls, who entered the school at eight and left at fourteen, were provided with a distinctive uniform (which seems to have remained unchanged until 1875) and were taught to spell, to read and to sew. (Of the £770 which covered the school's annual expenses in the early days, £300 was spent on clothing.) In 1845 a master was appointed to teach writing and arithmetic, and by 1850 history and geography had been added. The children attended service twice on Sundays at St Giles, Cripplegate, occupying a special gallery (which it was their duty to clean) and wearing their best uniform which they had to collect from the school on Saturdays.

In the 1870s educational needs were changing. Apart from the fact that the Cripplegate area was now far less of a residential area, the Board of Education was taking over responsibility for elementary schools, and the mid-Victorian mood was for better secondary education for girls. A 'middle-class' school was therefore opened in Hackney (then a pleasant suburb) in 1878, and the Redcross Street school kept for elementary pupils. The Cripplegate school finally closed in 1899 because of a dearth of pupils, a difficulty which was thirty years later to afflict the Lady Eleanor Holles secondary school, as Hackney became increasingly industrial and there were too few children for its schools. It was decided to re-establish the school far to the west, at Hampton, Middlesex, and in 1936 it left the old premises for temporary ones in Teddington, until the new buildings were ready in 1937.

That Lady Eleanor Holles could become a secondary school as early as 1878 is due to the fact that there was no boys' school on the foundation to take priority. Where there was, the history was very different. Take the case of the Merchant Taylors' School at Crosby, near Liverpool, for instance. The boys' school of this name had been founded early in the seventeenth century, from money left by a John Harrison to the Merchant Taylors in London to provide 'one free Grammar School for the teaching, educating and instructing of youth in the grammar and rules of learning, for ever, which shall be called by the name of "The Merchant Taylors' School", founded at the charge of John Harrison'. In this case it was laid down that by 'youth' 'male children only' was intended; however, the Taunton Commission's recommendation that girls' secondary schools, modelled upon the North London Collegiate founded in 1850, should be set up in all large towns, and the Endowed Schools Act of 1869 which empowered foundations to use their resources for this purpose, made the Merchant Taylors reflect. The boys' school at Crosby was bursting out of its old premises and needed new ones. Why not put girls into the old building? In 1874 it was formally resolved that this should be, and that three fifths of the income should be devoted to the education of the boys, two fifths to the girls. In 1878 the boys were moved to their new building. But the governors were heavily in debt and there was no money to adapt the old building for girls. They took legal advice and were told, to their infinite relief, that they could not be held 'chargeable with neglect of duty' if they postponed the establishment of a girls' school until they were in better financial health. Nor did they particularly wish this, it seems, and six years passed in which nothing whatever was done. In 1884 the Master of the Merchant Taylors Company himself tried to stir them up; the governors roused themselves sufficiently to have the building surveyed and estimates for alterations prepared. When it was decided that these would be extensive, the governors again felt profound relief and, though a committee had suggested borrowing the necessary money, they decided to do nothing until £1,000 had accumulated in the school's account. It was not until 1888 that the building was finally put in order, a headmistress appointed and the school opened.[28]

The Perse School in Cambridge moved even more slowly, but having started earlier was able to launch its girls' school seven years ahead of the Merchant Taylors'. Stephen Perse, born 1548, a Cambridge physician, had left in 1615 a parcel of land to endow 'a Grammar Free School'. After some two centuries of providing for boys, the governors began to have scruples and in 1837 a scheme was drawn up with new regulations to appropriate part of the income for the education of girls, and to let it accumulate until there was enough to provide buildings and accommodation for not less than fifty pupils. That consideration should have been given to girls' education so early is interesting – it was many years before reformers such as Emily Davies began to agitate for a better deal for women. But the finance was complicated and the resources limited, and it was not until 1873, prompted by the Endowed Schools Act of four years earlier, that a new scheme for the Perse School was drawn up which included provision for a girls' school. Little seems to have happened until 9 July 1881, when the governors applied to the Charity Commissioners for permission to appoint managers for the girls' school at once. This was granted on 6 August – the speed seems little short of miraculous when one considers that this was the middle of the Long Vacation – and the governors immediately set to work to appoint managers and find premises and staff. The school opened on 17 January 1882, with fifty pupils in a town house in Trumpington Street. Its first headmistress valiantly battled through those early terms with only three assistants (one of whom taught the kindergarten).

From the beginning, money was a serious problem; the history of the early struggles of the Perse to finance the new venture is typical of what many similar foundations were facing, and of the very small sums available. The Charity Commissioners had stipulated that £500 should be raised as an advance fund for initial expenses. £466 8s was subscribed, but out of this nine months' rent had to be found. The Perse Foundation was far from wealthy; they held the Manor of Frating (two farms and about 150 acres) and £6,228 2s 1d in Consols, but out of this £150 a year, or in lieu of it one quarter of the total income, was to be paid to the girls' school. But even this could not be wholly relied upon. The Frating property was sold in 1913 to buy a site opposite the boys' school and, though it had been originally valued at £20,000, it had depreciated considerably. Thus the state of the finances for a long time made it impossible to pay the full contribution to the girls' school. It was not until 1918 that the foundation, by altering its constitution, became eligible for a Board of Education grant, and dizzy with excitement at the prospect of at last having money in the bank, built itself an assembly hall (supposed to be temporary, but it lasted until 1950 when it gave way to the present one). Science rooms followed three years later and salaries were raised to the level paid at LEA schools.[29] Even now, while the academic achievement is as high as any school in the country, they are desperately short of space and housed in wholly inappropriate buildings, like 'student digs', as the *Good Schools Guide* put it.

In general, even when the governors of the ancient foundations were sympathetic to the cause of women's education (and many of them thought it was against nature, or at best of unproven value), they did not see how money could be spared from their boys. Where it was, there was often deep resentment. One master at King Edward School in Birmingham – where the boys were called upon to squeeze themselves into very confined quarters to make room for the new girls' school that opened in 1883 – adapting the words of Caligula, wished that 'all the girls of Birmingham had but one neck, and that had a rope round it'.[30] Leeds, the second-richest boys' grammar school in Yorkshire, told the Endowed Schools Commissioners dismissively that their income would all be needed for the proper support of their school. Dr Bartrum, the headmaster of Berkhamsted, returned a softer answer: 'I think we ought to be just to the boys before we are generous to the girls.'[31] Berkhamsted was an Elizabethan foundation that had just managed, after furious local opposition, to reduce the number of free scholars and to take in boarders, and Dr Bartrum did not see why the boys should be plundered of the swimming bath, fives court, carpenter's shop and smithy, reading room and library, museum and gymnasium that he considered was their due, and which would the better transform a country grammar school into a minor public school. Though it was agreed that £250 per annum should be provided for the secondary education of girls, it was settled that the governors should not apply to the Charity Commissioners until they felt ready to proceed. This took them ten years, and it was not until May 1888 that the girls' school could open.

The City livery companies often administered funds left by private benefactors for educational purposes. Some moved fairly swiftly after the Endowed Schools Act. The Haberdashers, for instance, who had used

Robert Aske's seventeenth-century benefaction for the provision of an almshouse and a boys' school, in 1874 enlarged the school buildings to take in three hundred girls. They also administered the estate of William Jones, who had died in 1615 leaving money to establish a 'free school' in Monmouth. Out of this bequest sprang Monmouth Grammar School, but proposals in 1890 to apply surplus income from the Jones bequest to the establishment of a girls' school met with local opposition; it was thought that the money should be spent on more almshouses rather than a school for the 'well-to-do'. (In fact, when the school opened in 1892, the fees were only £6 per annum and over a third of the pupils had scholarships or free places.) The most notable delay was with St Paul's, where in spite of the Endowed Schools Act the Mercers' Company managed to delay setting up a girls' school on Dean Colet's foundation (provided in 1509) until 1904, so that the school commonly held to be the most formidable of all the high schools, and certainly the one with the greatest self-esteem, was among the last to be founded. But the Mercers, for all the delay, provided handsomely in the end, and the spacious solidity of this Queen Anne-style building facing Brook Green in Hammersmith stands in marked contrast to the often ramshackle assortment of extensions that have grown up around high schools founded earlier but without a City company as benevolent patron.

There is one last school which, uniquely, can claim a Victorian benefactor in the style of the philanthropists of the past. This is the City of London School for Girls, which was established by the Corporation of London, following the wishes of William Ward, a coal merchant, who in 1881 left £20,000, a third of his fortune, for a girls' school corresponding as nearly as possible to the City of London School for Boys; 'making all proper allowances for the difference of the sexes [the school] shall provide for the religious and virtuous education of girls, and for instructing them in the higher branches of literature and all other useful learning'. This school, which opened in Carmelite Street near the Victoria Embankment in 1894, moved in 1969 to possibly the most spectacular position of any school – the Barbican where, said one awe-struck pupil, 'we had visions of a paradise of unlimited space, equipped with every conceivable facility . . . I remember a resolution made to work hard under these newer, easier conditions . . . the promises made seeing the gym and swimming pool (never kept!)'.[32]

Boarding Schools for the Middle Classes

The charity hospitals, as has been seen, originally provided elementary schooling for the poorest, as an alternative to the streets or the workhouse, and gradually during the Victorian period introduced secondary education. But there were girls from higher ranks in society whose predicament was almost as acute – children of huge clergy families where the father, like Trollope's Mr Crawley, scarcely knew even how to find food for them;

missionaries' children with their parents thousands of miles away; orphaned daughters of serving officers. As with the paupers on parish relief, in so many of these cases of genteel poverty the problem was the over-large family. In 1697 John Locke had pointed out how unwanted children were responsible for so much of the national deficit.[33] He thought that the ordinary labouring man and his wife could support two children, but most had far more and the parish had to take them over. Similarly, private charity had to come to the rescue of professional parents with families larger than they wanted or could cope with. One child of eleven, for instance, who applied for admission to the Royal School for Officers' Daughters in the 1860s, had six brothers and a sister and her mother's income was only £410 a year (her father, a colonel, had died of heat apoplexy in India after thirty-six years' service). Another was one of a family of nine; her father, a captain, was still alive but there was an invalid mother (probably worn out by repeated pregnancy) and an income of only £480. But even this was large beside the income of the poorer clergy, who might have to struggle to raise a family on £50 a year.

Schools were therefore needed to support these children, some of whom were 'pennyless' as the Adult Orphan Institution (now Princess Helena's) said sadly, and equip them to be governesses. In the days of rigid class stratification there was no place they could be taught except at an establishment that contained their own kind; from a brouhaha at the Royal School in the 1890s, one gets some idea of the horror that the professional classes felt at the idea of associating with those lower down even the middle-class scale. Parents had been complaining that the fathers of some of the pupils at this school for army officers' daughters had risen from the ranks, and the Duke of Cambridge, then the president, had to be called in to admonish the protesters; it was the school's duty, he told them, to accept the highest and lowest 'on the same candid and friendly footing as if they were all in the highest classes of society'. Initially it was fairly easy to drum up support for these hapless young things of gentle birth, though much more difficult to sustain it after the first flush of generosity. Altruistic clergy like the Revd William Carus Wilson, committees of well disposed ladies, brother officers – all set to work to find subscribers, with the backing of bishops, generals, admirals, sometimes royalty. Most of these schools came into being in the last century, but two were eighteenth-century foundations – the Godolphin School in Salisbury, which arose out of a benefaction made by Charles and Elizabeth Godolphin in 1707, and the Clergy Orphan Girls' School (now St Margaret's, Bushey) in St John's Wood, founded in 1749. Other clergy daughters' schools were founded in the next century: at Cowan Bridge – Charlotte Bronte's 'Lowood', now Casterton School; St Mary's Hall, Brighton, which was inspired by it; and St Brandon's in Gloucester. Missionary schools included St Michael's, Limpsfield (originally the Church Missionaries' Children's Home), and Walthamstow Hall. The Adult Orphan

Institution took clergy orphans and the daughters of serving officers and trained them to be governesses; and there were the Royal Naval School and the Royal School for Officers' Daughters. The two Howell's schools in Wales are in a category by themselves: opened in 1860 out of funds left by a Tudor merchant, they did not specify any particular social class or profession as the recipients of their charity.

None of the schools produced educational pioneers; as we noted earlier, the longer the establishments had been founded the less likely they were to be innovative. They were saddled with boards of trustees who were unwilling to change, and who were perennially anxious about money and thus unwilling to tempt providence by taking steps that might lose them subscribers. In any case, they encountered the same problem that had faced the charity hospitals when women's education came to be taken seriously: do you concentrate on providing a good education or on relieving distress? Do you consider children's need or their potential? The dilemma of the Royal School at Lansdown, Bath, illustrates the point.

It had opened in 1865, twenty-five years after its sister, the Royal Naval School, had come into being. The initial prospectus stated that the object of the 'Military Female School' was 'to bestow upon the Daughters of necessitous officers of the Army, at the lowest possible cost [a point that the Royal Naval School had also made], a good, virtuous and religious Education, in conformity with the principles and doctrines of the Church of England'.[34] (This last clause was to upset some supporters, and occasion a rebuke from the Prince of Wales, as it excluded Roman Catholics, who after all were members of the British army and were being admitted to Wellington, the school for officers' sons.) There were to be two classes of pupils: those who would only pay nominal fees (initially £12 a year), and those of 'competent means' who would pay £50. There was a junior establishment, Clarence House at Roehampton, where girls stayed until they were fourteen and were ready to move on to Lansdown. Joshua Fitch, who inspected both schools in 1875, was appalled at the antiquated system of teaching at Clarence House and the meagre educational attainments of the girls, who were accepted often without the most elementary schooling. He thought that girls who did not reach the required standard for Lansdown should be asked to leave; that since the object of the school was to help impoverished girls, then a liberal education was the best substitute for a fortune; and that in the long term 'the truest charity consisted of making the school a first-class place of learning', even if it meant excluding unsatisfactory pupils.

But this was a nettle that the administration could not bring itself to grasp. They may of course have had the case of Wellington in mind. This school, having listened to the criticism of the inspectors, had imposed an entrance exam, whereupon they were faced with such outrage and indignation from parents and subscribers that a Royal Commission was appointed in 1880 to investigate the matter. The Royal School went no further than telling parents in 1878 that they must prepare children better and that they should be 'not so far neglected as to be unfit to be classified with pupils of like age'. The inspectors who succeeded Joshua Fitch were to fulminate about the way army parents shrugged off their responsibilities, leaving daughters to begin their elementary education when they arrived at school at twelve, thirteen or fourteen (though in fairness to the army it has to be said that most of the high schools also recorded the problem of ill prepared pupils). It was a battle of ideals, between Mr Fitch and his kind who felt that the primary purpose of a girls' school was to turn out well educated women, and the tender-hearted who thought of the school at Bath as a refuge for the destitute daughters of their comrades-in-arms, and who held that the only desideratum was that they should become gentlewomen fit to be officers' wives. The Royal Naval School seems to have been much firmer. Early reports to the subscribers suggest that they were having difficulty with girls who had been badly prepared; when in 1872 it was pointed out that 'the admission of numerous very backward pupils will seriously delay the progress of others', the basic requirements (in most respects well below the present Common Entrance) for different ages were set out.[35] But even into recent times the Royal School continued to be bedevilled by the problem of low academic standards.

Most of the middle-class charity schools were in effect at the mercy of their subscribers, and all had anxious moments when funds were at a low ebb. The clergy daughters' school at Cowan Bridge, in particular, started in a very small way and had the added disadvantage of being sited in a remote part of north-west England, where Carus Wilson had his parish, and from which fund-raising was clearly difficult. As with other charitable foundations of its kind, the situation did not really become stable until the greater proportion of the pupils were paying fees at an economic level.

In the early days royal patrons could be a great help; the Adult Orphan Institution, founded in 1820, persuaded Princess Augusta, daughter of George III, to take an interest. They followed this up by working some embroidered ruffles, which they presented to George IV who had succeeded his father that year, and in return he subscribed £100 a year to the Institution. But their most enthusiastic royal patron was Princess Helena, third daughter of Queen Victoria. She was associated with the school for fifty-five years, for forty-three of which she was an active and devoted president of the board of governors. The school took on her name in 1879 and – an unusual distinction for a girls' school – was granted a royal charter of incorporation in 1886.

The Clergy Orphan Girls' School in St John's Wood (founded in 1749) received support from George III and another of his daughters, Princess Amelia. As well as ordinary subscriptions, there were unexpected donations like 'a portion of the offerings of the Knights of Bath at their installation in Westminster Abbey' (1787) and 'three shares in a Lottery Ticket sent by the post' (1801).[36] The Royal Naval School was always blessed with royal patrons: their presidents have included two monarchs, two royal dukes and one duchess, and Lord Mountbatten. These connections have brought in treats as well – George V gave them seats near Buckingham Palace for his coronation procession, and as Prince of Wales he had sent the school his birthday cake.

The Royal School at Bath struck lucky with the Duke of Cambridge (1819–1904), great-nephew of George III, a genial character who took a great interest. Not only did he 'drop into the City', as he termed it, to enlist the aid of City livery companies at a particularly lean time, but he also visited the school and bespoke holidays for the pupils. (It is recorded that the girls decorated the stairs with old-man's-beard, saying affectionately that it reminded them of his white whiskers.) Even the Clergy Daughters' School, remote on the borders of Westmorland, managed to secure a visit from Queen Adelaide, widow of William IV, who had been their patron since 1837. On a visit to Kirkby Lonsdale in 1840 there was a mishap to her carriage; the dowager was led to the school, and the chair she sat in is still treasured.

Subscriptions apart, there was a great deal of what might be termed sociable fund-raising. The Royal School tried 'Military Musical Services'. The first such event at St Paul's was so expensive to mount that there was little money left over, and the second one at Westminster Abbey brought in only £89. So they turned to bazaars, raising a few thousand pounds, enough to wipe off their debt. In 1879 Walthamstow Hall, in order to find money to build themselves a new school in Sevenoaks, held a 'Great Fancy Bazaar' at the Cannon Street Hotel. It lasted for four days; the hall was decorated 'like a Japanese village', the girls wore mob-caps and aprons, and Haydn's Toy Symphony was performed. £2,700 was raised.[37] But life for schools that could neither draw on endowments nor charge adequate fees was precarious. They had not the means to expand and thus attract fee-payers, nor could they afford to pay their staff properly, and the fact that they survived at all says much for the devotion and enthusiasm of headmistresses. Ultimately nearly all of them had to take the painful decision to shed old traditions on which much store, rightly or wrongly, had been set. Walthamstow Hall, for instance, after 1921 could no longer afford to keep itself as a private boarding school for missionaries' daughters; it applied for a grant from Kent Education Committee and agreed in return to take a quota of free-place day-pupils from local elementary schools. Most of those connected with the school were later to accept that this development was a good one; not only could the quality of the education be improved now that there was no financial anxiety, but the boarders benefited from the wider contacts. Nevertheless the break with the intentions of the founders must have given distress.

Three schools, however, did not have to face this sort of problem – the

Godolphin, and the two Howell's schools in Wales, which both had ancient endowments behind them. The Godolphin School seems to be unique among the Queen Anne charities in providing for the well born orphan, and therefore can be said to have changed less than any of its contemporaries. Charles and Elizabeth Godolphin, carrying out the request of their uncle, Sir William Godolphin, had made provision for the education of 'eight young gentlewomen between the ages of eight and nineteen, daughters of members of the Church of England whose fortunes did not exceed 300 l'.[38] They must be without either father or mother, and were to be brought up in Salisbury or some other town in Wiltshire, and taught to dance, work, speak French, cast accounts, understand housewifery and attend the services of the Church of England. Though Elizabeth Godolphin died in 1726 the school did not open until 1784, by which time the original scheme had been modified. By the time the Endowed Schools Commissioner visited it in the 1860s it had expanded to take in twelve orphans, and there were also twelve fee-paying young ladies. The school, with some three hundred pupils, still makes provision for orphans, offering six foundation scholarships (at 30 per cent of the fees) to girls who have lost one or both parents, though now the loss can cover separation and divorce, as well as death.

The two Howell's schools, as we noted earlier, spring out of a much older charity, and their history is an interesting illustration of how benefactions have to adapt themselves to changing social circumstances. Thomas Howell was born in Bristol in the late fifteenth century. He had business connections with Spain where he spent the latter part of his life, but for a time he lived in London and became a member of the Drapers' Company. His third and last will left 12,000 Spanish ducats to be held in trust by the Drapers' Company for dowries for orphan girls, priority to be given to Howell kin. It was a difficult benefaction for the Drapers to administer, and they were faced with many fraudulent claims; not the least of their difficulties was to discover where the Howell family had originated. The gentry of Monmouth managed to convince them that their county had the best claim, and in the succeeding three hundred years 1,208 orphans, mostly from Monmouth, did receive dowries, though not all of them were orphans and the kinship was elusive.[39]

But by the 1840s the position had changed. The charity was prospering, possessing valuable property in the City and an income of £2,000, the only outgoings being four annual dowries of £21 apiece. The Charity Commissioners ordered an investigation of the trust, and the Master of the Rolls pronounced in 1845 that the whole of the income must be used for charitable purposes. The Drapers therefore decided to establish two schools for orphans, and to site them in Wales, one in the south and one in the north. After tremendous local campaigning, Llandaff, on the outskirts of Cardiff, secured the former, and Denbigh the latter. The account of how these schools were set up is fascinatingly different from most of the charitable beginnings that have so far been described. Everything was on a very much more lavish scale: to begin with, the architectural plans for Llandaff were drawn up by Decimus Burton – admittedly after much bickering and acrimony, and he only got half the fee he asked for. (The building is a strange pot-pourri of different periods and styles: mediaeval and Tudor, English and French with perhaps a touch of German, at the same time representing what mid-Victorians considered appropriate for institutional use.) The premises were well equipped, and the Drapers had allotted £50 for laying out 'the Pleasure Grounds': thus there was a children's playground with a swing, and the staff had an elegant garden with lawn, shrubberies, roses and seats. There was a library (a most unusual feature), and plenty of pianos (it had been very hard for the committee that ran the Royal Masonic Institution to see the need for these), as well as a lavishly equipped kitchen. And there were sixty umbrellas for the children, as well as all the clothes that the foundation provided for them.

The two schools opened in 1860, with orphans and 'Pay Boarders'. The orphans would be entirely supported by the foundation for ten out of each twelve months, they would receive a good education, and when they left at seventeen could claim a dowry of £100 (ten times what the hospital children received) if their character and conduct were unblemished. Most unusually for the time, the foundation did not specify any particular rank in society , or profession; it is evident that at the beginning they got some fairly rough diamonds, and that manners and behaviour were not all they might have been. The first entry had been mostly children of small shopkeepers, clerks and farmers – and this was true of both 'Pay Boarders' and orphans – (in the Woodard Foundation this would have made it a 'middle school'). They were given a sound secondary education, nevertheless, and taught 'the Principles of the Christian Religion, Reading, Writing, Arithmetic, English Grammar, Geography, Biography, History, the Elements of Astronomy, Garden Botany, Music, French and Drawing'. But by the 1870s there was a marked change: clergy and army officers' daughters were taking up the places, and it seems that the governors' policy was to favour girls from 'homes where the refinements of the curriculum would be properly appreciated'.[40] Howell's had ceased to be thought of as a charity foundation.

What one also notices is the consideration with which the children were treated, strikingly different from the hospitals and from establishments like Carus Wilson's clergy daughters' school. This applied more to the Llandaff school than the Denbigh one, where an unlucky first appointment to the post of chief matron brought with it grave disorder and indiscipline. (The Schools Inquiry Commission noted 'the unfitness of the late headmistress for her position', which had had 'a most injurious effect upon [the girls'] moral character'.) But at Llandaff Miss Emily Baldwin – she had run a successful school of her own at Notting Hill – was on the children's side. It was she who realized that the children were far too young to make their own clothes in hospital fashion (which was what the Drapers had originally intended), and after a few years she insisted on prettier and more fashionable garments. She saw to it that there was good and appetizing food, storybooks in the library, carpets in the dormitories, bedding plants in the gardens. Discipline was strict – her counterpart at Denbigh, by contrast, was unable to cope with either staff or children – but that was the style of the times, and everything ran with admirable precision. The little girls were equipped with hoops, battledores and shuttlecocks, and skipping ropes, and as the architect's plans had provided for two large day-rooms (they occupied more space than the classrooms, in fact), there was plenty of room for recreation, even when it was wet. There were occasional festivities and entertainments to break the routine, and the children's 'Next Friends' (next of kin) were allowed to visit them one afternoon a month.

St Mary's Hall in Brighton for clergy daughters, which the Revd Henry Venn Elliott initiated in admiring imitation of his friend the Revd William Carus Wilson's similar establishment in the north, also seems to have been a friendly place. (It is notable for occupying the same buildings in which it started, most unusual for a girls' school of that age.) It opened in 1836 after three years of zealous fund-raising by Mr Elliott. His enthusiasm seems to have touched many: the Marquess of Bristol gave land, and the architect George Basevi made a gift of the plans. And one has to admire the courage and generosity of men like Elliott and Carus Wilson, who in pursuit of their ideal rallied supporters, lobbied the wealthy, dipped deep into their pockets, and devoted large tracts of their time not only to fund-raising but to administration. St Mary's was intended as 'a nursery for governesses for the higher and middle classes', and with rather more prosperous clergy families in mind than at Carus Wilson's school the fees were fixed initially at £20 per annum. For this girls would be boarded and partly clothed, and educated – they would be taught French and elementary music (drawing and more advanced music being charged as an extra). Though there was a board of eight trustees, the management was effectively in the founder's hands. He was an almost daily and always welcome visitor at the school, and though his fortnightly divinity lectures might include mild admonition of some fault he had noticed, he was a sympathetic presence, loved rather than feared; indeed, it is recorded that children were sometimes naughty on purpose, so that they could be summoned into his presence. He invited pupils to tea, played games with the younger, read to the older, and showed them his collections of curiosities.

The Revd the Hon. Horace Powys, who presided over the foundation of St Elphin's in Warrington, was of the same sort. This school for clergy daughters which opened in 1844 (taking its name from the Warrington parish church) owed much to Powys (later to become Bishop of Sodor and

Man), who contributed well over £4,000 out of his own pocket towards the building, furnishing and running of the school. He was evidently a merry little man who tested the service lift to the dining-room by coming up in it himself, to the delight of the children.[41] But Warrington grew increasingly industrial, and an outbreak of scarlet fever finally drove it in 1904 from its handsome Jacobean-style premises to Darley Dale Hydro, near Matlock. As a hydro, it was comparatively easily adapted to school use; it had the additional advantage of being set in beautiful grounds in glorious country.

All this is in great contrast to the Clergy Daughters' School that William Carus Wilson had set up at Cowan Bridge in 1824. The grimness of this establishment in its early years seems partly due to the Calvinism of its founder, which saw evil in what many would have regarded as innocent pleasures; to its situation in one of the bleakest and wettest parts of the United Kingdom; and to its remoteness, which caused a rapid turnover of staff. Since it was aiming to help the poorest clergy of all, the fees were set at £14 (in 1861 they had still not increased) to cover board, education and clothing, which meant that much must have had to come out of the founder's own pocket. In the end, though, his abrasive, high-handed manner made enemies, and among these was Charlotte Brontë. Many girls loathe their schools and carry their resentment of past humiliation and injustice even into old age, but few can have made such an issue of her grievances as she did. Mrs Gaskell herself, who was to make another very damaging attack on Cowan Bridge ten years after *Jane Eyre*, admitted it was hard that the errors Carus Wilson was supposed to have committed 'should have been brought up against him in a form which received such wonderful force from the touch of Miss Brontë's great genius'.[42]

William Carus Wilson was a clergyman of generous impulses, furious energy and overbearing temperament. Both Charlotte Brontë's and Mrs Gaskell's accounts of him were hostile – Mrs Gaskell, indeed, had to tone down passages in later editions of her life of Charlotte Brontë. But to anyone who knows the hectoring severity of Wilson's little Sunday school magazine, the *Children's Friend*, with its morbid, even prurient, catalogue of fatal accidents and divine punishments for naughty children ('in love to her poor little soul, [the Lord] caused the candle to set fire to her clothes'), the picture of Mr Brocklehurst may not seem a caricature, though Charlotte Brontë chose to ignore, or indeed may not have known, how much the school depended upon his financial generosity. He came of a Westmorland family of landed gentry, and in 1820 he had already established Lowood,* a charity school to train girls for domestic service. (Surprisingly for a school so limited in its aims, this survived until 1921, when it merged with the Clergy Daughters' School and the two became Casterton.) Then, conscious of the plight of fellow clergy of more limited means – there were many

* The name Charlotte Brontë was to give to the school in *Jane Eyre*.

whose income was less than £100 – he determined to provide their daughters with 'that plain and useful education which may fit them to return with respectability to their own homes, or to maintain themselves in the different stations to which Providence should call them'. There was already the St John's Wood Clergy Orphan Girls' School, and the Adult Orphan Institution in Regent's Park took a few clergy daughters; obviously, one was needed in the north, and casting around for a suitable place he settled upon Cowan Bridge, a hamlet in his own parish of Tunstall. Here he bought and enlarged an existing building to accommodate sixty children. The Cowan Bridge situation was later thought to be unhealthy (it was low-lying, and the drainage was no doubt inadequate), and in 1832 the school, by this time numbering ninety children from four to eighteen, was moved to Casterton. The fees were minimal, as mentioned earlier, and for this the children had to be housed for most of the year (the vacations were short, and some – such as missionaries' daughters – never left). So money had to be raised by subscription, though Wilson himself met much of the initial cost from his own pocket, and in the early days there was often financial anxiety.

Four Brontë sisters: Maria (born 1813), Elizabeth (born 1814), Charlotte (born 1816) and Emily (born 1818) were dispatched to the school at Cowan Bridge during its first year. Maria and Elizabeth, who had arrived weakened by whooping cough, died of consumption at home the following year. Mrs Gaskell attributed this to the spartan regime at the school, seemingly unaware of how high the death-rate from consumption was then at all schools, particularly the charity hospitals. Certainly, a strong physique would have been needed to endure the conditions, and the sisters were already delicate and consumptive. But though the location of the Cowan Bridge school, remote and surrounded by moorland, was particularly desolate in the winter, the cold and the poor food, the overcrowding and the shared beds, the relentless hours of lessons and absence of recreation were all characteristic of girls' schools well beyond that period.

The daily routine at the Adult Orphan Institution indeed seemed more taxing, with two hours of evening lessons from 6 until 8 o'clock on such subjects as arithmetic, history and chronology, geography and the globes. The early rising was nothing out of the ordinary, nor were the lessons before breakfast, the meals which consisted mostly of bread, and the punishments which sought to humiliate offenders (in *Jane Eyre* Helen Burns is made to wear a label saying 'slattern'). And the incident where Mr Brocklehurst demands that the girls with naturally curly hair must have it off had plenty of parallels in schools that insisted, even in this century, that curls were an affront to decorum and hair must be tightly strained back from the face. The headmistress of a Liverpool school in the 1930s, outraged by frizzy hair, would send offending girls to the cloakroom to wet it and tie it back with tape.[43] Where Carus Wilson's school seems different is in the severity of the punishments; corporal punishment for girls was most unusual, except at charity hospitals, but Charlotte Brontë had testified that Helen Burns (that is, her sister Maria) was birched, and another girl who had been at the school remembered that the younger girls were birched and the older ones locked up in an iron cage, or in a cupboard under the stairs (where the ventilation holes can still be seen).[44] And the repressive tone of the school is epitomized in the story of the fruit trees, planted to provide shade in the bleak garden. They flourished and bore fruit, but the girls were tempted to eat it and so the trees were cut down.

The most sombre account of the school, however, comes not from Charlotte Brontë nor from Mrs Gaskell but from Dorothea Beale, who taught there for a year in 1857. Those who knew her were doubtful whether her move to Westmorland was prudent; she was High Church and had spent seven years in the intellectually stimulating climate of Queen's College, Harley Street, the pioneer establishment for women's education. Nor was she used to boarding schools. As head teacher at the Clergy Daughters' School she found herself expected to teach scripture, arithmetic, mathematics, ancient, modern and Church history, physical and political geography, English literature, grammar and composition, French, German, Latin and Italian. But this was not the burden of her complaint. What she disliked was the Calvinistic atmosphere imposed on the school by its founder: 'its direct results on the education of the young were disastrous indeed. Hearts, by its agency, were turned to stone, or depressed into hopeless terror; worst of all, religious forms, phraseology, even emotions were assumed by those who were prone to self-deception, or over-anxious to please.'[45] She had found the school in 'an unhealthy state. There was a spirit of open irreligion and a spirit of defiance very sad to witness; but the constant restraints, the monotonous life, the want of healthy amusements were in great measure answerable for this.' She thought the school was too isolated, and the conventual atmosphere, the absence of family life and lack of contact with the outside world led to 'absurd worship of their teachers and to various extravagances'. The first headmaster of the re-established Merchant Maiden school said the same of the hospital system, and spoke of 'the want of ventilation ... They were so walled in and made impervious to outside influences, that bad customs and bad traditions lurked there and polluted the atmosphere.'[46]

Neither he nor Miss Beale at that stage of her life was experienced in the way of girls' boarding schools. They were then, and for many years to come, habitually conventual, since contact with the outside world could produce contagion both moral and physical, though it was the charitable foundations with very restricted vacations that suffered most. And it has to be remembered that the shadow of epidemics hung over all schools in the days before antibiotics; scarlet fever and diphtheria could kill a school as well as the pupils, and the Clergy Daughters' School suffered two serious outbreaks, one at Cowan Bridge of 'low fever'* and one of typhus in 1839 after they had moved to Casterton. Those early Victorian years were bad ones for the school; there was a rapid turnover of lady superintendents and head teachers – nine in five years – and the publication of *Jane Eyre* in 1847 was to bring much undeserved notoriety. Mrs Gaskell's attacks on the school in her life of Charlotte Brontë, in 1857, caused further trouble.

Wilson took a profound – perhaps too profound – interest in the school. He was capable of generous acts – he maintained a house by the sea, for instance, to which pupils in need of a holiday were taken (after being purged with senna and castor oil to prepare them for the journey); but he could not forbear meddling even in small domestic matters, and when he was for health reasons obliged to move south his assumption that his son-in-law would take office in his stead as school chaplain and member of the management committee caused furious dissension.

With a sad irony, the school did not begin to emerge into more tranquil waters until the death of its founder in 1859. This coincided with the appointment of a vigorous lady superintendent who was to stay thirty years, and a fund in memory of Carus Wilson which brought in much-needed money for additions and improvements to the buildings. At last there could be a playroom, for instance (admittedly in the cellar), for the younger children. The discipline remained very strict, however, and only one day a year (Saturdays, and of course Sundays, being as highly regulated as any other day) were the children relatively unsupervised. This was on the superintendent's birthday, when they were allowed to wear their own clothes and roam the grounds by themselves. Otherwise, the monotony of the timetable was unbroken by any extraneous events. When the next superintendent was appointed it was with a commission to relax the discipline, though even in 1913 the Board of Education inspectors were murmuring to the trustees that 'the early Victorian atmosphere still clings to the place'. With the amalgamation in 1921 of the Clergy Daughters' School with Lowood, the servants' school, Casterton moved out of the conventual seclusion about which Miss Beale had complained so long before. (As with so many schools, it was not finally shed until the 1960s). Casterton was not opened to children of lay parents, and as with all similar charities the fees to the clergy children have had to be increased to as much as half the normal rate, and the number of clergy places reduced (by 1963 there were only twenty-five in a school of 210); only thus could any sort of financial stability be achieved. It should be added as a postscript that, with a fine spirit of forgiveness, in 1921 Casterton named its junior school Brontë.

Casterton in its early days had taken many missionaries' children. With

* It has been suggested in Geoffrey Sale's history of the school that this disease was lethargic encephalitis.

parents in distant countries, their need for a home as well as education was as great as anyone's. The *Juvenile Missionary Magazine* said in 1844: 'parents have had to watch with anguish over the pallid looks and fading strength of their endeared offspring; and to commit them to an early tomb. The sweetest little buds of hope have withered away.' At St Michael's, Limpsfield, at least families did not have to be separated. Founded for children of missionaries of the Church Missionary Society, it began life in Highgate in 1850, taking both boys and girls, often very young: 'I was quite happy as I was in the care of my elder brother, aged five,' said one child.[47] But this was an unusual arrangement, and the sexes were normally divided. Walthamstow Hall, for instance, took missionaries' daughters, and Eltham College their sons. Indeed, in such abhorrence was the male sex held at Walthamstow that a special minute was recorded that 'no lady having sons shall be considered eligible for a resident post in the school'. It had begun in 1838, with five little girls in Marsh Street, Walthamstow, then 'a charming village, five miles from London'. Childen could enter at five and leave at seventeen, and though the whole of July was a holiday, and there was a fortnight at Easter, most in the early days stayed at school the whole year round.

At first, life was jolly: the ladies of the management committee were hospitable and took a great interest in the children; there were visits to the Royal Academy, the British Museum and the Crystal Palace and to friends' houses. Moreover, girls were then allowed to meet their brothers once a month and have tea with them. But after the school moved to Kent in 1879, 'we were not allowed to go out to tea for fear of infection'. Nor, later on, were the girls allowed into Sevenoaks to do their shopping. Instead, the headmistress 'added to her multifarious duties by undertaking once or twice a term, to buy in London anything we really wanted. The prefects prepared lists which she scrutinised and took up with her.'[48] (Farthing sweets, which had been such a joy to buy in former days, would not be considered 'real' wants, one fancies.) The first day-girl was not admitted until the Edwardian period – she would have seemed safe, as her mother was an old pupil. One always detects a sense of authority bracing itself anxiously when day-girls were about to be allowed into these enclosed communities.

Walthamstow seems to have been regarded with genuine affection by most, even in the days of iron discipline imposed by a headmistress who 'had no sympathy with wrong-doing; faults that nowadays would be considered as slight were regarded as crimes and severely punished'. Offenders were denounced at the Sunday evening service – but the headmistress nevertheless had enough tenderness to pick up the school baby and seat her on her lap. As at St Michael's, Limpsfield, it was expected that the girls would themselves enter the mission field. Learning was therefore desirable, but not too much, for 'the female character expands best in the shade'.[49]

This was a sentiment that was often repeated in governors' annual reports of the 1840s, the committee feeling that 'there is a danger whenever the female character is drawn from that shady enclosure, which is so favourable to the growth of those meek and quiet graces which are its chief ornament'. In 1844, though exams were held for the first time – these being oral in the manner of the times, and conducted in front of the committee – anything more public was felt to be unwise, since 'adventitious advantages of this nature' could only be purchased 'at the expense of infringing on the quiet and retiring delicacy of that modest refinement which finds its approved sphere within the home circle, and blushes to find itself the object of observation'. But in 1873 pupils were entered for the Cambridge locals, and after that it became a regular practice. Indeed, in the mid-Victorian period Walthamstow Hall must have led all the other charitable foundations, if not most girls' schools, in the variety of careers followed by its former pupils. Of those who were at the school between 1841 and 1878, fifty-seven were teachers, thirty-seven were wives of ministers or missionaries, and eighteen were missionaries; eight were doing clerical work, four were nurses and three were doctors; and there was one milliner, one school matron, and one wood-engraver.

3

The Day School Pioneers

Early Difficulties

'Coming into the school at the age of sixteen I saw its glaring faults and absurdities,' wrote Molly Hughes of North London Collegiate School in 1883.

> The whole seemed to me an elaborate machine for doing the minimum of useful things with the maximum of fuss. I didn't see then, as I saw later, that Miss Buss was faced by a herculean task. The endless anxieties she caused her pupils were as nothing to her own big anxiety. She was a pioneer, and almost single-handed, in getting some kind of systematic education for girls. She had no school to copy, no precedent of any kind.[1]

In the many summaries of the beginnings of higher education for women, these points are often overlooked: the initial over-reaction in the desire to give girls a boys' education; the fact that many people's experience at the early high schools was as disagreeable or tiresome as Molly Hughes's (at least until she reached the sixth form); and the enormous difficulties of running a school of five hundred girls when there were hardly any trained women to staff it. As mentioned earlier, the North London Collegiate School had started off in 1850 as a family venture, like so many girls' schools. Miss Buss's mother taught the younger children, and her father was responsible for elocution, drawing and science – 'His chemistry series was marvellous,' one of the original thirty-five pupils recalled, 'especially for smells and explosions.'[2] And her brothers Alfred and Septimus, both later ordained, took on arithmetic, Latin, drawing and divinity. It so easily could have remained a pleasantly idiosyncratic private school; there have been plenty of these, some of them still in existence, whose influence, often considerable, has been limited to its own pupils. But Miss Buss's ambitions went far beyond that: 'she planned for the future, often with amazing insight, for she realized emancipation was coming in any case, and that plans must be made to prepare for it'.[3]

Frances Buss was one of the nine women to give evidence to the Taunton Commission set up originally in 1864 to inquire into the subject of middle-clas education – others to do so were Dorothea Beale and Emily Davies.

Influenced by their representations, and especially impressed by Miss Buss, the Commission's report was to supplement its strictures on the wretched state of girls' education with a recommendation that schools run on the lines of the North London Collegiate should be founded on the outskirts of every considerable town. That was in 1868, and it was not until the 1880s that the high school movement – the term, said the first headmistress of Manchester High School, was in imitation of Edinburgh High School[4] – could really be said to be in full swing. The North London Collegiate was the mother of them all, and Miss Buss's confidence in her style of education is remarkable in view of the prevailing doubts about women's capacities and the physical damage they might do themselves and their reproductive systems through over-exertion at their lessons. A pupil at Oxford High School in the 1870s recalled the debate then going on about what women's health and brains would stand.

> Skulls were measured, brains weighed, nerves tested, and conclusions were usually accompanied by warnings . . . The more conservative element feared that the rightful place for these new claims was on the programme of anti-religious Liberalism . . . I remember one kind of argument in favour of preserving the *status quo*. It ran, a particular woman might be endowed with great gifts, but she was merely a trustee of these, she must not trade with them, but keep them in a napkin that she might one day hand them on unimpaired to a possible son.[5]

This meant inevitably that there was much anxiety when Cambridge University agreed in 1863, after strenuous campaigning by Emily Davies, to allow girls, as an experiment, to take their local examinations. When the Taunton Commission asked Miss Buss, who had submitted twenty-five candidates out of the ninety-one who sat that first year, whether she thought that the examinations would produce too much mental strain and excitement, and whether she feared vanity or publicity, she vehemently denied that they had any ill effect whatever. What she had noticed was the very businesslike way the girls had worked at their papers, and how they bore the stretch of the examinations: 'I could not detect any flagging of interest or any sign of weariness.' Cheltenham had also by the time of the Commission established its own system, and Oxford academics came down every year to examine the pupils.

The Cambridge Certificate was held to be a very high qualification in the days before it was possible for women to hold university degrees; Elizabeth Day, the first headmistress of Manchester High School, possessed this and was pronounced to be the best-qualified of all the applicants, with distinctions in divinity, French and Greek. Exams and the spirit of competition were from the start taken very seriously by the high schools, though there were exceptions, like the Mary Datchelor School in London which did not enter for any exams until the school passed out of the management of the

Datchelor trustees, the headmistress writing in the 1904 school magazine that working for public exams almost inevitably resulted in 'superficial, i.e., in dishonest work'. The private schools too were wary, and mostly took the convenient view that they were not necessary in a 'really good and well-conducted school'. These were the words of Miss Frances Martin, superintendent of Bedford College School, who also gave evidence to the Commission. She held that schools were fostering future mothers who would be responsible for 'the moral and religious training of the human race', and that no system of exams or certificates could test this.[6]

In fact, of course, schools in the past had habitually devised some form of examination, and the viva voce method practised by charitable foundations seems far more intimidating. It was essentially a public relations exercise in which the children were catechized in a wide array of subjects in front of an audience of their patrons, and financial support might well depend on whether or not these were impressed by the performance. On 24 June 1857, for instance, pupils of the Clergy Orphan Girls' School were examined in a huge array of subjects in front of the Archbishop of Canterbury. The walls were hung with their drawings, and they had to do exercises in French, German, Latin and arithmetic. The *Morning Herald* said that the children displayed 'a clear and expressive manner, intelligence and modesty' and that the exercise closed with 'Rule, Britannia'. Howell's School, Llandaff, held the same sort of function in the early days. Every class was examined and the audience was 'much gratified at the way in which the girls answered the questions'; one visitor spoke of 'the elegant and accomplished manner in which they played duets and sang, and of the purity and refinement of their accents when replying in French'. The 'Prize Day at the College at Llandaff' soon became one of the social functions of the Cardiff year; there was usually a little exhibition of art and needlework to admire, and the schoolroom and dining-room were tastefully decorated with ivy.

The Mount School, York, though not a charity school, from early times held an examination day at midsummer when the governors' committee questioned the whole school publicly. The desks were arranged in rows facing the examiners, each one of whom had a printed question paper. The classes were called up in turn, and any committee member might 'at any promiscuous moment suddenly dart on any girl in the class to read her answer to any particular question'. Though one representative of the Endowed Schools Commission found this sort of system 'highly objectionable' – for it 'tends to destroy delicacy and feeling; at the same time, it makes the boldest and least feminine girls the most likely to succeed' – the Endowed Schools Act of 1869 stipulated that there must be an annual examination of pupils by an outside academic, exemption only being granted if there was a Board of Education inspection, or if pupils were taking approved public exams. By the 1880s these were becoming routine at the day schools, at least; the Mount records the days when pupils were sent to the examination centre at

Leeds. The invigilator was courteous, and anxious that the female candidates should not encounter any hurly-burly. 'Young ladies, your places are by the door, so that you may leave first. I will cough as a signal for you to put up your papers, a few minutes before the general announcement.'

But overriding any fear about possible intellectual strain was fear of the dangerous class mix that must ensue at high schools. This was a time when it was axiomatic that contact with a lower social grade could only affect one's daughter for the worse. Clearly, there were from the start parents who could dismiss this as of less importance than the advantages of a properly structured education. 'The girls were of all social conditions in my time,' said one pupil at Notting Hill High School in the 1870s. 'I sat between the daughter of a publican and the daughter of a laundress, and I never succeeded in beating the former. The daughter of a viscount was at the bottom of the class.'[8] But there were plenty of parents for many decades to come who believed that 'anything in the nature of a pedigree was the best passport to life, and was a treasure to be guarded sacredly. It was better to live frugally in a quiet countryside than to rub shoulders with any sort of mixed crowd.'[9] They dreaded their girls picking up that infection known as 'high school manners'; hockey was one of the obvious stumbling blocks, a rough, unladylike game, conducive to injury and ungainly carriage. However, in 1922 the headmistress of St Paul's (a school that has always prided itself on its nonconformity), instead of enumerating the precautions taken to see that the social classes did not infect each other, could speak of their mingling as a positive advantage, something to be encouraged. She told an interviewer from *Queen* magazine that the school was 'most democratic, girls of very different social ranks sitting side by side and getting to know one another in a natural way that would help lessen the barriers between class and class'.[10] But for this very reason many parents elected to send their girls to schools where they could be confident the barriers would be sacrosanct.

Elizabeth Sewell (1815–1906), the Tractarian novelist who herself ran a small private school for girls, in 1888 set out her objections to the high schools which, she said with distaste, embraced children of every class and prided themselves upon it.[11] She asked if 'social intercourse is really furthered by the participation in intellectual advantages? Is it not true that care is taken to prevent such intercourse?' (Indeed, most Victorian high schools had very strict rules about conversation and friendship.) 'Equality before the law is one thing, social equality another.' Which was precisely the message that Charlotte Yonge, that arbiter of the behaviour of the young person, had for all her girl readers (though she was towards the end of her life to accept that high schools were there to stay). Both ladies, nevertheless, gave support to the promoters of Winchester High School which opened in 1884, but one suspects that while Charlotte Yonge had adjusted her views a little in accordance with changing attitudes, Elizabeth Sewell may have thought that a very different venture was proposed, something nearer to a convent boarding school.

There were plenty of others who condemned social equality as something totally unnatural, if not contrary to God's laws. In the early 1870s, when Emily Davies and Maria Grey were proselytizing on behalf of the National Union for the Education of Girls of all Classes above the Elementary, the organization out of which the Girls' Public Day School Company was to spring, they encountered ferocious opposition over the class-mixing inevitable at large day schools, which indeed was to be a central principle of the movement. The Duchess of Northumberland said she would rather see her daughters 'standing at a wash-tub than pupils in a High School', and the Bishop of Manchester, who had been invited to speak in support of the GPDSC when it was launched in 1872, confounded the organizers by warning the assembly that it would be an illusion to suppose that 'the children of fashionable people would be found sitting with the daughters of their grocers and bakers'.[12]

Another sticking-point for many was the undenominational nature of the new schools, again a GPDSC principle. This was an entirely new idea; even the North London Collegiate and Camden, the sister school, gave religious instruction in accordance with the teaching of the Church of England, though parents might withdraw their daughters from these lessons. Many churchmen (especially the Roman Catholics) deplored secular education. The Church Schools Company which was formed in 1883 subsequently founded several high schools in which they sought to rectify the move towards secularity. Undenominational high schools also meant that Jewish pupils could attend; Chelsea took its first Jewish girl in 1873, the year of its foundation, and there were many at Paddington and Maida Vale.

One of the first pupils at Oxford High School in 1875 could remember the social levelling that had to be accepted. Town had to mix with gown, and even within the university there were different factions; during the Franco-Prussian War of 1870–1, for instance, dons' families divided into two camps: the pro-Germans who carded lint for the German wounded and listened to propaganda against the immoral French, and the pro-French who were regaled in their drawing-rooms with stories about the iniquitous behaviour of the Germans. And there were religious differences, of course. There was one dramatic day when the girls and teachers who lodged at the house of a Balliol don came in tear-stained to morning prayers – from which his children were absent. The headmistress's exhortation that morning referred vaguely and oppressively to the very terrible thing that had befallen the don's family. What this was nobody could guess; some thought a fatal accident, others went further and suggested suicide, even murder. One form mistress enlightened her pupils: Mr Arnold had joined the Church of Rome. With all this went the infiltration of shopkeepers' children into the ranks of those who had never expected to be called upon to meet them socially. This same pupil at Oxford High School, who had been brought up to suppose that all tradesmen cheated, remembered the warfare between the 'university children' and the tradesmen's children, who shouted 'Gentry!' 'with such scorn and contempt as almost to imply *à la lanterne*. "Cads" called back a breathless victim, sprinting for safety. And now gentry and cads were to sit in the same classrooms!'[13] The school made a gallant beginning, staffed by those who had not themselves experienced school life, and who had to discipline a wild element, to fuse hitherto separate groups, and inculcate a corporate spirit and what was generally considered best in public school life.

When one considers the problems faced by the early high schools, the 'wild element' must be taken into consideration. 'Many of the girls who come to us have been allowed to grow up to 13, 14 or even 15 years of age without having done any difficult or serious work,' said the first headmistress of Redland High School, 'and in many cases they leave school for good after spending a year or a year and a half with us and before they have reached a higher form than the 3rd or 4th.'[14] They had to learn that regular attendance was insisted upon. One girl at Bedford High School was overheard saying: 'I never knew anything like this High School! If you go there you've *got* to go, and if they tell you to do a thing, you've *got* to do it.'[15] Most girls would in any case be going back to live at home until they were married. In the list of old members of Whalley Range High School in 1912 it is notable how few former pupils are earning a living.[16] Oxford High School, in an early prospectus, said bravely that the system was

> specially adapted to meet and correct the defects pointed out in the report of the Schools Inquiry Commission: want of thoroughness and foundation; want of system; slovenliness and showy superficiality; inattention to rudiments; undue time given to accomplishments; and these not taught intelligently or in any scientific manner; want of organization. Serious endeavours are made to train the pupils for the practical business and duties of life.

At Oxford the dons' daughters no doubt set the pace – particularly the Max-Müller girls, whose father, a polymath philologist, had a German's faith in examinations and never lost an opportunity to expound about their virtues – but other high schools had much to contend with, not the least of their difficulties being that the system was entirely new to everyone, including the headmistress and staff. The problem of finding adequate teachers was heightened by the strenuous efforts being made to assimilate the curriculum to that of boys' schools. It was believed then that if girls did not take certain subjects it was because they could not. Helena Swanwick (born in 1864) reflected on the state of affairs when she started at Notting Hill High School, which had only been founded in 1873:

> It was necessary to prove that a woman could be a Senior Wrangler or a Senior Classic before girls could feel really free not go in for being mathematicians or classical scholars ... So we were coached for the same examinations as boys in half the time that boys had, by women who were, in many cases, themselves studying in their spare time for degrees, and who had had no training of any sort as teachers. The little Latin I learnt at Notting Hill, for instance, was from a woman who did not know that there was such a thing as a false quantity.[17]

And Molly Hughes had been irked in the upper fifth at North London Collegiate by the teacher who kept a Latin crib on her lap. 'A fair copy on the desk would have been respectable, but a crib on the lap, hidden (supposedly) by the desk, was quite another thing.' There were other difficulties, such as absence of school editions, or cheap editions of any kind. 'To study the Ancient Mariner, for instance, one had to buy the complete works of Coleridge. Consequently it was unavoidable that teaching tended to become lecturing while the audience took notes as hard as they could', and that in geometry a lot of time was wasted writing out propositions.[18]

Rather surprisingly for someone so assertive and independent, so determined to earn her own living, Molly Hughes thought that Miss Buss had gone too far in her eagerness to expunge the ordinary feminine subjects from the curriculum, and that there was something to be said for the old idea that girls should aim to be pleasing to men. 'But instead of facing squarely the real needs of wives and mothers, as the vast majority of girls were to be, Miss Buss seized the tempting instrument at her hand – the stimulus to mental ambition afforded by outside examinations.' (Curiously, the entrance exam included the making of a button-hole – a test that Molly herself failed the first time – though the school did not teach any domestic skills.)

Very few high schools did concern themselves with domestic accomplishments; they supposed they were providing for the emancipated woman who had turned her back on them. But it was surprising how many of their pupils felt they were ill served by this. 'No one was interested in us as future wives and mothers,' wrote one 1920s Paulina. 'Apart from a little dreary sewing, there was no domestic training of any kind. The Paulines at the boys' school ... could have followed our curriculum and we theirs, I suspect, without noticing the difference.'[19] King Edward VI at Birmingham was one of the few that taught cookery in the 1890s. There was no suitable textbook, so the teacher wrote her own 'King Edward's Cookery Book', which many old Edwardians took with them when they married. Cookery was later to drop out of the curriculum, to be enthusiastically revived in the 1970s.

It was far more predictable that Elizabeth Sewell should find the new climate most objectionable. Disliking the system of public exams, she pointed out that the examiners were all male and did not understand the female mind. She queried the technicality of much of the modern teaching, the grammatical analysis, the concentration on a single period of history for a year, or a single literary work, and advanced mathematics. While all reformers mentioned with contemptuous loathing Mangnall's *Questions* and Mrs Marcet's *Conversations** as epitomizing the old-style teaching from which they sought to emancipate female-kind, Miss Sewell remembered them with approval, and also held it a great advantage that no one in her day thought of going beyond 'decimal fractions, interest and proportion'. 'What had we gained from our school life? The answer is easy – a deep and increasing knowledge of our own ignorance ... From that time we set to work to educate ourselves.'[20] This is a useful corrective to the automatic assumption that all women pre-Buss were badly educated, and that all was light thereafter. There were always women like Elizabeth Sewell and Charlotte Yonge who had acquired considerable learning from assiduous reading at home. Some of them were touchingly eager to build on such education as they had, and formed little societies for mutual improvement such as the diarist Francis Kilvert was invited to join in 1874 by a girl who deeply regretted 'the enforced apparent idleness of her life'.

One of the most poignant examples of these self-educated girls is Emily Shore, who died of consumption in 1839, aged nineteen. The journal that she kept from the age of twelve until a fortnight before she died is the record of a passionate quest for learning which becomes increasingly eager as she realizes how little time there is left to her.

> Emily Shore [said her editor] went to no High School, no Lectures, passed no Examination, and competed with no rivals; her teaching was that of Nature and of Love. Her education had two characteristics; it allowed her own individuality, with all its tastes and tendencies, freely to expand; and it was an education of pure and good home influences. Her sole instructors were her parents, especially her father; but much, very much, was done by herself. She made her whole existence a happy schoolroom.[21]

* Richmal Mangnall's *Historical and Miscellaneous Questions for the Use of Young People* was first published in 1800 and remained in print for some seventy years. Jane Marcet's *Conversations on Chemistry, intended more especially for the Female Sex* (1806) was followed by other books where instruction was imparted through conversation. Both Mangnall and Marcet were very popular with governesses and girls' schools, and pupils were expected to learn the text by heart.

The High School Movement

Whereas the schools that emanated from boys' foundations were almost invariably accepted reluctantly if not resentfully, the high schools founded by local groups of campaigners for women's education, though just as pushed for money, were launched on a flood-tide of enthusiasm. The high school enterprise of the 1870s and 1880s owes much, as every history points out, to the early initiative of Queen's College, founded in 1848. But though Queen's presented women, some of them to be future headmistresses, with serious learning – imparted by male teachers, thus for the first time confronting 'young women in a reasonable manner with reasonable men', as one writer[22] quaintly put it – it remained totally different from the schools that it was later to inspire, for Queen's was dilettante where they were in earnest, with pupils who were there to please themselves rather than to pass exams and who were mostly from the same (upper) class. (Bedford College, which started in the same year and in somewhat the same style as Queen's, with classes held in a private house in Bedford Square, rapidly moved up the educational ladder, and settled to give its pupils university teaching.) Somewhat ironically, Queen's began as an attempt to improve the status of governesses, especially those who used the Governesses' Benevolent Institution in Harley Street as a refuge between posts or while looking for them. One of the initiators was Frederick Denison Maurice, Professor of English Literature and Modern History at King's College, whose sister was a teacher and who knew how difficult it was for women to acquire any sort of solid learning. He had observed the pitifully low educational level of the Harley Street governesses, and indeed had some years before written a perceptive article on female education, attacking the 'mean and insignificant studies' which passed for learning in most girls' schools; 'The books which are put into young ladies' hands are amongst the worst that have been written upon every subject; but to make up for this deficiency, they have to learn them by heart.'[23]

Maurice had already arranged a series of lectures for women, given by himself and his male academic friends in the house next door to the Governesses' Benevolent Institution, and in 1848 the lectures were put on a regular basis and Queen's College began. The lectures covered a huge variety of subjects, ranging from mechanics to Italian, and though they were designed initially for governesses, they were open to any young woman over the age of twelve. It was an appealing prospect to girls who were thirsty for learning, and two hundred applied in the first term. Dorothea Beale and her sister were among the first, Dorothea taking additional private classes in trigonometry, conics, and calculus. Frances Buss, whose own education had stopped at fourteen and who by then was teaching in the little school in Kentish Town begun by her mother, went to evening lectures. A year after the foundation of the college the committee, realizing that the lecture method of instruction was unsuitable for younger girls who had had no proper grounding, opened a preparatory department (known as Queen's College School after 1860) for girls under fourteen.

Even at this early stage, well born girls whose parents desired them to imbibe culture of a sort that governesses could not impart predominated; it was an establishment for the leisured and wealthy. At the daily callisthenics sessions (one of the few things mandatory for all students) there was much emphasis on deportment and curtsying and exhibition dancing. There were certainly unrivalled opportunities to learn, but it was left to the individual to decide whether or not to work, and unless she had a solid background to build upon, the lectures, however distinguished the academics who delivered them, meant little, and the professors lectured to classes of very mixed ability. Dorothea Beale thought the system most unsatisfactory, and said that the younger girls needed far more attention and ought to be trained, watched and educated by ladies ('who alone can understand, and therefore truly educate girls');[24] these were the principles on which she was to organize Cheltenham Ladies' College. And in 1906 at least one of the professors felt he was casting his pearls before swine, and told the principal that most of the College students ought to be in the school 'which might be developed into a good type of High School – while the College should be filled with adults capable of understanding and appreciating the unique character of the lectures given by the professors'. (At this stage the college resisted exams, which were not introduced until 1916, and the few students who had university aspirations had to be specially coached.) But the then Lady Resident (who looked after the girls' welfare) begged the principal (who was responsible for their intellects) to let the college stay as it was and not to let it become 'an unsuccessful imitation of modern schools'. And this, Miss Camilla Croudace would be glad to discover, has never happened. The school, though it has lost its male professors and has a largely female teaching staff and, from 1932, a woman principal, remains a collection of individuals without a house system and without compulsory games.

In contrast to what might be called the gentrification of Queen's, the idea of lectures for women made a strong appeal in the north, the stronghold of self-education, and Liverpool, Manchester, Leeds and Sheffield all formed associations to promote what was looked on as the germ of university extension. The Leeds Mechanics Institution founded a Ladies' Educational Institution as early as 1854; it gave a practical education (equivalent to that in the 'modern' or 'commercial' schools of the time), and included as well as the basic subjects, classes in accounts and book-keeping. Moreover, the Mechanics made their school of art, laboratories and library available to senior LE pupils. (The school later became Leeds Modern School and was renamed Lawnswood High School when it moved to new buildings on the outskirts of the city.)

Edinburgh, never wishing to seem influenced by things English, waited until 1865 to form the Edinburgh Essay Society (later known as the Ladies' Edinburgh Debating Society), with a founder-president of only nineteen. The members, who were described as 'a galaxy of youthful maidens, eager for self-improvement', debated feminist issues, and went on two years later to set up the Edinburgh Ladies' Educational Association which organized courses of lectures to degree standard, taught by university lecturers and culminating in an examination. The Certificate in Arts granted by Edinburgh University to those who had successfully taken the course served in lieu of a degree until the Scottish universities were opened to women in 1892 – whereupon the Association, its end achieved, dissolved itself.

Some private schools tried to imitate the Queen's style – Miss Hannah Pipe's school, Laleham Lodge, for instance, described in Chapter 6, was notable for the distinguished academics who lectured there, and Tudor Hall in its Chislehurst days apparently also featured visiting lecturers. But at this level the system, as Queen's found for itself, was better suited to a finishing school. It is significant that although Miss Buss was a product of Queen's she, like Miss Beale, had no intention that her own school should resemble it. At the North London Collegiate there was not only a rigidly structured day and multitudinous rules, there was much emphasis on marks and achievement.

Margaret Fletcher, who was sent to Oxford High School in the 1870s, had been told by her father that all his children would have to support themselves, and that a high school education would best fit her for this; an aunt paid for Molly Hughes to go to North London Collegiate for the same reason. Margaret found the atmosphere highly charged, and like Molly Hughes thought that the teaching (at least in the lower forms) was not particularly good. 'We scribbled away taking notes of what was after all in the text-books. (There were no original interpolations.) At home we copied it all out neatly, margined and headed according to plan, and such was the hurry that there was little time to take in the subject matter.'[25] The fear of being late in the morning loomed very large. Little girls could be seen running along all the converging roads with anxious looks on their faces. 'There is no doubt that fear lurked just beneath the surface of our school life, which came from the personality of our headmistress [Miss Ada Benson, see page 216] . . . She lived in a state of righteous emotionalism which seemed to lack all sense of proportion.' After four years of this strained atmosphere it was felt that high school life was not suiting her, and she was sent to stay with cousins in Sussex. It was a staggering change; she was swept back to the world of her mother's youth. Her cousins were being gently taught at home by an amiable and conscientious governess, and the children learned general culture from Mangnall's *Questions*. After the competitive world of Oxford High School, full of earnest schoolchildren caught up in the stream of contemporary feminism, it was a haven of comfort and security and it was very tempting to stay in its shelter. But perhaps because of those painful high school years she could see that this life was an anachronism and would not last. She was to become an art student, and later to devote her life to moral welfare work.

But many girls' experience of the new high schools was happier. The bookish warmed to the intellectual atmosphere. 'The word "lessons" is misleading. They were adventures – discoveries ... But oh, how stupid I felt, accustomed only to learning by heart facts from the text book, Kings of England and battles of the Wars of the Roses. Now I was being asked to consider causes and results, to study characters and movements,'[26] said a girl at Winchester High School. 'We felt transported into another and a fairer land of learning. The ... Mistresses were regarded as perfect oracles of knowledge, and were revered as never before, or shall we say – since,'[27] said one at Manchester High School. And an early pupil at the Park School in Glasgow wrote of the heady excitement of setting the world to rights in the company of one's peers:

> Round the old stove there we sat in our tight-fitting bodices well whaleboned, high collars topped with scratchy frilling, voluminous, bunchy skirts, long hair confined by crock-combs or tied on top with broad black ribbon, arguing endlessly ... Round the old stove we made our first attempts to think for ourselves – we put a question to everything – Miss Kinnear's bodily presence was never seen to hover round the stove but her inexhaustible questing spirit permeated the whole atmosphere of the school. Her sudden flung and startling 'Whys' would set our dull minds groping for a reason for actions hitherto taken as a matter of course ... So beside the old stove we settled the affairs of the world, always to the slight smell of singeing wool we argued upon eternity; impossible to redd up the universe and remember at the same time not to venture too near the stove.[28]

For many there was a freedom they had never known at home. 'Dull piano practice, much tedious sewing, state calls, and receiving visitors – these were all crowded out of our lives by the engrossing claims of school.'[29] Joseph Chamberlain's daughter Beatrice at Edgbaston High School thought it was delightful to learn in a class after working alone with no one to measure oneself against. She even enjoyed the small details of routine like the cloakroom numbers with which all possessions had to be marked.[30] 'The novelty of it! They enjoyed every new experience – the pigeon-holes and pegs in the cloak-room, the desks in the class-rooms, the buns and milk at eleven o'clock, even the rule of silence, which made the fifteen minutes' relaxation in the middle of the morning such a delight,' said one of 'the First Brood' of eleven girls at the Alice Ottley School.[31] And the bleakness of the early schools could take on glamour. The girls' school at Berkhamsted opened in an austere house in the High Street with a great deal of stone flooring, but one child at least approved: 'Its very bareness made it appear to us like a real school, and we sang in our nursery of going to bare boards and stone floors as if no better fate could befall us.'[32] Miss Beale visited the school two years after it opened and told the girls that 'life was a serious business and we must be prepared to shoulder burdens'. But for all the seriousness, schoolgirls were allowed to be young – younger than they could be at home in the company of their mothers. The housekeeper at the new Blackheath High School, watching girls playing indoors in bad weather, was amazed: 'It's you great, big girls I can't help laughing at; you all ought to have been married, long ago.'[33]

And there was, of course, the excitement of taking part in a new venture. 'There was something very inspiring in working in a school that had no past and that was so full of promise for a glorious future,' said one of the new girls at Manchester High School when it opened in 1874.[34] Some of the pupils were girls of eighteen, nineteen or twenty who came of their own accord to supplement such education as they had. It was initially very difficult to sort out pupils of such different ability, few of whom had been taught anything properly. Manchester High School set an entrance exam to classify the applicants. (They had only expected five on the opening day, but sixty girls appeared, and the weight of the gold paid in advance fees was such that it had to be taken to the bank in a cab.) One of the girls in the 1899 school magazine remembered how extraordinary it was to sit down to printed questions about dreadful things like 'fractions', 'per cent' and 'stocks' when all they had learnt had been at home with a nursery governess or mother. 'Pens were bitten and fingers were inked to an alarming extent, but from time to time, a gleam of sunshine came into the room in the form of the Head Mistress, with the cheery question, "Are you getting on any better in here?"' The school later found it could assess pupils more accurately by getting them to talk about what they *had* learnt.

Manchester High School had opened in two rented houses in Oxford Road, in what Professor Sadler* called the Quartier Latin of Manchester near Owens College, later to be the university. Its beginnings were similar to that of many other high schools where local campaigners for a better education for girls had raised enough money to pay a few months' rent and buy some desks. Setting up a school then demanded comparatively little outlay; the Charity Commissioners, it will be remembered, had suggested that the Perse foundation should have £500 in hand before it opened its school for girls. But six years later, with great boldness, they laid the foundation stone of Manchester High School's imposing new premises. These were to cost £30,000, much of which had been raised locally. The balance was made up by a Mr Thomasson of Bolton who wrote offering to lend £10,000 on mortgage, saying he considered he had given something to

* Sir Michael Sadler (1861–1943), professor of education of Manchester, 1903–11.

the school in lending at so low a rate (though he hoped the committee was not going in for expensive ornamental buildings). The money was handed over in notes – 'a fine action, done simply, almost austerely,' commented the headmistress, who though not a Lancashire woman herself was becoming used to blunt northern ways.

Oxford High School started a year after Manchester, in the Judges' Lodgings in St Giles – a substantial early eighteenth-century building, originally the town house of the Dukes of Marlborough; the rooms were more spacious than Manchester's first home, but the school had to move out during the assizes. They were to get their own building in 1881, in the Queen Anne style then felt most appropriate for girls (and also for board schools). Chelsea, the earliest of all the high schools, began in 1873 in Durham House, once the home of Isaac Newton, an imposing house in its own grounds but in what was considered to be a very objectionable neighbourhood (it soon moved to Cromwell Road, and then to St Alban's Grove and was renamed Kensington High School in 1880). It was also in a very bad state of repair, and there was even doubt about the purity of the water supply – but Victorian schools lived in constant fear of epidemics.

Notting Hill and Bayswater High School, which opened a few months later, occupied a house in Norland Square, dark and depressing premises without a proper playground.

> No less than six classes of thirty or forty each were held in the big schoolroom [wrote an early pupil] . . . We had no playing-fields, but in the summer we used to be turned, at 'Recreation-time', into a small paved yard, where we could only walk round and round, while in winter we walked round and round a basement room, filled with pegs, upon which our outdoor clothes were hung.[35]

But some Notting Hill pupils enjoyed the chumminess of the single classroom. If bored by one lesson they could listen to another; if bored by that too they could always resort to plucking the fluff off the baize table-covers and use it for stuffing the pincushions which the more audacious presented to favourite teachers.[36] Croydon High School opened in September 1874 with eighty-eight pupils in a house in even worse condition, with 'defective ventilation, an inadequate playground and a singular shortage of earth-closets'. Some of the pupils were an embarrassment, two having to be removed for 'want of cleanliness'.[37] Numbers increased rapidly and six years later 230 pupils moved to purpose-built premises.

Chelsea, Notting Hill, Croydon and Oxford were among the first high schools established by the Girls' Public Day School Company, which the National Union for the Education of Girls had launched with an opening ceremony at the Albert Hall in June 1872, after an energetic publicity campaign conducted by Emily Shirreff, her sister Maria Grey, Henrietta Stanley (grandmother of Bertrand Russell) and Mary Gurney, four women of differing backgrounds who were all cultivated and largely self-taught. They were fortunate enough to have acquired a royal patron, Princess Louise, Queen Victoria's sixth child, who took her duties as president very seriously – indeed, she took great interest in women's education generally, and her name is often to be found in individual school histories. The GPDSC (it became a trust in 1906) began as a limited liability company with the purpose of establishing public day schools where girls would be given a good education at a low cost (though this was no charitable venture and the schools had to be self-supporting). The company aimed at raising a capital sum of £12,000 in 2,400 £5 shares, the capital to be used to purchase or rent buildings and to furnish them, a proportion being left for a reserve fund; there was to be a 5 per cent dividend payable from any profits. A prospectus was sent out accompanied by a letter signed by Princess Louise, and among those who took up shares were Frances Buss, Dorothea Beale, Joshua Fitch and the Marquess of Lorne (the husband of Princess Louise).

The company's schools would provide a high standard of education, with trained teachers as far as possible, and a class of student teachers attached to each school. The curriculum would include non-sectarian religious instruction, reading, writing, arithmetic, book-keeping, English grammar and literature, history, geography, French and German, the elements of physical science, drawing, class singing and harmony, and callisthenics. The senior department would teach in addition ancient languages, history, mathematics, the elements of moral science and logic, physiology as applied to the laws of health, and elementary economics.

In connection with the logic, it is of interest to recall that in 1887 the Revd Charles Lutwidge Dodgson offered his services to Oxford High School. The classes were very popular, but after three lectures he felt it advisable to test the girls' comprehension. He passed eight out of twenty-three; six he said he was happy to go on with 'if they are willing to go over some of the old work again before trying anything harder ... The others I would *advise* (but I do not *insist* on it) not to attend any more lectures at present, as I am sure they can spend their time more profitably in other ways.'[38] Mr Dodgson, being fond enough of girls to be able to tolerate their illogical nature, continued to visit the school and even invited some of the pupils to dine with him at Christ Church. Nor was his interest exclusively in Oxford girls, for it seems to have been extended to any high school he could reach by railway. He had a long-standing friendship, for instance, with Miss Alice Jane Cooper, the first headmistress of Edgbaston High School, which he visited in 1889 for a performance of *Alice in Wonderland*. ('*Possibly* I might wish just to be allowed to kiss the "Alice" of the play; but *that*, of course, would be an unheard of liberty, and not to be permitted on any account.'[39] It is not recorded whether he overcame these scruples.) He also visited the Alice Ottley School in Worcester in 1892, where he showed off arithmetical puzzles, gave a reading from his *Sylvie and Bruno*, and delivered 'a wise and thoughtful spiritual discourse to the staff and elder girls' in the evening[40] – something that Edgbaston had never been able to persuade him to do.

The success of the new high schools would be remarkable in any context, but becomes extraordinary when one considers the taboos that had to be broken down; the lack of experienced headmistresses (it seems that Miss E.E.M. Creak at Brighton was under twenty-one when she was appointed, and was worried in case the papers she signed were not legally valid); the mostly untrained teachers ('not conducive to a love of learning in the pupils', said one who had suffered under them[41]); the pitiful shortage of money and the wretched premises. 'We had to strive for years against continual opposition,' said the first headmistress of Kensington High School, comparing the advantages enjoyed by her profession thirty years later.[42]

Transport was another difficulty. However good the school, few Victorian parents, as we noted earlier, liked their daughters travelling by public transport to reach it. Huyton College was set up in 1894 in a suburb five miles east of Liverpool because one of its residents, when his daughter was nearly at secondary school age, realized that the nearest good school was in the city itself, which meant a train journey and consequent moral and social danger. Other residents had moved to be near a suitable school, but Mr Thomas Rogers wanted to stay in Huyton. He managed to find supporters for his scheme to start a girls' branch of Liverpool College, 'of the highest possible character and fit for any gentleman's child'. The high schools that sprang up in leafy London suburbs like Blackheath, Putney, Streatham, Dulwich, Clapham, Sydenham and Wimbledon reflect this Victorian need for girls to be able to walk to school. Some, of course, had to trudge quite a distance, carrying heavy satchels; one boarding house at Winchester High School used a donkey cart to carry these for the girls.

At Edgbaston the school provided from 1893 a bus to transport the Moseley children to and from school, and the behaviour of its passengers must have confirmed all the fears of those who dreaded 'high school manners'. For 'since the girls enjoyed the trip, and were, for a short time in their disciplined lives, free from the control of any adult except the driver, always a loyal friend, their audible shrieks and giggles brought discredit on the whole district of Moseley. It was not, said the censorious, a matter of economic standing, it was the *vulgarity*.' In the summer the girls climbed on to the roof and sat dangling their legs. If a teacher came out to remonstrate, the driver looked the other way and whipped up his horses. The bus took half to three quarters of an hour to make the journey, and in the morning this meant there was usually plenty of time to finish off your homework. 'But if things looked desperate – nearly at the top of Priory Road and still not finished – one could gain an extra ten minutes by accidentally dropping into the muddy road one of those complicated three-tier wooden pencil-boxes with all its pens, pencils, nibs and rubbers. If the bus were late for prayers nobody was ever blamed but the horses.'

One can only admire the parents who trusted their children to an untried system with hazards like the Moseley bus, and marvel at the speed with which such disparate elements were welded into communities with strong corporate feeling, each with its own personality. Good academic results were achieved remarkably soon. 'Some of us from the Upper Sixth were taking London Matriculation in June, 1888, and the Higher Certificate of the Oxford and Cambridge Joint Board in the following month,' wrote an early pupil at Redland, Bristol, which had turned itself into a high school only six years before. 'Not only had the work developed, but Games, School Societies, the School Library, with their respective Committees, were fully organized.'[43] But the examiners themselves wondered whether schools were not pressing their pupils too hard. A Dean of Durham feared that the girls at Durham High School might 'spoil themselves by being too eager . . . and sitting too long at their studies'. It would end in 'spectacles', he said dolefully.[44] And in 1880 an examiner from the Joint Board communicated his doubts to the GPDSC: 'Some of the forms come to me exhausted, having passed the Oxford Local Examination in June, and since done paper work for the Board before encountering this serious ordeal of a *viva voce* Examination. Some even contemplate the Cambridge Local in December. Much examining stimulates bad Schools, but cripples good ones.'[45] The GPDSC council were concerned, and instructed headmistresses to give out time sheets for homework, which the parents had to sign. St Paul's Girls' School is one of those that still keeps to the practice, but, as the pupils in a competitive school are the first to admit, it is no guide whatever to the time actually taken.

This earnest striving for good exam results was deprecated by many, and parents at the two Francis Holland schools in London were emphatic that they did not want them to be like high schools. Their founder, Canon Francis Holland, a man of great simplicity and charm who used to give the girls scripture lessons with the help of a concertina, had aimed to provide 'a good education, in which distinctive religious teaching should hold a high place, for the daughters of the well-to-do classes'. For as he told a later headmistress, 'he had discovered the crass ignorance in religious knowledge amongst the girls from this background'.[46] Apparently with St Cyr, the school founded by Mme de Maintenon for young French noblewomen, as his unlikely model, he set up the first school above the Baker Street railway tracks (it is now in Clarence Gate) in 1878; three years later he was asked if he would give his name and his blessing to a second school near Sloane Square. Both schools prospered, in spite of the insalubrious surroundings that the latter had to endure, but parents were adamant that their children should not be prepared for professional life or for earning any sort of a living, and some of them objected to the Cambridge local examinations. The schools were later to stand out against accepting any pupils from the state system, even though this meant that they alone of all the London high schools would be ineligible for government grants.

Talbot Heath, Bournemouth, is also a Church of England high school, and remarkable for the fact that it came into being not through any committee or limited liability company but as a result of the energy and generosity of its founder, Mary Broad. She had had a very short education, culminating in two years at Wandsworth High School where she took an Oxford local examination despite strenuous discouragement from her teachers who thought her poor spelling would let the school down. Later, fourth-formers at the school she founded were to find her joining in their Latin and maths as well as French and German lessons, because 'these were subjects she had not studied at school'. At the age of seventeen she became an assistant in a private school, and then in 1886, when she was twenty-six, joined with a friend to buy a small school near Bournemouth. Informal, happy and not particularly academic in its early days – Miss Broad apparently had less learning than any comparable headmistress – it seems to have been like many other south coast establishments of the late Victorian period. But Miss Broad (by now the sole partner) was determined to make it a high school, and an endowed one at that, and like Miss Buss, whom she had consulted in the matter, she sacrificed her own interest and future independence of action and turned it into a trust, putting it in 1898 (she was not yet forty) into the hands of the Winchester diocesan trustees. At first they insisted that it must be in return for a pension at a future date, but when it was found that this clause would be an obstacle to grants from the Board of Education, Miss Broad declared that she had wanted to make over the school as a gift 'and that if you allow the clause to stand it becomes a business transaction'.[47] 'Miss Broad's School' thus became Bournemouth High School, which in turn became Talbot Heath when the school moved to new purpose-built premises in 1935.

Miss Broad's school was remarkable for 'a minimum number of rules and a great deal of laughter'.[48] (There were in fact only two rules, more often broken than not: 'No talking on the stairs' and 'Keep to the right'.) In this it differed sharply from other high schools, which nearly all imposed a rigid discipline. Not only were inexperienced headmistresses dealing with children who in many cases had never been to school before and who were felt to need a strong framework of rules, but there was the problem of moving large numbers safely and quietly round buildings that had not been designed for such purposes. When awestruck inquirers asked the headmaster of the Edinburgh Educational Institution for Young Ladies, newly created in 1870 from the Merchant Maiden Hospital, how he coped with twelve hundred girls, he used to say that the immediate problem was to get them from room to room in an orderly manner. Accordingly he decreed that each class should always move as one, and on the hour they marched to their next destination to the sound of a harmonium.[49] Most schools felt, like North London Collegiate and Cheltenham Ladies' College, that silence was the answer; it was expedient, it taught self-restraint, and all authority was very much aware that 'evil communications corrupt good manners' and that the whole high school system was on trial. (There were ways round it at Christ's Hospital at any rate, where both boys and girls developed a sign language.) Total prohibition on conversation except in the playground was therefore the norm – to the extent that at Gateshead new girls who lost themselves in the building had to remain lost, as even if they had dared ask the way, no one would have broken the rule to tell them. Exchanges like 'Mary, were you speaking?' 'No, Miss A— , I was not speaking, I was only asking for a buttonhook', would be heard at Bedford High School, where one mistress at least thought the discipline might be *too* strict, and that some of the staff 'were in danger of treating a class as if it were a gang of convicted felons'.[50] There was also high moral earnestness, and when Blackheath pupils, after strenuous representation to the headmistress, were allowed to present tableaux to the parents, 'our anxiety was great lest the Sleeping Beauty should have her head turned, and one of us undertook to prevent such a disaster by explaining to her that she was chosen only because her hair was "rather nice"'.[51]

There were other high schools that were not under the GPDSC umbrella, but which were founded by local effort. Manchester has already been mentioned. Edgbaston was opened to provide a good non-sectarian education in a wealthy Birmingham suburb; like many schools of its kind it began as a limited liability company. Clifton, a prosperous Bristol suburb, opened its high school in January 1878. It had the good fortune to find as its first headmistress Mary Alice Woods, a young woman with academic qualifications and experience – she had been briefly headmistress at the GPDSC Chelsea High School, and it is tempting to infer that she found the physical conditions in those early days too depressing to wish to stay. She set out the three principles which were her desiderata for education. The first two were common to nearly all high schools: that there should be religious freedom and no class distinction. But the third, that it should be non-competitive, admitting no prizes, marks nor allotting of places, was unusual if not unique in a high school. Redland High School, also in Bristol, came into being in 1882 as a result of the enthusiasm of the Revd Urijah Thomas, 'the friend of the children and the poor city waif and stray', a public-spirited nonconformist for whom the bells of Bristol cathedral were to toll when he died. Having helped found the school, he served it until his death. Three years later the school moved to the nearby Redland Court, at first magnificently ill adapted to its new function. 'I well remember Latin lessons at a small table in the untouched but empty stable where the partitions for the horses, each with its manger, stood intact.'[52]

Many of these high schools originally had boarding houses, which in most cases have now been shed; boarders never predominated, the day element being the important one. One of the few exceptions was Winchester High School, which as St Swithun's (it took this name in 1927) now has a majority of boarders. It began as a church high school, with the blessing of both Elizabeth Sewell (though she may have given it reluctantly, as her stated wish was to see a system of good church *boarding* schools in the diocese) and Charlotte Yonge, whose name – somewhat ironically in view of her earlier views on education outside the home (see page 167) – was given to a scholarship to help girls go to Oxford or Cambridge. But even in the days when it occupied a site in the town (it moved to the Downs in 1931), boarders set the pace. 'Day girls were of a generally lower order than boarders,' as one of the latter said loftily.[53] A house system had been set up at an early stage; there was strong house rivalry and, pre-war especially, an unconscionable amount of games. As early as 1912 many felt strongly about the high school label, and a group of housemistresses wrote to tell the school council so:

> It has been brought home to us again and again since we last wrote, that we are losing girls for no other reason than that the school is called a High School and consequently now-a-days confused with the county schools and parents refuse to come and interview us on that account ... We are essentially of the Public Schools type and ought not to lay ourselves open to be confused with the county schools.[54]

After two years of debate the school dropped the 'high' that caused such social anguish, and became Winchester School for Girls, and then St Swithun's.

Scotland had its own problems, deriving ironically from the excellence of its secondary education which could in theory be used by both boys and girls, though in practice few of the latter received the classical education available to boys at the burgh schools. Complacency about a system that had served Scotland well, and extreme reluctance to appear to imitate England, meant that there was a long delay before girls' high schools of the GPDSC kind appeared. Glasgow was the first city to stir itself, but once it was convinced of the need it moved swiftly; a limited company was formed in 1880 to promote a school for girls, and the Park School opened that September, in premises less makeshift than most, since the building had been a boys' school. The company's directors included many of the university professors, and the school was fortunate in its early staff who, though none of them could have been graduates, possessed qualifications that were then unusual. The first headmistress, Georgina Kinnear, was a remarkable self-educated and much travelled woman who spoke French, German and Russian (there was a legend in the school that the diamond brooch she wore, and which was in fact a family one, had been given to her by a devoted Russian pupil). The Park as early as 1884 installed a chemistry laboratory – one of the first in any school – and many of its girls were to study medicine.[55]

Edinburgh, after the Ladies' Educational Institution had been formed in 1870, moved more slowly. Neither this school nor George Watson's Ladies' College (which had come into being at the same time, when the Merchant Company reorganized its hospitals) were what the professional middle classes desired for their daughters; they were held to be too big, too like education factories – with male teachers into the bargain. An early account of St George's stressed that it was the first Edinburgh school to have 'the advantage of a cultured lady as its headmistress'.[56] The Merchant Company schools were, besides, associated with 'trade', and the upper reaches of Edinburgh society were more English than Scottish in their exclusiveness. Nevertheless, to set up a high school of the English sort and thus deny the merit of the traditional Scottish system was abhorrent to many, and it was 1888 before St George's High School for Girls opened in Melville Street. It resembled the English high schools in its policy of providing a solid education for middle-class girls (who, however, like the Francis Holland girls, were 'not under the necessity of preparing for business or the professions'), but unlike them, there were to be no prizes, form lists or marks. It is a day school of a type only possible in Edinburgh, and like St Leonards, Fifeshire (a boarding school run on English lines), it stands apart from other Scottish schools.

Some high schools, as has been said, were founded as a corrective to the non-sectarian nature of the majority. The Church Schools Company, which came into being in 1883, runs seven high schools 'inspired by Christian Church principles'. Durham High School benefited from the enthusiasm of Bishop Lightfoot, who presided over the fourteen gentlemen (no ladies) at the initial meeting in 1883, and the school opened the following year. For eighty years, until it was forced to move by the building of a new road, it lived in Leazes House, which looked over a beautiful garden and the river to the cathedral and the castle. Worcester High School in its early days had an Anglo-Catholic atmosphere, more like a Woodard Foundation school or a convent. When Canon Butler, who had been the force behind the foundation of the Wantage schools (see page 194), arrived in Worcester in 1881, he saw a city 'ripe for educational development' and urged the need for a more thorough, specific and extended education for women. A limited company was formed and premises found (which form the nucleus of the present school), and the school opened in 1883 with ten little girls. These were soon joined by another, so that the group was always known as the 'First Eleven' or 'First Brood'. Canon Butler found in Alice Ottley a headmistress of the same Tractarian views as his own, and in her time the school was conducted within a religious setting which was unique among high schools (described at greater length in Chapter 6). Miss Ottley took the school motto, 'The white lily of a blameless life' (it was later to become 'Candida rectaque'), from Tennyson's Dedication to *The Idylls of the King*, which she deeply admired and which she expounded to generations of pupils. Nor did she have the usual high school aspiration to prepare girls for an independent life. Like Charlotte Yonge whom she resembled in many ways, she wished to encourage them to be 'good unselfish home-daughters' in 'these days of growing disregard for parents and neglect of home'. Though she continued as headmistress until 1912, in spirit she remained a Victorian, and a verse from the school's Latin hymn breathes Charlotte Yonge's ideal maidenhood:

> Shining white, and straight aspiring
>   As the lilies 'midst the flowers;
> White and straight, and fruitful growing
>   As the corn in ripening hours;
> These be watchwords ever cherished
>   Richest of all maiden's dowers.

The majority of the high schools, in spite of their air of brisk, forward-looking efficiency, were originally housed in premises like Durham's and had to endure temporary additions in the shape of corrugated iron class-rooms – Durham had an ex-army hut which served as an assembly hall – until redevelopment or wartime bombing finally drove most to put up buildings of their own. The North London Collegiate moved out to Canons Park in Edgware in 1940, the Treasury and the Board of Education having given their sanction for the completion of Professor A. E. Richardson's buildings, which had been roof-high when war broke out. Long before, the unsuitability of the school's site had been realized, with the Camden Road now a thundering, traffic-laden artery, and many of the Victorian family houses now tenements, or demolished to make way for factories. The Canons Park site had been bought as long ago as 1929, and parties of girls were sent out daily for lessons and recreation, but the Board of Education had required much persuading that it was right to move from the original site, which had been located to serve the needs of the St Pancras area.

The only school to have purpose-built premises from the start was Blackheath, which by local effort raised enough to build their own handsome Queen Anne style building whose assembly hall was adorned, unusually, by an undraped Venus de Milo, presented by the architect. Visitors who winced at her nakedness might well have felt that her presence epitomized the brashness and immodesty of 'the modern girl', the bugbear of the 1880s and inevitably associated by their detractors with the high schools. Few of them could offer much in the way of gracious surroundings. 'The woodwork was stained chocolate-brown,' said one pupil of her south London high school, 'and the corridors washed with a dull, heavy cream or a lifeless green. I can recall no paintings on the walls, only sepia reproductions of such pictures as the Mona Lisa, Holman Hunt's *Light of the World*, Burne Jones's *Golden Staircase*, and *The Last Supper* of Leonardo da Vinci.'[57] A few, like Durham and Edgbaston, started their life in pleasant old town houses; Redland, as noted earlier, moved in 1885 to Redland Court, a Georgian country house whose elegance and beautiful surroundings deeply impressed its pupils.

But of all the day schools, it was Worcester (later the Alice Ottley School) that tried hardest to distance itself from the high school stereotype. In gracious surroundings (a fine Georgian town house) Miss Ottley sought to shape gracious young women:

> The language of Worcester High School was to be as 'Court Language', the outcome of refined, reverent minds; such a thing as slang was not to be tolerated. The children were to show by their demeanour, even by the way in which they walked about both inside the building and out, that they were true gentlewomen, daughters of the King of kings . . . In the very early days the girls walked about the High School with their arms crossed behind their backs (a custom borrowed from the Oxford High School), but this was dropped before long, and a natural, easy but controlled way of walking, with hands by their sides, arms never swinging, never touching the banisters . . . was cultivated.[58]

None of the Moseley bus larkings would have been tolerated here.

The Twentieth Century

By 1900 the GPDSC had thirty-two schools with seven thousand pupils, but their very popularity brought financial problems. New buildings were needed to replace the dignified but unsuitable premises most had started in. Often a school had to wait for war or disaster for this (the headmistress of Wimbledon High School, which was burnt down in 1917, told a sympathizer to have no regrets – it was a chance to build something newer). Better equipment was needed, and more facilities, particularly for science. The school council was very unwilling to put up the fees (then about £16 a year), and after the Balfour Education Act of 1902, when municipal and county authorities were empowered to create secondary schools, they became increasingly aware of how poorly their staff were paid compared to what the local authorities were offering. The government grant for schools that taught science was very valuable – block grants in respect of the whole curriculum were substituted in 1904 – and it was in order to meet new legal requirements over these much needed grants that the GPDSC reconstituted itself and became a trust. The local authority secondary schools took most of their pupils from elementary schools; the high schools took a few, on scholarships, but after a prolonged and anguished debate that lasted for many years they resisted the much higher government grant that was offered if they would hold a quarter of their places for non-fee-paying children. (They would also have had to accept majority representation by the local authority on their board of management.)

So the early decades of this century were difficult for the high schools. Their prestige was not so high as in the pioneering days. They were losing girls to the local authority schools, where the fees were much lower; the GPDST was obliged to close down a couple of theirs and transfer others to the local authority. In the 1880s and 90s they had seemed to provide the newest and most dashing sort of education, so that ephemeral private establishments sometimes added the epithet 'high' to their own schools, and even middle-class parents were caught up in the wave of enthusiasm. But twenty and thirty years on, the high schools no longer seemed a new nor necessarily a very good idea, especially as there was an abundance of private schools to choose from, many of them begun by talented and cultured women who sought to provide something less rigid than the high school curriculum and more suited to the ordinary girl with no university aspirations. It was, for instance, a great shock to the Francis Holland School in Graham Street when their head, Miss Wolseley-Lewis, went to start her own very successful school, North Foreland Lodge, taking some staff and pupils with her. There was also the relatively new phenomenon of girls' public schools, which aimed to give a high school type of education while imparting *esprit de corps*. It has been shown how strongly the housemistresses of Winchester High School in 1912 felt they were part of a public school, not of something so socially lowering as a high school.

The high schools had not altered their determination to give girls the same curriculum as boys. In the 1920s and 30s they were still staffed by women who had been among the earliest to win university degrees and who thought it a betrayal of the cause not to strive for academic achievement. But matriculation, that hard-won passport to higher education for the early pioneers, became meaningless to a later generation, just a necessary number of credits that authority expected one to achieve in one's final exams. Miss Strudwick, the High Mistress of St Paul's, in 1937 deplored the fact that School Certificate, 'which should be a reasonable test of achievement after five years in a secondary school', should now be tied up with something completely different, the qualification for entry to a university.[59]

The headmistress's point of view, the genuine sorrow at the flighty rejection of the fountain of knowledge that a previous generation had fought so hard to unseal, can be seen in this lament of 1937:

> No small number of girls now in our secondary schools begin to pull away from [an academic curriculum] in their third or fourth year, not because they are unintelligent, but because they are bored by the logical study of disparate subjects which they 'will never need' . . . They make superficial compliance with our code of behaviour and they produce work of a kind, but growing up every week-end in Vanity Fair, and growing down again every

Monday with diminishing measures of goodwill, they eventually throw off all allegiance to our ideals. 'Drink, pretty creature, drink,' we plead, but having put their lips to the deep waters of learning, they turn away to some effervescent and sparkling beverage.[60]

But a girl at Nottingham High School in the early 1920s wondered to what end they had worked: 'We with our heads in the clouds, our six years of French and six years of Latin, just hadn't thought ahead.' It was Girton or Somerville for the extremely brainy; the local university for the less so; a teachers' training college or a secretarial course for others with parents who could pay. This girl, who took 'a very mediocre Civil Service exam' and got a job that was boring and monotonous, at the time had not realized that the school was educating its girls for jobs that did not exist.[61] Another, writing of the 1930s, thought that 'we were intellectually crammed and emotionally starved', and remembered school as 'a cloud cuckooland where nothing much mattered except sport, good behaviour and "honour"'. There was no streaming and very mixed ability, but everybody – even those of limited capacity – had to do the same Latin, maths and science. Many teachers were middle-aged or elderly, and there was an elderly headmistress.[62] The atmosphere was highly competitive; at Redland High School 'fortnightly, marks sheets for all the main subjects were placed on form notice boards and the Head Mistress made a brief visit to each form to comment on the marks of individual girls'. Oxford High School during World War I was remembered as very narrow, 'no societies, no clubs, no school expeditions'. Children started Latin in form I and no one had any domestic science teaching at all, nor was there any geography after the upper fourth. Being Oxford, 'some of the parents had a good deal of control over the school and some at least wanted girls to have exactly the same schooling as boys'. Nor was anything done 'to make us appreciate the fact that we were living in one of the most interesting and beautiful towns in Europe'.[63]

'I remember it as a place where one could not talk except in stipulated areas,' said an Old Paulina, 'and where regimentation was the commonly accepted norm. Individuality was frowned upon in dress and in attitudes. One had to be brave to be different . . . On the question of values I think the School strove to inculcate the quality known as "esprit de corps".'[64] Many complained that the schools never accepted that the majority of girls then would be wives and mothers and would rapidly abandon all thought of careers. 'Our education was good, but it was one-sided. We learnt to use our heads but seldom our hands. As in many schools, training in domesticity was crowded out by pressure of other subjects; or worse, looked upon as of no special importance.'[65]

But the occasional girl was aware of what high schools had achieved; one said of her own in the 1950s:

It made conformist citizens. We were not taught to question our next moves . . . [But] it gave its pupils a sense of belonging to a community of

> women who for generations had fought for the chance of education ... 'Knowledge is now no more a fountain sealed' – those words on the plaque in the Hall seemed to be more than a motto, more a battle-cry, and I still feel inspired by them.[66]

And the list drawn up by a proud Paulina of professions followed by members of the St Paul's League in the 1920s gives some idea of the new horizons that had opened for women (albeit for the most part single women): archaeologists; architects; authors; actresses; 'banks, in'; civil servants; church workers; doctors (a large section); gardeners; gymnastics mistresses; hospital almoners; hospital nurses; headmistresses; journalists; masseuses; music teachers; musicians; missionaries; nuns; poultry farmers; 'private schools, owners of'; poets; scientists; solicitors; school secretaries; singers; secretaries.[67]

The middle-class neurosis about contamination from the lower classes also reasserted itself in the 20s and 30s. This had been uneasily suppressed in the early days, partly because once it had been clearly demonstrated that there were virtually no other schools where a sound education was being given, professional parents were swept along by the tide of enthusiasm. It also seemed to them that, given the very strict rules about conversation and friendship, their daughters would be fairly safe from undesirable contacts. But as the high schools relaxed their discipline, and also took in more elementary schoolchildren, the middle-class doubts about infectious diseases, accents and undesirable manners returned. One of the first batch of 'free scholars' admitted to Nottingham High School remembered that, as they lined up to be interviewed by the headmistress, a parent remarked that they would ruin the tone of the school.

For the working-class child it was the key to a new life. One was considered fortunate in 1934 to have a grammar school education; the very uniform marked one off as someone distinct from the mufti-clad mob who didn't learn French or play tennis: school colours, a hockey stick, a tennis racquet, even doing homework and wearing black stockings made one feel different. The professional classes also wanted to distinguish themselves from the mob, and the 1920s and 30s saw the ultimate elaboration of school uniform (dealt with at greater length in Chapter 11): specially dyed Harris tweeds, subtly coloured shantung silk summer dresses, Liberty scarves, distinctive hats with or without cockades – these were worn at private schools that sought to show how different their pupils were from the gym-slipped crowd at the urban high schools. (The very term 'grammar school' became one used to rebuke boisterous or vulgar behaviour.) Uniform at whatever type of school you were at, though, was worn with a surprising pride. The Mary Datchelor School had wanted it so fervently at the turn of the century that they cut the badge of the Clothworkers (their trustees) from their exercise books and stuck it on their hatbands. (Hats were the first items of clothing to be standardized, long before anything else was.)

But most schools did not introduce uniform for anything except games and drill until after World War I. King Edward VI, Birmingham, was one of the first to wear gym tunics (to become the traditional high school garb) as everyday dress. 'The effect . . . on the appearance of the school was amazing. Instead of an odd collection of girls wearing out their old Sunday frocks on weekdays, we appeared as trim, neat schoolgirls.'[68]

Ironically, the high school headmistresses were doing all they could to turn their girls into ladies. 'She was interested primarily in moral conduct,' said the chronicler of a Liverpool headmistress of this period. 'Her concern [was] to promote ladylike behaviour in matters of dress, deportment, manners and speech.'[69] She added that in many respects the school's aims then differed very little from the private ladies' establishments in the area, and that this would not have been the case if parents and members of the local community had not apparently been more interested in discipline and appearance than in academic level. But deportment and appearance mattered a great deal to all high schools, who strove to stamp out giggling and loud behaviour on buses, eating sweets in the street, and a hatless or gloveless state. 'Hats parallel to the ground, hair must not touch the shirt collar, scarf tucked inside coat or blazer, and white gloves to be worn with your blazer in the summer,' Durham High School ordered. Walking with or talking to a boy was a very serious offence. The uniform identified one as a member of the school and to be seen behaving conspicuously, without gloves or hat, or with a hat worn in a rakish way, was to let the side down. Two boarders from Lady Eleanor Holles who encountered their headmistress while they were on an illicit jaunt to Twickenham escaped really serious consequences because 'she was so horror-struck at our being in Twickenham without our hats that it never entered her head that we shouldn't be there at all'[70] – which is comparable to the Birmingham headmistress who, finding two of her girls crouching in the street, wailed, 'Girls, girls, I say nothing about your playing marbles in the gutter. But *where* are your gloves?' Gloves were mandatory, even with summer dresses. The penalty at Clifton High School if you were caught without them was to be deprived of your hat-band for three weeks – felt to be a deep disgrace.

A new prestige was attached to the high schools and grammar schools when the whole education system was reorganized after the 1944 Education Act, and the Board of Education became a ministry. It had been settled that the secondary schools should be reorganized as three distinct types: grammar, secondary technical, and secondary modern schools, all to be maintained by the local authorities. The direct-grant schools with both fee-paying and non-fee-paying pupils were to act as a bridge between the independent schools and the maintained and voluntary-aided schools (at which all education would now be free). They could apply to remain within the scheme, but there were provisos: the first concerned their preparatory departments, which would be classed as independent schools; and the second, more important, condition was that every direct-grant school must offer the local authority each year no less than 25 per cent of the previous year's admission to the upper school as free places. The local authority would have the right to take up a further 25 per cent of the places, and the residue would be filled by fee-payers who had competed for their places.

It was a golden age for the direct-grant schools. The social broadening was an enormous benefit; the competition for the places was far greater than it had ever been, and the sense of achievement on the part of the professional classes when their children secured one completely extinguished any doubts they might have had about class differences. These were the years of meritocracy, when to pass the 11+ seemed to ensure a bright and prosperous future (and to fail it doomed you to be for ever an underdog). The high schools now took only children with academic potential – there had been many before who had been unsuited to the sort of education they offered. A few former direct-grant schools reluctantly decided at this stage that they would have to become independent. Clifton was one where the Bristol LEA would have insisted on a far higher degree of control than the school could have accepted, and it would in any case only be a temporary respite, for Bristol made it clear that it hoped to bring in a comprehensive system after a few years, at which point there would be no further use for a direct-grant school. Clifton therefore had to face the acute anxiety – at a time when all its energy seemed to be required for re-establishing itself after the war – of turning itself into an independent school. This it accomplished thirty years earlier than its sister schools did, though latterly they were all aware that their days were numbered. Not only was there strong political feeling about spending public funds on schools that were largely unaccountable, that were felt to be for the privileged and that creamed the most able from the state system, but there was burning middle-class resentment about the children (*their* children) who had failed to secure a grammar school education.

The end came in 1976, with a Labour government committed to removing the direct-grant status. The schools had three choices: they could elect to be independent, they could become integrated with the state system, or they could close. The GPDST chose the first, as did many schools of their kind. It was a decision that required great courage; few of the high schools had any endowments and they would now have to survive on the fees alone. All of them felt that since these would have to be greatly increased the first priority was to raise money to help in cases of financial need. Now there are scholarships and bursaries, and in 1980, under a Conservative government, an Assisted Places scheme was introduced to help bright children with school fees.

Nevertheless, the high schools which were intended to practise no class discrimination have inevitably become academies for the prosperous. Fees which once could be paid without much sacrifice from a middle- or lower-middle-class income now make a considerable impact on nearly all families. St Paul's is the most expensive, almost twice as much as the cost per capita in a London secondary school; fees which in 1960 were £38 13s a term (£50 including extras) thirty years later are twenty-five times as much. (The changes in the first sixty years of the school's life – the fees were £7 in 1904 – were not nearly so marked.) The GPDST schools, with their centralized administration, are able to keep costs to a minimum and their fees are, with only a couple of exceptions, the lowest of the high schools. Their number has dwindled a little since 1900, and now stands at twenty-six, two – Heathfield, Pinner (formerly Harrow High School), and Charters-Ancaster (an amalgamation of two private schools) – having recently applied to join them. Out of approximately seventeen thousand pupils 2,900 have Assisted Places and four hundred have bursaries. The high schools are still highly academic, though their syllabus and outlook is much wider than it was fifty years ago. Nearly 50 per cent of GPDST sixth-formers go on to universities, 15 per cent to other degree courses, and Oxford High School, to take only one example, would reckon to send fifteen or sixteen a year to Oxford or Cambridge. The thrifty ingenuity of the GPDST has always been notable. Many of their schools occupy cramped sites incorporating old and unsuitable buildings, and it has needed much juggling with space as well as money to fit in all the workshops, music and drama blocks, art centres and sports complexes that modern education demands. Four London schools have no facilities yet for teaching craft, design and technology (CDT), so a double-decker bus equipped to give nine- to thirteen-year-olds a foundation course in this new subject now visits them.

Though middle-class parents may reckon it an achievement to get a child through the entrance exam and safely launched upon a high school career, the schools themselves feel that they are competing for a declining number of children, both with other independent schools and with the maintained sector, particularly at the sixth-form level, when some pupils choose to go to sixth-form colleges and colleges of further education, as well as to boys' schools. In South London particularly, where the GPDST originally set up so many schools, a chill wind is felt to be blowing. Only one GPDST school, Sheffield, has tried to storm male bastions and take boys; and compared with the boarding schools there are surprisingly few headmasters, though as at all girls' schools, even convents, there is a large percentage of male teachers. The high schools will always attract those parents who feel that girls do better in a single-sex school, that the comprehensives are too large and not sufficiently academically demanding, but how much longer financial pressures and a diminishing birth rate will allow them to stay in existence is another matter.

4

Public Schools: The Gridiron and the Book

The System

The architect of Roedean, Sir John Simpson, was, it seems, something of a wag. After he had provided the buildings on the Brighton coast for the Misses Lawrence he devised a punning motto in two languages, 'Honneur aux Dignes', or 'Honour Roedean', and drew up a coat of arms with a collared hind chained to an open book, a gridiron upon its shoulder. His Olde Englysshe explanation runs thus:

> Thys Mounte upon a field of Silver and Blewe parted by a waving line signifieth the Dene whereon sitteth the Schoole aspected southerlie to the sea and skye. And the Hinde is for the young gerles therein for theie weare the Collar of wholesome Rule and are bound to the Boke of Lernynge by a golden Chaine of Kindnesse.
>
> (Yet are they free to move about the Mounte soe they forsake not their Boke.)
>
> And whereas the Hinde is charged upon her shoulder with the golden Gridiron of the blessed St Lawrence the Founders' Patron soe shall the gerles carry alway thro their lyves the mark of the Mistress' teachynge.

In spite of the disingenuous explanation of the gridiron symbolism, most who have been through the fiery furnace of six years in a public school must suppose that Sir John was intending another joke here. They may or may not agree about the 'wholesome rule' and the 'golden chain of kindness' or the freedom to move about, but all have been stretched on the gridiron – if not in their more senior years then certainly at the beginning. The original school hymn of St Catherine's, Bramley (founded 1885), included a gloomy catalogue of the pains of the saint's martyrdom:

> What to her the wheel of torture?
> What the dungeon's dreary shade,
> Hunger, cold and sharp temptation?
> She her willing choice had made.

This, of course, was apt to invite ribald comments from pupils who felt they themselves had little choice. The School of S. Helen and S. Katharine also sang about 'the wheel of torture' (and indeed still wear it on their blazers).

The sort of exhortation that public school headmistresses commonly used to address to their flocks also gives the feeling of a process of painful purgation.

> You are sent here [St Leonards] . . . in order that by dint of teaching and preaching, by discipline of mind and body, by force of example and mutual influence, you may at last grow up into the best type of girl and woman that your natural equipment allows you to be.[1]

It is difficult, as will be discussed, to decide which of the girls' schools can be categorized as 'public' and which are merely 'independent' formerly 'private', but other considerations apart, 'public schools' were at the beginning, having modelled themselves on boys' schools, usually tougher: Roedean and Felixstowe perched on their cliffs, swept by Siberian winds and with a yeasty sea pounding at the shingle below; St Leonards, on an equally wind-raked stretch of Fifeshire coast ('alarmingly efficient, sensible, competent and hard,' one girl wrote of her fellow pupils; 'their bony frames hurt if you collided with them'[2]); Wycombe Abbey, where the founder believed in daily cold baths and perpetually cold corridors ('Hot baths . . . were only available once a week. These principles applied as much to the mistresses as to the girls'[3]). Margaret Kennedy said of Cheltenham that the girls 'were kept most wonderfully busy, and in their subsequent careers they did [the headmistress] credit'; 'The governesses think of nothing but games,' complained two of the characters in her novel *The Constant Nymph*;[4] at Downe House the headmistress 'once preached a sermon on lack of nerve after the cricket eleven had suffered a severe defeat';[5] at Badminton – 'any idiot could pick us out from the rest of Bristol – hair scragged back, purple-cheeked, bull-necked, waistless and scabby-kneed with calves like cottage loaves';[6] at Malvern steel-mesh nets hang below stairwells to catch the falling bodies; at Sherborne – 'Run about, girls, *like* boys, and then you won't think *of* them.'[7] The St Trinian's scene is not exaggerated. 'Against a Stygian background of low leaden sky and greyish mud the blue-and-red faces of healthy English girlhood at play struck a note of crude but agreeable colour . . . Scourged by the icy blast of a late March afternoon, the First and Reserve hockey elevens were settling down to a practice match.'[8]

It has to be said at the outset that none of the girls' public schools can remotely compare in wealth and antiquity to Eton, Winchester, Westminster and Harrow, and by their side must look like private schools. With the exception of Cheltenham, all are half or at most two thirds the size, and though they may inhabit historic sites the history is not their own. Cheltenham with its eight hundred girls and ecclesiastical Gothic unity, and St Leonards with its ancient grey stones are probably the only two which in appearance could be mistaken for boys' schools. The others inhabit either purpose-built premises of varying degrees of grimness, or (the luckiest ones) erstwhile stately homes surrounded by beautiful parkland. Malvern comes somewhere in between the two, in a huge former hotel that looks like a turn-of-the-century infirmary. Many are a hotch-potch of random buildings, with more than a passing resemblance to this burlesque description:

> St Trinian's ... recognized, with a light shudder, by the Board of Education, and standing in extensive grounds on the beautiful Surrey uplands. St Trinian's is a towering and impressive pile ... of red-brick Gothic, a landmark for some miles.
>
> The main Gothic block, dated 1875, is today somewhat overshadowed by successive additions in the Neo-Renaissance, Prusso-Babylonian and Pure Functional styles ...
>
> The Chapel, a free adaptation in mauve-and-orange Doultonware by Jakes (1880–82) from the Baptistery of San Giovanni at Pisa, is undenominational. The interior frescoes illustrating Suffering, Joy, Heroism, Endeavour, Achievement and Ecstasy in the sphere of female Rugby football (1920) are by Bidet.[9]

Girls do not take easily to life in large institutions, and though at the outset founders spoke expansively of providing them with the same advantages as boys they did not in the main attempt to bring the numbers up to the boys' level. The whole idea of such a school for girls was an innovation in the 1870s. Founders wished to develop in pupils a strong sense of corporate unity and obligation to the community, and to kindle a flame that would be passed from generation to generation. 'What she wanted,' said an early Cheltonian of Miss Beale, 'was to make fine women who would influence their generation.'[10] By the 1880s preparation for a life of leadership and service was a required motive for those who initiated a new school. Thus the Revd Dr Joseph Merriman, addressing the sponsors at one of the early meetings to promote the school that became St Catherine's, Bramley, spoke broadly about the public spirit. And the founder of St Helen's, Northwood, chose the ox-eye daisy as the school flower because its massed florets symbolized 'that unity of purpose, that fair orderliness, that equability of all those who are working together for some common end, that close comradeship that we would have as characteristics'.[11]

Features of both the girls' and the boys' public schools were the house system; a bracing spirit imposed from above; and an excess of team games. But whereas the origins, history and character of boys' public schools differed sharply from private establishments, it is far more difficult to draw such a distinction with girls'. It is rare if not unknown for a privately owned boys' school to become a public one; but though a few girls' boarding schools – Cheltenham, St Leonards, Sherborne, Wycombe Abbey, St Swithun's (as Winchester High School, see page 73), and more recently Benenden, Westonbirt and Cobham Hall – and nearly all the day schools started as public companies, Badminton, Downe House, Felixstowe, Malvern and Roedean, which have been long regarded as public schools, began as small private ventures which later transferred to trust ownership. Now that all the 260-odd members of the Girls' Schools Association are charitable trusts they are in effect public schools, and certainly resemble each other more than they did fifty years ago, in that the older public schools are more feminine, and the small ones – now greatly increased in numbers and facilities – aim at turning out the same sort of robust, independent woman, prepared to do something worthwhile with her life.

Thus to categorize certain schools as more 'public' than others is to make a distinction that is now mostly historical. But the system originally introduced by St Leonards and imitated by many turn-of-the-century schools was a very potent one; its ethic affected all the schools discussed here (with the exception of Cobham Hall, the only post-war foundation in this chapter) and, modified, has to a large degree been adopted by the smaller, more idiosyncratic schools discussed in the next chapter.

Mostly, the public schools were not the pioneers of new learning for women; the day schools must take the credit for that, and had nearly thirty years' start. And though Cheltenham and St Leonards achieved remarkable academic successes – Agnata Ramsay, who went from the latter to Girton in 1884, was placed first in the first class of the Classical Tripos, beating all the male candidates and receiving the accolade of a cartoon in *Punch* – in general the day schools had the edge over them. Indeed, to a degree the public schools evolved in reaction to the strained, bespectacled and anaemic bluestockings that the high schools were felt to be turning out. There was far more to education than cultivating brains; it should prepare pupils to make the most of their talents, to work and play hard, and to take a responsible place in the community.

This was not a wholly innovatory idea. In a prospectus of 1770 the Canonesses of the Holy Sepulchre, when the school that was later to become New Hall was at Liège, set down their aims:

> Former le coeur des jeunes personnes du sexe à la vertu, leur faire aimer les pratiques de la religion, et les en instruire à fonds; leur inspirer le goût de l'application et du travail, de bon ordre et de l'économie domestique, orner leur esprit, and les accoutumer aux usages du monde poli et chrétien; tel est le but de tous les exercices de cette maison.

There would not now be so much emphasis on religious instruction, and domestic economy would not be mentioned, but the character-forming principle is the same. At the Clergy Orphan Girls' School, the rules in 1805 stated that the children 'be carefully taught the duties of true humility, of obedience and submission to Parents and Superiors, of gratitude to Benefactors, and of courtesy, affability and condescension to all'. The advantages 'arising from diligence, honesty and sobriety [should] be frequently pointed out to them, that they may thereby be able to live with credit and reputation in the world, and become useful members of the Community'. Here one has to discount the precepts peculiar to a Georgian charity school, but the hope that pupils should be well mannered, taught to work hard and lead useful lives is still expressed by most schools.

The emphasis on health, suitable clothing and adequate exercise was also entirely new. To be fair, some of the day schools had attempted to regulate these matters. Miss Buss had been vigilant about health: 'I hope your daughter wears woollen combinations. That is of more importance to her than passing matriculation,' she had remarked to one mother, and pupils were supposed to keep detailed records of the time spent on homework. But clearly at a day school it was impossible to guard against overwork, as Miss Lawrence was insistent that she did at Roedean (and where girls were actually penalized for finishing work too soon and moving on to something else). Most schools dispatched even their senior girls to bed soon after nine o'clock, and saw to it that they did not work after school hours. At St Swithun's in the 1930s this was carried to such lengths that even the sixth form, working for university entrance, were not allowed to do more than three hours' study (which included lessons and prep) after lunch.

This new breed of young woman, reared on fresh air, plain food, boys' games and cold baths, would become robust, of tireless energy, public-spirited and responsible. 'If only every girl would go to school and stay there long enough to learn the corporate virtues, in two or three generations we should realize Utopia,' the founder of Wycombe Abbey told the Headmistresses' Association. She envisaged her pupils dedicated to future lives of usefulness and to a broader sphere of action than merely the home – though in the early days there was, for the upper-middle-class girls educated in these establishments, little thought of professional careers. '[Father] is very strong about it being wrong for girls who live at home to take jobs from girls who need them,' said a character in Elsie J. Oxenham's *The School Without a Name* (1924). Nor was there any expectation that they would ever have to cope with the nitty-gritty of household chores; schools like Wycombe Abbey had an abundance of maids – the carrying of water to the dormitories for the morning cold splash alone must have required a vast and strong-armed workforce – and the girls remembered with distaste how they had to make their own beds on Sundays. Public schools saw themselves as pioneers of a more wholesome attitude to femalekind; their pupils were encouraged to shed such fetters of femininity as delicate health and corsets (Miss Lawrence of Roedean, who apparently wore none herself, was very strong on this, as Miss Buss had been). No doubt the slavish veneration of games was encouraged with the idea that the atmosphere of 'Oh-goody-goody-we-ought-to-do-well-in-lacrosse-this-term. Hurrah-for-the-house-and-I'm-so-glad-I'm-not-pretty' – the Good Moral Tone, in fact, that the best schools invariably boasted of possessing – would displace the gossip and prurient speculation otherwise endemic in a community of girls.

But though girls in these new establishments were to be given a boys' education, which meant they had to contend with a curriculum to which by no means all were suited and an abundance of team games which many of them detested, they had also to submit to a discipline that no one would have dared impose on boys – such as perpetual silence on the school premises (Wycombe Abbey was exempt from this), lack of freedom (however emancipated the school one was never allowed beyond the gate), constant employment and very little choice of how one occupied one's time, a plethora of rules and a general niggling authority. 'There are no petty rules or regulations,' a housemistress told the first pupils at Wycombe Abbey in 1896, 'for we shall depend on the discipline of the Sixth Form and your own sense of honour. But you are not, of course, allowed to eat butter and jam *together* with your bread as some of you did at supper tonight.'[12] The girl who recorded this tried to explain to her Eton brothers what an innovation Wycombe Abbey was:

> 'But how's it different from your Ladies' College at Eastbourne?' asked my brothers.
>
> 'We don't have rules' I would reply loftily.
>
> 'Oh yes, you do! You said you had to have cold baths and wear your hair in pigtails, and poor Ethel has to play lacrosse though she hates it. I call those rules.'[13]

Early Roedean was recorded as having the most complex (and otiose) code of rules of all, and Margaret Cole in 1907 lost her sub-prefect's badge and forfeited her access to the library because she finished her French prep too early and was reading Macaulay's *Essays* in the time allocated. 'A friend of mine, a sub-prefect . . . saw me and reported the sin to the head of the house.'[14] Even schools like Badminton (fictionalized in this extract), ambitious to turn out tough free-thinkers, and who prided themselves on their individuality and advanced attitudes, fell victim to this peculiarly female lack of sense of proportion:

> 'When the list for cold baths says 6.55 a.m. it does not mean 7. And it isn't as if your work was up to standard. Far from it. I am sure we will all have our work cut out if you're ever to pass Matriculation . . . And as for your untidiness! . . . How you'll ever become a responsible member of the community is beyond me.'[15]

It was the same at Downe House, which also saw itself as iconoclastic:

> Our good marks, for work, and our bad marks, for ill behaviour, were read out before the assembled school every Sunday after lunch. Miss Willis had a restrained dramatic delivery that was immensely effective. 'Number forty-five,' she would read out after my name, speaking in a low toneless voice, as if the words were too horrible to utter. 'Untidiness, forty-six, forty-seven, forty-eight, untidiness forty-nine, being late for Chapel, fifty, disobedience, fifty-one, bad manners to Mademoiselle . . .' I was forever plodding up the cloisters towards a floor known as Middle West, sent to Miss Willis in disgrace for exploding a balloon in a French lesson, or for whistling and banging my desk during algebra. Such behaviour was boring, childish and unnecessary, but it still seems to me that the pain and despondency that it occasioned among the staff was disproportionate. I was constantly made to feel that my soul was in danger, if not irretrievably lost.[16]

Few female establishments can apparently exist without a proliferation of rules; it is noticeable, for instance, how long governing bodies of all-female colleges at Oxford can debate such issues as who should be allowed to attend guest nights or use the SCR car park or fetch wine from the cellar, the principles governing these seeming to the protagonists to be of fundamental importance, as the cold baths and pigtails did to Wycombe Abbey. The rules about compulsory lacrosse which struck Winifred Peck's brothers as unfair were imposed, no doubt, to toughen the girls and to try to eradicate the drooping femininity which had been a characteristic of boarding establishments hitherto. And since team games for girls were still a very recent innovation, compulsory lacrosse may well have seemed exciting and revolutionary. The rule of silence which was a particular feature of Cheltenham Ladies' College (there are still vestiges of it there now) arose out of uncertainty about the whole concept of boarding schools for girls. Even in 1898 when Alice Zimmern was writing her celebration of the new learning available to women, *The Renaissance of Girls' Education*, and describing the excellence of such foundations as St Leonards and Wycombe Abbey, she was uncertain about the boarding principle, and wondered whether 'the gains to character really outweigh the advantages of family life'. And though one gets the impression that she would have consigned no daughter of hers to be a boarder, she does concede that 'without the excessive excitement of home gaieties and the distraction of domestic interests' study was facilitated. By this date it was becoming fashionable for upper-class families, who would hitherto have kept their daughters at home with governesses, to dispatch them to a public school where they would mingle with their own kind. Apart from anything else, as Winifred Peck pointed out in her memories of her own schooling, mothers now tended to absorb themselves in activities outside the home, which left little time for their daughters. Nor had there yet been literary exposures written by the disaffected of what boarding school life might entail, and few mothers had any idea of the dangers and moral evils, while fathers, if they remembered enough from their own days, would dismiss the possibility of the same thing happening with girls. By the 1920s and 1930s the more thoughtful parents were not so certain that they wanted such manly daughters – hence the plethora of individualistic private schools that sprang up all over southern England. And in 1962 when Cobham Hall came into existence, though it did not regard itself as 'progressive', it set out to discard most of the features which the founders of the earlier public schools had considered of prime importance. Organized religion, character-building discomfort, the house spirit, the rule of the prefects, team games – none of these were felt to be relevant to the 1960s, which was essentially the age of the individual.

The Schools

Cheltenham was and is still different from any other girls' public school. First, it is one of the few to have received a royal charter (granted in 1935, Roedean's following in 1938). It was an early Victorian foundation imbued with all the ardour and high seriousness of that era, from which in many ways it did not escape until after Miss Beale's death. It was also a pioneer, the first proprietary school for girls, a public company rather than the private venture that all girls' schools except the charitable foundations had hitherto been. Though after the 1880s it became predominantly a boarding school, it opened with eighty-two pupils on 13 February 1854 as a day college providing 'an education based on religious principles which, preserving the modesty and gentleness of the female character, should so far cultivate [a girl's] intellectual powers as to fit her as a wife, mother, mistress and friend, the natural companion and helpmeet for man'.[17] These were the words of the founders (who were unworldly, as can be seen, and did not foresee ribald misinterpretation). It is evident that they had the traditional role of women in mind (after all, it was early Victorian Cheltenham), and in the style of the times they also made it perfectly clear which classes they had in mind: 'the daughters and young children of Noblemen and Gentlemen'. The fees were fairly moderate, but at six to twenty guineas per annum, higher than the high schools were to charge, though music lessons were at first included. Those who lived too far away to attend daily lodged with suitable ladies in the town; the 'house' system thus grew out of an arrangement that was at first essentially a private one. The syllabus was much the same as the better sort of private school offered, but did include the elements of Latin. Cheltenham, a select spa town, has never been a milieu to countenance revolution, and the parents were adamant that they would not stand for anything in the nature of 'advanced' education. The school's education committee accordingly were placatory, insisting that they did not propose to turn out 'female pedants'.

The first principal, Miss Anne Procter,* had to contend with the low state of the finances as well as difficult parents (there were complaints of such matters as 'not enough conversational French' and 'imperfect knowledge in sewing and cutting out'). Numbers dropped and in 1858 she resigned and left to found her own school. It is at this point that Dorothea Beale enters the scene. She was twenty-seven when she was appointed Lady Principal, and her only experience of school was the brief period she had spent at a small private establishment at about the age of twelve, and a few unhappy months teaching at Casterton. The difficulties she faced were enormous: numbers were declining; the college was running at a loss; each quarter it seemed less likely that it could survive, until in the half-year of 1859 there were only sixty-five pupils and a few pounds in the bank. But this was to be the lowest point; the tide turned in 1860 with the presence of John Houghton Brancker on the college council, a man of great financial acumen and vision who over the next decades was to devote himself to the school he had helped to save.

The Cheltenham teaching, later to become so renowned, took longer than is generally supposed to raise itself above the ordinary level. Jane Ellen Harrison, later to become a distinguished classical scholar, thought little of the history-teaching, on which the college prided itself, when she arrived there in the late 1860s. 'It consisted mainly in moralizings on the doings and misdoings of kings. We did the Stuart period in tedious detail.' There were no books – the early difficulty in finding suitable textbooks has already been touched on; 'and what we had to feed on were the notes we took of lectures – a wretched starvation system'. Arithmetic and elementary maths, on the other hand, were admirably taught, but the teachers did not go very far.[18] Some twenty years later another girl considered the teaching 'old-fashioned and probably even then out of date', though she added that the teachers were women of culture and character.[19]

However, by 1865 Miss Beale's work was well enough known for her to be summoned to give evidence to the Schools Inquiry Commission, and this in itself earned the college considerable prestige. Instead of deprecating this development, the town of Cheltenham found itself taking a pride in being in the vanguard of the women's education movement, and there was great local support for the ambitious scheme to erect a building worthy of the college, though there were those who thought it was on a preposterously lavish scale. This building in the Gothic favoured by the newer boys' public schools, into which the girls moved on Lady Day 1873, is the nucleus of the present vastly extended campus. It was planned for 220 pupils (which then was thought to be absurd optimism), but by 1898 there were nine hundred, ranging from small children in the kindergarten to senior students who worked for external university degrees (and were to continue to do so until

* In fact her official position was 'Lady Vice-Principal', her mother, an army widow, being the 'Lady Principal', but the daughter was the real head of the college.

1924, long after the universities were opened to women), and those in the three teacher training departments – secondary, elementary and kindergarten. Such breadth is unique in educational history; it was comprehensive in the widest sense.

The decorated Gothic brick faced with Cotswold stone (described by Pevsner as an 'aesthetic disaster' for Regency Cheltenham) in which style all except the most recent additions were to be made, was, as has been said, characteristic of early and mid-Victorian educational institutions. It was also wholly appropriate for Miss Beale, an early Victorian Tractarian, who more perhaps than any other headmistress shaped the institution she served and formed it in her own image. The college was decked with works of art – statues, stained glass, paintings, the gifts of friends and former pupils – that she envisaged as a subliminal education, drawing those who passed them daily to higher things. The windows that adorn the tower entrance, commissioned in the 1880s, show Spenser's female knight Britomart, the personification of chastity and purity. The frieze 'A Dream of Fair Women' painted by a pupil of George Richmond's (J. Eadie Reid) in the Princess Hall shows Miss Beale's vision of woman as the sacrificer, steadfast, pure and faithful, but always submissive. Here is Andromache bidding Hector farewell as he sets off for war; Eurydice following Orpheus; Penelope unravelling her tapestry; Alcestis, who gave her life to redeem her husband from death; Jephthah about to be sacrificed by her father; the Indian Princess Savitri who wrestled with the Prince of Death for her husband's life; Iphigenia by the altar on which she is about to expiate her father's offence against Artemis; Portia, wife of Brutus, the ideal of a Roman matron; the Lady in *Comus* beside the sorcerer's magic which because of her innocence is powerless to harm her. Only Bradamante, the Christian Amazon from Ariosto's *Orlando Furioso*, shows a more militant aspect of womanhood, while the inclusion of Hat-Shephset, Queen of Ancient Egypt, a wise ruler and a great organizer, evokes the feminine type that the public schools as a whole have always most desired to mould.

This far-ranging choice of female exemplars gives some indication of the breadth of Dorothea Beale's reading and interests – the product of an upbringing in a fastidious and intellectual home, the sort of culture that can never be acquired at school. Ill health had meant that she had had to be taken away from her boarding school, and during the subsequent adolescent years she spent at home she found 'pasturage enough . . . dreaming much and seeking for a fuller realization of the great spiritual realities which make one feel that all knowledge is sacred'.[20] It has already been said that reformed education for women was not all pure gain, that there were many like Dorothea Beale who learned far more at home at their leisure than they ever could have working for exams. Charlotte Yonge, eight years older, who in many ways she much resembled, was another. Both had the same ardent seriousness, the same lofty idealism, but whereas Miss Yonge thought in terms of parish schools and bible classes and sought to influence the girls of her day in that direction, Miss Beale even as an adolescent had had a far grander vision of 'an air-castle school, with a central quadrangle, cloisters and rooms above',[21] where the woman of her dreams could acquire the ideal education. 'All knowledge is sacred,' she had said; learning for her started with religion. She taught Division I (the upper school and the university class) herself, expounding scripture to them, perhaps wrestling with the infinite number of meanings that could be extracted from a single line of St John's Gospel – a range of thought beyond most hearers – but imbuing them with her passionately held conviction that education was a pattern of receiving and giving, that the light one received should be passed on in service. Frances Buss, involved with a rather different social class, wanted to equip girls to support themselves; but though early Cheltonians certainly became teachers and doctors, Miss Beale's vision for her girls – was there perhaps here a hint of the upper-class prejudice against gentlewomen who earned money? – was more one of influence, service and leadership freely given in the spheres of home, the parish, perhaps settlements and the mission field.

The remarkable feature in the history of the college is that this singularly unworldly woman who abhorred competition should have achieved so much materially, and at every stage convinced her council that her vision, which inevitably meant the outlay of huge sums of money, was valid. She had no sense of finality, only of waiting for the next divine command to reveal itself, and it was not until 1898 that she felt the fabric of the college was adequate to its needs. She never retired, and when she died in 1906 she had been principal for forty-eight years. Her influence on education had been enormous, teachers from the college being sought by all the newer foundations, and by the end of 1897 the headmistresses of more than forty important schools, at home and overseas, many of them new foundations, had come from Cheltenham.[22] But it was an institution impossible to imitate, though some schools added 'College' after their name in emulation. Thus Miss M. M. Raven, the Cheltonian headmistress of Uplands, a small Suffolk school which had originated in Surrey, announced that as from January 1929 Uplands would become Felixstowe Ladies' College (a name later changed to Felixstowe College) under the aegis of the Martyrs' Memorial and Church of England Trust. Malvern, which began in 1893 as Ivydene, a small school for five little boys and five little girls, became Malvern Girls' College. However, it was the Roedean system that these schools, and Sherborne (founded 1899), adopted; Cheltenham could not have been imitated without a second Miss Beale.

Her achievement is all the more extraordinary in that, in the smaller details of life, she clung to the past. She had been reared on quill pens, so everyone in college must use quill pens long after steel nibs were available. 'The noise they made when a whole division was writing examinations in one hall was quite indescribable.'[23] Until 1914 there were two little page-boys in buttons whose duties included cutting down for use in Division II the quill pens that had been discarded by Division I. (Other duties included filling ink-pots and blowing the organ. Miss Beale allowed one boy in to scripture lessons, but he had to sit behind a curtain. He later became a missionary.) Her notions of propriety are reminiscent of early Charlotte Yonge. 'You are too young, and I hope too innocent, to realize the gross vulgarity of such a letter, or the terrible results to which it might lead,' she said to a seventeen-year-old, one of whose friends had sent her a postcard with the message 'Give my love to the examiners.'[24] Never requiring re-creation herself, she could not understand that anyone else should wish for it, and regarded the provision of tennis courts for the teachers quite superfluous (she spoke of tennis as 'playing archery'). Nor could she understand why any should wish to live out of sight of their work place. Even in the summer holidays she quite frequently chose to live in the sanatorium.

The girls in the early days seem to have been infused with Miss Beale's sense of purpose, and excited by the sense of being part of a unique educational venture. 'From our window ... we stand looking out over College, with its many small pinnacles silhouetted against the pale sky, like a miniature city ... and silence falls on another College day', runs an account of school life in the 1905 magazine, which proudly chronicles the features which the writers felt were unique to Cheltenham. Inevitably there was reaction. After Miss Beale had gone the busyness remained, but the girls no longer saw so much purpose in it. A Cheltonian of the Victorian period thought that there had been a great decline by her daughters' day, that games were overdone 'and the constant scurrying is bad for growing children. They never have a moment to themselves.'[25] She also thought that the girls were amazingly empty-headed, unable to take anything seriously except athletics and the cinema, and deprecated the type that the public schools now aimed to produce: 'The devil in the schoolgirl is thrown out, perhaps, by organized games, strict discipline, and such constant occupation that she finds no time to get into mischief. But to the swept and garnished vacuum what seven devils enter in, when she has left her carefully guarded scholastic establishment?' And Margaret Kennedy, a pupil before the First War, in describing 'Cleeve College' spoke about the belief that 'a uniform and most desirable type can be produced by keeping eight hundred girls perpetually on the run'.[26]

It was a characteristic of the public schools. 'The day was governed by bells,' said a Roedeanian who remembered the frenetic changing in and out of the required dress and the 'book' which had to be signed on time; 'and the lassitude which stretched us on our backs for most of Sunday came far less from using our bodies and brains than from the anxiety caused by a six days' race with time'.[27] 'We were never allowed to be idle,' said one girl who had been at St Leonards in the 1940s and found it 'totally absorbing and satisfying for the successful'; 'we were expected to work, and particularly to play, hard, whether or not there was any prospect of success'.[28] Louisa Lumsden, the first headmistress (and one of the first three women to take the Cambridge Tripos), had made that point twenty years before. Writing in the school's jubilee book in 1927 she said that she had wanted to provide a thorough and intellectual education, and play that was not frivolous, but as honest as work. Inevitably there were those who were wholly unsuited to this system – Winifred Peck categorized them as the artistic, the sensitive and introspective, the naturally yielding and feminine[29] – and it was the pace, the obsessional games and the lack of privacy that they most detested.

Like Cheltenham, St Leonards, the second public school to be founded, was not originally intended as a boarding school, but rather to serve the needs of the professional upper middle class in St Andrews who, following the example of other towns in the north and Edinburgh in particular, had formed a Ladies' Educational Association. A limited company, the St Andrews School for Girls Company, was floated, a capital of £3,000 subscribed, and a lease taken out on two houses. From the start a quarter of the girls had to board. Fifeshire, between the Firth of Forth and the Tay, has never been easily accessible. In order to reach St Andrews in the early days one of the founding pupils used to take a train from Edinburgh to Granton, cross the Forth by boat, get on to another train at Burntisland, sometimes changing at Thornton and always at Leuchars, and then take the horse bus through the town.[30] Now, though there are road bridges over the Forth and the Tay, there is no longer a railway link from Leuchars, and St Andrews seems remote indeed for parents outside Fifeshire who are called upon to arrange mid-term visits home. The number of English pupils at this school (which is held by the ordinary Scottish school to be unwholesomely English) has greatly diminished since the early days, when the records show that many were coming from the south (in 1911, for instance, a third of the new intake were from outside Scotland) to experience an innovatory education which originally could be had nowhere else.

The most innovatory element was not so much the games, which were not at all dominant to start with, but the democracy, or rather oligarchy. The girls, said Miss Lumsden, were to learn to govern themselves, to be worthy of trust and to be trusted, and the older and leading girls were to have a share in the government. This last feature was taken up enthusiastically by all the subsequent foundations, and was to lead to a peculiar tyranny of its own that many thought was worse than the teacher-rule of the older type of school. However, in this St Leonards resembled a boys' school, and this was held then to be the best model on which to form one for girls.

St Leonards also had the old grey stones that girls' schools so notably lacked, and in one sense a long-continuing tradition of education. It is a hauntingly beautiful place, standing on a promontory dominated by the tower which is all that remains of the church of St Regulus, by the ruins of the cathedral, abandoned after the Reformation, and the priory of Augustinian Canons Regular. This ancient setting, to which the school moved in 1883, held the first St Leonards, founded in 1512 for 'poor clerks' attending the university and enclosed by the wall erected in 1523 by Prior Hepburn to contain the monastic lands. The college survived the Reformation and continued to be a part of the university until 1747, when it amalgamated with St Salvator's, and its buildings and grounds passed into private hands. They were used briefly in the 1860s as a university hall of residence, and then were bought in 1882 by St Andrews School, which thereupon took on the name of St Leonards. The library, housed in a historic sixteenth-century town house (acquired in the 1920s) which once belonged to the chamberlain to the Earl of Moray, half-brother of Mary, Queen of Scots, and where each subject is accommodated in a different room, is among the finest of any school, and is remembered with deep affection by all who have read there. 'The St Leonards girl,' said the first school history, 'like her brother at Eton or Winchester, finds at her school the romance of tradition, the stimulus of a link with the past.'[31] By the time the school became St Leonards, Miss Lumsden had gone. She lacked stamina, it seems; she had left Cheltenham after eighteen months, exhausted by the quantities of elementary Latin she had to mark,[32] and by 1881 her health prevented her from continuing. She became first warden of the St Andrews women students' hall of residence, and was succeeded at St Leonards by Miss Frances Dove, who was to leave to found Wycombe Abbey in 1896.

Even after only ten years, it is clear that the school had a strong sense of its own past. Verses which appeared in the *St Leonards School Gazette* in 1887, while lame, show the sentiments of 'Forty Years on':

Comrades, let me speak a little – comrades, let me call you all,
You who were my mates, and you who gather now within the Hall.

Ten long years have passed away, and of the band who gathered erst,
Only two or three remaining from the last are now the first.

What of those who passing onward scattered into separate lives?
Still we see them – some are married, happy mothers, happy wives.

Some are pouring forth the learning that from Wisdom's well they drew,
Some are fighting still for honours, ever plucking laurels new.

Some have gone to foreign countries, travelled wide in distant lands,
Some remain at home in quiet, not, we trust, with idle hands.

The Gazettes of that period show that pupils were coming from such distant places as Coventry, Edgbaston, Bath and London, but also Gibraltar and Alexandria. One gets the impression of female Etonians (Miss Lumsden had always 'hoped that the Council did not intend to admit all social classes'); some of the leavers were taking the Girton entrance exam, and were distinguishing themselves in medical careers; some were studying music (from the beginning it was a very musical school); on the other hand, many were being presented at Court. In the 1892 gazette it was announced that Mary Crum had been accepted as a violin pupil by Herr Joachim in Berlin; that L. Garrett Anderson had begun studying medicine at the London School of Medicine for Women, and that E. Raffles Brooke had been acting in Dublin at the Gaiety Theatre – an astonishingly eclectic range at that time.

But until the 1940s (except for a brief period during and just after World War I), most girls had no thought of a professional career; instead, conditioned by the school's message of service, they devoted themselves to voluntary work, in settlements, play centres, nursery schools, the juvenile courts, the Guide movement. 'We left school with a strong sense of obligation to serve the community,' wrote one Senior (as from early days the old girls had been termed), 'and I think most of us were prepared for leadership.' Another Senior from the same between-the-wars period thought that 'school had put so much emphasis on doing things for others we almost forgot to do things "for ourselves" that we owed it to others to do. School always played up ... the public spirit, the team spirit.'[33] The 1920s and 1930s saw the girls' public schools at their best but also their worst, and in either case at their most extreme. The tradition of a male *esprit de corps* and conformism was firmly established; there was no room in it for eccentricity, and individuality was suspect. It was long forgotten that the schools had ever been experimental; their outlook was the norm for their many smaller imitators and for the myriads who wrote school stories – which were the most popular girls' reading of those years. At St Leonards, though, a change was under way in the late 1930s under a headmistress who deprecated the overexaltation of games and encouraged girls to be more feminine. 'It is a much kinder school than it was in the twenties,' wrote one Senior who returned to teach after the Second War.

Once the popularity of St Leonards had been established with parents of girls who, if they had been sons, would have been dispatched to Eton or Winchester, the need for a school nearer than Fifeshire became evident. 'Results seem to show that this class of school is one of the chief needs for girls at the present time,' wrote a commentator in 1898.[34] Accordingly Frances Dove, having in her usual meticulous style made everything shipshape at St Leonards and nominated her successor (Julia Grant, who had been the first house-girl and first head girl), went south to found an English St Leonards. One gets some idea of her phenomenal powers of work and organization from the fact that almost within a year of leaving Fifeshire she had succeeded in setting up the Girls' Education Company to finance the venture, and, having assembled a council of influential enthusiasts who would support and advise her, had persuaded them to put up enough capital to buy Wycombe Abbey in the Chilterns from Lord Carrington and adapt it as a school for a hundred girls. Weaker spirits would have delayed the opening until the premises were ready, but Miss Dove had no intention of losing a minute. The contract was only signed in May, but the first forty pupils (among them four prefects thoughtfully imported from St Leonards) arrived that September, and the repair of the dry rot, the installation of electricity (very daring in 1896) and all the repairs and renovations proceeded around them for the next three years – to the accompaniment of considerable financial anxiety, during which Miss Dove more than once had to wait for her salary because of more pressing commitments.

> We went back after Christmas [wrote Winifred Peck, who had been one of the first forty] to find builders, painters, electricians and plumbers in chief control of the building and even of Miss Dove. We were moved from room to room for meals and lessons. Draughts raged round us from newly opened doors or windows; we had, as we wrote home pathetically, often to break the ice on our cold baths.[35]

This, however, was commonplace in all boarding schools of the period, and central heating did not become standard until the 1960s; at North Foreland Lodge, for instance, there was a period when every pupil had to saw 240 logs a year to keep the fires burning. Miss Dove, moreover, had strong views about fresh air, cold baths and bracing exercise. While her aesthetic sense was finely developed – there were peacocks in the garden, tapestry and antiques in the entrance hall, Liberty curtains with Morris designs, and the everyday crockery was specially designed Rouen ware – and while there was an army of maids to wait upon the girls, she despised all yielding to creature comfort, so corridors and practice rooms were unheated and gales blew through the dormitories. She was impatient with ailments, and her attitude to fainting was much the same as that of a Guards RSM. 'Put your head between your knees at once,' she would hiss to any wilting girl. 'How she retained her belief in this remedy I do not know, for the horror of her voice and the effort to make any movement ended invariably in the victim's having to be carried or dragged out of the church unconscious.'[36]

But to girls like Winifred Peck it was all delightfully novel. Instead of being scolded as a tomboy she was praised for being good at games. There were none of Cheltenham's oppressive rules about silence, and the girls could chatter and laugh, even in the dormitories. The surroundings were satisfyingly beautiful, there were huge grounds to wander in, though a routine designed to fill every minute of the girls' waking hours did not give very much time for this. Ordinary lessons were sandwiched between periods spent on gardening, carpentry and physical exercise.

> Our lives were so full and lived at such speed, all our programme was so well-organized, that we had no idea of occupying ourselves in the holidays,

> and still less when we went home for good. We had worked for exams, played for our teams and lived to the calls of the school bell. Such leisurely enjoyment of music or literature as [those educated at home] knew was incomprehensible to me for a time.[37]

Miss Dove would have liked to see her girls go on to university, above all to Girton (she had not much thought of what would happen after that), but though there were candidates, it was not a burning ambition with most of the upper-class girls of Wycombe in its early years. There was a vague idea that college girls were earnest, bespectacled and dowdy swots, and in any case their parents were certain that it would ruin their chances of marriage. There were quite enough opportunities for a late Victorian girl from a wealthy background to lead a full and satisfying life without going to college.

When Miss Dove went south to establish Wycombe Abbey, Roedean, chronologically the third of the new-style schools, had been in existence for nine years. It had had a totally different beginning from the others, having started as a private venture and, like so many girls' schools, out of urgent financial necessity. That it did not remain a small south coast venture like so many vanished scores of its kind was due to the forceful personality of Penelope Lawrence (born 1857), the most dominant member of the trio of sisters who began the school in 1885. There were thirteen children in the Lawrence family (progeny of two marriages), and eight sisters were at one time or another on the staff, one going out to South Africa to found Roedean, Johannesburg. It was not a wealthy family. Mr Lawrence was a solicitor, later a barrister, whose health was not equal to the strain of supporting so large a family. There was money only to send Penelope to Cambridge, not for her younger sisters, though out of her early earnings as principal of the Froebel Training College Penelope paid for Millicent to go to the Maria Grey College to be trained as a teacher, while Dorothy went to Bedford College.

In 1881 their father was disabled by an accident and his income virtually ceased. Not only was the children's education threatened (there were still four under twelve), but the upkeep of the large house he had built in Wimbledon seemed impossible. The second Mrs Lawrence, a woman of charm and energy, rose resolutely to the occasion and took in pupils whom Dorothy and Millicent taught, side by side, as was the wont in large Victorian families, with their own small sisters. (Penelope herself was then living at home but teaching at Wimbledon High School.) After four years Dorothy and Millicent felt it was impossible to run a school with an invalid father and a tribe of young children in the same house, and in 1885 they persuaded Penelope to join them in founding their own school.

> The success that attended their enterprise was truly remarkable [their brother Paul was to say many years later], and resulted in rescuing the

family from the impending financial disaster which threatened it. Not only were my sisters from the first able to provide for their own maintenance but for the maintenance, education and advancement in life of all the younger members of the family and our parents were enabled to spend the rest of their lives in peace and comfort.[38]

It was at first a delightfully homely project, with Dorothy writing excitedly to Penelope in Madeira about the pupils they might get with a bit of bargaining, such as the two daughters of a local headmaster whom they might swop for two of their little brothers. Brighton was not their first choice, but an aunt told them that at Brighton 'all schools succeed', and so they set up their first establishment in a tall, narrow town house with a basement kitchen and a lot of stairs. Initially the three sisters did all the teaching themselves, supplemented by visiting teachers, though the prospectus spoke largely about the preparation for Girton and Newnham, as well as the rather less specific thorough education 'physical, intellectual and moral'. The numbers increased rapidly, and the Misses Lawrence acquired three adjoining houses in Sussex Square to which they gave the name Wimbledon House – hence the chorus of an early school song:

Wimbledonia, fair and free,
Health and strength belong to thee,
Felix Wimbledonia.

But by 1895 there were ninety girls and it was becoming clear that even larger premises would be required. This time the Misses Lawrence were ambitious that there should be 'a really suitable school building in which the school can have a permanent existence'. With a boldness and confidence that even now seem extraordinary (very few girls' schools at that date were housed in purpose-built premises, and no private schools), they settled for an eighteen-acre site high up on the Downs above Rottingdean; the Roedean Site and Buildings Company was formed, and the sisters began enthusiastically writing round to relatives, friends, old girls and parents asking for support. They did not always get it. A close friend of P.L. (as Penelope was always known) wrote:

I don't really *believe* in the scheme. I think you are sailing just now on a wave, because your school falls in with the popular sentiment for games and so forth, but I am not convinced that it has that about it that will last . . . I think so much that made the best part of its character, when it began, has got less as it grew larger that I do not wish to see it increased or kept up at this size.[39]

Roedean, a fortress in free Jacobean style that dominates that part of the Sussex coast, was a very different proposition from the informal family establishment down in the town from which the school finally moved in

1899. It was conceived on a grand scale, and whereas most schools are a piecemeal assemblage of buildings, often with a makeshift air, put up as needs dictated and funds allowed, Roedean is a magnificently solid unity, all its separate parts – teaching area, music school, living accommodation, even the chapel – under one roof. The Lawrences, however, wanted to preserve the family atmosphere, and each took over one of the houses: Dorothy in Number One, Millicent in Number Two, and P.L. herself in Number Three; their friend, Miss Hyde, presided over the fourth house. And the school all through the Lawrence regime was a family-run business; the Lawrences' brother used to write to them 'Dear Firm', and he himself (the Right Honourable Paul Ogden Lawrence, QC) was known throughout the school as Uncle Paul. The sisters were well aware that Roedean must eventually pass out of their hands, and to provide for its future they formed in 1920 a public company, Roedean School Ltd. In 1924 all three of them retired.

The promise to prepare girls for Cambridge had not been mere prospectus bluff; in the *Wimbledon House School News* of 1891 it was triumphantly announced that two old girls (who must have been in the original 1885 intake) had achieved good seconds at Cambridge, in Moral Science and in History. But the greatest emphasis was upon exercise, which was compulsory and strenuous, and though this seemed an adventure at first, many were to find it oppressive. Religious training had not been included in the aims set out in the initial Wimbledon House prospectus, and one early pupil remembered that she and her friends had discussed religious matters hanging out of the window, from a vague feeling that it was not proper to discuss such things on the premises.[40] The Lawrence family was Unitarian, though as Dorothy was a member of the Church of England an Anglican chapel was built. More than one pupil complained of the anti-intellectual bias, and the narrow outlook. Margaret Cole, who went there in 1907, remarked that though she and her contemporaries spent the best part of seven hours a day at their desks very few went to universities

> and the standards achieved would have shocked Miss Buss and Miss Beale and the founders of the Girls' Public Day School Trust. Perhaps this was because the Lawrences themselves, though first-class organizers, not to say advertisers, were no good as teachers and therefore not very good pickers; perhaps they were just giving their rich bourgeois clients what they wanted – some instruction, adequate Christian training ... discipline partly self-administered (by a prefectorial system and *plenty* of house and team spirit) and a frill of culture.[41] [It is only fair to add, however, that at least one Roedeanian of the period found P.L.'s history lessons 'inspirational'.]

The Board of Education's inspectors in 1912 to a certain extent bore out her strictures, their report saying that the girls had 'exceptional opportunities for the exercise of responsibility and the development of character arising therefrom. It is not so clear that they learn to face the difficulties of intellectual work.'[42]

Though Margaret Cole referred to the 'rich bourgeois clients', the public view always seems to have been that it is a school for the aristocracy – 'That's the school that's full of princesses and they all have a lady's maid,' Brighton residents are reputed to have said as they passed by – disregarding the fact that the aristocracy much more commonly select leisurely small private schools for their daughters. It is true that long before schools started wooing the East, Roedean had its quota of Indian maharajahs' daughters – acting on the advice, one supposes, of representatives of the English raj – and these would have mixed with the businessmen's and doctors' daughters remembered by Margaret Cole. But the fact remains that for some reason (perhaps because of the Lawrences' publicity talents) it is the only girls' school apart from St Trinian's that the person in the street has heard of and that comedians can lump in with Eton and Harrow.

Roedean, at one time the most extreme example of the girls' public school, excited much resentment, as might be expected, from those unsuited to the system. Olive Willis, a pupil in the 1890s, though not such a misfit as some, began her own school, Downe House, to correct what she felt was wrong with Roedean. She had not been particularly unhappy there, but she had a reflective mind and while still a pupil was aware of its faults. It was not just the exaggerated emphasis on games, but the lack of interest in the world outside; the rather ill-humoured rivalry between the houses; the over-elaborate prefect system and the emotional attitude towards the seniors, whose studies would be filled with hothouse flowers brought by their admirers. Above all she criticized the lack of religious outlook – though at the time the girls mostly gloried in the freedom from the irksome routines imposed by church schools. Her ideal school would be the antithesis of all this, and 'each individual would matter, life would be normal, and relations between people would matter'.

The school opened in Charles Darwin's former home, Downe House in Kent, in 1907 with five staff and one child who had brought her own dog. The child begged for a uniform, and so a purple blanket coat, made in Northern Ireland, was chosen, and a purple felt hat. Miss Willis had also imported the Roedean 'djibbah' – a tunic with short sleeves adapted from the garment worn by North African tribesmen, which Miss Lawrence had presumably chosen originally to conceal lack of corsets, strictly forbidden at Roedean. By 1908 there were six pupils and by 1910 thirty-six. In the light of the complacency Downe pupils were to feel about having been at a singularly 'unschooly' school, it is interesting to observe that a girl who was there in those early days classed it as no different at all from the harshest of its contemporaries. She loathed the cold, the food (tapioca pudding), the compulsory team games and gym, and thought little of the teaching (at that date the school took no public exams). And though the prefects might not be called prefects they behaved just as disagreeably. She was rescued from her misery there by a bout of pneumonia which seriously damaged her heart.

> It was unfortunate for me that I was at school at the time when it was thought proper that girls' schools should be as much as possible like boys'. Miss Carver who was 'in charge of health' had played hockey for England and did not, I think, believe in minor illnesses ... It was very cold that winter. We came in from playing games, queued in the bathroom where Miss Carver handed us each a towel wrung out in water 'to rub down with' and changed into 'evening' dresses in icy cold dorms. I was bad at gym so was made to do extra gym after breakfast. Directly after that there was 'Prayers' read by Miss Willis in the chapel. Kneeling, I prayed daily that I would not faint till I got to the passage, where my prayers being frequently answered I did faint; no one noticed, and I was only too thankful no one did.[43]

The curriculum was idiosyncratic, with the emphasis on English, history and French, and not much at first in the way of Latin, geography, maths or science. 'I used English literature as my chief material for lessons as I myself enjoyed books, poetry and prose, drama and fiction, ancient and modern, and I think that everyone in the first generation loved reading and being read to, and many of them wrote with considerable success.'[44] Individuals mattered more than a system, and when Elizabeth Bowen wrote about Maria – held by her aunt to be 'a motherless girl, sensitive, sometimes difficult, deeply reserved', and how at school all this was taken into account 'together with her slight tendency to curvature and her dislike of all puddings ... She was having her character "done" for her'[45] – it is possibly Downe, where she was herself, that she has in mind. Miss Willis understood some, though by no means all girls, as the pupil above would testify. Elizabeth Bowen was one whom she found *simpatica*: 'I was only too well understood,' she recalled, 'and when I left school my relations complained that my personality had made rapid and rank growth.'[46]

Miss Willis's strategy for eliminating the 'silliness' in girls, which other schools had tried to control by compulsory silence or by sheer exhaustion, was to outlaw it.

> The greatest crime ... was silliness. Or was it the crime of which one was most aware, as being the most dreary, the most mortifying? Some of us tried to get the silliness out of our systems by travestying it – mock cults, mock crazes, cultivated inanities of speech. The bad thing was to be 'affected' without knowing it – that was, without deliberately affecting to *be* affected.[47]

Miss Willis had been determined to have nothing of the conventional schoolgirl 'using rather silly slang and recognizing only trivial loyalties', and there was therefore no house system to break the community up into rivalries. There was no school song, no head girl, prefects, or badges, no prizes and therefore no annual prize-giving. It was considered boring to talk about games, and fashionable to be musical and impecunious. It was also fashionable to be a 'character', and high praise to be called 'rather eccentric'. 'We looked upon absence of mind and unpunctuality as proofs of intellect . . . We certainly did our best to establish our characters, and to avoid becoming what we imagined the average schoolgirl to be.'[48]

The Downe style had been established long before the school grew out of the Darwin house and moved to Cold Ash, near Newbury, a site high on the Berkshire Downs – indeed, even in 1914 Elizabeth Bowen was being told by her family that this school (only seven years old) was a very good one. The style owed much to Miss Willis, of course, but a great deal too to the girls' own backgrounds – the cultivated, literary ruling class. Publishers, academics, writers were well represented among the parents – categories who now could not afford, or would not choose to send daughters to, boarding school. One gets some idea of the prevailing mood from the pin-ups that flapped on the cubicle walls in the wind-swept bedrooms at the Kent Downe House: not dance-band leaders or athletes but 'Medici prints and portraits of Napoleon, Charles I, Rupert Brooke, Sir Roger Casement, or Mozart'. Or from the convincing scrap of conversation evoked by a member of the Cold Ash school:

> 'Would you,' we would ask each other, during those endless calm summer evenings looking down over the valley with its toy train and its stiff Noah's Ark cows, 'Would you, ever, really, actually, *be* someone else?'
>
> 'Not altogether. I would like to have a mind like Professor Gilbert Murray, and legs like Edna Best.'
>
> 'If you had a mind like Professor Gilbert Murray you wouldn't *want* legs like Edna Best.'
>
> 'How do you know? You've never been Professor Gilbert Murray.'
>
> 'Well superficially, of course, I haven't, but fundamentally . . . Shall we, after all, play tennis?'[49]

The merely rich or smart would choose a school that was larger, with a more resounding name, or smaller and more comfortable. Miss Willis was adept at detecting children who would not fit in, and had her own way of deflecting their parents, as this fictitious account shows:

> It's said that halfway through the conversation, she would ring the bell and send for that mythical list of vacancies and turn to parents saying, 'Oh, my dear – I wonder – look – we can't fit Vanessa in this year, but next year we would absolutely love to have her . . .' and they'd drive

away despondent. Vanessa would be fourteen soon and must be got in somewhere.[50]

Like the Misses Lawrence, Olive Willis was ambitious for the school's future, and in 1944, soon after the death of Lilian Heather who had been from very early days an unofficial partner, she transferred her ownership of the school to a public body with a board of governors. But this was relatively easy compared to severing herself from the school, *her* school, and in the end she could not bring herself to do it. She had chosen Brenda Sanderson, a member of the staff, as her successor, but when the latter discovered that Miss Willis after her retirement proposed to go on living in her house nearby, she felt she could not accept the post. Deeply hurt, Miss Willis offered to move away if the governors thought it best, thus putting the newly formed board into an impossible position. In the end Miss Sanderson departed to be headmistress of Badminton, and many of the staff resigned because of the outcome. Miss Willis did not finally leave the house until 1963, the year before her death, when a married headmistress was appointed and extra premises were badly needed for her family; Downe pupils in the post-war period invariably remember being dispatched to have tea with Miss Willis, and for Elizabeth North, writing about the school as 'Dames' in her novel of that title, it was in the 1950s still steeped in 'the Founder's' spirit.

Badminton, the school which had Miss Sanderson as headmistress in place of Downe, was in many ways comparable in spirit, with much the same sort of clientele, though tinged with a feminist leftism. 'Brenda's mother was an authoress, tossing off historical novels like shopping lists. Virginia was the daughter of a left-wing publisher, Ruth's father made the paper on which the books were printed, and Prunella's parents were colonels in the army.'[51] But this had not been the founder's intention, as had been the case with Downe. Badminton had begun in Bristol in 1858 as 'a small home school', and until Beatrice Baker ('BMB') became headmistress in 1911 it remained much the same for over fifty years, 'a good quiet, old-fashioned school . . . not coveting academic honours but giving a very fair grounding in at least English language and literature'.[52] Whether the retiring headmistress, Miss Bartlett, gentle and ladylike and much loved by her pupils (whom she protected from all newspapers), had guessed the power of the new broom she had brought to Badminton is undisclosed, but with the advent of BMB, girls were stripped of such things as corsets, veils to protect their complexions, and Sunday hats, and sent to play boisterous games on the Downs. More than that, they were expected to take part in debates, to be aware of current issues and to involve themselves with the outside world. Inevitably there were parents and girls who disliked the new regime, and for a time numbers fell, as did the bank balance, but the school became known outside Bristol and by the 1920s was very popular with upper-middle-class Fabians who, though their sons of course had to go to Eton or Winchester, felt that at least their daughters could be sent to an establishment where they could imbibe socialist principles; and it was favoured by the progressives, who, though they could not quite stomach Bedales or Frensham Heights, sent boys to Bryanston or Leighton Park.

BMB's message was internationalism: 'Those who did not belong to the International Club were lost souls.' Salvation was through the League of Nations; sixth-formers went forth to deliver leaflets on disarmament and to convert local residents, and every year school parties were dispatched to Geneva to study the workings of peace. BMB appointed a conscientious objector to be headmaster of the junior school, and some fifty years before it became fashionable (and financially necessary) to trawl for pupils in the Far East, Badminton was admitting girls from India (Indira Gandhi – then Indira Nehru – among them), Burma, West Africa and the West Indies. She wanted to build a community where different religions and different cultures could co-exist in a spirit of tranquillity and tolerance. During the Spanish Civil War Basque refugees were sheltered, and as World War II approached refugees from Germany and Czechoslovakia were taken in and educated. Nobody was too young to involve herself in world affairs; the juniors had newspaper lessons, the older ones current affairs, 'a test of one's observation, one's ability to discriminate between the relative importance of things, and to make judgements about them',[53] and all were expected to be able to converse about them with intelligent understanding. 'What are politics?' a first-former asked one of the staff. 'I am going to sit by Miss Baker at lunch . . . so I must talk about them but I don't know what they are.'[54]

BMB had formed Badminton; she was a compelling and dominant personality, and it is remarkable in the circumstances that the transition when Miss Sanderson (who inevitably became known as 'BMS') took over in 1947 was so smooth, especially as, with extraordinary irony, the latter found herself faced with exactly the same situation that had led to her refusing the Downe post – a predecessor living on the site: a triumvirate, what is more, since BMB operated with two close friends who had always shared her life. One supposes that BMS quailed at the thought of a second confrontation with a board of governors, but in the event it did appear to work out happily, though BMB was a far more formidable personality than Olive Willis – 'Bossy would be far too weak a word for what BMB was,' said Iris Murdoch, an old pupil, trying to convey her old headmistress's moral authoritarianism.[55] She was, moreover, often to be found on the school premises; 'she did not *try* to keep out of things,' said a member of the staff who watched her daily trudging up to the school. She was also still a governor. She had been admired and feared rather than loved, too impatient and frightening to be a good teacher; 'she kept us on our toes and opened our eyes'. BMS, in contrast, had the gift of the common touch; she took a sympathetic interest in each individual and under her the school was remembered for the easy, informal relations between staff and girls – unusual at that time.

Since she and BMB shared the same outlook, there was little break in continuity. The school continued in a whirl of extra-curricular activities: music (which reached a very high standard, the formidable head of music telling singers on one occasion that they had to be 'better than Glyndebourne'); pottery, weaving, play-readings, concerts, expeditions; involvement with the university settlement, with deaf and dumb schools and with the deprived generally – all standard practice now, but not common then. Political life was intense. 'It was essential to be left-wing,' said an autobiographical novel, 'dedicated to a lifetime of service, and above all a career woman, unencumbered by reactionary husbands. Implicit in this last virtue was a complete indifference to the pleasures of the flesh.'[56] Political thinking was shaped by the history mistress, whose lessons revolved round sufferings through the centuries under the oppressive rule of the rich. 'We pursued the enemies of socialism under the benign approval of the staff. Every morning a cluster of girls gathered round the *Daily Worker*, *The Times*, the *Telegraph*, the *Mirror*, the *Sketch* and the *News Chronicle*.'

But there were some who were beginning to question the system and the attitudes. It taught service, certainly, but did it after all lead to independence of thought?

> The strange thing is that while the main object of teaching at Badminton was to lead us to think for ourselves, I am not sure how far it succeeded – or how much we didn't merely adopt a 'Badminton' approach to things rather than say a 'Roedean' approach. Certainly, after leaving, I was very conscious of having to extricate myself from a cocoon of opinions, inhibitions and prejudices in which I had become wrapped during 13 years at the school.[57]

Others wondered if it was such a progressive, radical school as they had always been led to think. BMS might exhort them to break out of the mould and be unconventional, but no indication was ever given about what direction this should take, and the rules seemed just as strict as at any other girls' schools; talking after 'lights out' (8.30, even in high summer, and no curtains at the windows) was a heinous crime, and it was unthinkable that any girl should step outside the school gates, even to post a letter. And for all the vaunted socialism, and the duty to put something back in return for one's privileges, there was no fraternizing with the lower orders (social work apart). 'Matches were played or choral works sung with schools of similar status, and it was certainly not the boys from the secondary modern that were asked to the Summer Dance.'[58] This contradiction was implicit in the attitude of the parents, of whom Naomi Mitchison, socialist wife of a wealthy barrister, was typical. At the outbreak of war she had removed herself and her children from London to the family's Scottish estate in Kintyre, whence each term she dispatched a son to a prep school in the south in preparation for Winchester, and a daughter to Badminton (evacuated to Devon), while lamenting the necessity for so doing. 'Perhaps some case for College at Winchester as a kind of forcing place for the intelligent, more like a University really. But he does hate the lack of freedom at his prep school, and the assumption of bourgeois values, king and country and all that. But I have to let him go so that he can learn Latin grammar.'[59] The fact that there were plenty of Scottish academies who gave a classical education was ignored.

The informality of Benenden in the pre-war era comes as a dramatic contrast to the apparently inflexible systems of most of the foregoing schools. The founders joined in their pupils' activities with such relish that the Them and Us was forgotten. 'Can I have another butterfly net,' a child wrote home, 'because I have a friend called Birdie who will keep borrowing mine.'[60] This friend, Miss Bird, was one of the founders of Benenden; and with Miss Sheldon and Miss Hindle – none of them much more than thirty – had responded to the Wycombe Abbey headmistress's call, 'Will no one here start another school like this?' They had only £100 apiece, but when their advisers hesitated about backing the venture, Miss Frances Dove, the founder of Wycombe, chided them so vigorously for their lack of faith that it was agreed that if money, a house and a nucleus of pupils could be found, the supporters would form an educational company. By writing to friends and random names culled from *Who's Who*, *Crockford's* and *Whitaker's Almanack* they acquired promises of £2,000, and started looking, in off-duty periods at Wycombe, for a house 'with at least 70 bedrooms and large grounds'. In spite of the house-agents' interest this was difficult to find. But it is an indication of the immeasurable difference between the caution and expectations of parents now and the happy insouciance of seventy years ago that in 1923 twenty-three pupils, including three from Wycombe who were working for Oxford Entrance, were entrusted to a school without a name and without premises. They spent a term in temporary quarters in Bickley, and then in the nick of time were offered the tenancy of Hemsted Park, near Cranbrook, at a rental of £1,500 with an option to purchase at £22,500. Benenden School, taking its name from the village outside the gates, opened in January 1924, after a three-week flurry during which the founders and their friends painted, distempered, stained floors and made curtains.

The 1920s were boom years for independent schools. There was an abundance of dedicated teachers, their chance of marriage destroyed by the huge loss of life in World War I, and an abundance too of domestic staff – schools like Benenden required armies of maids. And since few girls were concerned with professional careers and there was no urgency to reach the right educational goal, headmistresses could concentrate on the subjects their staff enjoyed teaching (and which did not require expensive equipment). The fierce pioneering days when women's education had to prove itself were over. The schools which had started in that era found it difficult to shed the carapace of tough heartiness which they had been obliged to don; the newer schools could avoid these mistakes, and indeed cater for the parents who disliked the bouncing unfeminine hoydens that they were thought to turn out. Benenden was a gentle place, and though of course it is always difficult to assess atmosphere, since old pupils who contribute to jubilee compilations do so through a haze of nostalgia, it does seem to evoke outstandingly happy memories.

> There were gorgeous sunsets . . . and delphiniums to paint, all blues and purples . . . and you could learn anything in the world you fancied: Bellringing or Greek; Forestry or Pottery; or how to make salmon flies . . . Kindness mattered a great deal, and when I left I cried for a fortnight because I truly believed the best years of my life were over.[61]

The presence of the village just outside the gates was an enormous asset, allowing the school to be involved in its life in a way that was impossible in Bristol, High Wycombe, Brighton or Cheltenham; and with the huge grounds and the then largely unspoilt Kentish countryside the girls had an enviable freedom – the 1920s and 30s being probably, in any case, the safest period in history so far as women and children were concerned. Each of the three Benenden founders contributed her particular talent. Just as, at Roedean, of the three founding sisters Penelope Lawrence had taken the lead, Miss Sheldon – gentle, humorous and kind – had been seen as headmistress of Benenden from the first by her two colleagues. Miss Hindle managed the estate and the outside staff; she was also the musical one and persuaded the most eminent musicians of the time, from Fanny Davies to Solomon, to give recitals at the school. Miss Bird set herself to ensure that there was no one without a chance of being good at something, and created official duties for everybody – like showing parents round the school, or bell-ringing. She devised a school pageant (performed once every five years) in which the whole school had a part, and promoted hobbies. It was she who established the excellent relations between the school and the village, and on retiring she went to live in its main street. Her 'Angel' sermons (see page 153), so different from the hectoring tone of the traditional school assembly address, are perhaps the best guide to the Benenden style.

The last public school to be founded, Cobham Hall, which opened its doors in 1963, had a more difficult task than any of the preceding: it had to establish an ethic and weld itself together in an anarchic period when the old traditions and, indeed, authority itself were deeply suspect. The primary motive was to put historical premises to a suitable use; education was in the nature of an afterthought, so it lacked the visionary driving force, the sense of pioneering, with which the older schools had been established. The Bligh family, earls of Darnley, the owners of Cobham, by the 1950s could no longer afford to live there. The vast house – part Tudor, part seventeenth-century, with added Gothick work by Wyatt – was in a dangerous state of decay, and the Ministry of Works who acquired it in 1961 needed a tenant. Mrs Bee Mansell, the first woman Parsee to be called to the English Bar, was initially the moving spirit in launching the Westwood Educational Trust which first leased and then bought the house. But though she had strong views about what was wrong with girls' public school education, which she justly felt was too often a weak copy of boys', she did not have the long outlook and patience and persistence with which, say, Miss Beale had created Cheltenham. Moreover, she found it difficult to wrestle with the practical details of raising the money and making the premises habitable, and she was impatient with compromise. So in the end it was others who handled the day-to-day problems and acted as midwife.

It is interesting to compare the beginnings of Cobham and Benenden. Just over forty years separated them, but there had been a far greater change than there was in the thirty years between Benenden and Wycombe Abbey. To start with, the engaging amateurism with which most girls' schools had been launched was a thing of the past; far greater resources were now needed. It was not enough just to install beds and desks and hang Liberty curtains; one had to be able to assure parents that every subject in the educational spectrum was covered and that their daughters would be qualified to enter any profession. And since no parent was going to risk a daughter's academic future by sending sixth-formers to a new school, Cobham had to start with a mob of eleven- to thirteen-year-olds without any senior ballast. The Benenden founders had felt they could move forward when they had raised £2,000; Cobham needed something in the region of £200,000 – £50,000 of it admittedly for urgent building repairs, heating, plumbing and electricity. Inflation, however, was to bring even more rapid change in the succeeding quarter-century; the fees which initially were £160 a term are now in the region of £3,000.

Even more interesting is the difference in the stated aims. By the 1960s many of the English families which had thirty years before regularly dispatched daughters to boarding school were no longer able to afford it. Most schools now therefore rely on a substantial contingent from overseas to make up the numbers (and to support the latest appeal). Cobham from the outset would have had to be an international school even if that had not been Mrs Mansell's aim for it. The first headmistress's manifesto said the standard things about wishing to bring out the best in each girl, and to equip her for a useful role in society. But after that she had to tread very carefully. The old assumptions about discipline no longer held good in the 'swinging sixties'; and though 'surely at root [the young] are not so very different from their predecessors' they had, she admitted guardedly, 'a marked distaste' for authority. Thus the school would have 'a graded system of self-government', 'a contemporary approach to the distribution of responsibility . . . a commonsense training for the role of the individual citizen in a democracy'. Since Cobham Hall was multiracial any religious teaching was to be non-denominational, though it was hoped that each girl would be encouraged 'to be as thoughtful, sincere and good a member of her own religion as may be'.[62] That distinguishing mark of the public school, the house system, was in effect abandoned. Girls would belong to a house for the purpose of competitions, but would all live together under the same roof. Team games were not part of the new age: 'we feel that many girls prefer sports with which they are likely to continue after they have left school such as tennis, swimming, sailing, golf and fencing'. (Hockey and netball are in fact both played now, though hockey stops when the daffodils start pushing through on the pitch in the Easter term.) And though the manifesto did not mention it, there was to be a far higher degree of comfort than the older schools had thought appropriate – especially in the matter of warmth. (Indeed the Department of Education now decreed a minimum temperature of 60 degrees.) The cost of heating Cobham, with its acres of outside walls and windows with ancient leaded panes, must be astronomic, but a remarkably efficient system was installed, and during the severe winter of 1962–3 which followed the school's opening everybody was warm. There was one last break with tradition – there was no reference to the spirit of service which generations of headmistresses had preached; the emphasis was on the individual, and even the school's internationalism was presented to show the benefit it would confer on her.

The Gridiron

To some degree the public schools affected all the other girls' schools. They either adapted the ethos to their own purposes, or they reacted against it and invented their own. After St Leonards and Roedean had taken the initiative, schools could never be the same again; prefects, houses, uniform, team games now became the norm, and headmistresses at morning assembly urged service and sacrifice and the duty to return what had been given. Louisa Lumsden, the first headmistress of St Leonards, was the first to say that she wanted the girls to be worthy of trust and to govern themselves. Up till then girls' schools had relied on gaoler-like supervision. 'The girls seem to me over-governessed and over-superintended,' Simon Laurie, later to be Professor of Education at Edinburgh University, had said in 1868 when he was called in to give his view of the Merchant Maiden Hospital. 'I should think it impossible for them to move without the consciousness of some eye upon them.'[63] He assumed that this was because it was a hospital, but in fact it would have been true of most girls' schools of the period. Winifred Peck, at a young ladies' academy in Eastbourne in the 1890s, said that the headmistress's methods were 'perpetual watchfulness, espionage, draconic codes and regulations'. The real basis of school life was the rules. 'A hardened young cynic once said she had counted up to two hundred and fifty of these, and only stopped there because we did not learn to count any higher at Miss Quill's.'[64]

The trouble was that like Russia, wholly unused to freedom, the schools rejected one form of tyranny only to replace it with others. There was the tyranny of public opinion, as Margaret Kennedy's bohemian young Sanger sisters found at her fictional Cleeve College (Cheltenham). Here their failings 'brought them into collision with the other girls rather than with authority . . . They were persecuted for their own good and the honour of the school until they scarcely knew if they could call their souls their own. They could discover no smallest loophole of respite or escape; in class, at games, at bed and board the tyrannical, many-eyed mob were always with them.'[65]

There was the tyranny of the bells, which regulated the day, as in this fictional account of Harrogate College:

> Action was initiated and terminated by bells. At seven-thirty the rising bell; fifteen minutes later a devotion bell, which meant silence for a quarter of an hour, during which one could meditate, pray, or dash for the bath, according to one's disposition; breakfast at eight, and after it a very few minutes of blessed freedom during which, however, it was considered good form to turn out into the playground and practise lacrosse throws. Three bells, at five-minute intervals, announced the approaching time for morning assembly, and at nine o'clock, the whole school filed out into the lecture hall for prayers.
>
> Thereafter through the morning there was a succession of classes all regulated by bells. Long lines of girls filed about the corridors from one classroom to another, preserving the strictest silence, and respectfully turning to one side if a mistress passed, swaying in silent tribute, while she hurried by with fixed gaze as if in a determined effort to ignore the unavoidable tribute of outward respect.
>
> Lunch at one o'clock, a hurried change into gym clothes and a scurry to be on the field to report for lacrosse games by two-thirty . . . Half an hour to get back to the cloakroom, put away lacrosse sticks, change from running boots to house slippers, get to one's own House, stand in line waiting for a bath, and dress again, with slithering nervous fingers, so that one would be tidy enough to pass the eyes of the watchful matron at the head of the stairs . . .
>
> Classes followed after tea, until a seven o'clock supper, and the interval between its conclusion and eight-thirty bedtime was nearly always filled with something – darning, or a lecture, or perhaps more study . . . The bell again proclaiming bedtime, the devotion bell fifteen minutes later,

and then, last of all, the nine o'clock bell announcing 'lights out' and after that silence.

Then even an accidental remark was accounted an infringement of the rules, entered in a little black book, and read aloud to the whole school, with other sins of omission and commission, on Saturday mornings, after breakfast.[66]

The larger schools are still ruled by bells, or by electronic bleeps. A sixteen-year-old wrote:

For five disturbing years
The school bell daily clanged.
I went by hour
From house to school and back again,
Bullied by bells.[67]

There was also the tyranny of the prefects, who, well into the post-war period, were the commissars of school life. At least one headmistress thought that their power was dangerous, to themselves as well as to others:

Nearly every girl who rises to prefectship is distinguished by a well-marked love of power [which] . . . is given a great amount of free play in the most dangerous direction, viz, that of dominance over other human beings, at an age when cock-sureness and over-weening self-confidence frequently make the girl a perfect nuisance at home and in any society other than the school.[68]

In her own school, Wychwood, accordingly there was a system of self-government without prefects. Winifred Peck too was doubtful about the prefect system for much the same reason, feeling that a born leader developed her powers too early and too successfully at school, and afterwards, if she found no adequate outlet, became 'a bore in public and something of a bully in private life'.[69] 'Mistresses were far less important than prefects or games captains,' said Margaret Cole of Roedean, and prefect-rule was to spread to high schools (Miss Buss, in fact, had already introduced it to North London Collegiate) and private schools alike. At Edgbaston High School in the 1920s and 30s

the prefects were responsible for enforcing silence, single line, and no running in the corridors, for maintaining the insistence on hats and gloves and the prohibitions on sweets. They also had to chase the little girls out at break and lunchtime, however cold it was, and supervise them when they got there. They pounced on misdemeanours so trivial as hardly to be noticed today.[70]

'I enjoyed being head of the house,' said one girl who left Sherborne in 1931, 'as I was a priggish, bossy child. The one snag was, *no time* to oneself . . . endless piffling chores, supervising people, making lists, ticking people off – ugh! (I actually enjoyed it).'[71] They were in effect ADCs to the headmistress and housemistress, enjoying a prestige and authority that the 'ushers' in the old-fashioned boys' private schools never had. But some found the responsibility both demanding and exhausting. At St Paul's the prefects had no sanctions, except reporting a culprit to the staff. 'We tried to maintain discipline by personality alone. My mother once said the school was run on the prefects' nerves. (Two of our form had very serious breakdowns soon after leaving.)'[72]

Many schools have now abolished prefects and leave authority in the hands of the sixth form, who, preoccupied with A levels and university entrance and in any case living in their own separate sixth-form blocks, are not so willing as they used to be to undertake the 'piffling chores'. A St Leonards Senior noticed how the attitude to authority changed dramatically in the 1960s. 'When I arrived, older girls and staff were actually *venerated*. Most of us were very orderly. By the time I was in the sixth form (in 1968) it was impossible to keep order autocratically; one had to back up one's rulings with reason, firmness and diplomacy.'[73] And the relish for ticking people off has apparently disappeared. 'They don't mind having a jolly with the juniors,' said one headmistress, 'but it's no good any more asking them to do something about getting the Lower Fourths to tidy themselves up.' Mallory Wober in 1971 found it rare for girls to aspire to be prefects. Woldingham School, the secular relic of the Sacred Heart, Roehampton, however has introduced a system whereby senior girls apply to be 'ribbons' (prefects) and, as in a job application, have to submit an appropriate letter and be interviewed by a board that includes the headmistress. There are more enthusiastic aspirants than vacancies.

The tyranny of the games field was felt by many to be as oppressive as that of the prefects. To a certain extent its initial popularity must have been due to the feeling that team games were deliciously revolutionary; exercise in girls' schools until the late Victorian period had been restricted to decorous callisthenics, walks in crocodile or perhaps pacing round the garden. Rough team games would have seemed one in the eye for Mamma's and Grandmamma's generations, and as Chapter 10 shows there is plenty of evidence of the enthusiasm with which everybody whacked the ball in games of primitive hockey in the playground. Sport was not, however, part of early Cheltenham, where the girls were dispatched in crocodiles for walks and allowed to break ranks only when they reached the country; Miss Beale accepted organized games reluctantly, and though by the end of her life she agreed that 'the power of acting with others, and of rapidly judging, is [thereby] cultivated',[74] she refused to allow matches with other schools because she so disliked the spirit of competition.

Nor in the beginning were games paramount at St Leonards; it was merely understood that every girl should play at least once a week – cricket or tennis in the summer, 'goals' or rounders in the winter. Games were, as

1. An early Georgian orphan against the Bastille-like high walls and heavily barred gates once thought necessary for charity hospitals. The chapel, round which formal education was centred, can be seen in the background. From the frontispiece of *The Realms and Hymns at the Asylum or House of Refuge for Female Orphans* (*c*. 1775).

2. Detail from the painting by Eyre Crowe (1824-1910) of the schoolroom at Red Maids School, Bristol. The white linen tippets and aprons remained part of the school uniform for the first half of the twentieth century, and are still worn on formal occasions.

3. A Victorian photograph of St Leonards.

4. A view of Benenden.

5. Oxford High School, Girls' Public Day School Trust. One of the oldest high schools, which achieves notable academic success in bleak surroundings.

6. North London Collegiate School, Canons Park, one of the most splendidly housed of all high schools. The modern extension to the Georgian mansion can be seen on the right.

7. The Buss family with early pupils; Frances Mary sits in the centre, holding sewing.

8. Lydia Rous, superintendent of The Mount School, York, 1866-79.

9. Dorothea Beale, principal of Cheltenham Ladies' College, 1858-1906.

10. The founders of Roedean: Dorothy, Penelope and Millicent Lawrence.

below 11. Jane Frances Dove, the founder of Wycombe Abbey.

above right 12. Dr Sophie Bryant, successor to Miss Buss as headmistress of North London Collegiate School.

right 13. B.M. Baker, headmistress of Badminton 1911-46, with a Swiss guide, on a School Journey.

14. Dormitory cubicles at St Mary's Hall, 1920s.

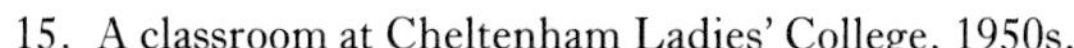

15. A classroom at Cheltenham Ladies' College, 1950s.

16. The domestic staff at Benenden, 1930s. The butler, Busby, is seen in the centre. Until the 1950s a large resident staff was taken for granted at all boarding schools.

17. Headmistress's room, St Mary's Hall, in the early years of the century.

HIGHFIELD

OXHEY LANE, WATFORD.

Principals :—MISS GERTRUDE WALLIS, MISS LAURA WALLIS.

'Phone and Telegraphic Address :—Watford 616.

HIGHFIELD is a Private Boarding School for the daughters of gentlepeople. Resident pupils only are received, and references or a personal introduction is required for all pupils.

The aim of the School is to train character as thoroughly as is possible during the comparatively short time of school life, so that the girls should leave Highfield prepared to take part in the wider life of home and country, and to prove themselves good, broad-minded, self-controlled, cultivated women. Highfield is situated on high ground in the picturesque country between Bushey and Pinner. It is served by lines of the L.M.S. Rly. and the Bakerloo Railway running from Euston and Baker Street respectively to Bushey.

The extent and general appearance of the School buildings are indicated by the accompanying illustration. The beautiful grounds of nearly sixty acres afford ample opportunities for Outdoor Games (Tennis, Hockey, Netball, Croquet and Lacrosse), and there is a large Open-air Swimming Bath. In wet weather the Drill Hall, which is fitted with adjustable gymnastic apparatus, serves for all purposes of recreation. Visits are arranged to galleries, concerts and historic buildings in London.

The curriculum is as wide and varied as is consistent with the ideal of thoroughness in essential subjects. The Principals are assisted in the work of teaching by a highly-qualified staff.

Prospectus on application to Principals.

323

18. From the Truman & Knightley Schools Directory, 1930, an advertisement very typical of its time. It will be noticed that the principals have no academic qualifications, and also the stress laid upon social class. By restricting a school to boarders it was felt a better 'tone' was maintained. The emphasis is on character training (the common refuge of schools who could not offer academic teaching), and on preparing girls for life at home and possibly voluntary work — certainly not for earning a living.

has been seen, part of the Wycombe Abbey routine from the start, but there were also more unusual activities like gardening and carpentry. Roedean was the school where games were a fetish. An early prospectus for Wimbledon House, Sussex Square, where the school began in Brighton states: 'Special pains are taken to guard against overwork, and the girls are encouraged to take an interest in Household Employments. From Two to Three Hours daily are spent in Exercise, Out-door Games are particularly encouraged.' The Misses Lawrence established a large playing field on what is now East Brighton Park, and the public way in which the girls played games there attracted much comment. (At Girton the students had had to wait until trees had grown up and the grounds were sheltered enough to conceal their activities.) Even the principals' brother thought the field was too exposed. By 1896 cricket (this was still an unusual game for girls) was so much part of the Roedean summer that Christabel Lawrence made scathing references to 'the innate frivolity' of players who absented themselves from practices – 'going to town, bathing, or even playing tennis'.

By the time Margaret Cole arrived some ten years later,

> the positive values ... were supplied from three sources – games, the prefect system, and religion, in that order. I put games first because their value was absolutely unquestioned, and without some sort of proficiency it was difficult for any but a very exceptional character to gain popularity – or 'influence' enough to reach the first rung of the ladder leading to authority.[75]

At Roedean, as at boys' schools, everybody played compulsorily every weekday afternoon, the whole school being divided by the housemistresses into about eighteen elevens which played one another three days in the week, and into house elevens which played on the other two. Thirty years later Katharine Whitehorn remembered the cricket practice on wet grass before breakfast. Games were impossible to escape; the authority that imposed them did not think of them as the recreation they once had been, but as a central part of education. At St Leonards each person spent an hour and a half daily on the games field, rather more on Saturdays. Everybody had to watch the matches; on the occasional 'surprise' holidays these could take the form of epic Scots v. English contests. To Miss Dove the different games were designed to develop different parts of the female character: lacrosse for grace, hockey for cheerful endurance, cricket for gentleness and courtesy.[76] Even at Downe House, which thought itself set apart from all other schools, though 'you didn't call it games [it was called 'Outdoors'], it *seemed* like games; you had two sides and played a thing they called lacrosse,' said one fictional account of the school.[77] (This was a game that Miss Willis held to be morally bracing.) 'A male system imperfectly adapted to female needs,' E. Arnot Robertson called it, recalling that at Sherborne a carefully fostered and almost entirely spurious interest in house matches was the main subject of conversation.[78] 'I do feel,' concluded Mrs Cole, 'that games-worship . . . gives some support to the complaint of anti-feminists that women ought not to be allowed to do the things that men do, because they have no sense of proportion and drive everything to death.'[79]

As at boys' schools, the greatest excitement was reserved for the house matches. (Because of the isolation of St Leonards these are the only matches that can be played.) Sherborne took them particularly seriously:

> On the eve of a house match the dormitory passages are festooned with house ties, bands and dark blue ribbons, and at night most of the house equipment is decoratively arranged in the captain's cubicle. On the way to the pitch the team are cheered by the house, who form an arch on the steps with the appropriate weapons. St Kenelm, our patron saint – a small orange cat with black stripes – is removed from his bed of blue velvet and religiously carried out to watch the match where, tradition has it, he whispers words of encouragement in the form of the House motto: *Res parva concordia crescunt*.[80]

At the Godolphin a pupil there in 1915–19 recalled that 'the House was the motive of every effort, and the crown of every achievement'. It was thought terribly slack not to turn up at fielding practice in break, and the spirit found supreme expression when the winning of a games cup was celebrated by drinking from it. A house-meeting would be called, and the cup filled with water and solemnly passed round. 'The water tasted of plate powder . . . but the significance of the ceremony was something which none of us could put into words.'[81]

But by the 1960s team games were losing their popularity and becoming supplanted, as at Cobham Hall, by sporting activities for the individual. St Leonards had noticed the difference as early as 1955, when a Senior commented in the gazette on 'the spirit of frivolity' which she now observed at a cricket match. In her day even the feeblest players had affected seriousness when they played. Six or seven years later it was clear that the new interest was gymnastics, that though there were still enthusiastic lacrosse and hockey teams, there was a general movement to demote games. Tennis (that game associated by Christabel Lawrence with 'innate frivolity') had supplanted cricket and in 1967, the year that a new swimming pool was opened, the game was dropped. Public school prospectuses now mention sports such as fencing, squash, judo, trampolining, canoeing; team spirit is no longer stressed as the greatest virtue.

Edward Thring, who became headmaster of Uppingham in 1853 and elevated a decayed midlands grammar school to the status of a reputable public school, is always given the credit for the initiation of the house system, so much a feature of the reformed public school. But whereas the schools who followed his example, and most of all the girls' schools, used the system to stimulate competition in work, games and good behaviour, his aim, initially at any rate, was more to provide an approximation of 'the civilization and gentler feelings of comparative home'. He had endured the brutal and comfortless barracks life in Long Chamber to which Eton scholars were subjected, and determined that units of thirty boys presided over by a master and his wife would be far more satisfactory. In fact, Eton Oppidans and Winchester Commoners* did already lodge with tutors in the vicinity of their schools, so that Thring's scheme was not completely innovatory, and the Cheltenham house system, as at Eton and Winchester, was in effect begun by the ladies in the town who took in boarders. Life in the Cheltenham houses, where there was no uniform scale of boarding fees, was kept apart from school life, and it was only gradually that responsibility for them was taken over by the college. It was not an easy nor a straightforward process, and in one case there was a protracted lawsuit. At St Leonards the houses were from the start under the control of the school, though until 1920 each housemistress (who, unlike Cheltenham, was a full member of the teaching staff) rented her house from the school council, furnished it herself and ran it with the help of her housekeeper.

Though there was a time when private schools were too small for it, nearly every school has now taken up the house system, though only the largest – the 'public' schools – physically separate their pupils, and some, like Tudor Hall, eschew the system altogether and group the girls according to age, as was the policy in the Ursuline and Sacred Heart boarding schools. Houses are given names appropriate to the foundation or their aims; thus Felixstowe's bear the names of Protestant martyrs, Queen Ethelburga's the names of Celtic towns of Ethelburga's time (which gives mouthfuls like Eoforwic), and St Felix, Southwold, which commemorates female pioneers, has a Thatcher house. Houses have an important motivational function. Instead of authority having to be perpetual watchdog and policeman, the spirit of competition (in theory, at any rate) inspires members of the house to do the barking instead. As a thirteen-year-old put it: 'All us little juniors have to slave away to get STUPID good house marks for the seniors. The teachers give bad marks as well as the seniors for bludy stupid reasons.'[82] But unexpected talents can pull one up: 'In my class a girl called Caroline was always getting into trouble and used to drag her house down in the league, but she did have a great advantage – she was a magnificent darner. So she cut holes in her lyle stockings and woollen socks and made such magnificent darns it was points to her house which knocked off her order marks.'[83]

Much is achieved by the moral disapproval of one's peers. One girl at St Leonards was so conscious that the romantic novel she was reading was considered unworthy of the house that she wrapped it in brown paper and wrote 'Bacon's Essays' on it.[84] Another said of St Swithun's in the 1970s,

* That is, pupils who were not scholars on the foundation.

where housemistress and prefects kept watch on 'posture and poise' and put up weekly lists of every girl's rating, that there was a feeling that 'one was continually being marked out of 10 and could never relax'. The house system, therefore, hardly provides the atmosphere of home that Thring had desired. Not only may one fall foul of one's housemistress (a fairly frequent occurrence from which there is no escape), but the companionship is limited in a system where one is not encouraged (and often actively discouraged) to make friends in other houses. At Christ's Hospital in the Hertford days this limitation in the choice of friends only broke down in the infirmary. At Cheltenham, the largest by far of all the girls' schools, it is possible to find yourself in a house where there is no one at all who is in the same form. Those who uphold the system speak of the advantages, chiefly those of endurance: 'For a great many of us now, probably fewer people are "impossible" because tolerance was thrust upon you at an early age.' '[It] taught me how to get on with the most irritating people.' But Mallory Wober's sixteen-year-old puts the other side more forcibly: 'one has to make friends ... with one or more of perhaps five or ten females, be they cretinous, bitchy, bloody-minded, "very nice" (rare) or whatever abilities they may possess. The moral of this is "IF YOU WANT A FRIEND DON'T COME HERE".'

Always in Victorian days a certain amount of anxiety had been expressed when a school was founded, lest this new style of education for girls should make them unfeminine. 'Of course there is no intention of making girls less feminine by bringing them under the influence of public spirit,' a school council chairman told an assembly of supporters. Thus along with the male-style curriculum and the emphasis on team games has gone concern about posture and good manners. (The lack of the latter among boys amazes girls' schools when they arrange joint social events.) Sometimes deportment was made part of the moral code: 'Straight words, straight deeds and straight backs,' said an early headmistress of Lady Eleanor Holles School. 'Courage, a natural happy everyday life and upbringing, sound work, friendliness, straightforwardness, good manners, *certainly* good posture' were Alice Baird's aims for her girls at St James's, West Malvern.

Good manners are, of course, difficult to define. There are few girls' schools which do not profess to try to instil them, but in some cases it may go little further than standing up when the mistress comes into the form room, or that preposterous rule, which at one time appeared to be standard at all boarding schools, that one might not ask for anything to be passed to one at table, but must wait for a neighbour to see the lack of it. Many schools teach you to write thank-you letters on every possible occasion – for being asked out to tea, for a housemistress's visit when one is ill, or to announce to one's headmistress that one has reached home in good shape: 'Dear Miss King, I have arrived home saffly', as one crumpled note picked off the cloakroom floor on the last day of term prematurely put it. Many schools stress the importance of powers of conversation, and to this end insist that girls at table must take turns at sitting next to a member of the staff, to amuse her.

> 'Where are you going for your holidays?' some brave person asks. After this subject has been explored to its full possibilities there is silence.
>
> 'Do you keep pets?'
>
> 'No. Do you?'
>
> 'We used to keep two mice, but one ate the other and we found the remains in the cage. Next morning the remaining one died of indigestion.' (Laughter, followed by silence.)
>
> ... 'I hope it does not rain,' says one girl, 'as we have games this afternoon.'
>
> 'Yes, it does look a bit overcast.' Pause, in which eating noises are just audible.
>
> 'Would you like some more?' asks the server.
>
> 'No, thank you,' is the universal reply.[85]

With enormous relief the table disperses and the normal style of talk is resumed.

Many headmistresses struggled to achieve something better. At Downe Miss Willis successfully instilled the habit of easy converse into her pupils – rather too succesfully, one of them was later to think.

> To be able to make conversation at table was regarded as a matter of personal prestige. To be dumb was to be a poor fish. The result was that making conversation became, in many of us, an ineradicable nervous habit. To this day, the briefest lull at a luncheon or dinner party is instantly filled by me with remarks of an inanity which startles even my children.[86]

And the power of the spoken word was held in such high esteem that the occupant of a bath-tub might even, if her chat to the waiting queue was riveting enough, manage to extend her stay there beyond the statutory time.

But for most schoolgirls this easy fluency used to be unattainable, especially if one was called upon to talk to one's elders about subjects other than school matters: 'those awful social evenings,' wrote one Kent College girl, 'when, if you had not opened a conversation then you had to stay behind until you did so.'[87] 'There is much complaint of the conversation of girls whose education is supposed to have been careful,' wrote a Sacred Heart head in 1912. 'The subjects they care to talk about are found to be few and poor, their power of expressing themselves very imperfect, the scanty words at their command, worked to death in supplying for all kinds of things to which they are not appropriate.'[88] And in the 1920s Miss Faithfull devoted one of her Saturday talks at Cheltenham to the importance of conversation, an art in which, she told the girls, they were deficient, if not lazy. 'You discuss your companions, your pastors and teachers, the personnel of the school. You discuss games with never-ending delight, and some of you no doubt discuss matters concerned with your work, but general conversation is concerned with little else beside.'[89] One Cheltonian told her how difficult it all was. For instance, she had found herself for a week sitting next to someone who was only interested in plays and poetry. 'I don't know anything about poetry, and I've left the subject alone, as the last time I got mixed up between Wordsworth and Shelley, and she looked daggers.'

But another, presumably older, correspondent put her finger on the real problem, which Miss Faithfull seems not to have grasped – the closed world of school with every minute filled for one. At home it was perfectly easy to talk, she said, but at school 'one has so little time to read the paper, and even if one has found time to read something interesting, probably no one else has done so.'

There was another consideration, which Miss Faithfull had not taken into account: the emphasis on conformity, the stifling of individual opinion. 'Treatment of those days was rather the suppression of the individual, and the training of the mass mind,'[90] wrote a Walthamstow Hall pupil, contrasting the diffidence of her contemporaries, all discouraged from making themselves conspicuous, with the confident way with which girls of a later generation were able to stand up and make speeches and do things alone. A different style of teaching, in which discussion and debate play a greater part than they ever did before, must be partly responsible for the self-assurance and easy manners of late twentieth-century adolescents, as well as the fact that they are now far less segregated at home from adults. From the early years of the last century travellers to the United States remarked with approval or distaste, according to their temperament, on the poise and confident conversation of young Americans, brought up on terms of equality with their elders and not banished to a separate nursery or schoolroom world. Until the upper classes in England made this change they could hardly expect social ease in their own young.

In earlier decades, girls from the grander public schools who were going to 'come out' would have had a year at a finishing school to try to turn them from ungainly hockey-playing Amazons with farouche manners into something tolerably elegant and polished. They had to be taught, among other things, to take an interest in their own appearance and how to converse with the opposite sex – neither of which had been encouraged while they were *in statu pupillari*. At some of the smaller private schools there was more scope for femininity. A few schools like Downe House, as has been described, looked for individuality; Badminton supposedly did, but as one girl perceptively pointed out, many were inhibited since 'ideas which BMB thought foolish were not well received'.[91] Schools often now allow senior girls to organize dinner parties and other social occasions; sometimes housemistresses give parties at which girls meet guests from outside. At Kent

College there were 'etiquette lessons' from the 1950s onwards, at which the lower sixth learnt 'how to sip sherry, how to get in and out of a mini with style, and how to set the table for a dinner party'. But schoolchildren now mix so much more with the adult world that formal lessons on how to do it are no longer necessary.

This sort of matter was of course peripheral to the grand central purpose of forming the character, but the public schools looked beyond the perfecting of the individual to service to others; it was the duty of those who had received so much to give something back. Headmistresses spent hours in eloquent exhortation to this effect, sometimes inspiring, but sometimes, it has to be admitted, antagonizing.

> Sunday evenings would often end with grim sermons . . . as we sat silent on the hard Riddlesworth Hall floor, with our attention riveted on the Headmistress, tears of remorse for our sins in our eyes. I remember one sermon about a giant Christmas tree which had thousands of babies sucking milk from bottles attached to the tree by red and grey ribbons – each one taking from the school and giving nothing in return.[92]

The preparation for responsibility was not an entirely new notion, though it had been in abeyance for many years during the pre-public school period. But at the Abbaye-aux-Bois where the French nobility in the eighteenth century sent their daughters, all the pupils had to undertake a variety of lowly domestic duties. They counted the linen and put it away, dealt with the household accounts, mended the vestments, acted as porters at the convent gate, gave out the provisions, cooked, swept the dormitories, tended the lamps, waited on the pupils in the refectory. 'It was a splendid training in responsibility. Hélène acting "Esther" before a brilliant audience . . . slips off quietly to change into her uniform that she may prepare the tisanes and the poultices for the infirmary.'[93] It has a very modern ring, but was a feature of Benedictine education for young noblewomen two hundred years ago.

All school histories record with fitting pride the good works that have been undertaken in their past, and it is an interesting aspect of social history to see how needs have changed. Leeds Girls' Modern School in 1863 held a three-day bazaar to raise funds for the relief of Lancashire textile workers, whose looms were at a standstill because of the American Civil War. Many school sewing guilds stitched clothes for the poor. The Brighton and Hove High School in 1886 'adopted' a street, visited the families weekly and took gifts of food, money and clothing. (One of its guild rules was that each member had to make at least one garment in the holidays.) The Francis Holland School in Graham Street also had a sewing guild, though by 1913 the headmistress was lamenting that too many bought garments were taking the place of the hand-stitched. In 1895 during a particularly cold winter they collected money to provide poor children with breakfasts. They wrote to slum children, sent zoo tickets and flowers, boxfuls of books, toys and clothes, and took their photographs. Haberdashers' Monmouth School concerned themselves with the workhouse over the road (now part of their own premises) and visited and entertained the inmates, and one headmistress, noticing how bare the graves were in the grounds outside, organized girls to decorate those that could be seen from the workhouse windows. At some of the smart private schools there was a *de haut en bas* note. At Tudor Hall when during the First War factory girls from the East End used to be invited, pupils were made to roll up their hair and wear hats – 'a precaution taken against the possibility of the visitors bringing some small unwelcome livestock'. Hayes Court School used to entertain girls from a Bermondsey club. 'Personally I can't recall having any genuine interest in their way of life. I suppose it was intended to broaden our outlook. After they had gone Nurse forbad the use of the loos until they had all been disinfected.' During the Depression, however, Hayes Court adopted a Rhondda school, with which they felt far more involved: 'We learnt a great deal that was new to us concerning the domestic conditions of the miners and their families.'[94]

All these are, however, traditional feminine acts of mercy. The public schools also saw women in a different role; they were to be more than helpmeets and comforters – they were to be leaders and initiators who would take their schools' message out into the world. Cheltenham from early days had its parerga – work that it carried on outside the school. There was St Hilda's College, Cheltenham, which trained teachers (Miss Beale thought of it as resembling a religious order, a body of women consecrated to the 'ministry of teaching'), and she set up St Hilda's Hall at Oxford for the same purpose. There was also the guild of old college members, based on the principles of 'continued self-education and service to the community'; they established the East End settlement of St Hilda's and the Missionary Study Circle. (It is interesting that, uniquely among associations of old alumni, membership of the guild was until recently select and limited to notable achievers.) 'Seniors were spread all over the world,' the St Leonards history recorded of the between-the-wars period, 'following diverse careers from helping in the Grenfell Mission in Labrador to medical work in the Straits Settlements of Malaya medical service; from teaching domestic service to girls in Nigeria to lecturing in a college in Nanking.'[95]

> They took in those in need [said Iris Murdoch of Badminton in the 1930s], no matter what the cost or what the Governing Body said. They took in Indira Gandhi when her father was in jail, and after 1933 they took in refugees from Germany and Austria until the school bulged at every seam. They did it with such conviction that no one ever felt patronised and no one ever had the nerve to object.[96]

And by this time the message of service had trickled down to the lowest level of private schools, where headmistresses who fifty years before would have been concerned only to drum the virtues of tidiness and decorous conduct into their pupils now talked about the duty of giving back what one had received – even though they could not tell their girls what to give, and no one was very clear what they had received.

But by the 1960s, as already noted, the young were more impatient. They did not want to wait until they had left school; if they were going to help they wanted to do something now. Apart from an annual jolly with a suitable deserving cause, the pre-war generation had rarely been brought into contact with the poor or the deprived; not even Badminton, for all its socialist principles, actually rubbed shoulders with the working class. 'In retrospect,' said a Benenden girl, 'I can see how well-informed we were on international affairs, and how little we knew about the economic realities of life in Britain. *Love on the Dole* was just another play.'[97] Now the schools which had cloistered and protected their pupils found they had to let them venture outside the school gates. But though there is no longer the terror of infectious diseases which in the pre-vaccine period haunted all boarding schools and led them to keep their pupils within the walls, it is not always easy to find outlets for this zeal. Some schools are too remote; some, like St Leonards and Sherborne, are faced with too few who want their services, and with competition from others; schools in localities like High Wycombe or Brighton are worried for the safety of their girls. But even if it means bussing the girls to the grannies, the schools try. To a certain extent good works are built into the curriculum, in that aspirants for the Duke of Edinburgh's award must have spent time in service to the community, but many do far more than the minimum required for this. Malvern, for instance, a school that has always had a keen social conscience, sends all its lower-sixth girls to work for a week with the mentally handicapped, with autistic children, with the disabled and the old, and runs a club for the elderly. All schools fund-raise for a wide variety of good causes, a fact which charities are well aware of.

What, then, is the effect of the gridiron on those who are subjected to it? The advantages are not primarily academic; though the public boarding schools' standards have greatly improved in the last two decades, the academic day schools in most cases probably still do better. As might be expected, the lasting results of the fiery ordeal are upon the character. It teaches endurance, of course; nothing later is usually as bad. 'Maybe the agony of exams, the discipline of doing the things we most disliked, and the conformity with others has made us more responsible citizens,' said one girl doubtfully of her day school[98] – a sentiment obviously doubly true when one is a boarder. One learns resilience, one can cope. 'The attitude conveyed by the staff was that it was just as possible, and part of a fully integrated life, to read the lesson in church, or give a talk at Sunday evening prayers as it was to make your bed properly or be punctual.'[99] The most striking outward sign used to be the resonant upper-class voice that had sent '*Don't* run!' or 'Take an order mark!' ringing down innumerable corridors. But this has vanished now that nobody cares a fig about order marks, and a hybrid mid-atlantic/South London accent is standard. There used also to be a toughness (perhaps concealed now) exemplified by the story with which a Wycombe Abbey headmistress sought to inspire school assembly at the time of the partition of India. Watching Hindus and Moslems bloodily massacring each other, a group of the English raj had tried to shield the only woman of the party from the sight. But, undaunted, she had pressed forward with the battle cry, 'Wycombe Abbey girls don't faint!'

'Living in a boarding school one learns not only to live with people – to deal with people – to be a peacemaker during lessons,' said one of Mallory Wober's more articulate witnesses, 'but more than all this you learn to be independent, and you learn to know what's going on inside people's minds.' The individual may be purged of eccentricity – 'It's safer to be like the others, then no one can laugh' – but very often she becomes a pioneer. In 1979 the Malvern Girls' College headmistress listed the school's achievements: these included the first woman judge, the first woman to reach top rank in the Civil Service, the first to be appointed to the council of the Institution of Civil Engineers, to command an RAF station, to qualify as a surveyor, to walk the floor of the Stock Exchange, to captain an air flight. But perhaps what is best in the public school aspiration is summarized in the Benenden school prayer: 'Grant, O God, that as the years pass by there may go forth from this place a great company, who, strengthened by Thy Grace, and inspired by Thy Spirit, shall serve Thee faithfully, for the welfare of their fellow-men, and for the honour of Thy great Name', and by the charge that is traditionally given to those who are leaving Christ's Hospital at the last chapel service of the school year:

> I charge you never to forget the great benefits which you have received in this place, and in time to come, according to your means, to do all that you can to enable others to enjoy the same advantages. Remember that you carry with you wherever you go, the good name of Christ's Hospital. May God bless you in all your ways, in the knowledge of His love, now and forever.

5

'Individuals, even Eccentrics': Private Schools before World War II

Freedom

> That was the real value of St James's, that we were allowed, even encouraged, to be individuals, even eccentrics, if we liked . . . St James's was an aristocratic culture. We were not forced into the narrow examination culture, but we had time to try our hands at writing, acting, and painting. The school gave us education for living, even if it did not fit us to earn our living. The whole system presupposed a comfortable private income.[1]

While the large public schools were at their most unattractive in the early decades of this century, and had a malign influence on both older establishments such as religious foundations and on the high schools who imitated the regimentation and the emphasis on games, a private school – a good one – gave far more scope for individuality. The writer quoted was at St James's, West Malvern, between 1917 and 1921, one of the many schools where wealthy girls could lead a delightfully happy life in supremely civilized surroundings until they were ready to be launched into society. (One early pupil married into the royal family and became Duchess of Gloucester.) And though the level of general culture at St James's would seem to be well in advance of what would have been attainable at, say, Roedean and its kind, academic success was clearly not one of its aims, nor was educational experiment.

Nevertheless, there were a number of private schools at that time which were innovators for, with a curious irony, the educational initiative in the first quarter of the twentieth century came from the private sector, from a type of school that the public schools had sought to replace. The founders were able to put their own particular vision into practice; those were spacious days, when there was no exam pressure or talk of a national curriculum. There was no need to be involved with the Board of Education at all. If one desired to put 'recognized as efficient' on the prospectus then there had to be a full government inspection which would take into account not only the quality of the teaching and the range of subjects offered, but also such matters as the food, the space in the dormitories, and the bathrooms and lavatories (there had to be a fixed number of these, a fact which stopped some of the more impoverished from applying for an inspection). Schools might drag their feet over implementing the inspectors' recommendations about buildings and equipment, but were in trouble if they did not act swiftly over matters of health and safety. The great advantage of 'recognition' was that it attracted qualified staff. But while the academically ambitious wanted to achieve recognition as soon as they could, there were those who felt they were above it, to say nothing of the mob – and any Kelly's Street Directory of the time will show how many there used to be of these – who were satisfied only to be registered, and no doubt Mr Squeers could have managed to squeeze on to that list.*

For every school like St James's there were forty or fifty inferior specimens, many consisting of a few desks in a town house with not even a playground, of a sort described savagely by Orwell in *A Clergyman's Daughter* (1935), where the children, whose parents had scraped together the few necessary pounds to keep them uncontaminated from the lower orders, daily prayed that they might become industrious, punctual and ladylike and 'not a disgrace like some schools of which Thou knowest'. The survival rate of schools like these, where the proprietors were only in the business to make a living and where the parents were only interested in class segregation, was very low indeed, and even the better sort of schools required much foresight and planning if they were to survive beyond the owners' retirement. Those who could bring themselves, like Olive Willis at Downe House and the Misses Lawrence at Roedean, to make the sacrifice of relinquishing their personal rule and transferring their creation to a board of trustees, were the exception. Many could not afford to do so and hoped to sell the property and the goodwill.

The catastrophic results of World War II are discussed more fully in Chapter 13; it had far more effect on private schools than the First War, and those that escaped being evacuated, requisitioned or dispersed were rare indeed. It particularly affected the innumerable schools in the invasion zone on the south coast; in 1913 there were eighty-seven boarding-schools in Folkestone alone, most of which sank without trace and have not been replaced. A few schools amalgamated with others. Hollington Park, for instance, founded in Hastings in 1860 as Winchester House, was forced out of independent existence in 1976 by the increasing expansion of a once rural area, by rising salaries and by the cost of fire-proofing, and with Lillesden (a prep school) joined Bedgebury.

Those girls' schools that survived have lost any idiosyncratic ethos they may have begun with. For one thing, they are now 'public schools' in that they have passed out of private hands; for another, the days are long past

* Government 'recognition' ceased in the late 1970s. The independent schools have set up a self-regulatory accreditation service which will inspect and report on new schools seeking this service.

when it was possible to spend five blissful years doing mostly English and history, dispensing with maths and science, and brushing aside exams as irrelevant. Nobody preaches salvation through eurhythmics or choral speech any more; modern conditions forbid interrupting the timetable if the weather seems too good for lessons, or allowing the children to sleep in the garden as was done when schools were small, life was safe, and summers were hot. The distinctive uniforms of specially dyed tweeds and velvets and shantung have been replaced by easy-care man-made fabrics in standard utilitarian shades of green, maroon, brown, navy-blue or grey, so that there is no difference in appearance between the child whose parents are paying £7,000 a year, and the comprehensive school pupil. The features which marked out some from the more traditional schools – the visits to art galleries and theatres, the music, the visiting lecturers – are now habitual practice in every state school; and since central catering units and even cafeterias prevail, and the separate tables with their abundance of white damask and flowers and maids to wait on them have gone for ever, mealtime conversation is no longer the gracious art it used to be. Everybody plays the same sports and is obliged to read the same examination texts, which leave little time for other books and certainly not for reading aloud; the inspired headmistress who formed one's literary tastes for life is a thing of the past. But on the credit side it can be claimed that if anyone now finishes her education without a certificate or a diploma it is not the fault of the school.

Sixty years ago the differences were marked. The early public schools and the high schools which had been the initial reformers, which had, as they thought, relegated the private schools to the Dark Ages, were by the First War the prisoners of their own systems, no longer in any way avant-garde. It was the dullest period of their history, when they were too near their beginnings to wish to make any change in an outlook which had seemed so innovatory thirty years before. But the wealthy upper classes did not necessarily want their daughters turned into beefy Amazons at the first, and many professional parents still looked askance at the class mix at the second, or felt there was something more to a girl's life than just exams. When *Queen* magazine in 1922 questioned various distinguished men and women about what form they thought girls' education should take, it was notable that not one of them would have sent a daughter to a public school or a high school, except Sir Oliver Lodge who did not believe in single-sex schools and had chosen Bedales for his. Countess Haig said that such schools crammed girls with too many subjects; Frederic Harrison deplored the craze for a crude copy of boys' education, Madame Albinesi the violent exercise 'harmful to health and injurious to feminine charm'. Violet Vanbrugh stressed the importance of practical matters, good manners and a religious background. Berta Ruck asserted that nothing that was going to be the slightest use to a girl was ever learnt out of a book. Her main thrust, however, was on the need for cleanliness. Until that branch of culture was attended to she wouldn't worry much about the theoretical side of education.

Private schools had always been more flexible, more responsive to parents' whims as well as bolder with educational experiments; the report of the Schools Inquiry Commission had singled this out in 1868 as one of the few points then in their favour. The public schools (it was referring of course to the boys') had the advantage of permanence, old associations, traditions; almost every grammar school had some history which acted powerfully on the imagination of its pupils, while private schools were essentially perishable. But on the other hand they were open to innovation, and could try out new methods of teaching.[2] However, these new methods were to be more in evidence in the next century, when the private schools – execrated at the time of the Commission – enjoyed a renaissance, an Indian summer that lasted until the outbreak of the Second War. There were schools for every sort and condition: for the débutante (St James's, Heathfield, West Heath, North Foreland Lodge, Tudor Hall); for the progeny of cultured families who were not averse to experimental methods (Prior's Field, Wychwood, Moreton Hall, Moira House); for girls in the suburbs whose parents distrusted the high schools; for towns that did not have high schools (The Laurels, in Rugby; Oakdene, Beaconsfield; St Anne's, now at Windermere); for delicate girls (some school perched on a Sussex cliff); for those whose parents lived in distant parts of the Empire ('entire charge' would be advertised in the prospectus, and they would often be described as 'home schools'). There were farm schools for those without strong academic inclination, and finishing schools for the late teens who had time on their hands and no particular purpose (except finding a husband) in view. Some of them specified that their pupils should be 'of good social position', or 'the daughters of gentlemen'; others, like Downe House (see page 104), had their own methods of sorting sheep from goats. The Truman and Knightley schools directory of 1930 lists hundreds of private schools, and it is noticeable from the photographs that advertise them how many occupy what appear to be town houses ill adapted to educational purposes, and how few of the principals have any academic qualifications.

It was also an Indian summer for the middle classes. Never again would they be able to purchase an education at so affordable a price, and never again would their daughters be so free from the constraints of exams and syllabuses, indeed from competition. 'Music and religion and good manners seemed to be the *most* important things, during my whole stay of eleven years,' said a girl who went to Moreton Hall in 1934. 'Some people were clever, and some people were not, but that, happily, did not seem to matter very much in those days.'[3] Another wrote of the school's 100 per cent failure when she and a friend were the only candidates taking School Certificate in 1942. But the war forced all school-leavers, however privileged, into jobs; after it was over even those who up till 1939 would have stayed at home until they were married thought if not of a career then of a job, and the qualifications needed before one could begin on a professional training, minimal in the 1930s, were to become more and more exacting. 'No child growing up now inherits security *outside* its own family circle,' wrote a Benenden senior who had begun her school life in 1936 and left in 1939. 'We did, we were the last to inherit the unthinking certitudes of upper-middle class Britain.'[4] And the writer wondered what had become of the contemporary who had planned to stay at home and do the flowers for a year, after which period her future husband would surely present himself. 'She had already begun to sew masses of trousseau lingerie, exquisitely – and baby-clothes.'

Ladies in Distressed Circumstances

It had always been easy to open a private school; indeed, it was usually the first thought of ladies in distressed circumstances, so that Prospect House Establishment for Young Ladies at Charlton near Blackheath in the early nineteenth century assured parents in their prospectus 'that the Misses Selby were not engaged with interested [i.e. pecuniary] views, but rather to satisfy their inclination (having a sufficiency of their own)'.[5] 'It was a common saying at one town,' said the Schools Inquiry Commission, who could find nothing whatever to commend in these establishments for young ladies, 'that if a woman did not marry by a certain age, she immediately opened a school.' And the report added that at the cheaper schools the proprietresses had not the slightest training, and that most had mistaken their vocation and should have become servants.

There is not the slightest doubt that remarkable schools could arise out of financial need. Roedean is the most famous example, but there is also Moreton Hall, dealt with later in this chapter, which was begun by a widow to educate her young children, and St Helen's, Northwood, which in effect had its beginnings in a business failure. May Rowland Brown, the school's founder, was a child of twelve when her father's printing business collapsed, and was deeply impressed by her mother's gallant courage in standing by him, teaching the younger children and securing an education for the older ones. In 1899, aged twenty-five, 'with a hundred borrowed pounds behind her and equipped with her own staunch character, her Christian idealism, her true love of teaching',[6] May embarked on her own venture. Nor was it easy going at the start; there were crises over finding pupils and over premises, and she seemed at the same time to have taken over responsibility for housing her parents, though her mother's housekeeping skills were an enormous help. (And with touching family piety the school was called St Helen's after the City church where Mrs Rowland Brown had been baptized, confirmed and married.) She had the support too of her youngest sister Doris, who came to teach French when she left Cambridge and was to become one of the principals until her retirement in 1945.

But though adversity spawned hundreds of girls' schools, few were of this calibre.

> Knowing what English female education is [wrote one acerbic critic in 1858], we know that the widow ladies and the clergymen's wives . . . are all stuff and nonsense – that the teachers are generally the wives of broken-down coal merchants, who contrive to hire a house and engage two or three housemaids, and get a few ignorant ushers to dub themselves masters, and call this sort of thing 'a Select Establishment'.

The writer added grimly that these wretched places, that appealed only to vanity and pride, 'could not be unless parents liked them'.[7] And right up until the last war one could get by with unqualified staff and the minimum of equipment, banking on the inflexible determination of middle-class parents to keep caste and send their daughters to a school where the pupils spoke with the right accents and came from an exactly similar background. From the 1920s onwards they would stand out from the rabble at the state schools by virtue of their elaborate, carefully designed uniforms; since the parents paid for this it appeared to be a hobby with some headmistresses, who had no intention of being lavish in any other direction, to dream up an extraordinary multiplicity of garments for every activity, from church-going to Greek dancing.

The unreformed Victorian private school has often been described in histories and autobiographies. One of the best accounts comes in Juliana Horatia Ewing's novel *Six to Sixteen*.[8] Mrs Ewing had not been away at school herself, but clearly had friends who had described it vividly, and she goes out of her way to castigate the system and set out her own views on education. It was not so much the actual teaching at Miss Mulberry's school, Bush House, that she represented as faulty, but the regime whereby thirty or so girls had in the fashion of the time to share beds (a Bristol school advertised in its prospectus that a single bed cost three guineas extra); were fed an unsatisfying diet consisting mostly of bread and butter; were cooped up together in a single schoolroom where they were kept at their lessons from breakfast to bedtime, with their only exercise a crocodile on the high road and a bare fifteen minutes of unsupervised recreation. Inevitably their health suffered. One of Mrs Ewing's characters mournfully contrasts her former school with Bush House: 'It wasn't everlasting backaches, and headaches, and coughs, and pains in your side all along.' And Mrs Ewing's brisk comment is that it is better to start life with a sound, healthy constitution and a reasonable set of nerves than to have one's head crammed and one's health neglected.

Miss Mulberry was typical of her kind, in that reduced circumstances rather than zeal for education had driven her into teaching; she had worked hard for many years, Mrs Ewing tells us, to support 'a paralytic mother and a delicate sister'. By the time the narrator reaches Bush House Miss Mulberry has achieved a modest degree of prosperity, and can afford to keep a French governess to do the hard teaching work and to keep the pupils under perpetual surveillance. But the French governess has the deepest distrust of girl-nature, and resorts to espionage in her efforts to detect misdemeanour: 'We suffered at Bush House from an excess of the meddlesome discipline which seems to be *de rigueur* in girls' schools. I think Miss Mulberry would have felt that she had neglected her duty if we had ever been left to our own devices for an hour . . . The *nag* of never being free from supervision was both irritating and depressing.'

Conditions, of course, varied and were often a great deal worse than at the fictional Bush House. Elizabeth Sewell, sent in 1819 at the age of four with her sisters to a school at Newport, Isle of Wight, spoke of the wretchedness of the bedroom which five little girls inhabited. It was uncarpeted and unlit except for a large horn lantern; they were forbidden to look out of the one window (the other two had been blocked up), and the only seats were their trunks on which they had to sit and learn their lessons until they were called down to breakfast on milk and water and bread. Lessons went on from morning until night, and one was never free of the extra lessons imposed for punishment – even for speaking ungrammatically in playtime, for instance saying 'Come here' instead of 'Come hither'. Once Elizabeth was seventy lessons in arrears. The children never used Christian names to each other, but said 'Miss' and the surname, which she thought was a sensible way of avoiding undesirable intimacy, since the school was mixed socially, with a few children of the professional classes and many whose parents were farmers and shopkeepers. 'The strictness of the school discipline was extreme. Not a word was spoken in school time; and as for disobedience, it never entered our thoughts as a possibility.'[9]

'My dear mother never knew, until we were grown up and had left the school, all we endured there,' Miss Sewell said of this establishment. But most of its features were common to all private schools of the time, and among the defects in boarding schools noted by a writer in the *Victoria Magazine* in 1876[10] were the long hours of study – nine or ten hours a day which started long before breakfast, with girls sometimes carrying textbooks to their meals to swot – and the single classroom in which twenty or thirty girls had to do all their lessons, the only exercise a languid walk two by two. Like Miss Beale, the writer thought far too many subjects were attempted, and deprecated the practice of making the girls talk French all the time: 'school-girls invariably coin a kind of base alloy, composed of French and English, fused rapidly, without the least respect to mood, tense, or general speech'. She was severe on the poor arrangements for physical health, the absence of washing facilities and bathrooms, the lack of ventilation, the overcrowded sleeping accommodation. And finally: 'we consider the nun-like seclusion of school-girls to be the very means of fostering unhealthy ideas concerning love and marriage'.

It was against all these errors that the reformers very reasonably reacted, devising a system where attention to health was stressed, where the girls took strenuous exercise and were continually on the run (this replacing conversation conducted in French as a means of keeping idle chatter at bay), and where a regime of trust and responsibility was encouraged. But, as has been seen in the previous chapter, all this was carried to extremes, and by the Edwardian period parents were casting around for an alternative form of education. Once again the private schools became popular with the elite (they had never gone out of fashion with the ordinary middle classes who merely wanted to keep their children out of the board schools), and though nearly all such schools had been to a certain degree affected by St Leonards, Wycombe Abbey and Roedean, there was far more room for idiosyncrasy. Indeed, one suspects that the most interesting teaching in the between-the-wars period was to be found at good private schools (perhaps from unqualified teachers), though the curriculum was inevitably heavily tilted towards arts subjects, particularly English. And there is no doubt whatever that girls at this time could be far happier in these relatively small communities than ever they seemed to be at the big public schools. 'No doubt it did not provide that prolonged and exacting type of education which is now the inevitable preliminary to any professional career,' Vera Brittain said defensively of her Surrey school, St Monica's. 'But such training was then mainly obtainable in schools which sterilized the sexual charm out of their pupils, and turned them into hockey-playing hoydens with gauche manners and an armoury of inhibitions.'[11]

But even in the earlier period of the *Victoria Magazine* denunciations, there had been exceptions. Constance Jones, later Mistress of Girton, was sent for a year in the 1860s to a small private school in Cheltenham, Alston Court, where she was happy, comfortable, and very well taught. 'The order and freshness of the place was charming . . . There was no tyranny, no fuss, no spying.' She was able to learn Latin and Greek, and some Euclid, and they had delightful history, geography, and English literature lessons from a visiting master. The girls were taken to concerts and readings, and in this way she heard Santley and Sims Reeves and Dickens.[12] This could never be done cheaply, as Elizabeth Sewell pointed out.[13] It presupposed not only first-class teachers, but an abundance of good domestic staff, and a considerable outlay on the premises, furnishings and general comfort. To skimp on any of these meant an inferior school.

There were schools, of course, that took note of the reforms being effected by the North London Collegiate and who tried to emulate them, albeit on a less ambitious scale. Such was the school that is now Wroxall Abbey, which began as The Laurels in Rugby, at the instigation of Dr Frederick Temple, then headmaster of Rugby School. He thought that there ought to be an establishment of suitable academic standing for the daughters of masters at his school. Miss Constance Woods took up his challenge and with her sister opened a school in her own house in 1872. For that date she was reasonably qualified – she could advertise in her prospectus that she had an honours certificate in the Cambridge Higher Examination. Her sister having departed for Clifton, she ran the school (which included twenty-five boarders) virtually single-handed for fifteen years, with visiting masters to teach Latin, art, music and gymnastics. She achieved remarkable successes, so that in 1890 a Laurels girl was accepted for the London School of Medicine for Women, and by the time she retired in 1898 there was a regular flow of pupils to the women's colleges in Oxford, Cambridge and London. Miss Woods was unusual in her encouragement of interests outside the school curriculum, and in theatricals and music; The Laurels was one of the very few schools where the violin was taught.[14]

But schools like The Laurels could only thrive then in an academic milieu; the expectations of the ordinary middle classes who chose a private school rather than a high school for their daughters focused on manners rather than on educational attainments. In an article about the Oxford school, Wychwood, in 1922 *Queen* magazine observed that one mother had sent her daughter there because the girls 'behaved like gentlewomen in the streets and public places'.[15] There was more to Wychwood than this, as will be seen later, but this was how most middle-class parents chose their daughters' schools. It was therefore a very easy time for unambitious private school owners, who were not even required to provide the accomplishments that earlier generations had demanded. The staff did not have to be qualified, as we noted earlier, and did not expect to be paid as if they were; the children were docile and amenable and did not question authority; the most expensive item was the uniform, which the parents provided.

Consider one Surrey school: Dunottar, Reigate, now a well equipped day school offering a wide range of subjects, but fifty years ago very different. It was opened in 1926 with a handful of girls in rented premises. As numbers expanded it moved rapidly from house to house in the neighbourhood, and at its fourth removal in 1933 settled in an imposing Victorian mansion in the classical style, with twelve acres of beautifully laid-out grounds. By this stage the proprietors had presumably overreached themselves, for there was very little money spent on adapting the premises to educational purposes. The founder and headmistress was a Scotswoman, a graduate of Glasgow University, but had none of her country's traditional zeal for education. She did not aspire to have the school recognized as efficient and in her time no girl went to university, nor indeed could have been prepared for any entrance exam, for the staff was not sufficiently qualified and there was no sixth form. Science was not taught, as there was no laboratory; mathematics was shared out among the staff generally; art was taught by the gym mistress, among others. There was no library; music (except for the very few who took piano lessons) was non-existent; there was no provision for craft or handwork, and very few textbooks (most were second-hand). The only foreign language taught was French; even English – the great strength of so many girls' schools – was pitifully inadequate and focused on the set books prescribed for School Certificate. Everybody learnt the same subjects; there was no question of choice. The general level of culture was unusually low and there were no out of school activities; no interest was taken in anything literary or aesthetic, or indeed in anything beyond the school walls. The emphasis was on handwriting (as in the school in Orwell's *A Clergyman's Daughter*, tremendous importance was attached to a good copperplate hand), neatness, diligence and good behaviour; and, most ironically, on achieving enough credits in School Certificate to obtain matriculation exemption, though few parents, and probably no pupils, had any idea that this was connected with admission to a university.

The founder retired in 1951 and after her death the parents bought the premises and the goodwill from her widower, turning it into an educational trust, and the school adapted itself to post-war educational expectations. Yet 1930s parents had been content with the system – Dunottar and its kind could not have prospered if they had not been. The premises were undoubtedly impressive, and they liked to see the girls in their distinctive royal-blue uniform; so they chose to send them there instead of to the local county secondary school with its excellent academic record where, in the home counties climate of fifty years ago, they would have lost caste.

That private schools could be ambitious, however limited the capital, is shown by the history of a neighbouring school, Greenacre, Banstead, begun by two idealistic friends in 1933 who wanted to put their views on education into practice: they felt that sound learning ought to be combined with experience, both cultural and social, of the outside world. They launched their school with breathless and endearing optimism, using an uncle's legacy to buy a house on the Banstead Downs and enough furniture for three rooms. When the photographer came to take pictures for the prospectus, children and equipment had to be borrowed. But during the six years before the war (when most of the pupils were taken to the West Country) there was considerable academic achievement, and the principals, determined to achieve recognized status as soon as possible, worked to bring education and premises to the required level. When the school was inspected in 1938, it was granted Board of Education recognition.[16]

But Dunottar conditions must have prevailed in many unrecognized between-the-wars schools set up to provide an income, and even in the better sort where girls had been sent for social reasons rather than for any academic expectation the brighter pupils often lacked intellectual stimulus.

> The main flaw in the contentment of many was the lack of provision for those girls of higher intelligence than the average. They suffered pangs of intellectual starvation, and were often irritated by the superficial character of the teaching ... Queenwood had always had good results in the

> various public examinations but never attempted to teach the only lesson worthwhile, *how* to learn, *how* to read, how to make use of the knowledge which would be presented to them in a wider world than school.[17]

The place of science in the curriculum is discussed at greater length in Chapter 10. Before 1950 few private schools of any sort concerned themselves with it. There was of course the difficulty of equipment and qualified teachers, but also a genteel prejudice against the subject, it often being thought lower-class and artisan, something that the high schools and the technical colleges could be left to tackle. English and history, however, were sometimes taught exceptionally well, and the inspectors' report in 1936 on Upper Chine School, Shanklin, in the Isle of Wight would have been true of the better sort of private school of the time. The oldest private school in existence, having begun in Folkestone in 1799, it had first applied for recognition in 1925, and by the time of the 1936 inspection had about 120 pupils of many nationalities, a quarter coming from outside England. (Except at convents this was then most unusual.) The inspectors were pleased with what they found. There was a sixth form, and three pupils were working for Oxbridge entrance. Though none of the English mistresses had a degree, 'spirited and sensitive work was seen', the girls read widely and intelligently, and had 'an independence of judgement which owes something to the courageous tone of the School'. History was also taught by a non-graduate, a former pupil, whose methods the inspectors praised as exceptionally good. French was average; 'the accent of the girls, except in isolated cases, is no better than the average British compromise'. There was a classics mistress, and Latin was taught though it was not compulsory. German was taught by the French mistress (though a German specialist would be appointed the following term), and maths by the geography mistress, 'with some help from various other members of the staff'. Over science, the inspectors were agreeably surprised: there was a laboratory with a fair supply of apparatus and nearly every girl took a general course which included chemistry, physics and biology. As far as art went, though the pupils were 'steady and commendable' there was little distinguished work; a wide variety of handicrafts was undertaken, however. The music was good, with well qualified teachers and a small orchestra; there were a lot of out of school activities including lectures, debates, Guiding and impromptu drama. And the inspectors spoke highly of the beautiful surroundings and the excellent balance between freedom and discipline.[18]

Women of Vision

It was possible, as has been said, for the middle classes in the earlier decades of this century to indulge themselves where daughters' education was concerned, and to let beautiful surroundings, emphasis on a favourite subject or the right atmosphere override any objections they might have to deficiencies in the curriculum. It was also a time when gifted women whose financial resources were in startling contrast to their enthusiasm and vision felt that they could express themselves in no better way than by building up schools of their own. Fewer careers were then open to women, of course, but one must also concede that education, in the middle-class sector at any rate, then seemed to offer exciting possibilities and opportunities to experiment that have now vanished. Financial rewards were not what they were after; it was their school that mattered. Miss Louise Watts who founded Oakdene School at Beaconsfield in 1911, like the Baird sisters who founded St James's, only allowed herself the most meagre personal income; Miss Doris Rowland Brown at St Helen's was reputed to sleep under the stairs so that there should be more room for the girls; and one remembers too Bronwen Lloyd-Williams, who sold a favourite horse so that the stage at Moreton Hall could be equipped with curtains. The schools that have survived and are now educational trusts owe it not only to their founders' vision and self-sacrifice but also to their qualities of doggedness and perseverance and business acumen. Hayes Court, for instance, a Middlesex school somewhat in the St James's tradition, where the pupils lived graciously and were interestingly taught, failed to survive 1939 because of the proprietor's lack of foresight and her financial incompetence.[19]

One of the most innovative early twentieth-century schools was Prior's Field in Godalming, founded in 1902 by Julia Huxley, the wife of Leonard Huxley and mother of Aldous and Julian. It started with six girls aged between seven and sixteen, and Aldous aged seven and a half. The atmosphere was informal; the house, designed for the Huxleys by Charles Voysey, was comfortable and homelike, and the Huxley family was much in evidence; the boys were about, and would join in the Saturday night dances at which Mr Huxley taught the girls to waltz. Mrs Huxley, who died in 1908, treated the girls with courtesy and consideration, crediting them with commonsense and a measure of adult judgement. They could go out for walks and bicycle rides and sketching parties, and were taken to the theatre and to museums. Such parents as Gilbert Murray, Maurice Hewlett and Sir Arthur Conan Doyle thought this of more importance than 'the mere accumulation of facts', which Mrs Huxley despised. To creative talent she gave great encouragement. When Enid Bagnold, for instance, wrote a precocious verse drama, Mrs Huxley sent it to Yeats and took Enid (by her own account an ungainly and self-conscious adolescent) to an evening party at his Bloomsbury flat, where she met Ezra Pound. 'She tried to transfer to us her great knowledge of literature and the arts,' said one of her pupils, 'sometimes at the expense of the more basic subjects, illustrated by the fact that most of us failed in arithmetic in the Lower Certificate exam.'[20]

Her successor, Mrs Burton-Brown, who was herself succeeded by her daughter Beatrice who did not retire until 1952 (there is still a Burton-

Brown as well as two Huxleys on the board of governors), carried on in the same style, preserving the Prior's Field ambience, concerned that the surroundings should be beautiful and the house full of flowers and pictures. Pupils remembered her lectures on Greek and Italian art and her history lessons. 'Her teaching gave to many of us – even the most philistine – a keen desire to see and understand more of great pictures, and sculpture, and architecture.'

Somewhere between Prior's Field and Wycombe Abbey came Runton Hill on the Norfolk coast, founded in 1911 by Janet Vernon Harcourt ('JVH'), a member of a distinguished Oxford academic family. She had taught briefly at Wycombe, which she deeply admired and wished to imitate though not in size, and Runton was deliberately kept small so that a family atmosphere – which she felt was lacking at Wycombe – could be maintained. As at Prior's Field, pupils were expected to behave with responsibility and good sense, and were allowed a considerable amount of freedom; they could go off on expeditions, and decide for themselves which church they should attend on Sundays. Like all east coast schools it was tough and bracing and unheated, and for the unsporting there was a great deal too much games – eighty minutes a day and two hours on Saturdays. There was also the annual marathon of the inter-house relay race, a cross-country scramble which bore a resemblance to the hare-and-hounds described in *Tom Brown's Schooldays* and involved the odd broken arm. Unexpectedly, however, music was also taken very seriously, and for some this compensated for the heartiness of the outdoor life.

Moreton Hall in its early days concentrated on the aspects of education which seemed relevant to its founders, the gifted Lloyd-Williams family, and blithely dispensed with the rest. Exams played little part in their scheme and many subjects were left out altogether, but the culture, especially the music, was rich. It was a school that arose out of financial need and a large family. John Lloyd-Williams, the headmaster of Oswestry Grammar School, died in 1913, leaving his widow with two sons and nine daughters. She began a school, at which three of her daughters were pupils, and then in 1919 with great courage and daring moved it to Moreton Hall, five miles away. Here three of 'Aunt Lil's' daughters did most of the teaching: Miss Mary dealt with music, history and divinity; Miss Grace with French; and Bronwen, who had been at Bedford Physical Training College, with English, dancing, games and gymnastics. Possessed of many talents – she was an international lacrosse player, a choreographer and an inspired English teacher – she left the school to spend ten years as a journalist, but returned to become principal when her sister Mary died in 1945. She herself died in 1973, by which time the responsibility was overpowering her. A fourth sister, Letty, was matron from time to time, going off for spells as a private nurse when the school got too much for her. English and music were the only subjects that were taken seriously: the choir was superb; piano lessons were part of the ordinary curriculum; and there were two orchestras even though there were under a hundred pupils, some of them very young. The whole school took part in ballets devised by Bronwen, while the more gifted tackled ambitious ventures like the Borodin Polovtsian dances or the Rose ballet from Gounod's *Faust*. In the 50s an outdoor theatre was built, opening with a dramatization of *Paradise Lost*. ('Couldn't we sometimes have Gilbert and Sullivan?' the more faint-hearted parents entreated.)

In the austere child-rearing style of the time, comfort was irrelevant; the winter cold was fearful, the electricity supply fitful, and the cook couldn't cook – the meals 'engendered in us a stoical ability to eat anything' – and everybody was expected to undertake long walks to church. But there was a delightfully happy family atmosphere. Ages ranged from eighteen down to eight or even younger. Miss Mary brought round sweets to the juniors when she came to say goodnight in the dormitories; Aunt Lil gave out half-crowns on people's birthdays, and Bronwen had the habit of saying comfortingly, 'You don't look very cheerful, darling. Come and have a piece of cake.' On impulse the principals might sweep everyone off on a picnic or a blackberrying expedition, or to go skating. 'I had twelve happy years there,' said one Old Moretonian, 'a splendid education, and a husband [met in the kindergarten] thrown in.' Another recalled being told that she was the only person in her university tutor's experience to have enjoyed boarding school.[21]

There is one girls' school that came into being as a result of a man's vision. Charles Ingham was an engineer who interested himself in teaching evening classes, and when his father-in-law's business failed 'the desire came to me of quitting a commercial life and adopting that of a teacher of the young'; he could also thereby provide work for his sisters-in-law. After he had studied American educational methods he opened a school in Croydon in 1875, calling it Moira House from the name engraved on the gatepost of the premises where it moved after the first few months. The first pupil was a young woman of nineteen, expansively spared to Mr Ingham by a colleague in New York. ('You shall have Jessie, she shall be your first pupil; let me know the date of the opening of the school and Jessie shall be punctually there.'[22]) The school from the start had unusual features: there were to be no marks or prizes, no rules – 'imposed restrictions inhibit the young from learning to control and guide themselves' – and no punishments; nor external exams 'to cramp and warp the intention of the teaching staff and to interrupt the smooth and even life of the school'. The only bell was a getting-up bell, and a gong for meals, and each class was taught in a separate room; the GPDSC were making a practice of this latter, but it was by no means common – at Cheltenham in the early days, for instance, everybody had their lessons in the same schoolroom. Charles Ingham also introduced cricket, and there were violin lessons, quite uncommon then in girls' schools.

By 1888 the school was established in Eastbourne, in a house designed by Mr Ingham himself. (There had been four years in Bournemouth, but this was not an area in favour with London doctors who considered it too relaxing, and since their good opinion was of paramount importance he moved to Eastbourne's more bracing climate.) He had evolved an educational philosophy which he elaborated in *Education in Accordance with Natural Law* (1902), in which equal stress was laid upon the formation of character, the unfolding of intellect, the development of the physical organism and the giving of knowledge.

The curriculum outlined by Gertrude Ingham (the Inghams' daughter, who succeeded her father as head), which was apparently long-established when she described it in 1925, made history the centre of the work scheme. Subjects were not separated but were dependent on each other; they were all approached historically and chronologically, and in six years the pupils would have passed twice through the three-year course, the second time at a more advanced level. There was 'setting' according to ability, and timetables were adapted to individual needs. Drawing and handwork were important, and after 1911 Dalcroze eurhythmics played a prominent part in the syllabus. The eurhythmic way of life – the training of musical understanding by movement to music – excited enormous enthusiasm among those who saw it demonstrated. (These included the Ingham family, some of whom later set up the London School of Dalcroze Eurhythmics.) In his introduction to *The Eurhythmics of Jaques-Dalcroze* Sir Michael Sadler claimed that Dalcroze had 'rediscovered one of the secrets of Greek education'; its disciples called eurhythmics an education in itself. It was taken up fervently by girls' schools in the early decades of the century – like the League of Nations and the Scout movement it then seemed the answer to the world's problems – but nowhere with more ardour than at Moira House, where girls were called upon to give demonstrations. The stoical calm with which they did so in London during a zeppelin raid in 1917 was regarded as a great tribute to M. Dalcroze's methods. Under Mona Swann, an old girl of Moira House who succeeded Miss Ingham as head, the emphasis was on spoken English and drama and on very little else, and it was not until the 1970s that the school, with a new headmaster, pulled the numbers up to an economic level and established the academic standards that are now so essential in a highly competitive world.

In 1918 Moira House introduced a system of self-government. After a crisis period when the school had suffered from the world-wide influenza epidemic, both staff and children wanted to preserve the unity that had emerged during those weeks. The school play the previous year had been an adaptation of *The Idylls of the King*, and it was decided that a league should be formed in imitation of the Arthurian court, where there would be knights (equivalent to head girl and prefects) elected by girls and staff, squires who had lesser responsibilities, with the rest of the school ranking as pages who aspired to rise higher. All would have votes, whose value was in proportion to their rank.[23]

Forms of self-government appeared at other schools. Sometimes it was only nominal, as at Hayes Court where 'the school was run on ostensibly avant-garde and democratic lines . . . but in fact Miss Cox was an absolute autocrat',[24] though others defended the scheme as giving valuable experience in committee procedure. It was more truly democratic at Wychwood in Oxford, to which many dons and literary parents sent their daughters in the days when it was possible to wander down to north Oxford from Boars Hill through cornfields and water meadows, 'and hear nothing but the tinkle of sheep bells and the splash of the stream', as a fictional account of Wychwood had it.[25]

Founded in 1897, Wychwood has always been a small school and still inhabits the same limited site in the Banbury Road to which it moved in 1918. The prefect system was found not to work in such an informal atmosphere where there was no particular dividing line between seniors and juniors, and at about the same time as Moira House was initiating its league, Geraldine Coster was developing a similar system at Wychwood. The school was divided into two categories: citizens, who had a vote, and minors who had not but who could express an opinion. The school council, to which each form elected a representative, met once a week and discussed punishments and complaints (though they had no power to vote on matters affecting curriculum, health or chaperonage – all-embracing categories which usefully covered many of the pupils' most burning grievances, like 'Why need we wear hats?' or 'Can't we go to bed later?'). There is still a school council, and Rye St Antony, a Roman Catholic school founded by two members of the Wychwood staff, also uses the procedure. The lack of seriousness about games – to a certain extent forced on it by limited space – appealed to many Oxford parents, who warmed to the music, drama, painting and handicrafts that were offered instead. It was also possible in the early days, before Banbury Road was so dense with traffic and when urban life was less dangerous, to give the pupils much more freedom than was customary in boarding schools, and they biked and rambled round Oxford and went punting on the Cherwell.[26]

None of these schools, individual though many of them were, can be called experimental in the way that certain co-educational schools such as Summerhill, King Alfred's and Beacon Hill (run briefly by Bertrand and Dora Russell) were in their time. There were a few freakish ventures, but they have not survived. One was a school for girls from five to fifteen, started in 1935 at Capel-y-Ffin in a remote valley of the Black Mountains, a spot where a succession of ardent souls had since mid-Victorian times tried and failed (human flesh never being equal to enduring the rigours of the site) to establish the perfect community. The last to be defeated had been

Eric Gill and various followers, who stayed for four years before the climate and the isolation drove them back to the home counties. 'The object of the school is to provide education and training for domestic and family life on the basis of the Catholic religion,' said the prospectus, and the curriculum included gardening and dairy work, cooking, housewifery, household accounts, spinning and weaving, needlework and an elementary knowledge of first-aid. Music was restricted to plain-chant, folk song and dance, violin and pipe, and Eric Gill visited at intervals to supervise drawing lessons. 'The buildings are of stone, and having been built originally for a monastery are admirably adapted for school use.' In 1930s style there was an elaborate uniform – though there was no one to see it but the sheep on the hills – which included holland tunics with belts, velvet cord jackets, velvet dresses and shantung blouses.[27]

The one school that does now seem to stand out as different – St Anne's, Windermere, which is cast in the Gordonstoun mould and is one of the international Round Square Conference schools* whose philosophy and ideals were inspired by Kurt Hahn – ironically started life in 1863 in Lancashire as a small venture where young ladies were taught accomplishments, presided over by two principals, one of whom was only eighteen herself. It had become a 'recognized' secondary school by the early twentieth century, but it was only fairly recently that it finally turned its back on its sedate urban past and took on its present outward-bound persona, though the opportunity had been there since 1928 when it moved to a superb location by Lake Windermere. Everybody from her first year now has to learn to swim, life-save, do first aid, orienteer and sail; the seniors include mountain rescue and conservation work with the Lakeland National Park wardens among their voluntary service activities. There are unusually good opportunities for field studies, and the terrain is regarded as challenging rather than as dismayingly isolated. Many schools in the past proudly boasted that they gave a boy-type education, but St Anne's is probably alone in offering the same opportunities for leisure activities – over seventy to choose from – as boys have habitually been used to.

A word should be said about St Trinian's. St Trinnean's was a real school in Edinburgh.[28] When Ronald Searle was stationed in Kircudbright in 1941 he was entertained by the Johnston family, whose two daughters were at the school. He made drawings to please them and sent them to *Lilliput*, the first appearing in October 1941 ('Owing to the international situation, the match with St Trinian's has been postponed', ran the caption), the second in 1946, and the remainder spasmodically between 1947 and 1952. Most of them were drawn in the Japanese prisoner-of-war camp where he spent the war years after 1942, and reflect the violence and cruelty which he was unconsciously trying, by associating them with English young ladyhood, to reduce

* The only other Round Square Conference girls' school in England is Cobham Hall.

to something acceptable ('Some little girl didn't hear me say *unarmed* combat'). However, his St Trinian schoolgirl, the hard-drinking terror of the campus – 'Hell! my best Scotch!' 'It means we must make sacrifices, darling. Help Mummy by cutting down your smoking' – which seemed far-fetched fantasy in the 1940s is now a sufficiently recognizable type to have lost much of her humour.

Growing up Gracefully: Schools for the Upper Class

'We believe that the art of living is greater than the art of earning a living,'[29] said the Misses Leeson who ran a finishing school in Wimbledon in the 1920s, and this was the ethos of such schools as St James's, Tudor Hall, North Foreland Lodge, West Heath and Heathfield between the wars. As we have seen, few private schools did much to equip girls for professional exams, but these took particular pride in holding themselves aloof from such matters. Like the Misses Leeson, they did not believe in 'forcing problems on young people before they are ready for them', and they wanted them to enjoy being young. The upper classes, as has been said, nearly always preferred small schools for their daughters, and a system which would not put them through academic hoops and turn them into dauntingly unmarriageable bluestockings. A few patronized St Leonards and Wycombe Abbey, but far more preferred a less hearty atmosphere where their girls could spend six years in gracious surroundings, making the right friends and being gently exposed to culture and prepared for the world outside.

> 'You are alone in your mother's drawing room,' [the dancing-mistress] would say crisply to some gawky pupil. 'The door opens and the maid announces a caller. What will you do? *Not*, I hope' (with infinite scorn) 'blush and run away, muttering something about fetching your mother. The maid will do that. No, you must rise gracefully, resting your weight on your back foot as you do so; you must come forward, put out your hand with an agreeable smile and say . . .' One after another, in pairs, we used to rehearse this and other social emergencies, dealing firmly with the Reluctant Dancing Partner, the Old Lady who has forgotten your name, the Person who has called for a charitable subscription. The dear woman, I am sure, never guessed that the world for which she was preparing us was doomed.[30]

The ambience, the unhurried pace, the congenial company all made it an enjoyable experience. 'The unintellectual fox-hunting gentry came away from it with a fundamental culture,' said one girl, and all the pupils at St James's remembered the extraordinary beauty of the place, not only the immaculately tended gardens with their banks of azaleas, grassy paths and flowering shrubs, but the fields and woods that stretched beyond to the distant blue line of the Welsh hills. There was leisure to appreciate it and a high level of comfort; strawberries and cream for breakfast, hair-brushing sessions carried out by pleasant, smiling maids. 'Luxury indeed ... but much was expected of us and so high were the standards of honesty, fastidiousness, decent kindliness and responsibility, that I challenge any system to do better.' The pupil who described those pre-1914 days forty years on admitted that she had often grumbled about lack of diplomas and certificates. And even in the 1920s outside exams were unheard of except for the brilliant few. 'When one of those rare spirits passed her matriculation the whole school was given a holiday.' But she felt that by the time she and her contemporaries left they were trained to govern a small British colony 'or at least a lesser archipelago'.

St James's (which in 1979 amalgamated with another Malvern school, the Abbey, to become St James's and the Abbey), like the North London Collegiate, Roedean and Moreton Hall, owed its being to a prolific Victorian mother. Alice and Katrine Baird, its founders, were two of seven daughters of a professional man who, unable to provide incomes for his children, urged them to capitalize on their education. The two sisters had never been to school themselves, and had little experience of teaching, 'but in those days ... wide reading and a great wish to acquire knowledge or skill could do a very great deal'. The immediate problem was that they had no capital. But somehow they scraped together enough to pay a term's rent on a house in Christchurch. 'And then we waited. I remember so vividly Kitty and I returning the calls of the other heads of schools ... and seeing the life in the buildings, and returning to our silent and sparsely furnished house, wondering when anyone would come.' But at half-term a day-girl came, and the sisters devoted themselves to her; next term there were three more, 'and it was not long before *we* had a band of chattering children'. They moved to Crowborough in 1900 and then to Malvern in 1902, when they were joined by other sisters and the school rapidly prospered – to the extent that when two of the sisters left to found their own school in Hertfordshire Miss Alice was able to spare fifteen St James's girls to start them off. Early pupils remembered the loving kindness that the sisters gave them, and the comforting presence of the old family nanny; as with Moreton Hall, the school history breathes content and a spacious way of life.

Inevitably the leisure has departed; St James's now aims 'to give to each girl that education which will best prepare her for a full life in the working world'.[31] Everywhere girls want to earn – paradoxically, the richer the pupils the more impatient they appear to be – and headmistresses of schools such as Heathfield lament that pupils are so confident of their marketing skills and good connections that they see no reason to take exams and professional qualifications very seriously. And only Heathfield now admits publicly to cultivating the social graces, though several schools in fact encourage them by organizing dinner parties and ensuring that their girls understand such matters as decanting the claret.

Heathfield, probably the best known of the débutante schools (it was the first to have a royal pupil), had its origins in a Kensington day school started in 1880 by Miss Beatrice Wyatt. It moved to Heathfield, Ascot, then a pleasantly rural area, in 1899. An ardent Tractarian, she had perhaps chosen the locality because of the proximity of Edward Pusey's Ascot community, and her first priority was to build a chapel whose Anglo-Catholic ritual would be the focus of the school's daily life. As with religious foundations such as convents and Woodard schools, the Easter ceremonies were the high point of the school year, and it was with great reluctance that between the wars the practice of spending Easter at school was abandoned. Miss Wyatt also burned to infuse her well-born pupils with the desire to help 'the struggling lives of those who are less happily placed than yourselves',[32] and in her day the school involved itself with slum children, missions and clubs for working girls. She walked fast and talked fast: one father said, 'I can't hear a word Miss Wyatt says but I know what she is saying is right', which is why, perhaps, she is remembered less for what she said than for the fact that she always wore a black lace mantilla so that she could make frequent visits to the chapel. It was she who introduced the 'lily badge' as a mark of a high order of merit, only attained after two stages of probation and held in such esteem that when one of its earliest holders died, aged eighteen, the badge was buried with her. 'We placed Audrey's photograph on a stand under the Lily Badge Board, surrounded by lilies of the valley,' the school magazine said sadly. Though after Miss Wyatt's death in 1942 the chapel has continued to mean much to its old pupils, the school is known to the world at large less for its religious affiliations than because Princess Alexandra was once a pupil. But it does have the unexpected distinction of having produced the first woman ever to read engineering at Cambridge.

Tudor Hall was intellectually tougher, at any rate in its early days. It had been founded in 1850 near London, in Forest Hill (it was later to move to Chislehurst, then during the war to Burnt Norton near Chipping Campden, and finally to Banbury), by a Scottish minister, the Revd T.W. Todd and his wife. Dr Todd himself taught, terrifying nervous girls by his violent temper in scripture lessons – 'Ha! Ha! I've led you on the ice, Miss X, and you've fallen in!' In addition to the resident female staff the Todds, perhaps influenced by Queen's College which had also been founded in 1850, employed visiting professors of considerable distinction to lecture in such areas as history and geology, and to teach music. (It had long been the custom in private schools to import masters to teach the subjects that the proprietress and her assistants could not cover – Mrs Ewing's Miss Mulberry, for instance, had visiting arithmetic and drawing masters – but the ones who came to Tudor Hall were on a different plane.) From the 1880s when the Todds' daughter, Miss Maud, came back with a first-class degree in history from Cambridge and gradually took over the school, it seems to have provided a Cheltenham-style education, with girls taking London degrees from school. It was, however, less enclosed and conventual and without the rigours of that establishment – though Miss Maud had apparently inherited her father's temper. 'In fact she gave the Upper School a university education,' one of her pupils recalled in the centenary number of the school magazine. 'It was a complete revelation to me,' said another, 'after three years cramming on standardised lines for Cambridge Local Examinations with minute study of set periods and books.' Instead she now found herself set to read historians such as Curtius, Mommsen, Stubbs and Grote.

It was a strenuous day for the seniors, lasting from eight in the morning until ten at night. Not only was there a very impressive array of visiting scholars who lectured to the senior forms, but the girls were taken on frequent visits to London museums and art galleries and to concerts and the theatre. Not all the lecturers were equal to the task – one, on being confronted with his audience, fled to the gym shed. Some were incomprehensible; 'the young maid's dream,' it was said of one of the German lecturers, 'the Gary Cooper of pre-film days [was] understood by very few, but what matter while we could gaze on his beautiful face.' It was also one of the first private schools to install a gymnasium, planned and supervised by a Herr Stemple who had his own in London. If Miss Maud had stayed and had organized the transfer of Tudor Hall to a board of trustees, its history might have been very different. As it was, she married the lecturer in Greek and Roman history, a young barrister who was to become a distinguished law lord. The school observed the development of the attachment with fascination: 'It was exciting to hang out of the windows to see them returning from the tennis courts after a strenuous game . . . [and] the Roman History lectures became thrilling when given the background of romance'.[33] Eight of Miss Maud's special class were bridesmaids at the wedding in 1892; 'all the same it was a bit sad for the retirement of Miss Maud was now a foregone conclusion'. She did not leave, however, until 1901. She had handed over the school to two members of the staff, old pupils whom she had trained herself, and afterwards seems to have taken curiously little interest – even when one of the partners withdrew because of ill-health, leaving the other, who was hardly more than a girl herself, to shoulder the whole burden. She rose to the occasion admirably, though, maintaining the academic excellence and also introducing the new public school spirit of responsibility and service; girls were called upon not only to give money to orphans and girls' clubs but to entertain them as well.

Tudor Hall was one of the schools that attempted the Dalton Plan, an educational ploy fashionable between the wars and only practicable in small, very well staffed schools since it needed a high level of organization and planning on the part of the teachers. Red Maids' School tried it, but not for long; many private schools, however, refer to practising 'a modified version of the Dalton Plan'. Emanating from the United States, it had first been tried in a school for the handicapped, and later in a public high school in Dalton, Massachusetts. Subjects were divided into academic and vocational groups, and pupils worked their way through an individual monthly assignment, known as a 'job' and made up of twenty units, each supposed to represent half an hour's work, in every subject; progress was recorded on job cards. The girls were free to plan their own work schedules, but had to finish each monthly job before going on to the next. 'Of course most of us did nothing for the first three weeks, or only did the things we liked best . . . then the fourth week there would be panic and despair when we realized we were bound to be given Extra Work on Saturday afternoon to get the assignment finished. If we did get it finished in the month we earned a half-holiday.'[34]

But as succeeding principals took over, invariably chosen from among old girls, the Todd ideal became diluted; besides, since universities were now open to women there was no demand for university classes in schools. Tudor Hall thus gradually turned into a friendly school for nice upper-class girls, many of them daughters of Old Tudorians. And when in 1935, after a period with a principal whose health and energy were not equal to the task, the school finally seemed on the point of extinction with no pupils at all, Old Tudorians summoned yet another of their members, Nesta Inglis, to refound it. It was, in fact, the war that restored the school's fortunes; transplanted from suburban Kent to the Cotswolds, it found itself besieged by parents who wanted a safe place for their children. Many stayed on in the holidays, and were joined by other members of their families. The five years at Burnt Norton, though not distinguished academically, were radiantly happy for the girls there, who later were convinced that when T.S. Eliot had written

> For the leaves were full of children
> Hidden excitedly, containing laughter

it had been prophetic. An unforgettable and wonderful childhood, one of them called it, adding: 'I asked [Dame Helen Gardner] if she thought Eliot, when he came to the house long ago in the early twenties when it was locked up and empty and no one else about, had somehow become aware of the future and of us playing here exactly as he described.'[35] The beauty of the gardens and the grounds affected them deeply; they were freer and involved with the local community in a way that was impossible in Chislehurst; they could even bicycle the twelve-odd miles to Stratford and back through the black-out. The school never returned to Chislehurst. Miss Inglis, even before the war was over, was casting round for suitable premises in the Cotswold region, and with that courage and imagination which so often feature as the decisive factor in a school's history, she decided that Tudor Hall must acquire Wykham Park, near Banbury, then still occupied by the army. Like other determined headmistresses before her, she managed to persuade friends and supporters to lend the necessary £10,000, and the school moved there in 1946.

North Foreland Lodge, founded in 1909 by Miss Wolseley-Lewis who had been teaching at the Graham Street Francis Holland School, and West Heath, founded in 1865, are similarly happy havens for the well bred (indeed, until recently the whole examination timetable at the latter was geared to the London season). They do not bother with prospectuses or advertising; the word is passed round the table at dinner parties and their numbers are kept up by the loyal and loving old members who send their daughters. West Heath began in the traditional way with a clergy wife, a Mrs Power whose husband's health had broken down, and who advertised that she received 'a few young ladies whose education is conducted on religious principles with that of her own daughters'. Special arrangements could be made for young ladies over nineteen who might wish to avail themselves of masters 'without being subjected to School Discipline'. It was an expensive school, charging 126 guineas a year (Cobham Hall a hundred years later was only charging £160), but perhaps this was what attracted its clients, for it flourished and was able to acquire handsome premises on Ham Common. Violet Markham, the daughter of a prosperous colliery owner, who was to devote her life to public service, recalled of her schooldays there in the 1890s, when it was still a small academy of some thirty pupils, that 'a liberal, if in some respects limited education was put within our reach; school discipline was sensible and not coercive ... There was an art room but no laboratory and no gym. We were taught no science, no economics, no social history. I cannot remember that the problem of poverty was ever mentioned'[36] – a picture of private school education that would have been true of many a school for the next forty or fifty years.

The school passed through the hands of various owners. The three sisters who had bought it from Mrs Power sold it to Miss Elizabeth Lawrence and Miss Margaret Skeat (daughter of the distinguished Cambridge philologist) in 1900. They found the West Heath young ladies a very different proposition from the girls they had taught at Bradford Girls' Grammar School: 'We *must* try to make the tone less petty,' Miss Lawrence wrote to Miss Skeat; 'We will stir each other up to be good to the girls. I don't feel drawn to them yet. I wish they were poor or had some sad features in their lot, but I am afraid they are prosperous and materialistic.' Nevertheless the parents accepted them ('a couple of old 'ens', the butler was overheard saying of them), and the school prospered. What was more the curriculum broadened; a carpenter's shop was added, a science room, a studio and a library. But after the death of Miss Lawrence in 1929 there is a curiously mysterious passage in the school's history which no one now seems able to explain. Miss Skeat, who had been the less assertive of the two, took on a new, young partner, Phyllis Elliott, but neither was visible when the school had a general inspection in February 1932, and the inspectors reported that Miss Skeat was confined to her room. The inspection seems to have passed off satisfactorily, but in the September, for no reason that is known, the whole school was moved to Sevenoaks to a far less convenient house with none of the amenities such as the splendid assembly hall that had been built in memory of Miss Lawrence. Here Miss Skeat, who did not die until ten years later, appears to have been virtually walled up with her little dog and was seen no more, while Miss Elliott, who suppressed all reference to the West Ham past, ruled supreme, an eccentric and an autocrat.* She did not retire until 1965, having provided for the school's future by making it an educational trust and having trained her successor, Ruth Rudge, over a period of fifteen years. Miss Rudge accepted the easy-going upper-class traditions – though as an Australian and a classicist she might have wanted to send the winds of reform blowing through the establishment – and, indeed, said that her principal aim was 'to give the children a happy time'.[37] A most endearing ambition, and one which rarely features in a school prospectus.

* One of her edicts was that the girls must eat nothing yellow (no custard, bananas or corn) – 'It is what I want, darling.'

6

Religion and Religious Foundations

Environment and Practice

'Most people in their hearts believe in God and enjoy the services excluding the serman. But most girls make out their athiasts when everyone knows there not. Many religious discussions go on after lights out where one's true beliefs come to the surface.'[1] Mallory Wober, a sociologist who conducted a survey of girls' boarding schools in 1971, noted the hostility among the girls towards institutional religion. 'CHRISTIANITY DRUMMED INTO US: PUTS US AGAINST IT,' one girl put on her questionnaire. Though older pupils might take a serious interest, 'at no school visited . . . did the group norms of the younger girls appear to include a dedicated orientation to divine worship'. What they *wanted* to worship, on the other hand, was pop idols. One girl calculated that 1008 days at school over 4 years, × 10 minutes on knees each day = 168 hours = 7 days exactly, and set down the more useful things that could have been done in the time. (And this excluded the time spent listening to religious discourse.) It was the convent he included in his survey which seemed to have the most success at getting across the idea that worship was of value in itself, 'partly because it directed human attention in awe at a mystery', and here he did find that the girls answering his questions attached importance to Christian principles. As for the rest, though the staff on average put religion fifth in the list of fifteen aims they were asked to arrange in order of priority, the pupils themselves rated it fifteenth.

One has to take into account, of course, that girls at a convent boarding school are more likely to have come from homes with firm religious convictions, whereas the majority of pupils at other schools would have only tenuous connections with any church. Not all public schools are religious foundations in the sense that they were established with the primary purpose of promoting a particular religious doctrine, but all attempt some form of worship and announce in their prospectuses what their religious policy is. Though the fashion now is, even in the case of many erstwhile convent schools, to describe this as 'Christian' or 'ecumenical' and to say that girls of all denominations (or none) are welcome, up to the 1970s the policy was, in the absence of anything different, firmly, rigorously and often joylessly Church of England. There are, of course, many schools which were founded to promote Church of England principles, and specific gradations of 'High' and 'Low' churchmanship at that.

The Anglo-Catholics were the first to take the initiative. St Dunstan's, Plymouth, opened in 1850; St Anne's, Rewley House (no longer in existence), run by the nuns of St Thomas, in 1852; St Mary's, Wantage (see page 144), in 1873, the same year as St Mary's, Calne, a school established for 'the express purpose of teaching children the primitive Catholic Faith as taught in the Catechism of the Church of England'.[2] At the time of the foundation of this last, hostility to the High Church movement was very strong in Calne, and it says much for the spirit of conciliation of its initiator, Canon John Duncan, the greatly loved vicar of Calne (who had been brought up as a Presbyterian but was by then a Tractarian), that the school never encountered local religious opposition; St Dunstan's had had unhappy experiences in this respect. Woodard schools followed in the 1880s, as described later in this chapter.

In due course, the evangelical wing of the Church tried to redress the balance. Feeling that 'Public School accommodation for daughters of gentlemen of small means was either started by, or had fallen under the control of, Roman Catholics, or of the extreme High Church Party', the Church Education Corporation, for instance, started several schools, of which Bedgebury (opened in 1920) is the only one surviving; and the evangelical Martyrs' Memorial and Church of England Trust, already responsible for several boys' schools, founded Westonbirt in 1928 and Felixstowe College the following year. The Church Schools Company was established in 1883, with the object of setting up Church high schools, the undenominational character of the recently founded GPDSC schools being regretted by many. But there were many which went in for Church of England practices because this was the expected formula.

Religious denominations have always wished to establish their own schools, where their particular view of the Divine Will could be imparted.

> For a religious environment is never without its influence [a bishop wrote of the Woodard schools]. A boy may leave school apparently unaffected, or even alienated, by the services he has attended and the instruction he has received. Yet, little though he may recognize the fact, he will have been in contact with something assured, unchanging, and victoriously dynamic; and the memory of it, at later moments of his life, may avail to call him home to [the] Church.[3]

Sober, reserved, temperate – many would see it as a typically Anglican statement. Only with 'victoriously dynamic' does the bishop allow himself to lapse into enthusiasm, but dynamic, alas, was not the adjective most would have used to describe the religion of their boarding schools.

> Each day began with Morning Prayer ... [and] ended with prayers conducted by the head prefect. On Sundays the whole school walked in crocodile to Chirk church for Mattins; in the afternoon there was Choral Evensong at school. On alternate Sundays the confirmed also walked, before breakfast, to Weston Rhyn for Holy Communion. We had a short religious lesson after lunch, and learnt the collect of the day by heart. RE – Divinity as it was then called – was also a regular examination subject. How much of the religion survived school days I don't know, but at least it provided us with valuable training in sitting quietly through agonies of ennui (the very highest standards of behaviour were required of us in church), it gave us a total familiarity with the beauties of the English prayer-book and bible, and a rich knowledge of church music.[4]

This routine at Moreton Hall, which was by no means a church school, was standard, and has probably only begun to waver during the last twenty years, though it would have been regarded as fanaticism by parents if the children had followed the same practices in the holidays.

Wycombe Abbey was in Winifred Peck's day far more strenuous: first, early service for the confirmed; after breakfast, 'stodge hour' when they read improving books. Then matins (and it always seemed to be Litany Sunday). After dinner a two-hour walk; after tea they had to learn collects and verses before evening church. A light supper, then prayers in Big School and all could only rejoice as they sang 'The day thou gavest, O Lord, is ended'.[5] But of pre-Victorian school Sundays, probably that spent by the clergy daughters at Cowan Bridge* in Lancashire seems to have been the harshest. After breakfast the girls set out over the fields to walk the two miles to Tunstall Church where their founder, the Revd William Carus Wilson, a zealous and authoritarian clergyman of the evangelical school, presided and preached. Since there was not enough time between morning and afternoon church to go home, they took a cold lunch with them which they ate in a room above the porch, 'a deathly cold proceeding in the middle of winter'. Very great attention had to be paid to the sermons, because on Monday a full account of both had to be written out (any note-taking on Sunday being strictly forbidden). The rest of Sunday was spent learning texts and hymns, and in the evening there was a third service, conducted by the superintendent.[6]

Perhaps the most sombre indictment of school religion was written by Joshua Fitch, who had covered the Yorkshire schools in the Schools Inquiry Commission of 1865–7. Speaking of the effect on pupils of the type of religion taught and practised at charity schools, he said:

> Yet the class to which these children belong is more completely alienated than any other in the community from the English Church. The scholars

* Charlotte Brontë's 'Lowood', which later moved to Casterton: see Chapter 3.

> whose attendance is part of the school discipline, almost invariably quit the Church for ever when they leave school. And no student of human nature can wonder at this. The hard aggressive teaching of Church dogma by creeds and formularies, and by compulsory church attendance, defeats its own purpose . . . Nobody ever comes in later life to love the Church as an institution because he has first been taught her doctrines and formularies as school lessons.[7]

But more disquieting than resistance to school religion, from which can often spring later gratitude ('I can thank her for founding my religious belief which has been a great strength in later years'), is the morbid religiosity sometimes encountered in certain girls' schools of the past, which usually finished in revulsion and contempt. In one Church of England public school fifty years ago (an establishment where girls were asked on arrival whether they were 'High' or 'Low', then dispatched to the appropriate place of worship, from which allegiance one could not swerve), everything was weighed up in terms of one's eternal life – even whistling on the stairs – and girls were forever uneasily raking their consciences. Everybody was very well behaved, very conforming, but nevertheless most were oppressed by guilt and fidgeted by moral scruples. The black sheep of her house, for instance, would bounce out of her dormitory cubicle and rebuke the girls she overheard pitying the punishment that had been meted out to her, and admonish the pair she saw laughing and throwing up their hats on Good Friday. In this particular case a housemistress ambitious to become a deaconess encouraged in members of her house the natural female tendency to over-scrupulousness. There was, as well, a tendency on the part of authority then to try to make religion do all their work for them: 'What is the use of your confirmation if you go on playing that prelude so badly?'

Much more than at a Catholic school with its ritual progression through the Church's year, the effect on the average pupil of the standard public school Church of England observance as practised up to twenty years ago depended upon the personalities of those who promoted it. Miss Willis, the founder of Downe House, had had an unorthodox upbringing, with parents who were nominally Anglican but had dabbled with Unitarianism and Theism. Though a practising Anglican from her undergraduate days, she had had to find and test her beliefs for herself. This fact made her school sermons at once convincing and compelling. 'What Blake called "the immortal man" in her always spoke to the immortal man in her hearers, as she stood there with uplifted face.'[8] 'She made Christianity seem exciting,' wrote one pupil, and another recalled that she once said: 'I have not found anything better than Christianity; if I do I shall certainly change my religion.' It was this approach, says her biographer, that made her Sunday classes so stimulating; here her pupils, as they grew to the age of scepticism, could truly feel that, as Dante said to Virgil, 'To doubt is not less grateful than to know.'

At Badminton, a progressive, non-denominational school with a humanitarian rather than an orthodox outlook, whose religion might be said to be 'internationalism' and scepticism, the headmistress Miss Baker (1911–46) used to insist that, when 'I vow to thee, my country' was sung, the girls must substitute 'the love that *does* ask questions' for the line 'the love that asks no questions'.[9] For the recital of texts, which still is a feature of the Quaker school, the Mount, Miss Baker had a secular substitute: 'Prayers [were] made hazardous by the fact that we were required to have ready a poem, learnt by heart, or (later) an item of up-to-date news which we might be called upon to recite in front of the whole school'.[10] Her successor, Miss Sanderson (1947–66), was cast in the same mould. Her readings at morning assembly were taken from unlikely secular sources (this is standard now, but forty years ago was unusual). Her 'scripture' lessons had nothing to do with Christian religious instruction but covered moral problems, politics and philosophical questions for the older girls; the identification and drawing of biblical plants and the study of Palestinian roof construction for the younger ones, whom she told passionately, 'I want you children to be sceptics, you must *question* everything you read.'[11] 'One didn't switch off Miss Sanderson. And if you did, the next moment there'd be a murmur of amusement all round, and you'd missed something good.' 'BMS always seemed to produce something compelling to listen to and think about – however negative one may have felt initially.' Her addresses and dicta are still remembered by her pupils in a way that the more orthodox must envy.

At Benenden also former pupils remember the school services with affection. The spirit of the three founders and the beauty of the setting fused to become a religious experience for many.

> We remember the peace of the evening garden [wrote a member of the school who left in 1939], sun and birdsong streaming in through the open windows, long shadows on the grass beginning. The choir, that oversang the birds, with the singular clarity of sound that is Benenden's trademark. The silence when we stopped shuffling, and prayed, so that all our memories of all our Sundays at Benenden merged into this one moment of Sunday-now. Did we find God? Some of us perhaps thought we had. Some of us who thought we had not, may indeed have done so.[12]

This was the generation who would have remembered the addresses given by Miss Bird, one of the founders. She invented the Benenden Angel, who made wry criticisms of schoolgirl foibles and gave wise, often humorous advice. 'I feel he knew us uncomfortably well, that Angel. I was surprised never to see him queueing with us for buns at break.' He counselled social virtues like kindness and tolerance and cheerfulness, and the addresses evoked so potently the ambience of the school and its traditions that past members had them reprinted in 1968, though their style was not one that a headmistress in the late 1960s could have used with any degree of unself-consciousness.

At other schools church services and religious occasions were inextricably entwined for many with happy memories of summer landscape, as they were for the girls at Haberdashers' Monmouth School eighty years ago who, boarding out at a local vicarage, used to go by boat to a village church on Sundays. Ascension Day, which was for most the greatest church feast that fell during school term, is celebrated with picnics and outings at many schools – though the specialness of these must have largely evaporated now that they have to be organized in buses along crowded roads. At the Godolphin School in Salisbury you could in the early days walk out on to empty Wiltshire downs for your Ascension Day picnic. The communicants' guild of the two Francis Holland schools in London was invited each year to Canterbury by their founder, Canon Holland, and those who went had a composite memory of cathedral services, meals in a marquee, picking bluebells and a final lantern-lit procession round the precincts to deposit girls at the homes of the various cathedral dignitaries who had offered hospitality.[13]

Nonconformist schools with no church feasts to celebrate did not do so well in the way of holidays. (Quakers and Methodists, among others, until comparatively recently saw even Christmas Day as no different from any other day.) There was, however, at Walthamstow Hall (in the days when it was still a home for missionaries' daughters) Exeter Hall Day, the occasion of the annual meeting of the London Missionary Society, when the older girls in their new summer hats and provided with sandwiches were taken in brakes to Exeter Hall for the four-hour assembly, while the younger ones had a holiday.[14]

There must have been many who regarded religion as an extension of lessons, designed to keep them occupied and, especially, to fill the empty hours of Sunday and give the staff a rest. 'Chapel or hall prayers twice daily, church twice on Sundays; scripture lessons a time for moral exhortation; extra Lenten addresses; confirmation at fifteen the norm with rigorous preparation taken by a suitably elderly and unemotional clergyman.'[15] The routine was much the same for all boarding schools, though in most people's experience the moral exhortation (which was frequent) would have come from the headmistress's rostrum, scripture lessons being devoted to exam subjects such as the Messianic prophecies in the Old Testament and the missionary journeys of St Paul. Despite the part that religious observance has always played in school life, it is rare to have a resident chaplain; usually the local incumbent comes in to take services and to prepare girls for confirmation, and the RE lessons are taken by members of the staff. To have one's own chapel, one that could seat the whole school, was from the start an indication of seriousness, and it is curious in this connection that Cheltenham has never had a chapel, the girls going out to local parish churches. Miss Beale was High rather than Low Church (indeed, had found the evangelical Christianity of the Clergy Daughters' School at Casterton, where she had spent a brief period, not at all to her taste, while they in their turn had thought her dangerously High), but religion at Cheltenham in her day was centred on her exposition of the scriptures – which she and the school treated with immense seriousness – rather than on sacramental worship. None of her successors felt strongly enough to repair the omission, and the lack of a chapel in a foundation that is of all the girls' schools most like a boys' public school seems a strange anomaly.

Though pupils at the time may have found the hours they spent in chapel inordinately long, there would for most have been a special moment: 'In the evening, when Chapel was voluntary, and there were prayers about "the fever of life being over" and, from the organ loft, they sang: "Come Holy Ghost our souls inspire" it meant more than anything else; more, perhaps, simply because it was not thrust upon us.'[16] And the passing years apparently bring nostalgia, if one can go by the record of old girls contributing memories to the school magazine for some jubilee celebration. Often it seems to be the Anglo-Catholic chapels that have meant the most. Here girls have acted as sacristans and sub-sacristans, laid out the vestments, lovingly arranged the flowers, and wearing chapel hoods and cloaks have sung elaborate settings of the mass. Many have memories of Easter celebrated at school, as was the practice at the Wantage schools, the Woodard schools, and Heathfield School, Ascot, whose small chapel, where the name of every past pupil has been carved on the stalls, is remembered with passionate devotion by the elderly.

Now, with far less time spent on communal devotion and with much of it vaguely humanistic rather than spiritual, feelings about school religion seem not nearly so definite, either for or against, as they once were: 'The Advent Service – oh that's the one where we come back for mulled wine' – a remark quoted in a recent school magazine – is more likely to be the attitude. School assembly, 1980s-style, is more often than not a DIY affair with every class in the school allowed to devise music, perhaps mime or dance; with readings from poetry or biographies (accounts of children who have died of cancer are particularly popular), silence or 'guided thinking'.

> School prayers give expression to the girls' own feelings about the world they live in. On one day a week, prayers are taken by the girls themselves, in various groupings: sometimes a form or a House, sometimes a society, with the Scientific Society debating the claims of science and religion, or the Modern Languages Society producing a hymn in French, and a reading in German. [The headmistress] herself varied the proceedings with readings from current Oxfam literature.[17]

'There is a continual awareness of the need to understand spiritual and ethical attitudes which are fundamental and not specifically Christian,' says another school, describing how, though the Bible is 'the central textbook', RE lessons now take the form of study of comparative religion or discussions of social problems.[18] Even church schools whose worship is sacramentally based, such as St Mary's, Wantage, devote substantial time to these.

Aesthetic experience plays a large part in memories of girls' school religion – chapel music, for instance; there is always keen competition to get into the choir. Those with a feeling for language remember the beauties of the 1662 Prayer Book. At Christ's Hospital in its Hertford days they sang daily and weekly through the psalms at morning and evening service: '[It] gave me a sense of security whatever happened, a trust in the power of God even after death which has never left me, even in the face of periods of doubt and disbelief.'[19] Though against this one has to set the memories of a boy who had been at Christ's Hospital in its Newgate Street days. He recalled his state of mind on Sunday evenings, after twelve hours of Bible-reading, prayer and inaudible sermons, as 'blank, cold, hungry, church-wearied, sermon-stunned, Xenophon-dreading, for-ever-and-everish despair'.[20]

Christ's Hospital had its own chapel and a strong sense of tradition and ritual continuous from the sixteenth century. These are both elements that affect most children more than direct instruction, so the Protestant reliance on The Word alone has been at a disadvantage when it comes to religious practice at school. (And a tax on those who preside over school assembly: instead of following the Church's year they have to find themes of their own round which to organize daily worship.) For most, sermons were an exercise in sitting still rather than a means of spiritual profit. Of the Methodist services at Edgehill, some forty years on an Anglican remembered the drone of prolix elderly preachers. Another wrote: 'Chapel has not left me with many memories, except perhaps a dislike of Temperance speakers . . . and a picture of a collection plate filled entirely with threepenny pieces.'[21] And the words that are remembered are mostly those of inspired headmistresses whose religious faith, expressed with passionate conviction, made a deep impact on their listeners – like those of Alice Ottley at Worcester High School, or of Miss Beale at Cheltenham, whose expositions of religious doctrine seemed to one pupil 'to set forth a spiritual construction of the universe, into which no spiritual truth learned afterwards could possibly fail to fit'.[22] A beautiful speaking voice was a tremendous advantage – many headmistresses are remembered for this. Many early pupils at Bedford High School said that they never knew 'how glorious were the Collects of the Book of Common Prayer until they heard them read by [Miss Belcher's] beautiful voice. A new meaning shone through familiar words.' And the older girls used to invite friends who wished to see the school to come to school prayers. 'The teaching of the Church's year, with its festivals and feasts, meant so much to the head mistress that gradually her school saw these things through her eyes.'[23] But inevitably there must have been others who regarded it all as one of their headmistress's fads, like Winifred Peck, herself a bishop's daughter, who said of her own headmistress at Wycombe

Abbey: 'If Father knew how High the Dove was getting he'd take me away, just when I had a chance of getting into the Eleven.'[24]

Like Miss Ottley, Miss Belcher herself prepared girls for confirmation. It was a tradition followed by many headmistresses, and was partly due to strong personal convictions, but also, no doubt, to the number of clerical headmasters of boys' public schools who were as much chaplains as administrators. Miss Ottley followed up her own confirmation classes with classes for communicants, which were latterly intended primarily for old girls, and all those within reach took advantage of them. Under her Tractarian influence and that of Canon W.J. Butler, who had already been responsible for the foundation of the schools at Wantage (see page 194), Worcester High School's day was set in a round of worship. It began with the psalm and hymn of the morning office (with a different, penitential, office for Fridays), a short office for midday, and evening prayers at four o'clock, with creed, confession and thanksgiving.

> Miss Ottley was extremely particular about the recital of the daily prayers. Her own example of devotion and of profound reverence in worship, the very way she said the prayers, carried with it a sense of the awe of the Divine presence, and she would have every detail of this special offering to God as nearly perfect as possible. The prayer desk was to be beautifully kept, with flowers renewed each morning; the movements, kneeling and rising, were to be 'as one man'; the responses, ringing and firm as from one voice; the Amens (as in early Christian worship) 'like a clap of thunder'.[25]

This religious framework was unusual at a high school; as we have seen, they were more often deliberately non-sectarian – Manchester High School was 'absolutely free of creed and religious persuasion', and morning prayers in the early days were read privately only to 'those few girls who wished to attend'. Religious instruction was more exam fodder than spiritual. Writing of Oxford High School – also non-sectarian – in the 1870s, Margaret Fletcher remembered:

> The subject called Divinity was upon the school programme. In this hour we took notes on the authorship of various books in the New Testament, according to current knowledge. We made diligent maps of St Paul's journeys in coloured inks. We were furnished with rationalistic explanations of all miracles except those performed by Our Lord Himself, and were introduced to watered-down versions of the new German Higher criticism. The whole subject was dealt with from an examiner's point of view.[26]

The high schools for the most part assumed that spiritual direction was to be left to the parents, and many pupils would not have welcomed it. 'Well, we were trained to "get up" books of the Bible,' said one member of

Blackheath High School. 'As to direct religious instruction, some at least of us would have felt highly embarrassed, almost outraged, had it been offered to us.'[27] Nor has it ever been standard practice to prepare girls for confirmation, though this has always played a large part in the religious instruction given at boarding schools.

It used to be very difficult, if not impossible, to avoid being confirmed if one was Church of England and at a Church of England boarding school. It has always been an important occasion, the nearest Anglican equivalent to the convent first communion preparation and ceremonies. ('Just think, the next big occasion will be our wedding!' a recent candidate remarked, standing with a flock of others outside an Oxfordshire church in school veils and looking, in her view, like 'war-help nurses'.) Great pressure was exerted by one's housemistress and one had to be strong-minded and determined indeed to try to step outside the system; for most girls it would be unthinkable. Besides, 'early holy' (as girls at the Royal School used to call it, to the horror of one headmistress who regarded the term as blasphemous) often let you off one church service on Sundays, and in some cases meant a late and leisurely breakfast. However, some hardy spirits were known to resist. E. Arnot Robertson, at Sherborne some sixty years ago, won her release because she took the mulish line that if the school said she must, obviously there was a catch in it somewhere. Prefects were deputed to walk her round the grounds after lunch on Sundays. 'They, poor conscientious girls, could find very few reasons to advance in favour of confirmation, except that the preparation classes were "simply topping"; but then so, I had been given to understand, was compulsory cricket, and I knew all about that.'[28] But the vast majority conformed, and though some of the more conscientious might have had doubts it was far easier to keep them to themselves. One Roedeanian, for instance, was prepared by Miss Dorothy Lawrence, her housemistress. 'Miss Dorothy' had recently returned to the school after a stroke and her instruction was unintelligible, but it did not occur to the girl to say she had not understood a word. 'I was no more disposed to a very active disbelief than to a very active belief,' said Margaret Thomas (later Lady Rhondda), worried about the nature of her belief.[29] And she must have been typical of most schoolgirls in that her main emotion was embarrassment – worry about whether people would look through the inadequately curtained door of her housemistress's study and see her with the Episcopalian clergyman (she was at St Leonards) who was preparing her, kneeling on the floor at the final interview. Typical, too, of the adolescent was the earnestness. The housemistress offered her and two of her greatest friends a chance to share a bedroom for the last few nights before the confirmation so that they could be quiet, but they all decided it would be dishonourable to accept, as they would only talk and rag.

Non-conformist Establishments

Roman Catholics, and to a certain extent Anglo-Catholics, long felt that a religious community ideally made the best background for education (the convent schools, their history and their ideals, are dealt with in Chapter 7). First, there was the great advantage of continuity, the prospect of children being taught by nuns who had known their mothers. And it was easier to accept the rigours of a system when one knew that 'the lives of the nuns had entailed a sacrifice, and that they were subjecting themselves to a discipline far more stringent than any that could ever face us'.[30] But the supreme advantage was the totally religious ambience and the single-mindedness of the aims.

Though many schools have a particular religious affiliation written into their charters and see to it that their pupils are provided with the appropriate form of worship and instruction in doctrine, only two types, in their early days at least, seem to resemble the convents in attempting to provide this total religious experience – the Anglo-Catholic Woodard schools, and the Quaker schools. From the very start, when most of their members were ragged radicals, the Society of Friends insisted that their children be instructed in Quaker schools where they could be guarded from the evils of the world. From the point of view of the history of female education the Society's policy was of supreme importance; Friends held that since women could minister equally with men, girls' education should be the same as boys' – indeed, the first schools were co-educational. In many respects we will find that Quaker schools anticipated standard educational practice by a century or more, and certainly the Mount School in York provided solid teaching for girls decades before any other school could.

However, so spiritual were Quaker aims at first that there was difficulty in finding suitable subjects to teach, or indeed books to teach from, because all seemed to be tainted too much with matters of this world. Interests could only be pursued if they had moral or religious ends; it was not enough if they gave mere personal pleasure or deepened human understanding, or offered intellectual or aesthetic satisfaction. This narrowed book-learning almost to vanishing point. English grammar was regarded as a safe subject, and the study of it became an end in itself. William Howitt at Ackworth in the early years of the last century received 'a very excellent English education' in that all pupils were well grounded in spelling and grammar and read the graded readers compiled by the American Friend Lindley Murray, who had left his native Pennsylvania to settle in Yorkshire. Otherwise there was elementary arithmetic, and that was about all – no Latin, French, history, geography or natural history – and much emphasis on practical matters; the children had many domestic duties and cultivated their own gardens. Nor, surprisingly, was there very much direct religious instruction; Mary Howitt (1799–1888), whose parents were particularly austere in their beliefs, had to sit through hours of silent Meeting without having the remotest idea of what it was all about. Her account of the religious atmosphere in which she and her sister were brought up conveys something of the spirit of the Friends' schools.

> Firmly adhering to the fundamental principles of George Fox, that Christ, the true inward light, sends to each individual interior inspirations as their guide to Christian faith, and that the Spirit, being free, does not submit to human learning and customs, [our parents] aimed to preserve us in unsullied innocence, consigning us to Him in lowly confidence for guidance and instruction. So fearful were they of interfering with His workings, that they did not even teach us the Lord's Prayer.[31]

They were, however, like other Quaker children, made to learn Robert Barclay's *Catechism and Confession of Faith*, supposed to be 'fitted for the wisest and largest as well as the weakest and lowest capacities', but which left Mary Howitt and her sister 'in the state of the perplexed eunuch before Philip instructed him in the Holy Writ'.

It was the religious ambience that mattered, 'evidenced not so much in words as in general atmosphere', the historian of the Mount School wrote of its predecessor in York. 'Esther Tuke's religion, we are told, "governed her steps, but was seldom the topic of her conversation".'[32] This school, established in Trinity Lane in Micklegate, very near that other great pioneer of female education, the Bar Convent, opened in 1785 with Esther Tuke as its superintendent. Most of the early Friends' schools were co-educational, but Bootham School, for boys only, having already been set up in York, it was thought fitting to provide one for girls. The staff resembled nuns in their dedication. Esther Tuke and her husband not only gave their services but paid for their board and lodging, and were expected to shoulder any financial deficit; 'and several religiously minded young women offered themselves as assistants in the school without salary'. For several years the only paid member of the staff was the sewing mistress, 'a pious young woman who served the institution very essentially for a small remuneration'.

The first prospectus advertised that children would be taught useful needlework, knitting, the English language, writing and arithmetic; the terms were fourteen guineas a year and no holidays. It concluded: 'In order that plainness and moderation, consistent with our religious Principles, may be attended to in the Education of their children, it is requested that such clothing prepared as is costly, or superfluous, may be avoided', adding the sternly practical rider: 'also such kinds as cause extraordinary trouble in washing'. But by 1796 salaries had been introduced and the curriculum was a little wider – this school and Bootham being for children of more affluent Friends than the other Quaker schools such as Ackworth, Sidcot, Saffron Walden, Wigton and Sibford, where practical skills were more emphasized. At the school in Trinity Lane the girls made their own beds, swept their rooms, and took it in turns to wait at table – it was another 150 years before this became normal in other boarding schools – but book-learning increased; and though 'such literary publications as unprofitably elate the mind and give a disrelish for the purity of gospel truths' were not allowed, French, history and geography were now taught, the latter being learned by embroidering maps on chenille. As at Ackworth, grammar was an end in itself, and for the Trinity Lane girls Lindley Murray, who was living nearby, wrote the *Grammar* that was to be a standard school textbook in America and England for the next fifty years. What was more, he gave the profits from the first edition to the school.

But these were not enough to keep the school going, and in 1814, with increasing financial difficulties – and even greater difficulty, after the death of Esther Tuke, to find anybody to run it – it was forced to close. There was a lapse of seventeen years before its successor began in Castlegate – the York Quarterly Meeting Girls' School, otherwise the Mount School. From the start, the curriculum was astonishingly substantial, more like that of a school of the reformed period and very unlike the superficial flitting over a myriad topics that was standard at the time. Thus a child writing home in 1835 talked about starting Greek lessons (as she also mentioned scanning Virgil, she was obviously learning Latin as well), and geometry and algebra. Courses of lectures on chemistry were being given in 1839. At Polam Hall, a private establishment for the daughters of Friends begun in Darlington in 1848 by Jane Procter and her sisters (it still exists, but not as a Quaker school), the first prospectus also offered good plain subjects such as English grammar and composition and needlework, with the option of German, Italian, Latin and Greek. Quaker education had the great advantage of eschewing instruction in accomplishments, and the thoroughness of the teaching was unique at the time. Joshua Fitch who reported on the Mount in the Schools Inquiry Commission of 1866 said: 'The curriculum of instruction is remarkable for the small proportion of effort devoted to accomplishments, and the large share to intellectual culture. Accordingly this school stands out in marked contrast to the majority of ladies' schools.' He remarked on the thoughtful reading, the general knowledge, the neatness and precision of the written work, the gentleness of the moral discipline, the professional attitude of the teachers.

The latter was in part due to the training college attached to the school, which took in girls hoping to be teachers at a reduced fee, and to Lydia Rous, the energetic and far-sighted superintendent (as the headmistress was then called) 1866–79, who introduced the girls to the theory and practice of teaching, and made them give specimen classes. They had an extra year of schooling and were then engaged as junior teachers. It was a scheme that had its disadvantages (the pupil-teachers, for instance, sometimes found themselves learning the school subjects beside far younger, abler girls whom they would later have to teach), and when university education became available to women it faded away. Lydia Rous, who was the last superintendent to be addressed thus in Quaker style, without the prefix 'Miss', also encouraged pupils to attend the university extension lectures at York Museum, where they were introduced to astronomy, geology and physical geography. In 1878 the first pupil from the Mount presented herself for the London matriculation exam, passed, took her degree in London and came back to be the first graduate on the staff.

The drawback of Quaker education was the lack of aesthetic experience. Mary Howitt had been hungry for beautiful things throughout her youth, and had stared longingly at even the houses in Croydon when her boarding school went out for its walks. Pupils of Lydia Rous complained that their visual sense was starved and that nothing had been done to bring home to them the beauties of York. And at that time no music was allowed. Indeed, early Friends regarded music with horror; whistling was akin to swearing, a boy at Sidcot was told. A girl at Sibford in the 1840s was made to wear the label 'I am not allowed to sing', and one overheard humming a hymn tune was severely rebuked for her wickedness and set to knit sixty rounds of stocking.[33] A new girl overheard singing at the Mount in the 1860s was sent to the superintendent, who sat her on her knee and told her what a dreadful thing it would be if all the girls followed her example. But, curiously, she asked the girl to repeat 'what had been such a grave offence downstairs', and even called her back once or twice to sing again. This same superintendent allowed the girls to do round-dances to the accompaniment of a Jews'-harp, and though her successor, Lydia Rous, implacably opposed the pleas of parents that music should be taught, singing was allowed during her time; one group used to call on a mimed accompaniment from a girl strumming silently on a bookcase. But in 1884 resistance broke down; seven pianos arrived and fifty-one of the sixty-two girls immediately took lessons. However, it was not until the 1890s that even teachers were allowed to go to concerts outside the school. There had been similar embargoes on the teaching of art, and even when drawing was allowed, the use of colour was forbidden. However, by Lydia Rous's time the girls all had their paintboxes, and made up for the aridity of lessons in which they were set to copy geometrical shapes by using colour copiously on their own creations, such as the decoration of texts. It was, said one pupil, their only aesthetic outlet.

The Mount, as Joshua Fitch had noted, was very gentle in its disciplinary methods, and one of the first schools to depute responsibility to the girls. For a century before any other girls' school had contact with boys – and at some day schools in this century girls were forbidden to walk even with their brothers – pupils were encouraged to visit brothers at Bootham, and brothers were allowed to come and see their sisters. And long before any other school had thought of such things, the combined pupils of the Mount and Bootham were in the last century organizing their own Meeting – the Wednesday Meeting at the local meeting house having had to be abandoned through lack of adult Friends to support it. 'The change was a success, especially when boys and girls grasped that this meeting for worship was theirs to make or mar by their use of it.'

Direct instruction, as has been said, played little part in the religious life of any Quaker school. There was Meeting of course, and some of the younger ones found the unstructured proceedings very tedious: 'Yesterday was a *horrid* day; it was so very long and tiring,' wrote one new child at the Mount in 1889 before the regime had been modified. She described a gruelling Sunday with Meeting in the morning followed by Preparative Meeting, scripture-reading, text-reciting; then lunch followed by a long reading about missions; afternoon Meeting – 'I nearly cried in the middle with tiredness' – then back at school, French and English hymns and more scripture-reading. The young ones had their own sedate methods of bringing Meeting to a close; when time was known to be seriously overrun one could try by yawning oneself to infect the adults opposite with strangling yawns. But many older girls found no tedium.

> We often felt very sorry when Meeting broke up, and wished it could go on longer. Our whole souls seemed full of prayer and peace and trust. And as we walked home we often spoke to one another of the words we had heard, and confided our longings to do right. We seemed to gain courage to speak thus from the deepening gloom that hid our faces and made it easy to break through the barrier of reserve which girls often feel in speaking about religion. We were sorry when the walk came to an end.[34]

Eighty years later, however, junior girls still felt oppressed, and, typically, thought of religious routine in terms of food.

> Wednesday breakfasts were a highlight because we had hot sausages. This was because we then set out to walk the mile and a half across the city to the Friends' Meeting House. The midweek service only lasted for half an hour and always started with a hymn. Then someone would give a short sermon. The Sunday meetings were quite another ball game. We had watery scrambled eggs for breakfast and then walked off to Meeting again. This was for an hour and was conducted completely in silence unless the spirit moved someone (occasionally an old man) to speak. The biggest excitement was when one of the girls fainted.[35]

But other girls have remembered the wonderful calm and leisure of Sundays, when there was time to read in the library, or take books into the garden, or just lie there staring up at the trees.

The one traditional practice that seemed to afflict them deeply – it began in 1831 and continues to this day – was the recital of texts.

> We wound ourselves round the gymnasium in a long crocodile in the set order which we would have previously ascertained from the weekly lists.

> The whole school would be standing there with linked arms and a member of staff would read out notices, lead us in a prayer and then pick on one girl to repeat the verse of text for the day. We were of course given these texts well in advance to learn by heart but only a few could be relied on to have done so.[36]

In the 1860s you could choose your own text, but this was open to abuse, since the occasional impertinent individual could either choose a very short one or something offensive like 'I have more knowledge than all my teachers.' In the 1890s occasional lines from poetry were introduced. Nobody seems to have found it easy, and it gave rise to a surprising number of anguished memories: 'It caused me real and frequent nightmares for over fifteen years after I left school,' said one. And another: 'I shook so before it came to my turn that I was unable to speak when my text was due.'

Unlike the Quakers, the Methodists were slow to interest themselves in women's education; 'Wesley never attempted to do for the daughters what he did for the sons of Methodism,' as a historian of Methodist secondary education phrased it.[37] Wesley, in any case, had strongly disapproved of large girls' boarding schools, and felt that wherever possible girls should be educated at home. Even the mid-Victorian rush of interest in women's education failed to stir Methodists, and when the Schools Inquiry Commission published its report with recommendations for the better secondary education of women, the attitude of *The Watchman* was that this was a matter which 'others must settle'.

But there was one distinguished Methodist schoolmistress of whom even Wesley would have approved, feeling as he did that if girls had to be sent from home it should be to some lady 'whose life is a pattern to her scholars, and who has only so many that she can watch over each'.[38] This was Hannah Pipe (1831–1906) who founded Laleham Lodge, called after Dr Arnold's first school. The daughter of a Manchester manufacturer and lay preacher who died when she was still a child, economic necessity drove her to teach. She opened a day school in Manchester in 1848, brought it to Clapham as a boarding school in 1856, and four years later moved to a larger house where she could accommodate twenty-five pupils, a number sufficiently small to keep under her own personal care. Here the school remained until its closure in 1908, Miss Pipe having retired in 1890. It was an expensive school, with fees of a hundred guineas a year at a time when the Casterton Clergy Daughters' School was charging only £14, and Penrhos College, a Methodist school, forty-eight guineas. Her ambition was to attract the daughters of newly rich Wesleyan parents, from 'homes more affluent in comfort than in culture';[39] she had realized what few of her Wesleyan contemporaries had acknowledged – the cultural poverty of Methodist families.

> My ambition was to get hold of those girls with money and without refinement from their earliest years, and to open their eyes to all that is best in this life and that which is to come. The inrush of wealth without the discipline of generations behind it was apt to vulgarise their minds.[40]

To this end she employed, as well as her resident staff, a team of distinguished visiting academics who taught music, law, economics, history, astronomy, science and mathematics. Conservative Methodists sometimes found aspects of this dangerously advanced, and one or two removed their daughters. But for most girls it was a profoundly formative experience, and one pupil who had come to Laleham from the more ordinary sort of mid-Victorian seminary spoke of the 'contrasting light, the breadth and space, which dawned for us' after the cramping, unintelligent ways, the unsatisfied craving for real knowledge, to which girls like herself had been used.[41] Since the girls were from wealthy families it was not expected that they would ever have to support themselves, and they took no exams, though between 1873 and 1893 ten Laleham girls went to Newnham and three to Girton. But it was not the sort of school that could well survive its founder, though it was in some measure the forerunner of Farringtons, founded in Chislehurst, Kent, in 1911, to fill what was regarded as a gap in Methodism. This school, too, catered for wealthy families, and when it opened there were only fourteen pupils to five resident staff.

Many Methodist families sent their daughters to the high schools that were founded in the 1870s and 1880s, but for those that wanted boarding schools there were Jersey Ladies' College, St Heliers, and Penrhos College, both founded in 1880; Edgehill College, 1884; Kent College, 1885; Queenswood, originally a small school for ministers' daughters but refounded at Hatfield in 1894, and Hunmaby Hall School, 1928. There was even a Unitarian foundation – Channing School, founded 1885, which long ago shed its Unitarianism – but these are all comparatively late and seem, like Laleham which accepted girls of any Protestant denomination, not to have adhered to strictly denominational religious teaching. For instance, the eight staunch Methodists who founded the Kent Wesleyan Methodist School Association in 1883 stated their object to be 'a sound education, combined with moral and religious training in the principles of the Wesleyan Methodist connexion, as set forth in the first four volumes of sermons of the Rev. John Wesley, and in his notes on the New Testament'; but, says the author of the *Kent College Saga*, it seems extremely unlikely that the girls were ever nurtured on the sermons of Wesley – rather, sound education was at the heart of the school's aims.

Very different from Laleham, which assumed that its pupils had no need of careers, was Milton Mount College for Congregational ministers' daughters, which opened in Gravesend in 1873 and aimed to prepare girls to be 'wives, mothers, teachers and missionaries', and to help girls who were looking forward to self-support. But it had perhaps the most elaborate class stratifications of any establishment of the period. Between 1873 and 1889 there grew up around the original college a high school, a middle school (a social rung higher than the first), a training college for teachers, the first technical college for girls in England (down a few rungs), and a training home for laundry maids (bottom). Milton Mount eventually left Gravesend for Worth Park, and then when Crawley New Town seemed on the point of swallowing it up, amalgamated with another school to form Wentworth Milton Mount at Bournemouth. 'This was bound to happen,' remarks its chronicler. 'Schools for ministers' daughters seemed less relevant in the context of an efficient national system of secondary schools',[42] and Congregationalists did not, any more than Methodists, feel themselves to be so different from other Protestant denominations as to need exclusive education.

Nathaniel Woodard and his Schools

George Fox had set out to give girls the same education as boys. This was no part of the policy of Nathaniel Woodard (1811–91); and though he ended by having several girls' schools within the Woodard Society, he started by strenuously resisting them, and they were forced on him in spite of himself. His remark that for the Society to own any 'would in no length of time take out of us any little dignity and self-respect that we may at present possess' shows perhaps better than anything else the abysmal reputation that girls' schools had in early Victorian days. But although he was married – indeed, his studies at Oxford were interrupted by 'the responsibilities of a husband and father', so that he only scraped a pass degree – he apparently held women in low esteem, describing them as 'so slippery' that it behoved one to be very careful in any negotiations with them. Nor did he at all approve of schools for girls; it was only because of 'the growing selfishness of society in all classes' that they had become necessary.[43]

In his mission to educate the middle classes he had to contend with the elaborate Victorian class structure – which was most passionately upheld by the middle classes themselves – though it was something that he accepted as part of the natural order of things. The terms of the foundation that he brought into being affirmed in ringing tones that

> For all future time the sons of any of Her then Majesty's Subjects should be taught, together with sound Grammar learning, the fear and honour of Almighty God, the Father, Son and Holy Ghost, according to the doctrines of the Catholic Faith as it is now set forth in the Book of Common Prayer and Office of Administration of he Sacraments of the Church of England.

But the daughters, if not the sons, were to be separated into social strata. This segregation was not confined to the Church of England; no religious denomination of the last century could afford to neglect it. 'Again and again I was told that it would be absolute annihilation to a school were it known that such a rule had been infringed,' said one of the Taunton commissioners in 1866, commenting on the need to exclude tradesmen's daughters from 'upper' schools.[44]

It was not just a question of different types of education for different needs; very often 'upper' and 'middle' schools offered the same. To understand the strength of feeling about 'trade' one needs to read the novels of Charlotte Yonge, who because of the dangerous social mix of girls involved opposed high schools as implacably as Nathaniel Woodard. Tradesmen's daughters could do nothing but harm to the daughters of the gentry, it seemed; Charlotte Yonge was even able to convey, by her description of the cut of a girl's dress, that she was 'trade', and the reader instinctively knew, therefore, that she was not to be trusted. But naturally she felt that gentry and aristocracy could mingle with profit to both sides. 'The "middle" class . . . did not wish its children to mix with all and sundry – at least, not with all and sundry of a lower social grade', as the historian of the Woodard schools pointed out wryly.[45] The various religious denominations tailored their schools to take account of these scruples. The Franciscan convent at Taunton, for instance, was reported by the Schools Inquiry Commission to have two schools – an upper school (where the average yearly bill for a pupil was £78), and a middle school where the charge was £16 and the teaching in the ordinary subjects was 'a little above that of a good national school'. 'The two schools never meet or see each other, even in Church.'[46] And when Ursulines came from France to open schools in Brentwood they were told by the local priest that the 'nobility' would not sit in class with tradespeople. So two schools were opened and were not amalgamated until 1918.

Woodard, when he set out to give the middle classes a religious education to fit them to give it to others in their turn, naïvely supposed that each member knew his appointed place in a society that after all was God-ordained, and would not attempt to move out of it. Therefore there must be upper schools for the upper classes (at which the education would go on longest), middle schools for the professional classes, and lower schools for the tradesmen – 'from the small huckster,' he said ardently, 'up, step by step, through third- and second-rate retail shops, publicans, gin-palace keepers, etc., to the highly influential and respectable tradesmen, whose chief dealings are with the higher ranks of society'. But as the century moved on, and the high schools got under way, the boundaries between the classes became less easy to define. Woodard had not been lavishly educated himself; the ninth of twelve children, he had not even been to school, it seems. He had supported himself as a tutor in a family and had saved enough to go to Oxford, though his studies had been curtailed, as has been said, by his marriage. He was ordained in 1841 and given charge of a parish in Bethnal Green, where he plunged almost immediately into waters both hot and deep by preaching a sermon about the benefits to be derived from what was then termed 'auricular confession'. Having fallen out with his bishop over this highly controversial topic, he found a curacy at New Shoreham where he seems to have become immediately aware of the lack of schooling available for the children of local tradesmen, and of the deep social ills that must arise from future employers having no education. There were elementary schools for the poor, some of them church schools where they would get religious teaching, but nothing except wretched private academies for the shopkeeping class. 'By neglecting the employer, you are, in the present pressure of civilization, hastening on a very general state of barbarism.' He thought of this education in solely religious terms, and his condemnation of all state education lost him a lot of support. It has to be remembered that this attitude was not unusual among the devout who felt that children should attend church schools only; Charlotte Yonge viewed the secular schools (as they were then called to differentiate them from church schools) with strong hostility; in one of her family chronicles we are shown girls stitching away for a bazaar by which it was hoped to raise money to suppress one such.

Woodard felt that his was a sacred mission. He had sold all his possessions – his furniture, even his watch – to establish a school in his own house, and then in temporary buildings in the churchyard, and he had two boys' public schools under way – Lancing and Hurstpierpoint – when he was in 1855 offered a girls' school. A Miss Rooper had founded a boarding school in Hove eleven years before and wished it to become a Woodard school. Swallowing his scruples, he accepted, transferred the school to Bognor, and invited Lady Caroline Eliot to be its first Lady Warden. The greater part of the school's original site and buildings was her gift. His scheme was that the school should be governed by a body of teaching 'canonesses' (thereby becoming as near to a convent as possible), presided over – since he distrusted the female mind – by the provost of Lancing. This held good until 1920. The class structure always being at its most complex and rigid where females were involved, there were three different entities: an upper school limited to eighteen young ladies, the daughters of gentlemen, with fees of sixty guineas per annum; a middle school for the daughters of 'the Clergy, Tradesmen, Farmers and others of moderate means', where the fees were twenty-one or seventeen guineas according to age; and an industrial school where girls over sixteen could be trained for domestic service, at an annual fee of £8. The upper and middle schools met for classes and at meals, but were otherwise carefully segregated and took their walks and amusements separately.

On this school, St Michaels (now moved to Burton Park near Petworth), the schools of S. Mary and S. Anne at Abbots Bromley in Staffordshire were modelled. Again, they were not of Canon Woodard's direct founding. By this time there was a midland division of the Woodard Society, and S. Chad's College at Denstone had been opened in 1873. Its provost, Dr Edward Clarke Lowe, wanted to extend the religious and spiritual benefits to girls; a house was acquired in Abbots Bromley for £500, and, the provost piously hoping that money to furnish it would be forthcoming, the school was launched forthwith, opening on St Mark's Day 1874 with nine little girls. It was inaugurated with much ceremonial, two bishops and the choir from Denstone and a procession up the village street.

Staffordshire being socially, it seems, a different kettle of fish from Sussex, there was no attempt to found a young ladies' school. S. Anne's was a middle school whose pupils were being educated to become governesses and schoolmistresses. Like all such schools, it was financed on a shoestring; the furnishings cost £308 9s 7d, the teachers took no salary, and at the first prize-giving the provost announced that while half the £800 debt was paid off, £2,000 was still needed. The school lacked even basic necessities; there was no proper water supply, and until there was a case of diphtheria in 1876, no drains. For his boys' schools Canon Woodard had been an indefatigable, not to say belligerent, fund-raiser, employing both tact and charm. 'It is a privilege to receive a begging letter from you,' Lord Halifax once told him. But Woodard was also capable of tearing up a cheque for £1,000 and refusing to leave until its donor, a rich man from whom he had expected more, had replaced it with one for £5,000. On another occasion he told an assembly of wealthy guests at one of his 'nice luncheons' that he was not allowing them to get up until they had subscribed ten thousand pounds. But girls' schools had not the same appeal, and money for Abbots Bromley came in in tiny subscriptions. However, though life in the school itself was spartan in the extreme, no time, money or energy was spared to make the chapel as beautiful as possible; its foundation stone was laid only a few months after the school opened, and it was completed six years later.

S. Anne's had opened with, in addition to the middle school, a little 'industrial school', where the girls were given a few lessons but were chiefly occupied with domestic work. 'It is certain that, if they did not drink deep at the fount of "Sound Learning", they were not stinted in their share of "True Religion",' said the school's historian sententiously.[47] But in order to make the school the three-tier system that its founder had all along intended, a third school had to be inserted between S. Anne's and the 'industrials'. This was S. Mary's, founded in 1882, and since S. Anne's was already a middle school, it was to be designated S. Mary's Lower Middle Boarding-School for Girls and catered for 'daughters of gentlemen farmers, tradesmen and others of limited means', preparing them to train as teachers. The education there differed little from that of S. Anne's, though the fees were initially only £21 per annum, and the pupils tended to leave earlier. Many of them went on to S. Anne's to do more advanced work, the teachers for S. Mary's being almost entirely recruited from S. Anne's. The first five pupils occupied a rented house in the village and lived a life if anything more frugal than at S. Anne's. There was no money, so one just had to do without. The staff, all ardent Tractarians, were unpaid; the girls slept in dormitories of a monastic simplicity with no cubicles and a single drawer for their possessions; and they took baths, in a bucket of water, once a week. The food consisted mostly of bread and suet pudding, and the girls fought an anguished battle with Dr Lowe, who insisted they should eat bread and milk for breakfast (the history of religious establishments is fraught with male meddling such as this). The headmistress eventually managed to persuade him that tea and bread and butter was cheaper.

Dr Lowe was anxious that the school should have its own premises. A site was bought for £475, and the S. Mary's children when they passed it, located well above the level of S. Anne's, used to say gleefully that now they would be the 'high school'. The money for the building accumulated in very small sums, in subscriptions of one, two and three guineas. Miss Coleridge, the warden, held drawing-room meetings and wrote endless letters soliciting sympathy and donations, and the girls did their share, taking home collection cards, begging money for the gravel paths which cost 2s 6d a yard. They made socks, baskets and basket chairs, and one member of the staff made babies' boots at 1s 9d a pair 'from the Archbishop of York's wife's pattern'. The school ceased to be advertised as lower-middle-class after 1900, and the two schools amalgamated in 1921, the little 'industrials' having long since disappeared.

The Woodard Society took a long time to work up the same sort of enthusiasm for girls' schools as they had for boys', but the Abbots Bromley schools pressed forward, making themselves more academic, widening the curriculum, sending a girl to St Hugh's, Oxford, in 1905, and winning open Oxford scholarships the next year. The buildings, all except the chapel, were shabby, and they lived plainly, putting religion and education first. It was the same with the two Yorkshire schools, Queen Margaret's, founded in Scarborough in 1901 (it left the Society in 1986) and Queen Ethelburga's. But the austerity of the early years was not easily shed. Queen Margaret's was very bleak when Winifred Holtby was there:

> The founders of church schools regarded neither beauty nor comfort as necessary aids to the morality and religion which they desired for the young women whom they set out to educate. Hence the old schoolhouse, with its huge draughty windows and tiny antiquated grates, was a cheerless study in green, white and brown. White butter-muslin curtains divided the bedrooms into small unlovely cubicles. Furnished with white-painted chests of drawers and heavy white counterpanes, they gave, like all cubicled bedrooms, the impression of a comfortless unpatterned disorder. Throughout the school the floors were covered with brown oilcloth, the

> walls painted a dark olive green. Its chill, stuffy, lysol-pervaded ugliness was more than sufficient to account for the late development of aesthetic standards in its pupils.[48]

'It must all have been the ideal training for life in large country rectories for the daughters of the poorer clergy,' said one old member, remembering the austerity of the school in the 1950s.

But Winifred Holtby felt she owed much to her old school. Vera Brittain tells us:

> The true spirit of the School was to be found not in its external appearance, but in its aims, the quality of its teaching, and its motto, Filia Regis. Its education was designed for middle-class girls of moderate means with their living to earn; even in Winifred's time it was assumed that the majority would follow some professional career to make themselves independent. Winifred never ceased to be thankful for this early inculcation of modern ideas, and in gratitude bequeathed her library to the school.

The Woodard girls' schools still hold their own, though their numbers have diminished now to four. But the fact that they are there at all is a curious reversal of the founder's original intentions.

7

Convent Schools

The Tradition

'Sight, hearing, touch, taste and smell were all used to make an indelible impression upon the soul,' wrote a former Sacred Heart child (they were always children, never girls), recalling her schooldays.[1] 'One has only to remember the great feast-days, the bowers of flowers around the altar, the softly carpeted chapel aisle, to be convinced of its truth.' (This school was in New Zealand, but there were Sacred Heart convents all over the world, all with identical traditions.) It is an adage of the Ursulines that religion is best caught, not taught, and convents hoped to make school an experience that would never slide away, even from the most frivolous. 'Then would the Old Children gather,' wrote one of them about the Feast of the Immaculate Conception, kept with great pomp by all Sacred Heart convents throughout the world, 'veiled hats perched on fluffy little heads, fingers with brittle polished nails, and muffled to the ears in fox furs, their clacketing high heels and shrill voices echoing down the long stone corridors. The odour of sanctity, scrubbed serge, mingled with Schiaparelli's "Shocking" and Chanel's "Numero Cinq" and the arum lilies'.[2] Antonia White also recalled the same combination of piety and frivolity – the 'old children' at reunions who 'displayed their Child of Mary medals hung on broad white ribbons over their beautiful worldly frocks', and who giggled and chattered and rustled round the study rooms.[3] Many of them, incapable of much spirituality, clung to the traditions. After four years at the Convent of the Five Wounds – the barely disguised Sacred Heart convent at Roehampton – Nanda Gray in Antonia White's autobiographical novel, *Frost in May*, the child of a convert, felt that 'she was part of the Church now. She could never, she knew, break away without a sense of mutilation. In her four years at Lippington, it had grown into every fibre of her nature; she could not eat or sleep or read or play without relating every action to her life as a Christian and a Catholic.'

A Catholic education was not a matter of lessons; it was a way of life, a process that went on for twenty-four hours in every day for which, properly, one needed to be part of a community, and this explains why, at a time when boarding schools were not the norm and the upper-class Protestant girl was usually educated at home by governesses, the Catholic girl of good family was sent to a convent, very expensively abroad if need be. Charlotte Jerningham, dispatched to the Ursulines in Paris in the 1780s, was costing her parents £200 a year (a huge amount, when one remembers that other convents were charging under £20). 'Sometimes,' her mother lamented, 'as we are not yet very affluent, Sir Wm finds it a good deal.'[4] And though nearly all teaching orders would have 'poor schools', as well as their boarding schools for the privileged classes, the former subsidized by the latter, they tended to prefer boarding to day establishments; boarders could fit into the pattern of the religious day more easily, especially with orders such as the Canonesses of the Holy Sepulchre whose Rule included daily public recital of the Office. In the days when nuns did all the teaching and fees were kept low, it used to be for non-Catholics one way of securing a cheap and ladylike education for a daughter. She might not emerge with much knowledge of higher mathematics, but she would have fair French and English, and would have been taught good manners and how to sew.

Frost in May, an account of a pupil who failed to come to terms with the system and who was cast out from it, is, ironically, the fullest description that we have of traditions and a way of life that had gone on for generations. It is not easy to discover the history of any individual convent school; each is so much bound up in the history of the teaching order of which it is a part, and the records even of these are scanty. 'They seem, in their humility, to have forgotten that those who came after them would have much valued some little account of their actions,' wrote one archivist wistfully of her forebears.[5] After the publication of *Frost in May* Antonia White received two letters from 'old children'; one had left in 1883, the other in 1927, but both were certain that the author, who had in fact left in 1914, had been their contemporary. 'Reverend Mothers and Mistresses of Discipline may come and go,' White wrote in 1934, 'but their characters affect the school very little. The real ruler is an invisible one – the French saint, who in the early part of the nineteenth century . . . laid down, once and for all, its code of manners and morals.'[6] 'A pattern [was] laid down for them in France in the early nineteenth century,' wrote Mary McCarthy, 'clipped and pollarded as a garden and stately as a minuet.'[7] The Sacred Heart convent that she attended was in Seattle, but 'at four o'clock on any weekday afternoon in Roscrea, Ireland, or Roehampton, England, or Menlo Park, California, the same tiny, whiskered nun was reading, no doubt, from *Emma* or *A Tale of Two Cities* to a long table of girls stitching French seams or embroidering bureau scarves with wreaths of flowers.' And all of them would be wearing the same blue serge dresses with white collars and cuffs, the same blue, green and pink moiré ribbons awarded for good conduct. They had the same traditional feast days, the same retreats and sermons, and sang the same French hymns. They processed to chapel in the same black veils – white net for feast days – and dipped the same low curtsies to nuns and visitors. The system that at the time seemed to be so immutable that there was no need to record it has, since Vatican II, nearly vanished from the educational scene, for neither the daily life of the convent boarding schools that remain nor the education they provide is now very different from that of their secular contemporaries; many are under lay management and all have largely lay staff.

It is only comparatively recently that they could compete academically with the ordinary girls' public school, or indeed that they concerned themselves with equipping their pupils for professional careers. 'If you want *that* sort of thing,' said a Mother Superior to a father who had made rash inquiries about university entrance for his daughter, 'you should have sent her to one of those pushy high schools.' Their children were to be prepared for eternal life, and as far as the fleeting life of this world was concerned there were two alternatives: they might become nuns or they might become mothers. 'To train the future mothers of [the middle classes] is to sanctify entire families and to sow the seeds of piety in whole congregations; it is to make friends for the poor of Christ, nurses for the sick and dying, catechists for the little ones, most useful auxiliaries in every good work,' Nicholas Wiseman (later to become the first Archbishop of Westminster) told Cornelia Connelly, foundress of the Society of the Holy Child Jesus.[8] 'Education leading up to the grand object of enabling a woman to stand alone . . . is, in point of fact, found in convents in exactly the same proportion as in the ordinary run of all other schools for girls, and that is a very small proportion indeed,' wrote one defender of convent schools.[9] But that was in 1874. Sixty years later, when most schools of any standing prided themselves on turning out girls who would take up professional careers, a Sacred Heart nun was pronouncing that 'the independence desired for a woman was not the fruit of a successful career, but rather the right and peaceful self-reliance of a mind which carried within itself resources for its own happiness and healthy occupation'.[10] And in 1912 Mother Janet Erskine Stuart of the same order had been gently sceptical of the uses of higher education for women, pointing out that degrees for men and women meant very different things.[11] For men at Oxford or Cambridge there was an 'atmosphere unique in character, immemorial tradition, association, all kinds of interests and subtle influences of the past'. But for a girl it was a final effort in the process of learning: 'either her life's work takes a different turning, or she thinks she has had enough' – unless she was going to teach, in which case university education was 'the key that fits the lock, for the gates to the domain of education are kept locked by the state,' said Mother Stuart somewhat bitterly, thinking no doubt of the cultured and cultivated nuns, including herself, who taught in the schools of the Sacred Heart without any university education.

Sacred Heart children were educated to be courteous, considerate and cultivated Catholic gentlewomen, with a love of the best literature and art and music (though there was danger in unbalanced preoccupation with any one activity). They were to be dignified and immaculately tidy, and carry themselves well. (One child still remembers with horror how her American mother let a piece of chewing gum slip on to the floor when Reverend Mother stopped in her stately progress to speak to her.) They were not expected to abjure the world and its pleasures, but to pass through it unsmirched to eternal glory. In the last century Mother Henrietta Kerr told her pupils that 'after a night passed in a ball-room, a girl might be quite as pleasing to God as if she had spent it in a church'. It was their duty to their parents to attend such functions, because it was the will of God as part of the duty of their social position.[12]

For the most part it was left to the Catholic grammar schools, for the children of far less prosperous parents, to pick out bright pupils who might make teachers and persuade their parents to let them go to universities. These independent day schools run by such orders as the Notre Dame and the Ursuline nuns, and now nearly all absorbed into the state system, were responsible for encouraging and helping many girls from families with no background of education. They do not come into the scope of this book, but, on a shoestring, they provided a sound education and shaped the lives of their pupils, putting before the working-class child the chance of a professional career. The tradition of the boarding schools, on the other hand, was to give to girls who supposedly would never be called upon to support themselves 'a thoroughly feminine culture along the lines of the past',[13] and they did not bother their pupils with external exams until some fifty years after these had been taken up by the high schools; New Hall had none until 1925, the Sacred Heart schools not until 1928. Though the Holy Child nuns, who for a long time were held to provide the best academic education of the convent boarding schools, had established a hostel at Oxford as soon as the university admitted women, many of the early pioneers of Catholic education – such as Mother Cecilia Marshall of the Institute of the Blessed Virgin Mary who built up St Mary's School, Ascot – had had no formal training except the schooling they had received at their various convents. By the 1920s and 30s other orders had followed the lead of the Holy Child. The Sacred Heart, which had been entering for London degrees since 1893 and had opened a training college in Wandsworth in 1874 (it moved to North Kensington in 1905), established a house in North Oxford in 1924 from which nuns could attend the university. The order had the satisfaction of seeing a member win the Chancellor's Essay Prize in 1933.

As far as the humanities were concerned, the teaching of the best convents was undoubtedly good. Antonia White, dispatched to St Paul's after she had been removed, disgraced, from Roehampton, found it unmemorable and nowhere near so cultivated as the Sacred Heart. (It has here to be remembered what a terrible humiliation St Paul's must have seemed, since the terms 'high school' and 'grammar school' were so often used by nuns as terms of opprobrium to point out the way that Sacred Heart children should *not* conduct themselves.)

> Languages, music, and the history of painting were taught with far more intelligence and efficiency at the Five Wounds than at any secular school and we also learnt such old-fashioned, but useful accomplishments as reading aloud and writing tolerable letters. Literature, it is true, was taught with many reservations, but well enough to give us a genuine love of it and the elements of a respectable taste.[14]

St Paul's might teach Latin and Greek and science and maths and prepare girls for professional life, but it did so without any grace. And the Sacred Heart prided itself that the education it gave was solid, with emphasis on clear thought and right judgement; philosophy and the elements of logic were taught in its schools and training colleges. 'Stress should be laid on the necessity of the formation of judgement. The children might be practised usefully in searching for varieties of reasoning in the course of a written speech or argument, or they might be asked to prove a thesis or refute an error in syllogistic form,' said a 1930s 'plan of studies'.[15]

But this is not to say that independent thinking was in any way encouraged.

> Through years of training the nuns had learnt to recognize the faintest sign of such an attitude, and it was severely repressed. They could detect it in the slightest thing – a straying curl, an inclination to 'answer back' and, most of all, in the faintest hint of speculation in matters of faith . . . Mental pride and physical vanity were considered the most dangerous of all our temptations and our mistresses were always on the watch for their appearance.[16]

Initiative counted as nothing, and Cornelia Connelly, presented with an exquisite piece of point-lace made by one of her nuns during the time that the community was supposed to occupy itself with tatting, threw it into the fire.[17] 'One of these days, if you're not careful, you'll be setting up your own conceited little judgement against the wisdom of the Church, which is the wisdom of God himself,'[18] Mother Frances tells Antonia White's nine-year-old Nanda, who she perceives after only a few weeks possesses obstinacy and independence, two attributes that had to be eradicated in a system where obedience, self-control and abnegation of the self were supremely important. '"Nuns are happy," I was told by a big girl, "because they have no wills. They try to make us happy by breaking our wills."'[19]

All study, of course, was dominated by the Faith, just as the school terms were structured not by work for public exams but by the progress of the Church's year, culminating in the ceremonies of Holy Week (within the memory of many, convents and church schools used not to disband for the holidays until after Easter). These were remembered by those who experienced them as the supreme moment of the year. Lent might be dreaded –

six weeks of boiled cod eaten in silence, with the nuns' temper uncertain because of fasting and penance. But the mounting drama of Holy Week left no one untouched: the Tenebrae psalms; the Messianic prophecies while the candles were one by one extinguished; the warmth and light of Maundy Thursday; the bare chapel on Good Friday; the lighting of the new fire on Easter Saturday, and then the splendour of the Easter Mass in a chapel filled with the white dresses of the girls, the gold of the vestments, the flowers and music.

The Sacred Heart school day was a version of a monastic one. Each girl was woken in her cubicle by a bell, the holy water stoup was presented to her with the words 'Sacred Heart of Jesus, Immaculate Heart of Mary' to which she responded, 'I give you my heart and my soul.' The whole day was punctuated by prayers. Besides the morning and evening prayers and the thrice-recurring Angelus, every day's lessons began with an invocation to the Holy Ghost and ended with a recommendation to Our Lady; there was, besides, daily mass for everybody. In the month of May, the whole school assembled to recite five decades of the rosary before supper, and there was usually a novena in preparation for an important feast, or a special intention. The day ended with prayers in the chapel and an examination of conscience. On Saturdays children were encouraged to go to confession, and in the evening there were special devotions in the vestibule of Our Lady of Good Success. On Sundays all the children attended mass with a sermon in the morning and went to Benediction in the afternoon. 'The first impression is that of being caught in a treadmill,' said one nun, recalling her schooldays, 'which one is terrifyingly powerless to control or direct.'[20] There was silence at all times except at meals and during recreation.

In early days convent pupils were regarded as members of the religious community; during their schooldays they did not go home at all, and at a time when only charity children wore uniform, they wore prescribed dark convent dresses. Short holidays in the summer were gradually introduced, and even then somewhat grudgingly:

> An uninterrupted course of Education being desirable, no deduction is made for absence from School, except in case of indisposition, but when circumstances lead a parent to consider a short vacation for a child necessary, this indulgence is allowed only from the 28 July to the 25 or 26 of August; and it is important that this regulation should be strictly observed,

said a nineteenth-century prospectus of the Bar Convent in York. And a letter addressed to a Miss Riley from the convent at New Hall in 1801 said pointedly: 'Long Vacancies are certainly very detrimental to all Young Persons but particularly so when Young Ladies are rather backward.'[21]

One Victorian writer who had experienced the system spoke about the 'prisonlike regime'. In time, she said, the girls got used to it; but to a newcomer 'the monotony, the enforced dullness and silence, the gloomy dresses and general bleakness of everything, were fearfully irksome'.[22] However, she did concede that there was ample space for recreation, 'and those who were inclined for outdoor games had every liberty to enjoy them'. The Sacred Heart up to a point encouraged high spirits at recreation, were wary of pupils who were too quiet and meek, and thought games important; at Roehampton they were playing cricket and tennis in the 1870s. (This was very advanced thinking; the Anglican convent of St Mary's at Wantage was reluctantly allowing younger girls to play cricket in 1895, but decreed that nobody over fifteen must take part.) Certainly the ceremonial and protocol, the preoccupation with minute detail, the attention to deportment, were formidable; one always curtsied to a nun; gloves were worn on every formal occasion; one was never allowed out of the sight of a *surveillante*, and one always played under watchful eyes, aware, one felt uncomfortably, of all character foibles; sins were made out of the most innocent actions.

But there were many feast days, especially in the summer term, when the community would abandon itself to pleasure. Corpus Christi was a special favourite, when the Blessed Sacrament was carried in procession and children in white veils and wreaths strewed flower petals before it. Feast days were holidays when you could talk where you pleased and as much as you pleased, and there were epic games of *cache-cache* when the school was divided into two camps, religiously preserved from year to year so that the secret of traditional hiding places should not be revealed. The young nuns might also play. 'Once they took the part of "ghosts" identified by a white sheet in a game of outdoor hide and seek in the dark. Our best sprinters and dodgers were soon bundled up into the "pound" by these young women with their skirts hitched up to their knees and held firmly in place by their aprons.'[23] There would be chocolates and weak currant wine at dinner, and the day would end with some splendid entertainment such as charades, or fireworks, or a ghost story, told in pitch-darkness, by one of the nuns. New Hall in the early days of no holidays had special treats on Holy Innocents Day, when the youngest children, dressed as prioress and sub-prioress, made a speech asking the real Reverend Mother for privileges. Then there was 'Kingtide'. This began on the Sunday within the octave of Epiphany and lasted until the Wednesday evening; all the school rules, except silence in the dormitories, were in abeyance, and a new set of customs came in such as eating sweets in class and playing cards.

At all convents tremendous effort went into ensuring that one's first communion should be an imperishable memory. The tradition of celebrating this landmark in a Catholic child's life apparently began with the Ursulines in Paris,[24] and only at a boarding school could one properly prepare for it. The first communicants were set apart, a privileged band who spent extra time in the chapel, had daily interviews with Reverend Mother, received special instruction, and would help with the vestments and with the altar flowers. The ceremony itself was preceded by a three-day retreat, and on the eve of the feast the children wore their white veils everywhere. In the evening they went first to their schoolfellows and then to the nuns' community room, to kneel and ask forgiveness. Then on the day itself they went to the altar dressed like young brides – or like nuns making their first profession.

All this became part of the fabric of their life: the real world beside which the world outside was shadowy indeed. In Antonia White's day twenty per cent of the girls were to enter the order. 'A vocation was to be more ardently desired and more warmly accepted than anything in the world. A secular life, however pious, however happy, was only the wretched crust with which Catholics who were not called to the grace of religious life must nourish themselves as best they could. A vocation followed was the supreme good; a vocation rejected the supreme horror.' The chaplain of an Anglo-Catholic convent in Oxford in the last century told the girls in a prize-giving speech that he hoped they would all join the Sisterhood, and that he would rather officiate at the funeral than at the marriage of any of them[25] (though at this particular convent all the girls of that year were to marry within a year or so of leaving school). Once the call had sounded it must be immediately obeyed in the heart, even though the actual dedication might be delayed; and the fear of being called hung over many who were unable to decide which was worse – the danger of hell which threatened those who were deaf, or the prospect of having to be a nun: 'there were nuns who had fainted with fear and horror when their vocation had been revealed to them'.[26] There must have been many who, like the little Irish girl at a convent of the Faithful Companions of Jesus in the middle of the last century, prayed fervently that God would protect her from a vocation and yet let her go to heaven when she died.[27]

At this convent in a small town in county Limerick little Sissy O'Brien, a farm child, was being educated 'as a gentlewoman, by gentlewomen', and taught how to give orders to butlers and footmen, how to reply if addressed by royalty or the Lord Lieutenant. 'A giggle, even a twinkle of the eyes between two girls over these exercises, would cause Mother Berchmans pain; loyalty to the Law of the Foundress must be upheld at all costs.' The system, of course, had its critics. 'What would happen to these girls who had thus been brought up as ladies?' asked one. They would find their own home background unbearable; they had been taught no housekeeping, cooking or plain sewing and could not obtain employment as governesses or teachers, 'for the convents had the monopoly of that profession'. The only future for them was to return to the convent. The parents who protested about the butler-footman and royalty lessons were told that the law of the foundress must be obeyed; just as she had decreed that the girls must wear scarlet *capelines* when they went for walks and turned-up sailor hats in summer, so she had laid down that all pupils – county, country or town – must be educated as gentlewomen. It was this sort of obedience (some might call it slavish), this thraldom to the past, that for so long kept convent schools in the rearguard of education.

Mary Ward and the 'English Ladies'

The foundress of the Faithful Companions of Jesus was a Frenchwoman; indeed, most of the teaching orders have been French, it being a curious fact that nearly all the religious orders have come to the rest of the world via France. One great exception was the Institute of the Blessed Virgin Mary (IBVM), which rose on the ruins of the congregation founded in the seventeenth century by the remarkable Yorkshirewoman Mary Ward, whose views about the education of women have already been mentioned in Chapter 1. If her spirit had been maintained the history of convent education would have been very different. Her community was suppressed mainly because of the hostility shown by the clergy of her own faith, who passionately resented her attempts to found an organization of uncloistered nuns in secular clothes, free to move about and serve the community where they were most needed – something she felt to be imperative at a time when there were penal laws in England against Catholics. And from the middle of the eighteenth century until the middle of the nineteenth, for the sake of survival the name of Mary Ward could not be associated with the Institute. The Institute as she had planned it was not confirmed until 1877, and the Jesuit constitution for which she had asked in 1620 was not granted until 1978.

She had founded her first school in St Omer, and the report for 1610 speaks of a day school for the young girls of the town.[28] They were taught, as Winefrid Wigmore, an early friend and companion, wrote, 'the sciences fitting our sex, all that became good Christians and worthy women. The English, in regard of the distance, lived wholly under their care . . . and were taught qualities to render them capable and fit to do God service in whatsoever state, religious or secular.' The members of the community, which was not enclosed, were known in St Omer as 'the English Ladies', a title that was to stick, and many daughters of notable English families were dispatched there to be brought up 'in the Faith and good manners'. About 1611 the first affiliated community was established in London at Spitalfields, and in the years that followed Mary Ward was travelling constantly in England, Italy, the Low Countries, Germany and Austria founding schools. When she returned to England towards the end of her life her friends and acquaintances entreated her, in Winefrid Wigmore's words, 'to receive their daughters, as she had done before, to train them and educate them. Among them were many of high birth and position. But Mary, whose kind heart ever yearned over the difficulties of the poor and needy, in spite of her poverty, added out of her own charity others to their number, who were unable to pay anything.'

Little is known of her school in those years; the times were too anxious and the community too harried for there to be any records, and it was finally broken up by the Puritans in 1642. But as Mary Ward's nineteenth-century biographer pointed out, the 'admirable characters and qualifications' of members of the Institute during the seventeenth century testified to the solid nature of their learning. They were taught Latin, German, French, English and Italian,

> and this not as a smattering only, but so as to be able to speak, read and write in each language, and also to study good authors in each. They were also instructed in a variety of general knowledge, music, painting and embroidery. But beyond all these mental acquirements were the careful culture and training of each mind and character, so that the best of the powers that God had bestowed on both were brought forth and perfected to the utmost. Habits of self-control and self-government were instilled and made strong in them, and above all they were instructed in the fear and love of God which were made acceptable to the pupils by the holy lives which they saw in their teachers.

It was not until 1686 that there was a school of any permanence, and miraculously it was to survive, even latterly to flourish, through a century of penal laws against Catholics. Mother Frances Bedingfield, a companion and friend of Mary Ward who had been present at her deathbed in 1645, bought for £450 a house and garden just outside Micklegate Bar in York. She was a woman of great learning, who had studied Greek, Hebrew and astronomy, but like so many of her kind was willing and able to take her turn at the washing-tubs, all night if need be. Because of her faith she also had to face imprisonment in 'loathsome holes, dark and verminous, with a poisonous atmosphere', the last time when she was seventy-eight.[29] Though it was illegal, the nuns took in 'young ladies of Roman Catholic families' and in 1699 opened a day school. They wore slate-coloured gowns rather than religious habits, were addressed as Mistress or Madam, and went out to feed and nurse the poor of York, struggling to survive by keeping sheep, cows and hens. Only in the later eighteenth century could they be said to prosper, when a dowry brought by one of their members, prudently invested, allowed them to embark on an ambitious building programme, which even included a chapel. It was still illegal for a Catholic to build one and there was the added risk of popular outbreaks of anti-papal feeling. But Mother Ann Aspinal, a woman of the same mettle as Mary Ward, was undeterred, and chose as her model a church near Rome, only modifying the plan by lowering the dome and concealing it with a slate roof so that the chapel merges into the complex of buildings and cannot be seen from the street. In case of danger a priest's hole was built under one of the transepts.

From 1778 the position eased in that priests were no longer subject to persecution at the denunciation of common informers, and the penalty of lifelong imprisonment for keeping a Catholic school was abolished. And after 1791 Catholic worship and Catholic schools were tolerated, so that the convent could offer hospitality to nuns fleeing from the French Revolution, including the Canonesses of the Holy Sepulchre who, forced from Liège in 1794, were to establish their own school at New Hall. But the Revolution and the Napoleonic Wars also meant that the Bar Convent was cut off from the sister houses that Mary Ward had founded in Italy and Germany; and, the convent's historian says sadly, it seems to have suffered a change of identity: 'Totally isolated, the community allowed an enclosed, monastic style of life, for which they were altogether unsuited and which they did not understand, to be imposed on them.' In the mid-eighteenth century they were still going out to minister to the sick and needy of York, both men and women; in the nineteenth they lived within their own walls and turned all men away. But even so, in the early 1800s members went out from the Institute to found the Irish Sisters of Charity, and the Loreto Sisters who were to set up many schools of their own.

The Bar Convent became a grammar school in 1929, then co-educational in the 1970s; in 1985 it amalgamated with two other Catholic schools in York to become All Saints' Comprehensive School. The Georgian buildings have been opened as a museum of the history of English Catholicism. The existing IBVM boarding schools are all of comparatively late origin, but it is to these Institute schools that the old Catholic families tend to send their daughters, following a tradition that started in the time of Mary Ward. St Mary's, Ascot, sprang from a school that began in Gloucester in 1862 and later moved to Hampstead. From this house nuns came down to Ascot and opened there in September 1885 with eighteen boarders, among them Cissie Marshall, to be Mother Superior from 1913 to 1959.[30] An heiress of some substance, she encountered fierce opposition from her brother and stepmother in her wish to become a nun in the convent which was more home to her than anywhere else. The considerable dowry that she brought when the Bishop eventually did give her permission to enter the order went a long way towards paying for the Ascot school's first buildings.

At the outbreak of the Second War the Hampstead community moved first to Sussex, then to Wiltshire. But even before the war was over plans were being made for the future. It was decided that Hampstead should only continue as a prep school, and that premises in the West Country should be found for the main school. Accordingly the nuns quartered the country, sallying out on bicycles and on foot. Eventually the Coombe House Hotel outside Shaftesbury, commanding views of the Dorset country which make it one of the most beautifully sited of all schools, was bought in 1945 for £16,000 (with the help of a loan from Ascot). It opened that September and has flourished, despite initial fears that it was too remote (the drive alone is three quarters of a mile long).

As has been said, the easing of the penal laws made it possible for religious communities driven out of France and the Low Countries by the French Revolution to take shelter in England, and Benedictine nuns (the first seen wearing religious habits since the Reformation) established a convent with a school, first at Bodney Hall in Norfolk in 1793, and much later at Princethorpe in Warwickshire. The Canonesses of the Holy Sepulchre arrived the following year – their vicissitudes during the flight from the French armies are described in Chapter 13. One of the most ancient of the orders of women (their oldest existing house, in Saragossa, dates from 1276), their own convent had been founded in Liège in 1642 by a young Englishwoman, Susan Hawley, born in 1622, who had been joined by other Englishwomen, many of them from Suffolk. Though there was a school from about 1650, there were seldom more than five or six girls until 130 years later when Mother Christina Dennett became prioress and 'set her heart on giving Catholic girls the same advantages which they would have in the great schools in England'. She recognized that for a lot of parents a godly upbringing was not enough, and that 'many would prefer a place where their children might have the means of improving their natural abilities or talents, to a convent where they would possess every advantage for their improvement in virtue and piety . . . though deprived of many advantages which others possess'.[31] So she set out to reconcile God and the friends of the mammon of unrighteousness – successfully, for the numbers increased to some forty pupils and the community embarked on new building. The education seems not to have been so solid as at the Bar Convent, but covered a wide range of formal subjects and accomplishments. The girls studied reading, writing, English, French and Italian grammatically; sacred and profane history; arithmetic, book-keeping, and 'all that belongs to epistolary composition in different ranks of life'; heraldry, the use of the globes, geography; 'the principles of natural history so far as may be found useful for girls'; embroidery and all sorts of needlework, and the art of drawing and painting flowers. Dancing, music and portrait-painting were all extra, as was miniature painting on ivory, and cost three guineas a year. The full boarding fees were seventeen guineas a year, plus the habitual two guineas for washing and two for writing materials.

But the turbulent period of the French Revolution was upon them and in 1794, with the invasion of the Low Countries, the nuns realized they would have to leave. 'It is more easy to conceive than express the affliction we all felt to be obliged to quit our dear convent.' After weeks of wandering (they left on Ascension Day and arrived at Gravesend on the Feast of the Assumption in August) the thirty-five nuns, fourteen lay sisters and fourteen pupils reached England and were given shelter by Lord and Lady Stourton at Holme Hall in Yorkshire. After a brief spell in Wiltshire, New Hall in Essex was bought for them in 1799 by a friend of the order, a large and splendid property which had once been owned by the Boleyn family and at which many Tudor and Stuart monarchs had been entertained. The school is still there, vastly extended, with some five hundred pupils, a third of whom are non-Catholic (there is an Anglican chaplain as well as a Catholic one). Though the headmistress is a member of the order only fifteen nuns work in the school, and there are some forty-five lay staff members, one third of them male.

American and French Connections

The Bar Convent with its record of three hundred years of history, even though its identity is now lost, and New Hall are unique in having English origins and in having educated English girls from penal times. The Holy Child convents, which originated in England, used to say proudly that they provided an English education for English girls in an atmosphere of freedom and simplicity (presumably in oblique criticism of the French-dominated convents that were the norm, and their watchful *surveillance*). But the foundress was in fact American.

The story of Cornelia Connelly is a curious one. Her husband, Pierce Connelly, who like her had begun life as a Presbyterian, was the Episcopalian rector of Trinity Church in Natchez, Mississippi, and there were three children when in 1835 he resigned his parish to join the Church of Rome. Cornelia followed him, and the family left the United States to live in Rome. By 1840 Pierce had resolved to become a priest, and asked Cornelia, then pregnant with their fifth child, if she would be willing to live in celibacy from then on. With much sorrow she acquiesced, and was given shelter in a Sacred Heart convent in Rome, where her daughter was a pupil, and where she received training as a religious in preparation for a still uncertain future. She took with her the youngest surviving child, who was then three. But in 1846, without as yet having taken any vows except that of celibacy, she was sent to England to devote herself to education. There the Catholic Church was expanding fast; the old Catholic families emerging from the isolation of penal days – Catholic Emancipation had come in 1829 – had been joined by a flood of converts, and, particularly in the industrial midlands and north-west, by thousands of Irish immigrants of the very poorest sort, fleeing from the famine of the 40s. Such schools as existed were not able to deal with them, and it is an indication of the Church's desperation that it should have turned for help to a penniless foreigner who had no experience of education or knowledge of English ways, nor friends who could help. Here was a Reverend Mother without a community, who had achieved her position without even being a novice and who had three living children, two of them in her care. (One should also spare a thought for the predicament of her wretched eldest son at Stonyhurst, where all his peers would undoubtedly have known that he was the offspring of a priest and a nun.)

Cornelia Connelly began her work in Derby, assembling a small community and organizing a parish school, and a small boarding school for young ladies. Unfortunately, as her work prospered so her private life became turbulent. Pierce, employed as a tutor with an English Catholic family, was having misgivings about celibacy. This was to culminate in an action brought before the Court of Arches for restitution of conjugal rights. He lost it, but he bore off the children (who had in any case all left their mother and had been consigned to boarding schools) and she never saw them again. Pierce spent the rest of his life as an Episcopalian, writing virulent anti-Catholic pamphlets; his wife was to devote herself to Catholic education.

In 1849 the mother house of the order of the Holy Child Jesus was established at St Leonards-on-Sea. Eventually there was to be not only a convent and a boarding school but a poor school and a training college as well, Cornelia Connelly realizing, long before any other teaching order did, the importance of making provision for a properly qualified staff. Her views on education were well in advance of her times, and the Holy Child schools shone at a time when the early excellence of the Bar Convent had diminished almost to vanishing point. Her methods with young children had been learned through teaching her own; lessons were based on games and stories, drawing and acting, and she realized the importance of plenty of activity. Arithmetic was taught partly as a game, with bricks and cards and weights; geography started with the making of maps of first the table, then the schoolroom, then the playground, then the neighbourhood; and she insisted that lessons should be related to each other and not dealt with in isolation. For older children she stressed the importance of explanation as against mechanical learning, of exciting interest, arousing curiosity, stimulating the imagination; they ought, too, to be aware of the outside world and be able to read a *Times* leader intelligently. (Even in the twentieth century many convents barred newspapers.) She encouraged acting, and felt strongly that drawing was not a mere genteel accomplishment but 'a Christian art, and one of the most important branches of education, second only to that of speaking and writing'; she gave her nuns minute instructions on how to achieve the desired effect in watercolours by the use of an old cotton stocking.

Not for her the pinched and cramped way in which girls were so often accommodated; in 1860, before it was general to teach classes in separate rooms, and when Cheltenham Ladies' College and the North London Collegiate still used a hall for several different groups, the St Leonards convent had a library, a studio, a hall and a desk for each pupil. (It seems that convents were often generous with their accommodation; a prospectus for St Margaret's Convent in Edinburgh for 1834, housed in a former stately home long before this became standard practice, announced the provision of separate classrooms.) At a time when convent life was formidably organized and austere, Cornelia Connelly dressed the children in crimson because she disliked seeing them in sombre, dowdy clothes, and introduced recreations such as waltzing and whist which she took part in herself. (It has to be remembered that waltzing had recently been described as 'the most degenerate dance that the last or present century has seen', and that fifty years later at the Sacred Heart, Roehampton, it was only allowed if the girls held each other at arms' length.) She deprecated the insistence of convents in the French tradition that girls should be kept under constant supervision. She went further: long before any other school she introduced a system of mutual responsibility whereby each class voted for its own 'badges', who were allowed to discuss school policy with the authorities. The syllabus itself was not remarkable, and resembled most other schools of the period in attempting to spread itself over far too broad a field. The first school prospectus advertised English, French, writing, arithmetic, geography, history, grammar, singing and the principles of church music, drawing, plain needlework 'and every kind of embroidery, tracing, point-lace together with the cutting out and making up of vestments'. Philosophy, logic, astronomy, geology, architecture, heraldry, Latin and Greek were also thrown in (one has to bear in mind that there is a lot of time to fill when there are no holidays). Most remarkable of all for a convent, and stemming perhaps from the American instinct to look to the future rather than to the past, was her desire that the system should be flexible and should 'change to meet the wants of the age'.[32]

Her own bishops might not always approve of her methods. As early as the Derby days Wiseman* had had grave doubts about French: 'The present French literature is so wicked that the temptation to read it is better removed.' And Thomas Grant, Bishop of Southwark, wrote in 1865: '*Confidential*. Enquire prudently as it is said that in one of your houses (either St Leonards or Harley Street) the pupils have been taught to *waltz* and *dance the polka* as well as to play Whist.' If it was true, it was to be stopped. Ever racked by scrupulous doubts, he could cause her much trouble by suddenly deciding to prohibit standard textbooks used in the school, and he expressed grave dismay when he heard that the nuns had been allowed to picnic. But her system pleased secular authority. In 1853 an inspector reported on the poor school attached to the boarding school at St Leonards: 'It is impossible to witness without admiration the results obtained in this very interesting school, in which consummate skill in the art of teaching, unwearied patience and the most persuasive personal influence have combined to accomplish all the rarest fruits of Christian instruction. The school is now one of the most perfect institutions of its class in Europe.'[33]

* Nicholas Patrick Stephen Wiseman (1802–65), first cardinal-archbishop of Westminster since the Reformation, at that time coadjutor to the vicar-apostolic of the central district of England.

Approval by government inspectors was far from standard; the Ursulines were very dashed in the early 1900s when they were told that their Brentwood school was under-equipped and the staff not properly qualified; New Hall failed its inspection in 1927 and did not get recognition until 1947. But the assistant commissioner employed by the Schools Inquiry Commission in the 1860s to visit Lancashire schools spoke of the courtesy and kindness he encountered at the convents; it would be unbecoming, he said, not to acknowledge it in the amplest manner.[34] He found that the internal organization of a community could be turned to good account for the purposes of education, and the fact that a religious order was an international institution was an advantage in finding teachers, but he did wonder whether it was a good thing that the pupils – though he conceded they seemed happy enough – should so frequently become 'a willing and almost passive instrument in the hands of those who guide them', and whether their character and opinions ought not to show more independence.

It is interesting that the convents he visited (they are not named) should have impressed him by their international nature, and this did not necessarily mean the nuns only, for long before economic necessity dictated that there must be a substantial leavening of overseas pupils, the Catholic schools had cast their nets wide. 'Our community was made up of all nationalities, of Brazilians even, to say nothing of Frenchmen,' wrote one old Stonyhurst boy, remembering his schooldays in the early years of the last century.[35] Antonia White met Spanish, Austrian, French and Polish girls at the Sacred Heart at Roehampton, and as a convert's child felt far more of an outsider than any of them. 'They might be inarticulate but the very way their trunks were packed, with a crucifix folded in the tissue paper among the dozen regulation calico nightgowns, was proof of "a good Catholic home" in the background.'[36] And it was at Roehampton that a present member of the order had the satisfaction of banging together the heads of two Hohenzollern contemporaries just before the outbreak of the last war. It was perhaps the French tradition in which the Sacred Heart was steeped – in the early days all the teaching was in that language – which made it so popular internationally. French culture and manners were the great desiderata among families who would have shuddered at exposing their daughters to the hoydenish heartiness of the ordinary English public school.

The foundress of the order of the Sacred Heart, Madeleine Sophie Barat (canonized in 1925), was born in 1779. She had had a formidably intellectual education, and a remarkable one for the time. Her brother, who was also her godfather and a stern taskmaster with high standards, insisted on her following at home all the classes that he did at school – grammar, rhetoric, mathematics, history, Spanish and Italian. When she accompanied him – he was by then a priest – to Paris in 1798 it was with the idea of becoming a Carmelite. But one Father Joseph Varin persuaded her that it was her mission to devote herself to education. (He was in fact passing on the vision of Léonor de Tournély – who had died the previous year – of an order of the Sacred Heart which should devote itself to education.) A small group of nuns was formed in 1800 and was sent to take charge of a girls' school in Amiens, and in 1802, though she was only twenty-three, Madeleine Sophie was elected Superior. The order spread rapidly, and in its heyday its schools were to be found all over Europe, the Americas, Australia and Asia, so uniform in their outlook and practice that there was no difficulty in moving from one to another. Its 'old children' are tenacious in their loyalty to the Sacred Heart, but with the gradual disappearance of convent boarding schools presumably even they will eventually be forced to disband, as the Old Contemptibles disbanded when members became too aged and arthritic to parade.

The first Sacred Heart school established in England was at Berrymead, near London, in 1842, when founding members came over from Paris with a handful of children. In 1850 it moved to Roehampton. Here it stayed until World War II, when it was evacuated first to Newquay, then to the midlands, and finally at the end of the war to Woldingham in Surrey, where it is now under lay management. Roehampton, which was badly bombed, has become a training college. A second boarding school was established at Hove in 1877, but closed in the summer of 1966 when the order felt it could no longer cope, in the 'swinging sixties', with the responsibility of looking after girls in such an environment. Tunbridge Wells, founded as a convent in 1915, is now under lay management and has a headmaster, and the only boarding school run by the order left in the United Kingdom is Kilgraston in Perthshire, though there is a comprehensive school in Newcastle which has evolved out of a boarding school closed in 1918.

The French tradition was strong, too, in the Ursulines. The oldest of the teaching orders, founded in North Italy in 1535 by St Angela Merici and established in Paris at the beginning of the next century, the Paris members took a fourth vow, after the habitual ones of poverty, chastity and obedience – that they should teach. (The order is unusual in that it is made up of several different branches with varying observances and ceremonial, loosely bound by the Roman Union of 1900.) By the end of the eighteenth century there were several hundred Ursuline communities in France, all to be swept away by the French Revolution, which drove the nuns into hiding or into refuge with their families. Though some of their schools were fashionable ones for young ladies, such as the one in Paris attended by Charlotte Jerningham two centuries ago, this was not the object of the four nuns, only one of whom could speak English, who came to England in 1851 at the invitation of Cardinal Wiseman, to work among the slum children of East London. It was a time when the Roman Catholic hierarchy had only just been restored; there were 'no popery' graffiti scrawled on every wall; the nuns needed a bodyguard of young men before they could walk to mass; and the windows of the wretched cottage where they lived behind barred doors were frequently broken by stones. The venture was not a great success; two nuns, only one of whom had a few words of English, were trying to teach two hundred children, many of them twelve- to fourteen-year-olds so ignorant of the rudiments of their faith that they could not even make the sign of the cross. As with the invitation to Cornelia Connelly, it is a measure of the desperation felt by Wiseman, recently created Archbishop of Westminster, that he should have thought it appropriate to ask the foreigners to come.

By 1859 there were nine Ursulines in England, some of them English, but by 1861 there was no money and nowhere to live, £400 that had been painfully raised in Belgium having gone on building materials for a grandiose scheme for church, school and convent in Barnet which never rose higher than a few courses of bricks. Sorrowfully the nuns returned to Belgium. But Wiseman had predicted that they would come back, and this they did the following year, establishing themselves in Upton, Forest Gate, on the outskirts of Epping Forest. Their task was easier in this rural area, and they set up an elementary school, and also a high school and a boarding school – a three-tier structure to satisfy the requirements of the highly sensitive Victorian class system that we have met in other church foundations. They prospered and expanded and by the early years of this century, in addition to St Angela's at Upton – which the remarkable Mother Mary Angela Boord as early as 1945 shaped into a five-form voluntary-aided multilateral school, able to provide grammar, technical and modern education long before it was government policy to set up comprehensive schools – they had high schools at Wimbledon, Brentwood and Ilford (which last, founded in 1903, is the only one remaining within the private sector).

In the wake of the anticlerical legislation in France during the opening years of this century and the expulsion of the Ursulines along with many other orders, various small private schools sprang up in England, their precarious financial state worsening as standards of girls' secondary education improved. The convent at Westgate-on-Sea, the only boarding school now left, derived from one that had to leave France at that time. It stemmed from a different branch of the complex Ursuline tree from the one responsible for founding Upton and the high schools in London – from the Congregation of Paris, which concerned itself more with education for the upper classes. It had begun at Boulogne-sur-Mer in 1624, and had educated many English, Scots and Irish girls in the penal days. Dispersed during the French Revolution, the nuns could not re-establish themselves until 1810. By 1842 they were prospering once more and had one hundred boarders and five hundred children in the day school, but in 1904 the French government again made it impossible for them to carry on, and the community with some of its boarders came to Westgate-on-Sea in Kent, where they first rented premises and then managed to buy a large house built by a prosperous solicitor some twenty years before and standing in its own land.

For the first twenty years or more it was still very much a French school. The children were expected to talk French, and ladylike accomplishments such as drawing, music and needlework, as well as the study of French, received much attention. Once a month the whole school assembled in front of the *Maîtresse générale* in the *grand parloir* for the *tableaux d'honneur*. Marks were read out – *très bien*, or *presque bien* – and the one who came top of her form wore a rosette. The costume was also French. Besides the curious genteelism which Sacred Heart children also had to endure, of gloves at all formal occasions such as mark-reading, the pupils wore long black serge dresses with Eton collars and bows, a black sateen overall in class, and black shawls and mittens to combat the cold.[37] Gallic traditions such as these remained in force until 1926 when, with the climate in France becoming more favourable to teaching orders, the French nuns went back, and Westgate was bought by Ursuline nuns from Bideford. Henceforward it was to be an English community; young nuns were sent to Bedford College to study, and the syllabus gradually broadened and was brought more in line with the Ursuline day schools in London, though it did not become a 'recognized school' until 1946. In 1940 it was evacuated to Rush Court, near Wallingford in Berkshire, but, unlike the vast majority of the private schools that in the 1930s clustered in such numbers on the south coast, it returned to its original home, in August 1945.

Something has already been said of the very great difficulties that nuns encountered when they first arrived in England, either driven out of their own countries by anticlerical legislation, or invited over to grapple with the problem of educating the huge new numbers of Catholics. Sometimes wealthy patrons came to the rescue and gave them at least temporary shelter; sometimes the nuns must have regarded those who offered help at best as doubtful blessings. Such was Louisa Catharine, Duchess of Leeds, who swept into the lives of the Holy Child nuns in Sussex and of the Assumptionists in Richmond, Yorkshire. 'Have nothing to do with Lou's orphanage,' said one of her sisters, rousing herself on her deathbed, 'or your hair will turn grey before its time.'[38] The duchess was an American, one of three beautiful sisters who all married into the English aristocracy. Her first husband shot himself at breakfast one morning after remonstrating with her about her frivolity. Her second husband, the seventh Duke of Leeds, esteemed her more highly, and was later to become a Catholic himself (attributing a lucky escape in the hunting field to a holy medal she had given him). She had met the Sisters of the Assumption (a French order founded in 1839) in London in 1849, and had invited them to send members to Yorkshire where she wanted to establish an orphanage for twelve girls to be trained as domestic servants. The orphanage faded away (it was difficult to get the right sort of children) but the poor school and the boarding school, which were started in 1850, grew in spite of the imperious and wayward nature of their patron (the bishop had warned the nuns that the duchess was the laughing stock of the local gentry and totally unreliable, to boot), and in spite of fears that the house she had provided was too remote and the climate too harsh for many to want to send delicate girls there. The school is still there in Swaledale, but passed into lay management in 1988, and is now the Assumption School rather than the Convent of the Assumption.

The Duchess of Leeds was to have an even more decisive effect on the future history of the Holy Child schools, though at the time her impulses must have seemed impractical to the point of madness. She had come to St Leonards to take the sea air, and, profoundly impressed by Cornelia Connelly, had asked if she could become a postulant. She was eventually deflected from this ambition and compromised by becoming a resident at the convent, from which she made the occasional foray to her Yorkshire home to harass the Assumption nuns. She set up two orphanages in the south, one of them under the aegis of the Holy Child, where she was to be a patron both arbitrary and parsimonious. She displayed eccentric notions of housekeeping, ordering a hundredweight of pepper and so much spice that it lasted the community well into the next century, but forgetting the bread, and allowing no more than two packets of sewing needles (each one of which had to be accounted for) for the whole community.

It was she who persuaded the order to send a contingent out to the United States to found a convent on land near Philadelphia which she had instructed her agent to buy for them. The Bishop of Southwark, with some reason, was doubtful about the whole scheme – for one thing, there was the American Civil War to be reckoned with. But five nuns set out, and though they succeeded in establishing a school in spite of appalling privations, their health failed and one of them died. Nevertheless, though it brought much suffering to the nuns, which ironically the duchess in England and even Cornelia Connelly knew nothing of, the project established the order in the United States.

A second dream seemed to have even more of moonshine about it. Mother Connelly had taken the St Leonards children on a Whit Monday picnic to the Old Palace at Mayfield, the picturesque ivy-clad ruins of the ancient palace of the archbishops of Canterbury, with a history stretching back to the tenth century when St Dunstan had built a wooden church there. When the farm that included the ruins came on to the market a few months later, the duchess bought it and presented it to Cornelia Connelly and the Holy Child with the proviso that the ruins must not only be preserved but restored. And as with the Philadelphia project, she succeeded in communicating her dream to others. Not only Cornelia but Wiseman himself was fired with enthusiasm to bring this ancient religious site back into the fold of the True Church, and Edward Pugin, son of A.W.N. and as zealous as his father in the cause of Gothic architecture, was employed to rebuild the ruins.

The fund-raising for this makes fascinating reading. Nuns feel no false shame in begging for an honourable cause, and with the consent and encouragement of Wiseman and even of the very scrupulous Dr Grant, Bishop of Southwark, they went out begging all over England and France, Belgium, Holland, Germany and Spain, even Canada, where they stood in snow to the knees. (All Hallows, Ditchingham, was another convent whose nuns had to resort to begging in the London streets in 1900 and 1901.) There were also raffles and bazaars, with prizes such as a cope valued at £200, 'an exquisitely beautiful Roman Mosaic Brooch, Mounted in Fine Gold, the Gift of His Holiness, Pope Pius IX; a handsome Brougham; a Russian Brocade Silk Dress; An Alderney Cow and Calf; the 14 Stations of the Cross brought from Jerusalem, engraved on Mother-of-Pearl Shells, the gift of the Duchess of Leeds'.[39] Bazaars, however, did not find so much ecclesiastical approval as begging, and Archbishop Manning told Mother Connelly as much, though he did give her the necessary permission.

With money in hand, the first necessity was of course a church, and by 1865 the ancient Synod Hall had become a chapel dedicated to the Sacred Heart, and nuns were teaching children of two Catholic families in the village. Beginning as a junior school, Mayfield expanded to take in seniors, and then in 1953, when it became evident that it was no longer practical to run two separate schools on parallel lines, it amalgamated with St Leonards to become St Leonards-Mayfield, St Leonards being the junior school and Mayfield the senior. The orphanage at Mark Cross about which the duchess's dying sister had uttered her solemn warnings flourished no better than the orphanage she had foisted upon the Assumptionists in Yorkshire. 'They will want to call it Mrs Connelly's orphanage, but they shan't,' the duchess said threateningly to her nurse on her own deathbed, when she was obsessed with the 'conspirators' who surrounded her (including, she felt, the Queen and the Russians).[40] When her will was read it was found that she had left the orphanage only £80, so that fee-paying pupils had to be taken and the nature of the school changed. But it survived – the duchess's projects had an almost supernatural life-force – and now, renamed Combe Bank and since 1972 independent of the order, it occupies a fine early Georgian house and parkland near Sevenoaks.

The Empress Eugenie, exiled in England after the fall of the Second Empire, was more restrained in her patronage of the school that was then called Hillside and was later to become Farnborough Hill. It was established by the Congregation of Christian Education in 1889 (a French order founded by the Abbé Lafosse in Normandy in 1821), who chose the neighbourhood of Aldershot because a school was required there for officers' daughters. The Empress lived at nearby Farnborough Hill, originally built by the publisher Thomas Longman, though as this Victorian mansion was to her eyes a mere cottage she felt obliged to extend it considerably. She took a keen interest in the convent and used to make a practice of attending its speech days, and had indeed contributed prizes herself. The prize-winners, clasping their massive silver trophies, would be crowned by her Imperial Majesty with a heavy wreath of white roses and ferns which would invariably lurch over one eye however firmly their hair had been adjusted to receive it beforehand.[41] There were also occasions on which she invited them back to tea. However, whether she would have approved of the convent acquiring her home for the school in 1927 is another matter; probably not, especially as her own bedroom was to become a middle school dormitory. Much of the imperial decoration remains: the magnificent chandeliers in the dining-room, for instance, and the vast carpet made by prisoners at Agra which runs the whole length of the gallery. (The Mother Superior had felt some scruples as to whether she would infringe the rule of poverty by buying it for £100, but the rector of Beaumont School had told her that even if it only lasted twenty years that would mean a mere £5 a year – hardly an extravagant sum, he thought.)

There are also, of course, Anglican convents. Margaret Nevinson remembered hers with no affection.[42] She was in the 1860s at a school in Oxford for clergy daughters – a school which she does not name but which is identifiable as St Anne's, Rewley House. In everything the Anglo-Catholic regime was more extreme than the Roman Catholic.

> The bell clanged at six, prime was sung at seven, followed by an hour of preparation for chilled and hungry brains, breakfast at eight, bed-making, lessons, matins. A walk, which most of us hated, in long crocodile ... dinner, some games in our high-walled sunless playground, lessons, piano-practice, tea, preparation, bread-and-water supper at eight, compline, bed.

The cold was dreadful, the food bad and insufficient, 'especially in Lent, on vigils and fast days; on Fridays, bread and water and tea was our sole sustenance'. The religious pressure was intense, and involved a secular confession of all misdeeds, great and small, to the sister-in-charge at the end of the week, as well as the formal confession in church, which Margaret Nevinson did not attend, though it was expected of all girls who had been confirmed. But in spite of a system which she disliked and resented, she was moved by the 'great drama of Holy Week [followed by] the mystical joy of Easter morning as we went to six o'clock mass at St Thomas' and, amid the scent of flowers and incense, sang the great hymn "O Filii et Filiae"'.

The first in the Tractarian revival of religious communities was St Dunstan's Abbey in Plymouth, founded by the Society of the Sisters of the Holy Trinity in 1850. The nuns had nursed the sick during a terrible outbreak of cholera in 1849, and had celebrated daily mass in a tent on the site of which the school hall now stands, thereby exciting alarm and hostility among the stout Protestants of Plymouth. The school was transferred to the

Community of St Mary the Virgin, 'the Wantage sisters', in 1907. The CSMV, founded by Canon William John Butler in 1850, had their own schools, of which the first was St Mary's, Wantage, which has a curious history. Many schools have diverged from the original purpose of their founders, and plenty of orphanages and homes for clergy daughters have become public schools, but St Mary's appears to be unique in evolving from a penitentiary for fallen girls. This had been set up by the Community in 1850. It was a project instigated by one of the founding members (who within a few months had left the Church of England for Rome), though Canon Butler himself had wanted the sisters to devote themselves to teaching. In 1854 the foundation stone of new convent buildings was laid, and when these were ready the magdalens were moved to it. A Mrs Dynham was appointed by the vicar to run a ladies' school in the house that the penitentiary had been occupying. The change of use must have deterred many parents, and it was clearly a seedy establishment. One girl who came in 1859 referred to it as 'Do-the-Girls Hall', a ramshackle building which was falling apart and where the girls were kept hungry. In 1872 the sisters resumed their occupation of the house, and opened it in 1873 as St Mary's School with fifteen boarders known as 'young ladies'. There was to be religion, and exams. The *Short Report of the Works under the Charge of the Community*, published in 1874, stated:

> We believe that nothing will be more useful or more acceptable at the present time than a school for girls receiving its religious tone and character from those who desire to work for Christ alone; and at the same time thoroughly well taught. We may mention in connection with this that three of our present girls passed successfully through the Cambridge Examination of Junior Pupils.

These 'carefully selected young ladies' plus some sixty day-girls (the 'middle' school that was a feature of the Woodard and other similar foundations) were all taught in a nearby schoolroom that had once been used as a dissenting chapel. Five classes were held there, and to reduce the noise, classes were taught in turns, only one voice was allowed to be heard, the voice of the teacher, or the pupil answering. The vicar would walk in and listen, and rebuke any girl who looked at him instead of at her teacher. 'If an elephant came into the room,' he used to say, 'you ought not to look up.' Gradually the number of boarders increased, and in 1894 a separate school, S. Katharine's, was set up to take care of the day children – Victorian schools, especially convents, having a deep-rooted suspicion of the effect that less carefully guarded pupils, exposed to the temptations of the outside world and very probably of a less elevated class, might have upon their boarders. In 1938, no doubt because the school was too small to provide satisfactory secondary education, the girls were transferred to S. Helen's School in Abingdon, becoming S. Helen and S. Katharine, a school of high academic standing, housed in splendid Queen Anne style buildings. They wear St Catherine's wheel on their blazers and keep St Catherine's day as one of the principal feast days of the calendar, celebrated with a procession, a Schubert mass performed by the chapel choir and the orchestra, and a chocolate biscuit handed out to each girl. 'We're the brains,' say the H. and K. girls, 'they [St Mary's] are the double-barrelled names.'

The regime of St Mary's, Wantage, was strenuous in the early days. A girl who came in 1874 said:

> We were expected to be down to Prime at 6.45, and if we were late getting up we were sent to bed early and supperless. Sext was said before dinner, and compline before going to bed; besides this we went every night to evensong at the church. When attendance at these services was given up I remember well the rhyme we chanted joyfully under our breath
>
> No more Sext and no more Prime
> No more Compline to waste our time.
>
> But there was still plenty for us to do. I well remember listening to eleven sermons (and long ones at that) in a fortnight. Canon Butler, then Vicar of Wantage, was very particular about the attention his congregation gave to his sermons, and he always expected to be looked at while he was preaching. Once when we girls seemed to him to have been inattentive he then and there called the Sister-in-charge to the pulpit and said 'I will not preach to the tops of heads.'[43]

Like other convents, for a long time it was not a school that took a very serious view of academic studies, or of preparing its pupils for professions. But no school in the 1990s, however strong its affection for the traditions of its past, can afford to neglect such matters, and like the rest St Mary's, Wantage, now has its careers room and careers adviser. There is less compulsory chapel. Up to 1967 every girl had to go twice daily; now there is a short morning assembly in chapel, a voluntary mass during the week, and a sung mass on Sundays. The community handed the school over to lay management in 1975.

In the late 1960s, in the wake of Vatican II, came a new freedom for Roman Catholic religious orders not only to reconsider their form of service, but to move outside their communities. At first their pupils noticed only the details: that the younger nuns were discarding their habits and appearing, often disconcertingly shabby, with cropped hair and in cheap lay clothes; that those who taught them English were now able to accompany them to the theatre. (One redoubtable Sacred Heart headmistress borrowed a wig from the school acting box to go to see *Hair* with her sixth form, and was only recognized by one of her former pupils by her voice.) But soon it became evident that there would be fundamental changes. Many communities questioned whether they should be involved in providing private education, and the direct-grant schools nearly all decided to join the maintained comprehensive rather than the independent sector, when government support was withdrawn in the late 1970s. Many also recognized that the old-style convent turned out 'dangerously innocent and naive people into the world',[44] and that girls must be prepared for professional careers and encouraged to serve the world outside rather than devoting themselves exclusively to religious practice within the convent walls. There was also the problem of rapidly diminishing numbers of nuns (from 889 teaching in private schools in 1977, they have now dropped by a half), and fewer still who wished to dedicate themselves to the privileged classes. Thus at St Mary's, Ascot, where in 1955 there was a community of sixty strong, now there are twenty nuns, only six of whom are active in the school. Most erstwhile convents are under lay management; all have a largely lay staff. And all, however guileless they were about accounting in the past, now charge economic fees and make proper provision for pensions and endowments. Convent schools are now as businesslike as their lay contemporaries, and the education they give their pupils is no different from any other school's.

8

Boarding School Life

'I have boarded since I was eight,' writes an eighteen-year-old in her last school term, 'and to many parents it will seem inconceivable to send a girl away so early. A friend of mine went home for an exeat not long ago, and at the end her younger sister presented her with the visitor's book to sign.'[1]

> I don't like being away from home, and I don't like having to get up at 7 o'clock and strip my bed and air it and then make it neatly . . . Work starts at 9 o'clock and there are eight lessons a day. The main subjects are boring and it is difficult to get from place to place because the school's so big. They expect you to know when to hand your work in and if you forget you get told off . . . Some of the older girls are nice and some are horrible.[2]

(This eleven-year-old's impressions of boarding school life had to be dictated to her mother because she was suffering such agonies of homesickness, even in the holidays.) Very few indeed appear to think that they gained a superior academic education by being sent away from home; some value the friendship, beautiful surroundings; more reckon that it taught them qualities like endurance, tolerance, ability to eat any food however unpalatable, or small talents such as darning. 'How to do "hospital corners" when I made my bed was, in addition to darning, one of the more useful legacies of my time at Westonbirt,' says one girl of her 1950s schooldays.[3]

The numbers of those who are dispatched to boarding school at the age of eight to spend ten years away from home are declining. What used fifty years ago to be an automatic procedure in many families is now financially possible for far fewer, and many are questioning whether it is worth spending £7,000 a year for a child to be homesick and learn to strip a bed and do hospital corners if the other subjects in the curriculum can be taught nearer home. 'My mother had a strong and not altogether unjustified feeling that daughters growing up in the home were liable to quarrel with their mothers,' wrote Margaret Cole to account for why she had been dispatched to Roedean. Dorothea Beale put it less bluntly, saying that anxious mothers who suffered from their children's faults of temper and disposition were tempted to give up the training into other hands. Sometimes this was unavoidable; 'but how frequently, without necessity, is the burden of parental responsibility temporarily cast aside, only to press with tenfold weight in later years.'[4] Edward Thring in a paper written at an early stage of his teaching career pointed out that the upper-class Englishman traditionally sent his children from home to be educated by strangers. Lessons and skilled teaching could easily be provided, as they were in other European countries, without sending them away. But England preferred boarding schools, the reason being not the teaching but the training.[5]

But this belief in the virtues implanted by exposure to boarding school life is departing. Good exam results and a place at a university are the top priorities for late twentieth-century professional parents, and these can be achieved at a day school, or perhaps with two years in a sixth form as a boarder. Increasingly pupils come from families domiciled abroad; from parents who are divorced, perhaps remarried, and who find it difficult to provide a proper home life; or from the elite in the Third World who still have a touching belief in the English system of education. Headmistresses lament how 'the nice, ordinary girls' have been crowded out, but one doubts whether even if the fees were within their parents' reach they would now choose to send their daughters away. Boarding school for the upper-class boy has been traditional for centuries; with girls it was always less general, and their public school life, as has been seen, only began in the 1870s. While many middle-class parents believe strongly in single-sex schools and the virtues of the independent system, they are less sure about sending girls away from home. And many of those who staff boarding schools have their doubts about the system – 'Don't the parents realize what girls are *like*?' said one housemistress, referring to the gossip, the bitching and the smut which passes for conversation among younger girls. Others have spoken of the unnatural system of condemning children to the undiluted society of their peers, and the effect of adolescent subculture upon the personality. 'Mamma did not know what school was like when she sent me here; it makes me a great deal worse than I was before,' says a child in Elizabeth Sewell's *Laneton Parsonage* (1844). (Miss Sewell had suffered at boarding school and herself ran one, and understood the moral perils.) Charlotte Yonge came to the same conclusion: 'It is a curious thing, but of universal experience, that while most boys are improved by free intercourse with their own kind in large numbers – generally the larger the better – girls as certainly deteriorate in proportion as the sense of family life is lost.'[6]

Uniformity and regimentation are inevitable in an institution, and, as Miss Yonge had properly noted, girls take to it less easily than boys. Orphanages and workhouses knew their children by numbers; so did many large schools, who insisted, for instance, that one's number was marked in nails on one's shoes. It makes administrative sense, but it symbolizes negation of individuality and is often resented. 'From the first time we were given our Westonbirt name tapes, which had to include our house number,

I had the sense that my personality was lost,' writes a girl who had been very happy at her previous school, a convent, where she felt there was considerable respect for the pupils as individuals.

> Even the language private to the pupils was imposed from above and I learned it on the train journey from Cardiff, repeating it dutifully ... The Prefects were called the Parlour, as that was the room sacred to them. The large square in front of the main entrance was called Piccadilly. You didn't have a crush on someone, you were 'pipped' on her. Even that intimate feeling was pre-arranged and organized. When, that bewildered first evening, I was asked who I was going to be 'pipped' on and was nonplussed, but mentioned, hopefully, the splendid tall figure of Imogen, our just-glimpsed Head of House, I was told brusquely by my mentors that too many people had her already; I was to have Ann, the lacrosse captain in the Fifth. She was greasy-haired, insensitive and hearty and I was an unco-ordinated non-starter at any team game. A worse match could not have been chosen yet I quickly and anxiously conformed, learning to blush and giggle whenever she approached.[7]

Undoubtedly there was once a glamour and excitement about new public schools, for a generation brought up by governesses or in old-fashioned seminaries. Winifred Peck, a natural tomboy, was delighted to be freed from the constraints of young ladydom and to be sent to Wycombe Abbey. Angela Brazil, too, thought she would have liked that sort of life:

> When I go to see modern girls' schools, and know what jolly times they have with games and acting, I feel I have missed a very great deal. If we had had prefects, and had ever been taught the elements of citizenship and social service, and that our school was a world in miniature where we might help each other, it would, I think, have brought in a totally different element.[8]

She made up for it by evoking these jolly times in forty-nine novels of schoolgirl life, which, along with contemporaries' efforts in the same vein, must have done a lot in the 1920s and 30s to make boarding schools very desirable to eleven- and twelve-year-olds. In that era immaturity was prolonged to seventeen or eighteen, and, segregated from the opposite sex, girls appeared to enjoy to an advanced age strenuous group activities and fierce loyalties to the institution in which they found themselves and to their own particular age group. All this features in the school stories of the period, for which the early twentieth-century girl had an apparently inexhaustible craving. These were, however, abhorrent to headmistresses, and Angela Brazil, particularly, came under an almost universal ban.

> [Miss Gray] told us, with fire in her voice, that one of her prefects had been given an Angela Brazil as a Christmas present from her godmother ...

> The said prefect then took a pair of tongs and put the book on the kitchen stove! This Miss Gray held up to us as a wholly admirable action, displaying proper horror of such unhealthy literature.[9]

This was St Paul's. But not all Paulinas were thus right-minded, and on the first day of the autumn term of 1936 Miss Gray's successor, Miss Strudwick, told the assembled school that she would like to have a public burning of all the works of Angela Brazil. At about the same time Mrs Elliot-Pyle at Dunottar was forbidding girls to read them, thereby sending many, who had not heard of her before, to investigate this apparently subversive author. It is difficult now to see why authority should have been so united against Miss Brazil's works, which are strikingly moral and upright and promulgate the *esprit de corps* which was such a feature of the public school system and which she yearningly felt had been lacking in her own school life. Though they are full of highly coloured slang, the element of romantic friendship is less febrile than, say, in the works of Elsie J. Oxenham and L.T. Meade.

Nor does the Brazil type of ideal schoolgirl differ much from what the schools of the period hoped to turn out. The fictitious heroine is fearless and truthful and looks you straight in the eye. She may break rules – school chroniclers of many real-life headmistresses say firmly that they had a weakness for the naughty children – but she always owns up and never lets anyone else take the blame: 'Retta Garnett was tall for her fourteen years, well made and healthy from much outdoor exercise . . . This big pretty girl with her tanned cheeks and bright fearless eyes, which gazed at strangers frankly as a boy's . . .'[10] This is very near the ideal type described in an autobiographical novel based on Downe House. (There is the added element of the donnish, literary background which was a distinguishing mark of early Downe clientele.)

> And here was Harriet, Head Keeper, new to the job, the third of five Shields children and having so many relations at Dames that she can remember going to Founder's Birthday every year since she was three . . . Her father was the Master of an Oxford College, they had a cottage in the Lakes. Her great-grandmother bought the cottage and knew Wordsworth, Coleridge and Dorothy. (Her mother knew Virginia Woolf.) . . . Harriet, straight-nosed and clear of eye, and clean, no doubt, of conscience, having had a super time these holidays and romped in friendly fashion with her brothers and cousins in the tarns of Westmorland. On the wet days they played intellectual games, and cricket in bright periods.[11]

Lack of sophistication in those days, immediately post-war, was still held to be an advantage; it set the privileged middle-class girl apart from teen-agers forced by circumstances to earn their living. One working-class girl sent with a scholarship to Wycombe Abbey in the 1950s thought when she came home that her sisters' teenage fashions looked flashy and cheap; she stuck to jeans and the demure dresses approved by school authority.[12] 'There was nothing wrong in powdering faces, it was quite true,' a school story had said some twenty years earlier, 'but they'd always despised people who did it, just as they'd always despised people who couldn't play games, and people who wore queer clothes. It was – oh, fussy and finicky and affected, to powder your face.'[13] 'Many of the present generation are to be pitied,' said a Paulina writing in 1975. 'They seem to have missed a whole section of life, being adolescents at twelve and having adult preoccupations at fifteen or younger. We had no use for the occasional girl whose mind was on fashions, jewellery and boys.'[14] Even eighteen-year-olds were given very little in the way of adult privilege. Bedford High School in the 1950s thought that it was being unusually liberal when it announced in the school history that prefects now had new freedom: 'they may go to the cinema if they wish (a privilege which they use with discretion) and they make their own coffee in the cookery room in break. Once a week a prefect reads the lesson [at prayers].'

The new teenage development of a sense of identity with adolescents everywhere was curiously delayed. It did not follow a war, like the 1920s cult of youth; indeed, the 1950s showed unexpected continuity with the 1930s. Though the great majority of schools had suffered disruption during the war, and had been evacuated, dispersed or made to share their premises, any informality that this had induced disappeared after conditions had returned to normal, so that Roedean, for instance, went back to its rigid segregation of girls into houses.

Writing of boys' schools, John Rae spoke of the tight framework of compulsion that remained in the early 1960s:

> It was still the norm that a boy had to attend chapel every day and twice on Sunday; play the major sport whether he liked it or not; join the Combined Cadet force; and wear a school uniform, every item of which was prescribed in the school rules. He was probably compelled to attend the play and the school concert. His movements were strictly controlled by bounds and bells. Fagging and corporal punishment were common practice; in many schools the prefects had the power to beat other boys. A hierarchy of prefects or monitors kept the machinery of compulsion running and in return enjoyed privileges that allowed them to escape the more disagreeable aspects of the machine themselves. For all pupils, whatever their position in the hierarchy, the secret of success – and survival – was to conform.[15]

Remove the fagging and the corporal punishment, and the situation was precisely the same in the girls' schools, and in boarding schools has still probably not changed so very much. If you go into a sixth form from outside you will no doubt have to play hockey or lacrosse or whatever the statutory team game is, regardless of whether you know the rules or not.

('Even if you are off swimming you must report at the swimming baths,' says one current set of senior house regulations, having reminded girls that games and swimming are as much a part of the school curriculum as lessons.) The bells, the bounds, the compulsion and the uniform are still there (relaxed for sixth-formers), although prefects no longer wield so much authority; it is in any case an office which some schools have abolished or handed over to the lower sixth in order to allow their seniors to devote all their time to their studies in the A-level year.

Very few school histories record the 'teenage revolution' of the later 60s – an active hostility to the adult world and authority, a desire to be identified with other young people regardless of class. Perhaps, anyway, it was less marked in girls' schools than it was with boys, though the new informality between teachers and the taught, the greater freedoms (including links with home), the slackening of compulsory chapel, can all be said to date from that epoch when there was a general revulsion against uniforms, conformity, tight discipline and restrictions that were increasingly out of step with the life lived at home. With some the revolt was genuine idealism – conformity seemed a mark of a privileged class; marks and prizes favoured an elite and were out of place in a free and caring society – but most of the rebellious teenagers wanted an easier, more comfortable life. It was the era of the Beatles, of mini-skirts and long hair for both sexes (opposed passionately by parents, schoolmasters and schoolmistresses, who saw it as the chief symbol of defiance); of desert boots and the 'young student' image, when commercial interests were able to tap a wholly new market, the teenager, and girls who had hitherto relied on their parents supplying them with pocket money looked around for ways of earning the records, the clothes and the independent travel abroad that they now wanted.

It was at day schools where all this was most evident, though boarding schools, too, noticed a falling off in *esprit de corps*. 'To be a prefect,' wrote one headmistress with some bitterness, 'was for some boarders no longer an honour, it was an unwarranted imposition: "I'm here to get good A levels, not to supervise Upper Fourth's prep."' Many day girls, she added, 'were more concerned to keep their Saturday morning jobs in the supermarket than to be chosen to play in the first hockey eleven'.[16] But much as headmistresses might regret it, school no longer came first in adolescent loyalties. A fifth-former writing in 1987 of the current teenage scene says: 'It seems that affiliation to a movement is part of growing up. During the transition period of the teenage years, the person is finding his feet in society, becoming more independent, and growing apart from his family. For many people, however, a substitute family is needed at this stage.' She divided the adolescent population into punks, casuals, psychobilly [sic], mods and Sloanes, of which she clearly considered the first to be the most satisfyingly original and the last – 'they are notorious for having coming-out balls and behaving badly . . . Diana, Princess of Wales, is the ultimate

Sloane' – the most dreary. 'Therefore it can be seen that as well as the psychological need to belong to something, one of the main reasons why young people become numbers of a unit is as an act of rebellion.'[17] A contemporary pointed out that 'the horror-face oldies' who looked askance at punks with Mohican haircuts had probably been Teddy Boys or rockers or flower-power hippies in their time; her own grandmother had been a flapper in the twenties and her mother 'was into Trad-Jazz. She wore yah-yah skirts and had her hair in a bee-hive.'[18]

Fashions may have changed, but the uniform effect that boarding school produces has not. 'Everybody seems the same,' said one sixth-former going to a new school as a boarder for the first time; the schools which admire eccentricity and individuality – as Downe did fifty years ago – are rare indeed. One anonymous headmistress spoke of

> this community influence, strong in all schools, but most particularly so in boarding schools [which] may well destroy individuality. The girls have all the time to live up to a certain standard and dare not often be completely natural. Even at home the boarding school girl does not always feel at home; she is a holiday visitor, politely adapting herself to interests not really hers, while of all the absorbing interests of her school life – which is really her life – she dare not speak too much.[19]

Another teacher spoke of watching newcomers lose their individuality and change into indistinguishable members of a mob.[20] Mallory Wober quoted a thirteen-year-old's recipe for success as a new girl: 'Have good taste in clothes and be fun; be exciting with lots of new ideas . . . *hate* games and *love* pop music. One must not be *too* hygienic. Must wear hair loose and not with a hairband . . . don't be horse mad, hearty, too bumpseous; don't take notice of the clothes list . . . do know the facts of life.' Fit this stereotype, and your initiation as a new girl will be easier.

Wober found that the youngest girls were the happiest, that the novelty of community life soon wore off, and that a nadir was reached by the age of fifteen. But this does not take into account the terrible homesickness that afflicts many at the start. 'I don't think I did much practising,' wrote one girl who used to shut herself into a piano cubicle, too wretched even to cry, and frightened, besides, that there might be awkward questions about red eyes. She used to pray: 'Oh God, take me away from this prison-house, don't let me stay here any longer; what have I done for such a punishment? Was it for throwing away my medicine? If so, I will go home and tell them. Only let me go home; how can I bear it till Christmas? Let something happen.'[21]

But bed is the obvious place to cry

> My most vivid memories are of crying quietly by myself, till my head throbbed and my lips burned; of a pillow soaked with tears and the

> shivering fit that would follow. Of the sullen inexpressive wretchedness next day. They do grave wrong to children who underrate their power of suffering and the effect upon them. The griefs of grown people are as nothing to those of a child, who cannot see beyond them, and who has not yet the strength to control them.[22]

This eloquent account was written sixty years after the event by Helena Swanwick, who had been sent to a French boarding school in 1874. 'If you can get through your first month at Rickmansworth,' an old schoolfriend told another at a crisis in her life, 'you can walk this one!' A surprising number have confessed that they tried to run away, but since they were inevitably wearing school uniform and did not know anything about the locality outside the school gates they were rapidly returned.

> I arrived at the station and asked the stationmaster how far I could go for one shilling and sevenpence. He was a kindly man and took me to his railway cottage where his wife made me bacon and egg. The Matron and another teacher arrived and I wasn't allowed to finish the meal but promptly went back to school. I was locked by myself in the sick room. I contemplated the fire escape, but the idea was rather frightening. My parents came, and my mother, with myself present talked to [the headmistress]. She asked me what I wanted to do ... I was really torn between duty – knowing how my mother had gone round all the relations collecting clothing coupons, and the money spent sending me there. My parents said I could have a dog if I stayed, so I stayed. Never got the dog as we only had a backyard. However if it taught me one thing in life it was to stick a thing out and hang on.[23]

The worst moment of all for this writer seems to have been when she was summoned by her housemistress (who was one of her main causes of misery) and asked why she had run away. Inevitably she answered, 'I don't know.' 'One other girl copied me the following year and was expelled. Pour encourager les autres.'

Experience of boarding at a prep school can help a little with homesickness but, informal, relaxed and happy, they are very different places from a large public school. 'All good things must come to an end,' said one pupil sadly leaving Butterstone House (which she said bore the closest resemblance to Enid Blyton's Malory Towers that any school possibly could). Her next school was St Mary's, Ascot: 'It was terrifying driving up to the front door to see half the school hanging out of upstairs windows to watch the new girls arrive.'[24] Some large schools have a junior house in which the new intake spend their first year, but this has the disadvantage of isolating the homesick from those who have settled down, and one teacher has referred to the difficulties of teaching children who are 'shell-shocked with misery'. Most schools allot a new girl a guardian or housemother (St Anne's,

Windermere, calls them 'shadows') – an older girl who will take charge in the first few weeks.

> My 'minder' thought me tedious and stupid from the word go – and I suspect she was right. Accustomed to boarding school life from the age of 8, she dragged me (usually long-faced and not infrequently snivelling) from House to meals, to class, to games – twitching with impatience while I – the perpetual slow-change artiste – lagged in the pavilion or the swimming pool.[25]

Even for a day-girl the hustle of a large community is at first overpowering: 'the clanging of bells and the roar of voices; the rush and scurry; the insistence on punctuality. I had nightmares in which I seemed to hurry, breathlessly, along unending corridors and up and down stone staircases, fearing always to be late.'[26] Many remember 'the anxiety caused by a six day race against time', and few are so imperturbable that they have not experienced some sort of angst during their school career. For some it was the horror of being called upon to recite a text, as at the Mount; for others it was dreaded food that they were made to eat up. One terrified child at Walthamstow Hall in the last century cut up her best dress and tried to dispose of it piece by piece because she suddenly realized she had forgotten to hand it over to her housemistress at the beginning of term, as ordered. If a whole school was new together, there were different problems. At Bedgebury Park in January 1920 five girls assembled for the beginning of the first term. 'That first meal was terrible, everyone was extremely nervous, not knowing what to talk about or how much to eat.' There was 'a regular bombardment of questions, the ones that are asked when there is nothing else to say, such as "Have you been to school before?" "How old are you?" "Do you play hockey?"'[27] At the school that was to become Benenden twenty-four girls assembled for the first supper and everyone was too shy to speak, except to ask for the salt in inaudible whispers.

Once over the first miseries of homesickness, the newcomer has to contend with the lack of solitude. 'Solitude was an eccentricity the school was at pains to discourage,' wrote one girl of Wycombe Abbey, but she could have written it of any other boarding school. Even a cubicle can help, but these are rare. One girl at Walthamstow Hall just after the First War remembered hers with gratitude:

> Those wooden partitions that gave you your own sanctum did not at the same time cut you off too completely from the sense of neighbourliness; there could always be a friendly tap, or even a whisper through a chink . . . They may not have been the most artistic of backgrounds, but they sustained adequately all one's earliest attempts at decoration – from *Dignity and Impudence* to *Faithful unto Death*, and one's first bookshelves. It was a wise and refreshing plan that we could spend the whole of

> Sunday afternoon alone, each in her own cubicle, or perhaps with a sister, doing quite quietly whatever we pleased. Here, and in other ways too, we escaped from what can be the tyranny of boarding-school life.[28]

The high degree of organization is also hard to get used to. There is rarely more than half an hour daily that is not accounted for on a timetable – sometimes not even that; and it is a very unusual school where a pupil can find a place to be alone. 'Our days were organized to the last five minutes – rising bell, prayer bell, first and second gongs, breakfast, bed-making, cleaning, formrooms, prayers . . . The days all continued at the same speed . . . there was simply no time for idleness and no room for choice.'[29] The routine at Wycombe Abbey in the 1950s ran like this:

> 7.00 a.m.: rise from bed in an open dormitory shared with five or six other girls; 7.30: breakfast, followed by bedmaking; 8.30: early morning lacrosse practice or running round the lake; 9.00: chapel; 9.20: three periods of lessons or prep; 11.20: break for buns and milk; 11.40: two periods of lessons or prep; 1.00: lunch; 1.40 approximately: a house meeting in which each of thirty-six girls had to inform the housemistress of her activities for the afternoon, and other house business was discussed; 2.00: lacrosse (tennis, cricket, running) or, if the weather was bad, country dancing, or, with luck, a shampoo; 3.20: wash and change into non-uniform clothes; 3.45: tea; 4.00: four periods of lessons or prep; 6.40: house prayers; 7.00: supper: 8.00 or 8.30 depending on age: half an hour to be spent in chitchat with the housemistress in her room; 8.30 or 9.00: bathtime followed by bedtime.[30]

The writer also mentioned the intimidating system of house order, to be found in other schools of this sort, where all the girls in the house were graded from one to thirty-six, the criterion being the individual's worth to the community – and, in practice, how well she got on with her housemistress. Sheila MacLeod had come to the school from a working-class background under the post-war 'guinea-pig' scheme whereby local authorities paid the public school fees of suitable bright children. The grant covered the fees only, and her parents failed to supply her even with the basic necessities such as toothpaste and stockings, so that although she appreciated the teaching and the companionship, her early years at the school were 'a mixture of deception and humiliation' as she struggled to be like other girls.

There are many literary and autobiographical accounts of despairing efforts to be accepted in such an environment. Elizabeth Bowen has a short story which ends in suicide.[31] Two girls, both ugly and 'queer-looking', form an alliance against the hostility which their companions feel for them. 'There were about eighteen other girls, but none of them liked us. We used to feel we had some disease – so much so, that we were sometimes ashamed to meet each other.' But when one is gradually accepted, the other is left to endure total isolation: 'It was as though everything I had got free of had fallen on her, too: she was left with my wretchedness. When I was with the others I used to see her, always alone, watching me . . . I was so frightened of being lost again; I said terrible things to her. I wished she was dead. You see, there seemed to be no other world outside the school.'

In real life Margaret Cole's misery at Roedean was wholly unexpected. She had always got on well with her contemporaries before, and was to do so again when she reached Cambridge. Forty years later when she was describing her unpopularity, she was still at a loss to account for it; perhaps she was unintentionally uppish, spoke before she was spoken to, or, unbidden, asked for a part in the house play. Whatever it was, she was made to feel she was an outcast, and described the horror of being in a residential community with no privacy

> where you can never, for thirteen long weeks at a time, get away from seeing your own personality mirrored in the eyes of others – or watching them move away from the vision in repulsion. To have no one – no one at all – who wants to speak to you, to giggle with you, or to be seen alive or dead with you; to find any group to which you try unobtrusively to attach yourself melting mysteriously away, leaving you in naked and patent quarantine; to hear voices saying 'Margaret Postgate? No, thank you; not with a barge-pole!'; to dread the weekends, when you had ironic liberty to sit where you liked and next to whom you liked, and to pray for Monday morning, when at least you had your desk, a place assigned to you by authority, and could not be roughly or politely asked to move out and make room for some more desirable Dorothy or Nellie or Sybil – all this is enough to make a pretty average hell for a poor dog who only asks to be liked.[32]

Then there is the tyranny of games. The organized team games introduced by the pioneer public schools in the last century rapidly lost their spontaneity, and instead of recreation became part of the timetable (an unwelcome part for many). 'For the ungifted,' wrote one who had endured long hours of lacrosse at St Swithun's, 'it was a cold and dreary ordeal. Cricket games were less traumatic, and at least it was usually warm; but being stuck sometimes at the far end of a practice net, with ferocious women launching fast balls at one could be an alarming experience.' Another at the school spoke of the compulsory house games practice, and going into school with stinging hands after 'enormous beefy girls had been hurling or bouncing cricket balls at junior girls grouped around them. It was no use trying to avoid the pain by deliberately missing the ball; they went on firing at you until you had stopped enough balls to satisfy them.' In one particularly sporting house the members were made to learn the fixture list by heart.[33] Katharine Whitehorn complained that schools such as Roedean were far too slavish in their imitation of boys' public schools: 'Girls have to flog round the lacrosse field working off a whole lot of physical urges which they do not in fact have – even at a time of the month when they *do* have an urge to crawl away into a quiet corner.'[34] (Roedean was specially tough, however; other schools had a record kept by Matron and one was 'off games' at monthly intervals, or less: 'I think Queen Ethelburga's had the most irregular periods in the north of England.')

One sees the advantage of compulsory team games for boarding schools; it is the easiest and most economical way of getting lazy teenagers into the open air, and of knowing where everyone is. Schools like Cobham Hall which go in more for individual sports, or like Bedgebury where you can bring your own pony, have correspondingly higher fees. Compulsory games every afternoon is still an almost universal feature of boarding school life, though sometimes sixth-formers have some latitude, and it may be possible to arrange one's music practice to cover a certain amount of the time when one is supposed to be pounding up and down muddy fields. It is often obligatory to watch matches. 'Last weekend a girl in my house handed in a red ticket, the worst form of conduct mark. "What did you get this for?" I asked her in my best stern voice. "I went to Sunninghill before going to watch the match" came the answer.'[35]

To be plunged into institutional life straight from home is traumatic for the toughest – the bells, the hubbub, the press of people, the inexorably timetabled day are all exhausting in themselves. There is no one to help you with your homework or your practising. Many remember the awe-inspiring size of the buildings, the crowds always around you, the difficulty of getting to sleep in uncurtained dormitories. Mealtimes seem like a battlefield for eleven-year-olds faced with a cafeteria system, impatient queues and older girls who shoulder one out of the way. Even when one adjusts to the school day there is the blankness of the weekend spent entirely in the company of one's age group. 'Hearth is missing here,' reflects one of the characters in *Dames*, a fictional account of Downe House, surveying her contemporaries cooped up in their form room on a Saturday afternoon 'with nothing much ahead except the supper which was always sausages on Saturday and afterwards a lecture by a man on (big deal) planting trees in the Sahara'.[36] Twenty-five years ago hearth was missing for thirteen weeks in each term. Whereas now a five-day break at half-term is standard, and parents may take children home for some weekends (some schools have unlimited exeats), in those days even half-term holidays were usually lacking in the Easter term, and some schools, Felixstowe College for example, did not allow girls to sleep at home at all during the term. In fairness, one must suppose they were afraid of infection, but the attitude of schools towards parental contact with children even twenty years ago is reminiscent of the charity hospitals of the last century:

> On the very rare exeat days, girls could be taken out by parents from two o'clock until seven o'clock on Saturdays, or after Mattins on Sundays until the time of the Evening Service. With so little time to spare, it was

> not posssible for girls to go home so an exeat usually meant being taken by one's parents to the Felix Hotel ... In those days the Felix was a very grand railway hotel, full of potted palms and prim elderly ladies, with a string ensemble, dainty triangular sandwiches and little iced cakes ... Dinner was taboo because it was after exeat hours.[37]

Much of Sunday was then spent in compulsory worship, as described in Chapter 6. Saturday was given over to prep, letter-writing, games and mending (the darning of woollen and lisle stockings could absorb a lot of time).

But middle-class adolescents then were used to structured routine and a fairly spartan home life, and were less irked by school conditions than they tend to be now. 'With so many restrictions and so little liberty, it might be expected that the girls were unhappy,' said the Felixstowe historian of the 1930s regime, adding that this did not seem to have been the case and that most girls remembered the life as pleasant. Weekends were certainly much easier to organize when the sort of programme cited above was standard, and when it was accepted that girls were cloistered for a whole term on end with very little contact with the outside world. Weekends now present girls' schools with problems. At boys' public schools staff live on the premises and run extra-curricular activities with enthusiasm. Very few married teachers live on the premises at girls' schools, and boredom at weekends comes high among girls' grumbles. They want neither to be compelled to take part in group activities, nor to loaf around in a form room with everyone else, and they resent the necessary restrictions on their movements. They would like the sort of wide-ranging choice that is clearly impossible in a small school, plus the liberty to come and go as they please that they have at home. Girls who go to boys' public school sixth forms seem more satisfied, and Christ's Hospital girls, newly absorbed into the boys' school at Horsham with its huge campus, remembering their cloistered, limited life at Hertford, speak ecstatically of all the opportunities they now find. Schools that are remote have the greatest problems of all. Shopping is a great pastime, but to do this on a Saturday afternoon it is often necessary to send out pupils in fleets of taxis. Westonbirt, near nowhere at all (one headmistress who later went to Cheltenham admitted to being much oppressed by the isolation), is the hardest-hit and has to take the girls some thirty miles to Bath or Bristol.

But most children are amazingly resilient and adaptable, and settle down.

> You learned to survive, to have your own circle of friends, and as you moved up the school life was better: small bedrooms for three or four in the Lower Sixth, cubicles in the Upper and even studies. By then the authorities had decided that for those who didn't see the importance of House Spirit and School Spirit it was too late to keep exerting power.[38]

And there are compensations. Like sundials, school histories tend to record only the sunny hours, but such recollections seem genuine enough. In the lives of most adolescents there are, for all the periods of gloom and boredom and angst, moments of great happiness, often associated with beautiful surroundings and with empathy between individuals.

> On winter nights Prid and I used to walk round the playground [of St Leonards] together . . . We loved the cool, dark playground; the grass under our feet, as, wrapped in our long hooded cloaks, we strolled round the cricket field; the great stretches of empty space spreading out round us up to the old encircling abbey walls, which we could just see here and there looming up in the darkness. We loved the fresh air blowing in clean and salt and tangy from the North Sea . . . But above all we were enabled, evening by evening, to engage on a discussion of the whole world.[39]

Sometimes it is the excitement of discovery, playing *Don Giovanni* on a wind-up gramophone behind the gym, first encounters with Jane Austen or Dostoevsky, trying to teach yourself heraldry. The summer is by far the happiest term, as Mallory Wober discovered. In the winter, cooped up indoors, resentments and friction rise to the surface; in the summer, lessons are often outdoors (some schools, when the world was a safer place, even allowed pupils to sleep outside), and one does not feel so jostled by one's fellows.

Above all, there is companionship. In the early days when girls were so often mewed up at home it was exhilarating to be allowed to mix with contemporaries. Elizabeth Sturge, who was sent to a Quaker boarding school in the 1860s, did not find the teaching very stimulating, but said of her sister who was educated at home: 'I think she suffered from the want of that intimate association with companions of her own age which is one of the advantages of boarding school life.'[40] Sometimes the proximity of so many contemporaries, irksome at other times, can be headily exciting.

> Sunset on hills across the valley in the afternoons of autumn terms . . . You came in fresh and hot, or sometimes very cold, and washed and changed and brushed your hair, had tea and wandered down into your form rooms for the later lessons of the day. The steps, the cloisters, past the chapel door, the practice cells, the lower steps, the library, steps echoing up to a high glass roof, and voices too as you walked with friends.[41]

Boarding school solidarity is considerable. 'They're close, girls are; they'd call it loyal,' said a housemistress bitterly, referring to the cover-up job that the young invariably do for each other: the rubbish left lying around of which no one claims knowledge, the absentees about whose movements friends are totally ignorant. Cooped up together for thirty-six weeks of the year, even relatively incompatible elements grow together to present a

19. The days before school uniform: Winchester High School (now St Swithun's) VI form, 1897. The blouses and tight belts emphasised female curves and made girls look very much more mature than when they were clothed in form-concealing gym tunics.

20. St Mary's Hall tennis team, 1920s, the sexless ideal familiar from the schoolgirl stories so popular between the wars.

21. Middle school pupils at the Sacred Heart, Roehampton, in the 1890s. Convents had uniform long before this became general at secular schools. The children's medals signify that they are members of the Angels Congregation; the centre three wear the ribbons awarded for specially good behaviour.

22. The cricket team at St Leonards, 1891. Sports clothes were for most schools the earliest uniform.

23. The high noon of uniform, Moreton Hall juniors, 1950s. Notice the hats all worn at a prescribed angle; the standard length of coat; the gloves, ankle socks, and 'Cromwell' shoes peculiar to Moreton.

24. The casual look of the 1980s. Three Oxford High School juniors model alternative styles of uniform, which can include - unusually - corduroy trousers.

25. Roedean, wearing the djibbahs devised for the school by Penelope Lawrence, march to salute the flag on Empire Day. This annual ceremony, which was followed by a picnic, was a tradition which lasted until the 1960s, and seems to have been the equivalent of the Ascension Day outings at other schools.

26. Olive Willis in 1915 with Downe House seniors wearing the djibbahs she had adopted in imitation of Roedean (though in other respects the schools were poles apart). Note the dog, one of the many ill-behaved animals to which she, like other headmistresses, was peculiarly addicted.

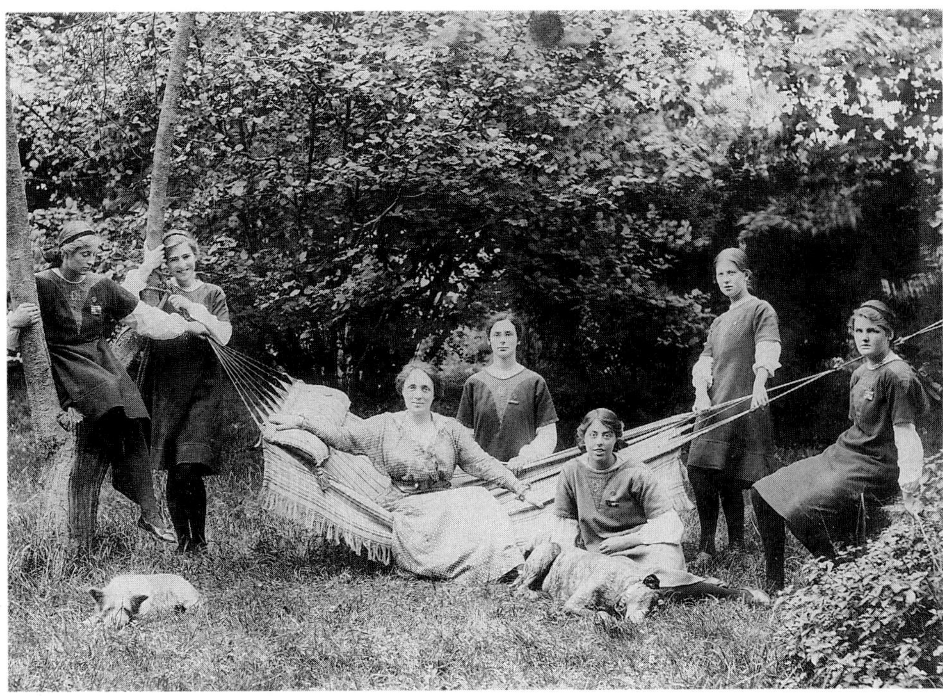

27. Heathfield Chapel Choir about the time of World War I, wearing the chapel caps and capes devised for them by the school's founder, Beatrice Wyatt.

28. School of S. Mary and S. Anne, Abbots Bromley. Commemoration service, 1958, led by Bishop Mortimer, President of the Woodard Corporation, 1954-73.

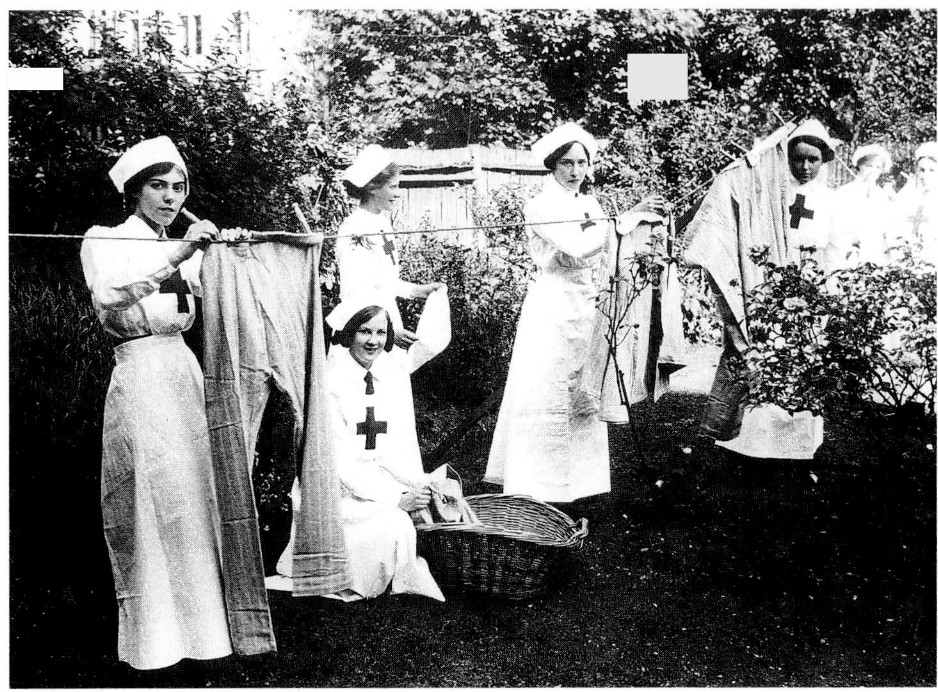

29. Red Cross cadets at Cheltenham Ladies' College, 1911.

30. Wycombe Abbey, Mission Day, 1904. Social service was a feature of the public schools, and many undertook mission work in slum parishes. The Wycombe Mission was in Camberwell, and every year the school invited large parties to the Abbey for a day's holiday.

31. A 1920s dancing class at St James's West Malvern.

32. Piano quartet, 1980s, North London Collegiate School. The professional approach to music and the laid-back style of dress contrast with the dilettante formality above.

33. A 1940s production of Maeterlinck's *The Blue Bird* at Tudor Hall.

34. Oxford High School and the Oxford University Experimental Theatre Club in *Living Creation*, 1985, written for them by Francis Warner. The professionalism of much recent school drama is in sharp contrast with the old-style productions which tried to give a part to as many pupils as possible.

united front against authority. They support one another in trouble; a prep school headmistress said that when she had to break bad news to a girl she would tell close friends first so that they could rally round. In one school, confronted with a companion in distress, friends each contributed £10 of pocket money towards an abortion. No day-girls can ever expect to reach the inner rings of this rapport.

> I always liked meeting the day girls each morning and they were very kind inviting us out to tea with them at weekends, but you could never really become so friendly with them as you could with people who lived in the same house with you, borrowed your hot water bottle, or kept you waiting for your bath.[42]

There is pleasure in the unthinking, giggling sort of camaraderie of one's early days: 'Pattie was very amusing and had an artificial eye, which she used to take out and show to privileged friends.'[43] Or just in straight enjoyment of life:

> April 22. Dr Broadribb married Miss Capper. Greek, Latin, German, etc.
> April 23. Snow! Read Vanity Fair.
> April 29. Toffee; it boiled over all the grate etc.
> May 19. School. My spider is known as Livy.
> May 20. School. Livy's leg went in the inkpot![44]

There is St Trinians-style knockabout fun. A 1980s school magazine reminisces about enjoyable moments: 'It is inevitably in the house where the majority of fun is had by the girls. One evening's events resulted in a fourth year being locked in one of the cleaners' cupboards for ten minutes. There was another occasion at the end of term when several resident staff were thrown into baths by some fifth years.' There is the satisfaction of shared enthusiasms; a turn-of-the-century pupil at the Godolphin School remembered 'the staircase where we sat in serried ranks from 7 to 7.30 p.m. when any new "craze" took the House – chip carving, paper-hat making, drawn thread work and all the rest'.[45] However, a middle school girl quoted by Mallory Wober gives probably a more accurate picture of the realities of communal life in leisure periods:

> At weekends the form is awful. Radio (recently allowed), record player (form privilege this term) blaring . . . sweet papers on floor, waste paper baskets overflowing, desks upside down, hunks of bread and butter all over the place, cakes, bottles of pop, biscuits etc. on desks, rags being around, records being on the floor, and everybody screaming.

'I remember we always seemed to be hungry,' said a weekly boarder at Durham High School. 'I was more fortunate than the termly boarders as I used to stoke up with food when at home during the weekend. Our favourite school lunch was sausages with baked beans and mashed potatoes which we smothered with jugs of fat which came out of the sausages during cooking.'[46] Food – usually of a sort that adults would find repellent – evokes an almost lustful response from the adolescent. 'Thank you. The schoolgirl's appetite is notorious,' says one of Elizabeth Bowen's fourteen-year-olds,[47] coyly accepting yet another of the iced cakes which her elders have spurned. And contributions by younger writers to school magazines never forget to catalogue the food that accompanies an educational outing; in a recent record of a retreat, 'the sandwiches, crisps, biscuits, and several other bits and pieces' were obviously of more significance to one participant than any spiritual reflections.

Until as recently as thirty years ago – until, in fact, Britain was fully clear of the austerity period that followed the war – school food was mostly carbohydrate. The amount of bread consumed by schoolgirls was prodigious; it formed the basic ingredient of breakfast, tea and supper. Meat was eaten at the main meal of the day, accompanied by root vegetables only, followed by suet or perhaps milk pudding. The dietaries of charity schools of the last century differ very little from boarding schools of the earlier decades of this, and it is worth remembering that the current preoccupation with fruit, salads and raw vegetables as the basis of healthy eating is a very recent one. John Locke in *Some Thoughts Concerning Education* (1693) had prescribed 'plenty of bread, milk, milk pottage, water gruel and flummery [cold porridge] at breakfast and supper, all very plain', and his precepts were followed for 250 years, long after his name had ceased to be associated with them. The main meals for the week at the Clergy Daughters' School, Casterton, in late Victorian times ran as follows (in country style they seemed to eat their pudding first, to take the edge off the appetite): Monday: baked rice and 'pie of odds and ends'; Tuesdays: treacle pudding and hot roast meat; Wednesdays: suet pudding and hotch-potch; Thursday: rice and treacle and hot roast meat; Fridays: baked rice pudding and hot-pot or pie; Saturdays: hot boiled beef with milk pudding and potatoes; Sundays: baked rice pudding with no raisins and cold boiled beef.[48]

The 'pie of odds and ends' seems to have featured at every school, and to have been viewed with loathing. At Benenden in one house it was known as Cuddy Pie (after their housemistress's late dog), until the death of Stalin, when the name was changed to Stalin's Remains. Moreton Hall took the same view of their Saturday stew, which they called Ichabod;* Nottingham High School called theirs Pterodactyl's Hooves. But worse even than Charlotte Brontë's description of Lowood diet is the food recalled by a pupil at the school that was to become St Mary's, Wantage, the Do-the-Girls Hall referred to earlier, where the girls were so hungry that they used to eat the bread provided for rubbing out at drawing lessons: 'I will not attempt to

* Hebrew: 'The glory has departed'.

describe the awful *black* mince of Tuesday's dinner, or the weird and horny Saturday pie – nor was the bread without fault, often uneatably bitter, hungry as we were, and Ann the cook who made it had sometimes to do so in gloves as she suffered from warts and gatherings on her fingers.'[49]

The girls at this establishment used all their pocket money, such as it was, to buy ships' biscuits 'as the most sustaining to be bought for the money'. Their suffering must have indeed been great if none of it went on sweet things, which is what most children crave as the dipsomaniac craves his bottle. These extracts from letters could be parallelled in a thousand others.

> *1948, June*: Did you say the jam you brought when you took me to the Dentist was to last to the end of Term? If not, will you please send me some more in two weeks' time as I have not finished it yet, but it is so I may have it later.
> *20 June*: Could you send me some sweets for this month then I will not bother you for a long time perhaps not before the end of term.
> *23 September*: I am not asking for tuck but I do want some.
> *October* [no date]: When I come back for half-term I shall want some butter and sugar . . . I want some more sweets.
> *October* [no date]: We need not write letters as we saw you so this is not very long.
> Please will you send me some photos and some sweets.
> *7 Nov.*: Isn't it wizard about the sweets, or don't you know? The sweets that are under sixpence are off ration on 5th December. And the others on New Year's Day.[50]

The difference forty-odd years later is that tastes have become slightly more sophisticated. In a survey made in 1985 at a convent school where all the pupils listed their preferences the favourite drink was revealed as gin and tonic, and joint second were wine and Coca Cola.

9

Authority: Headmistresses and their Staff

Flaming Catherine Wheels

'Sometimes a girl would stand so long outside that door without the courage to knock,' wrote an Old Paulina of a High Mistress before the First War, 'that a passing mistress would stop, rally her, and knock for her.'[1]

In those days the power of headmistresses, their seeming ability to read one's very soul and to quell by their appearance alone, seemed something divine. It was said of one headmistress of Wycombe Abbey that she was the only person who had any control over a ferocious pair of swans on the lake in the school grounds who attacked all passers-by, and that she achieved it by her voice alone. 'I had a private conviction that she had some sort of direct communication with an avenging Jehovah, who would point us out to her if we didn't own up . . . Without raising her voice she reduced us to objects about the size of a mosquito,'[2] said a girl detected in some peccadillo outside the premises of Clapham County Secondary School. A pupil at the Mount remembered saying loudly, '"Well! I hate her!" A voice outside said calmly, "Whom dost thou hate?" There was an awful stillness and I could not answer. She said, "That girl must come to me before she leaves this room."' This particular all-seeing, all-hearing presence was Lydia Rous (the Mount being a Quaker school, she had no prefix to her name): 'all feared her, most respected, some dreaded, and a few adored her'. She did not punish the girl, who was too frightened even to confess; she merely remarked 'But I think I can guess who it is by thy unwillingness to tell me.' 'If correction had to be given, a look was enough, a word was more than enough,'[3] the same writer commented, and this then would have held good of most headmistresses, who well into this century ruled by fear – not of punishment, but of rebuke. A word was enough. Miss R. M. Haigh Brown, headmistress of Oxford High School, overhearing a girl say 'Hurrah' to the announcement that she would not be presiding over the usual divinity lesson, sent for her. 'She said, "I am *surprised*" in the saddest of voices. I apologised again. She said "I *am* surprised." I departed, and feel to this day that she secured an unfair effect with unfair economy.'

The terror that headmistresses inspired is recorded over and over again in school histories. Very occasionally astute pupils could discover an Achilles heel, and were sufficiently level-headed to use it in an emergency, as with the Victorian headmistress of Red Maids' who could be sent clambering on to her chair by the whisper of 'mouse', but this sort of good fortune was rare. Girls at the Royal School between 1898 and 1910 had to face a pre-breakfast ordeal of shaking hands with the Lady Principal. Sometimes she might smile and say 'Good morning, dear'; sometimes it was 'Good-morning-your-stocking-is-coming-down-go-and-dress-properly.' Other times it was 'Good morning' with averted head; worst of all was when there was silence and her hand was withdrawn. The school committee, all military men, approved, one commenting 'I am sure we must all feel as soldiers that the importance of discipline in the school cannot be overvalued. Miss Blake has paid special attention to that point.'[4] But military-style discipline was a commonplace at schools of the time:

> To be sent to her room was an ordeal, at the memory of which Old Girls seemed to quake sixty years later. It seemed she knew just how long to keep one waiting to allow any residual defiance or bravado to ebb out of one, so that when one finally went in and faced her across the desk a few well-chosen words were all that was needed to complete the humiliation.[5]

And if one forgot to say good-morning, or prefaced a remark with 'Well', then the carefully prepared speech had to be started all over again. (Girls at this Birmingham grammar school would struggle back after two days' illness because after a third day an absence note would have to be taken to the headmistress.) 'Known, respected, feared and loved by generations of Ascot girls,' said a chronicler of one convent headmistress,[6] 'a figure of great dignity, able to inspire awe by her very appearance.' Many have described their headmistresses in the same terms; for generations the ability to inspire fear seemed an integral part of the office. 'Miss Belcher would not have been so much loved if she had not also been feared,' said one admiring pupil of a Victorian headmistress of Bedford High School. It is only recently that sympathy, diplomacy, tact and ability with public relations have seemed greater desiderata than awe-inspiring presence. A distinguished politician recently recalled that he had once been goaded to complain to a particularly authoritarian High Mistress of St Paul's that no prime minister had ever dealt with him in such a high-handed manner.

Their very mannerisms seemed threatening. Miss Louise Watts, the founder of Oakdene, had 'a great deal of Queen Victoria, a slightly menacing touch of the Red Queen, with more than something in her appearance which recalled Mrs Noah'. Tightly upholstered, she wore 'a tortoise-shell case pinned on in front from which she could draw a pince-nez and fix it on the bridge of her thin nose, nostrils made thinner than ever by the indrawing of breath which always prefaced some rebuke . . . When she had finished, she removed the pince-nez and let it snap back into its case.'[7] Often sheer size made headmistresses threatening. Victorian photographs show women whose formidable busts are made more emphatic by leg-of-mutton sleeves. An early headmistress of Edgehill College 'was a big woman with a large bust whose very presence made one obey school rules with alacrity'.[8] An intimidated first-former at Laurel Bank thought the principal

> was the largest, darkest lady, with the largest, darkest eyes in the whole world ... I had the distinct impression that there was twice more of her than there was of any ordinary woman. Her appearance created a lasting awe ... I can never remember Miss Watson either scolding or being fierce. Once when some of my class were sliding on the banisters they heard a voice behind them say: 'Be careful, girls, or you will fall,' and the shock was worse than a ferocious row.[9]

Sometimes, of course, they were both fierce and scolding, like Ada Benson, first headmistress of Oxford High School, stern sister of a stern headmaster (later Archbishop of Canterbury), who no doubt thought she was following his practices at Wellington:

> Nearly every morning after rollcall and brief prayers she delivered an oration, and as the eloquent denunciations swept on, the smallest offence became a crime, which the punishment never fitted; or when there was no need to denounce, only to exhort and uplift, she wielded the words of St Paul, 'Whatsoever things are pure,' etc., until they too became a bludgeon full of menace. It was hard to forgive her when we saw members of the staff, and the whole staff had our devotion, leave her office in tears.[10]

But, she added, the children themselves did not cry. 'I think we regarded her much as we should a runaway horse, a thunderstorm, or any "act of God", as something for which no one was responsible and which did not really touch our lives.'

Most people over forty-five remember those orations, which were particularly awe-inspiring when it was considered that pupils' bad behaviour had let down the school (leaving the way open to much gloating by rivals). Angela Brazil included one such in *A Patriotic Schoolgirl* (1918), which conveys the tone perfectly. The excited crocodile of girls has broken ranks at the sight of Captain Devereux, the great French airman who has just flown over from Paris and has been looping the loop, and they have begged for his autograph.

> So far, at Whitecliffe, the name of a Brackenfield girl has been synonymous with perfectly and absolutely ladylike behaviour. The inhabitants or visitors at Whitecliffe will naturally notice any party of girls who are proceeding in line through the town; they will note their school hats, observe their conduct, and judge accordingly the establishment from which they come. Every girl when on parade has the reputation of

> Brackenfield in her keeping. So strong has been the spirit not only of loyalty to the school, but of innate good breeding, that up to this day our traditions have never yet been broken. I say sorrowfully up to to-day, for this very afternoon an event has occurred which, in the estimation of myself and my colleagues, has trailed our Brackenfield standard in the dust. Sixteen girls, who under privilege of a parade exeat visited Whitecliffe, have behaved in a manner which fills me with astonishment and disgust. That they could so far forget themselves as to break line, rush out on the shore, passes my comprehension. And this under the eyes of two other schools . . .

The old-style headmistress could be very domineering. An unusually candid account of one such was given in the history of Merchant Taylors' School, Crosby. Miss Emily Fordham (1922–39) was a forceful and energetic personality whose predecessor had been culpably lax, though much loved. 'It was clear that Miss Fordham believed that only by controlling *all* areas of the girls' lives could she achieve her ideal Merchant Taylors' product.' 'You will take Botany, Zoology and Chemistry in Higher School Certificate, proceed to Liverpool University, take a degree, and become a sanitary inspector,' she told one pupil. But normally she stressed social rather than academic qualities. She ironed out the local accent, she demanded immaculate deportment off the premises as well as on them, she kept a stern eye on pupils' leisure activities. Her insistence on straight hair has already been referred to (see page 49); one girl suspected of trying to induce an artificial bend in it was told 'she was no better than a street-girl, although we'd no idea what that meant'. She inspected girls' underwear to make sure they were wearing navy knickers with linings; she expected the staff to be soberly clad in navy or grey costumes with long-sleeved blouses – no short sleeves were allowed, and a member of staff who appeared at school in fawn stockings rather than the statutory black would be sent home to change.[11] Though insistence on uniform dress was unusual, plenty of other head-mistresses of the period exerted a formidable degree of control over the lives of their staff, who did not think it unusual to ask permission before they shingled their hair, or to be told that sleeves must cover the tip of the elbow. One high school head summoned a teacher and reprimanded her for smoking in her lodgings; it was an unpleasant habit which might bring discredit to the school and was, besides, too expensive a taste for a young woman.

Their pupils' attitude to these autocrats, at least by the time they were old girls writing in the official school history, was usually adulatory, and one forms the impression that many girls (up to the 1960s, at any rate) expected to be dominated, and reverenced dominating women. Miss Marcia Matthews, who built up St Mary's, Calne, from its thirty-nine pupils and four teachers in 1923 into a major public school, terrified many by her outbursts of temper and her withering sarcasm, and the clerk to the governors recalled that she had been rescued from libel actions more than once. But she had extraordinary influence, an influence which many pupils and staff reckoned to be the major force in their lives. Her vigorous standards, said one girl, 'meant some rather painful hammering into shape. It meant some searing public reprimands, some bad minutes waiting for a private word after Chapel ... [She] could never have got away with it, never inspired such respect and personal loyalty unless we had been so completely confident that she practised what she preached.'[12]

At the time, they may have been more resentful than they remembered in later years. 'I have heard it said since by her colleagues that Miss Gwatkin was a fine headmistress. It may be so. I saw her with the emotions of hostile adolescence. For me she was a cold, domineering woman who took pleasure in disparaging timid girls.'[13] The same writer remembered with distaste the headmistress's open-work crocheted jumpers in artificial silk, and the way she would fiddle with the cuffs as she addressed a class – and it is certainly true that girls have a critical eye for clothes and mannerisms even while they are enduring crushing rebukes. 'We *hated* her boned collars and the way her front hair wobbled when she was emotional,' said one girl of her St Swithun's headmistress fifty years ago (a woman, sadly, who had been regarded as supremely elegant when she had first come in 1916). Conversely, they are delighted by stylish clothes; one Badmintonian bought a 'blue-grey velvet coat with swirling skirts' in flattering imitation of Miss Sanderson, whose sense of fashion came as a revelation after the Quaker austerity of her predecessor. It was customary, too, to assume that the headmistress was impossibly out of date. 'They sang some songs from "South Pacific" and she said they were most unsuitable and she was perfectly certain that none of our parents would take us to see any American shows in London, they were most unsuitable. Honestly she must be simply ancient if she thinks none of us have seen "Annie" etc.,' wrote a disgusted St Felix girl to her parents in the 1950s.

The old-type headmistress was expected to have presence – style was unnecessary – and was often compared to Queen Victoria. Miss Watts of Oakdene was one, Miss Beale another.

> She was short [a Victorian Cheltonian said], but her dignity was marvellous. The only person of her generation whose dignity was greater was Queen Victoria. She had large penetrating eyes and great humour in the corners of her mouth ... It was a sight to see her come up the long hall and fall upon some luckless child who had caught her attention from the furthest end.[14]

'We were convinced beyond any shadow of doubt that she was the greatest headmistress, and that [Cheltenham Ladies' College] was the finest school in existence,' said another. 'If she spoke to us, we experienced a sinking sensation, a combination of diffidence and awe.'[15]

I thought I saw upon the Throne
A flaming Catherine wheel.
I looked again, and found it was
The glory of Miss Beale.
'Take off those shoes, at once,' she said.
'That's far too high a heel!'

was a verse written in many Cheltonian autograph books.

There were many girls who, like the St Mary's pupils, felt that their headmistress was a major influence on their lives. Sometimes it was their religious faith, as with Alice Ottley, Miss Belcher at Bedford High School (see page 156) and Miss Beale, of whom an early pupil said: 'I shall never forget the impression I received as quite a young girl when I heard her read the first chapter of St John's Gospel. It was quite electric, one felt that this woman was reading the thing she considered the greatest in the world and that she was somehow putting over to a class of little geese that it was immensely important.'[16] Sometimes it was the way that they formed pupils' tastes, kindled intellectual excitement by lending books and reading aloud. 'It was then that I learned to love poetry,' said an old pupil of Downe House, one of many who remembered Miss Willis's reading. Their precepts and punctilios were often ineradicable – it is impossible for girls from one Oxford school now to address an envelope with the house name in inverted commas or with a comma after the street number. 'There was no aspect of our daily lives that she was not interested in, whether it was the right way to walk into a room, or how to hold a book.'[17] These women were also – and still are – astute and penetrating, and often had a surprising knowledge of each girl's character and capabilities. In real life headmistresses had none of the phenomenal gullibility of their school story counterparts, who were always the last to recognize the true nature of their girls.

A surprising amount of kissing went on. A boarding school headmistress no doubt regarded herself as a surrogate mother, and that it was incumbent upon her to kiss her pupils goodnight at least once a week. Some of them even tucked the girls up at night. Penelope Lawrence at Roedean kissed her entire house goodnight every twenty-four hours, and on Saturday nights the whole school – a strange custom in a school that prided itself on its masculine approach. At the Mount in the 1880s the headmistress went round all the dormitories on Saturday night and kissed every girl. Many found this odd; a few shuddered. 'Whether one would have welcomed this caress if one had had love and admiration for the head, I cannot say. For myself I rather think not. The only chance of escape in this weekly kiss of peace . . . was to feign sleep, but this was a risky device and not to be tried except on rare occasions.'[18] Forty years later Miss Cox of the now defunct Hayes Court, an elegant and original woman and certainly not a mother-figure, administered a daily 'Proustian good-night kiss, resented by some, intimidating for the new girls'.[19]

Tough and resilient themselves, the old-style headmistresses tolerated no weakness in others. Miss Beale once threatened to cut off the hair of the next girl who fainted in church, since the weight of it was clearly too much for pupils who had been collapsing in too great numbers. 'You must never allow a girl to faint,' Miss Buss said angrily to a pupil who had helped a friend out from the weekly sermon at North London Collegiate. 'Once I was in church with a pewful of girls. I noticed that one of them looked like fainting. I leant across to her, shook my fist at her, and said: "You *dare* faint." And she didn't.'[20] Coughing was similarly forbidden by many. 'We might go purple in the face with efforts to restrain a cough, and our neck muscles stand out like tree-roots: if we did let one escape, we were first scolded and then led off to the medicine cupboard . . . to be dosed with the hated cinnamon.'[21] 'I owe to Miss Baker the unusual ability to suppress a cough during a public performance whatever the cost,' said a Badmintonian, remembering how a contemporary with a bad cold was arraigned at assembly and sent sobbing out of the hall. 'That this talent was born of a moment of pure hatred, and some real terror has sometimes depressed me, but I nevertheless value it very highly.'[22] Many headmistresses insisted on cold baths, though probably only Miss Dove in the early days of Wycombe Abbey extended this edict to the staff as well. At Badminton Miss Baker shared a bathroom with some of the girls in her house. If the bottom of the bath was warm to her feet, she knew why and summoned the offender. She also regarded hot water bottles as a deplorable sign of decadence, and at the beginning of one Lent gave a sermon about renouncing self-indulgence and doing without them. 'Many of us came out of Assembly determined to be strong; but it was a cold Lent indeed.'[23]

Sometimes it was their all-pervading presence, their seeming ability to be everywhere, that made these headmistresses so god-like. Lydia Rous 'organized, disentangled, surveyed, decided . . . Time-wasting people and things were moved out of the way, extinguished. Amused, annoyed, detached, she fronted them, then dealt with them, and left them, with no backward glances.'[24] Autocrats of this breed required to be involved with the smallest detail, from choosing the tennis team or the hymns for morning assembly to ordering the menus and pronouncing on whether conditions underfoot necessitate galoshes outdoors. Some, like one Durham High School headmistress, patrolled the corridors and stood listening outside classrooms. 'One would suddenly become aware . . . of a figure standing still outside the formroom door. Backs straightened up, a more intelligent attention became apparent, probably thus warning the mistress in charge.'[25]

Some, like Margaret Spurling, Alice Ottley's successor at Worcester, inspired awe by 'a deadly accuracy of judgement. She could sum up a girl's abilities and weaknesses in a few moments, and her judgement was unerring.'[26] Many had an infallible gift for deflation. 'I suppose you are only reading that to make an impression,' said one headmistress in a crowded railway carriage, spotting a former pupil who had Macaulay's *Essays* on her lap. 'Do you mind not being a success?' said another to a young actress making a début appearance. ('I always knew when she was in the audience as soon as I made my first entrance,' said that particular pupil. 'I immediately felt tawdry.') Olive Willis was another who specialized in character analysis. Each member of the school was discussed at the last staff meeting of the term, and each came to her for an end-of-term interview, known as a 'jaw'. 'She told me things about myself I never knew, and all true,' wrote one girl, gratefully it seems – though others might well have resented this clinical exposure of one's naked inner self. She was certainly kind and generous; a typical letter to an old pupil gave news of a hamper of food dispatched to her Florence *pensione*, instructed her in sixteen sides of paper what sights to see, but included some stringent comments on her character.[27]

There was, too, the benevolent despot, like Alice Ottley who tried to resign many times but was always overruled, and continued to govern until the very end. As she lay dying she helped choose her successor, and then sent for every member of staff separately, begging some to remain for a year to see in the new regime, suggesting that others, unlikely to be compatible, should move on. An intensely spiritual woman, she used to read devotional books to her staff while they did their needlework after staff meetings. Her concern for her girls' welfare lasted long after they had left school: 'I take it for granted that no Guild girl reads story-books in the morning.'[28]* Lydia Rous at the Mount had a similar concern for the spiritual welfare of the teachers, most of them very young and former pupils. She told them that *Jane Eyre* was a book which they should not read until they were twenty-five. And most headmistresses would have considered it part of their duty to give guidance in post-school behaviour: 'She spoke to us chiefly about our clothes – how not to be extravagant and yet not to neglect our appearance. She said that those of us who were going to the university would be tempted chiefly by the latter, and those of us at home by the former.'[29] 'One has read elsewhere of these powerful Heads,' said the Mount historian, considering Lydia Rous, 'Heads who dominate the wills and emotions of staff and girls.'

Private schools, as has been said, suffered less from such women. The Lloyd-Williams family at Moreton Hall, Mrs Huxley at Prior's Field and the Inghams at Moira House have already been described in Chapter 5.

* Like other headmistresses, notably Miss Beale, Miss Ottley had formed a guild of old members which met regularly and undertook good works.

There was also Alice Baird, the founder of St James's, West Malvern, gentle and humorous. Children would say to her at the end of the holidays, 'Oh Miss Alice, I'm so glad to be back.' And she was always delighted to see them, even if they had been sent to her room for some misdemeanour. In a typical gesture she swept girls dismally afraid that they had failed university entrance (they had) off on a shopping expedition, and instead of a final 'jaw' such as Miss Willis delivered she dispatched head girls who were leaving with a set of valedictory verses, invariably affectionate and appreciative.

One headmistress whose pupils wilted under her lashing tongue told them they should be grateful to be told of their faults; when they were adult, people would just discuss them behind their backs. Miss Alice, on the other hand, tried to give them confidence. Mary Aylett Broad (1860–1942), the founder of Talbot Heath, had a similar aim – and an ebullient sense of humour which delighted in mimicry. No one was afraid of her. A child whom she discovered dancing on the landing said in horror, 'Oh you did give me a fright. I thought it was Miss X.'[30] Pupils enjoyed her company and competed to sit next to her, and though they had great respect for her they were so little afraid that one threatened to pick her up and carry her downstairs if she refused to give a holiday. The child did so, to the great joy of two watching children who applauded and called, 'Do it again.' It should not be forgotten, either, how much the lives, interests and social activities of the unmarried, old-style headmistress were focused on the school. The scrapbooks of Bedgebury School, for instance, are full of the wedding invitations sent by old girls to the first two headmistresses, together with cuttings from newspapers and society magazines with such headlines as 'A Polo Bride' or 'Fashionable Wedding in Peebles', and pages of birth announcements.

But perhaps of all headmistresses Sophie Bryant (North London Collegiate 1895–1918) differs most sharply from the stereotype image. She was an Irishwoman of such compelling charm that, if she was invigilating, examiners had to be warned not to spend untoward time in her room. The daughter of a Fellow of Trinity College, Dublin, she had very little education in her youth except that which she picked up from her father's books. She was sent to Bedford College when she was sixteen, but married when she was eighteen. At twenty she was a widow. Miss Buss offered her a part-time job and she lived with her mother in London, looking after her younger siblings. In her spare time she worked for a degree, and achieved a First in Mental and Moral Sciences in 1881 and a DSc (the first ever to be awarded to a woman) three years later. Not only did she manage to write ten books in addition to full-time teaching and administration, but she also campaigned for Home Rule, and pursued recreations – rock-climbing, mountain-climbing and bicycling – with the same indomitable spirit. Sir Michael Sadler said of her that she could melt solemnity, prejudice and irritation 'with the magic of her good humour, by her caressing voice and by her adroit use of phrase and tone'.

School was, of course, for many generations of women one of the very few areas where they could rule, and as many heads themselves had found with prefects, it required a very strong character to resist being corrupted by the sense of power. The private school heads, founders of their own establishments, were less affected by it; the informality and family atmosphere which many such schools retained long after the early years precluded absolutism (though the staff, as will be seen, could fare worse than the girls). At the large public schools it was more often the housemistress who wore the jackboots, and the girls had little contact with the head. Margaret Kennedy in her novel *The Constant Nymph*, with her own school, Cheltenham, in mind, wrote of Miss Helen Butterfield MA, and the impression she made on the wild young Sanger sisters, sent to Cleeve College for their first experience of English boarding school life. One of them relates:

> She used to read prayers in the morning in a black cloak, with a queer blue thing round her neck. And she had a most beautiful voice . . . And she saw people – bishops and parents and people – and she saw the girls if anybody had died, or if they'd done anything perfectly dreadful. And she used to give addresses to us on Fortitude and Friendship and things like that. She was very nice looking and had lovely clothes. She very nearly knew our names.

But at the high schools, after the pioneering days were over, the newly appointed principal found herself in control of a large organization where her word was law to a staff who desperately needed their jobs and to girls who expected authoritarianism. In the pre-1939 days such schools were relatively easy to run, and many of those in charge must have gained the illusion of omnipotence. Miss Georgina Tarleton Young (headmistress of Edgbaston High School 1899–1924) was a very *grande dame* who devised her own ceremonial for taking morning assembly. She would sweep through the hall, bowing to each member of the staff, lined against the wall, the head girl carrying her Bible and prayer-book on a cushion. In total silence she would mount the platform and address the school – 'Good morning, g(u)erls' – and the school would reply, 'Good morning, Miss Young'.[31] Autocracy prevailed. 'She knew what she wanted,' a former pupil said of the dictatorial Miss Fordham, 'and she and the girls got it, and no Education Authority, Governing Body, Parents, Staff, had the slightest effect on her.'[32] When Edith Creak, the first head of King Edward VI School, Birmingham, retired she had been in authority for most of her life, having become principal of the Brighton GPDST school before she was twenty-one. Notable at the beginning of her career for her *joie de vivre* and sense of humour, by the end of it she had become domineering and irritable and she drove rather than led. She had been one of the most distinguished of those early pioneers who set out to give girls the sort of academic education hitherto reserved only for boys; unlike so many women heads she abhorred fuss, and encouraged responsibility and self-reliance in the older girls, one of whom spoke of the 'large and spacious freedom accorded to us as we got older'.[33] But in the end the eminence of the position seems to have destroyed her, and when she retired at the early age of fifty-four she disappeared into an obscurity from which it seemed few of her old associates or pupils sought her out.

To be a headmistress at such an early age was not unusual in the days when it was very difficult to find any woman suitable to fill such a post. When the Girls' Public Day School Company was establishing its first schools, therefore, they had either to appoint the very youthful who had the Cambridge Higher Local Certificate (the only qualification then possible for women, and only available from the 1860s) or older women who had had experience as governesses or with small schools of their own. They often showed amazing adaptability. Miss Harriet Morant Jones, for instance, was forty when she became the first headmistress of Notting Hill High School. She was an able woman who had had her own school in Guernsey, but she was no scholar. At Notting Hill, to begin with, it would have been very little different from such a private establishment; she had one assistant and ten children and taught most subjects herself (arithmetic excepted). But when she left in 1900 the school had four hundred pupils and some twenty teachers, and a record of high academic achievement.

Some heads were unusually enterprising: Miss Alice Jane Cooper, headmistress of Edgbaston High School 1876–95, undertook a journey to the United States in 1882 to visit American schools; in seven weeks she saw about sixty educational establishments. Others had an unexpected background: Miss Georgina Kinnear, first headmistress of the Park School, Glasgow, 1880–1900, had been a governess in a private family before she was persuaded by friends to apply for the post at the new school. The child of prosperous and bookish parents, she had acquired her very considerable learning at home, largely by her own efforts; she never went to school. As governess to a diplomatic family she had travelled extensively, and must have been unique among contemporary headmistresses for her knowledge of Russian. She had lived for many years in St Petersburg, latterly as governess in the family of one of Alexander II's ministers. Her only experience of schools had been the brief period she spent at St Leonards (head-hunted by Miss Lumsden) before the Park opened three years later. She was a formidable woman. 'Her wrath at bad behaviour or destructiveness was terrifying; her eyes flashed and her diamond brooch did the same',[34] but her pupils felt that though a lot of her teaching was above their heads she was a stimulating and exciting presence (see page 65).

Most early principals had a full timetable of teaching; this was essential when the schools had so little money, and to pay someone merely for administration would have seemed the grossest extravagance. At a charity boarding school they had to combine every function. At St Brandon's School for clergy daughters the first headmistress was 'responsible for the entire education of the children, their religious and moral upbringing, and all domestic matters. She was not able to spend even a night away from the school without the permission of the Committee because her place was in the dormitory.'[35] Mother Clare of the Ursuline convent at Brentwood 'took a more than fair share of classes in the school; she kept the accounts . . . she read to the community at breakfast, took the Children of Mary sodality, and looked entirely after the novices. When extra work was necessary such as washing curtains or rearranging rooms, she took the main share.'[36] For all this, good health and enormous physical stamina were required, and not all could summon enough. Miss Unwin, headmistress of Walthamstow Hall 1878–98, for instance, taught throughout the school and attended to every detail of household management and of the girls' daily lives, temporal and spiritual. She was up at seven and did not go to bed until two; she did the work of three ordinary people, and did it easily. Her successor was broken by this regime, and lasted only two terms.

But even Miss Unwin's record pales beside that of Miss Alice Olivey, who died in 1982 aged eighty-five. She had been headmistress of Hemdean House School, Caversham, from 1926 to 1972, having entered it as a little girl of five in 1902 and become a pupil teacher at the age of fifteen or so. (Apart from this, she appears to have had no formal training.) Domestic staff was difficult to find and she was nanny, cook, bursar and teacher. She got the boarders up, lit the boiler and cooked the breakfast. She took time off from the morning's teaching to cook the pudding for lunch, and served the meal. At the end of the afternoon she cut the bread and butter for the girls' tea and swept out classrooms that the cleaners had not been able to reach. She supervised the homework, marked her books, read the little boarders a bedtime story and put them to bed. Then she dealt with the accounts. She continued working thus until she was seventy-five, but she also delivered the parish magazine and played badminton and tennis.[37]

Miss Olivey's lack of formal qualifications would have been unusual at that date in a high school, but was often encountered at private schools. Nesta Inglis, for instance, whose association with Tudor Hall began as a pupil in 1911 and who became headmistress in 1935, said she never took any exam in her life. Some early headmistresses came from families able to afford (and willing to contemplate) education for their daughters. Others had had to struggle by themselves. Alice Ottley was one of many contemporaries whose distinguished career in education had its beginnings in an over-large family and dire need. Born in 1840, she was the fourth of the fifteen children of a Yorkshire clergyman. She had very little education, and after a few months as a 'parlour boarder' in a London school she and her sister came home to help teach their younger siblings. In 1861 her father died, leaving twelve surviving children, the youngest only eighteen months. Mrs Ottley, a semi-invalid by this time, moved to Hampstead and took in a few girls who could be educated with her own youngest daughters, and for the next twenty years of her life Alice devoted herself to a succession of girls aged between fifteen and twenty. She had no privacy, not even a room of her own, and most of her reading was done on the horse bus that took her to University College for classes organized in preparation for the Cambridge Higher Local. Only when her mother gave up the Hampstead establishment did she find independent employment, and in 1881 went at the invitation of Canon W. J. Butler to be headmistress of the new high school in Worcester.

Jemima Leys, headmistress of the Royal Naval School 1883–1904, an austere character who had lost her mother in infancy, lived on her father's ship at Chatham where her education was limited to learning Mangnall's *Questions*. Efforts by brother officers after her father's early death secured her a place at the Royal Naval School. After she left she worked as a governess to three families, and then spent every penny of her savings to go as a private student to Bishop Otter School. She was forced to retire at fifty-three from the RNS because of rheumatoid arthritis. Kate Harding Street, headmistress of the Perse School 1881–1909, began her teaching career at the age of sixteen as a student-teacher at a London private school; at nineteen she had her first full-time teaching post at the Clergy Daughters' School, Casterton. Dissatisfied with her lack of learning, she and a friend went to live in London so that they could attend university lectures. (They lived 'very economically', the school history says laconically, which no doubt meant they half-starved on meagre savings.) After teaching at the newly reorganized Grey Coat School, they both went to the Perse, Miss Street as principal. Here she kept up a full teaching timetable as well as doing all the secretarial work. She was a forceful and formidable woman, and one supposes that it was due to an excess of these qualities (she did not hesitate, for example, to set examiners right when she saw fit) that numbers started declining and the managers asked her to resign. She was, however, voted a pension of £75 – generous when one considers that it had to come from the school's very limited resources.

School histories are reticent about failures, which undoubtedly do occur, though Miss Street's is an unusual case. It is the unassertive and yielding, the muddlers, who are more commonly defeated.

> She was a kindly, sentimental person ... She seems to have been a good teacher, and her Scripture lessons are reported to have been most interesting, on the rare occasions when they actually happened as promised on the timetable ... What with poor health, and one thing and another, things reached the point when poor Miss Collier not only missed her

> Scripture lessons but was late for Prayers, forgot to enter girls for examinations, and failed to keep appointments with parents, even the grandest. Various stratagems were tried. But nobody could give her the warm uncritical affection and support for which she had always sought in vain. There was some relief when . . . she resigned in order to apply for a post as an Inspector of Schools.[38]

Some heads, having lost their nerve, become reclusive and refuse all contact with the school. One such was forced to resign by her governors, and then promptly married the chairman, but this was a bonus out of the ordinary. A recently retired headmistress said sadly that she had watched several boarding school heads come to grief, not in most cases because they were inefficient. Sometimes they had underestimated the enormous commitment and stamina that were required; sometimes they had not recognized the power of human emotion, or if they recognized it, had not been prepared to cope with it; 'there is nothing like the intensity of an entrenched society such as a girls' boarding school'.[39]

Very occasionally the governors' attitude conflicts with that of the pupils and their parents, as in the case of the predecessor of the overbearing Miss Fordham at Merchant Taylors'. At a time when there was more usually a vast abyss between the rulers and the ruled, Miss Shackleton had established a warm rapport with her pupils; indeed, 'any function that we hold is not the same, unless she is with us,' they said. But she was less than good at administration and finance, and failed to establish any authority over the staff, who became lax and disaffected, and the governors had to insist on her resignation in 1921. At the farewell ceremonies parents, girls and the local community made it clear that they unreservedly deplored her departure. Honours boards recording scholastic achievements during her reign were unveiled, gifts and illuminated addresses were handed over. 'It is certain,' said the local paper, 'that a more remarkable demonstration of affection and confidence has seldom, if ever, been accorded to a retiring Headmistress.'[40] The school historian surmises that much of the trouble emanated from the staff, who made Miss Shackleton the scapegoat for some of their own shortcomings.

An incoming principal is usually aware that no headway can be made against a staff that is in opposition, and most with reforming zeal have to wait for the retirement of the old guard before they can effect much change. It is in any case daunting even to the toughest to have to enter a community deeply rooted in its own traditions and on the alert for any sign that the newcomer will tamper with them. Margaret Popham, facing her first college prayers at Cheltenham in 1937, told the huge assembly of a cartoon of a small terror-stricken dog confronting a menagerie of wild beasts and saying, 'If I wag, will you wag back?'[41] One headmistress reminded her fellows of how carefully the newcomer had to tread. It was always to be hoped, she said, that one was not succeeding a first-rate head, and in any case it was far better not to have known her, or to have a very critical attitude. However, it would not be the outgoing head who would oppose change, but the sixth form, the staff or the old girls.

> It is almost impossible to tell by inspection which of the outward, and apparently trivial, forms are embedded in unreasoning emotional loyalty. Beware of such things as school dress, the form of the magazine, the election of officers, the privileges of the Sixth, the peculiar ritual of school prayers, of prize-giving, of the fetchings and carryings of books, of notices on the Staff Room board. On no account express any amusement at any of them.[42]

Now, at the end of the twentieth century, authority and good learning are not enough. Academic qualifications, teaching experience, and dignity must be augmented by public relations skills and pastoral care, both of which now take up so much of a headmistress's time; and few will be able to spare any for teaching. School no longer consists just of lessons; a huge variety of extra-mural diversions now have to be organized and co-ordinated. And the teachers are no longer dedicated spinsters; most of them are married and their priorities nowadays are different. Heads not only have to lend a sympathetic ear to staff problems – the change-over to the GCSE exams has brought particular strain, involving staff training, reorganizing class sizes, new textbooks, extra teachers – but they also spend much time listening to the marital and financial troubles of parents. Girls too are far more ready to confide than they used to be. Heads have to cope with continual changes in legislative, curriculum and educational policy which their predecessors never knew. Financial stresses are nothing new (though appeal campaigns are now conducted on a much larger scale), but the effort to keep up numbers by recruiting foreign pupils is a very recent phenomenon, and many heads go on regular trawling trips to Hong Kong and other parts of the Far East.

Boarding school headmistresses are always on call, and are obviously under far greater strain than others. More than one has spoken of the loneliness and isolation accentuated by the knowledge that one is on the wrong side of the staff-room door, that laughter and jokes fade as one comes into the room. There is also the knowledge that the volcano that is a girls' boarding school may erupt at any moment, at the worst bringing media representatives round the premises like hornets. In a crisis like this it is the other boarding school headmistresses who prop one up; 'However bad it seems, it always turns out that worse has happened to someone else.' Married boarding heads are a minority; and even where there are husbands, they do not fall easily into the conventional wife role. This may be hardly surprising, but it is a wife that a head really needs, which is why perhaps there are a surprising number of headmasters in residential girls' schools

(John Hunt at Roedean being one of the earliest) compared with day schools. (The GPDST, for instance, has not, to date, appointed a male head, though they regularly receive male applications.) Reactions of female heads to the new species vary. Some of them doubt whether a man could cope with the human predicaments. 'I bet they wouldn't get the same sort of confidences as I have to deal with,' was one comment. But the mildly flirtatious manner that many of them adopt with their senior pupils, of whom they are touchingly proud, seems to be enjoyed by the girls, who clearly feel they are gaining thereby experience in handling future male colleagues. It seems in any case that there will be increasing numbers of headmasters, since there are fewer and fewer women willing to undertake this particular form of responsibility.

Custodians and Teachers

> She was one of the old, pioneer type of school mistress, getting on for sixty now, inclined to be stout, with grey hair strained back from a great forehead above a jutting nose . . . As each batch of wild people from the Upper Fifth arrived under her sway, she drilled it into shape and turned it out polite, responsible, considerate, fit to join the ranks of Prefects the following year.[43]

'The staff of our wonderful school were all dedicated women, all unmarried. Miss Stainer, our English mistress, once remarked: "We have no children of our own; *you* are our children."'[44] The writers (the first in a fictional account, the second an actual reminiscence of a high school) are describing a breed, now disappeared, of dedicated spinsters to whom the school was all, whose personality and life indeed depended on it. 'She could find nothing to say to me now that the context of work and discipline was gone,' said Mary McCarthy of her former Latin teacher.[45]

Evidence of the devotion of those *in loco parentis* has often been recorded; we find it in the Great Fire in September 1666, when Christ's Hospital masters worked frantically to rescue the children and to find them shelter elsewhere; it was the same 320 years later when, after snow storms blocked the roads – 'we were living wondering if each meal was to be our last,' said the Bedgebury school magazine – staff trudged miles to look after the needs of children in Kent boarding schools; and in 1987, when a hurricane swept over southern England bringing a similar state of emergency. The dedication is still there, but what one headmistress who retired in 1988 noticed was a new attitude to pay: 'talking about what they feel they deserve would never have occurred twenty-six years ago'.[46] Forty years before that,

> teaching posts were so hard to come by that one promised to do *anything*; for every post advertised there were shoals of applications . . . [we] had to be satisfied with posts in the private sector, mostly in boarding schools

> where the average salary was £100 per annum and could be as low as £50 with board and residence but no laundry. It is odd to remember that we did not feel in any way ill-used ... We accepted our lot and never dreamed of staging rebellious demonstrations, nor did it occur to us ... to be unpleasant about spending weekends supervising games on icy playing-fields and taking children in crocodile formation for long walks on which they did not wish to go.[47]

As has already been discussed in earlier chapters, the great difficulty the new schools faced in the mid-Victorian period was the lack of qualified teachers. Miss Beale in the early days found that though Cheltenham was offering unprecedentedly high salaries of from £80 to £100, there was a dearth of suitable candidates. The only certificates of competency then were those from the College of Preceptors and Queen's College. A little later in the 1860s, when women were allowed to sit for it, the Cambridge Higher Local Certificate was the best qualification available, but very few schools at first could prepare for this. In the 1880s and 90s girls often took a teaching job at a day school as a temporary expedient so that they could save money for more training. Some early headmistresses prepared themselves in this way, as has been seen, and at Channing School (and there must have been many others), pupils and teachers worked side by side for matriculation.

For the first generation of university-educated women – those who needed to earn a living – teaching was the only outlet, and some remarkable and gifted people were to be found in the profession who now, if they were ambitious, would probably look elsewhere for a career. Mrs George du Horne Vaizey, a writer of novels about school life who was always concerned to put the teacher's point of view, in *A College Girl* (1913) could see the sad difference between the undergraduate from a family with means and her contemporary who needed a degree so that she could earn a living.

> She would study and cram for examination after examination, go through agonies of suspense waiting for results, and as she passed or failed, obtain a good or second-rate appointment in a suburban school. Henceforth work, work, work – teaching by day, correcting exercises by night, in a deserted schoolroom, with three months' holiday a year spent at home among brothers and sisters whose interests had necessarily drifted apart from her own. As the years passed she would become staid and prim with a schoolmistressy manner; the girls would speak of her by derisive nicknames.

Miss Sandys, an early housemistress at St Leonards, who today might be found in the higher echelons of the diplomatic service or running her own publishing firm, had, one surmises, private means, for she was able to live in an unusually lavish style. She joined the school in 1886, when girls' public schools were an exciting new idea and St Leonards in particular offered an entirely new approach, providing opportunities that girls had never had before. She was rumoured to buy her clothes in Vienna, she had a fine taste in pictures, glass, antique furniture, food, wine and books; she played bridge and she smoked. 'The House took a pride in her as a woman of the world,' said one of her girls.[48] She was also a supremely capable housemistress and it is surprising perhaps that she did not become a headmistress.

The headmistress of Lincoln High School spoke in 1937 of the state of affairs thirty years before, when one needed a supplementary income if one was to have any sort of material comfort; otherwise one had to get a zest, as the end of term drew near, out of seeing 'how good a dinner could be had for fourpence'.[49] Indeed, the pitifully small income (and no pension at the end) that teaching brought in features in many memoirs. Often the salary was barely enough to live on, but few dared to raise a voice. One who did so at Newcastle High School in the 1920s was told by the head, horrified at such unladylike behaviour: 'I suppose all your private affairs will be public property now.' And that was the end of it until one mistress, who was helping to support a widowed mother, fainted with hunger, and it was found she could not afford the school dinner.[50] Even the most conservative of her colleagues then agreed they had reached a point at which pressure must be exerted to improve salaries.

The unqualified, of course, fared far worse: 'I was Form Mistress, Gym Mistress, Games Mistress and Music Teacher to the duds and I was so hard up on £25 to £65 a year that I often took my form out on half-holidays on a Paper Chase or to visit something interesting locally so that my expenses were paid by the school,'[51] said one young woman who had been a pupil at the Royal Masonic School and returned there to teach after World War I. The greatest number of unqualified were to be found, naturally, at the private schools, and their life there could be harsh indeed. One of the best accounts of a teacher's life in the early years of this century is given by Amy Barlow in *Seventh Child* (1969), and the conditions she describes would have held good in such schools until after the Second War. The school was one of many in a fashionable Lancashire seaside resort, and 'the staff were underpaid, overworked and badly fed'. The children, she thought (one is doubtful about this), were on the contrary very happy. Her bedroom was part of a room divided into three. She had to teach in addition to her own subjects of Latin and English anything where there was a shortfall, including science and sewing; 'before my Higher Local history lessons, I used to pray fervently that I might die in the night'. There were no free periods, and duties included supervising children at all hours of the day and at the weekend. The food was so bad that staff used to save to eat out; the staff-room was 'a horror'. When she went to Bedgebury, a school run on far more generous lines, she was incredulous not only at the beauty of the place, but at the comfort, and the consideration with which she was treated; 'it didn't seem like a school but more like a luxurious country house full of friendly and helpful people'. (Bedgebury School, then as now, was very spacious, with vast grounds where children could ride, row on the lake, swim, skate and roller skate, and where the headmistress would let them do anything, however unusual. No greater contrast to her previous school can be imagined.)

Amy Barlow's description of the rigours of the typical penny-pinching private establishment before World War II is borne out by other teachers. Winifred Lear remembered the minute unheated bedroom carved out of another room where the only chair was a cane-bottomed upright one, and the cold – '[we] sat marking with old cardigans swathed round our legs and hot-water bottles on our laps as we were not permitted to use the gas-fire from the beginning of May onwards . . . From time to time we broke off to massage each other's numbed fingers.'[52] She had been hired to teach history and English at Brighthelmston School in Southport, but found she was also expected to teach algebra and geometry to matriculation forms. Like Amy Barlow, she had to supervise the children all their waking hours, and she and the rest of the staff seemed as intimidated by the headmistress as the pupils, and fully as apprehensive when they were caught about to make themselves a post-supper nightcap of cocoa.

> Miss Allbutt, never able to resist looking to see what other people were reading, turned to this cupboard where our jug gleamed white against dark-backed library books and dictionaries . . . She picked it up, distastefully as though it were something obscene.
>
> 'What's this?' she demanded.
>
> All eyes fastened stupidly on the article in her hand. For a long moment no one spoke, then Domakin put on her glasses, peered over the top of them and said: 'It looks to me like a jug of milk.'[53]

Austere though the lives of teachers such as these might have been, they were outdone by what was expected at a convent. One Sacred Heart nun in her first term at Woldingham School just after World War II (at that stage she was totally untrained) was allotted thirty-two teaching periods a week. She had a dormitory to supervise, in which she also slept. She was mistress of files (which meant she had to control the movements in and out of chapel and so on); twice a day she had to supervise recreation. Her day started with an hour's meditation; she then got her dormitory up, dressed, washed and tidy. After mass, and breakfast with the community, she went back to oversee bed-making. Then a full teaching morning, fifteen minutes' prayer and lunch with the community. There was a free half-hour before community recreation at 1.30, the only respite that she had. At 2 o'clock she said office; then taught from 2.30 to 4.30, snatched five minutes for tea and went out to the children's recreation. From 5 to 6.30 she corrected books, prepared the next day's lessons, and prayed. At 6.30 there was spiritual reading, at 7 o'clock office, followed by supper, and then she went to the dormitory to put the children to bed, after which she retired to her own cubicle to sleep.

Sleeping in the same dormitory as the girls had always been a commonplace in the charitable establishments, and even elsewhere. In 1933 the Board of Education's inspectors were strongly critical of the staff bedroom accommodation at Kent College, which in the case of five teachers consisted of dormitory cubicles, and said that the minimum requirement for a resident member of staff should include suitable window space, heating, an armchair, a desk and provision for books (all luxuries, especially the heating, which few private schools before the 1950s would have attempted to provide). In 1953 the inspectors said of Red Maids', which was then finding it difficult to recruit staff, that the accommodation they offered 'was much below what one normally finds'.

At the Royal School in the 1890s the demands made of the teachers differed little from that exacted at convents; they were with the children during all leisure hours, supervising their play, taking them for walks, showing them how to darn, helping with their hobbies. They also had to carve for their particular table at lunch (again, this was not unusual), and the headmistress inspected the joints in the larder each morning and reprimanded those who were responsible for any gross mutilation. Teachers had to put their lights out at 10 o'clock, and any who failed to comply or who were found outside their cubicles were severely reprimanded. Such rigours were accepted by teachers up to the last war. Very few in private schools belonged to the NUT – it would have been thought subversive, political, by the heads, and in any case not many could have afforded the subscription. Of all the schools, Cheltenham probably provided the best conditions for the teaching staff, since Miss Beale from the very beginning had been determined that they should not be responsible for the children out of school hours, and also took steps to ensure that they lived comfortably, were well looked after and properly fed. Of few schools until relatively recently could all this be assumed.

The Fisher Education Act of 1916 made some provision for pensions, and many teachers in their memoirs have blessed it. But it was the Burnham salary scale that made the greatest difference to their lot. It was directed only at the maintained schools, but was adopted by the high schools, the public schools and more prosperous private ones. There were still plenty of schools, though, that could not afford to pay at these rates – and knew that their parents would not stomach the consequent raised fees. The first Burnham committee had met in 1919 with the purpose of securing 'the orderly and progressive solution of the salary problem in public elementary schools by agreement on a national basis'. The original scales were recommendations only, and post-war financial difficulties meant that they could not be implemented; only in 1925 after arbitration were the scales adopted, at a reduced level. Women had to wait until the mid-1950s to be paid on a parity with men, a step which like the Burnham recommendations meant a financial crisis in many schools, in spite of the fact that they were allowed seven years for the implementation of equal pay. Inevitably fees went up – indeed, it is obvious now that the middle classes before that had been purchasing cheap education from sweated labour, that the children had in effect been parasites sucking the life blood of thousands of underpaid women.

Nevertheless, at no time was there any shortage of applicants, and reminiscences in many school histories pay tribute to the excellence of their teaching. One of those who made a great impact on her pupils was Lucy Soulsby, who taught at Cheltenham before she went on to be an early headmistress of Oxford High School: 'the ugliest woman I have ever seen. She must have been about six feet two inches and every single thing about her was ugly, ungainly and badly made. With a huge mouth and shapeless nose, there was nothing to recommend her, but most of her class learnt to worship that ugly face.'[54] She taught even the most insensitive to find pleasure in poetry; she had the whole form in tears over such matters as the execution of Charles I and Rossetti's *King's Tragedy*; she imbued them with a love of the Bible, but also drove home to sceptical upper-class Victorian girls that knowledge of housekeeping and the direction of a household were important to all women, whoever they were, and taught them 'enough of public affairs to be able to discuss them with [their] menfolk'. She was also very human, and at a time when there was usually a vast abyss between girls and authority she 'read our poetry and criticized it, even my impassioned love lyrics she did not laugh at too much, but tried to show me how to prune them, and we carried all our private troubles to her as well'.

It is this warmth and zest, this power to stimulate and awaken intellectual excitement that is remembered in teachers by their pupils. Said a Manchester High School girl of her history teacher:

> She vivified each person she named. She set us essays that meant us having to think and made us look forward with keen anticipation to the half hour she returned our work. Sometimes she asked that the best essay should be read aloud, but always gave her own racy comments on our blunders, so genially but so decisively that we avoided such blunders in future like poison.[55]

English and history teachers seem to be the ones most remembered for these qualities, and also, perhaps surprisingly, classics teachers. Thus Miss Neild of the Mount cared so much for Greek history that she was said to weep *real* tears over the Battle of Thermopylae. 'We had the feeling she must have been there, it was so real.'[56] Of a Nottingham High School teacher a pupil remembered:

> She taught us classics as if she had personally discovered them . . . She was positively tiptoe with a never-flagging, joyous amazement that Homer

> lived, that Xenophon fought, and even, in our first faltering days, that a noun declined, a verb conjugated ... She actually instilled in me a respect for accuracy, a realization that inspiration without discipline is like a bird with wings but no feet. Before you can love Virgil, you must *know* him, the message seemed to run.[57]

French mistresses, sometimes German ones as well, brought dauntingly high standards which the average schoolgirl was unused to. 'Her standard was perfection and the grammatical slackness of the ordinary young English girl was anathema to her,'[58] wrote Miss Willis about one Downe teacher, adding that most lessons used to end in tears. The Swiss lady who taught at King Edward VI, Birmingham, before World War I was of the same breed, fanatical about pronunciation, knitting frenetically while she taught, and from time to time hauling a fob watch out of her bosom and wishing that the gong would release her from these imbeciles. 'Often she must have felt like a French race-horse asked to drag a plough through heavy English soil,' said one girl at St James's, West Malvern, with rare intuition, commenting on the formidable figure of Mademoiselle Eva Delpierre, 'small, sallow, tight-lipped, always ready to strike'.[59] Nor did these foreigners play by the accepted English rules. 'If exercises showed three or four mistakes she would count one of them several times over so as to be able to refuse it. Her nickname in College was Scratch,' said a Cheltonian writing of a German teacher 'of a thorough-going Prussian strictness quite untempered by mercy'.[60]

Terror was inseparable from institutional life at least until the 1950s (it was the same in hospitals, where the mere appearance of Matron or Sister could paralyse a probationer, and the more irascible surgeons threw trays of instruments at clumsy theatre staff). 'The most audacious were reduced to meekness before her. It was impossible for the younger ones to speak to her without stammering or saying the wrong thing. One child when asked who she was said with a gulp "Please, I'm a girl."' This senior mistress at Cardiff High School (1895–1919) could enthral, amuse, inspire, but also 'stun, deftly snub, slaughter even, when exercising the intentional rudeness a lady may indulge in'. The terror inspired by one maths mistress at Nottingham High School was such that when a look-out recognized her footsteps a whole form fled into a lavatory cubicle and locked themselves in. A voice boomed, 'Lower Vc, come out!', and to her astonishment nineteen girls emerged. When they were asked what induced them to do anything so imbecile they could only say, 'Well, we always run away from you; it's sheer habit.'[61] Frequently such women prided themselves on the fear they caused: one Cardiff tyrant, remembered for 'her biting tongue', 'her dilating nostrils, her scarlet flush', who could reduce eighteen-year-olds to tears, told one class who were appalled to find her as their form mistress, 'If there's a dragon round the place you might as well have it on your side.'[62]

There were, of course, the exceptions. Gym mistresses were younger and less formal; indeed, with so much leg exposed it was impossible for them to keep up the full degree of imperious dignity which was such a feature of the longer-skirted members of the staffroom.

> In her gym tunic, cut short like a tabard, the girdle worn daringly only a few inches above the hem, dark hair in a page-boy bob and legs long and elegant in their black woollen stockings [PT staff often wore tights, long before these were standard], she had the allure of a mediaeval armour-bearer in a Gozzoli battle scene, and with her deliciously cold, no-nonsense air of command was everybody's dream of a P.T. mistress. Pashes abounded (a decade later they were called crushes) so hockey practice was also at a premium.[63]

Informal relationships between teachers and the taught fifty years ago were of sufficient rarity for an invitation home to stand out. 'She took us to her home and gave us real evening dinner and her dear old husband would pour a glass of wine for us as if we were ladies at a finishing school. We learnt to think that we weren't just hockey players, but women as well, in a world starved of male influences.'[64] Even French teachers sometimes unfroze: 'she took all her girls under her wing, was totally unshockable, firm as a rock and would happily introduce us to all the "dirty bits" in classic French authors'.[65] But headmistresses, especially in the high schools, insisted on a suitable distance between girls and staff. One told a teacher that she would never be able to keep order in the classroom if she played tennis without a hat; another was warned that friendliness out of school was unwise. The Edgbaston High School chronicler noticed freer relations growing up in the 1930s, and from 1939 wartime conditions broke down most barriers, though Katharine Whitehorn's experience of Roedean evacuated to the Lake District was that 'contact with teachers as human beings was entirely prevented by the knowledge that you would be thought a filthy little sneak if you were seen talking to them'.[66]

The private schools in the pre-reform period had always imported visiting masters for extra subjects such as drawing, music and French which their own governesses were not equipped to teach at an advanced level. Indeed the Schools Inquiry Commission had said that it was generally accepted that elementary instruction was best taught by mistresses, since they know more 'about the disposition of the girls, and are able to act and speak more freely to them. On the other hand, the higher parts are best taught by masters, the girls being usually more willing to exert themselves to please them, and having more respect for their opinions.'[67] There were male teachers at the Mount in mid-Victorian times, the former headmaster of Newton School teaching maths, Greek and Latin there. His successor introduced science (including chemical experiments which often failed to work) and, most unusually for the period, psychology. The Royal School had a much loved English and history master who taught there from 1866 to 1899. 'Our own thoughts, however crude and badly expressed, were of more value to him than the neatest and glibbest summary of what we supposed to be the proper thing to say . . . His attitude to us assumed we were girls – even women – of intelligence.'[68] Men were usually credited with a more easy-going style and with not so much regard for punctilio.

There was a story of one at Queen's College who came upon a small girl about to pour water down a stair well. Seeing one of the worst female dragons of the establishment advancing towards them he enveloped the child in his gown and college business was discussed while the child clung to his legs. When she could finally be safely released he merely said, 'Now don't do such a naughty thing again.' Men could on occasion be more easily disarmed: 'She made a false quantity which always upset him, and he opened his lips to administer a rebuke, when she raised her eye from her book and shot a dazzling smile at him. He paused, his frown fled, and he gently made the correction.'[69] And girls have always been swift to grasp the unmanning effect of tears. 'But she *cried*,' said one headmaster recently, trying to explain his lack of adequate response to a girl sent to him for outrageous rudeness.

There was of course in the early days meticulous chaperonage and the utmost propriety during classes conducted by men. At the small mid-Victorian boarding school described by Juliana Horatia Ewing in her novel *Six to Sixteen* (1875), where there is an arithmetic master besides the standard drawing master, the girls are instructed not to wear their muslin bodices when the former gives an evening class – 'Should the young ladies of this establishment expose their shoulders in the transparency of muslin to a professor?' Two generations later, at Christ's Hospital after the First War, an Old Blue[70] remembered how the chaperon sat knitting during singing lessons, never taking her eyes off the class, as much to ensure the girls did not sing conversations instead of the words of the songs, as to detect incipient impropriety on the part of the master. A Cheltenham chaperon in the Victorian period knew how to subdue the temperamental Domenico Barnett, who was given to tearing his hair and hurling music on to the ground in agony at his pupils' imperfections. '"Mr Barnett!"' and a lifted finger from behind the partition, were enough to restore composure.'[71] Teachers such as these were visitors rather than part of the regular staff. At Casterton during the 1950s the presence of the elderly chemistry master was held to be so undesirable in a wholly female staff-room that his meals were given to him separately on a tray. Scottish schools accepted men on an equal footing long before it was standard practice – visiting masters apart – in England; the reorganization of the Merchant Maiden School in Edinburgh was handed over to a headmaster, as described in Chapter 2. Now, of course, headmasters are commonplace, and even at convents there is a substantial proportion of male teachers on every staff.

The area which still is exclusively controlled by women is the boarding house. The housemistress, in a large school, has far more impact on a girl than a headmistress.

> In the house you were at the mercy night and day of the housemistress, who could be a motherly soul or a sadistic tyrant. The former would coddle the ill, find distraction for the home-sick, sustain the hardworking with late night cocoa, and let the little ones keep guinea pigs. The sadists insisted on every regulation cold bath, that no word should be spoken in the dormitories at night no matter how near death you felt, and went in for peculiar tortures like House Order. This was an order of seniority worked out by the housemistress according to her personal assessment, her pets at the top, bêtes noires at the bottom.[72]

The best can indeed be very good, a surrogate mother. Cecily Steadman wrote about one who had been in charge of a Cheltenham house in 1889: 'Dear Mrs Smith! There never was a child so homesick and forlorn that she could not bring it comfort and very soon charm it out of its misery, nor was there ever one so naughty that she had no room for it in her big warm heart.'[73] She established an excellent rapport with seniors as well as juniors, and was remembered for her sense of fun, her moments of indiscretion, and the way that everyone felt they could go and confide their woes. 'If we felt like grumbling, we went and grumbled to Mrs Smith, for no child was ever afraid to say to her exactly what was on its mind.' Miss Sheldon and Miss Bird, founders of Benenden, could also provide this sense of comfort and security: 'She offered to telephone for a taxi and provide a train ticket home, should life at School become unbearable,' said one girl in Miss Sheldon's house, while another remembered of Miss Bird that when an illicit pet, a tamed grey squirrel, rushed up her leg while she was showing visitors round the school 'she was marvellous and behaved as if it was an everyday occurrence ... which only goes to show what a fabulous Housemistress we had'.[74]

The impact that Miss Sandys made on her St Leonards house and the pride they took in her style have already been described. She too took a great pride in the house and their behaviour, and, like many another housemistress, would from time to time deliver a collective 'House-row', a favourite theme being want of backbone. The rows usually started calmly, but she would get more and more indignant until 'the whole room seemed to be enveloped in the flashing blue lightning of the storm'.[75] Like the best housemistresses, she fought for her young, and there was a story of her defying a teacher who she reckoned was being unfair to one of her flock. The former, coming to supervise the detention which she had ordered, found herself confronting Miss Sandys, who had replaced the girl.

This sort of internecine warfare between housemistresses and academic staff can still arise. Miss Beale from the very beginning had been insistent that the mistresses in charge of houses (which were, as has been discussed, at first private houses which were not under the aegis of the college) should not be part of the teaching staff, and this still pertains at Cheltenham. There are advantages in the arrangement, one being that there is more time for the role of surrogate mother. The teaching housemistress is under heavy pressure. 'This, of course, was only the husk,' said one former housemistress, describing the routine of supervising the girls, attending to their welfare, exhorting, admonishing and consoling in a day which stretched from 7 a.m. to 9.45 p.m.; 'the kernel of every day was some five hours' teaching, the preparation of lessons for the morrow and the correction of up to sixty written exercises'.[76]

But there are drawbacks. Housemistresses, made to feel second-class citizens, can take it out on teachers by refusing to co-operate. And quick-witted, intelligent girls are swift to notice if their housemistresses are not of the same intellectual calibre as those who teach them, or even as themselves, and resent the constant nagging which some women mistake for authority. ('They're an easy lot this year, so I find myself nit-picking. But that's the way, isn't it.') If all in charge of houses were like Mrs Smith or Miss Sandys, school life would be happy, but this is rarely the case, and many boarding school girls have unhappier memories of their housemistress than of anyone else.

A typical story of forty years ago is of the small girl woken in the dormitory because of a terrible enormity – a decayed piece of bread and jam, rejected from supper some weeks before, had been found in her locker downstairs. After a suitable interval spent cooling her heels and shivering outside the housemistress's room, half-asleep and completely ignorant of what was wrong, she was confronted with the evidence of her crime and harangued about the sin of wasting good food. Conversely, the life of the housemistress is one of terrifying responsibility with no relaxation possible. 'One should never be surprised by anything a girl can and will do,' said one, writing in a school magazine,[77] going on to elaborate about the various ordeals for which one must be prepared. There were the relatively minor ones that could be discussed in such a journal: the bathwater continuously cascading down the stairs or through the ceiling; the fire risk – and the difficulties of getting seventy-two excited girls back to bed after fire practice. Then there were the lost possessions; the impossibility of settling a dormitory at night – 'What is it that transforms ten or so charming girls into raving lunatics after lights out? Why after 16 hours of close daylight contact do girls need another 8 hours to exchange confidences after dark?' – and the exhaustion of waiting up until after midnight for a school expedition to return. The writer did guardedly refer to the 'undesirables' who must be kept out of the house, but did not mention the inmates who might try to get out to meet the undesirables. One 1980s housemistress, in a school with a boys' establishment nearby, spoke of her certain knowledge that girls were absconding at night for sexual encounters, but felt that she could no longer stay awake after 12.30 listening for windows to open. ('Oh it was only the two or three you knew about anyway,' one of her house said to her after she had left. 'The rest of us were too exhausted to do anything but sleep.') There are also the new problems of drink and drugs, of pregnancy (one house games captain miscarried on the cloakroom floor after a particularly strenuous match), of anorexia, of divorced parents ('Tell the child last thing at half-term, put her on the train and leave it to us to cope').

There are still faithful people who are willing to undertake the responsibility of caring for other people's daughters at a particularly vulnerable stage of their lives, and some of them are as good at it as Mrs Smith and Miss Sandys, but they are increasingly difficult to find. In boys' schools to be a housemaster is a step on the ladder to promotion; in a girls' school this rarely holds – indeed, many are only glorified matrons. Housemasters may also have wives who more often than not give a helping hand, but though some girls' schools are now experimenting with providing married quarters, a married housemistress is torn by loyalties to her own family. There are plenty of divorced women who see a housemistress's job as a way out of their own problems, but this is rarely the right solution from anyone's point of view, and headmistresses find the recruiting of suitable people to fill the posts one of their most difficult tasks. Indeed, one wonders if boarding schools for girls may yet founder not through any political move to suppress them, nor through lack of pupils, but because of the increasing dearth of responsible unmarried staff to man them out of school hours.

There are plenty of others in a school community besides the teachers and the taught. 'Their life of prayer was confined to service to the needs of the house and the children,' said one Sacred Heart child of the lay sisters at her convent. 'Their example was no less pervasive than that of the Choir Nuns, and we adored them. They were our refuge in time of trouble, our consolation, our link with home and the mundane.'[78] Secular schools could never be so rich in sympathetic peripheral staff, and although before 1939 there were multitudes of maids in every school there seems to have been little fraternizing in this quarter; indeed, many schools had strict rules that girls must never under any circumstances speak to servants. The matrons are curiously little remembered – except for their severity. The traditional armour-plated sister who inspected drawers and handed out order-marks for hairs found in one's comb is now virtually extinct, largely replaced by young foreigners, students, failed actresses, under the control of a trained nurse who attends to health.

The old-style disciplinarian ruled by fear. 'She assured us repeatedly that she was not hung up on the wall to do this, that or the other for us, although we frequently wished she were hung up in other ways.'[79] The girls of Louie Angus's 'ward' (house) at Christ's Hospital so loathed the matron, who always wore a hat decorated with a stuffed squirrel, that one day they put the squirrel through a mangle whence it emerged flat. (In contrition at her grief they bought her a new hat, with poppies.) The best of them seemed to be fierce with the healthy, kind to the sick: 'A wonderful figure,' one Mount girl said of an Edwardian matron, remembering the marvellous armour in which her unbending and prim contour was cased. 'Most of us were afraid of her, at any rate to begin with; she had a sharp way, and was quick to detect fussing or shamming, though wonderfully kind if one was really ill.'[80] Much better loved than any matron was 'Clarkie', the Baird sisters' old nanny, who came with them to St James's to look after 'the young ladies' and teach them to sew. She seems to have filled the role of a convent lay sister, and her room was a comforting refuge – 'like creeping back to the nursery', said one girl who remembered with much affection her gentle 'Come in' and the creaking of the basket chair as she greeted one.

Gardeners, butlers (the best schools had these) and odd-job men are also lovingly remembered – indeed, a wall bracket perpetually filled with flowers in the Oak Hall at Prior's Field commemorates two much loved gardeners of many years ago. Sometimes they had quirks and eccentricities: one gardener at Walthamstow Hall used to call the girls, all missionaries' children in those days, by the country they came from. Sometimes they were felt to be allies against authority, like Conde the odd-job man at Moreton Hall, 'always ready to co-operate in our clandestine purchases of Mars Bars and meat pies for those dreadful midnight feasts no one really wanted to eat in the chilly darkness'.[81] And there were those who seemed part of the essence of the school, like Busby and Purver, butler and head gardener respectively at Benenden, who were there from the very beginning. One girl remembered 'Busby's welcoming smile at the beginning of each term'. He also looked after the fathers – 'If they looked worn out at Speech days and Hobbies days, I used to look after them in my room and just give them a dram'[82] – and when the school was in Newquay during World War II he was left in charge, dispatching delightful letters of news from the Kent front.

There are characters who fit into no single category, like the redoubtable Anna Bramston who with her lifelong inseparable friend Aimée LeRoy was the moving spirit behind the foundation of the Winchester High School, later St Swithun's. They were never on the staff but always identified themselves closely with the school, and entertained schoolgirls at their home – visits which were not without dread on the girl's side. But outstanding among all school characters was Maria Nickel of Downe House. Nobody knew what her origins were – except, possibly, the Foreign Office official who interviewed her when during World War I she was suspected of being a spy. She was originally engaged to teach, but her efforts in this direction were erratic, and as she had an affinity with mechanical things (except her car, which she drove with reckless abandon), she took over the care of all the heating and electrical apparatus. Later, she turned herself into architect, builder and general handywoman, running up classrooms, even a chapel, as needed. It was held to be a great saving to have an architect in residence, even though her roofs leaked and on one occasion a half-finished block of classrooms had to be pulled down because of an error in design. Her loyalty was ferocious. 'No liver for visiting dogs,' she proclaimed in the kitchens, jealous in case Miss Willis's dogs should be deprived; and, scorning a room of her own, she slept in Miss Willis's bathroom.

Downe House was alive with dogs; the first pupil had brought her own. 'Walks punctured by vain cries for unheeding dogs were to be the lot of Olive's companions in all the years to come,' remarked her biographer. And this seems to hold good for the great majority of headmistresses; they are the doting owners of peculiarly badly behaved dogs. 'I cannot truthfully say that Major really appealed to me. He wasn't beautiful, nor particularly affectionate,' said one member of the Badminton staff who had suffered from Miss Baker's dog, who had to be taken for walks on which he invariably disappeared. The first headmistress of Haberdashers' Monmouth School had Pomeranians (a small, yapping breed) which rode about on the train of her dress. (This school also had a morose donkey who was supposed to take the equipment up to the weekend cottage, though he expected the girls to push the cart up the hills.) The splendid Miss Sandys, the pride of her St Leonards house, was also partial to Pomeranians; there were never less than three of them barking and scampering round her. At Moreton Hall there was Ross, a 'poor pedigree half-witless grey Irish wolfhound who wandered about disconsolately with straws in his hair' (a fire practice could always be predicted when he was seen being locked up), and 'whole generations of Cardiganshire corgis, much loved though some were of uncertain temper, ready to nip the heels of those they disliked'.

Tudor Hall had its share: 'Magic trotting around the typewriters; wonderful Joey tearing round the History Room table totally destroying any hope of a serious history lesson; Wasp, always on the wrong side of the door; patient Fudge snoring loudly throughout the English lessons; Geordie, permanently hungry, and last, but not least the notorious Viking'. For lonely and unhappy children a dog, it has to be admitted, is a great solace; however witless or uncertain of temper, it cannot hector or criticize. 'Belinda the Grate Dane' was a source of great comfort to generations of children at the preparatory school for St Mary's, Wantage. Given to the school by the grateful parents of a child who had unexpectedly passed Common Entrance, she was at first a doubtful asset but came fully to earn her keep. 'She could not bear to see or hear a child cry' – probably every school should aim to have a similar presence.

10

Work and Play

Curriculum

'Monday is such a horrid day for me because horrible French class, villainous music lessons, brutal dancing lesson, and disgusting Italian class besides fearful French geography and ditto history which we have regularly every day.'[1] These comments on lessons in the 1870s show how little has changed in the schoolgirl's attitude to the learning her elders wish her to acquire. This school, Queenwood, which later moved to Eastbourne, was at that time sited in France (albeit with English proprietors), hence the emphasis on things Gallic. But French had always been the dominant subject for boarding school girls, and though the day school pioneers introduced a broader-based syllabus with the classics and mathematics necessary to put them on a level with boys, French, joined by English, remained paramount at the privately owned schools. Such schools in the 1920s and 30s might not bother with maths or science or with any other language, ancient or modern, but French invariably had a prominent place on the timetable.

Early schools, before the educational reforms of the 1870s, had attempted to cover a multiplicity of subjects at a very superficial level. This was sometimes imitated across the Atlantic. 'Whenever one of our girls gets a "European education",' an American remarked to an Austrian immigrant in 1839, 'an attempt is made to make her a walking encyclopaedia of arts and sciences.' And a product of a fashionable New York school described the curriculum she had endured:

> We had reading, writing, spelling, arithmetic, grammar, geography, history, maps, the globe, algebra, geometry, trigonometry, natural philosophy, chemistry, botany, physiology, mineralogy, geology, and zoology in the morning; and dancing, painting, French, Italian, Spanish, and German in the afternoon. Greek, and the higher branches of mathematics, were only studied by the *tall* [presumably senior] girls.[2]

All this was taught by the proprietors themselves, for, said the young lady, 'they wouldn't allow a gentleman to enter the house'. According to the author, the purpose of this ferocious curriculum was not so much for the sake of developing a girl's mind, 'as to make her "superior" to other girls, whom she is to outshine in society'.

The English seminaries for young ladies, on which this school was modelled, expected their pupils to have a smattering of every subject that could be picked up from textbooks: 'the catalogue of a child's library would contain Conversations on Natural Philosophy, on Chemistry, on Botany, on Arts and Sciences, Chronological Records of History and travels as dry as a road-book,' said Catherine Sinclair in her preface to *Holiday House* (1839). The educational reformers of the middle years of the century all deplored the shallowness of this teaching, the emphasis on accomplishments. Queen's College, founded in 1850 to correct such errors, in fact offered the same dilettantish spread of subjects: there were lectures in arithmetic, drawing, English literature, French, German, English grammar, Latin, geography, history, mathematics, theology, Italian, mechanics, method in education, physical geography and geology. Originally designed for governesses, the course was in fact most popular with the upper middle classes, who wanted culture for their daughters and not the means of earning a living. The Adult Orphan Institution (later Princess Helena's), which had been founded in 1820 to educate army and navy officers' and clergy daughters to be governesses, had a more workable curriculum, aspiring to teach each pupil, who was admitted when she was fourteen and stayed until she was twenty-one, 'to be mistress of the English language and Arithmetic; to write and read French grammatically; to be well-grounded in Sacred and Profane History, Chronology, Ancient and Modern Geography and the use of the Globes; perfect in the Rudiment of Drawing, the Theory of Music'. After 1843 instruction in German was added and also Latin so that pupils would be qualified to teach boys. All pupils had a further skill to fall back on in hard times: they learnt 'the manufacture and spinning of lace thread as a means of constant employment'. (In charitable institutions for the less privileged this would have been contract work, and the remuneration part of the school income.) The Bishop of London was the Visitor and oral examiner – exams, as described in Chapter 2, were a regular feature of the charity school year.

Charitable establishments were bound to pare down the syllabus to the essentials, but the fashionable school (such as Queen's became) continued to spread itself over a huge variety of subjects. Even in the 1870s when schools were improving, a critic of boarding school education thought that far too many subjects were still attempted: music, French, German, perhaps the elements of Latin; drawing, arithmetic, history 'with its comprehensive sections of sacred, ancient and modern'; English literature 'embracing elocution, composition, grammatical analysis and learning of poetry'; geography political and physical, astronomy and the use of the globes; natural philosophy and botany and geology, sometimes chemistry; 'heathen mythology', biographies of historical celebrities. 'Let us remember that each of these classes is held at least once in the six days, and entails no small portion of close reading, writing of notes, abstracts and themes, drawing out of tedious chronological and genealogical tables and charts, and commission to memory of a mass of dates, facts, rules and formulae.'[3]

The writer was clearly referring to the more ambitious sort of boarding school, influenced by the educational reformers but still burdening its pupils with a curriculum that contained elements from the past (like astronomy, heathen mythology and the globes). The curriculum would also have been textbook-based, with no opportunities for practical work, and included the music without which no young lady could enter society. 'The acquisition of piano-forte playing is made almost compulsory to every school,' the writer complained, 'regardless of ability or lack of it.' 'Why should not a few hours of each week be abstracted from the "ologies" and devoted to a practical acquaintance with cookery and plain sewing? . . . An intelligent study of the preparation and nature of food-stuffs, the best means of house-ventilation and cleaning' would raise housekeeping to the level of an interesting science.

This point was often made, but until the reformers felt that they had satisfactorily proved that women could do the same work as men they were clearly on the whole reluctant to include purely feminine subjects in the curriculum, especially as practical subjects were associated with the charity hospitals. However, Miss Buss did include a subject called 'domestic economy' for the lower forms at North London Collegiate, though these lessons were entirely theoretical 'as there was neither kitchen nor laundry at our disposal, and I darkly suspected that our teachers had never entered such places'.[4]

The early efforts to compete with men, as has often been related elsewhere, were strenuous and exhausting. In 1866 Emily Davies, who had been trying to persuade London University to allow girls to matriculate, was offered a special 'women's examination' which she indignantly turned down, deciding that she must open her own college which would provide the same opportunities for young women as Oxford and Cambridge did for young men. Thus Girton came about, whose students, without any of the educational background of the men, set out to study the same university subjects and sit the same exams (even the ones that in an unreformed Cambridge the men habitually did not bother about) within the same time limits. 'Three years and one term was . . . the time allowed to men in which to take the Tripos, and Miss Emily Davies scorned all compromises and her students must conform to the same rule.'[5] In 1872 three Girton women successfully passed the Tripos exams and, though they could not be awarded a degree (and had not been able to attend university lectures), it triumphantly proved that women, though lacking the educational advantages of men, could still do creditably in their exams.

The effect that this determination to compete with men had upon the high schools and their curriculum has already been touched upon in Chapter 3. But though the aim of pioneers like Miss Buss was to provide girls with the same educational advantages as their brothers, they never attempted (presumably realizing that parents would never stand for it) to follow the older boys' public schools and restrict the curriculum to Greek, Latin and mathematics. (Winchester did not take on its first specialist English master until the 1950s; until then any classics don was regarded as capable of coaching boys in the Shakespeare necessary for passing School Certificate or of teaching the beginners German – this, not French, being the standard modern language.) No girls' school was ever as narrow as that, though Winifred Peck found to her great joy at the new Wycombe Abbey in the 1890s that 'English grammar and geography, those hated subjects, were things of the past. They were not, it appeared, taught at public schools.'[6] (Geography, indeed, until the later decades of the twentieth century, tended to be dismissed with contempt by academics in the older universities as a woman's subject.) Euclid and algebra appeared as not very welcome substitutes, and were inadequately taught as even Miss Dove had not been able to find experienced teachers. French and English were outstandingly well taught; history – at first at any rate – was the usual study of the Tudors which Winifred had endured at her day schools, and 'in scripture we still pursued the Acts and the Kings of Israel'. They devoted a great deal of time to Latin, and at fifteen began either Greek or German. But a precocious boy, like her brother Ronnie (Monsignor Ronald Knox), would have begun Greek at nine or ten and Latin at seven – Ronnie, according to family tradition, was reading Virgil at six – which has never been possible for any girl unless she has gone to a boys' prep school; girls have habitually approached classics with this great disadvantage.

Attempts to give girls a sound education in the early days were made difficult, as has been said, by an absence of people qualified to teach and by the tremendous lacunae in the learning of the pupils themselves, who more often than not were ill equipped to begin secondary schooling. The Royal School had experienced this with army daughters, but the problem was not confined to this school; Miss Beale in 1866 said that of forty-seven children of over fifteen who aspired to enter Cheltenham Ladies' College, and who claimed to have learned specific rules of arithmetic, only two got the simple sums set for them right; in the English paper, only three out of forty-four were able to write correctly the few tenses set, and one seventeen-year-old and one fifteen-year-old failed to write a single word correctly. These were, she said, the daughters of army officers, gentlemen of means, clergymen and the learned professions. The standard in a local church school was far higher.[7]

No doubt for these reasons sixteen-year-old Molly Hughes, when she entered the upper fourth at North London Collegiate in 1883, found the education dull and elementary. The teaching was 'text-book-and-water'; and though there was a large range of subjects including English, French,

German, history and geography, they were all drearily taught and involved much learning by heart.

> Of all the lessons French was the dullest. It is barely credible to-day that hardly a word of French was spoken. We had to buy an expensive and appallingly dull book by Van Laun, and prepare the French at home for his stupid exercises. When we came to class we had to write out two or three sentences selected to test us . . . The bulk of the lesson consisted of so-called translation.[8]

The method of teaching English was bad too; they had to be word-perfect in the footnotes given in their texts, these consisting of the paraphrasing of lines thought to be obscure. (This emphasis on learning useless information by heart was long to remain a feature of many girls' schools; at Casterton in 1902 the inspectors felt that the whole approach was too 'bookish' and that there was no opportunity for experiment or practical work in the little science that was taught; in the 1940s the classical sixth form at one of the better-known schools was still being made to prepare for Oxford Entrance by committing pages of their ancient history textbook to memory.) Latin was not studied until the fifth form, but political economy was, and there was an innovatory subject called 'Laws of Health', where 'we had to draw lovely skeletons and lungs and hearts' and a life-size model of the human trunk was brought in to demonstrate the processes of digestion.

Molly Hughes was disparaging about Miss Buss's system of education, complaining that she had overlooked the needs of future wives and mothers and concentrated too much on exam success. But in this she was less than fair; the subjects might be poorly taught but they ranged over a wider field than the almost wholly classical curriculum of Eton, Winchester, Harrow, Westminster, Charterhouse and their kind then did. As Winifred Peck said, comparing the education she and her sister received with that of her four brothers at the turn of the century: 'While girls' schools all over the country had felt some influence from the educational pioneers in women's education, boys' day schools still breathed out the last disenchantments of the Middle Ages.'[9]

Before she went to Wycombe, Winifred Peck had been a day girl at the Ladies' College in Eastbourne, 'a good girls' high school of the period', and she set down 'the attainments of an average child of twelve' then. She knew a lot of the Bible by heart, many Old Testament stories, the order of the kings of Israel and Judah. Her father (a bishop) complained that they never seemed to study any books but the Acts. 'I suppose I knew more, and understood less, of the Bible than any child today.' Of arithmetic: 'we would boast that we had "got to" or "done" some type of sum'. But she had not the faintest idea of what she was doing, and in fractions what the point was of the line between the denominator and the numerator, and failed arithmetic three times in School Certificate. In French 'a complete knowledge of Henri Bué's *First French Primer*' was demanded, and the teacher took exception to her moderately good French accent, urging her to speak plainly and unaffectedly. 'So I settled down to speak honest unaffected Stratford-atte-Bow French for the rest of my life.' English included 'the nightmare of grammar' with its parsing and clause analysis. But it also meant poetry, and much learning by heart which she valued. She began Latin and learnt the regular nouns and verbs. Geography involved learning the principal islands, capes, bays, mountain ranges and lakes of the world. 'The Tudors, I suppose?' her father had said about her history. He was right, and she had 'clear if extremely partisan pictures of the Tudor monarchs and their leading adherents . . . Of the story of the English people as a whole I had no idea at all; they were just "the mob" who died of the black death, rioted under Jack Cade, or stood by at burnings and executions and coronations.' There was also music, of course: 'Every little girl learnt the piano in those days, and though my fingers were stumpy and I had no ear, I could thump the "Merry Peasant" with the best of them.'[10]

This style of education (though not music, which was to become the exception rather than the rule) held good for the lesser sort of privately owned girls' school for the next fifty years, and not just at the twelve-year-old level. At Eastbourne Ladies' College, Winifred Peck would have moved on to more advanced work; at hundreds of private establishments up to the 1940s she would not have learnt very much more, though she would without doubt at the end of it have passed School Certificate, since that could then be achieved by learning by heart. As far as history went, older children would have studied the Stuarts, but the eighteenth-century political scene was too complicated, and the Victorians apparently too close to one's own time. They would have read one or two Shakespeare plays, and would have learnt a fair amount from Palgrave's *Golden Treasury*. Maths would have included solving equations, using logarithms and writing out Euclid propositions, though they would not have had the remotest notion of what the purpose of any of this was nor how it could be put to any practical purpose. The only science they would have encountered would have been botany or biology, taught in the classroom without any apparatus; few would have ever looked through a microscope. For the girls at these schools education had not improved since the Victorian era; it might even have deteriorated, in that the religious education was less solid, the only language taught was French and there was virtually no music. Nor at such schools was there any attempt to send girls to university – which in any case at that time meant only the few women's colleges at Oxford and Cambridge, the red-brick universities being completely disregarded by the schools outside their particular area and used mainly by the local high schools. There were, of course, some interesting and idiosyncratic schools, discussed in Chapter 5, with inspired founders who formed the tastes of their pupils and made a lasting impression, but here the curriculum was almost inevitably one-sided, heavily arts-orientated, and special individual coaching in Latin and maths would be needed to bring a girl up to university entrance level.

Until well after World War II many headmistresses had the same prejudices as the older boys' schools about the great superiority of a classical education, though as far as they were concerned it had to be an arts education and English and French substituted for Greek and Latin. (Latin was taught at a low level, Greek almost never; one would have to go to a high school or to Cheltenham, Wycombe Abbey or St Leonards for that.) Quite why French should always have featured so prominently in the female curriculum in a blatantly xenophobic country is not clear. Until comparatively recently at the older boys' schools modern languages came a poor second to ancient ones, and Thomas Day (educated in this tradition at Charterhouse), in his *History of Sandford and Merton* (published 1783–9), put what one would have thought was the view of the ordinary English paterfamilias. In this educational treatise, Day's ideal of sensible young womanhood, Miss Sukey Simmons, an unaffected, no-nonsense girl, is shown as commendably ignorant of foreign languages. 'My niece is to marry an Englishman,' declares her uncle and guardian. 'To what purpose then should I labour to take off the difficulty of conversing with foreigners, and to promote her intercourse with barbers, valets, dancing masters, and adventurers of every description?' He doubted whether the English would ever gain much by adopting either the manners of the French or their government, 'and when respectable foreigners choose to visit us, I see no reason why they should not take the trouble of learning the language of this country' – which for centuries has been the received English view. But Thomas Day was regarded as an eccentric, which he undeniably was in every respect, and a knowledge of French (even if it was only limited to irregular verbs) was a requisite for all women in polite society. Indeed, it was this that was latterly to separate the lower-middle-class girl who went to a backstreet private academy from the children at council schools.

As has been seen, it was standard for Victorian schools to insist on their girls talking only in French. Frances Power Cobbe (1822–1904), at a very superior boarding school, was obliged to be trilingual and to talk French, Italian or German all day long; only at six o'clock was English allowed. Bad marks were given for the wrong language, 'and a dreadful mark for bad French, which was transferred from one to another all day long, and was a fertile source of tears and quarrels, involving as it did a heavy lesson out of Noël et Chapsal's Grammar on the last holder at night'.[11] (She had always resisted formal lessons. At the age of five she had indignantly written 'Lessons! thou tyrant of the mind!' on the gravel path, preferring always to explore books by herself in her father's library. Thus when she was at last free of school she took up Greek and geometry, read the Greek and Latin classics in translation, and dabbled in architecture, heraldry, philosophy and eastern religions.)

The Churchillian accents of the Englishwoman who had spent ten or more school years sweating over French grammar and irregular verbs without ever acquiring any conversational fluency used to be marked and ludicrous. Most pupils remember taking turns to sit at the 'French tables' which were a feature of boarding schools, but even if there was a French mademoiselle few thereby learned to be articulate. At Hayes Court

> Mademoiselle Moisson owned an ample figure, a round face covered by wirewool hair, a slow deliberate dignity, and appeared to exude a quizzical, almost cynical, nature of which you were instinctively wary . . . At lunch one was placed for a week at the French table in the hall where she presided in terrifying silence, waiting for one of us to utter some stilted platitude in French, and she was completely merciless in never coming to the rescue, or starting up a subject herself.[12]

It was, as Winifred Peck said, considered by most of one's contemporaries to be very affected if one attempted to speak with a French accent. Janet Erskine Stuart of the Sacred Heart remarked aptly:

> an English accent in a foreign tongue has been for some speakers a refuge for their shyness, and for others a stronghold for their patriotism. The first of these feared that they would not be truly themselves unless their personality could take shelter beneath an accent that was unmistakably from England, and the others felt that it was like hauling down the British flag to renounce the long-drawn English A-o-o.[13]

(French was traditionally the great strength of convents, many of whom in any case had French nuns in the community.) Though many schools appeared to rely on teachers who had never left the country, there were some, as has been seen in the previous chapter, which employed Frenchwomen – whose standards of precision and accuracy were far higher than English children were used to. 'At [Downe] we had a truly wonderful French teacher, Mademoiselle Agobert, who struck awe into her pupils. Stories abound about her teaching and her violent efforts to rouse and hold the attention of classes. Her methods were drastic and more than two mistakes necessitated the return of the work.'[14]

But specialist teachers were not common, even fifty years ago. Marcia Matthews was struggling with very limited resources at St Mary's, Calne, in the 1920s, and appointed a French mistress who had also to teach maths throughout the school, some Latin, and needlework. (Miss Matthews herself taught English, history and divinity.) Some of the high schools taught German, but the present range of languages available – Italian, Spanish and Russian, as well as French and German (Heathfield even offers Modern

Greek) – was unknown until well into the second half of this century, and has blossomed particularly since the 1970s (when there was much fund-raising for 'language laboratories', which then seemed the ultimate teaching aid).

English was traditionally a woman's subject (and was despised on that account by boys' public schools, who would not recognize as a serious discipline something that they felt was part of the heritage of any well bred gentleman), and until there was an abundance of specialist teachers for other subjects, it was probably the one best taught. Lessons were given in literature, in what was known as 'composition', and in grammar, which seemed to be the girls' substitute for the Latin complexities with which their brothers wrestled – 'the awful morass of adverbial and adjectival subordinate clauses and indirect extension of the predicate in which we waded forlornly', as Winifred Peck wailed.[15] (She thought of all the parsing and analysing of sentences into clauses as a shocking waste of time, but educationalists apparently regarded it as a mind-training exercise rather than as a useful end in itself.) The result was that girls often emerged as far more fluent on paper than boys, though the content of their essays may not have been particularly apt or informative.

But many remembered English literature, in the earlier decades of this century particularly, as strikingly well taught, and were grateful for teachers who had opened windows on to new terrain and formed tastes for a lifetime. A Laurel Bank tribute is typical: 'Miss Spens – I can still hear her reading to us of "rosy-fingered Dawn" from Lang's translation of the Odyssey . . . Everything she touched upon she made to glow with life and beauty. She planted in us a seed of love for beautiful literature which has gone on increasing at least in all *my* life – and in how many more?'[16] Very often headmistresses were a formative influence in this respect. 'She read *Villette* so that even the most restless were soon under her spell, and sad when it was time to go,' a Badmintonian said of her headmistress's weekly reading periods.[17] Few Downe pupils who wrote about Olive Willis failed to mention her informal readings, which might range from Browning to *archie and mehitabel*. 'She taught us to know and love books,' said one pupil at Hayes Court of Katherine Cox, 'and above all to discriminate. And at the same time, and equally important, we learnt how to write, and also how not to write, the pitfalls to be avoided, such as trite and hackneyed expressions, not to mention the split infinitive.'[18] At this school Virginia Woolf and Lytton Strachey were among the headmistress's greatest enthusiasms, and one child was unwittingly the cause of much mortification when, without her knowledge, a page from her composition book was torn out by an over-zealous relation and sent to the *New Statesman*, which printed it as a remarkable effort by a child of fourteen. It was in fact a passage from *A Room of One's Own* which Miss Cox had herself dictated to the class.

Music had featured in nearly all Victorian young ladies' schooling. This was restricted to piano-playing, and indeed the equivalent of the school orchestra was massed pianos. At the Royal Naval School in 1867 the *Middlesex Chronicle* reported an astonishing achievement, the performance of the overture to *Euryanthe* by twenty performers on ten pianos, 'the music mistress glancing at her pupils with a look of pardonable pride'. In Bath, Royal School concerts took much the same shape; sixteen girls might be heard playing duets on eight pianos, twenty girls on five pianos, and finally in 'The Grand Smash' thirty girls would go into action on ten pianos. At St Anne's School (now in Windermere) in its early, urban-sited days so constant was the piano practice that owners of an adjacent house moved out and the school was able to acquire the premises.[19] But no doubt as a reaction to this force-feeding of music to everyone, however unsuited, school music fell to its lowest level in the first half of the century. There was a certain amount of singing (schools with their own chapels and choirs scored here, and several proudly record singing in the ripieno choir at London performances of the *St Matthew Passion*), and a small minority worked their way through the lower grades of the Associated Board piano exams. Occasional schools offered violin-teaching, perhaps even cello, and there with few exceptions it rested: 'I have memories of the school orchestra continually playing a march from *Carmen*,' said one Edgehillian of the 1940s. 'It seemed to be the only piece they knew.' Even schools now as musical as Oxford High School had very little music except singing and piano.

There were exceptions, of course. Worcester High School had Elgar as a visiting violin teacher in 1887. He was then at work on *The Dream of Gerontius* and used occasionally to bring the score to school and play over passages to some of the teachers. A generation later a music teacher 'brought the orchestra to such a pitch of enthusiasm that many stringed instruments and even a clarinet were now studied, and with some augmentation from friends . . . concertos by Bach and Mendelssohn were given good performances'.[20] St Paul's, which was a byword for musicality at a very sterile period, had Gustav Holst as its director; 'we abused his gentle ways by behaving disgracefully,' one Paulina said remorsefully of his singing lessons. Another remembered playing a two-piano arrangement of 'The Planets' suite, proof-reading for him, and preparing his orchestral scores by writing the names of the instruments, clefs, key-signatures and bar lines. 'Sometimes he would play a bit of what he was writing, "trying it out on the dog", as he said.'[21] St Leonards took music seriously from early days (here the strong house system gave it a competitive element), as did Haberdashers' Monmouth School where in 1946 there were 170 instrumentalists and Thomas Dunhill came to conduct a performance of his *John Gilpin*. Badminton was a very musical school, increasingly so after Miss Sanderson became headmistress in 1947, and in 1958 gave the first performance of a cantata by Tippett, *The Crown of the Year* for choir and orchestra, commissioned by a parent.

The more expensive schools such as Benenden had visiting celebrities to play to them – Jelly d'Aranyi, Elisabeth Schumann, Casals, Cortot, Myra Hess, Solomon, and Leon Goossens (who seems to have dedicated himself entirely to schools, so frequent were his appearances); the more progressive smaller schools took pupils to outside concerts. But at Moreton Hall, as has already been described in Chapter 5, music played an exceptional part. Indeed, it was in terms of music that most people who were there in the Lloyd-Williams family's day remembered Moreton. They sang and they danced ambitious ballets, and acted; an enormous amount of time was devoted to rehearsing for these performances, which the founders felt were of far more importance than exams.

> We were continually exposed to the world's greatest treasures, of music and literature, art and drama, our days pickled and steeped in culture, our eyes opened and our appreciation stretched. And we were not just passive ingestors of performances by visiting artists, but we were active participants and interpreters. Looking back, I am astonished at what we tackled. With the help of stalwarts from the Weston Rhyn Male Voice Choir we soared and roared majestically through the Messiah, the Bach Passions, *The Childhood of Christ*. We acted Molière in French (yes, really), and Milton in sonorous English.[22]

Everyone learnt an instrument; there was a school orchestra (augmented by local talent) at a time when this was most unusual at a small school (only fifty-four pupils, ranging in age from seven to eighteen in 1939), and several of the girls were given the opportunity to play concertos. 'I don't think I should have learned to love music without Moreton,' said one. And another: 'My career in medicine has its foundations in music, dancing and literature.'

The Moreton Hall curriculum in the 1920s, 30s and 40s relied heavily on what the Lloyd-Williams family could teach, as has been described in Chapter 5. An outsider was imported for mathematics, botany and geography, 'and some very elementary science. No attempt at a lab in those far-off days.' Though few, if any, of Moreton's contemporaries would have achieved anything like such a high standard in music, the somewhat meagre curriculum in other respects has already been seen to be characteristic of the privately owned school. In those days School Certificate – even the coveted matriculation exemption given for credits in stipulated subjects, including English, maths and one science – could be acquired by painstaking attention to textbooks; diligence, accuracy and neatness were what examiners were looking for then, rather than insight and understanding. Many smaller girls' schools took the Oxford local exams, this being the examination board that favoured English and was supposed to be easiest for maths. The Oxford Junior, which one sat at fourteen, was sometimes taken as a preliminary canter for the Senior two or three years later. Cambridge locals were held to be the most scientific, and the Joint Oxford and Cambridge Matriculation Boards the most testing, only attempted by really academic schools.

Even reputable schools, however, were remarkably casual about seeing that pupils were gathering up the right subjects to take them to university. The best-known account of the struggle to qualify for Oxford is Vera Brittain's.[23] She had been at a small boarding school for wealthy girls in days when 'girls' private schools attracted but few parents possessed of more than a half-hearted intention to train their daughters for exacting careers or even for useful occupations', and had to find the necessary coaching in Latin and maths by herself. This was 1913, but twenty, even thirty years later girls would still find that no one had ever warned them – or perhaps no one had known – of the necessity for taking these subjects. Debating whether a 1947–56 Badminton education was a suitable preparation for life, one girl said she had acquired

> a lot of English, Classics, French and Music, a little Science and less Maths. Even the science was an afterthought, an 'O' level Biology achieved by the nervous, persistent patience of Miss Stanley when it was discovered that a science was needed for university entrance and I didn't appear to have one. I shall never forget how she wept into her hankie, like one recently bereaved, when I outlined to her the questions and how I had handled them. 'The earthworm is *not* an amphibian, Shirley. How could you! O, how *could* you!'[24]

In the privately owned schools there was on the whole a marked absence of science before the 1950s. Even for those who proposed to take up scientific careers, the entry qualifications were not demanding. 'No physics or chemistry,' said one 1940–7 Moretonian who left to go to the Royal Free Hospital and qualify as a doctor, 'but Mrs Richards did try to teach me and Jill Murray biology in what was the tool shed'. There had been no science while she was there; nature study was as far as anyone ventured. It was of course expensive to equip laboratories, but there was another factor: it seemed something that could be airily dismissed as pertaining to technical colleges, at best to high schools, and in such a class-ridden society as pre-World War II England this was an important consideration. 'Science doesn't matter,' said one Surrey headmistress in the 1940s to a mother (a doctor) who had expostulated about the lack of provision for teaching anything except botany, and that at a wholly theoretical level. (It was interesting that, even so, the parents preferred not to break caste and send the child to the local county secondary school.) Many apparently felt that science had no educational value, that it was merely a matter of acquiring techniques with bunsen burners and the like. The first headmistress of Manchester High School 'had grave doubts as to the suitability of science teaching, especially chemistry as then taught, as an educational training, and did not see how to increase the teaching without reducing the amount of time devoted to languages'.[25] (The teaching mostly consisted of botany and physical geography, with a little geology and elementary physics for some.) One Sacred Heart headmistress in 1912 wrote as though the teaching of science was a once trendy fad now discarded. It had seemed important at the end of the previous century, she said, when laboratories were fitted up at great expense, and the enthusiasm had reached a peak in 1904 and 1905.

> Then disillusion seems to have set in and the tide began to ebb. It appeared that the results were small and poor in proportion to expectation and to the outlay on laboratories . . . The links between this teaching and after life did not seem to be satisfactorily established . . . It begins to be whispered that even in some boys' schools the laboratory is only used under compulsion or by exceptional students, and the wave seems likely to go down as rapidly as it rose.[26]

A few schools took science seriously from the start. The Park School in Glasgow, as has been noted in Chapter 3, acquired its first laboratory in 1884, only four years after the school had opened. It cost in the region of £60 to equip, and being on the top floor, there were disastrous results when enthusiastic chemists left the taps running. 'Such episodes added greatly to the gaiety of the girls.'[27] But this was soon replaced with a safer room, one of the first laboratories in a Scottish girls' school and the envy of some of the boys' schools. St Leonards was another pioneer, teaching science right through the school, not only to the seniors; many of its girls were to read medicine. The professor of chemistry from St Andrews who conducted an examination of the school's science in 1885 reported that the work of the lower sixth and fifth forms for the London matriculation exams was extremely good. In the fourth and lower fourth forms he was 'particularly struck with the accurate answers I got to questions on Hydrostatics. Most of the girls had perfectly clear ideas about the nature of solids, liquids and gases; of the transmission of pressure by fluids; of pressure on surfaces, etc.' The third and lower third forms did extremely well. 'Many of them are very young, but they have been already taught to observe, and have acquired a considerable amount of knowledge about the chemistry of common things.' But the report by the mathematics examiner was not so enthusiastic. The girls had been carefully taught but showed diffidence in answering questions, were afraid to try equations, and could none of them solve the rider he had set in geometry. 'Some of the students seem to have but a confused idea of what a geometrical demonstration consists of.' (Winifred Peck had admitted that although she could learn Euclid propositions by heart, if the letters on the diagrams were changed she was totally lost.)

In England, Redland High School (founded 1882) had a strong science side from early days and was 'one of the few girls' schools to take physics in public examinations, at one time entering for heat, light and sound, and electricity and magnetism as two separate subjects . . . How we got through so much in that one small laboratory under the art room I still wonder.'[28] But few schools were properly equipped. At Oxford High School in the early years of this century

> There was an acute lack of apparatus, particularly physical apparatus, and when I took my scholarship examination at Cambridge, I had never used most of the pieces of apparatus with which I was faced, though I knew their pictures and the theory of their use. This shortage of apparatus cut both ways, for we became ingenious in constructing home-made things and got a great thrill when they worked, and we certainly understood the fundamental principles underlying their construction far better than many pupils of today who have only to plug in a terminal or touch a switch to get what they want.[29]

St Swithun's achieved a separate chemistry lab as early as 1895 (by dint of leaving a particularly smelly flask of chlorine in a classroom where the Visiting Committee were bound to encounter it), and the first candidates were entered for Joint Board chemistry practicals two years later.

> In those days a 'don' was in charge in cap and gown. An enterprising examiner had given red phosphorus as the unknown substance. About ten minutes after we had commenced a nervous candidate dropped a glowing match on the 'unknown' – result, a wild flare and we all 'knew'. Hardly had the invigilator extinguished this when it was discovered that a pile of dusters was on fire; this in turn was extinguished. Then suddenly the bottom came out of a medicine bottle improvised to contain sodium hydrate, devastating a varnished table and all the candidates' papers. Wearily our friend came for the third time to the rescue, remarking, 'My life is insured – I only hope yours are!'[30]

But even high schools were often late to include science in the curriculum. Miss Joyce Brown, headmistress of Durham High School 1933–8, appointed a mistress to teach science 'properly' for the first time.

> The appointment was made on the steps of the British Museum. Miss Jackson had been expecting less than perfect conditions but was not fully prepared for the laboratory consisting of a sink, two marble-topped wash-stands and a gas-ring. She stayed for six years though . . . After starting with School Certificate Botany and achieving encouraging results here she then introduced Chemistry in a laboratory largely of her own design which was also used as a form room . . . Laboratory facilities were moved in the 40's to an outbuilding.[31]

Other schools recognized the need for science teaching, but had no money or had other priorities. At Huyton College, for instance, in the 1920s the headmistress had been concentrating on building a school chapel. Since the laboratory space was inadequate, most of the teaching was done in the ordinary classrooms, and any girl aspiring to study physics had to go to Liverpool University. But a biology and a chemistry lab were opened in 1927, and a science foundation course for junior girls was established, covering botany, zoology, astronomy, geology, hygiene, physics and chemistry, and seniors were able to specialize in chemistry and biology – provisions that were not at all common at that time. Indeed, at Red Maids' until the 1950s any girl wanting to study any form of science had to be sent to one of the other Bristol schools.

Upper Chine, as has already been discussed in Chapter 5, was one of the very few private schools to take science seriously. Throughout the early decades of the century inspectors were to try to persuade schools to improve their science teaching, and no doubt many proprietors chose not to ask to be inspected because they had no intention of making good such deficiencies. But this Isle of Wight school was advertising in the 1920s that it taught biology, physics, chemistry, physiology and hygiene, and was commended by the inspectors in 1936 for its 'science scheme of work', which seems to have been taught throughout by a single member of staff who 'although not a graduate, completed a three year degree course in the subject at Reading University'. The maths, however, was not so warmly commended. 'The top Set is taught by a Visiting Mistress, and the bulk of the rest of the teaching is undertaken by the Geography Mistress, with some help from various other members of the staff. None of these teachers included Mathematics in their degree course, and the standard of work is not high.'[32] This would have held good for most schools except the high schools and the better sort of public school. As mentioned earlier, there had been much Victorian controversy over whether the study of mathematics would not actually do lasting damage to the female brain, and Janet Erskine Stuart of the Sacred Heart felt there was no shame in saying that the aptitude of girls for mathematical study was generally less than that of boys and that the subject meant much less to them in after life. 'The mathematical teacher of girls has generally to seek consolation in very rare success for much habitual disappointment.'[33]

School Certificate, as it was then called, was for most the end of their school career. Only the very academic schools concerned themselves with Higher Certificate, and girls spent their sixth-form years doing a broad general course. The lightweights might go off to finishing school, perhaps abroad, or to such an establishment as Ivy House in Wimbledon which *Queen* magazine investigated in 1922. It was run, they said, in gracious surroundings with girls who entered when they were fifteen or sixteen, and who might stay until they were nineteen or twenty. They had a daily French lesson, elocution lessons, debates on political topics (though the Misses Leeson did not believe in forcing problems on young people before they were ready), and learnt dressmaking, housewifery and cooking – about which a

Roumanian visitor commented: 'The thanks of the bachelors of all nations are due to you for this fine work you are doing!' (a comment perhaps obliquely directed at the appalling state of English cooking then).

Domestic science was inevitably a Cinderella subject at the ordinary school, and associated with the duds, who might, as at Harrogate College at one time and at Cheltenham, be accommodated in a special domestic arts wing, the implication being that one was fit for nothing else. There were attempts from time to time to reinstate it; Francis Holland School, Clarence Gate, for instance, at one time ran a householder course where seniors (and old girls) were taught about day-to-day matters like rents and rates, income tax forms, mending fuses, changing washers and elementary plumbing as well as the duties of citizenship. Domestic science was part of the duties of charity pupils; as late as 1937 the inspectors wondered if it was really necessary for girls at Red Maids' to have 'to peel potatoes for about a hundred people every day'. But the inclusion of home economics as a subject at A-level has given it a new status; it is in the regular syllabus at many schools for the first two years, becoming optional later. At St Leonards, leisure cookery is offered as an extra subject to senior girls, ranging from dinner party menus to survival cookery for university, and at plenty of boarding schools sixth-formers cook meals for invited guests.

Girls at the smaller independent schools (and at many of the so-called 'public' schools) had to wait until the 1960s for a significant change in academic standards. After the war a system of grants had made a university education accessible to social groups who had never before been able to afford it. But it was the report of the Robbins Committee in 1963 that made the real difference, with its acceptance 'as an axiom that courses of higher education should be available to all who are qualified by ability and attainment to pursue them and who wish to do so', a principle which heralded the establishment of new universities and polytechnics, and in its turn huge new building projects at schools to provide laboratories and new classrooms. School Certificate (replaced in 1951 by the General Certificate of Education) with matriculation exemption was no longer enough to secure access to universities and professional training; A-levels became imperative for anyone who wanted higher education, and the easy-going, comparatively undemanding life of the sixth-former disappeared for ever. For many girls the glamour of being able to go to one of the prestigious men's colleges, as Oxford and Cambridge gradually abandoned sex segregation in the 1970s, must have been a great incentive to hard work in their last two years. And schools that had drifted along without seeing need for change had to reconsider their whole outlook.

Schools have changed more in twenty years than throughout the preceding seventy. The curriculum they all offer is now standard; so far as what is studied goes, there is little difference now between boys and girls, between a high school and a small school like Heathfield, which offers divinity,

English, Latin, history, geography, French, German, Italian, Spanish, economics, mathematics, biology, chemistry, physics, art and music at GCSE level (this exam having replaced the former GCE in 1988), though the boarding schools often have better provision for art and practical subjects (which latter St Paul's, for instance, hardly bothers with). Craft design technology is now an important subject, and schools are busy building themselves CDT centres. Roedean carries it as far as anyone; in the physics department girls have been encouraged to make such things as satellite dishes and an electric car; sponsored by an oil company, they even built a hovercraft. The endearing amateurism seen in so many pre-war schools has given way to a highly professional approach; on the campus of Moreton Hall for instance there is now a science school, a home economics school, a computer centre, a music school, a library building and careers centre, and a specialist mathematics school, most of it added since the mid-70s.

This professional approach is found everywhere. It can be observed in the art turned out by the children, which in the 1930s was usually restricted to formal drawing of the sort necessary to pass the Royal Drawing Society's graded exams. Now pottery is commonplace and there are opportunities for sculpture, fabric-printing, print-making and photography, as well as weaving and embroidery. (In effect, one might say, the pendulum has swung back to the myriad accomplishments taught in early Victorian schools.) Music has dramatically improved; many girls play two instruments, and all schools of repute have to be able to offer tuition in strings, woodwind and brass, sometimes harp and timpani (St Leonards offers bagpipes, in addition). Schools field several orchestras, send choirs abroad, produce competent soloists. A-level music, like history of art, is an increasingly popular subject. Youth Enterprise, whereby schools learn business expertise, is a working proposition, and uncovers some remarkable entrepreneurial skills; girls who used to go off to finishing schools are now equipped to start their boutique in Knightsbridge, or fast-food chain in the West Country. Sometimes schools choose an easy option, like marketing biros or school photographs. Moreton, more ambitious, opened a seventeen-acre farm and learned by sweat and tears what hard work a smallholding is.

The children have also changed. Authority can no longer rely on unquestioning submission, on *esprit de corps* and loyalty to the flag. They are far more confident and more articulate, with views on most world issues. The difference can be illustrated, perhaps, from the accounts of debating societies. In the past the Mount managed better than most, as they had had an essay society since the 1840s where girls assembled to hear each other's work, so that when a debating society was started in the late 1880s they were used to expressing opinions. Indeed, in 1901 the question of over-representation in Ireland raised the Irish members to such a pitch of turbulence that some had to be expelled from the meeting. But at Worcester High School in 1906 the mistresses had to do all the speaking, as the girls were too shy. 'The Club has had its barren seasons, when silence has brooded heavy and terrifying over its meetings,' said a member of the S. Anne's, Abbots Bromley, debating society at the same period, and its Berkhamsted contemporary had to be disbanded because the members were too frightened to speak freely. Nottingham High School tried fining those who would not speak; on 26 October 1917 nine out of eleven girls were each fined a ha'penny. Bedgebury School in 1920 decided to initiate debates – on simple issues like whether cars were better than horses:

> When we were all in the drawing room Betty stood up and the few things she had to say she said with a rush, then for the rest of the two minutes there was an awful silence, and suddenly everybody burst out laughing.
>
> When Mrs Horlock had succeeded in restoring order, she called upon Peggy to second the motion. So Peggy said 'I second the motion.' But she could get no further; till at last her time was up and Helen started to oppose, but even she could not last out for two minutes.[34]

But the middle school at S. Helen and S. Katharine in 1969 announced that they had had many fruitful discussions on subjects ranging from the Pope and the Pill to the colour of pillar boxes. '[The Chaplain] has been very tolerant although our opinions often differ.'[35] And Bedgebury in 1987 debated with great articulacy such issues as euthanasia, whether homosexuality should remain legal, capital punishment, abortion – topics on which most had views. For all the boldness of theme, the opinions expressed, if one examines school magazines over the years, are often conservative; debating societies at the beginning of the century tended to vote against women's suffrage; in the 1950s most appeared to feel that the place of married women was in the home, and in the 1980s the feeling was against the ordination of women and for the restoration of capital punishment. In mock elections the Tories mostly win, though not at West Heath in 1986: 'We were all seriously fighting against Labour gathering seats throughout the country; but voting for the Labour candidate in school as we felt it would be the only time we could ever vote Labour.'[36]

Extra-curricular

'Our lives were so full and lived at such speed,' said Winifred Peck of her schooldays at Wycombe, 'that we had no idea of occupying ourselves in the holidays, and still less when we "went home for good." She felt there should be some effort made in every school to encourage pupils to find interests and hobbies. 'For what,' the old Scotswoman asked a niece who could not knit, 'wull ye do when your faculties commence to decay?'[37]

One or two schools applied themselves early on to filling this need. St Leonards, perhaps mindful of the long northern nights, encouraged needlework from the start. There is still a Golden Thimble award, and many examples on show of exquisite stitching of the past. They also in early days took up *slöjd*, a type of woodwork which originated in Sweden and was held to be of great educational value, 'inculcating in children by a method calculated to appeal to their intelligence such qualities as patience, perseverance, self-reliance and accuracy'. At Badminton, under Miss Baker (1911–47), not only were art and hobbies promoted (there were opportunities, for instance, to do pottery, at that time a very exotic pastime), but reading was taken seriously. There were regular reading periods and most girls 'adopted the habit of reading, and appreciated it'. Benenden, whose founders had made a special point of encouraging everyone to have their own special talent, from early years had a Hobbies Day in which all members of the school took part, contributing music, drama or crafts according to their tastes and abilities. One of the first pupils had reared a brood of ducks. But one of them turned out to be a drake who could not pay his way by laying eggs. 'So very tearfully, under Miss Whyte's guidance, I killed "Frida", plucked him, drew him and trussed him, exhibited him for Hobbies, and won a First!'[38]

The early seminaries for young ladies filled every waking moment with lessons, which began even before breakfast (a fact of which medical opinion was highly critical). At the school described by Mrs Ewing in her novel *Six to Sixteen* the girls had fifteen minutes' recreation daily, usually curtailed by the appearance of 'Madame'. The only exercise was 'a promenade in double file under the eye and ear of Madame'. One difficulty about recreation may, of course, have been lack of space. Most of these establishments would have been housed in the proprietress's own home, with all the pupils crammed into one classroom and no space for a playroom. Even the clergy daughters at Casterton, with much more space, did not have a playroom until 1871, at about which time swings and see-saws were installed in the playground for the younger children. The Mount from early on had a playroom with a swing that could take four, even five, at a time. (The great ambition when swinging alone and standing was to kick the high ceiling. There was also 'a pulley with a cross bar on which we could sit and swing off from a table underneath, and a nice jumping board'.[39]) This sort of imaginative provision was rare, and so was the initiative shown by two new members of the school in 1879 who collected money for cricket bats, wickets and a ball and, without asking permission (it would not have been given), prepared a pitch and organized practice. Manchester High School showed the same sort of spirit in the 1880s, when the girls clubbed together to buy a barrel-organ so that they could dance when the weather was bad. In the end they became tired of dancing but used to churn away at the organ until it finished its life with a fall downstairs.

One school, the Adult Orphan Institution, was reported by the Taunton commissioners as having a library, which must have been so unusual in the 1860s that they recorded its contents. But it would seem to be for work rather than for leisure. There were over four hundred volumes, consisting of 'judiciously selected works of approved authors'; these included: theology, works of British essayists, poets and historians, travels, Saturday and penny magazines; French authors such as Racine, Corneille, Mme de Sévigné and La Fontaine, Noël et Chapsal's French grammar (much groaned over by pupils on whom it was inflicted); Tasso, Dante, Metastasio; Virgil, Cicero, Caesar; the prose works of Schiller, and *Undine*.[40]* (The Merchant Maiden Hospital which, being Scottish, did not come within the scope of the inquiry, had had a small library since 1832, the governess being directed by the governors to distribute books 'according to her best direction' and occasionally to entertain girls to tea in order to converse with them about their reading.) By the 1890s more account was taken of leisure reading, and the *Winchester High School* (later St Swithun's) *Chronicle* reported proudly that they too had a library, of some three hundred volumes, but here there was fiction, including Kipling, Stevenson, Anthony Hope, Stanley Weyman, Conan Doyle, Rider Haggard, Jerome K. Jerome, and, curiously, Zola.[41] However, Cheltenham Ladies' College about this time took the view that 'the average girl fresh from school, reads the magazines, but little else. She cannot be said to have a favourite author, for she thinks little of the writer, so long as what she reads amuses her. Poetry she never touches, and solid prose of any kind she finds too difficult.'[42] Nevertheless, even at that time Cheltenham had a remarkably fine library, more like a university's, with rare volumes donated by distinguished scholars.

The best schools have separate reference and leisure libraries. Of all school libraries St Leonards' is remembered with the greatest affection, housed, as has been described in Chapter 4, in a sixteenth-century town house each of whose rooms holds a different subject. Unlike some libraries, it is open on Saturday and Sunday afternoons as well as during the week.

> Oh you have been a well to me from whence
> I drank great peace in deep cool draughts, and quenched
> The thirst of discontent and pain; and you
> Have been a garden full of lovely things,
> Amongst whose flowers I wandered . . .[43]

wrote one sixth-former in 1936.

The Mount, a pioneer in so many areas, seems to have had school societies long before anyone else. We have already noted the essay society and the debating society, and there was an astronomical society by 1897, 'wildly popular', a contemporary reported. 'The older ones have to teach the others. I have learnt to take the sun's transit and have looked at Saturn's

* *Undine* by the German author La Motte Fouqué, first published in 1811, was a story very popular with Victorian readers as various as Charlotte Yonge and George MacDonald.

rings and Jupiter's moons and several coloured doubles besides sun-spots and mountains on the moon. It is glorious!' And an archaeological society was founded a little later. A 1920s pupil said enthusiastically that it had taught her to understand maps and plans and to appreciate old York. This was at a time when it was most unusual for girls to be allowed to leave the school premises; pupils of both Nottingham and Oxford High Schools complained of how little they knew of their cities. The Park School in Glasgow was particularly rich in clubs in the Edwardian period. Many of them were literary societies, and there was a Latin club that met each Friday, 'when Latin quotations we had found during the week in the newspapers and our general reading were translated, thus the subject was given reality and a correlation with life'.[44] Badminton was a conventional young ladies' seminary when the formidable Miss Baker arrived in 1911, and one of her first moves in reshaping it was to inaugurate clubs and societies. A debating society came first, then archaeological, dramatic, reading and nature clubs, and the Settlement Guild, to help with Bristol slum children.

Societies now proliferate, as is evident from any school magazine. They cover intellectual activities, and most sporting ones. Pupils compete in music festivals and in public speaking competitions. There are religious fellowships and groups involved in social service; Malvern has clubs for martial arts, caving and bridge; at Benenden there are Young Farmers, and at nearly every school older pupils take part in the Duke of Edinburgh Award Scheme. However, these do not always keep boredom at bay. At girls' schools far more than at boys' it is difficult to find staff willing to supervise weekend activities, and often the expensive and lavishly equipped studios and craft rooms are closed out of school hours. As one girl said bitterly, at a school where weekend boredom was acute, 'Everybody has to join two societies, but it doesn't follow that they do much. The Jewellery Society only meets twice a term, and what's the good of that?'

Most country schools make full use of their environment. At a few, such as Bedgebury, you can bring your own pony and riding scholarships are among those offered. Activities at St Anne's Windermere, as has been described in an earlier chapter (see page 141), take advantage of a superb location in the Lake District. St Felix at Southwold has no mountains, but runs a two-year scheme whereby younger girls learn practical skills like camping, map-reading, orienteering, first-aid, ecology and interior decoration; and social services, a run-up to the Duke of Edinburgh Award work which has now largely replaced Guiding – its scheme of social service being far more demanding than the Guide movement, in the days of more cloistered girlhood, ever thought possible. The official Girl Guide movement started in 1911, but several schools, feeling that something was missing in the ordinary boarding school curriculum, had anticipated it. Pioneer scout patrols were formed at St Mary's, Wantage, at the time of the

Boer War, before Baden-Powell had started the Scouts.

> We were divided into Patrols. Sister set the special work for the day, and a written report had to be sent in by each patrol, which was marked like a school exercise. Sometimes we had to report on the possible defences of a village, or on the people we met. Sister read us Baden-Powell's little red book on Scouting for Soldiers, and that was our only textbook.[45]

At Roedean the scout scheme devised by Millicent Lawrence in 1909 antedated the official Guides. As might be expected under the Lawrences, it was compulsory, and took in the whole school with prefects as leaders and a member of staff as scout mistress. It was not until 1926 that membership became voluntary, though by this time it was affiliated to the national Guide movement and renamed. There seems at that time, and particularly during World War I, to have been a great female longing for a quasi-military organization. The girls at the Ursuline convent at Brentwood formed themselves into 'The Royal Grangers' during the early months of the war, providing themselves with hats, ties, belts and poles – all this quite unknown to the nuns, whom they invited to a display of drill and signalling. Many headmistresses felt in the early days that Guiding was an essential part of character-training. 'Could you, with a good conscience, run your school *without* Guiding?' Alice Baird of St James's, West Malvern, asked another headmistress. St James's girls came from particularly privileged homes, and like Miss Wyatt at Heathfield, she wanted them to go out into the world prepared to do work among the less fortunate. Three Guide companies were started at the school, with the expectation that many of the girls would go on to be Guiders, and that 'the talents, aptitudes, training and opportunities' would be conveyed to others. St Margaret's, Bushey, did even better, and by 1936 had four Guide companies. Now it is comparatively rarely found in any school, the enthusiasm for uniform and military-style organization having waned.

One of the earliest extra-curricular activities was drama. It had long been traditional at convents. New Hall had 'conversations' performed at speech days – two dialogues, one in French, the other in English, composed by the nuns on some literary, historical or scientific subject, and recited with gestures. The children, who in the early days lived a semi-enclosed life, rarely going home for holidays, also performed a play for each other at 'Kingtide' (Epiphany), a time when most rules were in abeyance. Sacred tableaux were a great feature of Sacred Heart convents; the performers used to kneel together in the green room before the curtain went up, to pray for a successful performance. 'I can still see . . . the Immaculate Conception, seeming to stand amongst the clouds, and the lifelike and tender impersonation of the Sacred Heart, blessing the nations of the world.'[46]

Some schools resisted, feeling that the stage was the devil's cockpit. 'A suggestion has been made that I should permit the girls to act a charade or two at the festival *without any change of dress*,' wrote the Dean of Queen's College to one of the Lady Visitors (chaperons) in 1864. 'The objections of the Lady Visitors and the Council, if I understand them rightly, were chiefly directed against the *costume* of performance and the theatrical display which it involved.'[47] The charade was not performed. Sherborne, being an evangelical foundation, banned acting and dancing at first; only the kindergarten was allowed to give small plays. The senior school had to use its ingenuity to devise entertainments that came within the law, and devised *tableaux vivants*, living statuary, and shadow plays. 'The theory seemed to be that it was not wrong to dress up and act a scene if you did not speak, nor to speak a scene if you did not dress up and act.'[48] But when one house produced scenes from *A Midsummer Night's Dream*, this was the thin end of the wedge; others quickly followed, and in 1924 came the first school play. Finally Sherborne was set on the same course as all the other schools, and now takes drama as seriously as any, which is very seriously indeed. No longer is it a matter of squeezing as many pupils as possible into a production, or of contenting oneself with *The Merchant of Venice*, perhaps *Dear Octopus* or *Quiet Wedding* on an improvised stage. St Paul's and Wycombe Abbey in the 1980s both opened lavishly equipped theatres, where highly professional performances of ambitious plays are staged; Westonbirt has one of the most beautiful theatres of any school, in the old Orangery. Benenden took the bold step in 1987 of having an actor-in-residence, whose brief was to introduce workshop drama at all levels, with visiting actors, designers and players. The first of these introduced the girls to circus skills, and 'for an entire day, the hall was full of trainee clowns, jugglers, high-wire walkers and people falling off stilts'. The school magazine reported 'a noticeable drop' in the number of hobbies submitted that year.

Gardening used to be popular; at St Leonards, the Godolphin, St Mary's Hall and several other schools children could have their own gardens, and one distinguished alpinist said that her interest stemmed from her school garden at Hayes Court, the only subject where she could get ten out of ten.[49] These have now nearly all disappeared, some under new buildings or playing fields, but others seemingly abandoned through lack of interest. The botany gardens at James Allen's Girls' School, Dulwich, established in the 1890s by an inspired teacher so that classroom botany could be combined with practical work in the grounds, are one of the very few remaining. She had wanted to be able to show town children different plant habitats – such as heath, chalk downs, pebble beach, sand dunes, oak wood, lanes, ponds and so on – and created all these on London clay. By 1914 more than three hundred girls were helping with the work, and the site was visited by many London schools. Inevitably during the last war any work on it was impossible;

it became overgrown and the distinctive regions were lost. But since 1984 the school has been hard at work reclaiming them, and they are again a resource for other London schools.

School expeditions are now standard for everyone; from primary schools upwards, parties are taken skiing, to study classical civilization in Greece, trekking in the Swiss Alps, sightseeing in Italy, on Mediterranean cruises. They go to Russia often, to China occasionally (Cranborne Chase took one of their dramatic productions to various Chinese schools), on school exchanges and field trips. Before 1950 this was very rare – as was, indeed, any family holiday abroad. The School of St Clare, Penzance, took a party of ten to Brittany in 1931, where their appearance at the Dinard Casino in white dresses and black woolly stockings made a sensation. Redland High School girls, from the beginning, were intrepid travellers, but they were the exception. One fourth-former wrote about ten days spent in Paris in 1890, laconically cataloguing the disasters.

> There was a slight fuss at Bristol Station on account of a misunderstanding about the Saloon Carriage that was to convey us to Paddington, and in the confusion one of our number got left behind . . . The [sea] passage was not a pleasant one to some of our party. Dieppe did not impress me very favourably. At Dieppe, we took a train to Paris, our train collided with another one and the boiler burst, but after sundry stoppages, and much exercising of patience, we arrived.[50]

But Cranborne Chase's experience of Chinese trains in 1987 was very different: 'If one in every five British Rail employees were to see Chinese trains, their slogan "We're getting there" might become "We've got a long way to go".'

Physical Education

'The older view of physical culture for girls had been concerned with grace and posture rather than with health and activity,' recalled one school chronicler. 'Walking and perhaps riding were the only actual exercise, and apart from that the girl was trained, as it were, more like a plant than an animal, by fastening her to various sorts of rigid framework.'[51] Girls were made to lie on backboards, had their chins held up by iron collars, their backs pulled back by steel bands. Mary Martha Sherwood (1775–1851), author of *The History of the Fairchild Family*, one of the most famous evangelical children's classics, in childhood was made by her father to translate fifty lines of Virgil every day, standing in stocks to straighten her back, with an iron collar round her neck.[52] As has been said, the only exercise taken by the old-fashioned seminary was walking in crocodile (a term which seems to have first been used about 1870). When the Mount abolished their crocodiles in 1900 one girl, at least, felt nostalgic: 'I rather liked walking in a crocodile, it felt friendly and rather important.' But it was held to be a nuisance to passers-by in York, though for a time it was thought to be enough if the girls went into single file when they met pedestrians. 'We then practised in the garden, the seniors, armed with coal pans and other impediments, meeting the croc at various corners.'[53] A few schools had callisthenics classes, but Mr Fearon, appointed by the Taunton commissioners to report on the metropolitan area, found that of a hundred private schools for girls, sixty provided no form of exercise other than 'walking abroad, croquet and dancing', and thirty-two provided only a form of callisthenics, which was often unpopular with parents as it was an expensive extra.[54] He attributed much female ill-health to lack of exercise, and stressed in his report that proprietors of schools 'ought to provide their pupils with games which shall be sufficiently difficult to thoroughly divert their minds'.[55]

Two of the headmistresses who gave evidence to the Commission were themselves aware of the importance of exercise. Miss Buss told the commissioners that at North London Collegiate callisthenics was compulsory for everyone, four days a week, and the younger children were encouraged to take exercise in the playground.[56] Miss Beale said that at Cheltenham they had 'a room specially fitted with swings etc. It is to be wished that croquet could be abolished, it gives no proper exercise, induces colds, and places the body in a crooked posture; besides, as it does not fatigue, girls are able to go on for five or six hours and induced to be idle.'[57] A few headmistresses like Alice Ottley feared that games might rub off the delicate bloom of femininity. She detested women's cricket, for instance, which she allowed only the little girls of her school to play.

In the absence of trained female instructors, schools often had to import army sergeants to drill the girls. 'We had a sergeant from the Barracks who came to teach us drill,' a founder member of Norwich High School recalled. 'His voice was terrific, and one day the Headmistress came in and said "My good man, will you please modulate your voice?" at which he took a deep breath and shouted louder.'[58] The tradition of the army sergeant survived into the early years of this century at The Laurels (Wroxall Abbey), where the girls were taught by the Rugby School instructor, a veteran from the Boer War. He made the girls sing 'Oh fighting with the Seventh Royal Fusiliers' as they lunged right and left in dumb-bell exercises, insisting that the unsuitable words were to aid correct breathing.

> He used to love devising competitions for his pupils, and became more excited than the competitors in the heat of a contest; if a favourite was beaten by an outsider, he would shake his head and say wistfully 'Why do they allus lose their 'eads in a fight?' 'Oller yer backs!' was always his cry when the girls were standing to attention.[59]

But by this time Swedish drill, taught by experts, was fashionable. It reached the smarter schools via the elementary schools. (The latter were obliged by the terms of the 1870 Education Act to provide two hours of physical education for boys, and were in effect the pioneers of PE as a universal subject.) The method was brought over to England by Madame Sofia Helena Bergman (she married Dr Per Österburg in 1886 and was subsequently known as Bergman-Österburg), who had studied at the Royal Central Gymnastics Institute in Stockholm the Ling methods of exercising each part of the body in turn, taking care not to develop one part at a different rate from the others. In 1881 the London Schools Board appointed her Superintendent of Physical Education in Girls' and Infants' Schools, and the following year she organized a drill display in which hundreds of London schoolchildren took part, watched by a large and distinguished audience including the Prince and Princess of Wales.

In 1885 she opened a gymnasium (which later became the Dartford College of Physical Training) to train teachers. But though the girls played team games, Madame Bergman-Österburg never grasped their rules, and if she did attend a match was apt to be unclear whether the players were supposed to hit or kick the ball. She felt passionately that her mission was to improve the lot of women:

> I try to train my girls to help to raise their own sex, and so to accelerate the progress of their race . . . If [women] studied the laws of health and lived free, untrammelled lives, with plenty of physical exercise, they would not be the sickly, careworn beings so many of them are at present.[60]

When the drill sergeant at Mary Datchelor School was displaced in favour of a Bergman-Österburg trained instructor he told her forcefully that the dresses of the pupils were 'too tight to carry out the practice in a proper manner', and in 1891 there was a ferocious indictment in the school magazine of the clothes worn at the drilling lessons, dresses often so tight that the girls could hardly breathe, so small in the armholes that they could not move their arms, and with skirts so tight that it was difficult to move at all. The older girls were urged to leave off corsets and wear jerseys on drilling days, and many schools devised a gymnasium dress (as described in Chapter 11). At Kent College in the late 1880s, where there was a gymnasium, drill was taken by a sergeant and the girls wore

> gym tunics made of very heavy serge trimmed with a light blue band around their yokes, and with high necks with a pleated frill of light blue flannel. The sleeves were long and had elastic at the wrists and were also faced with light blue flannel. We wore belts either of serge trimmed with a blue band or hand-knitted woollen girdles with heavy tassels at their ends. Our knickers were down to our knees and had elastic round them with frills of light blue flannel like our cuffs. We were very proud of them and later wore them as bath costumes. But we didn't swim.[61]

In 1891 the brother school at Canterbury (both were Wesleyan Methodist foundations) described in their magazine a gymnastics display given by the girls, under the sergeant. It consisted of 'marching, mazing, and exercises with rings, clubs, dumb-bells and trapeze rings' by about thirty performers in 'becoming gymnastic costume and with musical accompaniment'. The display ended with a jumping contest in which the winner cleared 4 feet 10 inches. The sergeant then proposed a tug of war, in which the boys were decisively defeated. There was however a return match, and the tug of war for a time became a feature of the school calendar.[62]

Though Edward Thring had installed a gymnasium and a swimming pool at Uppingham in the 1850s, for girls the former was not by any means usual. Kent College's, purpose-built in 1886, must have been one of the earliest. The headmistress of the Lady Eleanor Holles School, then at Hackney (Julia Maria Ruddle, 1878–95), is supposed to have begged the governors not to build a gymnasium because such exercise was unladylike. As late as 1923 Mother Clare of Brentwood Ursuline Convent was reporting with grim satisfaction that inspectors were beginning to show 'disapproval of much that takes place in the drill lessons'. She picked out somersaults, cart-wheels, leap-frog and tunnel-ball as particularly undesirable. A Catholic inspector had remarked that she could not understand superiors of convents allowing such activities. Simple Swedish exercises were quite enough, with pupils being taught how to walk and dance gracefully.[63] Dancing, of course, had been a feature of the old-style seminary, but this was a social accomplishment rather than an outlet for exercise, and dance as part of physical education did not appear until the latter became more sophisticated. Some schools in the early part of this century took up English country dancing – it features in many of Elsie J. Oxenham's books[64] – and Greek dancing and eurhythmics were fashionable in the 1920s and 30s. Ardent disciples claimed much for both. In Greek dancing

> Not only are the physical powers developed; the sight of the unhastening movements of the dance gives rest to eyes tired with the unrhythmic kaleidoscope of modern life, the sound of great choric odes or divine melodies brings peace to ears weary with the harsh noises of machinery; the contemplation of the arts of the ancient world soothes the spirit and sets it free from the confining walls of cities, to roam in the great spaces of nature and of the human soul.[65]

Eurhythmics, the system of combined muscular and musical instruction developed by Emile Jaques-Dalcroze (see page 139), is intended to make feeling for rhythm a physical experience. It teaches the interpretation of music through movement, and at one time at schools like Moira House was a way of life in itself. Greek dancing had been started for a few of the older girls at Mary Datchelor School in 1927, and the 'green tunics and elegant hairbands' inspired such envy that it was introduced for all, 'and now girls disport themselves as nymphs and butterflies and seagulls and heaven knows what else'.[66] Both of these were supplanted in later years by the Laban free dance system. Rudolf Laban, who had escaped from Nazi Germany in 1938 and settled in England, evolved a whole philosophy of movement as a means of human expression. His free dance was a useful antidote to the constricting formality of the classical ballet taught at independent schools from the 1920s onwards, which only the advanced who had fully mastered the technique could use for self-expression.

But dance tended to belong to the smaller, more idiosyncratic school. In the public schools it was games that mattered. It is both sad and salutary to remember that what was to become such tyranny started off as fun. Writing in the Francis Holland, Clarence Gate, magazine in 1892 the hockey captain earnestly invited her readers to try the game, adding 'All who have played it declare it to be one of the most exciting and exhilarating games they know. It is as thrilling as football without the strong element of danger ... Hockey is not in the least dangerous; with the exception of a few trifling bruises, no one is likely to get hurt.' Her girlish enthusiasm, and the notion that you played games because they were fun, is a far cry from the hectoring severity of the school's lacrosse captain writing in the magazine forty years later.

> One or two girls, shirking the drudgery, have given up the game altogether. Let them clearly understand that this is not showing a sporting spirit. In future all slackers will be turned out of the Club, so that its members may be looked upon as earnest, hardworking players – who play, play up, and play the game.

At first games were spontaneous, initiated by the girls themselves (though the girls of the Royal School in the 1880s got no further than buying a football and learning to blow it up). The Misses Lawrence and later Miss Dove at Wycombe Abbey incorporated games into the curriculum from the start, but this was unusual. Even at St Leonards it was optional and unorganized in the early days. There was merely a games club with a rule that 'any members failing to play at least once a week for three weeks, without proper excuse, will be fined the sum of 2d'. The club lapsed, and an elected school captain was made responsible for seeing that everybody played at least once a week; there were many who never did more than that. 'Goals' and rounders were played in the winter; cricket and tennis in the summer. 'Goals' was able to accommodate any number of players. The weapon was a cross between a heavy walking stick and a shepherd's crook, and the only copy of the rules was in the captain's pocket and open to the widest interpretation.

Bedford High School in the late 1880s and the 1890s played the same sort of game.

> The goal posts were two sticks at one end and the large chestnut tree and the privet hedge. We had practically no rules, except that we always changed places after a goal was scored; if the ball went out, whoever reached it first threw it in, and we played with the stick in either hand as we liked, and with the front or the back of it. With the arrival of Miss Lea we began to learn that there were rules, though we must have been extraordinarily difficult to teach, as I remember how keen we were on our own peculiar game.[67]

Similarly the upper sixth at Worcester rebelled against being pulled up in their rushings to and fro. They indicated that they had never played games like that, and if they were going to be ordered about so much the game might as well be called a lesson. At Blackheath High School an 1880s pupil said there appeared to be no limitation on numbers at their games of hockey; it seemed as if the whole of the upper school took to the field at once. There were no rules, except a vague one about offside. 'Goals were generally scored from a confused mêlée, in which the ball was pushed over the line by sheer weight of numbers . . . I do not know when I have enjoyed any game more.'[68]

Like Miss Ottley, Miss Beale required a great deal of persuasion before she would allow games to be a regular part of Cheltenham life. 'She greatly valued in women a gentle and dignified courtesy of manner, and she did think it possible, and even likely, that this grace might be lost beyond recall if women took up men's sports. She felt too that the use of slang expressions was encouraged by the excitement of the games.'[69] Miss Creak, the first headmistress of King Edward VI, Birmingham, refused to allow her girls to play them, convinced, like her medical adviser, that they ran the risk of injury to vital parts. But in spite of Miss Beale's reservations, the school council in 1891 decided to rent a piece of land for a playing field. It was not ideal: a farmer pastured his cattle on it when the girls were not using it; it was worked for drainage purposes into ridges between which the water lay, and the cattle trampled the ground into a bog. There were no prescribed clothes; girls wore their outgrown Sunday clothes and their least respectable boots. They played with ash sticks, like walking sticks, which cost 4d, and there was very little organization; a girl who had played with her brothers taught the rest the rules. Nevertheless, it was such a success that the field was bought, together with neighbouring land, and tennis courts were laid and a cricket pitch levelled.

Brighton and Hove High School in 1886 was playing football in the same carefree spirit, but with a greater degree of organization. Their playground was a mass of stones and gravel which quickly wore out leather, and the game was often interrupted by the ball bursting – 'Our balls get done for very much more easily than they otherwise would,' said the school magazine.

But the writer reckoned that their game had improved, though she had criticisms:

> A few of the smaller members of the Club have a great tendency to hop over the ball, instead of kicking it; whilst others are terribly afraid of it and think only of getting out of the way of kicks; others make gallant dashes at the ball, but, on second thoughts, think they had better leave it to their opponents.[70]

But by 1900 the carefree abandon had gone out of team games (except at small schools like Prior's Field, where 'we could not very well play hockey with only six girls, so we purchased a football, and all of us . . . used to have the most exciting times with it'.) The City of Cardiff High School magazine gave hints on the clothes that should be worn ('Hard hats and hat-pins are dangerous, but a cap may be used. The shins may be protected by shin-guards or gaiters'), and pointed out that it was a 'sanitary necessity, often neglected by women', to take a 'warm (not hot) bath' afterwards.

> In conclusion, it may be remembered that one of the chief defects in present girls' play is a certain slackness; they are not quick enough in 'bullying', or in taking their places at a 'throw-in', or in getting on to the ball from a corner-hit, or in following up their own hits. Further, in playing matches, they have not sufficient knowledge of the game to divine the weak places in the game of their opponents . . . They should also learn to stop the ball otherwise than with the skirt.

And twenty years after those gloriously ad hoc games at Blackheath, the school had settled down to the ritual of matches. 'We appeared at morning school in our black skirts and "wasp" blouses, with the yellow ties that were the "colours" . . . our hair was plaited with a tightness that was more utilitarian than beautiful, and tied with yellow ribbon. At Prayers we sang "Fight the Good Fight" with great feeling.'[71] St Swithun's in 1896 at their first outside match, against Queen Anne's, Caversham, had been suitably daunted by the professionalism of their rivals (who had won). The team who 'were all dressed in scarlet and looked to us very burly and experienced' had declined suet pudding at lunch time, and according to St Swithun's tradition, were discovered afterwards 'lying on the floor resting in preparation'.[72] But in this year The Laurels won its first away match.

> I only know the feelings of those who stayed at home – we waited in almost breathless anxiety till the telegram came. And how we cheered the victors back to the Laurels, and what a welcome we gave them, as we ushered them in with the well-known strains of 'See the conquering heroes come'.[73]

The stage is now set for the grim earnestness with which games were taken at the larger girls' schools in the early twentieth century. But even in 1906

Dr Jane Walker at the Conference of National Women Workers was warning 'against making physical health and strength the principal aim of our national well-being'. Games were no longer fun; they were an important part of the curriculum – too important, some were beginning to feel. Even Miss Faithfull (a one-time committee member of the All-England Hockey Association) said at a Francis Holland, Clarence Gate, prize-giving that she was always 'rather sorry to see that a large number of girls want just to be physical training teachers and nothing else'.

And the girls themselves tended to take games with painful seriousness. 'Brenda is a good player, with very reliable stickwork and tackling,' the Paulina lacrosse captain wrote of her team in 1927. But she could not say the same of anybody else. 'Dorothy showed her lack of experience in keeping the team together.' 'Horatia lacks pace and is slow in passing.' 'Barbara's catching is weak and her shooting wild.' 'By unnecessary running round in circles [Joyce] muddles the rest of the attack.' 'Barbara has been a hard-working and conscientious captain,' commented the games mistress, 'but inclined to be over-anxious and sometimes too easily discouraged.'[74]

However, at St Paul's work came before play (this could not be said of some of their contemporaries). The High Mistress, interviewed by *Queen* magazine in 1922, said that if a girl was not up to the standard of work in her form, she was not allowed to represent it in the team. 'We do not place skill in games higher than intellectual achievement. We discourage excessive talk about games and we are very careful that girls shall not over-exert themselves.'[75] This would have pleased *Queen*'s educational correspondent, who a few months later wrote that too much exercise made girls thick-set and clumsy.

> I shall never forget watching a large party of public schoolgirls coming by two's into church. They were delightful girls with frank, fresh faces, but their figures one and all ran to breadth not height, and the less said about the way they walked the better.[76]

Queen had also interviewed Miss Penelope Lawrence – Roedean having been originally founded to promote health through exercise at a time when this was a revolutionary principle. She was guarded, perhaps feeling that Roedean was under attack on this score. 'I do not assert that games teach all the virtues . . . but I do think that an hour's organized outdoor sport a day is essential for the harmonious development of mind and body.'[77]

The Sacred Heart nuns had always put great stress on the importance of innocent recreation, and at Roehampton they were playing cricket and tennis in the 1870s. The game of *cache-cache*, peculiar to them alone and remembered with ecstasy by all 'old children', was held to have peculiarly beneficial effects on the character. 'Few school games are as fine a training in endurance, self-control, discretion and chivalrous honour,' claimed a member of the order.[78] You had to restrain your excitement when twenty or thirty of you were lying in a haystack or some outbuilding, or up in the rafters, while enemy spies crept round nearby. You had to control the urge afterwards to boast about the superb new hiding place, and you never, never looked, when the game was over, to see where the other side was coming from.

Cache-cache seems to have been universally loved, which was more than can be said for most team games. Cricket, now played by very few girls' schools, even St Leonards having abandoned it in the 1980s (one of the reasons being that few games mistresses now have played the game themselves), was particularly disliked by all except the very capable. 'Playing cricket and hating it', someone gave as her worst memory of Benenden. 'Much more fun making daisy chains at Long Stop (is there a position there any more?). Certainly seemed the safest place, as far away from that hard ball as possible.'[79] Curiously, it seems to have been the earliest team game played by girls. Miss Susan Kyberd, giving evidence to the Schools Inquiry Commission in April 1866, said that at the Chantry School in Somerset, a small boarding school, the girls played cricket, though 'no girl is allowed to play without her parents' permission, and without a proper dress'. It was also played at Moira House in the 1870s, a fact so unusual that *The Times* commented upon it. At first girls seemed to want to play cricket, though others than Miss Ottley felt it was only suitable for the younger ones. At St Mary's, Wantage, a small girl brought a 'cricket set' to school in the 1890s, but it was decreed that no girl over the age of fifteen should play. At Edgbaston High School authority allowed it, but when a match was played against a neighbouring school in 1881, the *Globe*, a Birmingham paper, remarked disapprovingly: 'We must confess to a preference for those less pretentious places of education where English lasses used to be taught modesty, if little science.' It was a game only played by the larger schools – despite its appearance in the small establishments much loved by the school story writers of the 1920s and 30s; for one thing, a great deal of space is required.

Lacrosse – that game of unparallelled ferocity which English schoolgirls play with the minimum of protective clothing while in Canada, where it originated, men appear in armour – traditionally was first played at Ladybarn House, a Manchester prep school for boys and girls, as early as 1886,[80] the headmistress (who had to import the sticks from Canada) feeling that it was suitable for both sexes. St Leonards records matches in 1890; Withington School in 1891. Dame Frances Dove thought it an admirably character-building game, requiring skill and perseverance, powers of organization, 'good temper under trying circumstances, courage and determination . . . rapidity of thought and action, judgement and above all things unselfishness.'[81] A game, in short, that seemed designed in heaven for public schools. It was played from early days at Wycombe Abbey;

Malvern Girls' College took it up in 1917, and in the 1920s was one of the schools involved in the actual development of the game. 'Miss Newbold, the architect of the game, would come to us for a day and try out new ideas, leaving us to master and perfect them till her next visit.' Netball, which the smaller schools and younger girls played, is a version of basket ball, invented in the United States in 1891, and first introduced to England in 1895 when an American taught it to students at Madame Bergman-Österburg's college in Hampstead. The game was played in the gymnasium at first, with the walls as boundaries and waste-paper baskets as goals. In 1897 the students were taught the way that American women played the game, and in 1901 the college formulated and published rules that are now standard.

Individual schools had their own traditions. Wroxall Abbey played rugby football from time to time, the rumour being that when the school was in Rugby it played on the Rugby School fields. And at Runton Hill an epic game called 'valley ball' used to be played, invented by the headmistress, Miss Vernon Harcourt.

> The entire school would turn out, and stand shoulder to shoulder in two lines, like a crocodile ... The object of the game was for one house to touch down the ball in the opposing house's camp on the top of the opposite hillside, having crossed the valley ... Miss Vernon Harcourt would hurl the ball into the air and the game would be on. The game raged down and up the steepest valley that JVH could find in the Roman Camp. One might run with the ball, but when tackled one had to pass, but backwards, as in Rugby football. I used to spend most of the game face downwards in the bracken, all breath knocked from my body, while the two teams, North and South, tramped heavily by on my shoulder blades. But I was fairly well off. Frances sprained an ankle. Viola had long scratches down her face. Even JVH, bounding high in the air, tooting on her whistle, occasionally hurt herself. I imagine that for the rest of the girls of Runton Hill, valley netball has a great nostalgic significance, like the Eton Wall Game.[82]

Swimming lessons were to be added to the curriculum comparatively late. Christ's Hospital was one of the earliest girls' schools to possess its own swimming bath, from 1916. The girls were all provided with long-legged red cotton romper suits, with frills and white braid round the arms and legs and collar, and a belt to keep the whole in place in case they swam out of it. St Paul's, another early possessor of a covered pool, had a similar costume, in navy blue.

Organized games have changed less than any other area of the curriculum. Girls still have to spend as much time on the playing fields as ever they did, athletics now adding an extra dimension to the outdoor life, and though there are more individual sporting activities – trampolining, fencing, judo and so on – they are extra, not a substitute for the hearty activities that no one can escape. 'I get tired after ten minutes on the hockey pitch,' said one thirteen-year-old dolefully. 'That's before the game has started.' Perhaps the great difference between now and fifty years ago is that it is no longer a necessity to pretend to like games.

11

Discipline

'What did they do to you when you were naughty?' the elder two Sanger girls were asked by their fascinated siblings, curious about the ways of English public school life, in Margaret Kennedy's novel *The Constant Nymph*. 'They seemed at a loss to explain, but they intimated that it was something awful. It was not so much what was done as what was said. "I know what it was," put in Sebastian wisely. "They said 'Naughty girl Sanger! Don't do it again!' And you cried for the rest of the day. That's the way they do at girls' schools."'

This puts the matter in a nutshell. The Taunton Commission was told by Miss Buss that as far as discipline was concerned 'we do not find any difficulty'; indeed, all the headmistresses questioned in 1864 answered in much the same fashion, saying that punishment was minimal. What the commissioners did not state in their report, of course, was that probably more anxiety and fear could be generated by the moral disapproval of authority than by the corporal punishment at boys' schools. Nor did they refer to the multiplicity of rules without which few female establishments seem able to operate. Ironically, these were carried to their most extravagant lengths at the supposedly emancipated North London Collegiate School in Miss Buss's day.

> Almost every day a new one appeared in a corridor, in large sprawling home-made lettering – such as 'Broken needles must not be thrown on the floor'. There were so many that they ceased to attract attention and got caught up into the decorative scheme ... We were forbidden to get wet on the way to school, to walk more than three in a row, to drop a pencil-box, to leave a book at home, hang a boot-bag by only one loop, run down the stairs, speak in class. As for speaking, it would have been easier to enumerate the few places where we were permitted to speak than those where talking was forbidden. The ideas were sensible, but why make rules about them? One felt that if a girl were to knock over the blackboard by mistake there would be a rule against it the next day.[1]

The punishment was to have one's name recorded in the Appearing Book, something which might appear of ludicrous insignificance to ribald brothers, but which smacked of the Day of Judgement to the culprit. And those who appeared too often would be summoned by Miss Buss for 'a jaw'. 'But I don't believe any boy since the world began has ever known what a jaw can be. It needed Miss Buss to give a full content to the term. I never experienced it myself, but heard tales enough of poor girls reduced to sobs and almost hysterics as they bent under the storm that went on and on and on.'[2] It was not, of course, just Miss Buss. 'A notice on the board in the Verandah reading "So and so, speak to me! DRB" was enough to reduce one's knees to jelly and a robust lecture from Mrs Broadbent in her study was often as effective as any penalty she might impose.'[3]

'It was clear to Miss Buss,' said the school history in 1950, 'that character requires discipline; that slackness, untidiness, forgetfulness, unreliability, unpunctuality, must be checked, otherwise the development of the individual and the community was in danger.' Most girls at single-sex schools have listened to headmistresses waxing eloquent on variants of this theme, in which the moral consequences of small peccadillos have been magnified to monstrous proportions; indeed, examples have already been given in Chapter 4. 'The rules that had crept into being as necessities became to [authority] character-building virtues. They elaborated on any system of rewards and punishments until life became a minefield. A moment's carelessness – stepping out . . . in indoor shoes or leaving a book out on the table might turn you into a major criminal.'[4] Even an apparently enlightened headmistress could make a weighty moral issue out of a minute lapse in propriety, such as when a Notting Hill High School girl waved her hat and coo-eed at a friend in the street 'like a butcher's boy'. 'Suppose the whole troop of you coo-eed and waved your hats, what do you suppose would be the effect on the actual butcher-boys?' The writer, then in her seventies, felt that this specious argument traditionally used by authority was 'wise and witty', and demonstrated a 'beautiful submission to the fitness of things'. She concluded slavishly: 'she made me feel the beauty of order and fitting into one's place in one's society, one's country, one's world'.[5]

Admonition could be attended by much emotion. The anonymous writer of 'Reminiscences of the Ladies' College, Cheltenham' in the mid-1870s described the brouhaha over a transgression of young ladydom. For some weeks she had supposed that her housemistress's unwonted coldness towards her was because she had been noisy, but at last she elicited that it was because of her 'use of slang and unladylike expressions'. She was made to write to her mother to explain why she had been moved into another room. At this stage not very much troubled, she tried to compose a letter 'penitent enough for Miss Beale and yet nothing extraordinary to people at home'. Sitting at class in the hall, she saw the housemistress take this missive to Miss Beale on her throne. 'I watched them while they read it, every now and then one would point out a passage to the other and then they would shake their heads and look down at me in anything but an approving way.'

She was told that this effort was not good enough and that she must write another letter. There was one painful interview with the housemistress when she 'cried awfully' and said she had never used these expressions before she came to college, and another with Miss Beale who questioned her closely about the prevalence of slang among members of her house. Schoolgirl honour prevailed and she denied what was apparently a commonplace. Miss Beale 'made me cry a great deal' and when she finally 'put her arms all round me and kissed me so beautifully' the delinquent was melted and promised to be a reformed character. It is an interesting example of how authority allows itself to be deceived, and how emotion can prevail over truth and reason.

The North London Collegiate chronicler conceded that there were dangers in Miss Buss's emphasis on rules:

> Whereas detailed rules for the guidance of conduct had a part to play when girls were unaccustomed to life in any sort of community larger than the family, both experience and psychology showed them in many cases to be harmful, fretting the over-sensitive, concentrating the attention of girls and staff alike on detail rather than the broad principles of conduct, and tending to confuse small transgressions with real moral failure.[6]

This has long been a characteristic of schools, particularly girls' schools, so that no room is left for the really serious failings. 'At best the children learned to be good in a negative sort of way,' said one teacher, recalling the pettiness of the regulations at the boarding school where she had taught, and in particular the uproar when a little girl was found to have hidden some biscuits in her shoe locker.[7] Louie Angus, interviewed by the Christ's Hospital headmistress when she arrived at Hertford some seventy years ago, was asked what was the worst thing any schoolgirl could do. She guessed lying, then cheating, then stealing, and could think of nothing else but murder and adultery, but did not know what the latter meant and was afraid she would be asked. '"I don't know anything else," I said. "The worst thing a school girl can do," announced Miss Robertson solemnly, "is to pass notes in class to another girl."'[8]

'There were many pitfalls in the path to virtue,' said a girl of her 1950s boarding school. 'No girl might go up or down stairs more than one at a time. Possess food other than sweets or fruit. Send or receive letters from boys. Use a postbox out of school or use day girls to post letters. Run up and down the banks on the lawns or climb trees. Talk when lining up for a meal.'[9] A female organization feels safer when life is decently shrouded in a network of rules. A former head girl recalled among a multiplicity of supervision duties 'one particularly time-consuming and thankless chore'. She had to work out the walk-list for the weekend and submit it to the headmistress. 'What with girls who couldn't be allowed to go together and prefects who could be trusted only with the most amenable girls it was a nightmare.'[10]

A hundred years before at a teachers' training college where some of the pupils had been as old as twenty-five there had been sixty-nine rules, read out every Monday morning and most rigorously enforced, with a system of fines which rated unpunctuality at one penny, slamming doors or not walking in or out of the dining-room in proper order, at twopence, but 'each time the surname is repeated unnecessarily' and 'kissing, except on birthdays' at sixpence.[11] (At Margaret Nevinson's Anglo-Catholic convent in Oxford in the last century the rules were similarly read out once a week before breakfast.) The directives to the teaching nuns at St Mary's, Wantage, in 1900 included a list of the points ('last detached villas in Manor Road') where the crocodiles out for a walk could break rank, and the only activities (blackberrying was one) where girls might remove their gloves. Even the number of words that could be uttered when saying goodnight was specified.[12]

That rules at day schools could be fully as complex as at boarding schools has been seen from Miss Buss's code. Silence was enforced with the same rigidity in the early days; as we saw earlier, girls might not walk home with their friends until they had permission from their parents, nor be seen in the company of any male. At Norwich High School pupils had to move around the premises with their left hands behind their backs, and when they sat at lessons they had to have both hands behind them, to encourage good posture. Those who imposed such laws no doubt felt that these played a vital part in developing responsibility to oneself and the community, and that they had a religious duty to turn pupils out into the world as disciplined and faultless as five or six years' watchfulness could make them. One redoubtable art teacher at the City of Cardiff High School (1897–1930) held that 'the true appreciation of art required the true appreciation of discipline'. Before any lesson started she therefore inspected nails, stockings for holes, feet that might be illicitly wearing gym shoes, and only when all was in order would she march her class, single file, to the studio. 'The headmaster of the Boys' High School remembered meeting the procession, each girl holding blocks and rulers in the same hand, eyes front, and not an eye daring to flicker to the boys' party.'[13]

It is clear from current rule lists that though attitudes to such matters as gloves and hats may have changed, the nagging desire of female authority to cover all possible contingencies has not. A few schools, the smaller ones, manage to keep to matters of commonsense and courtesy, like More House School (245 girls), which says in its prospectus that there is no need for an elaborate structure of prohibitions. But most cannot dispense with these, and once rules are made they have to be enforced: 'Students are aware that some staff are more effective than others,' says one staff handbook reproachfully. 'Consequently girls add or remove jewellery between lessons and meals depending on the members of staff they are likely to encounter ... All members of staff share responsibility for ensuring that girls are appropriately dressed.' There is no subject too insignificant for rule books. All contemporary ones have stern warnings about the consequences of being found with drugs, cigarettes and drink; forbid make-up and jewellery; give rulings about exeats, correct clothing, the use of electrical appliances and the telephone, and about which shops in the locality are in or out of bounds. (Harrow in the 1960s also issued instructions to proprietors of the recognized shops about their staff: they had to have characters of appropriate rectitude, and if female might not be young.) But there is considerable additional detail, varying from school to school, about such matters as changing one's underpants and socks (and what to do with the soiled ones); about where sun-bathing is permitted and when, and the clothing that may and may not be worn for it; about ballpoint pens (forbidden), and the correct way to date one's work. (At least one school has helpfully provided an index for the anxious inquirer.) There are directives such as 'each girl should always have a College library book to hand' and 'at the end of a lesson the blackboard should be cleaned'. One school sees danger not in walking with a boy (permitted), but in meeting a recent old girl (forbidden unless an adult is present). Woldingham School presents its rules with a preliminary apologia: they are to 'enable each one of us to grow in respect for self; to encourage respect and concern for others; to maintain the safety and well-being of everybody'. Cheltenham points out that 'if you keep your desk tidy it helps you to work efficiently'. Other schools just list the do's and don'ts, which are often many and bewildering.

In contrast, a feature of some of the small private schools of eighty years ago, such as Prior's Field, Runton Hill and Wychwood, was the absence of rules and the freedom to move around the locality unsuperintended, in deliberate reaction to the over-regulated public schools. Even the Godolphin School, still very small at the turn of the century, then had very few (though a pupil of 1861 had complained that the discipline was 'more like a reformatory'). 'If you left your books in the cloakroom, or your goloshes were unmarked, you just took the consequences of your carelessness as people do in the real world.'

> There were ... no marks, either for work or conduct. Coming fresh from a school ruled by conduct marks and such accessories as silence in the passages and cloakrooms, it was indeed a revelation to find such a natural happy freedom, and such a sense of proportion in our school life. The life of many a girls' school has been crushed by a mass of detail, and insistence on niggly, worrying little rules and penalties, but from that the 'great red Godolphin', even in the nineties, was conspicuously free.[14]

But as soon as schools ceased to be small family units where the headmistress knew all the children personally, the rules crept in. In the 1920s and 30s they were accepted with docility, and made for tea-cup dramas in the school stories that were so popular in those two decades. Most pupils 'did not mind never being allowed to see any relatives during term time; never entering any shops; never writing more than one letter home a week; never speaking to anyone not a pupil or staff . . . The rules that had crept into being as necessities became to them character-building virtues.'[15] And the rules themselves were often cherished as Holy Writ by staff to whom the school was life itself. 'Once [the rules] were considered advisable and established,' said one pupil of a formidable martinet, 'she took them to her heart and loved them, as she did the girls for whose good they existed. Accordingly, she endured the rigours of their administration with comparative ease.'[16]

To an outsider the English girls' boarding school system still is amazing. Americans, particularly, find it like nothing else they have ever encountered.

> Coming from a co-ed school where no one wears a uniform and we all complain bitterly about having to wear shoes (well, sandals) from the age of thirteen or so, I was absolutely astounded to find everyone calmly accepting more rules than I would have had the imagination to invent. 'No make-up,' they told me. I couldn't believe it. 'Whose business is it if I feel like wearing make-up?' I told myself. But then, why bother at a girls' school? 'No jewelry.' 'No nail polish.' 'Tie your hair back.' I was beginning to feel like an old maid. 'Walk on the left.' 'Stand up when the teacher comes into the room.' 'Sit down when you're told.' I wasn't in a school, I was in a prison! I was sure of it. 'There must have been some mistake,' I thought. But there hadn't been, and after a few weeks I even began to think that some of the rules were pretty sensible. As a matter of fact, they were all so sensible they depressed me.[17]

Rules and a system of shaming those who broke them were felt to be a necessity in a set-up where there could not be corporal punishment. Trust is perhaps possible where the numbers are very small, but, as a fifteen-year-old sagely remarked: 'I think this does not work because (a) we are not in fact completely trusted, (b) we are not completely trustworthy.'[18] But girls, Mallory Wober concluded, are not law-breakers on any great scale, and do not develop a large-scale 'underlife' as sometimes happens with boys. Boredom and peer pressure may make them break out and do things that would never tempt them if they were living at home, but they are undertaken in a lack-lustre way and often with a marked lack of competence. 'Sister Michael told us later that it would never have occurred to her that [the girl] was out of bounds without permission if she had not tried to jump into a non-existent ditch,' said a convent prefect about a junior who had ducked out of watching a hockey match. 'My knees were like jelly,' another girl recorded in her diary about a limp escapade with a friend. They had plotted to go into Bristol to see a film, but the presence of a member of staff on the bus meant that they had to devise an elaborate alibi to explain why they were out of bounds. So they spent meagre resources on a box of chocolates and walked miles through the suburbs to deliver it to an invalid one of them conveniently remembered, and were too late for the film. 'We found that we would have to pay 2/6 to see the last half of Mutiny aboard the Bounty so we decided not to go.' The highlight of the whole affair was 'I saw my first parking meters. One was about ¼ hr overdue.'[19] (They were hauled over the coals, but, in the manner of girls' schools, the heinous sin was not to have been wearing hats.)

It is the fourths and lower fifths who feel the greatest urge to kick over the traces. This also applies to the equivalent in prep schools. At all schools it seems that the middle forms are the tearaways; the new intake is awed by the strange environment and anxious to please, while the top form is preparing itself for the next stage. Louie Angus (Christ's Hospital 1916–25) remembered the anarchic attitude of her fourth-form contemporaries:

> We were impervious to reason at that stage, largely because we found it much more fun to be in rebellion however mild. Successions of monitresses and Black Aprons tried to stop having to punish us, tried to get us to co-operate with them ... But the conference over, we would go straight back to our top shelf eyrie and think up our next devilment.[20]

The only cure was, she concluded, growing up and discovering more intelligent interests. This 1980s fifth-former found the same:

> Saturday afternoon is the highlight of the week. In Lower V the trendies among us began to visit Windsor each week. To do this one has to be seen leaving school in uniform, as if walking to Sunninghill, carrying 'Windsor kit' in plastic bags. On to the train, off with the uniform and on with miniskirt and make-up. Once in Windsor the danger of breaking rules is far from over. You may meet [members of the staff] in the High Street, doing their shopping. And of course the whole purpose of the trip is to meet the Etonians. This is a fearsome breed of young men, to be found in abundance in Macdonald's, 'The Graveyard' and the station. However, once in Upper V we became older and wiser, and Windsor lost much of its attraction.

Drugs apart, most of the subversion at girls' schools is of this order. Sustained, highly organized exploits such as occur with boys – like the sale of spirits manufactured with a home-made still, setting up as a bookmaker, organized prostitution, playing the stock market – are rare, though one girl was expelled from her convent for organizing a restaurant service (with wine) in the boiler room. At Burlington School, founded as a charity hospital in the eighteenth century, 'sullenness and indiligence' were the chief crimes, and 'indecent practices', which meant writing letters to the boys at Tenison's Chapel School. In Edinburgh in 1806, three Merchant Maidens who had assaulted some girls from the Trades Maiden Hospital were reprimanded 'in the presence of the whole family' and put in solitary confinement.

The most spirited account of schoolgirl mischief is not English at all but comes in the diary of the little Polish princess referred to earlier, who was sent in 1772 at the age of nine to the aristocratic Abbaye-aux-bois in Paris.[21] There were midnight feasts and the usual squabbles, and some vivacious pranks. On one occasion the girls poured a bottle of ink into the holy water stoup, and as it was dark when the nuns passed by for matins two hours after midnight nobody noticed the state of the others' faces until dawn. Another day Hélène and her friends tied their handkerchiefs to the bellrope so that the bells for matins never sounded. But their initials on the handkerchiefs gave them away, and they were made to kneel in their nightcaps in the middle of the choir at High Mass the following Sunday, and to recite seven penitential psalms during recreation. However, authority declared that the princess's frolics 'always bore the stamp of gaiety and wit', and it would be a loss to the convent, they thought, if she and her boon-companions became steady.

She also records a barring-out, something that was commonplace in boys' public schools in the early nineteenth century, but is exceedingly rare, if not unknown, among girls. Incensed by the behaviour of one of the mistresses, the girls barricaded themselves into the kitchen building, ejecting the lay sisters, though prudently keeping one of them to do the cooking. From the kitchen they presented a petition to the headmistress, asking for the dismissal of the unpopular mistress and a general amnesty for the past, 'and that we have eight days' recreation, to rest our bodies and minds after the fatigues we have undergone'. The authorities, somewhat perplexed about how to handle the situation, sent for the mothers of the ringleaders and asked them to remove their daughters, and the rebellion faded away with no retribution towards those who remained. 'About thirty of the pupils had not joined in the insurrection . . . and they were simply wretched. They were tormented and run down by the whole class; they fancied they would gain great credit by their conduct; but [the headmistress] did not like them any the better for it.'

But the crimes that girls mostly describe – together with the punishments that followed, usually still remembered with smouldering resentment – are of a pitifully minor sort, like being seen hatless, 'selecting a less crumby piece of bread and butter', going up the stairs two at a time, talking in a forbidden place. One epic saga at St Swithun's fifty years ago arose out of a postcard surreptitiously dispatched from the sanitorium begging a friend to bring books (Gray and Hardy) because 'the san. is a god-awful place and I'm bored'. The card was intercepted – ironically the sender supposed that it would be as unthinkable for authority to read other people's correspondence as it was for her to – and in a drama that involved the headmistress, the housemistress and all the girls in her house, who were forbidden to speak to her, she was stripped of her office of sub-prefect. The house felt so degraded by the whole episode that it could not take part in the house plays.

Girls have always been capable of disrupting the classes of the weaker teachers. There are various ploys: one can pretend the radiators are leaking, get behind the blackboard to roll it round, fake a nose bleed. Sometimes they have been more imaginative. 'We used to play "cricket". The idea here was to move to a different seat in class without the teacher seeing (when she was writing on the blackboard) and every time you did this you scored a "run".'[22] At St Mary's, Wantage, a favourite pursuit in German class 'was for the front row to slide their desks forward and pull up the ones behind so that on turning round from the blackboard the mistress found the whole form gazing up attentive and solemn just under her desk'. (Sacred Heart nuns in the course of their teacher-training learnt never to turn their backs on a class.)

The dormitories, of course, traditionally have offered the greatest opportunity, as this eighteenth-century story about school life shows:

> Sometimes we are so merry you cannot think, we all get out of bed, and play at blindman's buff, or dance about in the dark; then if we hear any noise, and think any body is coming, away we all run helter-skelter, to get into our beds; then we knock our heads against the bed-posts, and sometimes push one another down in our hurry, for if we are found out of bed my governess is very angry, and the next morning we have nothing but dry bread and nasty poison water-gruel.[23]

Few twentieth-century schoolgirls would venture as far as this; merely talking after lights-out is a heinous offence, and authority takes what seems a disproportionately severe attitude towards it. As for the more larky activities, accounts of midnight feasts cast an extraordinary spell over the generations that read school stories, and impelled younger pupils to try to organize their own. Few seemed to enjoy them. 'Pork pie in a soap dish and watery jelly in my tooth mug are my two main recollections.'[24] Headmistresses had various ways of dealing with them. Some harangued weeping rows of penitents. Miss Broad at Bournemouth High School lamented that she had not been asked too. The headmistress of Channing School sat the culprits down in the dining-room to eat their provisions off plates. Miss Willis said if only she had known that was what her pupils wanted she would have arranged the occasion herself – and did so the following week, waking up the whole school at midnight to eat dry biscuits. At Wychwood sixty years ago it was an altogether more formal affair, where one invited the staff who duly appeared in dressing-gowns.

Slang was a matter of much concern to authority in the earlier decades of this century. At Roedean words like 'ripping' and 'rotten' were banned, as was the use of animal names; a new chum called a sub-prefect 'a lamb', and since it was a Roedean point of honour to report even one's best friend she was promptly served with a discipline mark. ('Girls and staff at Roedean were without exception high-minded, pure-souled conformists,' wrote one of them. 'Anyone who caught anyone else doing anything sneaked sanctimoniously to the staff.'[25]) At the Woodard school of S. Anne's (soon to be amalgamated with its sister school S. Mary's) all slang was forbidden in the 1920s and parents were begged to co-operate by discouraging its use in the holidays. In this period too Miss Faithfull devoted the whole of one of her Saturday evening addresses at Cheltenham to the same subject.[26] She used a letter composed for her with some ingenuity out of expressions heard round the college at that time.

> Dear Old Bean,
>
> Empire Day turned out a colossal stunt after all. Some blighter came and gassed for nearly an hour about the sun never setting on the All Red Route, and though most of it was utter tosh it was not pure pi-jaw as we'd expected.
>
> It was a whole hol after that, so we buzzed off on our own and had an absolutely hectic day out. Sis had putrid luck though; she took a toss off her bike and got badly biffed in the upper story. Doc says she is fairly done to the world and must go slow for a tidy bit, which is pretty rotten. The bike has simply gone west in small pieces. But are we downhearted? Not much! We were fed to the teeth with swatting up for the Stinks exam so felt we'd earned a razzle-dazzle right there. . . .

It finished 'Yours to a cinder'. The letter aroused much interest, and in a subsequent collection of her talks Miss Faithfull quotes extracts from the resulting comments, some of which were far better argued than her own case against slang, which rested on its being lazy, slipshod and impoverished and not what you would use to the Queen. Much of it also derived from the hunting field or from the trenches, she said, and was therefore inappropriate for the female sex. But as one of her critics pointed out, where the expressions came from was immaterial – many French, Latin and Greek phrases were incorporated into the English language, and, besides, many words not slang were used universally in different meanings from their original one.

Hair was something else over which authority expended much time and energy. As fast as girls take up the latest fashion, authority moves in to try to stamp it out. ('But please no teen-age fashions like shiny macks and white boots,' said one Oxford school in the late 1960s after conceding that sixth-formers could wear home clothes.) It has always been thus; when Queen Alexandra popularized the fringe most schools forbade it. (At this time it was still generally accepted that the individual had very little say in her appearance, and that when the headmistress decreed that it was time for a girl to put away childish things she submitted. 'Miss Unwin would suddenly decide it was time for hair to be turned up, and a sixteen-year-old (or younger) with her long skirt and hair in a bun, became old in a day.'[27] But after 1918 such edicts became impossible; bobbed and shingled hair was all the rage, and therefore deplored and resisted by authority. Permanent waves were regarded with even more hostility; indeed, any attempt to put a curl into straight hair was disapproved of – 'Princess Elizabeth would *never* curl her hair,' one Nottingham High School girl was told. But once short hair was accepted as the norm the battle was against hair below collar length. One nun at St Mary's, Wantage, remembered how she had always been in trouble about her hair, which refused to conform to the style in which it was decreed pupils' hair should be worn. ('Hair like a little guttersnipe,' one of the staff had said furiously.) But when she became a member of the community herself she admitted that she was just as inflexible, and thundered at Assembly that she kept a school, not a zoo, and that unless hair was tied back or kept short enough to clear the collar she would cut it off herself.

Hair could not be washed when one liked, and of all grievances this one seems to rankle the most. Those who were at school before 1950 complain passionately about the greasy hair that they were obliged to endure, and also about the lack of baths and the frequent ban on 'lustful deodorants'. In the days when hair was worn long and hot water was not plentiful, the washing and drying of it could not be lightly undertaken, and a hairdresser very often attended to conduct the operation – he was known as 'the Hairy Man' at St Leonards. The ceremony did not take place often, sometimes only twice a term; at St Mary's, Wantage before the First War only once, as the same sister recalled. On one occasion she and a friend rebelled and washed theirs in the bath, but were detected. 'Had we been guilty of some serious moral lapse we could not have been in more dire disgrace.' This curious embargo on cleanliness persisted long after hair was worn short. At one Malvern school in the 1960s hair could be washed every six weeks. If girls desired to do it more frequently then they had to get a doctor's certificate, but they also had to forgo chocolate. At schools now there can still be trouble if one is seen with a damp head on a day that is not the right one.

Uniform is so much a cornerstone of the independent school system that it is often forgotten that it was introduced relatively recently. At first it was only convents and charity schools that wore it, and, as has already been said, one private school imposed the wearing of charity hospital uniform as the ultimate disgrace (see page 23). At the Assumption Convent in Richmond a nun aged 102 recalled in 1980 that in her schooldays 'we always wore a uniform which was exactly like the dress that the postulants wore'.[28] This was black for weekdays, blue for Sundays, with a white dress for processions and feasts, and had changed very little from forty years before. Nearly all the early convent schools were run by French teaching orders and dressed in French style, which later English superiors managed to change. Thus when the first superior at Hillside College (later Farnborough Hill) was succeeded by an English nun the black uniform was changed for navy blue, and the black felt hats with feathers gave way to boaters with school colours, with sealskin caps for winter. Cornelia Connelly, as we have seen, disliked dull colours for children and dressed the Holy Child girls in red; at New Hall, run by an order which had been founded in the seventeenth century by an Englishwoman, the style from the start was far less formal than the French tradition: bright red merino in the winter, pink print in the summer, with white for Sundays, though after about 1852 this latter was altered to blue, a colour that in 1870 was adopted for every day. But uniform for girls was regarded with such distaste by the ordinary parent that one ex-convent girl in 1874 felt bound to defend it and ask whether 'the pounds and pounds of unpleasant false hair, the pouf, the high-heeled boots, the fantastic assortment of gaudy rags' in which the ordinary middle-class Protestant Englishwoman arrayed herself were any better.[29]

Charity school uniform has already been described in Chapter 2. It was provided not only by the hospitals, but at such places as clergy daughters' schools, and Rickmansworth Masonic School and Christ's Hospital still equip their pupils themselves. Emily Baldwin at Howell's School, Llandaff, insisted on pretty and becoming clothes for the children, but this was most unusual; the garments normally provided were intended to be serviceable, to distinguish the children as recipients of charity, and to discourage vanity. Clergy daughters, who partly paid for their clothes themselves, fared a little better. At St Mary's Hall in 1836 the school provided frocks, tippets, cloaks, shawls and bonnets and asked the children to bring underwear, a Bible, a prayer-book, a *new* umbrella and 'also, if convenient, a Silver Dessert Spoon, Tea Spoon and Fork, which will be returned'. (This was a standard request at early schools, as was the demand that the umbrella should be new.) An account of Casterton in the early Victorian period describes the purple winter dresses, purple capes, with green plaid cloaks for bad weather, and pattens, later replaced by clogs – an attempt to keep their feet dry in that wettest part of north-west England. Summer dresses were of buff nankeen, and for church everybody wore white dresses and white bonnets trimmed with purple ribbon.[30] (This feeling that white was the appropriate colour for Sundays seemed to have been unconsciously derived from the convents, and many schools specified a white serge suit in which their pupils would process to church. On 10 June 1905 the *Folkestone Herald* wrote: 'Last Sunday morning the young ladies attending Kent College were uniformly attired in white with hats to match. As the scholars walked two by two down the Sandgate Road to the Wesleyan Church they attracted much attention.') 'I remember thinking how lovely we looked that first summer Sunday walking in crocodile to chapel,' wrote an Edgehillian of the white-garbed church parade with its panama hats. At this Methodist school, uniform had been introduced during World War I, 'a godsend to daughters of the manse' who usually owned one best dress and a second best which was mother's passed on.

At Christ's Hospital, as mentioned earlier, the uniform was changed in 1870 but continued in this mid-Victorian state for the next fifty years. It began with impressive layers of underclothes.* (Though many have recalled the elaborate underwear of their youth – and it has to be remembered that all schools were very cold until central heating became standard in the 1960s – these were excessive by any standards.) Underneath everything else were long-legged, long-sleeved woollen combinations which tortured the skin. Over these came Liberty bodices with buttons to support stockings and 'garments' (a euphemism for knickers). The stockings, standard until World War II, were of thick black ribbed wool and must never be taken off, however hot the weather or whatever the activity. The 'garments' were of unbleached calico, which the girls had to stitch by hand, and over these went 'blues', by 1920 comparatively modern in design; some even had elastic. Next came petticoats, grey flannel in the winter, blue and white stripes in the summer, worn even under gym tunics. Then thick flannel blouses, and inside them clerical dog collars. Finally, tunics and white pinafores so that the older girls looked like surpliced clergymen. The seniors wore black aprons, a sign of authority. For playing they wore short double-breasted monkey-jackets; their top coats were caped rather like eighteenth-century coachmen. They crocheted their red caps themselves, often misshapen from their inexpertise, though these were later replaced by navy-blue caps with yellow piping and crests which were still being worn in the 1950s. The straw boaters, criticized by the school inspectorate as ugly, and impractical because of their shallow crowns, were replaced in the early 1920s by panama hats. The uniform now is the most attractive of any school; it is one of the few with any elegance and possibly the only one that is still worn with pride. Consisting of a white blouse with pendant white bands at the neck, a loose pleated navy-blue skirt topped with a silver-buttoned jacket which is worn with a loose leather belt, it is both dignified and practical and suits all figures; it also complements the boys' long Tudor coats.

Long before there was uniform headmistresses had tried to make girls dress sensibly. Both Miss Buss and Miss Beale insisted on low heels; many tried to outlaw tight lacing. Edgbaston High School's magazine *Laurel Leaves* described how the model late Victorian schoolgirl should comport herself.

* The uniform at the time of World War I is described at length in Louis Angus: *Blue Skirts into Blue Stockings*, ch. 3.

And though her figure may be slim
  Her boots alone she laces.
Her books, but not her skirts, she straps,
  Her steps are light and free ones.
Her heels are low, except perhaps
  Her going out to tea ones.

The earliest uniform item at most schools was the hat. The motley appearance of their school on church parade seems to have led many headmistresses to try to standardize headgear at least, and the accounts of what schoolgirls took with them to Cheltenham and St Leonards in the early days – 'a felt hat with a wing; a velvet hat with an ostrich feather'; 'a fine black straw, about the size of a small tea-tray, handsomely trimmed with black velvet ribbon and ostrich feathers' – make one sympathetic to their efforts. But the replacements were often grotesquely ornate. At Badminton in the 1880s there was winter Best Hat (worn for two terms), and a summer Best. Both were resented with fury by the pupils, and the parents complained of their expense. The winter hat was cream felt with a great deal of satin ribbon, the summer one straw with even more ribbon, in loops. 'I never heard of anyone wearing these creations in the holidays – they were too frightful, especially on the younger children. We were all hatted identically, from nine to nineteen.'[31] St Leonards adopted sailor hats for all in 1887 after Miss Dove had decided at a picnic that the school looked unbearably patchy.

School or house colours came next, and by 1901 Heathfield could announce that it had its 'own colours in ties and hat-bands. These are worn with white flannel shirts, dark blue skirts, and white sailor hats.' But this is unusually early. At the Alice Ottley School there was no uniform for the first thirty years except, latterly, hard straw hats in the summer and blouses right up to the neck in all seasons. Drill tunics of navy-blue serge edged with velvet were introduced in 1912, blazers in 1923 (though pocketless, so that 'no one could stand about with her hands in a slovenly or disrespectful attitude'. However, there was a standard prize-day dress, white with blue silk sashes, half of the school wearing them over their left shoulder, half over the right, so that when they were carefully grouped 'the sashes met in chevrons, or capital V's in honour of the Queen'.

For most schools uniform began in the gymnasium, where a specially designed costume was required. (When one reads Cecily Steadman's description of the boned dresses she took to Cheltenham in 1889, with their very full skirts, lined and equipped with 'a sort of horsehair pad about the size of a bicycle saddle' to give them the proper set, one understands the urgent necessity for some alternative.[32]) Many found it very daunting. 'It was a terribly shy and self-conscious experience for some of us to expose our hitherto secreted calves, and the otherwise inexpressible joys of jumping unfettered were entirely damped by the knowledge that our knees were visible,' said a girl at St Mary's, Wantage.[33] One senior hid in her cloakroom cupboard, ashamed of showing so much leg. (At Burgess Hill School the tunic was required to be six inches above the knee and senior girls had to wear coats when they walked through the streets after the residents complained that they looked indecent.) St Leonards adapted their first games wear from that worn in a Belgian school. It consisted of a tunic to the knee worn with either knickerbockers or trousers underneath. Staff wore it to encourage the more timid, and one fourteen-year-old celebrated the uncouth new garb in a set of verses that shows how strong the classical tradition was at the school then. When the heroine supposedly goes home after her first term

> On heavens! did you ever see a waist
> Half to compare with hers? and what a figure!
> Caesar we'll throw aside, and we will seize her
> And make her leave off Pindar till we've pinned her
> Into a pair of stays, and soon the strain
> Of Anacreon will be Anne-a-cryin' with pain.[34]

The St Leonards costume evolved into a blue serge tunic and knickerbockers worn with a loose belt that in the early days had a steel ring in it so that the instructor could seize girls to help them on the trapeze or bar. A silk handkerchief in the house colours was also worn. When these became uncomfortably hot they were torn off and tucked into the belt, and latterly were to stay there, known as 'tails'.* Wycombe Abbey, the daughter school, also took up the practice.

But the most reformed garment was the djibbah which the Misses Lawrence introduced at Roedean for games. As mentioned earlier, Roedeanians were forbidden to wear stays, and the djibbah admirably concealed the fact. It was waistless and knee-length, made of thick blue serge, and the style was later extended to evening and weekend wear – though here girls could at least choose the colour and length. Other schools adopted it; Miss Willis, herself a Roedeanian, took it to Downe House where it was so popular that pupils resisted her attempts to adapt it. At Oakdene too they wore it. One girl thought the single pocket 'which gave you away if you put more in it than a hankie' was a disadvantage, 'but the garment had one outstanding asset. You could slip it on over your head while running downstairs, and appear quite tidy at the bottom. It had no fastenings at all.'[35]

The gym-slip which later became standard wear was derived from the costume designed by one of Madame Bergman-Österburg's students at her Hampstead gymnasium. But it took some time for this to be accepted, and

* This item of uniform was discarded a few years ago.

in 1910 a letter printed in the *Hockey Field* expressed great distaste. The correspondent quoted a letter received by a county player from her fiancé: 'If there is any chance of your wearing kit like that my foot comes down bang and you have no more hockey.' From about 1920 onwards it became everyday uniform, not just for games, particularly at grammar schools. It concealed a lot, including books (only you had to knot your girdle tightly to prevent them crashing to the floor). With their three box pleats fore and aft they were not becoming.

> Gym tunics were very short, waists and busts were definitely out. I was, to my shame, a big-busted girl, and took tucks in my liberty bodice to try to conceal the fact. As waists were almost indecent, one stayed out as far as one's top half came out. The girdle was loosely tied round the tunic, a few inches above the hem, and the collar of one's blazer was always turned up at the back.[36]

The gym tunic was admirably adapted to an epoch which adulated immaturity and which treated girls as children until they left school at eighteen, since it concealed the burgeoning female form and gave all wearers a bolster shape. (A Walthamstow Hall pupil recalled how the advent of uniform tunics made everyone seem so much younger, since it eliminated the curves that Victorian dress had accentuated.) Authority spent much time and energy ensuring that it was of a seemly length, and disciplining girls who wanted to wear it too short or too long.

But private schools, ever class-conscious, were determined that their girls should not be mistaken for the denizens of high schools or maintained grammar schools. They rapidly discarded the gym-slip, except for games for which it would be dyed the school's own colour, and the two decades before World War II saw more whimsy and self-indulgence on the part of headmistresses (who of course did not have to pay for the outfit) than one would have thought parents would have endured. There was a separate costume for each term, and special clothes for every activity. In addition, there were winter hats and summer hats and garden hats, umbrellas in the school colours, sometimes even satchels likewise; blazers and topcoats and raincoats, a special suit for the Sunday church parade and another for travelling, all of it often made up from material that had been dyed or woven to the school's own specification, and more often than not wholly impractical – cream tussore silk, for instance, for summer dresses that creased like corrugated cardboard. Boarders changed into special off-duty uniform, very often made of silk or shantung, with a separate long dress for gala occasions. Many still have nightmare memories of trying to scramble into a complete change of clothing for the next activity with far too little time allowed. (Short cuts like putting on one's black games stockings under one's brown school ones would meet with dire retribution at Roedean.)

Headmistresses who spent much time trying to stamp out girls' attempts to be fashionable had no scruples about imposing their own notions of elegance. At Oakdene the founder, Miss Watts, made the girls twine Liberty scarves round their panama hats or navy felts. And every other year she chose a new type of Sunday hat to go with the white suits or coats. 'I remember best a most elaborate wide-brimmed affair, with masses of baby-ribbon bunched round the crown and the underside of the brim lined with net.' Moretonians were distinguished by their blue tweed coats with black velvet collars, and 'Cromwell' shoes, very conspicuous with square steel buckles, which amazed foreigners; they also wore white to church with beige striped stockings. Old girls of other schools remember such outré items as brown Harris tweed suits with pale pink viyella blouses; Liberty old-gold shantung dresses (supposed to tone with the school's oak panelling); wide-brimmed straw hats with a wreath of roses (known as 'rosy pearls'), worn with cream serge coats and skirts on Sundays; different-coloured overalls for every activity; long-sleeved green serge dresses worn with scarlet silk sashes, flowing ties and green hair ribbons, and over them scarlet cloaks or green golf jackets. The oddest is probably the extensive wardrobe required for a progressive school in a remote Welsh valley. It prescribes not only wellington boots, riding breeches and oilskins, but also velvet dresses and a Christopher Robin outfit of brown holland overalls for both boys and girls.

Cloaks, often with the hoods lined in house colours, were an item which distinguished boarders from day girls and survived longer than most others on the uniform list. A few schools still use them, very often bequeathed by leavers, but they have become prohibitively expensive, and Heathfield has had to discard theirs. They were much loved, and were very useful in dramatic productions – particularly for shepherds watching their flocks in Nativity plays. There were other advantages. The Durham High School boarders hid tuck in the hoods to smuggle into prep or the dormitories, and in addition 'they were lovely and warm and completely enveloped us and often doubled up as a blanket if we were cold in bed'.

Some uniform items were always detested. At Runton Hill on the North Norfolk coast, presumably as a protection from searing east winds, 'we had the most hated, self-conscious-making headgear – a grey knitted pixy hood with ear flaps edged round with green wool and tied under the chin'. (This school, which was unheated until comparatively recently, had out-of-the-ordinary uniform items to combat the cold: arctic trousers, anoraks, and fishermen's jerseys.) Few schoolgirls took kindly to gloves, but these were *de rigueur* before 1939, and there was always a member of staff or a prefect to check that each pupil was wearing them when she left the premises. Nobody had much affection for their hats. '"Keeping one's beret on out of school" was one of the strictest rules, disliked and broken by nearly everybody. Indeed, in the days of "beehive" hairdoes (achieved by vigorous back-combing) in the early sixties, the problem became not keeping one's beret on but where to put it in the first place.'[37] This school finally abolished its beret (which had replaced pudding basin velours and panamas) in 1969, a time when most schools finally abandoned compulsory head wear. It had always been time-consuming to enforce, and when it was abolished staff and prefects must have found themselves with a great deal of extra leisure.

There was also the question of *how* hats were worn. 'We were always in trouble for wearing our hats twisted into all sorts of shapes to try to make them more becoming.' This was Durham High School with their 'pudding basin' or 'paddy' hats which were a compulsory part of school uniform until the 1980s. There was constant friction over the angle that girls wore their hats, which rarely coincided with what authority considered seemly. They were either tilted at the back of the head, or rakishly on one side, or a tuck was taken in them. Boaters were not regarded with much affection. You could not sit back at church in them, the juncture of crown and brim scored a red line on the forehead, and it was kept on with elastic that was either so tight that it bit under your chin, or so loose that you had to knot it. Winter and summer at high schools, black woollen stockings were often mandatory (indeed a summer uniform at day schools was very rare before 1930); 'the modern schoolgirl,' said one wearer, 'has never been forced to ink in the patch of pink leg where she has just torn her stocking on the nails in her desk'. The more exclusive schools wore beige lisle stockings (only small girls were allowed to wear socks). 'As they aged they washed paler and paler, and they had powerful twisting instincts throughout their lifetime.' Much time was spent on Saturdays darning these. Galoshes were a frequent cause of irritation. Many private schools thought it was the ideal way of keeping feet dry and passages clean, but they were always being mislaid, kicked across the cloakroom, found to have a flapping sole or to be the wrong size for the shoe underneath. And some days might be dry enough to discard them, but one could never be quite sure and there was always the risk of an order mark.

The changing style of uniform is epitomized by the history of Burgess Hill's. The school was founded in 1906. There was no uniform until 1914, though girls were required to wear a straw hat with a hatband in the school colours. There were also small enamel brooches (depicting a skylark and the motto 'I am, I can, I ought, I will'). In September 1914 navy-blue gym-slips were introduced and remained, with various alterations in style and length, until 1921 when they were replaced by brown djibbahs, worn for everything from games to pottery, with black stockings and black shoes. A blazer was added in 1922. The djibbah lasted until 1940, when white Aertex shirts and navy shorts were adopted for games. Over the years the shorts became culottes, then a wrap-over skirt with a navy track suit to be worn over it, and a grey sweatshirt with the school logo. Grey kilts for everyday were introduced in 1971.

Tremendous sacrifices were made to maintain the usual standards during

World War II, and there were very few concessions. Indeed, one day-girl at S. Helen and S. Katharine remembered the blasting she received from the headmistress because she arrived in ordinary school uniform for a weekend expedition and had not equipped herself with the boarders' walking-out suit. Standards have dropped since, and there are very few schools left who nowadays dare ask parents to equip their daughters with a lavish idiosyncratic wardrobe made out of exclusive materials. Clothes have to be hard-wearing and easy to maintain. Silks, alpaca and cashmere have disappeared, but wool too is rare, and most schools appear in the standard school outfitters' shades of dark green, brown, grey, navy-blue or maroon terylene, with everything possible made uncrushable and drip-dry. There is now little that is distinctive about the appearance of independent school girls. The 1920s pride in uniform, when it was a novelty, and the satisfaction of the class-conscious 1930s at being marked out as a member of an elite, have departed. A few schools – St Paul's is one – have abandoned it altogether; some, like Queen's College, have never had it. Others, like Oxford High School, allow so much latitude that the general appearance is of a collection of individuals. Most schools (there are exceptions, of which Cheltenham is one) allow their sixth form to wear their own clothes – though this presents problems when it comes to school outings and a motley collection of gipsy grannies and *midinettes* straggles out. (For this reason a few, like Rickmansworth Masonic School, have devised a special sixth-form costume.) But most girls concede that uniform of some kind is desirable – indeed, that it makes life easier; though few – Christ's Hospital being the shining exception – wear it with any apparent pride, but then few schools have a uniform that brings any pleasure to the wearer or to the onlooker.

Standards now have slackened, but struggles to make reluctant girls wear their uniform in the manner that authority desired used to be one of the weightier disciplinary preoccupations at girls' schools. It was axiomatic that pupils would seek to be in fashion and that headmistresses would implacably resist and seek to eliminate all signs of precocious sexual awareness. Indeed, most elders would like schoolchildren to be frozen in a state of sexual immaturity while they are *in statu pupillari* – a state which seemed apparently to have been achieved in the 1920s and 1930s when uniform regulations were most strictly imposed and girls were docile. 'Ain't they plain but ain't they neat!' an admiring local called out as the Godolphin girls paraded through Salisbury in their straw 'boards', and plain but neat and several steps behind fashion has always been the great desideratum. Thus at Norwich High School in the 1920s gym tunics had to be calf-length, but as soon as girls *desired* to wear them thus in the New Look period the rule was changed to make them three inches above the knee.

But girls' schools, as has been said, can afford to worry away at details such as this since they mostly only have minor problems of law and order to deal with. Punishment has taken the form of humiliating or frightening the perpetrator, and this has proved very effective in that while a boy shrugs off and forgets a beating, the victims who have had their names in the school's Black Book or Appearing Book, who have lost their 'characters' or their 'house order', usually remember the incident for life. Frances Power Cobbe described how her expensive Brighton school dealt with malefactors in the 1830s, but there would have been parallels in most schools a hundred years later.

> On Saturday afternoons, instead of play, there was the terrible ordeal generally known as the 'Judgement Day'. The two schoolmistresses sat side by side, solemn and stern, at the head of the long table. Behind them sat all the governesses as assessors. On the table were the books wherein our evil deeds of the week were recorded; and round the room against the wall, seated on stools of penitential discomfort, we sat, five-and-twenty 'damozels', anything but blessed. It was at this ceremony that pupils were told if they had 'lost a card' – for such offences as not finishing a lesson or practising, had stooped or been impertinent, had had a lesson returned, or been convicted of 'disorder' (e.g. having a shoe string untied). If three cards had been lost in a week there was a fearful public scolding, and the transgressor had to sit in a corner all evening.[38]

'I dreaded it more than many people do hanging,' Lady Jerningham recalled to her daughter in 1785, describing how her French convent made wrong-doers kiss the floor in the middle of the choir.[39] 'The awarding of a conduct mark was almost as frightening as expulsion,' said a pupil at the Royal School before World War I. A girl who received one for writing a note of thanks to a maid who had good-naturedly made her bed for her recalled how the whole school was assembled, the accusation made, and how she felt she was 'standing in the dock awaiting sentence to be sent to the gallows'. Another girl received one for writing to a choirboy. One of the onlookers said: 'It seemed terrible to us, like hearing a sentence of death. I can see the girl's face now.'[40]

Public humiliation at early schools might take the form of wearing asses' ears (for bad work), or a red tongue (for lying or making false excuses). At Red Maids' intractable girls were made to wear the Black Cap and put in solitary confinement. As has been said, the punishment at charity schools was notably harsh; girls could be put on a diet of bread and water; Burlington School had handcuffs (still in their possession) which were apparently used until 1850. At the Royal Naval School in the 1880s a dose of Gregory powder (an explosive purgative) was given for bad behaviour ('You must be unwell to have been so naughty'), and pink Gregory powder (more explosive still) for very serious crime. Misplaced belongings were hung round one's neck, and girls writing home might be told to include some phrase as 'Miss Leys is shocked at my spelling'. One such letter dated

1881 and with the air of having been dictated was written home from St Mary's Hall. 'My dearest Father,' it begins, 'I am writing to tell you that I am again separated from my class for trifling and hindering conduct. This want of diligence and want of respect is so serious because it is so hindering to the other children in my class.' She had been interviewed by Canon Babington, she said, and yet she was again reported for disorderly conduct. 'I am now doing sewing in the Nursery [the sickroom].'[41]

Corporal punishment for girls was rare, though foreigners might expect otherwise; indeed, the headmistress of Edgbaston High School received a letter from an interested parent in Buenos Aires in 1924 which inquired about it for his two daughters: 'Supervision and discipline is very strict? Whipping punishment is practised when the temperament of the pupil requires it?' It was, however, a commonplace with charity children; at Grey Coat Hospital, indeed, it was very severe (see page 27), and though it is not recorded at any other clergy school, birching seems to have taken place at Casterton, where trouble-makers were also imprisoned in a 'cage' under the stairs. Christ's Hospital had, in addition to the red tongue, a steel collar for those who hung their head and bands with 'Beware the thief' and 'Gossip'. There was also 'the Mark'. A monitress who detected some fault on a Monday could tell the offender to 'take the Mark'. But the girl could pass it on to another whom she caught in the same fault, and she to another, and the wretch landed with it on Saturday afternoon had to forfeit her pocket money.[42]

Long after the handcuffs and the red tongue had been abandoned, the practice of publicly shaming culprits was standard. Most schools had a system whereby miscreants who had collected order, discipline, or conduct marks – whatever the terminology used – were catechized about them in assembly. At the Clergy Orphan Girls' School in the last century the upper school had to make their confessions in French, which furnished 'moments of rejoicing to a disrespectful Junior listening to the struggles of the Seniors with that evasive French accent, not pitying even the trembling maiden who lost her ticket "pour avoir fixement regardé Mademoiselle"'.[43] At the School of S. Mary and S. Anne, Abbots Bromley, staff inflicted 'characters' on their pupils – 'careless', 'rude', 'dishonourable' and so forth – recorded in a book of judgement laid before the headmistress on Saturday mornings. The record was read out and each girl had to stand up and explain her misdemeanours; decades later this labelling was still remembered with burning resentment. But one of the most dramatic occasions recorded in any school history was when two girls were publicly expelled from the Royal School. The chairman of the governors (a general) was summoned down from London to preside over the execution. The whole school was assembled, without explanation, and in silence he and the headmistress mounted the platform. After a long and infinitely terrifying pause he addressed them, telling them over and over again that there was a certain subject that no 'nice girl' ever spoke about. Then two girls were called up to the platform by name and expelled. They left the same day. Nobody knew what their crime had been and the more anxious children suffered greatly, wondering if they too had transgressed unwittingly. The explanation, pieced together long afterwards, seemed to be that they had been overheard wondering how babies were born.

But anguish would arise out of much lesser occasions. Winifred Peck could be amusing about the weekly inquest at 'Miss Quill's' establishment, but other pupils were tormented. At this school those whose names appeared in the register of misdeeds wrote out a confession of what they had done. 'It was better to restrict oneself to such faults as speaking in a forbidden area or forgetting to put a pair of shoes away, than to let Miss Quill loose on such topics as "I laughed in Bible reading."' There was also a box of fines for slang, usually made up of halfpennies which was the tariff charged for 'awfully' or 'jolly'. But one day a sixpence was found in the box, and the bad girl of the school admitted to having said 'damn it'. 'Miss Quill wept, the mistresses hid their faces in their hands and the girls sat in stunned silence.' After that it was tacitly agreed among the girls that all fines, however large, should be paid in coppers.[44] At Margaret Nevinson's convent the more conscientious kept 'sin books' in which they jotted down any transgression; these were confessed to the sister-in-charge at the end of the week. Typical of girls' schools was to put people 'on their honour'. When a few girls cut singing lessons at Nottingham High School, the whole form was punished by being put on 'honoured silence' for a week. This meant that all, innocent and guilty, were on their honour not to speak in the school buildings except to teachers. It was much resented: 'I felt it was unreasonable to expect us to honour a compact to which we had never freely consented.'[45]

A headmistress of Christ's Hospital in the early 1920s had her own method of making culprits confess. She would send for them and ask them why they were there. 'You thought of all your latest misdeeds and suggested one of them, only to find she wanted you for something quite different ... but by then you had given yourself away.'[46] Sometimes humiliation was achieved by loss of privilege. At Roedean in the Misses Lawrences' day a detention mark

> carried more actual worry and inconvenience than anybody could have guessed who had never earned one. It meant that for the rest of the term all concessions and privileges were forfeit. The recipient came last on every list – could only bath ten minutes before the breakfast bell, had a 'hairbrushing' which overlapped tea, was not allowed to go into town with a prefect on Saturday afternoons, had her life in fact made thoroughly uncomfortable.[47]

The punishment for the St Swithun's girl who sent the illicit postcard was along the same lines: she lost her 'house order' so that in effect she became a non-person, a ghost presence without any standing or position. Humiliation for petty misdemeanours is still a feature of girls' schools. In the 1960s at S. Helen and S. Katharine the girl who talked on the way to chapel was made to scrub the steps publicly for a week; in the 1980s the girl who would not eat her pudding at her Oxford public school was sent with it to stand outside the headmistress's study, weeping into the plate. The punishments devised by children themselves, however, might be even more severe; at Milton Mount the school parliament formed in the 1920s decreed that a girl found talking should wear a handkerchief round her mouth at break, and that those who left possessions around should have them tied to their persons for several days.

Rewards for good conduct are far fewer, and it seems that it was the convent schools, always the most imaginative when it came to devising celebrations, that made them most memorable. The Sacred Heart had their system of awarding ribbons – blue, green and pink – to the well behaved and those deemed worthy of responsibility. At New Hall silver medals were given for success in studies. They were attached to a blue ribbon and worn on Sundays and feasts. It was not easy to achieve one, but if kept through three successive examinations they became the property of the winner. A very good 'medal dinner' of chicken and plum pudding, followed by a half-holiday, was provided for winners, a custom which was gradually discontinued after 1855, and replaced with book prizes. Some schools provided a treat for a form that had comported itself specially well, though this was rarely on the level of a chicken and plum pudding dinner. In Miss Buss's day a form at the North London Collegiate who had managed to get through half a term without any offence against discipline was awarded a 'Gratification' – a half-hour in which they could do as they pleased. Molly Hughes remembered choosing 'a romp', and the form went to the gym and amused themselves – probably the best that could be done within the time limit.

About the really serious offences such as drink and drugs schools are reticent. 'Few, if any [boys'] public schools were entirely free of the problem,' said John Rae about psychedelic drugs in the 1960s, '[and it was] exacerbated by the authorities' ignorance of the subject and by their unwillingness to discuss it. At meetings of headmasters in the late sixties almost any subject was discussed other than the pupils' use of drugs; no one wanted to admit in public that his school was affected.'[48] A headmistress of a North London school writing in the 1980s said she had never needed to consult the many handbooks showered upon schools about teenage drug-taking, nor did she feel she should take up the invitation to visit the local police station to recognize the smell of cannabis. 'Informal questioning of Sixth Formers in the mid-60's did, nevertheless, reveal which were the Hampstead coffee bars where cannabis was to be obtained, and that this information was generally known; also that the use of soft drugs was frequent at private parties in Highgate and Hampstead.' School rules invariably state that the penalty for being found in possession of drugs is instant expulsion. As John Rae observed, it was the schools that took action that tended to acquire the reputation of having a drug problem. One gets the impression that the worst is now over, as far as schools are concerned, and that pupils have been convinced by the strenuous propaganda organized by authority: the lectures by police and the medical profession, the documentary films and the evidence of ex-addicts.

Alcohol seems a greater problem. Again it is a recent one; the only reference to drink in a school history concerns a freakish episode in the last century when the mother of a Royal School pupil was caught smuggling wine to her daughter. Middle-class parents drink far more themselves than they did a generation ago, and children who would once have been satisfied with lemonade or ginger beer now expect not only wine but spirits. They also have the means to buy it, whereas in the past even a senior's pocket money would only run to the occasional cream tea. School rules naturally prohibit alcohol (though some allow celebrations on a birthday or a bottle of wine at dinner parties organized by house mistresses or the head – the female equivalent of the bars that many boys' schools now provide). But many admit that it is smuggled in, in shampoo bottles if necessary, even hidden under the floor-boards. Some girls may have a genuine taste for hard drink; some are experimenting – as, presumably, in the recent case of a teenage boarder who starved herself for twenty-four hours before downing half a bottle of gin and collapsing unconscious. Suspension is the usual penalty, though one headmistress, seeing drunken offenders lurching through the school grounds, told them briskly how stupid they looked and imitated them.

Smoking was an offence long before authority had to worry about drink and drugs, and would seem to demonstrate bravado among young children anxious to make their mark as much as genuine addiction among older girls. Some high schools allow it in the sixth form common-room; most forbid it anywhere, though there is one school that provides a suitably dreary room for properly attested addicts. Expulsion is the usual penalty for being caught *in flagrante delicto* for the third time, and at least one headmistress has wondered whether the exhaustion of trying to catch and discipline the offenders is worth the candle, and whether if smoking was permitted the problem would disappear. But boys' and girls' schools alike take a firm line against it, a line that has been strengthened since the realization that those pupils who were caught smoking cannabis had almost invariably been in trouble first over ordinary smoking. The connection between smoking and health is indisputable; the danger of communities such as boarding schools is that children through boredom and resistance to authority may experiment and catch a habit that otherwise would not have appealed to them.

12

Sex and Emotion

Febrile Friendships

'I find it quite impossible to imagine anything more sexually obsessed than a restrictive boys' public school in 1890 (or 1930 or 1960),' wrote Jonathan Gathorne-Hardy in his study of these, proceeding to devote two chapters to the boys' activities.[1] But with girls there is no evidence of anything like this. Indeed, there must be many whose experience of boarding school before the 1960s was the same as Katharine Whitehorn's. Of her wartime schooldays she said:

> I cannot be the only girl who is absolutely unable to persuade advanced friends that I got through six schools without ever finding out even the meaning of lesbianism or what the clerics call solitary vice; or even having heard any of the serious swear words. No boy could go through school in such ignorance . . . Girls are moony and sentimental and emotional and giggly and stupid . . . Even their cruelty – which is as bad as a boy's or indeed a ferret's – is mental cruelty; teasing, insults, leaving a girl out of things. They rarely go in for what Molesworth calls 'tuoughing up'.[2]

Though women did write of the lesbian passions of schoolmistresses, as in *Olivia*,[3] readers seem to have looked upon these as curious exotica that related to nothing they had themselves experienced at school. And the steamy sex that rampages through *Children, Be Happy* (1931),[4] a novel by a twenty-year-old, recognizably set in her London day school (it resulted in a libel action) – 'I want her. Terrifically. This waiting's driving me mad . . . I can't stand it . . . God! she's tantalizing . . . she's lovely . . . I can't stand it' – is about as convincing as *The Young Visiters*.

Emotion there is, though, and plenty of it, always ready to erupt and overflow, together with a superabundance of silliness. No doubt this is the reason for so much games at boarding schools, to exhaust the girls physically and suppress the sort of hysteria that could be far more damaging than the physical manifestations of sexuality at boys' schools. One girl remembered her first experience of this. The sixth-formers at her school had put on an impromptu entertainment for their juniors, and were pretending to be guitarists, strumming their lacrosse sticks. But a wave of hysterical excitement, palpable and unnerving to the performers, ran through the audience, and the headmistress rapidly brought the proceedings to a close. It was spontaneous, totally unexpected, and seems to have frightened the participants themselves by its force. This sort of excitement is associated nowadays with pop stars, but it used to be just as possible for preachers to arouse it (there is, of course, plenty of evidence of mass hysteria at revival meetings). One twelve-year-old at the Mount in the 1850s remembered the impact made by a temperance orator. 'We all vowed eternal hostility to alcohol, and after the meeting, when it had been intimated to the hero of the evening that we would like to shake hands with him . . . our enthusiasm reached its topmost height . . . The glove I had worn on that occasion was for long a priceless treasure.'[5]

Normally authority is on the watch for signs of hysteria, fully aware of how contagious it is, but to one school, when George VI died in 1952, it denoted perhaps a patriotic fervour that ought not to be curbed. (His death was notable for the demonstrations of grief recorded in school histories; Churchill's in 1965 seems to have passed unremarked.)

> How we all cried! It was the first time I had allowed anyone to see me cry in public, but I remember not minding as everyone was doing it too. Miss Butler, the headmistress, told us we could go to the library and cry there (VI form only, that was) and I remember the sounds of grief, from loud cries to muffled sobs. After a while we were told that there was to be a service in Chapel, which we all attended, but we found it hard to sing properly.[6]

The founder of Wycombe Abbey would have been more cautious. 'Much care is needed,' she said at one point, 'more particularly if there is decided musical taste, to begin with composers who appeal least to the emotional nature.'[7]

Excitement, of course, is infectious, and authority must always be on the watch for signs of control breaking down. Sometimes ordinary high spirits can boil over into hysteria, as in this novelist's account of her old school:

> Some nights – you never could tell which nights it would happen – there was something in the air about the place, and children's voices rose and laughs and screams rose high to echo round the panelled ceiling of the dining-room, along the gallery, seeming to cry out for space in which to spread. Perhaps this grew from child to child or was already in the crackling atmosphere, or one child sensed it and conveyed it through some heightening of spirits to another and another and another. Towards mid-term it built up, spilt and spattered. Children ran much faster in their cloaks through cloisters and through corridors, banged doors and

> shouted to each other on the outside paths or ran through the pinewoods flapping cloaks and leaping for no reason, juniors stamping in their socks and bouncing balls and chucking quoits and bumping bags of books about.[8]

Sometimes it takes on a morbid aspect. Readers now are amazed by the tempestuous passions described in the earlier school stories. Girls at the turn of the century were in any case very much more demonstrative than they later allowed themselves to be: 'I remember my dismay seeing the hordes of girls prancing round the playroom embracing each other the first night of the Half,' said one newcomer to the Mount in the 1890s. At Edwardian Roedean they used to kiss and call each other 'lovie', and Evelyn Sharp's Becky, arriving at school for the first time in *The Making of a Schoolgirl* (1897), notices how much the girls kiss each other; she is not surprised, it only bears out her brother's gloomy warnings. (One teachers' training college (see page 280) had a rule that there should be no kissing except on birthdays.) L.T. Meade's school stories were highly popular then, and the most overwrought of all. In *The Rebel of the School* (1902), to take a typical example, Irish Kathleen O'Hara confesses publicly in school assembly that she is the promoter of a subversive secret society, a crime for which her friend Ruth is about to be expelled.

> No one quite knew what happened next. Some of the girls went off into violent hysterics; others rushed out of the great hall half-fainting, while others controlled themselves and listened as best they could. The scene was vivid and picturesque. [One of the governors] sobbed quite audibly, and took hold of Ruth's hand and even kissed it. But as she did so Kathleen herself came near and flung her arm round Ruth's neck.
>
> 'If you mean to expel Ruth you will expel me,' she said.

It was a favourite situation in the school story. Elsie J. Oxenham concludes *Expelled from School* (1919) in much the same way with a chapter called 'Clearing the Air', where 'that Italian cad' Giulia is shown up for the base worm that she is and the atmosphere is thick with the sound of girls sobbing and hissing 'Sneak!'

The School Favourite (1908), also by Meade, is a story of febrile friendship and jealousy. ('"I want you! I want you!" [Poppy] said with a sob.') The girls on one occasion go to bed together, 'Elizabeth's arm flung round Poppy's neck, their cheeks touching, their young figures close together', and the book ends on a note of high emotion with Elizabeth making a public confession (a favourite theme with the author): 'She writhed in her emotion. The great depths of her heart were broken up. Her proud nature underwent an anguish which would be inconceivable to one of a less proud spirit.' Meade was a married woman with three children and no doubt would have been profoundly shocked if she had been accused of writing about lesbianism, even if she had known what that meant. Stories of passionate school friendships between boys, such as E.F. Benson's *David Blaize* and Horace Annesley Vachell's *The Hill*, were the vogue then, and Ernest Raymond who had written one himself said fifty years later that he marvelled at 'the indubitable but wholly unconscious sexuality in it'. So that it was possible for Elsie J. Oxenham in her popular Abbey series to write of female partnerships which take on the aura of marriage.

> 'We've been engaged ever since the Coronation, Miss Macey,' Jack [Jacqueline] explained eagerly, 'just to see if we liked it, you know! We've decided that we do, so we're going to go ahead.'
>
> 'And get married,' Jen [Janet] supplemented . . . 'If you ever call me Janet, Jack, I'll – I'll get a divorce.'[9]

And in another book in the Abbey series 'Norah and Connie were a recognized couple. Con . . . was the wife and home-maker; Norah . . . was the husband, who planned little pleasure trips and kept the accounts and took Con to the pictures.'[10] Elsie Oxenham was clearly writing for a generation whose chances of marriage had been blighted by the huge loss of life in the First War.

Bosom friends abound in school stories, but though characters might blush and turn dizzy with emotion if a favoured older girl spoke to them, the formalized ritual of being 'pipped', as described by the Westonbirt girl not even allowed to choose her own object of worship (see page 199), plays little part in these books. At Tudor Hall they were called 'gone cases', at Cheltenham 'raves'; Wycombe had 'pashes', at Roedean ('I think we were specially prone to these complaints'[11]) you were 'gone' on someone, and those who were not afflicted kept books which recorded 'gonages' and their 'gonees'; at Benenden 'you had your cracklet who pressed soggy biscuits into your hand and made your bed. You had to have them to tea in your study and say goodnight to them and talk to them on their beds in return.'[12]

Nor was it just a feature of boarding communities; plenty of girls at day schools remembered it. 'One aspect of school which was very familiar was the crush, or pash,' said a girl at King Edward's Grammar School for Girls at Handsworth. 'This adoration and idolisation of an older girl or a young and pretty member of staff, frequently one of the games department, seems today [1983] totally to have disappeared.'[13] Just to know their Christian names and whisper them in the playground gave great delight, and the more daring might follow them home to their digs, and hang about hoping for 'a glimpse of the beloved before being parted for sixteen hours'. A crush on a member of staff did not necessarily result in good behaviour. Two wartime St Swithun's sixth-formers had a passion for the classics mistress ('though half of us knew she was a silly goose'). It took the form of outrageous outbursts in their coaching sessions with her, inevitably followed by a visit to her afterwards to abase themselves (there is often, as has been said, a masochistic impulse in girls). They always hoped that this would lead to a heart-to-heart talk and a baring of the soul ('What makes you behave so badly, Mary and Imogen?'), but it never did.

At St Paul's, where a crush at one time was almost a social obligation, it was more likely to be on seniors, the possessors of the white girdle awarded for gymnastics or games: 'Sheila and I used to wait for hours on railway stations as dreary as Willesden Junction, in the hope of meeting our ruling passion.'[14] At Nottingham High School a sixth-former's diary for 1949 said: 'At dinner-time two of my "pashees" were serving and said they wanted to kiss the food before they gave it to me!'[15]

Sometimes it was just hero-worship of a junior for a senior, as Tom Brown admires 'the head of the eleven, the head of big-side football', Old Brooke. In Mrs George du Horne Vaizey's novel about Cambridge, *A College Girl* (1913), the second year feels this for the third year, each of whom after her Finals is carried off 'by her special second-year adorer to a cheery little tea-party ... Here the tired senior was soothed and fed, and her self-esteem revived by an attitude of reverence on the part of the audience.' Sometimes it was, as has been said, in the nature of a recognized social custom: 'Being in her first year she soon had to decide upon whom she had a pash. It might be Erica, she thought.'[16] But on occasion, emotion overwhelmed you in spite of yourself, as this school story account of a sixth-former's feeling for her science teacher, which the author, Josephine Elder, who 'gets closer to the atmosphere of a real school perhaps than any other girls' writer of the period',[17] is at pains to distinguish from the common or garden crush.

> She had been afflicted with G.P.'s [*grandes passions*] in her youth, but always mildly, with her tongue in her cheek, because she could see the funny side of them, she had seen other people afflicted very badly, and thought what idiots they were! This was not a bit like that. She liked the Gypsy tremendously. Liked her enough to be reduced to stuttering, blithering pleasure when they met unexpectedly, and to look forward eagerly to the next time they should meet. She liked everything about her, her looks and her splendid brain, and the sensible humorous way of looking at things ... That was the difference. A person with a G.P. didn't know what her Worthy Object was really like – didn't care either, was just bewitched by her.[18]

The same author took a poor view of seniors who deliberately sought for admiration: 'To encourage "kids to suck up to you" was a most despicable sin, whether in a girl or a mistress. It hardly ever happened, because public opinion was so much against it. Admirers accepted "squashes" as a matter of course, and admiration either withered under them or continued, circumspectly, in spite of them.' And of a senior who broke this unwritten law: 'She's letting the whole Sixth down ... She smiles that toothy grin of hers at them, and puts her paws on their shoulders, and they nearly faint with joy. It's most *horribly* undignified.'

But writers saw nothing more reprehensible than loss of dignity in such behaviour, and apparently nothing unhealthy. In Mrs du Horne Vaizey's *Tom and Some Other Girls* (1901), a self-centred and vain schoolgirl falls in love with her housemistress, whose influence on her is a thoroughly good one. The latter visits her pupil's home, and in spite of the love passages between them – '"Kiss me!" replied Miss Everett simply, lifting her dark eyes to the girl's face with an appeal so sweet that it would have touched a heart of stone' – she becomes engaged to the brother. Rhoda is not jealous, but delighted. 'My own sister! And I can take care of you always.'[19]

Headmistresses had different ways of dealing with adolescent emotion. Sometimes the atmosphere of the school totally precluded it. At the Alice Ottley school 'No words were strong enough to express [Miss Ottley's] condemnation of the morbid kind of sentimental affection not worthy of the name of friendship, which tends to sap the spiritual life and lower the spiritual standard, and lead to selfish neglect of home and duty, to a craving for admiration, and to jealousy.'[20] In Sacred Heart schools 'the rules were very strict, their principal object being to dry up all the natural springs of affection in the human heart,' wrote one pupil bitterly of her experiences at a Paris Sacré Coeur in 1828.[21] 'We were kept under the most strict *surveillance*,' said Antonia White, 'and, even when we believed ourselves alone, a nun would appear from nowhere, in her noiseless list slippers, to make sure that we were not getting into mischief. On the assumption that "when two are together, the devil makes a third" we never walked in pairs but always in trios.'[22] But another, later pupil thought these were wise precautions:

> There was none of the sentimental wandering about in pairs with linked arms, which spoils the healthy public life of many girls' schools. And not only was there no encouragement to idealize friendships which were founded merely on transitory attractions and motives, but active discouragement was meted out to any demonstration of partiality.[23]

Olive Willis's was the most original approach. She had always deprecated silliness, and when there was a fashion for falling in love with members of the staff she commissioned a play making fun of it. The part of the girl with the crush was played by herself with plaits and a lovelorn expression, and the object of her passion was a woman of farcically grim appearance. But she refused to take this sort of problem very seriously, telling the staff on one occasion that so-and-so was such a selfish little toad that it was a relief to find her able to care for anyone but herself. Similarly, when the staff were worried by an outbreak of lavatory humour she reminded them that it was like puppies rolling in mud, a stage that children soon grew out of (very different from another headmistress, who harangued her whole school because

35. The gridiron: Wycombe Abbey pupils stretched on the gym ribstalls, *c.* 1902. Like St Leonards and Roedean in early days, Wycombe made a point of hardening its pupils with cold baths and strenuous exercise.

36. Informal hockey, 1890s, at Winchester High School in the days when games were a recreation rather than an inescapable part of the school system.

37. Early Girl Guides at St James's, West Malvern. The Guide movement was very popular with schools in the first half of the century as a method of teaching leadership. St James's, a small school, at one time had four companies.

38. As in the Army, bedmaking at girls' schools, in the days before duvets, was a solemn ritual with much attention paid to hospital corners. A dormitory at Moreton Hall, 1950s.

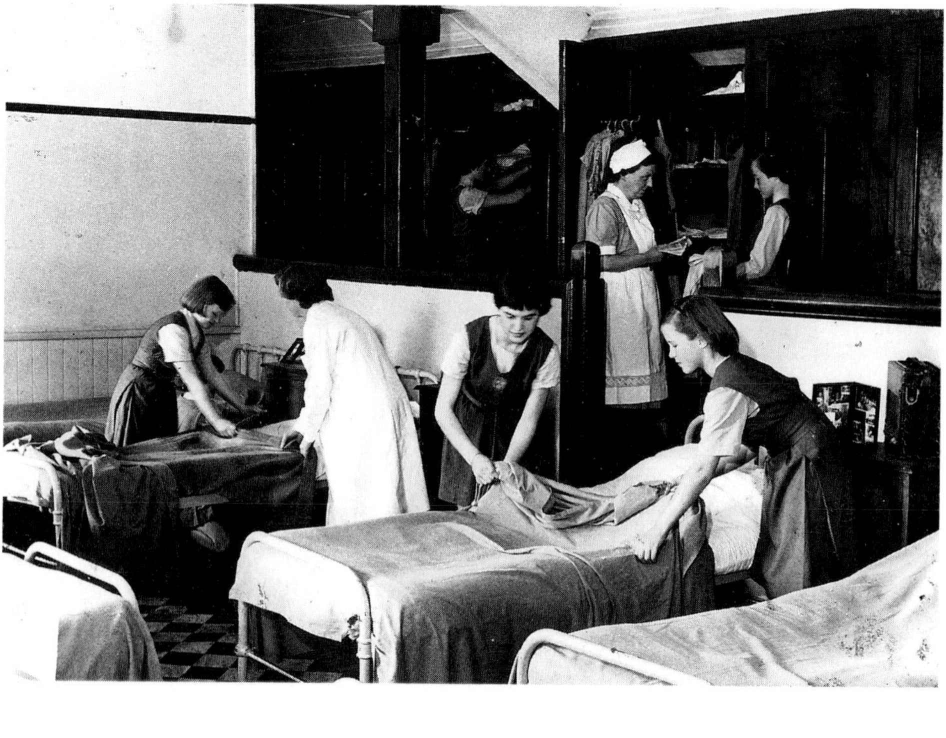

left 39. A changing cubicle in use as a study at Cheltenham Ladies' College in 1940 when all the school buildings except the swimming bath were requisitioned.

right 40. A lacrosse house match on the sands when Benenden was evacuated to Newquay.

41. A wartime class at St Brandon's School which was evacuated from Bristol to the Bishop's Palace at Wells. As can be seen, the room was also used as a dormitory.

42. Pupils at St James's, West Malvern.

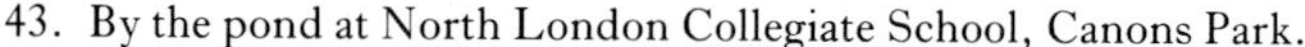

43. By the pond at North London Collegiate School, Canons Park.

44. Friends at Walthamstow Hall.

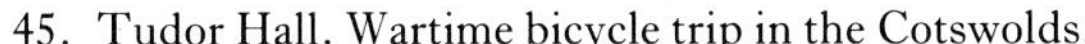

45. Tudor Hall. Wartime bicycle trip in the Cotswolds.

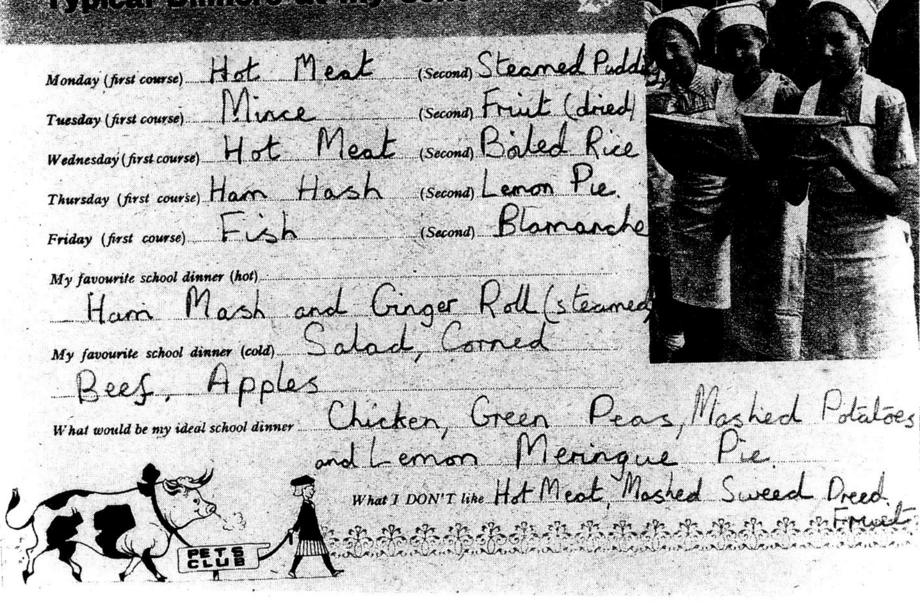

Typical Dinners at my School

Monday (*first course*) Hot Meat (*Second*) Steamed Pudding
Tuesday (*first course*) Mince (*Second*) Fruit (dried)
Wednesday (*first course*) Hot Meat (*Second*) Boiled Rice
Thursday (*first course*) Ham Hash (*Second*) Lemon Pie.
Friday (*first course*) Fish (*Second*) Blamanche

My favourite school dinner (hot) Ham Mash and Ginger Roll (steamed)

My favourite school dinner (cold) Salad, Corned Beef, Apples

What would be my ideal school dinner Chicken, Green Peas, Mashed Potatoes and Lemon Meringue Pie.

What I DON'T like Hot Meat, Mashed Sweed Dreed Fruit

46. The schoolgirl view. Record by Letitia Opie, aged 10, of school food in a school diary issued with *Princess*, February, 1960.

47. Drawings from St James's, West Malvern, Junior House scrapbook, with signatures of pupils.

48. Drawings from *The Book of Bedgebury*, Christmas, 1923, by a Bedgebury School VI former, showing progress from tear-soaked new girl to poised young woman carrying luggage marked SELF-CONTROL, MANNERS and KNOWLEDGE. (The artist has admirably absorbed authority's ideals for the young.)

49. English boarding schools are increasingly multi-national. Overseas pupils at the School of S. Mary and S. Anne, Abbots Bromley, 1973; Malaysia, Nigeria, Norway, Sierra Leone and Uganda are represented.

50. Modern technological achievement. Roedean VI formers and their teachers with the electric car that they built.

of graffiti discovered on a desk, the punch line being 'She actually used the word LOVE').

When Miss Faithfull at Cheltenham in the 1920s decided it was time to do something about 'false friendships', as she termed them, she made them the subject of one of her Saturday evening talks ('What do you call them now? Is it still "raves"?' Chorus: 'Yes!'), and said that it was an emotion that 'catches hold of you and is a roaring fire all in a minute'. It seemed to her to be more serious then than it was in her own schooldays, leading to 'a great deal of nervous interest and mental instability' which might spoil a year or more of school life. And the great risk was that it should become so fashionable that a girl felt abnormal if she did not succumb.[24] The seniors apparently responded indignantly and told Miss Faithfull she was impugning the good sense of the college, but from the younger girls she gathered that 'you can have as many as seventeen [raves] and three is quite usual'.

Both Miss Willis and Miss Faithfull were much more adroit than Miss Lawrence, who commanded the Roedean games captain to put a stop to all the nonsense. The blushing games captain told the similarly embarrassed assembly that she knew all about the whispers of '*Isn't* she sweet?', 'Look out, *she's* coming!', the rush to open doors, to take off their idols' cricket pads – and wasn't it ludicrous and revolting? 'There must be no more of this sickening *nonsense*. The school itself was getting a name for it, and had we ever thought how bad it was for the school?' That night in obedience to the games captain all the gonees went round to bid farewell to their gonages. One of the juniors could not accept total severance from the beloved.

> 'Goodnight, Stella. Stella –'
> 'Yes?'
> 'May I still go on making your bed, please?'
> 'Yes, – if you like!'
> 'Oh thanks – *awfully*' . . .
>
> Then . . . things lapsed back into much the same state as usual . . . It was better that the old enthusiasm and devotion should go on than that brutality should have been used to destroy them.[25]

And as Theodora Benson remarked, absurd and distasteful as it all was (she had gone late to Cheltenham and was amazed at the heroine worship she found there), it was no more than a phase of growing up. Raves were of no significance in the post-college life of the girls. 'There was nothing sinister about them. We must all be silly sometimes.'[26]

Emotional friendship between contemporaries is recalled later, by those who went through it, as essentially absurd; females, unlike males, apparently have never had a wish to invest it with a Hellenistic haze of romanticism. A girl at St Swithun's fifty years ago remembered how she and a contemporary, temporarily soul-mates, used to creep out of bed and meet for searing sessions of self-analysis, the aim being to discover if each had been truly sincere during the day. Mostly they found they could not claim to be, but on one notable occasion they decided that they had achieved a state of perfect sincerity, and each solemnly pinned a badge on the other's pyjamas. But they were caught by outraged authority and closely questioned, and asked if they had ever kissed. 'I was astonished, and revolted.'

A girl at St Paul's remembered a similar friendship.

> So romantic was my friendship with Maire that we were unable to speak to each other at school as we were too shy. So we wrote long letters nearly every day . . . We might have kept diaries and exchanged them – but chose instead this intensely personal and introspective correspondence. We debated whether a time would come when we could actually talk to each other like other people by daylight 'on the leads' [a terrace which opened out of the hall]. We exhorted each other to achieve stability. 'The calmness,' Maire wrote, 'which we are both cultivating – with some success – will also help us towards universality. In these last weeks of infinitely personal thought I've almost forgotten that universality was once our aim.' We thought we might allow ourselves to go for walks together at some future point, but not meet together after dark.[27]

Authors of school stories often wrote about bosom friends, though anything more than superficial treatment of this theme is exceptional. But Lucy Kinloch's *A World Within a School* (1937), a romantic account of Harrogate Ladies College (called here 'Danbury College'), is a more serious study of the sort of friendship that may flourish in a single-sex community, and comes nearest to boys' school fiction like *The Hill*. The author describes tangled politicking and jostling for position, since apparently one can only have a single *real* friend. It also throws an interesting light on the schoolgirl code of conduct then.

New girl Nora as soon as she arrives at Danbury is drawn to the immensely popular Bobby, the games captain, but falls foul of Joan, Bobby's bosom friend. Joan is the ringleader in the persecution of the new girl, but the form mistress guesses the truth, and Joan has to face the headmistress's wrath and contempt. Far worse than this, however, is 'the dreadful fear of losing Bobby's friendship'. Joan tells Bobby that the truth was only known because Nora sneaked, and Bobby feels that this is a far greater crime than Joan's efforts to get Nora into trouble and her consequent lying, and cold-shoulders Nora. But weeks later, Nora gets the chance to set the record straight, and begs Greta, her own friend of the moment, to tell Bobby the truth, which the code forbids her to divulge herself.

> 'Greta, Bobby thinks that I told about Joan in that row over the books and things. Will you tell her the truth?'
>
> Greta looked at her friend in silence. What irony was this which had chosen her to demolish the barrier that kept these destined friends apart?

> She had no illusions; she could give these two back to each other, but she would lose Nora. The pause was only her silent farewell, but as if her thoughts had cried aloud Nora suddenly understood. Never had Greta been so close, nor seemed so dear. All Nora's generous nature rushed to the surface, as she caught Greta's hands in hers.
>
> 'Oh, Greta dear, I shouldn't have asked that! Never mind, don't tell her; I don't want you to after all. If she can believe that of me, let her.'

Bobby now realizes the truth of the matter, but loyalty dictates that as long as Joan is in the school she must be *the* friend. Once she has gone, Nora and Bobby spend a happy year in close friendship. Then Bobby herself leaves for Edinburgh University. Nora, tremulous with excitement, goes to visit her there the first Christmas holidays. But Bobby is different, totally absorbed in a new life with new friends. She has even forgotten which term the house matches are played; worse still, men friends have taken the place of girl friends and she whirls away on the back of someone's motor bike. 'Bobby had gone. The longed for, looked forward to meeting was over, and the light had gone out of their precious friendship like a snuffed candle. It was unbelievable, it was unbearable.'

She goes back to school desolate, and droops apathetically throughout the term. Her housemistress guesses the trouble, and in trying to put things into perspective puts her finger on the artificiality of boarding school life, its isolation and remoteness from the world outside.

> 'If you think about it, you must realize that one of the drawbacks of our public school system is the way in which the entire life of the people is compressed within its horizon. Your friends are here, your interests are here, your work and your games are all-absorbing. You go home for the holidays, but scarcely for long enough to catch up even with family life. Frequently you spend the holidays with a school friend, or she with you. The school, in other words, is, for the length of time you are in it, the core of your life. You keep its rules so automatically that in time you hardly realize you are under continual restraint. Try, then, to imagine what it is like to have this life, this centre of your existence, suddenly cut away from you. The new life has much wider horizons, far fewer restraints; its possibilities are boundless, immensely exciting. By comparison, life at school suddenly shrinks, and all the things that mattered there no longer matter at all. You are free. You are emancipated.'

Lucy Kinloch was devoted to her old school but in this passage, at least, recognized its limitations as a way of life.

Physical homosexuality is never mentioned in either memoirs or schoolgirl fiction. But authority latterly has been watchful, it seems. In the early years of the century schoolgirls apparently kissed each other freely; in the 1920s and 30s they might not kiss but they walked around arm in arm, but at Wycombe in the 1950s girls 'were not allowed to share wash-cubicles, hold hands, or walk along arm-in-arm, and the washing of another's hair – a fairly frequent happening – was severely punished. Close friendships with girls a few years older or younger than oneself were actively discouraged.'[28] The author did not know of any lesbian relationships, but rumours were rife, as they inevitably would be; gossip is the main pastime among girls at boarding school. At many schools now friendship between girls who are in different forms or houses is frowned upon.

It would seem that a sense of the ludicrous has inhibited women writers from making these unconsummated emotional experiences the subject of adult novels about adolescence. They have preferred instead to write about the love of pupils for their teachers, as in *Olivia* by Olivia (1949), where a sixteen-year-old falls passionately for a teacher at her French finishing school (it is an account of jealousies, rivalries and politicking as much as of love); or Clemence Dane's *Regiment of Women* (1917) and Christa Winsloe's *The Child Manuela* (1934, about a German school), both of which end tragically with the girls throwing themselves from windows. In Rosalind Wade's *Children, Be Happy* (of which very few copies can remain, since as the outcome of two separate libel actions the publishers were ordered to recall and destroy the entire edition), one girl is seduced, another has a heady affair with her teacher (who breaks off her engagement on this account), and the thwarted spinster mistress who denounces them hangs herself. The twenty-year-old author reckoned that envy and bitterness underlay the behaviour of those who taught: 'We're jealous of you, your youth. You see, life's been unkind to us, and we think we'll get back on it by doing this to you, by ruling red pencils through your exercises and by giving you bad marks. Don't think too badly of us; it's just because we've failed so hopelessly ourselves that we've simply got to take it out on someone.' This smouldering resentment about past injustices, which features in the Dane and the Winsloe novels, seems more characteristic of women's memories of their schools than does the heady nostalgia that so many men apparently feel about theirs.

Boys and Girls

'One might have been introducing a striptease dancer to the Athenaeum,' said John Rae of the consternation caused in 1966 when, newly arrived as headmaster of Taunton School (now co-educational), he proposed to take his wife to the school chapel service.[29] Until well on in the 1960s official contact between boys and girls during the school term was minimal, and Wykehamists, indeed, were accused of not realizing there was a second sex. 'The opposite sex is despised and hated, treated as something obscene,' Robert Graves wrote of public schools before the First War. 'Many boys never recover from this perversion.'[30] As we have noted, at the earlier girls' schools there were visiting male teachers for specialized subjects, but women became increasingly competent to teach these, so that at many boarding schools between the wars girls might not see any male for twelve weeks on end (exeats then being almost non-existent), except the gardeners and the clergyman who took the service on Sundays. 'Discounting the rector and the doctor, the only male company around from the beginning to the end of term was Timothy, the sixth form's skeleton. He hung from a nail and was for anatomy,' said a girl at a midlands boarding school in the late 1930s, adding: 'We were so fenced in and cut off from all male company that our attention focussed, intensely and hopelessly, on a fair curly-haired gardener's boy who used to push a roller up and down the lawns.'[31] When she had gone to boarding school at fourteen she was used to brothers and at ease in male company, but after three years in this atmosphere she was so shy that she blushed if a male spoke to her. Even when pupils in the 1950s were allowed more freedom to move outside the school premises there were elaborate rules, if there happened to be a boys' school nearby, about which streets one might walk down so that the sexes never coincided.

At day schools the same segregation was attempted, and was largely successful in that the sexes rarely met for social purposes. And indeed many girls seemed to have shared the views of a Victorian pupil at Notting Hill High School, who said that though she and her friends enjoyed romantic poetry and fiction they 'dismissed as disgusting any evidences of schoolgirl flirtations and premature passions'. Besides, 'for those years I disliked the company of boys. I felt vaguely that they "spoilt things".'[32]

At King Edward VI, Birmingham, when the formidable Miss Creak was headmistress (1883–1910) and the boys' and girls' schools shared the same premises, brothers and sisters did not dare to approach together. At Nottingham it was much the same.

> It was never recognized that girls might know boys ... They were condemned as an unhealthy distraction. Every year we held an all-female dance. It was said that the headmaster of the Boys' High School regularly suggested joint dances, which Miss Philipps as regularly rejected. Of course ... some girls had boy-friends, but they were a decided minority. Other girls used to 'collect' policemen and bus-conductors, and used to rush to each other first thing with breathless reports of conversations.[33]

There were also the standard 'crushes' on other girls, and when the next headmistress arrived in 1935, she found the school 'a welter of emotion'. Day school embargo on any contact with boys was standard. A pupil at King Edward's School, Handsworth, in the 1920s was banned from the school playing fields for a whole year for bringing a nine-year-old boy to the sports day (eight was the upper limit), and after a girl had been seen talking to a boy on a bus the headmistress addressed the whole school at assembly saying how serious this offence was and that if the girl would come and speak to her privately she would explain the dangers involved. But by the post-war period there were dancing lessons for the Nottingham High School sixth form one evening a week with the Boys' High School.

> Today, the tension, giggling and even terror generated by these occasions seem so disproportionate to the actual correctness and formality of it all, as to be absurd. I never found a boy friend on these occasions for the simple reason that I found these youths absolutely unattractive, not at all like real men (Heathcliffe, for instance, or Mr Rochester).[34]

(Which is matched by a Durham High School girl's comment, 'Boys aren't really as exciting as you think they will be.') Many others recall the agony of conversation with the opposite sex. A member of Nottingham High School described the 'experience of acute embarrassment all round' when, during World War II, the French mistress decided that as a substitute for school trips to France the school would entertain French sailors by showing them the city and taking them out to tea in the Mikado Café.

> With true British reserve, we refused to chatter in French . . . We spoke only when spoken to, and, as we walked along the pavement in a bunch, I remember skilfully dodging so that I was not hemmed in on both sides by amiably grinning Frenchmen. Unfortunately – not all that skilfully; Miss Tucker soon hauled me back into position.[35]

At boarding school it was normal in the 1940s and 50s for all incoming mail to be scrutinized. 'If you received a letter with a boys' school crest on the envelope, it meant disappearing on Sunday afternoon to explain satisfactorily,' said a Felixstowe girl of the 1930s. But in that between-the-wars period authority got closer to persuading girls that they were sexless than at any other time. Most of the older schools had experienced some sort of trouble over boys, and Elizabeth Sewell, who ran a small private school herself, was well aware of what might arise when girls congregated together – 'not so much actions as conversation'. One surmises, however, that this was probably no more than 'unhealthy views on love and marriage', as a contemporary put it.

The charity hospitals often recorded more serious episodes. At Grey Coat conditions were such that it was not often possible to do more than exchange notes with the Archbishop Tenison boys, but at the Merchant Maiden Hospital girls were arraigned from time to time for consorting with youths, and on one dreadful occasion for climbing over the garden wall and going out with them. The culprits were put in solitary confinement for six weeks and fed on bread and water, which was the punishment a few years later when four others had escaped to dine with some young men in a tavern. (As this time it was January, the surgeon was consulted 'on the proper mode of fitting up the apartments, that no injury might arise to them from the season.[36]) Some boys at Sedbergh School in the 1830s had the audacity to send valentines to the clergy daughters at Casterton, and then to come in person to see how these had been received. (In fact they had been burned.)

Nor were convent schools immune. Margaret Nevinson remembered that at her mid-Victorian Oxford convent 'a great deal of romantic flirtation went on . . . and I learnt that certain stones and hollow trees called "post offices" were used for letters by amorous undergraduates'. At a later French school she was horrified by the coarse talk and jokes of girls who had been so zealously guarded from the world that they could not even cross the road unchaperoned, with every book chosen for them. She said that at the Oxford convent, 'except for some innocent nonsense of the kind mentioned', she heard nothing that might not have been heard or seen 'by the Vice-Chancellor and the whole Bench of Bishops'.[37] The nuns, however, were very watchful; not only did the trimmings of hats have to be the very plainest, but hair, even pigtails, had to be concealed when the school was out walking. It was the same at St Mary's, Wantage, and when it was discovered by the sister-in-charge that the senior girls had persuaded one of the curates to write in their birthday books these were confiscated, 'and from that time onwards on our daily walks two big girls had to walk with one small girl between them to act as gooseberry!'[38]

The school story books so popular in the first four decades of the century, though regarded as subversive twaddle by authority, in fact did valiant and unrecognized work on authority's behalf. They not only ardently promoted the *esprit de corps* on which the whole public school ethic was based, but they did their best to deny that girls could be sex objects and to deny their femininity. Their heroines were honorary boys; it is interesting to see the ambivalence of the attitude of Evelyn Sharp (1869–1955), an ardent worker for women's suffrage who went to prison twice in the course of her campaigning. She was the ninth of eleven children, and in her family and school stories the heroine (invariably spirited, intelligent and much put-upon – as, one infers, she saw herself) usually has a dominating brother full of contempt for the female sex which the heroine seems half to share herself. In *The Youngest Girl in the School* (1901) Barbara's rich aunt says:

> Do you want to go on being a boy for ever, reading all sorts of books you have no business to read, and banging people on the head when they offend you, and looking alarming old ladies in the face without flinching; or do you want to be combed and brushed and smoothed into a young lady, and taught to rave about art and music and poetry, and told to look down when you are spoken to and never answer back if the truth is unpleasant?

In this and in *The Making of a Schoolgirl* (1897) the heroine goes to boarding school primed with a brother's contempt for such establishments ('You don't call a girls' school *school*, do you?'), expecting to find 'girls who minced their language, and minded their clothes, girls who put lessons before larks, girls who told tales, and girls who giggled, and all of them incipient drawing-room visitors'.[39] Indeed, both heroines find all of that, as well as the ferret-like cruelty which is – as Katharine Whitehorn so rightly says – the peçuliar speciality of girls. But there is also a like-minded friend, a tomboy like herself, and a headmistress who is 'as reasonable as a jolly sort of boy'; and there the author lets the matter rest, leaving it unresolved whether her heroines are going to stay in tomboyhood for ever or move into the drawing-room, but making it very clear where she felt most at ease herself. And in an essay supposedly written by the heroine she indicates her contempt for what a girl understands by friendship.

> Friendship means kissing, and writing letters about nothing at all, and quarrelling so that you can make it up again. Friendship is very beautiful and touching, but being chummy is ever so much jollier. Chumminess means liking the same sort of things, and keeping the same sort of animals ... But you don't say you are fond of each other, because, of course, that's granted; and you don't kiss at all; at least not often. It is boys who understand being chums ... Girls don't understand chumminess at all.[40]

Many later authors similarly advocated boy ideals; their heroines were 'madcaps', 'harum-scarum' (these epithets were great favourites), or perhaps 'Irish', which invariably meant that they were wild. But their escapades were boyish ones; only the bad girls of the book (who often turned out to be foreigners) thought about their appearance and clothes, and even they rarely if ever went so far as to involve themselves with the other sex. If young males put in an appearance it is made clear that they see schoolgirls as a different sex from women; they giggle and cannot be objects of desire. This is the view of the young officer who arrives, intent upon clearing his family's name, at his old home, now a school, in May Wynne's *The Honour of the School* (1919): 'A regiment of Huns would have been easier to face than thirty giggling schoolgirls.' 'No fear of their coming out is there?' he says to the girl who accompanies him, 'or I shall scoot.' For he doesn't see *her* as a girl: only as a necessary guide in his task. As for the girl herself, when she first meets him 'she was not in the least shy, because she never thought of herself at all; and after having been "comrade" all her life with Dad and Dad's many friends, who were her friends too, she really regarded this khaki-clad young hero far more as a boy than most girls of her age would have done.' And in the same author's *Carol of Hollydene School* (1926) there is a boy who is a 'chum' of four schoolgirls and they all 'run wild like so many colts', all apparently regarding each other as of the same sex.

It was perhaps with stories such as these in mind that Lilian Faithfull in one of her Saturday evening addresses to Cheltenham girls in the 1920s warned them to avoid the temptation of flaunting their athletic prowess, though she conceded that when boys at the age of sixteen or so began noticing girls they liked them 'to be good at games, and nice looking and well dressed ... At this point the boy wants good fellowship, not what he would call "anything silly or sloppy".'[41]

A few schools, notably the Mount, had always had a policy of letting girls meet their brothers at weekends. During 1835 they even went, ten at a time to tea at the Friends' Bootham School, and saw chemical experiments, 'poked around into every corner' including the boys' bedrooms, were given 'quite an elegant supper', and were escorted home by some of the boys. 'I spent the pleasantest evening I have had since I came,' wrote one girl enthusiastically. But this easy fellowship was not at all usual, and when boy/girl events began to be countenanced in the 1950s nobody appears to remember them with much pleasure. 'I personally was scared stiff. Boys were bunched up at one end of the hall, girls huddled at the other; on the command, the boys tramp in a body to pick their partners, and you trundle, stumble, whirl or kick your way round the floor.'[42] The prefects at Channing School, reluctantly, it seems, felt obliged in 1965 to reciprocate the hospitality of Mill Hill and Highgate schools. 'I remember that nouveau brick wall of the New Hall splattered with stuffed prunes which those well-bred young men had seen fit to lob rather than consume.'[43]

At first mixed dances were incorporated into the school system rather like athletic fixtures, with clearly defined limits and regulations to restrict prolonged absence from the dance floor. (One school presented each girl with a carnation button-hole; 'Was it to ensure that one came home with it uncrushed?' one of them speculated afterwards.) Later, vigilance was relaxed and a certain amount of flirtation was tolerated, even expected. ('Snog, girls, snog. I don't see any snogging going on,' one Mother Superior used to call out at such dances, striding up and down the outfield.) But plenty of schools found the behaviour of their male guests anaphrodisiac. One girl at a Berkshire convent in the early 1970s disliked the assumption that the girls wanted heavy petting sessions. (The nuns had instructed them on what to avoid and what led to danger.) Marlborough boys had had to be banned because they had tried to shin up drainpipes to reach the girls' bedrooms, but Radley, when they organized a reciprocal dance (though 'organized' was an inexact term since they had failed to take any trouble at all), surrounded the dance floor with mattresses, which the chaperoning nuns appeared to ignore. But the boys' loutishness may of course have been sheer perversity, as a reaction to the girls' feminine attention to detail, like the boys who had been invited to debate against a girls' school in the days when such fixtures were a daring novelty, but had responded to the girls' earnestness and weighty argument with elegant and laid-back frivolity.

'Keep the Girl a Child'

Authority tried hard to protect the girls in its charge. At some convents the modesty inculcated was such that girls were made to bath in long white shifts so that they never caught sight of their naked bodies, and patent leather shoes were said to be forbidden because they might reflect what dwelt above. (But it also might have been that the nuns, being women of good taste, thought they were deplorably bad style.) At the Feast of the Immaculate Conception the Sacred Heart children processed with much ceremony carrying flowers, and 'two by two we curtseyed low to the image of a Heavenly Queen and placed our blossoms in great jars that stood ready to receive them, saying "O Mary, I give thee the lily of my heart, be thou its guardian forever"'.[44] It was a moment of great solemnity, which may have acted as a talisman – certainly more than the rosebuds which one RE teacher at Cheltenham suggested girls should embroider on their underwear to preserve them from impurity. And it was not only convents that would not allow girls to wear male clothing when they were acting; Miss Gray, High Mistress of St Paul's, was also excessively modest and forbad trousers on the stage unless covered with an overcoat. At gym when a Paulina turned upside down on the wall bars, another had to stand by her holding up her gym tunic in case her knickers could be seen.

But in the 1920s and 30s the chief protection of girls was the unique state of immaturity in which prosperous parents kept their young. (It was very different, of course, for the children of the poor.) Even the 'innocent nonsense' that Margaret Nevinson remembered was rare. The state seems to have been achieved partly by shielding the young from everything in the adult world, and partly by clothing that emphasized their youth (tunics and djibbahs that concealed the burgeoning female curves; shorts until thirteen or more for the boys). Diet may have been a contributory factor: there was much farinaceous food, limited protein, everything was cooked very plainly and meat served only once a day – a regime recommended by paediatricians of the period, apparently with the object of delaying the onset of puberty. The longer that this could be put off the better. 'Keep the girl a child in her physical habits as long as possible,' said a child-rearing manual in a chapter about the problems of adolescence. 'Introduce her to camping, volley ball, folk-dancing, etc. to counteract the tendency to loll, stay in the house and act like a lady . . . counteract any tendency to bad habits by athletic ideals, early rising, morning baths, big projects, and much activity.' 'Bad habits' of course was the masturbation about which there had been so much hysterical Victorian warning, but which by the 1920s seemed of so little importance that this textbook gave it only the briefest reference in a page of general advice. The author was also fully in favour of encouraging the girl to be a tomboy. 'A pair of black bloomers and a high fence . . . ought to give a girl every opportunity to do in the friendly tree or on the trapeze all the stunts that attract her brother.'[45] A contemporary, however, remarked that the ideal of sexlessness held up by many parents could be almost as harmful as the other extreme, and that prudery and sentimentalism were not desirable standards.[46]

'The principle should be to broaden by retarding,' said G. Stanley Hall, the American psychologist whose *Adolescence* (1904) was regarded by his contemporaries as epoch-making. He was referring to intellectual activity, but the general retarding process was very much in evidence at least until the end of the 1940s, and applied most of all to what the middle-class child was allowed to know of the world beyond home and school. Boarding school girls in particular might be said to have been in a state of suspended animation until they were eighteen. It has been seen that Badminton was an exception to this. At Christ's Hospital after World War I Louie Angus's housemistress was appalled 'at the parochialism of our conversation and interests'. She had the fourth-formers to her sitting-room, and evenings were devoted to reading leading articles from different newspapers and evaluating them. At Benenden there was an attempt to inform pupils about world affairs:

> Every Saturday morning we repaired to the Entrance Hall for [Miss Bird's] Current Affairs. We sat on the floor, or on the stairs and there was usually a bumble-bee droning against the diamond panes and amongst the pots of gloxinia. Birdie gave us a crisp summary of the week's events and read bits from the papers, particularly what Wickham Steed had said in the *Spectator* the day before and the Stephen King-Hall Newsletter.

But it would seem that most of the pre-1939 generation were happily self-absorbed. 'Some of us looked forward with apprehension to the University, and others with serenity to Coming Out – Presentation in ostrich plumes, and "doing the flowers for Mummy".'[47] This particular writer had remembered the Slump, and pinch-faced men in the streets, and she and the more perceptive of her contemporaries 'cared passionately that March about Czechoslovakia, Chamberlain's "small country far away"'. For them there was a sadness about their last term, 'the first touch of frost in the air'.

This was unusual. At other schools past pupils marvelled at how isolated and ignorant they had been. Many had similar experiences, as the girl who said of her 1930s education that 'we were woefully ignorant of world affairs (for History only gave us William the Conqueror to James II). World War I was never mentioned and . . . we had no idea what caused it . . . We knew nothing of Lloyd George.'[48] At St James's, West Malvern, 'our only contact [with world affairs] had been with dear old Mr Jerram on alternate Thursday evenings, who lectured on Current Events – a pleasant, restful period during which we were allowed to knit, provided we did not drop our needles too often'.[49] At the Sacred Heart, Roehampton, the only newspaper available even to the nuns themselves was *The Times* (the centre pages), but that was removed from them during the 1936 abdication crisis. Nor did matters change very much until the advent of television.

> We led very protected, insular lives and had little notion of the realities outside our strata of society or sex [said a post-war schoolgirl]. We never heard the news nor saw any newspapers. I remember my father being quite horrified several weeks after the North Atlantic Treaty was signed – I arrived home for the holidays never having heard of NATO. The only item of news which I remember being announced was the death of George VI.[50]

At Westonbirt in the 1950s it was the same.

> No television, of course, but also no radio except in the House Drawing Room, where the Fifth Years had the treat of the Sunday evening radio Classic Serial. Also, in the main school we had no access to newspapers. The Sixth Form Common Room had selected papers: the Times, the Telegraph and, daringly, the Mail, but during the Lord Montagu case these appeared with large pieces cut out, with the inevitable result that copies were brought in by girls from leave and we learned for the first time of the existence of homosexuality. We were, on the whole, remarkably uncurious about the world outside. Every Monday evening the Upper School was gathered together for a half-hour session called News in which the housemistresses in turn told us of the events of the week suitable for us to hear and we were inevitably bored. Once during a General Election we held a Mock Election, amazed at the bravado of the girl who stood for Labour. She was, of course, soundly defeated. It was not until I got to Oxford that I seriously considered other political points of view.[51]

There was similar reticence about the facts of life. Margaret Popham, principal of Cheltenham (born 1884), as a girl had asked her mother where babies came from. 'Well, dear, I really don't know. God starts it, and the doctor does the rest.' 'This was the entire extent of sex knowledge vouchsafed to me. In any case, we just never talked about sex at school – it was never in our minds.'[52] A generation later Louie Angus admitted to the same ignorance: 'The day before I was fourteen, while walking up and down the bridge over the platforms at Liverpool Street Station my mother had told me what she considered I needed to know about the probable onset of menstruation. I have never been so surprised again in my life.' She remembered the only conversation she and her friends had on birth: 'Dulcie said that her mother had told her that babies grew inside their mothers. We roared with laughter, we nearly fell off the shelf, and we said, "Oh Dulcie, if you'll believe that you'll believe anything."'[53] Margaret Mackworth (Lady Rhondda) said she had worked out the main facts for herself at the age of twelve 'with the aid of a donkey in foal, *Midshipman Easy*, the Bible and an older cousin ... If they had only concealed all knowledge of geography from me as carefully as they did all knowledge of this, how hard and how eagerly I should have worked at geography!'[54] But Victorian books of physiological information for the young – one or two of which sought to make the subject more acceptable by treating the body as a machine or a house – even if they very daringly dealt with the elimination of waste, totally ignored the process of reproduction.

One trouble seems to have been that all the anatomical terms in the latter were apparently taboo, except for the medical profession, who could not bring themselves to use them for the laity. This applied even when writers set out to give technical information to young husbands or wives; they devoted far more space to the reproduction of plants and the lower forms of animal life, and dodged the main issue with astonishing agility. When it came to writing for the young there was, of course, even more emphasis on flowers and birds and fishes – 'the Papa and Mamma natures united in the oyster,' said one pamphlet for boys[55] – and even more reticence, so that no more is said to prepare a girl for menstruation than that she will feel 'a strange weariness, perhaps headache or backache' and may be irritable and nervous.[56] There was difficulty even in using the word 'breast', so that we are told that the baby derives milk 'from outside the mother'. But the main purpose of the books was to warn against what was always referred to as self-abuse.

> When I see a little girl or young lady wasted and weak and listless, with great hollow eyes and a sort of sallow tint on the haggard face, with the red hue of the lips faded, the ears white like marble and the face covered with pimples, I dread lest they have committed the sin which, if not abandoned, will lead them down to death.[57]

Like Dean Farrar's thunderings about 'Kibroth-Hattaavah' in *Eric or Little by Little* (1858) – an allusion to an obscure Old Testament place-name which literally means 'the graves of desire' (but how many of his readers would have been able to understand the Hebrew?) – the warnings are never specific and must have baffled and worried many anxious readers. They moderated in the next century, but the hazy vagueness, the assumption that children could infer the human reproductive process from accounts of ferns and oysters, persisted. One of the most curious examples of sex instruction comes in Edith Howes' *The Cradle Ship* (1916), where Mother and Father, Win and Twin, fly away to Babyland to find out where babies come from. (They all have to turn themselves into flower fairies first; Father elects to be a red hot poker. One assumes this was a Freudian slip, rather like Angela Brazil naming two passionate friends Lesbia and Regina in *Loyal to the School*.) Here they have the mandatory encounters with trees, flowers and butterflies before the children grasp that 'baby grew in a silky baby-bag under your heart, Mother' – though, compared with assertions in other books of the period that babies had been brought across the rainbow or out of flowers by the fairies, this is an unusually scientific statement.

The adult allusions to flowers and pollen and bees, only half-understood by their hearers who, however, grasped that they were in some way charged with hidden meaning, meant that for many girls the whole subject of botany was a minefield of embarrassment. Elizabeth Bowen imagined one adolescent dilemma:

> At her confirmation classes they had worked their way through the Commandments: at the seventh an evening had been devoted to impure curiosity. She had been offered, and had accepted, a very delicate book and still could not think of anything without blushing. She felt she had erred in accepting the delicate book when she lacked impure curiosity, but the other candidates, all averting their eyes, had held up their hands for it, and she did not like to be out of anything. So that now flowers made her blush, rabbits made her blush excessively; she could no longer eat an egg. Only minerals seemed to bear contemplation.[58]

The high schools were just as reserved. At Merchant Taylors' in the 1930s 'the embarrassing fundamental study of reproduction was avoided. The biology mistress had to face this problem when "sex raised its ugly head in frogs and rabbits"; her solution was to study reproduction only in "biological drawings" – discussion on such an embarrassing subject was avoided like the plague – even in the Sixth Form'.[59] 'On one occasion,' said a girl who was at Oxford High School 1935–42, 'the VI form were summoned to the Biology Room to see a particularly successful dissection of a pregnant rat . . . It was instructive but inadequate.'[60] But it has to be borne in mind that schoolgirls themselves then were very modest and terrified of embarrassment: 'Had to read Lady Macbeth in English today but don't know how I dared Act I Scene 7 – very vulgar', ran one 1940s diary entry.[61]

Even in the late 1960s instruction was often held to be inadequate. 'Sexual education, very bad,' said one girl questioned by Mallory Wober. 'We don't get *any* help and learn from experience of very exaggerated form from others. Should be given by housemistresses *I think*, but mothers should do much more . . . otherwise it is very unfair to the girl – she doesn't "get" all the filthy jokes going around.' But another girl thought that juniors 'are adequately taught in the dormitories, the first thing found out about new girls is how much they know'.[62] By the 1980s, sex education had started at primary school, with long-term projects on 'my body', and explanation of menstruation to the older girls. Younger teenagers learn about the changes of puberty, and are shown films about the conception, development and birth of a baby. The older ones are taught about contraception and sexually transmitted diseases, discuss 'personal relationships' and such issues as abortion. (Very often this spills over into RE, along with drug abuse and alcoholism, leaving not very much room for Bible study.)

'The Pill,' said Elizabeth North in a fictional account of her own 1950s schooldays, 'too late for Sister, luckily. It won't be for Sister to find the first recorded flattish pack of pills with Monday, Tuesday, Wednesday printed on the foil, hidden beneath a pile of handkerchiefs in the drawer of – of all things – a Keeper [head prefect]! No wonder that girl was Off Games so regularly, thinks the successor to Sister.'[63] 'Great advances in the technique of birth control,' said the headmistress of Malvern Girls' College in 1984, 'and the consequent weakening of old forms of sanction, far from simplifying, have only made the problem of moral choice more difficult for girls.' She was one of the very few to face the situation unequivocally. Most choose to ignore it, though one school is rumoured to slip in with the uniform list a stipulation that all sixth-formers must be on the Pill. Schoolgirls in uniform, all jewellery and make-up forbidden, can look neat and chaste – one young American who spent a year at an English boarding school was amazed at how the appearance of these desexed objects changed when they were in home clothes – and, always provided they do not break bounds, they consider that what they choose to do with their boyfriends is their own affair. The Catholic Marriage Advisory Council attempts to give more positive guidance (that this is needed, even at convent schools, is shown by the Council member who asked her daughter to find out how many of her contemporaries were sleeping with their boyfriends; at first the girl thought three, but then telephoned to say it was eight). They organize sessions at schools on request: the better sort of school is anxious to inculcate a sense of responsibility; the lesser sort, frightened by a pregnancy, try to ensure that it won't happen again on their premises. The Council takes along a panel of experienced people, including a woman doctor; the girls, divided into groups, discuss the pros and cons of first smoking, then drink, then sex, and are urged to take responsible decisions and not to be hustled into conforming with their peers. They are taught to recognize the sort of party where drugs are passed and when pregnancy can result from drink. The disadvantage is that only sixth forms are involved, by which time it may be too late to form a satisfactory outlook on such matters.

As far as awareness of the world outside goes, the difference in the last decades of the twentieth century is very marked. From kindergarten onwards it is now impossible to escape involvement with disaster, disability and deprivation. Nobody is under the illusion that the world is a safe or pleasant place, or that there is an easy solution to any of its problems. Schools in the between-the-wars period, unless they were exceptional, limited themselves to vague and undirected appeals for public spirit (which often appeared to mean belief in the League of Nations): 'Only by the spirit of service can the social and international troubles of the present time be removed. The world is crying out for a generation of men and women who, forgetful of themselves and their own ambitions and inclinations, are ready to give themselves wholeheartedly to whatever work needs to be done.'[64] Sixty years later it is very much more specific. Benenden, to take only one instance, included among its sixth-form lectures in 1987 such topics as 'Understanding Industry', 'The Shape of Work to Come', 'VSO and Nigeria', 'The Work of the NSPCC', 'AIDS', 'Opportunities in Management', 'Higher Education', 'Genetic Engineering', 'Bereavement and the Work of CRUSE', 'CND Presentation,' 'The Case for a Nuclear Deterrent'. And an eleven-year-old wagged her finger at her prep school headmistress and asked, 'What are you going to do about AIDS? *I'm* all right, I've read the pamphlet.'

13
Crises

Finance

The girls' schools that have survived have all, almost without exception, endured crises that have extinguished the less fortunate – financial difficulties, epidemics, the 1930s Depression, dispersal during wartime; perhaps fires, internal ructions (inadequate heads do no great harm to a well established school, but divided loyalties may), and, latterly, the threat from the boys' schools who have opened their sixth forms to girls. The courage and resourcefulness with which the schools have faced such crises would in fact form a starting point for one of those headmistressly addresses which seem now to have gone out of fashion, as would the fact that good has so often sprung out of evil fortune – for instance, the solidarity (and business acumen) acquired by organizing bazaars to raise money for a new lease; or, on a more prosaic level, the disappearance during a disastrous fire of the antiquated pianos that have long irked teachers and players; or the splendid sixth-form accomodation that has resulted from the need to keep seniors from straying off to join boys' schools.

The boys' schools have been threatened by epidemics and fires, it is true, but, usually with more resources behind them, they have not had to endure so much in the way of penny-pinching or money worries. Few, if any, of their public schools have grown out of private ventures; it has already been seen how many girls' schools did, from Roedean (which achieved the status of a public school very early) to the small schools which took a long time to move out of private hands and become charitable trusts. Much has already been said in the histories of individual schools of the extraordinary optimism and courage with which women with a missionary zeal to communicate learning set out to found their own establishments without any capital, relying on fees only to see them through the first terms. Some schools, the high schools in particular, did not start out with a company of shareholders behind them (though Talbot Heath, once Bournemouth High School, rose out of 'a very nice little school' bought by a young woman of twenty-four, one of the most remarkable headmistresses of her generation, who shaped it into the school it now is). Some were offshoots of charitable foundations already providing for boys (and had to wait until the boys were properly provided with gymnasia and carpentry shops and rifle ranges before money could be disgorged for their most basic needs). But most owe their existence to individuals with courage and vision.

Rich and powerful patrons are very few, and though histories of girls' schools touchingly remember individual benefactions, these are on a relatively small scale. There was the uncouth eccentric who appeared at the clergy school of St Elphin's in its Warrington days and produced wads of banknotes from under his hat; the philanthropist who gave not only money for scholarships and prizes to the Royal School, but the far more imaginative gift of a box of chocolates to each girl. (This was so rapturously received that next year he gave two boxes.) City companies were often benevolent godfathers who might provide treats. The Clothworkers who had founded the Mary Datchelor School in 1877 celebrated the golden jubilee in 1927 by inviting the whole school to Clothworkers' Hall to partake of a feast of strawberries and ice-cream served out of their ceremonial silver bowls – 'Surely there was never such another banquet in Christendom!' The culminating imaginative touch, the school's chronicler thought, was when the bowls were put down among the girls and they were enjoined to finish it all up. The Freemasons were particularly generous in their provision for Christmas and Twelfth Night at the Royal Masonic School (and George VI was one of the habitual contributors).

This school, indeed, has been the focus of more royal interest than any other. Any royal visit to a school is recorded with inordinate, even obsequious, reverence as a highlight in its history; no other guest, however illustrious, gets a tithe of the attention. Even for minor royalty there are weeks of preparation, with obsessive attention to detail that can verge on the ridiculous. When the Duke of Cambridge, a grandson of George III, visited the Royal School in 1897 it was, for everyone, a great occasion. The girls were lined up, facing each other, from the bottom of the red stairs to the steps of the terrace. As the duke reached the top of the steps, the girls burst into the national anthem, curtsying simultaneously three times:

Down on – 'God save our'; up on 'Gracious Queen'
Down on – 'God save our'; up on – 'Noble Queen'
Down on – 'God save'; up on 'The Queen'

Unfortunately one girl was so carried away that she went on curtseying to the end of the verse.[1] (Girls' schools specialize in this sort of attention to detail; of a visit by the Chief Guide to Upper Chine School in 1944 the Guide captain later wrote: 'We had to practise for three weeks, running out from every doorway, neuk and cranny to welcome the Chief Guide in front of the house. The idea was to make the welcome look entirely spontaneous and unrehearsed!'[2])

But distinguished patronage does not necessarily mean enhanced funds, and most schools have scraped together the wherewithal to survive through the self-sacrifice of their founders, who often resolutely refused to accept any personal income except to cover the barest necessities, and who might, as in the case of the founder of St Helen's, Northwood, even give up their own rooms so that they could be used for school purposes. One school, at least, faced by the predicament of premises outgrown, found the answer through prayer. Mother Roantree of what was then Hillside Convent School asked her girls to pray for a special intention that concerned them all (there was added incentive in that the headmaster of a neighbouring prep school had promised them an outing and a delicious tea if their prayer was answered). The girls prayed to such purpose that next day they were told that Reverend Mother had succeeded in buying Farnborough Hill, the former home of the Empress Eugenie (widow of Napoleon III), and that they would be moving into the imperial apartments the next term – and the aforesaid headmaster expressed some alarm at what might happen if the interests of their two schools should ever conflict

On a more modest scale, St Helen's, Northwood, owed its beginnings as a boarding school to prayer. It had been started by May Rowland Brown, then aged twenty-five, in 1899, 'with a hundred borrowed pounds behind her and equipped with her own staunch character, her Christian idealism, her true love of teaching'. There was one small boarder, and 'the effects of a thunder-storm made me realize her need of companionship'. But more boarders were not forthcoming, though Miss Rowland Brown sought them all through the summer term and the holidays.

> The thought came that a second boarder might not be the Divine Will, and I knelt in submission. Immediately I heard the words 'Go and see Mrs Gollmick.' That was all, but I rose and went. I had not mentioned my desire to anyone in Northwood. On the doorstep, I realized how unusual my visit was, so I simply said on seeing the lady, 'Mrs Gollmick, I have come to tell you I want a boarder.' The immediate reply was 'and we want to send you one.' So she came, a clergyman's daughter from Whitney-on-Wye . . . It was remarkable that from that September, other girls came to live with us.[3]

Something has already been said in Chapter 6 of Woodard's methods of fund-raising for his schools. Other religious foundations were also partially funded by small contributions from the faithful. Collections were taken in Baptist, Congregational and Presbyterian churches to try to put the finances of Walthamstow Hall, originally founded for missionaries' children, on a sound footing, though in 1921 the *Christian World* was lamenting the precarious financial state that this and its brother schools of Eltham and Sevenoaks were in. The historian of Channing School, a Unitarian foundation, commented that 'the recurring theme . . . was shortage of capital funds, appeals for support, and indebtedness'. Until well into the 1960s the termly deficit was about £1,000. On just how narrow a margin many schools must have operated in their early days can be seen from a laconic letter sent in 1912 by the school secretary of St Mary's, Calne, to the chairman of the governors:

> My dear Archdeacon,
> I have just got in the last fees that were due for last term . . . and can now let you know how things stand. After paying the extras on the old account we have £7 8s in hand . . .
>
> Sincerely yours,
> A.L. Scott
>
> P.S. The Bank overdraft on the old account is £268 15s 7d.

To which the Archdeacon replied enthusiastically:

> My dear Dunne,
> Isn't this excellent news? And we have seven new boarders coming tomorrow, losing none, so that we ought to be all right, and then in August we shall lose two or three of the older ones who have been on the non-paying or scarcely paying fees and replace them by full-fee pupils . . .[4]

In spite of the Archdeacon's heady optimism, it was not until 1918 (the school had been founded in 1873) that the governors could feel tolerably secure.

The smaller the school today, the greater the problems. This is a recent development arising out of the late twentieth-century demand for schools properly equipped to prepare pupils for a wide range of professional careers. The Woodard School of St Clare, at Penzance – the most westerly borough in England – has never found life easy. Founded as the Penzance Church of England High School in 1889, it went into liquidation in 1927 and was handed over to the Woodard Corporation and renamed the following year. It still struggled, and in 1930 there was a gas explosion in which a maid was killed and several girls injured, due to 'the deplorable condition of the antiquated system of gas lighting'. The Board of Education inspectors, who had visited the school a few weeks before the disaster, were to include in their report a strong recommendation that electric light should be installed, but £717 was required, and 'the financial circumstances of the times' totally precluded the outlay of such a sum. The change from gas to electricity was not achieved until 1935, largely as a result of fund-raising by the girls themselves. Money was always tight – the school could congratulate itself if at the end of the year there was even £85 in the bank, and during the 70s and early 80s it was faced with falling numbers and a rising financial deficit. Those years are marked by desperate attempts to extricate themselves from disaster by selling off assets and by warnings that the school might have to close. In all this it is touching to note that the girls themselves between 1976 and 1981 sent a proportion of their charities money to Lancing

School's rose window fund, for a vast exercise in stained glass that celebrates Woodard, a man who had never wanted girls' schools and had great distrust of women. The school was only rescued by a new headmaster in 1986 and the decision to enlarge the junior school end and increase the numbers of boy boarders, thereby turning it into something very different from the Penzance High School as which it had started in 1889.

The North London Collegiate School had its anxieties in the early days, particularly in trying to secure backing to endow it for the future (vain appeals were made to the City companies and to people of influence, and it was a £50 donation by Princess Louise, Queen Victoria's fourth daughter, that eventually turned the tide), and there were moments when Cheltenham, its pioneering sister, looked unlikely to survive. In the 1850s the Camden area of London was far more ready to accept the revolutionary notion of solid academic education for girls than were Cheltenham parents, who dreaded 'advanced' teaching and anything 'of a more public character' than the ordinary private school.[5] When Miss Beale became Lady Principal in 1858 the college was in dauntingly low water. Her predecessor, Miss Procter, feeling that the school council showed a want of confidence in her, had resigned. Many of the older girls had left with her and those that remained were 'fiercely loyal'. There was no money to buy furniture for the principal's rooms; there was even difficulty in providing books, for the school had relied on Miss Procter's library. The situation was so precarious that it was felt the lease on the school premises must be replaced by a yearly tenancy; and one of the founding members of the council resigned and sold his shares. Three years later the crisis was receding, largely through the gentle but impressive determination of Miss Beale and the dedication of John Houghton Brancker, who had joined the council in 1860. As has already been described in Chapter 4, it was his financial acumen and affectionate loyalty that steered the college through to prosperity. 'He was the Mr Greatheart of those early days,' the school history says in the chapter that it calls 'The Hill Difficult'. No detail was too small for him – he would turn his attention to inadequate stoves, to desks and to the elimination of draughts, as well as searching for a suitable Oxford academic who would come over to examine the girls at the end of the school year.

Even St Leonards has never had any endowment. The school was built up on a small capital distributed among a number of shareholders. Gifts have been made by Seniors and friends of the school, usually collected in small sums for such things as books for the library, the organ and the clock tower, and the actual property was provided by putting every penny beyond the fixed dividend to the shareholders into improvements. Girls' schools have mostly had to rely on their own efforts. Professionals may be employed now, but until very recently fund-raising was a wholly personal endeavour. Walthamstow Hall's Great Fancy Bazaar in 1879 (it realized £2,700, a most remarkable sum then) paid for the new school at Sevenoaks.

> We worked very hard at our fancy-work for the School Stall at which [the headmistress] presided. I was one of the fortunate ones to be chosen to help on the first day. We carried things round the room to sell to visitors and stall-holders. Each of us wore a mob-cap and a pretty apron with fancy Dresden work on it. There were side shows given by various friends, and we girls gave the Toy Symphony. There were some very good tableaux, especially 'Where are you going to, my pretty maid?'[6]

The Francis Holland School, Graham Street, similarly invoked the help of all pupils and parents in 1920, when they had to renew the lease of their premises in Belgravia. Their sister foundation in Baker Street had been blessed with £11,000 in compensation for the diversion of the London Underground under the school buildings, and had been able to move to something far better in Clarence Gate, but Graham Street had no such luck. The Grosvenor Estates, though willing to renew the lease, stipulated that extra houses in the vicinity (including a derelict laundry) must be taken on at a vastly increased cost. £11,800 had to be found, and £6,000 of this was achieved, mostly in small sums, and by the school itself in bazaars, concerts, lectures, collecting miles of pennies, and such individual efforts as knitting, selling eggs, forgoing expensive school prizes, and 'the gift of a dear and most precious guinea pig from the son of an Old Girl, which was auctioned for a large sum, and then restored to its bereft owner'.[7] The remaining £5,000 was added by the school council, and Francis Holland School after forty years could now at last provide itself with a playground, 'heating apparatus that heated, light that lighted' and a sufficiency of windows and ventilation, to say nothing of a gymnasium and rooms for science and art. Bournemouth High School went about raising money to erect its Talbot Heath buildings in much the same way, with the added incentive that anyone who collected 10s or more was entitled to buy and lay a brick.

Individual effort by parents also saved the London Catholic day school, More House. It had been founded in 1953 by the Canonesses of St Augustine, but in 1969 the nuns decided to withdraw, and in spite of pleas to Rome from parents who were both articulate and eloquent it seemed as though the school would inevitably have to close. The children themselves organized a march from Cromwell Road to the archbishop's palace in Westminster ('Martyrdom made our feet light'), and an older girl was overheard telling a little one, 'If he gives you orangeade and a holy picture, don't look pleased; that's not what we're there for.' In the event Cardinal Heenan gave the deputation miraculous medals and the promise of his prayers and support, and these seem in the end to have achieved the desired outcome, for the parents decided to take over the school and formed themselves into a charitable trust. Premises were found at the former Monkey Club finishing school in Pont Street, supporters gave money and interest-free loans to buy it, and the parents themselves got down to the job of sanding the floors, washing the paintwork and serving the lunches. It is unique in London for the close association between parents (who form half the governing body) and school. There are no endowments or trust funds, and it is entirely dependent on the fees.

The histories of schools abound in bold and decisive actions such as More House's acquisition of the Pont Street premises, which must have seemed risky if not foolhardy at the time, but which have proved to be far-sighted and wise. When Nesta Inglis towards the end of World War II set out to find new premises in the Oxfordshire region for Tudor Hall, she was able to acquire Wykham Park near Banbury, then still occupied by the Americans, for a mere £10,000 which she raised in the form of loans from well disposed supporters. A far more extreme example, which must have seemed a chimera even to her supporters, was the Duchess of Leeds' dream, described at greater length in Chapter 7, of restoring the ruins of the archbishops' palace at Mayfield to make school premises for Cornelia Connelly and the Society of the Holy Child. Of course, it is not always possible to be bold, even if one sees the virtue of it. The Ursuline Mother Clare, having opened a school at Brentwood, wrote in her diary five years later in 1905, 'Everybody says BUILD.' But there was no money at all; nor could it be borrowed without security which the Ursulines did not possess, and in the event all she could do was to buy the neighbouring house and connect it with the existing one by a corridor.[8]

History mostly records survivals, and there must have been many schools that failed through financial ineptitude. The father of a pupil at Hayes Court in Middlesex, a leisurely establishment for the wealthy and fastidious, was asked in 1939 by the desperate proprietor if he could lend her £40,000 (a huge sum for that period) to take the school out of the danger area. 'Father told me afterwards that even if he had had it to lend her, he wouldn't, as her financial affairs were in such a mess, and the debts were so huge, that much more than that would have been needed, terribly sad. I loved Hayes Court. But my father said, he understood at last why I had failed School Certificate maths, twice!'[9]

One of the peculiar problems that faced the school that had started under private ownership and had been formed by a single strong personality was how it should carry on. It has already been shown (see page 105) how difficult it was for Downe House to find a successor to Olive Willis and how the headmistress-elect declined to take the post on discovering that Miss Willis planned to go on living near the school. Much the same situation arose at Runton Hill, the Norfolk school founded on Wycombe Abbey principles in 1911 by Janet Vernon Harcourt, daughter of an Oxford don. It was a small school (even now there are under two hundred pupils) and she looked upon it as an extended family. Her brooding presence just outside the school gates after she had retired presented her successor with daunting problems, and finally in 1958 the latter resigned, and most of the teaching staff with her, by which time the number of girls had dropped to seventy-eight with only a single sixth-former. Muriel Kilvert, the new headmistress, not only had to recruit an entirely new staff but found herself confronted with mutinous seniors who suspected she was plotting to deprive them of their former privileges and would jettison the school traditions. It took two taxing years to restore confidence and build up the numbers.

However, while the formerly privately owned school faced problems such as this, it was easier in the early stages for the far-sighted individual like Miss Vernon Harcourt or Miss Willis to take bold steps into the dark which a prudent board of governors would feel bound to discourage. We have already seen instances – particularly among the charity hospitals, Red Maids' being the extreme example – where timidity and caution kept schools in the nineteenth century. The historian of Merchant Taylors', Crosby, commenting on the need for an assembly hall, explains the familiar difficulty of the erosion of an already congested site. 'The school will be housed in an even greater assortment of buildings of all periods. There is no feasible solution to the situation; as early as 1911 a report to the Governors recommended the building of an entirely new school . . . But no action was taken on the proposal. In the late 1980s such a rebuilding would be prohibitively expensive.'[10] There have been opportunities to buy neighbouring property but never the money, nor the courage to throw caution to the winds. But the successful have always done just that.

Schools' early struggles to establish themselves had barely, for most, been surmounted when the Depression overtook them in the 1930s. Many schools record gratefully how the staff at this time willingly accepted, indeed often proposed, salary cuts; but for most there was no alternative, as there certainly would have been no other jobs available. There was crisis again with World War II (dealt with later in the chapter), but the most recent has been over the exodus of sixth-formers into boys' schools.

This is an issue over which all headmistresses feel strongly and refer to repeatedly. It began at Marlborough in 1969 when John Dancy was Master. His motives, as quoted by John Rae,[11] were not economic nor cosmetic but rather a matter of principle; he was anxious, he said, that boys' schools should continue to jettison 'the barbarities and absurdities' associated with the public school ethos, and he believed in sexual desegregation. Other headmasters who followed suit gave the same reasons, though at that stage none of them was willing to carry the desegregation below the sixth form. 'Another possible motive should not be ignored. Headmasters . . . hope to leave their mark. In the wake of Marlborough's example, the introduction of girls became not only possible but fashionable; it was a significant reform for which the headmaster would take the credit in the school's history, and, as reforms go, it was painless.'

The great trouble was that girls were eager to transfer. They usually reach their secondary school at the age of eleven (with boys it would be a year or more later), and after five years at the same establishment are often restless; before ever the boys' schools were open to them, they were going off to colleges of further education or to day schools or crammers to prepare for A levels. Headmistresses, in their emotive appeals to parents to keep their daughters from leaving as fifth-formers, would speak of the advantages of staying 'where the staff knew them'. But it was precisely because girls felt they were too well known, and resented the long memories of those who had taught them, that they wanted to start elsewhere with a clean slate. ('How is Margaret?' one husband, a distinguished physicist, was asked by a schoolmistress who had taught his Paulina wife. 'Better behaved, I hope, than when she was in the Upper Fourth.') Boys' schools were held to have stronger academic traditions, to provide better pastoral care and far more in the way of extra-curricular activities.

The high-flown arguments summoned up by both headmasters and headmistresses to support their case sound specious to the detached observer. Undoubtedly the former are benefiting by the injection of new talents and are finding the girls a civilizing influence; the extra revenue is another considerable bonus, so to imply altruism by talking about the preparation that co-education gives for university life and about the importance of parental choice is unconvincing. The headmistresses feel justifiably betrayed and deeply resentful that the boys' schools, who already have so much and who for so long benefited at the expense of girls, should try to snatch more. What they *say*, however, is that girls do not flourish in mixed sixth forms and need the care of their own sex. Undoubtedly girls need to be tough to endure the first couple of terms among adolescent boys, but it is often forgotten how tough one has to be to endure boarding school of any sort, especially at the beginning; and in a competitive world one needs to learn the technique of dealing with aggressively chauvinistic males at some stage – if not in the sixth form, then at university. One can also in a mixed school learn to have friends who are boys rather than boyfriends. And as far as pastoral care goes, girls have shown themselves surprisingly ready to confide in masters. The headmaster of Oakham School, now wholly co-educational, is warm about the benefits it has brought: 'The hobbledehoy masculinity of a boys' school ... is at once muted in a co-educational school, while the limited spinsterial vision of a girls' school is enlarged and the stressful emotional atmosphere and attitude defused.'[12] In short, once Marlborough had taken the first step, and it was seen how popular this was, it was inevitable that other schools should follow. Whether out of pity, or charity, or remorse for what had happened in the past the boys' schools should have resisted the girls' evident wish to join them, is another matter.

Natural Disasters

When the local medical officer of health heard in 1887 that during the thirty-seven years the Church Missionary School (later to be St Michael's, Limpsfield) had spent in London only six children had died he reportedly said: 'Yours is the healthiest school in or near London.'[13] Just how cataclysmic infectious diseases seemed in a close community, at a time when there were no antibiotics and little knowledge of how infection was spread, can be seen from a teacher's account of an outbreak of diphtheria in the last century at the Woodard school of S. Anne's, Abbots Bromley. One of her colleagues was the first to catch it.

> Rose and I and Dr Earlem were in her room, and he said *that word*. We didn't speak, we were turned to stone. It was the end of everything! There was no panic, we were not of that sort, but it was a great shattering. Think of what it meant! No infirmary at St Anne's, no telegraph nearer than Rugeley, messengers hard to get, a very elementary knowledge of disinfectants, not thousands of skilled nurses as there are now ... We had to act promptly. The girls, staff, servants, save one, were sent away ... I undertook the nursing till a nurse came ... It was a responsibility, for in those days most of those who had diphtheria died.

Infectious or epidemic illnesses were the schoolmaster's most serious risk in grouping numbers of boys together, said the biographer of Thring of Uppingham.[14] In 1875 'low fever' (later referred to as 'enteric fever' and later still as 'typhoid') had broken out. 'Immediate and practically irretrievable ruin stared Uppingham in the face.' And Thring himself supposed a few months later that this was the beginning of the end for the prestigious public school that he himself had built up out of a decayed Elizabethan foundation. The school was built in 'an elevated situation' above the town, and Thring had equipped it with a separate infirmary building, an advanced step for those days, but the town drainage was far from satisfactory, as was the water supply, since the ratepayers 'dreaded the heavy expenses of the sanitary engineer'. In the event the whole school was evacuated to North Wales, and stayed there for a year until the ratepayers stirred themselves to attend to the drains and the locality was declared safe. Some years later Wellington was similarly driven out of its own premises.

As we saw earlier, drains were the first to be suspected when infectious diseases broke out, and this could be a crippling expense to schools who had nothing in hand for unwonted emergencies. The Clergy Orphan Girls' School at Bushey had to pay £320 for an inspection of the drains in 1889 after a case of scarlet fever, and the chairman of the governors at the Royal School compared the effect of outbreaks of measles and scarlet fever to the devastation caused by the Jutes and Vikings. In this case the school had closed down entirely for the Easter term of 1897 while new drains were put in, at the enormous cost of £2,000. It was imperative to take some sort of action, and by making a start with the sewerage system the authorities were shown to be in earnest, so that when diphtheria broke out at New Hall in 1893 during a long hot summer the school decided to renew all the drains, even though they were found to be in perfect order. No one then thought of contaminated milk, though the Misses Lawrence advertised their school for girls, Wimbledon House, in 1885 as possessing 'its own laundry which is a great safeguard against the introduction of infectious diseases'.

Diphtheria was possibly the most dreaded of all. Diphtheria toxoid to counter it was not developed until the late 1930s, and inoculation only became standard in 1941, so that in 1935 64,084 cases were reported in Britain, with 3,408 deaths. When a case appeared, any school that could disperse its pupils did so at once. At the Sacred Heart in Roehampton in 1882 the doctor confirmed two unmistakable cases at midnight, and

> before 4 a.m. Mother Kerr was organizing all arrangements for the immediate break-up of the school. This was no easy matter, as the parents of many children lived at a distance, some even abroad, yet by the following morning there remained only three children whose parents before leaving England had asked Mother Kerr to keep them under her own charge whatever happened.[15]

Two children died in that outbreak. But some schools could not disperse, such as the home school for missionaries' children, St Michael's, Limpsfield. No cause could be found for their epidemic of diphtheria in 1891, since the drains seemed in good order. The children who had relations willing to take them in were sent away, but the rest had to stay and were nursed in the school hospital by the staff; the director and his wife (who nursed the children, becoming white-haired under the strain) gave up their house to the convalescents.

Preoccupation with drains as the source of disease was a feature of the 1880s; the children's writer Juliana Horatia-Ewing even wrote a story about tainted drains – 'Sunflowers and a Rushlight' – in 1883. An adequate sewerage system was not general until late in the century, and far too often domestic water-closets had no traps and were linked to cesspools from which noxious gases poured into the house. Such was found to be the case at the Royal Naval School, then at Twickenham, in 1882, after an outbreak of scarlet fever in which it was a matter of great thankfulness that none of the thirteen cases had resulted in death. After that all the water-closets were provided with proper traps and ventilation, at a cost of £700. (An appeal to meet this crippling sum went out to naval officers, who responded so nobly that there was £300 left over for the next emergency.)

The best-known of any school epidemic is of course the 'low fever' of 1825 at the Clergy Daughters' School, then at Cowan Bridge. Described thus by Charlotte Brontë, it still has not been certainly identified, but might possibly have been a virulent influenza, or lethargic encephalitis. No girls actually died at school, but there were six deaths among the nineteen who went home. The school was moved to a healthier situation at Casterton, but in 1839 and early 1840 suffered a worse crisis, when typhus, a disease associated with the overcrowded conditions encountered in jails and emigrant ships, broke out in the village and spread to the clergy daughters. There were eighty cases all told, and two girls died at the school and others took back the disease to their homes. People all over the country gave generously to the school in its trouble – not only money amounting to £1,300, but gifts in kind. But in this instance the drains were not suspected, and indeed were not put in order until 1892, when a damning report by a sanitary engineer made at the insistence of the retiring headmistress stirred the trustees to take action. Casterton was one of the last schools to have an outbreak of scarlet fever, in 1944, though by then it was not the killing disease it once was.

Death at school was once a commonplace. In the archives at St Mary's Hall, the school for clergy daughters in Brighton, there are frequent references to pupils who died. Of Selina Carpenter, 'a dear girl who stood at the head of the first class, and had passed through the school almost without a fault', who died at home in 1854, the school said: 'Blameless and harmless, the child of God, without rebuke, she departed early to the kingdom for which she was early ripe. May the first class be always like her!' The charity hospitals fared worst, of course, for there the children never went outside, and though this meant that they escaped some infections, any disease that was caused by poor drainage or living conditions spread like fire through these closed communities, as did skin troubles like ringworm and itch. This is hardly surprising when one considers that at the new buildings in Bristol to which the Red Maids moved in 1843 there were only two dormitories, one holding ninety-five and the other seventy-six beds. Fourteen deaths had been recorded at this hospital between 1780 and 1840, there being a particularly severe influenza epidemic in 1828. When the cholera epidemic reached Bristol in 1832 the charity took extensive precautions and lost none of their girls, though there was a terrible death toll among the children at St Peter's Hospital nearby. The headmistress herself died in an epidemic in 1843. At the Merchant Maiden Hospital the record was rather worse; from 1823 to 1828 there were eleven deaths, from 1834 to 1838 seven. The following year, 1839, was particularly bad with one death from typhus, one from water in the head, and three from consumption. Nevertheless, far greater comfort was provided for sick children at this hospital than at most, and certainly more than the Clergy Daughters' School could offer; the food was clean and wholesome, care was taken to warm the buildings, and there was a sickroom with a trained nurse and plenty of medical attention.

There was little that could be done in cases of severe illness. Red Maids' used much chloride of lime to try to avert cholera, and were successful, but all Carus Wilson's efforts to fumigate the school at Casterton with 'oxyd of Manganese' in 1839 as a prophylactic against typhus were of no avail. The Merchant Maiden Hospital spent lavishly on medical care, and a surgeon's bill for 1724/5 lists antifebrile powders, herbs for fomentation, blisters, plasters, vomits, liniments, pectoral decoctions, barley water, cordial mixtures, juice of liquorice, camphorated spirit, balsamic syrup and much else.

But the Scottish children were always remarkably well looked after compared to their English counterparts, and at St Elphin's School in the 1890s medical treatment consisted of nitre for a cold in the head, a tallow plaster for a cold on the chest and Gregory powder for all other ills. The Royal School ran to a couple more nostrums: the housekeeper toured the dormitories each morning with an attendant maid who bore a tray with a bottle of water, a box of compound rhubarb pills, liquorice and Gregory powder, powdered alum for gargle and blackcurrant lozenges. Remedies were simple then: 'I attribute the School's clean bill of health partly to [the caretaker] who keeps us so scrupulously clean,' said the headmistress of Francis Holland School, Clarence Gate, in 1893, 'partly to the large amount of eucalyptus and Sanitas with which the rooms are saturated during all my spare moments.'

By the 1920s and 30s, however, attention to health had become obsessive. Memories of those terrible epidemics of the past led schools to stress in their prospectuses their high situation and bracing air (very often on an exposed cliff top somewhere on the Kent or East Sussex coasts), their immaculate drainage system and the purity of their water. 'The sanitation is registered as perfect,' said more than one school in Truman and Knightley's schools directory for 1930, and nearly all had a trained nurse to oversee the pupils' health. The then headmistress of Manchester High School said that in 1879 she and colleagues of the Headmistresses' Association had devised a specimen health certificate, and schools took up this procedure, which attempted to ensure that children were not bringing infectious diseases into the community, sometimes in the wake of a particularly severe epidemic. The Royal Naval School, for instance, introduced health certificates after the 1883 scarlet fever epidemic. By the beginning of this century they were standard. *Public Schools for Girls* said in 1911 that 'one school, greatly daring, uses no such certificates, but pupils are examined on entrance by the doctor and the gymnastic mistress' (the latter functionary was always being called in to cope with health crises, from fainting to sprained ankles).

But the standard procedure in the early decades of this century was that no private school would accept children back at the beginning of term unless their parents could testify that they had encountered no infection for three weeks. As no one could be certain about what diseases might be lurking in public places, it meant for the scrupulous that there could be no visits to plays or cinemas for half the holidays, and certainly these were out of the question during term. Walthamstow Hall put an embargo on all visits by boarders to day-girls' houses. If one had been in contact with a known case of infection then one was put in quarantine, isolated even from brothers and sisters, until the incubation period was safely over (three weeks in the case of mumps and German measles). Boarders usually had their temperatures taken morning and evening. Some schools did this only for the first three weeks of term, but Mallory Wober discovered that at one school in 1971 the temperature routine was still carried out daily, 'except on Sundays and Ascension Day' when for some reason girls were considered immune. It seemed that the procedure served as a valuable opportunity to scrutinize each pupil at close range.

Constipation was another great preoccupation in the between-the-wars period. *Public Schools for Girls* pronounced that 'daily relief is frequently neglected by girls; in many cases to the life-long detriment of health', but ten years later it had become an obsession, so that a whole chapter of Arthur Marshall's compilation of school memories is devoted to bowel movements and to authority's methods of discovering whether you 'had been'.[16] At one school you reported whether you'd been 'very well', 'quite well' (in which case you'd be told, 'Pull it') or 'fairly well', 'badly' or 'I can't go', in which case syrup of figs or liquid paraffin was produced. At another school it was senna pods and a spanking for failure.

It was held as axiomatic that children must be hardened early. Margaret Fletcher, recalling her own Victorian upbringing, remembered that all medical opinion, and therefore all responsible parents, declared war on softness, laziness, and all forms of self-indulgence. Children must not sit by the fire or loll in easy-chairs. They must have cold baths every morning whatever the weather, they must not eat sweets or cakes, but must finish everything that was put on their plates, however much they disliked it. They must lie on very hard mattresses over which the coverings must not be excessive.[17] These were, though she did not realize it, the same precepts that John Locke had laid down in 1693 in *Some Thoughts Concerning Education*, and had been standard practice in the well conducted home ever since. Certainly they were all part of the boarding school ethos until at least the mid 1950s, when with the gradual introduction of central heating life became more sybaritic. The cold in all schools was remembered with horror, and there are few accounts of pre-1960 schooldays which do not mention agonizing chilblains. Plenty of schools, as has been mentioned elsewhere, insisted on cold baths. At the Royal School (evidently not run on a system of trust) the girls' baths were inspected each morning in the 1880s to make sure that no weakling had skipped hers. Some girls kept brown paper specially to make the water look dirty. Beds were, probably still are, of an amazing hardness – 'I'm sure the *whole* of the bed was made of iron – bedstead, mattress and pillows,' said one pupil of the Woodard school of S. Mary and S. Anne. This may have been economy, but probably reflected the views of many physicians of the period that soft luxurious beds led to impure thoughts, and that children who were tempted to lie abed in the mornings might indulge in impure actions. Many schools, including Benenden, still use the black-painted iron bedsteads traditionally associated with boarding school dormitories, and while authority has given up the battle against cakes and sweets there is still an anxious watch on children's plates, though now this happens through fear of anorexia. One girl sent from a working-class home to a public school as a scholarship pupil in the 1950s, often quoted in this book, has written a long account of how she became anorexic;[18] she felt an outsider both at home and at school, and was revolted by menstruation. At that date the school was not apparently aware of the reason for her weight loss, though they weighed her anxiously and tried to supervise her food. But the condition is now so well known that every housemistress is on the look-out for it.

As already described, infectious diseases were far and away the greatest natural disaster that could hit a school. Throughout, fire seems to have been feared far less, though some of the histories record devastating ones. St Catherine's, Bramley, was struck by lightning during the Easter holidays in 1907 and a greater part of the building was destroyed. But the governing body decided to carry on, putting up temporary buildings in the grounds and lodging the boarders in private houses nearby. At Sherborne in 1910 fire consumed the newly enlarged hall. Edgehill was totally destroyed in 1920, a catastrophe that is now remembered as mildly farcical, as the fire alarm was sounded with such ferocity that the apparatus jammed and wouldn't stop ringing; there was first no water and then so much that the main burst and the firemen were reduced to using the school's portable garden pump. The bystanders particularly remembered the school pianos falling through the burning floors, twangling faintly as they went. A new school was not ready until 1928, and until 1927 the girls used to celebrate bonfire night round the old ruins. There were accidents in borrowed premises in World War II: one school evacuated to Knill on the Hereford/Radnor border managed to burn Knill Court to the ground; and Queen Margaret's (now at Escrick Park), evacuated to Castle Howard, woke up to find fire roaring through the house. Girls and staff managed to salvage some of the pictures, but the whole of the central block was gutted and most of its contents lost.

Felixstowe suffered a crippling disaster in 1973, with a fire started by a local arsonist which destroyed among much else the library and its entire stock of six thousand books, five classrooms – including a new one that had not yet been used – sixth-form studies and common-room, and the school offices. Writing not long afterwards, the headmistress recalled the details of how the school had tried to reorganize itself in the face of so much loss; the 'horrible burning smell' that permeated everything; the relief when it was found that the lower sixth's files of notes for the past year were still readable; the miseries of the ensuing autumn term in makeshift, often unheated quarters, with most of the equipment and books borrowed. But by 1976 the school had provided itself with a set of new buildings which in many ways were an improvement on the old. As the Head Mistress looked at the Red Hall, quite restored to its former appearance and with the Honours Boards intact, remembering the chaotic horror of that night in 1973, she also recalled the verse which she had read to the school when they assembled in chapel for the first time after the fire. It seemed, she thought, to encapsulate the spirit which had always guided the endeavours of the College – *Fide Constantia* – Constant in Faith.

Upon the wreckage of thy yesterday design the structure of to-morrow.
Lay strong corner stones of purpose and prepare
Great blocks of wisdom, cut from past despair.
Shape mighty pillars of resolve to set deep in the tear-wet mortar of regret.
Work on with patience, though thy toil be slow.
Believe in God – in thine own self believe.
All that thou hast desired thou shalt achieve.

Hazards of War

In World War I few schools were directly affected as they were to be in 1939 with evacuation. Queen Margaret's, the Woodard school then at Scarborough, was one of the few that had to leave, after the famous incident in December 1914, vividly described by Winifred Holtby, when Scarborough was shelled. Writing about it to a friend, she began: 'When I got up on Wednesday morning, if somebody had told me it was going to be the most exciting day I ever had, I should have laughed and said "Rats".'[19] The first shell struck as the girls sat at breakfast ('I never tasted the porridge'). But the headmistress calmly told them all to put on coats, tammies and thick boots; they were going for a walk in the country. So the forty-odd girls (most of the school had already been removed by their parents) joined the refugees stumbling out of Scarborough (a sight to be familiar enough in France and Belgium later in the war) – the very old and the very young 'running for [their] lives in the chill twilight'. As always in emergencies such as these, the headmistress and the staff rose magnificently to the occasion, remembering to snatch up some sort of breakfast for the girls, making arrangements – even while running along the road – to dispatch them home (one of the mistresses had provided herself with a train time-table). Winifred finished her letter with 'Don't you wish you'd stayed at school?' The school spent the rest of the war at the Atholl Palace Hotel in Pitlochry. They had to leave Scarborough again in 1939, as parents remembered the bombardment of twenty-five years before and had started withdrawing their girls, and this time they went to Castle Howard. A land-mine fell on the school, which had only been rebuilt in 1932, and it finally moved to Escrick Park in 1949.

In some ways schoolchildren were perhaps more painfully conscious of the horrors of the First War than of the Second. In the latter, many of them were evacuated or spent night after night in the shelters, but there was not the same awareness of the sufferings elsewhere, and certainly not of the exhausting efforts their elders put into trying to ensure normality for them; and throughout there was a calm optimism that Britain was going to win.

Nor, of course, was the loss of life in the armed forces anything like so great. A former Red Maid admitted after World War II that she had been 'much more afraid of the opinion of Miss Humphreys on the pathetic state of my maths than of anything Hitler could do'. This reaction from someone who must have spent a lot of those years in air-raid shelters – for Bristol was badly bombed and Red Maids' stayed in its own premises – is typical, and in some ways reflects the protective attitude of adults towards children then. 'Reading the magazines of the time, one finds surprisingly few references to the conflict raging in the world outside school,' says the Kent College historian, referring to the school (evacuated from Folkestone to Pembury) in those years as 'a cosily isolated community'.[20] And this would have been true of the majority of contemporary schools. The wish to keep children young by shielding them from the world, which seems to have been a reaction to the horror of World War I, was at its height in the 1930s and persisted through the 1940s. There was plenty of war work, of course, but for most it was like a hobby, or inter-house competition. 'As in the First World War, they knitted – this time mufflers for merchant seamen – and at Pembury there was extra gardening – some experienced the "hard labour" of digging potatoes. Others have memories of extra domestic chores with brooms and dusters, and of their regularly taking over the kitchen . . . when the maids had a half-day off.'[21]

The young, perennially self-absorbed, can brush off much, and did so even in the First War when there were not many households without some experience of bereavement. Their own danger mostly elates them: 'I don't believe I have ever enjoyed myself so much', was one Kent College child's reaction to a zeppelin raid. 'Revolution in Russia,' wrote one schoolgirl laconically in her diary for 16 March 1917. 'Had to do my hair with parting down the middle and wear a black tie for drill.'[22] And there were others who resented the moral blackmail of their elders.

> The infuriating aspect of the war was the Holy Lecturing given by dear Chud. If we left our books about, talked after lights, spoke English on a French-day, arrived late for a lesson, it was always the same. 'Discipline! Think of our Tommies in the trenches, up to their knees in mud: *they* do their duty, *they* obey their officers, *they* have a sense of honour' . . . You could hardly raise a hand, make a remark, or glance at a just-convicted sinner, but she clapped on you 'an hour's silence' like a pair of handcuffs.[23]

But in contrast, the middle school at Francis Holland, Clarence Gate – stirred into seriousness and aware, probably for the first time, of the lives of people outside their own sphere – wrote of their aspirations for after the war that they and everybody else thought could never be fought again: 'There are many things we want to abolish – slums, sweating, selfishness, all dangerous work, all sickness which could be prevented, lock-outs, drunkenness, gambling, and the hire and credit system which encourages people to live beyond their incomes.'[24] During this First War there was a poignant episode when the head girls of the Royal School and the Royal Naval School (schools which, despite their similar background and names, have never had much to do with each other) exchanged letters of sympathy after reverses in the war which had brought heavy loss of life. Girls at the Mount were aware of 'big issues bearing down upon us, when we were old enough to realize and appreciate them, but not old enough to grasp them'. Louie Angus, whose own two brothers had been war casualties, realized that very few of the soldiers who visited their home ever came back, that most were killed before they even had leave from the front. All children then would have known the significance of the orange envelope brought by the telegraph boy, and at Haberdashers' Monmouth School the older boarders who had got up at 5 a.m. one day to cheer a detachment of the Monmouthshire Regiment on its way to France found, when it passed, that none of them could raise a voice but just stared blankly at the men who they realized were marching to their death. (At school they had 'put on hospital white and rolled bandages in the library; studied very elementary first-aid, learnt to sing, rather dutifully, the politer sort of war-song and a patriotic cantata', but that was play, and this was reality.)

Food in the latter stages of the First War was very much worse than in the Second: 'These husks do bring the war home to one,' a girl said grimly at Walthamstow Hall, faced with the coarse porridge (for which there was no sugar or milk) that served as breakfast; and many schools such as the Godolphin and St Paul's dug up playing fields and planted them with potatoes or kept pigs. As in World War II, the civilian population occupied itself with efforts that were morale-boosting but of dubious use, like making treasure bags for soldiers and knitting curious garments, but Francis Holland, Clarence Gate, listed occupations some of which went beyond this, together with the numbers who had engaged in them: economizing, 39; needlework, 35; knitting, 29; entertainment, 25; collecting herbs, 11; collecting sphagnum moss, 8; canteen work, 6; swabs and dressings, 5; parcels (of comforts for troops), 5; orderly, War Department, 1; sandbags; 1; keeping one's temper, 3.[25] From which last it will be seen again how useful a war is as a stick for authority to brandish at youth.

Many schools record the celebrations of Armistice Day, though at some, as at Walthamstow Hall, these were muted because of the influenza epidemic, during which two members of this school died. At Christ's Hospital when the news came the girls sang a tearful Te Deum in the chapel. Blackheath High School showed tight-lipped restraint: 'On Armistice Day . . . Miss Gadesden, passing through the library, remarked that although she sympathised with our interest in the great event, we need not neglect our work to talk about it.'[26] At Cardiff High School as the city sirens and hooters sounded pupils came pouring out of their classrooms with shouts of joy;

flags were hoisted, the headmistress read them the official announcement, 'and then we sang Praise God from whom all blessings flow, and God save the King'. The Girl Guides on the platform supporting the flag, the whole school marched past, saluting, and was then dismissed for the day. The Lord Mayor had declared a general holiday for all schools for a week, but this school felt that this was excessive. 'Some of the staff suggested a voluntary sewing class to help the destitute districts of northern France and Belgium, which had suffered in the retreat of the Germans, by making children's clothes. About 100 girls responded.'

But the main celebration came the following summer term, 1919, when the school presented a moving pageant of peace, long remembered, with words taken as far as possible from the poets of the countries involved.

> When Serbia called upon the Allies for help – this part was played by a Serbian child who had suffered in the invasion of her country – we remembered the retreat; when Belgium lifted bleeding hands for aid, we heard once more the dreadful beginnings of War, with the flight of the refugees from their ravaged cities and towns; when France kissed the hilt of her raised sword in immortal dedication of her will to oppose the enemy to the death, we thought of Verdun; when Canada, Australia, New Zealand came marching to England's aid, we remembered the landings at Plymouth, the mud of Salisbury Plain . . . One of the loveliest pictures of the evening was the arrival of Peace, who came through the audience with purple-cloaked and martial Victory, her arms filled with great white hollyhocks that gleamed mysteriously in the fading light against the white and silver of her dress.
>
> . . . But I think the most impressive and solemn moment was reached when the recital took place of Rupert Brooke's beautiful tribute to his comrades: Blow out, ye bugles over the rich dead. The audience rose to its feet as the piercing sweetness of the Chopin Dead March, to which we were so sadly accustomed, rolled softly and solemnly out on the night; and in the hush that preceded and followed the delivery of those heart-stirring lines a bugler sounded the Last Post to an audience which remained standing.[27]

World War II affected schools in a way that the previous war had not, and the girls' public schools far more than the boys'. A few – St Leonards, Sherborne, Moreton Hall, St Mary's, Calne – stayed in their own premises, but these were the exceptions, and the threat of bombing or of invasion dispersed great numbers of home counties establishments, while those that were in safe areas were very often requisitioned. Some disbanded altogether, some never went back – the south coast is now almost denuded of the schools that in the 1920s and 30s formed a large proportion of the population; a few prospered, either because they were already conveniently sited in a safe area and found themselves taking in evacuees, or, having removed themselves to a pleasant country house, as Tudor Hall did, they were besieged by parents desperate to find a safe haven for their children.

But what strikes the observer now is how once again girls' education suffered then at the hands of a male-dominated society. High-ranking government Etonians, Wykehamists, Harrovians and Carthusians – perhaps feeling that it was the boys who would have to do the fighting – saw to it that their old schools were never requisitioned. But Wycombe Abbey, Cheltenham, Malvern, the Royal School, St Swithun's and many smaller schools were given only hours to take themselves and all their pupils somewhere else – the government department or army unit did not in the least care where – and one gets a distinct impression of officialdom getting a savage satisfaction out of an opportunity to crack the whip in a way that had never before been possible.

Wycombe suffered the most, since for four years it ceased to exist, and the nominal rent that was paid for the use of the property did not approach the level of the fees that were lost, or compensate for the making-good that was required after the occupiers moved out. As with nearly all girls' schools, there were no reserves to fall back upon and the financial loss was severe. The headmistress was notified on the last day of the spring term, 1942, that the premises were to be requisitioned and she had sixteen days to get out. Since the Chilterns were regarded as a safe area, the school had made no plans to take itself elsewhere, and indeed was accommodating girls from St Paul's. All other suitable premises had long ago been taken over, and it was felt there was no alternative to closing down the school. Though Miss Crosthwaite broke the news to the staff, the parents and children could not be told until after the school council had met. So on the last day everyone was instructed to go through the usual ceremonies as though the school would be reassembling there again in a few weeks' time. The teachers later had to gather together all the books and schoolwork that pupils had left behind, and a generation to whom Wycombe was their whole life were then faced with looking for new jobs. The girls found places in other schools; they did not care for Malvern or Sherborne and, least of all, for Cheltenham, where they lamented the lack of a school chapel and were oppressed by the silence rules, the patrolling prefects and the house system with a mistress in charge who did not teach. But they enjoyed St Leonards, Benenden (evacuated to Newquay), Queen Anne's, Caversham; and Headington. The twelve or so seniors who went to the last considered themselves particularly blessed because they were accommodated in Oxford in the Master's Lodgings at University College, and they rather guiltily admitted to having thoroughly enjoyed themselves. But Wycombe was determined that after the war was over the school would resume. Miss Crosthwaite stayed near the school; the council continued to meet and the school gazette was published regularly. By May 1946 the buildings had been released (but only with much reluctance and after a question had been asked in the Commons) and the school could re-open. Sixteeen former members of staff and six of the original pupils came back; all the rest were new, though many of them were daughters, granddaughters or sisters of former members.

Cheltenham's troubles were over sooner, though they were both irksome and costly. On Christmas Day 1938 the principal, Margaret Popham, received official and secret news that, should war break out, the entire college buildings would be requisitioned. She was allowed to inform the retiring chairman and his successor but no one else, and since they were bound by the Official Secrets Act they could make no preparations in advance. The most that could be done without arousing suspicion was to secure Lilleshall Hall in Shropshire, which eventually housed 120 girls.

When war did break out the staff, then on holiday, were recalled by telegram, and came back to find that all the buildings, including the houses, had been commandeered and – with the exception of the principal's house, the college secretary's office and the swimming baths – were to be vacated within a few days. Miss Popham was determined that the college must stay in Cheltenham, so houses had to be found for over five hundred boarders and teaching premises for the whole college, and equipment and furniture moved and reassembled. But term started on the appointed day. The parish church of Christ Church was lent for prayers and religious teaching. The swimming baths were floored over and became the lower hall, where several classes were taught simultaneously as in the early days, and the dressing cubicles were used as private studies and for coaching. Other classes were taught in sixteen army huts; a games pavilion was converted into a laboratory, friends lent rooms for classes, for music and for a library, and the librarian wheeled along essential books in relays in a pram. Some of the girls had gone to Shropshire, but accommodation was found in Cheltenham for everybody else. Despite all the urgency that had been stressed, only the individual houses were being used, and the main college buildings remained empty. There were diplomatic approaches, and after a personal visit from the Minister of Works first the college and then the houses were handed back, and the school could reassemble in its own premises at the beginning of 1940. The school chronicler's response to this useless disruption, evidently produced by civil service ineptitude, was typical of the calm optimism with which girls' schools have faced vicissitudes and setbacks: 'It was a revealing experience, showing how little the spirit of a community is tied to its surroundings . . . Detached from their house loyalties and flung at a moment's notice into new places and situations, they responded with almost unbelievable steadiness and gaiety.'[28]

Children of the 1920s and 30s were brought up to understand that this was a war to end all wars, and, as we noted earlier, were in general so sheltered – except at schools like Badminton which made a point of keeping pupils abreast of world events – that few of them even saw newspapers. But the events of 1938 could be hidden from no one, and to many Neville

Chamberlain's journey to Munich was the first intimation that there could be a repetition of 1914. A sixth-former at Nottingham High School remembered that in 1938 the headmistress had referred to the First War, saying she was sorry that the girls' lives were likely to be blighted in the same way as her generation's had been. 'No one in my hearing had ever admitted before that another world war was almost certain.'[29] But as another at the same school said at a later stage: 'Whilst the fate of the free world remained uncertain, the end of term examination results, the score made by the hockey First XI and the results of the Drama competition were all felt to be of paramount importance.'

This time it was clear that the civilian population would be far more closely involved and that widespread bombing was likely; schools in danger zones therefore started prospecting for suitable country accommodation. Channing School even had a trial evacuation in 1938, to hotels in Ross-on-Wye, which must have been costly in every way. It is not clear whether they felt they had gained experience from this, but when the school did take itself to Ross again the next year it was to different hotels. To school proprietors and governing bodies it must have been a time of terrifying anxiety. If you stayed, would parents support you or would the school dwindle to vanishing point? Some who stayed were in fact to pick up custom from those who vanished, but no one could bank on this. If you delayed, all suitable properties would be snapped up by others. If you went, would there be anything to come back to, and what could be done with the premises when you were gone? For many schools there were in any case no financial reserves to cover the cost of removing a whole establishment; all the assets were in the buildings left behind; the fees could not be put up, and now there was rent to be paid and the extra burden of day-children who of necessity were boarders but whose parents could not afford to pay accordingly.

Nearly all London schools went, but there were some in the suburbs and in places like Bristol which could not escape the bombing. The children were resilient and usually treated it all as an adventure, a welcome break in routine, and had a cheerful confidence that lessons and meals would arrive at the usual times; it was the staff, struggling to see that this was indeed so, who suffered most:

> those broken nights, and constantly interrupted days, when one continued one's lessons in the shelter (with five or six other people giving lessons around one), or was interrupted at one's meal in the dining room and had to get the food conveyed down to the shelters and then the dirty plates collected again . . . Extra complications such as illness or an epidemic of whooping cough all had to be dealt with. During exams records were sent to the Oxford and Cambridge Joint Board of 'time lost during air raids'.[30]

If a school was evacuated the first problem was of sharing wholly unsuitable premises with possibly hostile owners. No householders could be expected to welcome invasion by strangers.

> It would be idle to suggest [said the biographer of one headmistress who moved her school from Hampstead to a Sussex mansion] that the arrangement was an entirely happy one. On the one hand, the chatelaine, accustomed to living in something like solitary splendour, found it difficult to adjust herself to the presence of scores – it must have felt like hundreds – of healthy, noisy children about the place. On the other hand, a stately home is scarcely the ideal structure for school-life.[31]

Malvern, which had been told that in the event of war they would have forty-eight hours to leave, distributed pupils in various premises in Somerset; they found one of their landlords uncooperative and resentful, until he was disarmed by the school calling its houses after his ancestors.

Property owners only endured school invasion because of economic circumstances, or to avoid getting something worse. This was what happened to Greenacre, which moved from its site in Banstead which was too near London for comfort, to a house in Dorset where the owner had snatched at the chance of a private school because he was threatened with mothers and children from Southampton. But when he discovered that these were refusing to be moved, he became increasingly fretted by the presence of the schoolgirls he had unnecessarily taken. By December he had issued a year's notice to quit, and in appalling weather conditions the headmistresses, one crippled with sciatica, had to tour the West Country looking for alternative accommodation.

Even if the householders accepted the situation with a good grace, their servants might not. At Longleat the housekeeper fought a last-ditch battle to preserve 'his Lordship's beautiful house' from the invaders, in this case the Royal School. 'Her distress when she saw the battered school furniture that was to stand cheek by jowl with Longleat's treasures was pitiable.' The girls, too, were struck by the incongruity of black iron bedsteads and green slop pails standing on polished oak boards with painted cherubs looking down on them, in a setting of long-fringed curtains and hand-painted Chinese wallpapers. In the event it was to work out very well. Lord Bath gave them the free run of his entire house, keeping only four small rooms himself, and wrote to the headmistress a few months after the girls' arrival, 'It is twenty-five years since I had children running about the house . . . I love hearing children all over the place – in fact I keep my door open on purpose.' They took him slices of birthday cake, sent him valentines and birthday cards, asked him to their concerts, and he in his turn would read a lesson at the carol service, attend their matches, and on one memorable occasion offered 10s to any cricketer who could hit a ball over a nearby clump of trees. One member of the staff was lyrical about the Longleat ambience:

> The children were everywhere. They ate their meals in the gold-brown, book-lined library. They slept under intricately wrought Italian ceilings, in immense rooms draped with Flemish tapestries or papered with Spanish leather or Genoa velvet; or in corridors hung with pictures in heavy gilded frames.
>
> They laughed and chattered and read their books in the banqueting hall. They stared at Tudor portraits and folios of Shakespeare, at the dolls' house, the Sèvres china and the gilded marriage chests. They collected chestnuts and fir cones; wild flowers, feathers, and the pellets of owls. They painted pictures in the orangery and spread them to dry on the floor, or they sat outside on the steps, chipping lumps of alabaster.[32]

But it is only fair to say that the girls appear to have remembered the beauty of the place less than its isolation, the cold, the inconvenience, the war work which included gathering nettles with numbed, gloveless fingers, and – despite the size of Longleat – the cramped conditions in which they worked, lived and played.

For some schools evacuation worked remarkably successfully, and town children had their first experience of country life. Half Nottingham High School was removed to a country house, Ramsdale, and pupils who had expected to be day-girls all their lives found themselves boarders with staff who, like them, were unused to the life. Everybody had to turn their hand to chores: many found themselves doing things like milking, planting vegetables, sawing wood. In the bitterly cold winter of 1939–40 they skated on the pond and hauled supplies along the mile-long drive on their sledges – oil, too, one day when the tanker stuck in a snow drift and the house oil tanks were nearly empty. In the spring there were wild daffodils, and there were always wonderful views. 'I loved the autumn mists, the country round about, the woods, and, oddly, the companionable washing-up . . . I liked, too, the break-down of age-groups . . . It was the lack of privacy that finally defeated me.' King Edward VI High School, evacuated from Birmingham to Cheltenham, remembered the unwonted freedom. 'We were fully aware that no one was wholly responsible for us. In Birmingham there were our parents; the school was responsible for education, our Cheltenham hosts gave us homes – but to a large extent we were free, to spend our time as we liked. We bought chewing gum and fourpenny schoolgirl novels.'[33]

There were advantages, not least the far more relaxed atmosphere inevitable when staff and children were living at close quarters; one member of the Sacred Heart felt that the formality and distance between children and nuns, once so impossible to cross, disappeared for ever when the segregation traditional in pre-war convent schools was no longer possible. But clearly there were constant difficulties, which put enormous strain on the headmistresses. The problem of finding suitably qualified teachers when a school was deep in the country was considerable, of course, though at a time when few girls' schools took science or maths seriously this was not as great as it might have been, and it was probably extras like music that suffered most. Finance, plans for the future, domestic staff must have been equally exhausting worries. The large numbers of troops very often stationed near schools presented fewer difficulties than might be supposed. 'Sometimes the proximity of the troops caused problems. One of the village children took a short cut through the Hall grounds and was found murdered,' said one school chronicle tersely in Harry Grahame style.[34] After that the girls were only allowed out in fives, two to stay with the casualty and two to run for help. But there were surprisingly few incidents of this sort, and, it seems, little trouble with girls so much less sexually aware and more biddable than they are today. When Miss Popham discovered that American GIs were stopping college girls in Cheltenham and talking to them, she asked to be allowed to address the men. She told them she understood the American fondness for children but that the girls in green uniform were her pupils for whom she was responsible, and she could not possibly allow them to talk to strangers, however charming. 'From that moment onwards we had no more trouble.'[35]

Problems of morale mostly affected only the erstwhile day schools evacuated to premises far from home. One senior from a London school noticed the homesickness of the younger children, 'the undercurrents of unhappiness and possibly unconscious resentment which sometimes seemed to undermine co-operation', and thought that traditions of behaviour and order depended on buildings and a routine to which everyone was accustomed.[36] This particular school was occupying two hotels in Ross-on-Wye. Roedean took most of its pupils to Keswick in 1940 (a party of fifty had already left for Canada), where they took over a hotel. Into its one hundred bedrooms were crammed twice that number of girls, plus the offices, the staff commonroom, the reference library, two classrooms and a laboratory. The rest of the classrooms were scattered round Keswick; there were even some at the railway station, where 'there were frequent interruptions from anxious passengers'. The formality of the house system, perhaps more rigid at Roedean than at any school, broke down in these conditions – 'there was a much more united feeling among all the girls', one of them commented – but was resumed when they returned to Brighton in 1945.

Benenden left Kent in 1940 when France fell and the buildings were shaking with the thunder of guns over the Channel, and it was realized that the school was only forty miles from the German advance. The girls were sent home on 24 May, and two of the principals went west to try to find an alternative home. A week later a notice appeared in *The Times* saying that the school would reassemble at the Hotel Bristol, Newquay, the following week, and there Benenden stayed, for five and a half years in a modern hotel with no grounds, on the edge of the cliffs. The Sacred Heart school at

Roehampton had also experimented with Newquay, but the sheer danger that cliffs and rocks and sea presented to their pupils had driven them away ('One only had to ask to go to the "cloakroom" in a boring old class and one was off down to the beach where, dodging the tides in caves and blow holes at great risk to life and limb, one was unfindable until driven in by hunger. Very difficult for nuns still hampered by wimples, long black skirts and rosaries clanking at their sides.'[37]) This school found a haven in 'a nice safe park in the Midlands' where the only stretch of water was a reedy mere.

But Benenden established a happy community life in Cornwall. One fifteen-year-old wrote ecstatically that life was 'one long roar of laughter at the moment, because everything we do is so unusual and frightfully funny ... I can't help saying "Gosh, this *is* lovely" (I have said it all day but honestly ...!) Actually we deserved something jolly nice after leaving such a glorious place as Benenden.'[38] The buildings were taken over by a military hospital, and one of the three principals stayed behind, together with the much loved Busby, the school butler, to try to supervise what was left. In one of his splendid letters to Newquay to keep them in touch with Kent, Busby wrote: 'Miss Bostock has written for her bicycle. I have tried hard to retrieve it for her, but up to now have not been successful. Seeing a bicycle with two flat tyres, no brakes and half the bell missing, quite naturally I thought it was a School bicycle.' And he gave a laconic account of one of the dottier inspirations for winning the war, the brain-child of the school's chauffeur.

> Pa Smith has just been in asking me to draw him an aeroplane with a steel gate hanging from its tail, so that he can send it to Lord Beaverbrook. The idea is to stop this night bombing. Our planes will fly over the German planes in the dark, of course they won't be able to see the gate. When they have crashed into it, the pilot pulls a lever and down goes the German with a steel gate on his propellor.
>
> My best wishes for a very good term, and I hope you will all be home again soon.[39]

The convent schools suffered particularly through enemy action, but for many of them it must have seemed something of a repetition of what their orders had suffered generations before, fleeing from harassment in France or the Low Countries, whether during the Revolutionary Wars or the later anticlerical legislation at the turn of the century which led to the expulsion of the religious orders. There is a poignant account by one of their number of how the Canonesses of the Holy Sepulchre left their convent in Liège in 1794 to journey by coal barge to Rotterdam and then to London.[40] They left at 3 o'clock on Ascension morning, their habits covered so that they would not be conspicuous, 'in deep silence, all crying most bitterly and many not having seen the outside of the Inclosure door for many years'.

There was an uneasy moment when they reached Gravesend and two customs officials came aboard. Strict instructions had been given that no one should show herself to be a nun – these were still penal days. But one of the stoutest of the company, allowed on deck for the first time for a fortnight, prostrated herself in front of the priest who had accompanied them and implored his blessing. 'Indignant at this address in the presence of such guests, he hurled her down again.' However, their troubles were nearly at an end, for once landed, old Catholic families came to their rescue and sheltered them until they acquired a permanent home at New Hall.

Something has been said in Chapter 7 of what the teaching orders had to endure when they first came to England, in the way not only of poverty but of hostility. The nuns of Jesus and Mary who came to Ipswich in 1860 to care for the children of the Irish soldiers garrisoned there found themselves, two years later, facing anti-Catholic riots whipped up by 'the lectures of a worthless renegade to the Catholic Church named Baron de Gamie'.

> One of the boarders speaking of that eventful evening describes a great fright the children had before their evening recreation. All day they had been talking of Baron de Gamie and had in their so-called brave moments threatened him with no end of suffering if they could only lay hands on him. One Irish girl among the rest, named Miss Levi, stood out as the bravest champion of all, casting all the rest in the shade as to what she would do, if she could only have her revenge on him. On going to make their little visit in the church before recreation, they had all knelt down to begin their devotions with only the lantern lamp to give them light, when on a sudden a knocking was heard at the church door. Of course they all thought it was the Baron and his followers come at last and with one bound they tumbled pell-mell over each other, foremost in the scrummage being the brave Miss Levi, only too anxious to be the first to save herself. They found out when it was all over that the cause of the noise was nothing more than Sister St Didier nailing medals on the church door.

However, the mob, having stormed the presbytery and wrecked that, broken all known Catholic windows, and hurled stones at the magistrates' houses, then advanced on the convent. The police were powerless to stop them, and though ironically there was an Irish Catholic regiment in the barracks, the authorities dared not call it out because of the fearful bloodshed that would have ensued. All the convent windows except those of the children's dormitory were smashed, but the mob failed to break down the gates. As they were expected to return the following night, the nuns, wearing disguise (clothes borrowed from the boarders), were told to take the children to safety while several hundred special constables were sworn in to keep the peace. Their presence had a sobering effect; there was less trouble that night and the ringleaders were caught and imprisoned. The Mother General of the order came over from France to comfort the community and told them that 'no doubt the Devil was enraged at the work of the religious and was the instigator of the riots, therefore not to grieve over the smashed windows, as God would send as many children for them to instruct as there had been panes of glass broken'.

Convents had to face more than broken glass in World War II. Incendiary bombs destroyed much of the Sacred Heart at Roehampton, and burnt down the new Trinity wing of the Ursuline High School at Brentwood. The greatest loss was at the Bar Convent in York, where a delayed-action bomb killed five sisters who had gone to the help of an invalid nun. It demolished the east wing and badly damaged the rest of the oldest convent in England. But schools in general suffered more in disruption than in actual damage by enemy action, though of course there were grave losses. A land-mine destroyed Kensington High School, and though new premises were found these were inadequate for the numbers, and the senior school, refused permission to rebuild on the old site, was forced to close in 1948. Of the GPDST schools, Bath High School received a direct hit, and Blackheath was damaged by a rocket, as were Croydon and Portsmouth High Schools; Sydenham High School, which had returned in 1940 from evacuation to Brighton, endured flying bombs and rockets but escaped extensive damage; most of the main school at Streatham Hill and Clapham was destroyed by a flying bomb; Wimbledon High School, which had stayed in London, was so badly damaged by a flying bomb in the holidays that at first it was thought the school would have to be moved to Scotland. But heroic work by staff, girls and parents meant that term could start only three weeks later, although there were no windows or doors.

Both Francis Holland schools were temporary casualties: forty-seven girls had gone to Roedean at the outbreak of war, but when Roedean itself had to leave Brighton Francis Holland ceased to exist. In 1944 the school council decided to reopen both schools. They appointed a headmistress for Graham Street (now Graham Terrace), but there was no building, no staff, and no pupils. The headmistress and the appeal committee raised £3,500; fourteen pupils aged from eight to twelve were collected, and met in the drawing-room of the lieutenant-governor of the Royal Hospital, while the headmistress struggled to get possession of the badly damaged school, where there was no water, no windows, no telephone, no electricity. The council wished her to live in the building, and she did, carrying buckets of water from the church across the road, getting up in the night to tip water off the tarpaulins that covered a gaping hole in the roof, scrubbing and cleaning, sorting out the furniture abandoned at the outbreak of war. But the school opened its doors on 16 January 1946 with five staff and seventy-one pupils, and workmen still repairing the hall and the top floor. The school history comments: 'Since during the war people had learned to do without, the pitiful inadequacies did not seem to matter so much then as they would now.'[42]

Schools that had been requisitioned usually suffered badly. Even if the occupiers had behaved in a responsible manner – and in many cases, the damage done by the requisitioners was more extensive than the bomb damage – there were losses that had to be made good out of very low funds. Wycombe Abbey, returning after four years, found the school in reasonable structural order, but all needing refurbishment at a time when even to replace the crockery was a financial embarrassment. Roedean had been very fortunate. It had been occupied by both the army and the navy, and senior officers had issued stringent and detailed instructions about the care that must be taken. Nothing was to be stuck on the walls, no sliding on the floors, no short cuts to be taken over grass banks: 'We are now living in an extremely fine building and it is the duty of every man to see that no damage occurs.' But this sort of consideration must have been unique, and most schools came back to painfully dilapidated premises, to soldiers' cartoons 'of an indelicate nature', several years' accumulation of rubbish and filth (even when, as in the case of the Royal School, the buildings had been occupied by women), inches deep encrustations of mud and grease, holes in the walls and the floors, dry rot, derelict gardens. The saddest case of all was Upper Chine, which had been occupied by Divisional Headquarters.

> I opened the front door to find bindweed halfway across the bare hall. It had forced a passage into the drawing-room and was flourishing gaily. The walls were a mass of holes where small fittings had been wrenched out, bringing the plaster with them. The ceilings all over the building had suffered similarly where electric fittings had been torn down . . . In the study the wreckage of the gas fire was scattered on the hearth – deliberately smashed to pieces, and to my horror, there was what remained of Wordsworth table reduced at its untimely end to an ill-used workshop bench. Standing by the window was the skeleton of an upholstered chair – stark and naked; one wonders why it had not been burned; that seemed to be the fate of all loose woodwork, cupboard doors, shelves etc. And so on throughout the building – dirt and destruction everywhere.[43]

'Which side is the War Office on?' a pedestrian in Whitehall is supposed to have asked in World War II. To which the red-tabbed staff officer he had just accosted replied with much feeling, 'By God, I often wonder myself.'

14

Envoi

To us the word 'education' embraces a wider horizon than is usually accorded to the term. To us education is not merely to impart knowledge; it is to train you, to fit you to meet every emergency which life may call upon you to face. The spirit of loyalty and obedience, of which we are so proud, is the result of a discipline that has slowly been absorbed by each member, and has built in you a foundation which will stand firm against the tests of the larger social and public life which you are about to meet ...

The games to which you give so much of yourselves are more than a struggle for supremacy and a test of skill. You have learnt to put the team before the individual; you have learnt that to play well, and be a good loser is a sweeter thing than victory without good sportsmanship.

In your life with each other you have learnt the joys of comradeship, the sweetness of sharing. In your work you have found the quest for truth and beauty, and have known the joys of competing with keen intellects; and in these, our Chapel Services, we have woven the love of fine music and the inner sense of spiritual security so deep into the fabric of our everyday life, that nothing will ever entirely efface it.

These are the weapons with which we gird you to meet the world. Go forth, and may good fortune attend you.[1]

This speech delivered by a headmistress to her school-leavers must have been typical of hundreds such. Only in the last twenty years or less has the fashion changed. Though it comes in a piece of fiction, it may well have been actually delivered, since the novel is a thinly disguised account of Harrogate College and an act of homage to Margaret James, headmistress 1898–1935. It is dedicated to '"the best school of all" and particularly to MEJ, who for many years held aloft the torch at which so many kindled the little flames that were a light to them through life'.

What strikes the outsider is the way that authority on such occasions used the system that expedience forced upon them as though it was one they had themselves specially devised to bring out the virtues that they most yearned for in their pupils. If one is going to herd two or three hundred adolescents together in constricted space and keep them out of mischief one must impose a stringent discipline, maintain a constant watch, and try to exhaust them on the playing fields. 'Comradeship' is inescapable in these circumstances, and many have found it excruciating rather than joyful; at best, they say grimly, it teaches endurance. Of the disadvantages of such a system – at any rate as it was in Miss James's time when the pupils were closely guarded from the outside world and the opposite sex, guarded too from the possibility of taking any initiative, and allowed no privacy or time to themselves – nothing, naturally, is said. Many loathed the regime which Miss James held to be so beneficial and felt they had gained little from 'the spirit of loyalty and obedience of which we are so proud'. 'Didn't we work twelve hours a day?' demanded a fictional 1940s Badminton fourth-former, comparing her lot to Industrial Revolution workers whose harrowing lives were being studied in history lessons. 'Weren't we lashed by tongues, exhausted by cold baths and compulsory games and to top it all not a drop of gin in sight.'[2]

And few would agree that boarding school was much of a preparation for life. Even day school pupils often feel that nothing afterwards can be quite so bad, though part of the trouble is, of course, just the pain of being an adolescent.

> Why then, in retrospect, does school seem so unrelated to life? The answer is that at no other time, except perhaps in prison or the army, is one so hopelessly subject to the whims of authority. Rules assume the proportions of moral laws; teachers an Olympian omnipotence. To the child, the school seems made for the rules, education is not the awakening it should be, but an obstacle race on the way to examinations . . . Obliged to remember it now, I realize that rarely in life since have I had such moments of acute happiness or undiluted wretchedness . . . I was always tired, my hands were always dry with chalk. I was too tall, too thin, too spotty.[3]

Many others, as has been seen in other chapters, complained of the tyranny of the mob with whom they were imprisoned for thirty-six weeks of every year. A Victorian old Cheltonian wondered whether anything had changed since her day or if a new generation of girls was 'being gradually moulded into the tragic pattern of the British schoolboy, the ideal of headmistresses, the member of the herd, with the herd mentality, the herd consciousness, ashamed of everything but herd instincts'.[4] They lamented how little they knew of anything outside the school walls – even at establishments like Badminton, which prided itself on looking beyond them.

> I know the arguments about girls achieving more in single sex schools [wrote a pupil who was there in the 1950s], but I've retained an intense dislike of that unnatural system. My daughter has come through co-

> education wanting to read engineering. She certainly would not have found herself aged 16 unable to raise her eyes above a sea of knees as happened to me when I first got to Salem on a term's exchange to the predominantly male German school.[5]

The priorities in Miss James's speech are interesting. For her it is the gridiron that matters, not the book; the vision of Penelope Lawrence rather than of Mary Ward. First comes loyalty, obedience and discipline, then the games field, and finally 'the quest for truth and beauty' and the chapel services. Many schools might have given a higher place to religion, but nearly all then would have agreed that academic matters were of secondary importance. The pupils, too, from the start used to be made aware of the true purpose of the regime to which they were being submitted. 'Oh, awful and awe-inspiring day,' wrote a schoolgirl in 1916, one guesses after a beginning-of-term exhortation from her headmistress: 'Meredith and I come to a bording [sic] school for the first time. Our future lives and characters will be moulded here!!!!'[6]

The structure of boarding school life has not changed so very much, though there are fewer attempts now to present what is merely expedient as a supposedly lifelong inspiration to those fortunate enough to participate. Nevertheless the emphasis on character-forming remains. Analysing 1970s prospectuses, Mallory Wober found that aspects of social responsibility were the aims most stressed. Schools wanted their pupils to be useful, considerate and dependable. Many of them also spoke about realizing the full potential of the individual and developing self-confidence and powers of leadership. Third on the list came a thorough and broad education avoiding extreme specialization, and fourth were courtesy, self-control and discipline. In all this such establishments feel that they differ markedly from the academic day schools which, in their opinion, only concern themselves with passing exams. (But the cynical might also observe that in prospectuses the most eloquent pronouncements about character-building usually come from schools who feel that they have less to say about academic achievement.) A typical 1980s statement from a minor home counties school runs thus:

> The aim is to enable each girl, in a happy and controlled environment, to achieve her full academic potential. She will be taught and encouraged to work hard, to discipline herself, to make the most of her opportunities, while recognizing and responding to the needs of others. High standards of behaviour are expected.

Here one senses that the governors are trying to reassure parents fearful of the state secondary system, which, they suspect, provides an uncontrolled, undisciplined, mannerless environment where pupils are not encouraged to work and where the weaker flounder and sink. Schools do not expect such pronouncements to be minutely analysed, and the more prestigious ones on the whole do not make them, no doubt feeling that their reputation should be sufficient – nobody asks Eton or Winchester to state their aims. They must also be perfectly aware that the eyes of parents slide over prospectus clichés, and that schools, especially boarding schools, are chosen for very different reasons.

Academic success, as has been said, is of much more importance than it was thirty years ago. Certain of the larger boarding schools are chosen with that in mind, though there is far greater competition for places at day schools like St Paul's, with parents struggling to get their four-year-olds accepted by the prep schools with the best entrance exam record. (There is similar pressure at prestigious nursery schools, which expect parents to register before their child is born.) In schools such as these, as their history has shown, parents have always been less influenced by social criteria when making their choice, though the size of the fees now precludes the sort of class mix that their founders had hoped for. But social considerations still play a large part when parents come to choose a boarding school for a daughter who is not an academic high-flyer. Sometimes Mummy has been there, sometimes the daughter of a friend that Mummy trusts or of one of Daddy's partners or fellow directors. Usually the accessibility matters, since there are now frequent exeats and weekends when the child requires visits, so that English girls now rarely get sent to one of the oldest and most prestigious public schools, St Leonards, far north on the Fifeshire coast. Ideally, the school should be near enough to those chosen for the boys in the family to make joint visits feasible, should have the right social mix *and* a record of academic achievement; but if the latter is shaky there is always the possibility of a sixth form elsewhere. The philosophy of the school, so carefully formulated and laid out in prospectuses, is mostly irrelevant to those who are making the choice, who, if they gave the matter any thought, would assume that such aims were common to all. From the school magazine they would get some insight into the clientele. Faced with names like Camilla, Victoria, Henrietta and Arabella the upper classes can be confident that their daughters will mingle with their own kind; if they see there are Samanthas, Kims or Karens on the school roll they know the reverse.

As to the 'tone' of the school, the magazine gives nothing away. All who write for it invariably project the same image of happy, united communities working together for the common good. Even though we may know that a particular school has been in the national newspapers over the contraceptive advice that it wishes its medical officers to give to the senior girls, that there is a serious drink problem, and that one of its more unmanageable houses has eaten four housemistresses in five years, we will find in the school magazine the same composite picture of healthy, clean-minded girlhood that pertained sixty years before. The fifth-form chroniclers of house activities subscribe to the convention, saying that their house has gone from strength to strength, is happy and friendly. They list proud successes in games and drama, Halloween celebrations, Christmas parties, scrumptious food; they catalogue ecstatically received gifts ranging from advent calendars to electric toasters, and convey thanks to matrons and housemistresses who are invariably kind and cheery and with whom they are always on the best of terms. 'Bar convents and MI5,' said Siriol Hugh-Jones, 'English girls' schools are the most closely guarded national mystery in existence, a conspiracy entered into with verve by English womanhood in the shape of staff, mothers, and non-communicative, enigmatic, schoolgirls.'[7]

A little more can be deduced from the pages devoted to old girls, though even here they tend to present the sort of news that they feel is expected of them. There is scant reference to divorce; nobody mentions the current boyfriend until she is actually married to him – if she is sharing a flat then it is with a school friend. But the activities and choice of careers are often revealing. At the best-known débutante school, for instance, they specialize in entrepreneurial skills. If anyone wants a portrait painted by a husband who was a pupil of Annigoni, wants a book published, their drawing-room rag-rolled or stippled, then ring Arabella, Tiggy or Camilla. Prue is still running her children's clothes business 'Nannie knows best'; Emma has begun 'Petals', her own flower-arranging business; Louise has launched another new company which designs modern mediaeval tapestries. Annabel and her husband drive a palomino pony tandem, resulting in many spectacular crashes. At Roedean they are more soberly professional: they teach, practise medicine or law, are heavily involved with voluntary activities and local affairs. At Benenden many write from farms, and there is news of husbands and children, bell-ringing, stewarding in cathedrals, voluntary work and fund-raising. At the Mary Erskine School in Edinburgh they are very businesslike: all chatter is eliminated, and news consists of a statement of one's husband's job and one's own, and lists of offspring with their ages. West Heath and North Foreland Lodge enlarge on their children's talents, their dogs and ponies, the derelict houses they are reclaiming. St Leonards Seniors confine themselves more to news of their careers. And a snippet from a 1934 Surrey school magazine evokes between-the-wars suburbia: 'Rosemary S. could not be with us on the 24th as she was going to a dance given by the Storrington Foot Beagles. She had a lovely tour of the West Coast of Ireland in the summer. Her time is taken up by Beagling twice a week, Badminton, Golf, and attending social affairs in the village.'

'Our girls make friends for life,' say the headmistresses, and from old girls' news items in the magazines it is clear how many are sharing flats, back-packing together in far-flung places, godmothering each other's children, and seeking each other out for reunions. It is with this in mind that so many parents appear to set about choosing their daughters' schools. It is a priority that other cultures might find eccentric, but which the children themselves sometimes find of lasting importance long after all memory of what the school itself has taught has disappeared. 'We had all three arrived at St

Paul's together,' wrote an Edwardian Paulina, 'because it was accepted amongst those who cared for education as the best girls' school in London. That the education it provided was not nearly so good as it ought to have been was not generally known. What was certain was that there one met the children of the intellectual élite.'[8] Every school has its devoted band of old girls whose golden memories dominate the official history. Many of these feel that they were formed by their days there or by one particular headmistress. In a shaky hand at the beginning of a manuscript account of her childhood a Paulina has written: 'with everlasting gratitude to St Paul's Girls' School for all they gave me during my school days and for the rest of my life'.[9] Beautiful surroundings have made a lasting impression on many. 'How deeply the beauty of the place struck into the souls of the young who were taught there,' said Anne Ridler of Downe, 'can be seen from many a callow poem and prose piece printed in the school magazine, the stumbling expression of a heartfelt joy.'[10] St Leonards has always evoked a similar response.

> I went to look at things for the last time. I climbed the steps of the old ruined tower set in one corner of the great wall which gave such a good view of the big cricket field and the sea and the lovely west cliffs. I went down to the end of the old grey quay by the side of the tiny harbour and looked out over the sea, and up to the land where St Regulus and the ruined cathedral stood out against a pale blue sky. I walked far along the west cliffs . . . and, looking east, I saw St Andrews blocked black against the pale grey hills beyond, like an etching come to life: the square tower of St Regulus, the twin towers of the ruined cathedral, and running down from them the prickly profile of the town itself, ending in the sheer drop of the castle rock into the sea. That is the most beautiful view I know.[11]

Even Margaret Cole, desperately unhappy at Roedean, could take pleasure in the beauty of the Downs and the sea 'rolling in with great green combers edged with white'. The Godolphin lauded the buildings and their surroundings in the school song:

> What is the loyalty deep in our hearts,
> That bursts into song in September?
> All hail to Godolphin, set high on the hill,
> 'Franc ha leal eto ge' we remember.
> We remember the colour of bricks and of leaves
> Now red in the rich Autumn weather,
> We remember the Dolphin, the weathercock gold,
> And the look of the place altogether.

Some remember ritual and traditions:

> The famous 'Lines' in which eight hundred girls walk swiftly and in

complete silence along the marble corridor and into the Princess Hall for Prayers is sometimes quoted as an example of soulless regimentation. I remember that hushed morning walk, past the glass doors, the green lawns, the willow-tree, as a time in which I first realized that I was a living creature, and the physical conformity itself to that silent precision of movement seemed to lend a kind of ecstasy to the awareness of a secret life within.[12]

Some, like Antonia White, whose feelings about school when they were there were ambivalent, melt into nostalgia as they recall the dawn of their lives, a lost innocence. Going back for a school diamond jubilee celebration of the Feast of the Immaculate Conception, the day when Sacred Heart old children traditionally met for a reunion, she wonders whether the procession of the present generation will move her as much as it did in the old days.

And then the lights are dimmed, the candles flicker into life, the first notes of the Immaculata are softly intoned – and suddenly there is not a lump in my throat; I am crying. Will those children down there, filing slowly past in their blue dresses and white veils, carrying their lilies, ever know how exquisitely beautiful their reverent faces look in the light of their candles? Is it possible, I wonder, looking around at my contemporaries, that we could ever have looked like that? What a cruel contrast there is between those faces which are like virgin pages and our own, on which time has scribbled the record of every experience we have lived through since our school-days.[13]

But few, if given the chance, would elect to go back.

If I end by saying that no experience since has been so bad as school, I should leave entirely the wrong impression. Yet from one point of view it is the truth. Schooldays were not the happiest days of my life; nor did I hate them or spend them in utter misery. There were good days and bad days; one could say, glibly, it was life in microcosm, and there would, again, be some truth in that. Certainly I am not exaggerating when I say there has never been anything quite so bad as the worst parts of school. In that sense, I suppose, [school] provided a good basis for life.

If you could survive it you could survive anything.[14]

Glossary

Assisted Places Scheme established after the Education Act, 1980, to give help with fees of children at independent schools whose parents could not otherwise afford to send them there.

Board of Education Constituted by Act of Parliament in 1899 to superintend education in England and Wales. Upgraded to Ministry of Education in 1944, and merged with the Ministry of Science in 1964 to become Department of Education and Science.

board school The Education Act of 1870 created school boards, local authorities to 'fill the gaps' in the existing system of voluntary schools. These were empowered to establish elementary schools, thus known as 'board schools'.

British school One founded by the British and Foreign School Society, a non-denominational organization set up in 1814 for the poor.

charities, educational The Charities Act, 1960, gave charitable status (and thereby tax relief) to educational institutions, even though the beneficiaries are not necessarily needy. The criterion is that they must be for public, not private benefit. All schools in the Girls' Schools Association (q.v.) and the Headmasters' Conference are educational charities.

charity schools Schools founded by individuals or groups of benefactors to provide elementary education for poor pupils.

charity hospitals Institutions where children of the poor were housed and given an elementary education.

council school See *maintained school*.

county school A primary or secondary school maintained out of public funds.

direct-grant school A school receiving funds direct from the Department of Education and Science in return for a proportion of its places being allocated free to local children (known as grant-aided schools in Scotland). After 1976 these were phased out, and schools had to decide whether to become fully independent or fully maintained, or to close.

Education Act, 1870 The first to make the provision of elementary education compulsory. It established school boards, and provided for schools to be built with funds from rates.

Education Act, 1902 Introduced a co-ordinated education system in England and Wales. It abolished school boards, and set up local education authorities, the larger of which had to provide elementary, secondary and post-secondary education.

Education Act, 1944 (Butler Act) Established the three-part system of primary, secondary and further education under the responsibility of the Minister of

Education. The school-leaving age was raised from fourteen to fifteen (to be raised to sixteen as soon as practicable).

Education Act, 1976 Made all local education authorities submit plans for the reorganization of secondary schools into comprehensive schools, thus abolishing the system whereby children had been divided at the age of eleven into those who would receive an academic education, and those who, having failed the 11+ exam, went to secondary modern schools.

endowed schools Chiefly grammar schools founded by benefactors. Winchester and Eton were among the earliest. Many, such as these two, turned themselves into boarding schools for the wealthy.

Fleming Report, 1944 The report of an inquiry into how the public schools might be more closely integrated into the state system of education. It recommended that assisted places in independent schools should be made available to children from maintained schools.

Girls' Public Day School Trust An organization of girls' high schools, founded in 1872 as the Girls' Public Day School Company.

Girls' Schools Association An association of the principal schools providing independent secondary education for girls. The male counterpart is the Headmasters' Conference. All the 260 schools have to be educational charities (q.v.) and there are minimum requirements as to number of pupils and academic achievement.

grammar school A secondary school providing an academic education. Originally established in the sixteenth century or earlier, often by private benefactors, for the teaching of Latin grammar.

Headmasters' Conference See *Girls' Schools Association*.

high school A secondary day school, an appellation often used by girls' independent schools. Manchester High School was apparently the first girls' school thus to style itself.

independent school A fee-paying school, not maintained by public funds. The educational standards are set by the school alone and it is not obliged to conform to any government standards.

maintained school A state school, maintained by public funds.

national school A school run by the National Society for the Education of the Poor in the Principles of the Established Church.

private school A term sometimes applied to any independent school, generally used in this text to indicate a school in the ownership of a private individual.

public school The term is loosely applied to the more prestigious independent secondary schools, and refers to those that are not owned by private individuals but which are run as educational charities (q.v.). The distinction between public and private schools is discussed at length in Chapter 4, under 'The System'.

recognized school One that has been inspected and recognized as efficient by the Secretary of State for Education. The term 'efficient' refers to the number of pupils, which must be sufficient for economical administration; to the teachers, who must be suitably qualified; and to the premises, which must be in good order and properly equipped.

voluntary-aided schools The Victorians used the term 'voluntary' for schools founded by voluntary bodies such as the National Society and the British and Foreign School Society. Voluntary-aided schools today are usually church schools, funded partly by the local education authority and partly by the voluntary bodies who founded them.

Notes

Chapter 1 Introduction

1 *Schools Inquiry* [Taunton] *Commission Report*, 1868, vol. I, p. 297
2 Christine Flemington, letter to author
3 Sara A. Burstall: *The Story of the Manchester High School for Girls*. Manchester: University Press, 1911, p. 13
4 Alice Zimmern: *The Renaissance of Girls' Education*. London: A.D. Innes, 1898, p. 38
5 Annie E. Ridley: *Frances Mary Buss and her Work for Education*. London: Longmans, 1895, p. 38
6 V.E. Stack (ed.): *Oxford High School, Girls' Public Day School Trust, 1875–1960*. 1963, p. 75
7 Sir John Otter: *Nathaniel Woodard*. London: John Lane, 1925, p. 274
8 Burstall: op. cit., p. 15
9 Priscilla Bain: *St Swithun's: a centenary history*. Chichester: Phillimore, 1984, p. 21.
10 Mary James: *Alice Ottley, First Head-Mistress of the Worcester High School for Girls, 1883–1912*. London: Longmans, 1914, p. 213
11 Elsie Bowerman: *Stands There a School: memoirs of Dame Frances Dove, DBE, founder of Wycombe Abbey School*. 1965, p. 16
12 R.M. Scrimgeour (ed.): *The North London Collegiate School, 1850–1950. A Hundred Years of Girls' Education*. London: Oxford University Press, 1950, p. 112
13 Mary Catharine Elizabeth Chambers: *The Life of Mary Ward*. London: Burns & Oates, 1882, vol. I, p. 410
14 C.S. Bremner: *The Education of Girls and Women in Great Britain*. London: Swan Sonnenschein, 1897, p. 2
15 Lucien Perey (ed.): *Memoirs of the Princesse de Ligne*. London: R. Bentley, 1887, p. xii
16 M. O'Leary: *Education with a Tradition*. London: University of London Press, 1936, p. 66
17 M.G. Jones: *The Charity School Movement*. Cambridge: University Press, 1938, p. 81
18 H. Winifred Sturge and Theodora Clark: *The Mount School, York, 1785 to 1814, 1831 to 1931*. London: Dent, 1931
19 Sheila Fletcher: *Feminists and Bureaucrats*. Cambridge: University Press, 1980, pp. 118, 114

20 Quoted by Sara A. Burstall and M.A. Douglas (eds): *Public Schools for Girls*. London: Longmans, 1911, p. 11
21 Evelyn Sharp: *Rebel Women*. London: A.C. Fifield, 1910, p. 111
22 George R. Parkin: *Edward Thring*. London: Macmillan, 1898, vol. II, p. 484
23 Sheila MacLeod: *The Art of Starvation*. London: Virago, 1981, p. 58
24 Betty Boyden (ed.), *Call Back Yesterday: a collection of reminiscences to mark the centenary of the Nottingham High School for Girls, 1875–1975*. [1976] p. 97
25 Lilian Faithfull: *You and I*. London: Chatto & Windus, 1927, p. 4
26 *The Story of the Mary Datchelor School, 1877–1957*. London: Hodder & Stoughton, 1957, p. 106
27 Geoffrey Willans and Ronald Searle: *How to be Topp*. London: Max Parrish, 1954, p. 47
28 MacLeod: op. cit.
29 John Rae: *The Public School Revolution*. London: Faber, 1981, p. 157
30 Elizabeth North: *Dames*. London: Cape, 1981, p. 194

Chapter 2 Little Eleemosynaries

1 Joshua Fitch: 'Charity Schools', *Westminster Review*, April 1873
2 *Schools Inquiry* [Taunton] *Commission Report*, 1868, vol. I, p. 476
3 *The Christ's Hospital Book*. London: Hamish Hamilton, 1953, p. 7
4 Frances M. Page: *Christ's Hospital, Hertford*. London: Bell, 1953, p. 84
5 Margaret K.B. Sommerville: *The Merchant Maiden Hospital*. Edinburgh, 1970, p. 2
6 Quoted in Jean Vanes: *Apparelled in Red*. Bristol, 1984, p. 46
7 Charles Dickens: *Dombey and Son*. London: Bradbury & Evans, 1848
8 Daniel Defoe: *Everybody's Business is Nobody's Business*. London, 1725, pp. 26–30
9 William Lemprière: *A History of Christ's Hospital, London, Hoddesdon and Hertford*. Cambridge: University Press, 1924, p. 7
10 Sister Clare Veronica: 'A century of Catholic education in Richmond, North Yorkshire'. Assumption School, Richmond, 1984 (unpublished)
11 [Dorothy F. Chetham-Strode]: *History of the Grey Coat Hospital, Westminster, 1698–1959*. London, 1960.
12 Vanes: op. cit., p. 46
13 Quoted in Richard Ollard: *An English Education*. London: Collins, 1982, p. 23
14 David Pryde: *Pleasant Memories of a Busy Life*. Edinburgh: Blackwood, 1893, p. 129
15 M.G. Jones: *The Charity School Movement*. Cambridge: University Press, 1938, p. 103
16 Alexander Law: *Education in Edinburgh in the Eighteenth Century*. London: University of London Press, 1965, p. 130
17 [Chetham-Strode]: op. cit.
18 Marion A. Burgess: *A History of Burlington School*. [1938?] p. 41
19 R.M. Handfield-Jones: *The History of the Royal Masonic Institution for Girls, 1788–1974*. 5th edn, 1974
20 E.H. Pearce: *Annals of Christ's Hospital*. London: Methuen, 1901, p. 21
21 *Westminster Review*, art. cit.

22 Louie Angus: *Blue Skirts into Blue Stockings*. London: Ian Allan, 1981
23 Vanes: op. cit., p. 94
24 See *Schools Inquiry Commission Report*, 1868, vol. I, p. 565
25 Dorothea Beale: 'On the education of women' – paper read to the Social Science Congress, October 1865
26 Sara A. Burstall: *The Story of the Manchester High School for Girls*. Manchester: University Press, 1911, ch. V
27 K.M. Westaway (ed.): *A History of Bedford High School*. 1932, p. 16
28 Sylvia Harrop: *The Merchant Taylors' School for Girls, Crosby: one hundred years of achievement 1888–1988*. Liverpool: University Press, 1988
29 M.H. Cattley: *The Perse School for Girls 1881–1981*. 1981
30 W.I. Candler, Ailsa M. Jaques and B.M.W. Dobbie: *King Edward VI High School for Girls, Birmingham*. London: Benn, 1971, p. 18
31 Sheila Fletcher: *Feminists and Bureaucrats*. Cambridge: University Press, 1980, p. 85
32 *Barbican* (City of London School for Girls magazine), 1969
33 John Locke: *Report of the Board of Trade Respecting the Relief of the Poor*. London, 1697
34 Honor Osborne and Peggy Manisty: *A History of the Royal School for Daughters of Officers of the Army, 1864–1965*. London: Hodder & Stoughton, 1966, p. 16
35 Philip Unwin: *The Royal Naval School, 1840–1975*. 1976, p. 32.
36 Dorothea L. Pullan: *The Record of the Clergy Orphan Corporation School for Girls 1749–1949*
37 Elsie Pike and Constance E. Curryer: *The Story of Walthamstow Hall, 1838–1970*. 1973, p. 28
38 M.A. Douglas and C.R. Ash: *The Godolphin School, 1726–1926*. London: Longmans, 1928, p. 4
39 J.E. McCann: *Thomas Howell and the School at Llandaff*. 1972, pp. 25, 26
40 ibid., p. 143
41 Margaret L. Flood: *The Story of St Elphin's School, 1844–1944*, p. 9
42 Elizabeth Gaskell: *The Life of Charlotte Brontë*. London: Smith Elder, 1857
43 Harrop: op. cit., p. 86
44 Geoffrey Sale: *The History of Casterton School*. 1983
45 Elizabeth Raikes: *Dorothea Beale of Cheltenham*. London: Archibald Constable, 1908, p. 4
46 Pryde: op. cit., p. 131
47 *St Michael's, Limpsfield: Times Remembered* (n.d.)
48 Pike and Curryer: op. cit., p. 31
49 ibid., p. 16

Chapter 3 The Day School Pioneers

1 M.V. Hughes: *A London Family 1870–1900*. London: Oxford University Press, 1946, p. 179
2 K. Anderson: 'Frances Mary Buss, the founder' in *The North London Collegiate School, 1850–1950. A Hundred Years of Girls' Education*, ed. R.M. Scrimgeour. London: Oxford University Press, 1950, p. 32
3 ibid., p. 111

4 Sara A. Burstall: *The Story of the Manchester High School for Girls*. Manchester, University Press, 1911, p. 35
5 Margaret Fletcher: *O, Call Back Yesterday*. Oxford: Shakespeare Head Press, 1939, p. 55
6 *Schools Inquiry Commission Report*, 1868, vol. V, p. 263
7 Joan E. McCann: *Thomas Howell and the School at Llandaff*. 1972, p. 123
8 H.M. Swanwick: *I Have Been Young*. London: Gollancz, 1935, p. 75
9 Fletcher: op. cit., p. 52
10 'St Paul's Girls' School', article in *Queen*, 8 July 1922
11 Elizabeth Sewell: 'The reign of pedantry in girls' schools', *Nineteenth Century*, February 1888
12 Josephine Kamm: *Indicative Past*. London: Allen & Unwin, 1971, p. 47
13 Fletcher: op. cit., p. 46
14 Joan Bungay (ed.): *Redland High School 1882–1982*. [1982] p. 6
15 K.M. Westaway (ed.): *A History of Bedford High School*. 1932, p. 38
16 Florence A. Field and G.B. Birdsall: *The Coming of Age Souvenir of the Whalley Range High School*. 1912
17 Swanwick: op. cit., p. 75
18 F. Cecily Steadman: *In the Days of Miss Beale*. London: E.J. Burrow, 1931, pp. 43, 44
19 Diana Hopkinson: *The Incense Tree*. London: Routledge & Kegan Paul, 1968, p. 39
20 *Nineteenth Century*, art. cit.
21 Emily Shore: *Journal*. London: Kegan Paul, 1891, p. vi
22 F. Myers, writing in *Macmillan*. Quoted by Alice Zimmern: *The Renaissance of Girls' Education in England*. London: A.D. Innes, 1898, p. 49
23 Elaine Kaye: *A History of Queen's College, London, 1848–1972*. London: Chatto & Windus, 1972, p. 24
24 Josephine Kamm: *How Different from Us: a biography of Miss Buss and Miss Beale*. London: Bodley Head, 1958, p. 29
25 Fletcher: op. cit., p. 47
26 Priscilla Bain: *St Swithun's: a centenary history*. Chichester: Phillimore, 1984, p. 7
27 Burstall: op. cit., p. 69
28 Joan Lightwood: *The Park School, Glasgow, 1880–1980*. [1980] p. 32
29 Mary C. Malim and Henrietta C. Escreet (eds): *The Book of the Blackheath High School*. 1927, p. 28
30 Janet Whitcut: *Edgbaston High School 1876–1976*. 1976, p. 38
31 Mary E. James: *Alice Ottley, First Head-Mistress of the Worcester High School for Girls, 1883–1912*. London: Longmans, 1914, p. 55
32 *Berkhamsted School for Girls 1888–1938*. 1938, p. 8
33 Malim and Escreet (eds): op. cit., p. 28
34 Burstall: op. cit., p. 56
35 Swanwick: op. cit., p. 36
36 Janet E. Sayers: *The Fountain Unsealed: A history of the Notting Hill and Ealing High School*. 1973
37 Kamm: *Indicative Past*, p. 61
38 Morton N. Cohen: 'Lewis Carroll comes to school' in *Ad Lucem* (Oxford High School magazine), centenary number, 1975

39 Whitcut: op. cit.
40 Valentine Noake: *History of the Alice Ottley School, Worcester*. 1952, p. 43
41 Malim and Escreet (eds): op. cit., p. 30
42 Kamm: *Indicative Past*, p. 57
43 Bungay (ed.): op. cit., p. 36
44 Joan Trowbridge (ed.): *Durham High School: a centenary celebration 1884–1984*. [1984] p. 11
45 Kamm: *Indicative Past*, p. 83
46 Elsie Quarrie: *The School that Refused to Die* (Francis Holland School, Graham Street). 1981
47 *The Jubilee Book: Bournemouth High School – Talbot Heath, 1886–1946*, p. 29
48 ibid., p. 41
49 David Pryde: *Pleasant Memories of a Busy Life*. Edinburgh: Blackwood, 1893, p. 138
50 Westaway (ed.): op. cit., p. 39
51 Malim and Escreet (eds): op. cit., p. 38
52 Bungay (ed.): op. cit., p. 10
53 Bain: op. cit., p. 38
54 ibid., p. 21
55 Lightwood: op. cit., p. 20
56 Nigel Shapley: *Women of Independent Mind: St George's School, Edinburgh, and the Campaign for Women's Education 1888–1988*. 1988, p. 35
57 Elizabeth Hamilton: *A River Full of Stars*. London: Deutsch, 1954
58 James: op. cit., p. 70
59 Ethel Strudwick in *The Headmistress Speaks*, ed. Christine Arscott. London: Kegan Paul, 1937
60 Christine Arscott, in ibid.
61 Betty Boyden (ed.): *Call Back Yesterday: a collection of reminiscences to mark the centenary of the Nottingham High School for Girls, 1875–1975*. 1976, p. 98
62 ibid., pp. 116, 117
63 Violet E. Stack (ed.): *Oxford High School, Girls' Public Day School Trust, 1875–1960*. 1963, p. 84
64 *Paulina*, no. 159, 1978–9
65 Hamilton: op. cit., p. 108
66 Fletcher: op. cit., p. 189
67 St Paul's Girls' School archives
68 Winifred I. Candler, Ailsa M. Jaques and B.M. Dobbie: *King Edward VI High School for Girls, Birmingham*. London: Benn, 1971, p. 62
69 Harrop: op. cit., p. 108
70 *The Holly Club Commemoration Magazine* (Lady Eleanor Holles School), 1986, p. 18

Chapter 4 Public Schools

1 Mary Bentinck Smith: *Ad Vitam: papers of a head-mistress*. London: John Murray, 1927, p. 218
2 Winifred Peck: *A Little Learning*. London: Faber, 1952, p. 147
3 Elsie Bowerman: *Stands There a School* (Wycombe Abbey School). 1966, p. 41

4 Margaret Kennedy: *The Constant Nymph*. London: Heinemann, 1924, p. 178
5 Anne Ridler: *Olive Willis and Downe House*. London: John Murray, 1967, p. 142
6 Anne Valery: *The Edge of a Smile*. London: Peter Owen, 1977, p. 22. The school is called 'Greenglades' in this autobiographical novel
7 E. Arnot Robertson: 'Potting shed of the English rose' in *The Old School*, ed. Graham Greene. London: Cape, 1934, p. 153
8 Timothy Shy and Ronald Searle: *The Terror of St Trinian's*. London: Max Parrish, 1952
9 ibid.
10 Annabel Huth Jackson: *A Victorian Childhood*. London: Methuen, 1932
11 Rosalind Onians (ed.): *St Helen's: The First Eighty Years, 1899–1979* (St Helen's School, Northwood). 1980, p. 112
12 Peck: op. cit., p. 111
13 ibid., p. 117
14 Margaret Cole: *Growing up into Revolution*. London: Longmans, 1949, p. 27
15 Valery: op. cit., p. 17
16 Priscilla (Hayter) Napier, in *Downe House Scrap-Book, 1907–1957*
17 Elizabeth Raikes: *Dorothea Beale of Cheltenham*. London: Archibald Constable, 1908, p. 87
18 Jane Ellen Harrison: *Reminiscences of a Student's Life*. London: L. and V. Woolf, 1925
19 'Lilian Mary Mott', a memoir by her husband (privately printed, 1956). Cheltenham Ladies' College archives
20 A.K. Clarke: *A History of the Cheltenham Ladies' College 1853–1979*. Saxmundham: John Catt, 1979, p. 34
21 Raikes: op. cit., p. 81
22 Clarke: op. cit., p. 47
23 F. Cecily Steadman: *In the Days of Miss Beale*. London: E.J. Burrow, 1931, p. 56
24 Harrison: op. cit.
25 Jackson: op. cit., p. 146
26 Kennedy: op. cit., p. 207
27 Rachel K. Davis: *Four Miss Pinkertons*. London: Williams & Norgate, 1936, p. 29. Roedean is thinly disguised as 'Sutton Weald', and the Misses Lawrence appear as the Misses Vaughan.
28 *St Leonards School, 1877–1977*, p. 46
29 Peck: op. cit., p. 140
30 *St Leonards School, 1877–1927*, p. 1
31 Julia Grant, Katherine H. McCutcheon and Ethel F. Sanders (eds): *St Leonards School, 1877–1927*. London: Oxford University Press [1928?], p. 24
32 Martha Vicinus: *Independent Women*. London: Virago, 1985, p. 179
33 *St Leonards School, 1877–1977*, p. 33
34 Alice Zimmern: *The Renaissance of Girls' Education*. London: A.D. Innes, 1898, p. 156
35 Peck: op. cit., p. 119
36 ibid., p. 220
37 ibid., p. 139
38 *A History of Roedean School, 1885–1985*, p. 9

39 *The Founders of Roedean*. 1935
40 This was Olive Willis. See Ridler: op. cit., p. 31
41 Cole: op. cit., p. 27
42 *A History of Roedean School, 1885–1985*, p. 17
43 May Wedderburn Cannan: *Grey Ghosts and Voices*. Kineton: Roundwood Press, 1976, p. 48
44 Olive Willis in *Downe House Scrap-Book, 1907–1957*
45 Elizabeth Bowen: 'Maria' in *Collected Stories*. London: Cape, 1980, p. 408
46 Elizabeth Bowen: 'The Mulberry Tree', in Greene (ed.), op. cit., p. 49
47 Elizabeth Bowen in *Downe House Scrap-Book, 1907–1957*
48 Jacobine (Menzies Wilson) Sackville-West, in ibid.
49 Priscilla (Hayter) Napier in ibid.
50 Elizabeth North: *Dames*. London: Cape, 1981, p. 77. Downe House appears as 'Dames' in this novel
51 Valery: op. cit., p. 19
52 *Badminton School, 1858–1958*
53 ibid.
54 Jean Storry (ed.): *At Badminton with B.M.B.* 1982, p. 20
55 ibid., p. 51
56 Valery: op cit., p. 20
57 *Badminton School, 1858–1958*
58 Joanna Turner (comp.): *B.M. Sanderson and Badminton School, 1947–1966*. Bristol, 1988, p. 112
59 Naomi Mitchison: *Among You Taking Notes*. London: Gollancz, 1985, p. 93
60 *Portrait of Benenden, 1924–1974*, p. 67
61 ibid., p. 78
62 Mary F. Edmonds (ed.): *Cobham Hall: the founding of a new public school*. 1987, p. 11
63 Margaret K.B. Sommerville: *The Merchant Maiden Hospital*. Edinburgh, 1970, p. 108
64 Peck: op. cit., p. 66
65 Kennedy: op. cit., p. 208
66 Lucy Kinloch: *A World Within a School*. London: Warne, 1937, p. 4
67 Quoted by Mallory Wober: *English Girls' Boarding Schools*. London: Allen Lane, 1971, p. 112
68 Geraldine Coster: *Self-government in Schools*. Oxford: Blackwell, 1923
69 Peck: op. cit., p. 140
70 Janet Whitcut: *Edgbaston High School, 1876–1976*. 1976
71 Cordelia James: letter to the author
72 Charis U. Frankenberg: *Not Old, Madam, Vintage*. Lavenham, 1975
73 *St Leonards School, 1877–1977*, p. 57
74 Dorothea Beale: *Does Modern Education Ennoble?* London, 1905
75 Cole: op. cit., p. 29
76 Dorothea Beale, Lucy H.M. Soulsby and Jane Frances Dove: *Work and Play in Girls' Schools*. London: Longmans, 1898, pp. 405–7
77 North: op. cit., p. 38
78 E. Arnot Robertson: 'Potting shed of the English rose', in Greene (ed.), op. cit., p. 154
79 Cole: op. cit., p. 30

80 *Sherborne School for Girls, 1899–1949*
81 M.A. Douglas and C.R. Ash: *The Godolphin School, 1726–1926*. London: Longmans, 1928
82 Wober: op. cit.
83 Christine Flemington: letter to author
84 [Margaret Haig Mackworth] Lady Rhondda: *This Was My World*. London: Macmillan, 1933, p. 53
85 Susan Hicklin: *Polished Corners, 1878–1978. A hundred years of contemporary life in and out of Francis Holland School, N.W.1.* 1978
86 Priscilla Napier in *Downe House Scrap-Book, 1907–1957*
87 Margaret James: *The Kent College Saga, 1886–1986*. 1986, p. 25
88 Janet Erskine Stuart: *The Education of Catholic Girls*. London: Longmans, 1911, p. 132
89 Lilian Faithfull: *You and I*. London: Chatto & Windus, 1927, pp. 9, 10
90 Elsie Pike and Constance E. Curryer: *The Story of Walthamstow Hall, 1838–1970*. 1973, p. 34
91 Jean Storry (ed.): *At Badminton with B.M.B.* 1982, p. 9
92 Elizabeth Manners (ed.): *Felixstowe College, 1929–1979*. 1980, p. 5
93 Lucien Perey (ed.): *Memoirs of the Princesse de Ligne*. London: R. Bentley, 1887, vol. I, p. 116
94 Roma Goyder: *Hayseed to Harvest: memories of Katherine Cox and Hayes Court School*. Colchester: 1985, p. 38
95 *St Leonards School, 1877–1977*, p. 32
96 Storry (ed.): op. cit., p. 50
97 *Portrait of Benenden 1924–1974*, p. 86
98 Betty Boyden (ed.): *Call Back Yesterday: a collection of reminiscences to mark the centenary of the Nottingham High School for Girls, 1875–1975*. 1976
99 Ursula Roberts (ed.): 'Memories of Moreton' (unpublished)

Chapter 5 'Individuals, even Eccentrics'

1 Alice Baird (ed.): *I Was There: St James's, West Malvern*. 1956, p. 270
2 *Schools Inquiry Commission Report*, 1868, vol. I, p. 299
3 Ursula Roberts (ed.): 'Memories of Moreton' (unpublished)
4 *Portrait of Benenden 1924–1974*, p. 86
5 From prospectus in the John Johnson Collection, Bodleian Library
6 Rosalind Onians (ed.): *St Helen's: the first eighty years, 1899–1979*. p. 11
7 From an unidentified cutting of an article on girls' schools, dated November 1858. Education Box 48, John Johnson Collection, Bodleian Library
8 Juliana Horatia Ewing: *Six to Sixteen*. London: Bell, 1875, chs 13–16
9 Elizabeth Sewell: *Autobiography*. London: Longmans, 1908, chs 2, 3
10 'Thoughts on some of the present defects in boarding schools for girls', *Victoria Magazine*, 1876, vol. XXVII, p. 43
11 Vera Brittain: *Testament of Youth*. London: Gollancz, 1933, p. 37
12 E.E. Constance Jones: *As I Remember: an autobiographical ramble*. London: A. & C. Black, 1922, p. 36

13 Elizabeth Sewell: *Principles of Education*. London: Longmans, 1865
14 Barbara Bourke (ed.): *The Laurels 1872–1972 Wroxall Abbey*
15 *Queen*, 5 August 1922
16 *The Story of Greenacre School*. 1987
17 Dorothy P. Carew: *Many Years, Many Girls, the history of a school 1862–1942* (Queenwood School, Eastbourne). Dublin: Browne & Nolan, 1967, p. 142
18 Jocelyn Logan: *Upper Chine*. 1987, pp. 37–47
19 Roma Goyder: *Hayseed to Harvest: memories of Katherine Cox and Hayes Court School*. Colchester: 1985, p. 97
20 Sybille Bedford: *Aldous Huxley*. London: Chatto & Windus, 1974, p. 9
21 Roberts (ed.), op. cit., passim
22 *The Shuttle* (Moira House magazine), January 1925
23 Transcript of an interview with Mona Swann, 1982 (Moira House archives)
24 Goyder: op. cit., p. 73
25 Joanna Cannan: *The Misty Valley*. London: T. Fisher Unwin, 1922, p. 35. Wychwood appears as 'St Anne's'. Kathleen Gibberd also describes it, under the name of 'Wyngates', in *Politics on the Blackboard*, Faber, 1954
26 M.L. Lee: *A Brief History of Wychwood School, Oxford*
27 These three extracts from the prospectus in the John Johnson Collection, Bodleian Library
28 Kaye Webb: *The St Trinian's Story*. London: Perpetua Books, 1959
29 *Queen*, 5 August 1922
30 Baird (ed.): op. cit., p. 140
31 *Independent Schools Yearbook*. London: A. & C. Black, 1988, p. 112
32 Message to pupils in first issue of *Heathfield Magazine*, January 1942
33 *Tudorian*, 1950, p. 79
34 ibid., 1985, p. 27
35 ibid.
36 Violet Markham: *Return Passage*. London: Oxford University Press, 1953, p. 43
37 For all this information I am indebted to the present headmistress, Mrs Lavinia Cohn-Sherbok.

Chapter 6 Religion and Religious Foundations

1 Quoted by Mallory Wober: *English Girls' Boarding Schools*. London: Allen Lane, 1971, p. 62
2 Kay Stedmond: *St Mary's School, Calne, 1873–1986*, p. 18
3 K.E. Kirk: *The Story of the Woodard Schools*. London: Hodder & Stoughton, 1937, p. 115
4 Ursula Roberts (ed.): 'Memories of Moreton' (unpublished)
5 Winifred Peck: *A Little Learning*. London: Faber, 1952, p. 137
6 [Mabel Williams]: *Notes on the Clergy Daughters' School, Casterton*. 1935
7 Joshua Fitch: 'Charity Schools', *Westminster Review*, April 1873
8 Anne Ridler: *Olive Willis and Downe House*. London: Murray, 1967, p. 101
9 Jean Storry (ed.): *At Badminton with B.M.B.* 1982, p. 20
10 ibid., p. 8

11 Joanna Turner (comp.): *B.M. Sanderson and Badminton School, 1947–1966*. 1988, p. 85
12 *Portrait of Benenden, 1924–1974*, p. 71
13 *Graham Street Memories*, ed. Beatrix Dunning. [Francis Holland School, SW1] 1931, pp. 44, 45
14 Elsie Pike and Constance E. Curryer: *The Story of Walthamstow Hall, 1838–1970*. 1973, p. 22
15 Felicia Lamb and Helen Pickthorn: *Locked-up Daughters*. London: Hodder & Stoughton, 1968, p. 66
16 Julian MacMaster, in *Downe House Scrap-Book, 1907–1957*
17 Janet Whitcut: *Edgbaston High School, 1876–1976*. 1976, p. 158
18 Winifred I. Candler, Ailsa M. Jaques and B.M.W. Dobbie: *King Edward VI High School for Girls, Birmingham, 1883–1970*. London: Benn, 1971
19 Louie Angus: *Blue Skirts into Blue Stockings*. London: Ian Allan, 1981, p. 109
20 Frances M. Page: *Christ's Hospital, Hertford*. London: Bell, 1953, p. 97
21 A. Mary Shaw (ed.): *When You Were There. Reflections on Edgehill College, 1884–1984*. p. 87
22 Elizabeth Raikes: *Dorothea Beale of Cheltenham*. London: Archibald Constable, 1908, p. 264
23 K.M. Westaway (ed.): *A History of Bedford High School*. 1932, p. 66
24 Peck: op. cit., p. 133
25 Mary E. James: *Alice Ottley, First Head-Mistress of the Worcester High School for Girls 1883–1912*. London: Longmans, 1914, p. 65
26 Margaret Fletcher: *O, Call Back Yesterday*. Oxford: Shakespeare Head Press, 1939, p. 50
27 Mary C. Malim and Henrietta C. Escreet (eds): *The Book of the Blackheath High School*. 1927, p. 41
28 E. Arnot Robertson: 'Potting shed of the English rose', in *The Old School*, ed. Graham Greene. London: Cape, 1934
29 [Margaret Haig Mackworth] Lady Rhondda: *This Was My World*. London: Macmillan, 1933, pp. 72, 73
30 Mary Don: 'Memories and thoughts on a convent education' (letter to author)
31 Mary Howitt: *An Autobiography*, ed. Margaret Howitt. London: W. Isbister, 1889, p. 47
32 H. Winifred Sturge and Theodora Clark: *The Mount School, York, 1785 to 1814, 1831 to 1931*. London: Dent, 1931, p. 13
33 W.A. Campbell Stewart: *Quakers and Education*. London: Epworth Press, 1953, p. 141
34 Sturge and Clark: op. cit., p. 151
35 Priscilla Quayle: letter to author
36 Sturge and Clark: op. cit., p. 160
37 F.C. Pritchard: *Methodist Secondary Education*. London: Epworth Press, 1949, p. 270
38 John Wesley: *Works*, 1872, vol. VII, p. 84
39 A.M. Stoddart: *Life and Letters of Hannah E. Pipe*. Edinburgh: Blackwood, 1908, p. 62
40 ibid.
41 *In Memoriam: Hannah Elizabeth Pipe 1831–1906*. Privately printed, p. 9

42 Clyde Binfield: *Belmont's Portias: Victorian non-conformists and middle-class education for girls*. London: Friends of Dr Williams's Library, 1981, p. 29
43 Sir John Otter: *Nathaniel Woodard*. London: John Lane, 1925, p. 274
44 *Schools Inquiry Commission Report*, 1868, vol. VII, p. 70
45 Kirk: op. cit., p. 16
46 *Schools Inquiry Commission Report*, 1868, vol. VII, p. 76
47 Violet Mary MacPherson: *The Story of S. Anne's, Abbots Bromley, 1874–1924*, p. 30
48 Vera Brittain: *Testament of Friendship: the story of Winifred Holtby*. London: Macmillan, 1940

Chapter 7 Convent Schools

1 Mary Catherine Goulter: *Schoolday Memories*. London: Burns & Oates, 1922, p. 2
2 Mary Don: 'Memories and thoughts on a convent education' (letter to author)
3 Antonia White: 'A child of the Five Wounds', in *The Old School*, ed. Graham Greene. London: Cape, 1934
4 Egerton Castle (ed.): *The Jerningham Letters*. London: R. Bentley, 1896, vol. I, p. 34
5 *History of the New Hall Community of Canonesses Regular of the Holy Sepulchre*. Roehampton, 1899
6 White: 'A child of the Five Wounds', in Greene, op. cit.
7 Mary McCarthy: *Memories of a Catholic Girlhood*. [1957] London: Penguin, 1963, p. 89
8 Mary Andrew Armour: *Cornelia*. Society of the Holy Child Jesus, 1979
9 'A word for the convent boarding-schools', *Fraser's Magazine*, October 1874
10 M. O'Leary: *Education with a Tradition*. London: University of London Press, 1936, p. 165
11 Janet Erskine Stuart: *The Education of Catholic Girls*. London: Longmans: 1911, p. 220
12 John Morris, SJ: *The Life of Mother Henrietta Kerr*. Roehampton, 1886
13 O'Leary: op. cit., p. 166
14 White: 'A child of the Five Wounds', in Greene, op. cit.
15 Quoted in O'Leary, op. cit.
16 White: 'A child of the Five Wounds', in Greene, op. cit.
17 Juliana Wadham: *The Case of Cornelia Connelly*. London: Collins, 1956, p. 244
18 Antonia White: *Frost in May*. [1933] London: Virago, 1978, p. 49
19 Mary Carbery: *The Farm by Lough Gur*. London: Longmans, 1937, p. 101
20 Goulter, op. cit., p. 11
21 New Hall archives
22 'Convent boarding schools for young ladies', *Fraser's Magazine*, June 1874
23 Don, op. cit.
24 O'Leary: op. cit., p. 67
25 Margaret Wynne Nevinson: *Life's Fitful Fever*. London: A. & C. Black, 1926
26 White, *Frost in May*, p. 54
27 Carbery: op. cit., p. 102

28 Mary Catharine Elizabeth Chambers: *The Life of Mary Ward*. London: Burns & Oates, 1882, vol. I, p. 267
29 *The History of the Bar Convent*. Godalming, n.d.
30 Thomas Corbishley, SJ: *The Life of Reverend Mother M. Cecilia Marshall IBVM*. London: Hamish Hamilton, 1969, p. 48
31 *History of the New Hall Community of Canonesses Regular of the Holy Sepulchre*
32 Wadham: op. cit., p. 20
33 ibid.
34 *Schools Inquiry Commission Report*, 1868, vol. IX
35 [Percy H. Fitzgerald]: *School-days at Saxonhurst*. Edinburgh: A. & C. Black, 1867
36 White: 'A child of the Five Wounds', in Greene, op. cit.
37 Mary Winefride Sturman: *The Ursulines of Westgate-on-Sea 1904–1979*
38 Wadham: op. cit., p. 238
39 *Mayfield Centenary 1863–1963*
40 Wadham: op. cit., p. 284
41 Dorothy A. Mostyn: *The Story of a House: Farnborough Hill*. 1980
42 Nevinson: op. cit., p. 29
43 *St Mary's* [Wantage] *School Magazine* (jubilee number), 1923
44 Sister Mark Orchard, interview with Simon Midgley, the *Independent*, 16 March 1989

Chapter 8 Boarding School Life

1 Cecily Don: 'The best years of your life' (letter to author)
2 Frances Knight: letter to author
3 Marjorie Morris: letter to author
4 Dorothea Beale: *On the Education of Women* (paper read to the Social Science Congress, October 1865). London, 1866
5 George R. Parkin: *Edward Thring*. London: Macmillan, 1898
6 Charlotte M. Yonge: *Womankind*. London: Mozley & Smith, 3rd edn 1878, p. 31
7 Marjorie Morris: letter to author
8 Angela Brazil: *My Own Schooldays*. London: Blackie, 1925, p. 149
9 From Old Paulina 1919–1925, in *Paulina*, no. 159, 1978–9
10 Elsie J. Oxenham: *Expelled from School*. London: Collins, 1919, p. 9
11 Elizabeth North: *Dames*. London: Cape, 1981
12 Sheila MacLeod: *The Art of Starvation*. London: Virago, 1981, p. 56
13 Josephine Elder: *Evelyn Finds Herself*. London: OUP, 1929, p. 202
14 Charis U. Frankenberg: *Not Old, Madam, Vintage*. Lavenham, 1975
15 John Rae: *The Public School Revolution*. London: Faber, 1981, p. 96
16 A. Mary Shaw (ed.): *When You Were There. Reflections on Edgehill College, 1884–1984*, p. 132
17 Louise Minet, writing in *Bedgebury*, 1987, pp. 68–9
18 Rebekah Jackson, in ibid., p. 64
19 'The aggressive reserve of adolescence', anonymous article in Walthamstow Hall archives
20 Elizabeth Hamilton: *A River Full of Stars*. London: Deutsch, 1954, p. 171

21 Margaret Nevinson: *Life's Fitful Fever*. London: A. & C. Black, 1926, p. 22
22 H.M. Swanwick: *I Have Been Young*. London: Gollancz, 1935, p. 48
23 Christine Flemington: letter to author
24 Don: op. cit.
25 *Machio* (Rickmansworth Masonic School bicentenary magazine, 1788–1988), p. 13
26 Hamilton: op. cit., p. 104
27 'The Book of Bedgebury' 1920 (unpublished), school archives
28 Elsie Pike and Constance E. Curryer: *The Story of Walthamstow Hall, 1838–1970*. 1973, p. 47
29 Anne Wells and Susan Meads (comps): *S. Mary and S. Anne: the second fifty years*. 1974
30 MacLeod: op. cit., p. 59
31 Elizabeth Bowen: 'The Apple Tree', in *Collected Stories*. London: Cape, 1980
32 Margaret Cole: *Growing up into Revolution*. London: Longmans, 1949, p. 26
33 Priscilla Bain: *St Swithun's: a centenary history*. Chichester: Phillimore, 1984, p. 38
34 Katharine Whitehorn: 'The playing fields of Roedean', in *Roundabout*. London: Methuen, 1962, p. 125
35 Don: op. cit.
36 North: op. cit., p. 178
37 Elizabeth Manners (ed.): *Felixstowe College, 1929–1979*, p. 9
38 Marjorie Morris: letter to author
39 [Margaret Haig Mackworth] Lady Rhondda: *This Was My World*. London: Macmillan, 1933, p. 46
40 Elizabeth Sturge: *Reminiscences of My Life*. Bristol, 1928, p. 140
41 North: op. cit., p. 38
42 Gwen Farish and Miriam Napier Jones (eds): *Acorn to Oak: some memories of Oakdene School 1911–1959*. 1962
43 Walthamstow Hall archives
44 Charis Barnett's diary, St Paul's Girls' School archives
45 M.A. Douglas and C.R. Ash: *The Godolphin School, 1726–1926*. London: Longmans, 1928, p. 91
46 Joan Trowbridge (ed.): *Durham High School: a centenary celebration 1884–1984*
47 Elizabeth Bowen: *To the North*. London: Cape, 1932
48 [Mabel Williams]: *Notes on the Clergy Daughters' School, Casterton*. 1935
49 *St Mary's* [Wantage] *School Magazine* (jubilee number), 1923
50 E.M. Saunders: *A Progress: Channing School 1885–1985*. 1984, p. 78

Chapter 9 Authority: Headmistresses and their Staff

1 Dodie Smith: *Look Back with Mixed Feelings*. London: W.H. Allen, 1978, p. 12
2 G.E. Evans: *So Hateth She Derknesse: a biography of Edith A. Willey, 1895–1970*. London: Whitefriars Press, 1971, p. 94
3 H. Winifred Sturge and Theodora Clark: *The Mount School, York, 1785 to 1814, 1831 to 1931*. London: Dent, 1931, p. 100

4 Honor Osborne and Peggy Manisty: *A History of the Royal School for Daughters of Officers of the Army, 1864–1965*. London: Hodder & Stoughton, 1966, p. 76
5 *King Edward's Grammar School for Girls, Handsworth, 1883–1983*, p. 80
6 Thomas Corbishley SJ: *The Life of Reverend Mother M. Cecilia Marshall IBVM*. London: Hamish Hamilton, 1969, p. 114. He was speaking, however, not of Mother Cecilia but of a colleague, Mother Ignatius.
7 Gwen Farish and Miriam Napier Jones (eds): *Acorn to Oak: some memories of Oakdene School, 1911–1959*. 1962, p. 43
8 A. Mary Shaw (ed.): *When You Were There. Reflections on Edgehill College, 1884–1984*, p. 32
9 Elspeth Mitchell (ed.): *Laurel Bank School, 1903–1953*. Glasgow, 1953, p. 123
10 Margaret Fletcher: *O, Call Back Yesterday*. Oxford: Shakespeare Head Press, 1939, p. 48
11 Sylvia Harrop: *The Merchant Taylors' School for Girls, Crosby: one hundred years of achievement 1888–1988*. Liverpool: University Press, 1988, ch. 4 passim
12 Kay Stedmond: *St Mary's School, Calne, 1873–1986*, p. 113
13 Elizabeth Hamilton: *A River Full of Stars*. London: Deutsch, 1954, p. 105
14 Annabel Huth Jackson: *A Victorian Childhood*. London: Methuen, 1932, p. 132
15 F. Cecily Steadman: *In the Days of Miss Beale*. London: E.J. Burrow, 1931, p. 99
16 Jackson: op. cit., p. 148
17 *Rye St Antony School Magazine*, 1968, p. 7
18 Unpublished recollections of Emma Catherine Childs (Pollard). Somerville College, Oxford, archives (From extract printed in Somerville College Report, 1988)
19 Roma Goyder: *Hayseed to Harvest: memories of Katherine Cox and Hayes Court School*. Colchester: 1985, p. 15
20 Quoted by M. Vivian Hughes: *A London Family 1870–1900*. London: OUP, 1946, p. 191
21 Farish and Jones (eds): op. cit., p. 54
22 Joanna Turner (comp.): *B.M. Sanderson and Badminton School, 1947–66*. 1988, p. 31
23 Jean Storry (ed.): *At Badminton with B.M.B.* 1982, p. 16
24 Sturge and Clark: op. cit., p. 103
25 Joan Trowbridge (ed.): *Durham High School: a centenary celebration 1884–1984*, p. 20
26 Valentine Noake: *History of the Alice Ottley School, Worcester*. 1952, p. 94
27 Anne Ridler: *Olive Willis and Downe House*. London: Murray, 1967, pp. 140–3
28 Mary James (ed.): *Alice Ottley, First Head-Mistress of the Worcester High School for Girls, 1883–1912*. London: Longmans, 1914, p. 246
29 From Charis Barnett's diary, St Paul's Girls' School archives
30 *The Jubilee Book, Bournemouth High School – Talbot Heath, 1886–1946*, ch. IX
31 Janet Whitcut: *Edgbaston High School, 1876–1976*. 1976, p. 84
32 Harrop: op. cit., p. 108
33 Winifred I. Candler: *King Edward VI High School for Girls 1883–1925*. London: Benn, 1928, p. 50

34 Joan Lightwood: *The Park School, Glasgow, 1880–1980*, p. 32
35 *St Brandon's School: 150 Years 1831–1981*
36 John Berchmans Dockery OFM: *They That Build: the life of Mother Clare of Brentwood*. London: Burns & Oates, 1963, p. 84
37 Molly Casey: *Hemdean House School, Caversham*. 1984
38 Whitcut: op. cit., p. 114
39 Patricia Lancaster: 'The human predicament', in *On the Map* (GSA newsletter), autumn 1988
40 Harrop: op. cit., p. 74
41 Margaret E. Popham: *Boring – Never!* London: Johnson, 1968, p. 110
42 D.F.P. Hiley: *Pedagogue Pie*. London: Ivor Nicholson & Watson, 1936, p. 14
43 Josephine Elder: *Evelyn Finds Herself*. London: OUP, 1929, p. 59
44 Betty Boyden (ed.): *Call Back Yesterday: a collection of reminiscences to mark the centenary of Nottingham High School for Girls, 1875–1975*, p. 46
45 Mary McCarthy: *Memories of a Catholic Girlhood*. [1957] London: Penguin, 1963, p. 140
46 Lancaster, 'The human predicament', in *On the Map*
47 Winifred Lear: *I Like This Place*. Southport, privately printed, 1980, p. 21
48 [Margaret Haig Mackworth] Lady Rhondda: *This Was My World*. London: Macmillan, 1933
49 L.E. Savill, in Christine Arscott (ed.), *The Headmistress Speaks*. London: Kegan Paul, 1937, p. 59
50 Evans: op. cit., p. 35
51 *Machio* (Rickmansworth Masonic School bicentenary magazine, 1788–1988), p. 8
52 Lear: op. cit., p. 48
53 ibid., p. 159
54 Jackson: op. cit., p. 150
55 Sara A. Burstall: *The Story of the Manchester High School for Girls*. Manchester: University Press, 1911, p. 125
56 Sturge and Clark: op. cit., pp. 180, 181
57 Boyden (ed.): op. cit., p. 168
58 *Downe House Scrap-Book, 1907–1957*
59 Alice Baird (ed.): *I Was There: St James's, West Malvern*. 1956, p. 192
60 Steadman: op. cit., p. 147
61 Boyden (ed.): op. cit., p. 152
62 Catharine Carr: *The Spinning Wheel: City of Cardiff High School for Girls 1895–1955*. 1955, p. 28
63 Lear: op. cit., p. 61
64 Shaw (ed.): op. cit.
65 ibid.
66 Katharine Whitehorn: 'Down with skool', in *Only on Sundays*. London: Methuen, 1966, p. 159
67 *Schools Inquiry Commission Report*, 1868, vol. VIII, p. 48
68 Osborne and Manisty: op. cit., p. 40
69 Lightwood: op. cit., p. 30
70 Louie Angus: *Blue Skirts into Blue Stockings*. London: Ian Allan, 1981, p. 65
71 Amy K. Clarke: *A History of the Cheltenham Ladies' College 1853–1953*. London: Faber, 1953, p. 79

72 Felicia Lamb and Helen Pickthorn: *Locked-up Daughters*. London: Hodder & Stoughton, 1968, p. 65
73 Steadman: op. cit., p. 29
74 *Portrait of Benenden 1924–1974*, pp. 81, 114
75 [Mackworth]: op. cit., p. 58
76 Kathleen Gibberd: *Politics on the Blackboard*. London: Faber, 1954, p. 51
77 'Further confessions of a house-mistress', *Moretonian*, 1986–7, p. 121
78 Mary Don: 'Some memories and thoughts on a convent education' (letter to author)
79 Shaw (ed.): op. cit., p. 92
80 Sturge and Clark: op. cit.
81 Ursula Roberts (ed.): 'Memories of Moreton' (unpublished)
82 *Portrait of Benenden, 1924–1974*, p. 14

Chapter 10 Work and Play

1 Dorothea P. Carew: *Many Years, Many Girls: the history of a school 1862–1942* [Queenwood School, Eastbourne]. Dublin: Browne & Nolan, 1967, p. 9
2 Francis J. Grund: *Aristocracy in America*. [1839] New York: Harper Torchbooks, 1959, p. 68
3 'Thoughts on some of the present defects in boarding schools for girls', *Victoria Magazine*, vol. XXVII, 1876, p. 432
4 M. Vivian Hughes: *A London Family*. London: OUP, 1946, p. 186
5 Constance Maynard: *Between College Terms*. London: Nisbet, 1910, p. 180
6 Winifred Peck: *A Little Learning*. London: Faber, 1952, p. 124
7 Dorothea Beale: *On the Education of Women* (paper read to the Social Science Congress, October 1865). London, 1866
8 Hughes: op. cit., p. 173
9 Peck: op. cit., p. 36
10 ibid., pp. 86–8
11 Frances Power Cobbe: *Life*. London: R. Bentley, 1894, vol. I, p. 66
12 Roma Goyder: *Hayseed to Harvest: memories of Katherine Cox and Hayes Court School*. Colchester, 1985, p. 57
13 Janet Erskine Stuart: *The Education of Catholic Girls*. London: Longmans, 1911, p. 154
14 *Downe House Scrap-Book, 1907–1957*
15 Peck: op. cit., p. 87
16 Elspeth Mitchell (ed.): *Laurel Bank School, 1903–1953*, p. 106
17 Joanna Turner (comp.): *B.M. Sanderson and Badminton School*. 1988, p. 107
18 Goyder: op. cit., p. 51
19 *Stannite* (St Anne's, Windermere magazine) 1983
20 Valentine Noake: *History of the Alice Ottley School, Worcester*. 1952, p. 100
21 *Paulina, 1904–1979*
22 Ursula Roberts (ed.): 'Memories of Moreton' (unpublished)
23 Vera Brittain: *Testament of Youth*. London: Gollancz, 1933, ch. 2
24 Turner (comp.): op. cit., p. 98
25 Sara A. Burstall: *The Story of the Manchester High School for Girls*. Manchester: University Press, 1911, p. 107

26 Stuart: op. cit., p. 120
27 Joan Lightwood: *The Park School, Glasgow, 1880–1980*, p. 20
28 Joan Bungay (ed.): *Redland High School for Girls, 1882–1982*, p. 79
29 V.E. Stack (ed.): *Oxford High School, Girls' Public Day School Trust, 1875–1960*. 1963, p. 79
30 Priscilla Bain: *St Swithun's: a centenary history*. Chichester: Phillimore, 1984, p. 10
31 Joan Trowbridge (ed.): *Durham High School: a centenary celebration 1884–1984*, p. 64
32 Jocelyn Logan: *Upper Chine*. 1987, p. 42
33 Stuart: op. cit., p. 118
34 'The Book of Bedgebury' (unpublished). Bedgebury School archives, 1920
35 *S. Helen and S. Katharine School Magazine*, 1969
36 *West Heath School Magazine*, no. 75, 1987
37 Peck: op. cit., p. 139
38 *Portrait of Benenden, 1924–1974*, p. 56
39 H. Winifred Sturge and Theodora Clark: *The Mount School, York, 1785 to 1814, 1831 to 1931*. London: Dent, 1931, p. 40
40 *Schools Inquiry Commission Report*, vol. X, p. 303
41 *Winchester High School Chronicle*, 1899–1900
42 *Cheltenham Ladies' College Magazine*, 1905
43 *St Leonards School, 1877–1977*. 1977, p. 24
44 Lightwood: op. cit., p. 60
45 *St Mary's* [Wantage] *School Magazine* (jubilee number), 1923
46 Mary Catherine Goulter: *Schoolday Memories*. London: Burns & Oates, 1922, p. 39
47 Elaine Kaye: *A History of Queen's College, London, 1848–1972*. London: Chatto & Windus, 1972, p. 101
48 *Sherborne School for Girls, 1889–1949*. 1949
49 Goyder: op. cit., p. 41
50 Bungay (ed.): op. cit., p. 28
51 Janet Whitcut: *Edgbaston High School, 1876–1976*. 1976, p. 49
52 Sophia Kelly (ed.): *Life of Mrs Sherwood*. London: Darton, 1857, p. 51
53 Sturge and Clark, op. cit., p. 189
54 *Schools Inquiry Commission Report*, vol. I, pp. 548–9
55 ibid., vol. VII, appendix XII, p. 587
56 ibid., vol. V, p. 265
57 ibid., vol. V, p. 740
58 Prunella R. Bodington (ed.): *Norwich High School 1875–1950*, p. 40
59 Barbara Bourke (ed.): *The Laurels 1872–1972 Wroxall Abbey*, p. 29
60 Jonathan May: *Madame Bergman-Österburg*. London: Harrap, 1969, p. 52
61 Margaret James: *The Kent College Saga, 1886–1986*, p. 70
62 ibid., p. 14
63 John Berchmans Dockery OFM: *They That Build: the life of Mother Clare of Brentwood*. London: Burns & Oates, 1963, p. 138
64 See Mary Cadogan and Patricia Craig: *You're a Brick, Angela*. London: Gollancz, 1976, pp. 162 et seq.
65 Ruby Ginner: *The Revived Greek Dance*. London: Methuen, 1933, p. 20

66 *The Story of the Mary Datchelor School, 1887–1957*. London: Hodder & Stoughton, 1957
67 K.M. Westaway (ed.): *A History of Bedford High School*. 1932, p. 49
68 Mary C. Malim and Henrietta C. Escreet (eds): *The Book of the Blackheath High School*. 1927, p. 108
69 F. Cecily Steadman: *In the Days of Miss Beale*. London: E.J. Burrow, 1931, p. 83
70 M.G. Mills: *Brighton and Hove High School 1876–1952*. 1953, p. 39
71 Malim and Escreet (eds): op. cit., p. 115
72 Bain: op. cit., p. 9
73 Bourke (ed.): op. cit., p. 15
74 *Paulina*, March 1927
75 'St Paul's Girls' School' in *Queen*, 8 July 1922
76 ibid., 14 October 1922
77 ibid., 1 July 1922
78 Goulter, op. cit., p. 37
79 *Portrait of Benenden, 1924–1974*, p. 57
80 Margaret Boyd: *Lacrosse Playing and Coaching*. London: Nicholas Kaye, 1959
81 Jane Frances Dove in Dorothea Beale, Lucy A.M. Soulsby and J.F. Dove: *Work and Play in Girls' Schools*. London: Longmans, 1898
82 Nancy Spain: *A Funny Thing Happened on the Way*. London: Hutchinson, 1964, p. 31

Chapter 11 Discipline

1 M.V. Hughes: *A London Family 1870–1900*. London: OUP, 1946, p. 165
2 ibid., p. 166
3 Rosalind Onians (ed.): *St Helen's: the first eighty years, 1899–1979*. 1980, p. 77
4 Felicia Lamb and Helen Pickthorn: *Locked-up Daughters*. London: Hodder & Stoughton, 1968, p. 64
5 H.M. Swanwick: *I Have Been Young*. London: Gollancz, 1935, p. 79
6 R.M. Scrimgeour (ed.): *The North London Collegiate School, 1850–1950*. Oxford: University Press, 1950, p. 203
7 Kathleen Gibberd: *Politics on the Blackboard*. London: Faber, 1954, p. 51
8 Louie Angus: *Blue Skirts into Blue Stockings*. London: Ian Allan, 1981, p. 22
9 A. Mary Shaw (ed.): *When You Were There. Reflections on Edgehill College, 1884–1984*, p. 94
10 ibid., p. 95
11 M.A. Douglas and C.R. Ash: *The Godolphin School, 1726–1926*. London: Longmans, 1928, p. 42
12 Sister Phyllis CSMV: *St Mary's School: a personal history*. Wantage, 1973, p. 19
13 Catharine Carr: *The Spinning Wheel: City of Cardiff High School for Girls 1845–1955*. 1955, p. 37
14 Douglas and Ash: op. cit., p. 84
15 Lamb and Pickthorn: op. cit., p. 64
16 Carr: op. cit., p. 65
17 *S. Helen and S. Katharine School Magazine*, 1969

18 Mallory Wober: *English Girls' Boarding Schools*. London: Allen Lane, 1971, p. 118
19 Diary of Dorothy Christmas, 1963–4
20 Angus: op. cit., p. 102
21 Lucien Perey (ed.): *Memoirs of the Princesse de Ligne*. London: R. Bentley, 1887
22 Joan Trowbridge (ed.): *Durham High School: a centenary celebration 1884–1984*, p. 62
23 [Dorothy Kilner]: *Anecdotes of a Boarding School*. London: Marshall, 1790
24 Shaw (ed.): op. cit., p. 94
25 Nancy Spain: *Why I'm not a Millionaire*. London: Hutchinson, 1966, p. 18
26 L.M. Faithfull: *You and I*. London: Chatto & Windus, 1927
27 Elsie Pike and Constance E. Curryer: *The Story of Walthamstow Hall*. 1973, p. 33
28 *Prospect* (Convent of the Assumption school magazine), 1980
29 'A word for the convent boarding schools', *Fraser's Magazine*, October 1874
30 [Mabel Williams]: *Notes on the Clergy Daughters' School, Casterton*. 1935
31 *Badminton School, 1858–1958*
32 F. Cecily Steadman: *In the Days of Miss Beale*. London: E.J. Burrow, 1931, p. 47
33 *St Mary's* [Wantage] *School Magazine* (jubilee number), 1923
34 Julia Grant, Katherine H. McCutcheon and Ethel F. Sanders (eds): *St Leonards School, 1877–1927*. London: Oxford University Press [1928?], p. 100
35 Gwen Farish and Miriam Napier Jones (eds): *Acorn to Oak: some memories of Oakdene School, 1911–1959*. 1962, p. 11
36 *King Edward's Grammar School for Girls, Handsworth, 1883–1983*, p. 64
37 *The Story of Queen Elizabeth Girls' School* [Barnet], *1888–1988*, p. 25
38 Frances Power Cobbe: *Life*. London: R. Bentley, 1894, vol. I, p. 61
39 Egerton Castle (ed.): *The Jerningham Letters*. London: R. Bentley, 1896, vol. I, p. 29
40 Honor Osborne and Peggy Manisty: *A History of the Royal School for Daughters of Officers of the Army, 1864–1965*. London: Hodder & Stoughton, 1966, p. 77
41 *St Mary's Hall Magazine* (centenary number), 1936
42 Frances Page: *Christ's Hospital, Hertford*. London: Bell, 1953
43 Dorothea L. Pullan: *The Record of the Clergy Orphan Corporation School for Girls 1749–1949*
44 Winifred Peck: *A Little Learning*. London: Faber, 1952, p. 70
45 Betty Boyden (ed.): *Call Back Yesterday: (cf. p. 393) a collection of reminiscences to mark the centenary of the Nottingham High School for Girls, 1875–1975*, p. 119
46 Angus: op. cit., p. 22
47 Rachel K. Davis: *Four Miss Pinkertons*. London: Williams & Norgate, 1936, p. 28
48 John Rae: *The Public School Revolution*. London: Faber, 1981, pp. 98, 99

Chapter 12 Sex and Emotion

1 Jonathan Gathorne-Hardy: *The Public School Phenomenon*. London: Hodder & Stoughton, 1977, p. 381

2 Katharine Whitehorn: 'The playing fields of Roedean', in *Roundabout*. London: Methuen, 1962, p. 127
3 [Dorothy Strachey Bussey] Olivia: *Olivia*. London: Hogarth Press, 1949
4 Rosalind Wade: *Children, Be Happy*. London: Gollancz, 1931. There is a copy of this rare book in the Opie Collection of Historical Children's Books in the Bodleian Library.
5 H. Winifred Sturge and Theodora Clark: *The Mount School, York, 1785 to 1814, 1831 to 1931*. London: Dent, 1931, p. 71
6 St Michael's, Limpsfield: *Times Remembered*, p. 44
7 Jane Frances Dove in Dorothea Beale, Lucy A.M. Soulsby and J.F. Dove: *Work and Play in Girls' Schools*. London: Longmans, 1898, p. 423
8 Elizabeth North: *Dames*. London: Cape, 1981, p. 180
9 Elsie J. Oxenham: *The Girls of the Abbey School*. London: Collins, 1921, p. 61
10 Elsie J. Oxenham: *The Abbey Girls Win Through*. London: Collins, 1923, p. 9
11 Rachel K. Davis: *Four Miss Pinkertons*. London: Williams & Norgate, 1936, p. 69
12 *Harpers & Queen*, July 1980
13 *King Edward's Grammar School for Girls, Handsworth, 1883–1983*, p. 60
14 Diana Hopkinson: *The Incense Tree*. London: Routledge & Kegan Paul, 1968, p. 40
15 Diary of Nina Bryan, in Betty Boyden (ed.): *Call Back Yesterday: a collection of reminiscences to mark the centenary of Nottingham High School for Girls, 1875–1975*, p. 159
16 North: op. cit., p. 102
17 Mary Cadogan and Patricia Craig: *You're a Brick, Angela*. London: Gollancz, 1976, p. 196
18 Josephine Elder: *Evelyn Finds Herself*. London: Oxford University Press, 1929, p. 207
19 Mrs George du Horne Vaizey: *Tom and Some Other Girls*. London: Cassell, 1901, p. 278
20 Mary James: *Alice Ottley, First Headmistress of the Worcester High School for Girls 1883–1912*. London: Longmans, 1914
21 *The Recollections of a Northumbrian Lady, being the Memoirs of Barbara Charlton*. London: Cape, 1949, p. 67
22 Antonia White: 'A child of the Five Wounds', in Graham Greene (ed.), *The Old School*. London: Cape, 1934
23 Mary Catherine Goulter: *Schoolday Memories*. London: Burns & Oates, 1922, p. 53
24 L.M. Faithfull: 'Real and counterfeit friendships', in *You and I*. London: Chatto & Windus, 1927
25 Davis: op. cit., p. 78
26 Theodora Benson: 'Hot water bottle love', in Greene (ed.), op. cit.
27 Hopkinson: op. cit., p. 43
28 Sheila MacLeod: *The Art of Starvation*. London: Virago, 1981, p. 46
29 John Rae: *The Public School Revolution*. London: Faber, 1981, p. 128
30 Robert Graves: *Goodbye to All That*. London: Cape, 1929, p. 40
31 Barbara Bourke (ed.): *The Laurels 1872–1972 Wroxall Abbey*, p. 142
32 H.M. Swanwick: *I Have Been Young*. London: Gollancz, 1935, p. 74

33 Boyden (ed.): op. cit., p. 118
34 ibid., p. 170
35 ibid., p. 137
36 Margaret K.B. Sommerville: *The Merchant Maiden Hospital*. Edinburgh, 1970, p. 56
37 Margaret Nevinson: *Life's Fitful Fever*. London: A. & C. Black, 1926, p. 25
38 Sister Phyllis CSMV: *St Mary's School* [Wantage]: *a personal history*. 1973, p. 10
39 Evelyn Sharp: *The Making of a Schoolgirl*. London: Marshall & Russell, 1897, p. 105
40 ibid., p. 101
41 Faithfull: op. cit., p. 51
42 *Holly Club* [Lady Eleanor Holles School] *Commemoration Magazine*, 1986
43 E.M. Saunders: *A Progress: Channing School 1885–1985*, p. 99
44 Goulter: op. cit., p. 33
45 William Byron Forbush: *A Guide Book to Childhood*. London: Hutchinson, 1921, p. 417
46 William A. White: *The Mental Hygiene of Childhood*. London: Heinemann, 1919, p. 121
47 *Portrait of Benenden, 1924–1974*, p. 85
48 Margaret James: *The Kent College Saga, 1886–1986*, p. 53
49 Alice Baird (ed.): *I Was There: St James's, West Malvern*, 1956, p. 273
50 A. Mary Shaw (ed.): *When You Were There. Reflections on Edgehill College, 1884–1984*, p. 87
51 Marjorie Morris: letter to author
52 Margaret Popham: *Boring – Never!* London: Johnson, 1968, p. 50
53 Louie Angus: *Blue Skirts into Blue Stockings*. London: Ian Allan, 1981, p. 85
54 [Margaret Haig Mackworth] Lady Rhondda: *This Was My World*. London: Macmillan, 1933, p. 48
55 Sylvanus Stall: *What a Young Boy Ought to Know*. Philadelphia, 1897
56 Mary Wood-Allen and Sylvanus Stall: *What a Young Girl Ought to Know*. Philadelphia, 1897
57 Lyman B. Sperry: *Confidential Talks with Young Women*. Philadelphia, 1894
58 Elizabeth Bowen: *To the North*. London: Cape, 1932, p. 61
59 Sylvia Harrop: *The Merchant Taylors' School for Girls, Crosby*. Liverpool: University Press, 1988, p. 105
60 V.E. Stack (ed.): *Oxford High School, Girls' Public Day School Trust, 1875–1960*. 1963, p. 98
61 Diary of Nina Bryan, in Boyden (ed.), op. cit., p. 158
62 Mallory Wober: *English Girls' Boarding Schools*. London: Allen Lane, 1971, p. 59
63 North: op. cit., p. 222
64 Katharine M. Westaway (ed.): *Seventy-five Years: the story of Bedford High School, 1882–1957*

Chapter 13 Crises

1 Honor Osborne and Peggy Manisty: *A History of the Royal School for Daughters of Officers of the Army, 1864–1965*. London: Hodder & Stoughton, 1966, p. 73
2 Jocelyn Logan: *Upper Chine*. 1987, p. 60
3 Rosalind Onians (ed.): *St Helen's: the first eighty years, 1899–1979*. 1980, p. 14
4 Kay Stedmond: *St Mary's School, Calne, 1873–1986*, pp. 52, 53
5 Cheltenham Ladies' College, Fifth Annual Report
6 Elsie Pike and Constance E. Curryer: *The Story of Walthamstow Hall, 1838–1970*. 1973, p. 28
7 Beatrix Dunning (ed.): *Francis Holland Church of England School for Girls. Graham Street Memories*. 1931, p. 96
8 John Berchmans Dockery OFM: *They that Build: the life of Mother Clare of Brentwood*. London: Burns & Oates, 1963, p. 69
9 Roma Goyder: *Hayseed to Harvest: memories of Katherine Cox and Hayes Court School*. Colchester: 1985, p. 97
10 Sylvia Harrop: *The Merchant Taylors' School for Girls, Crosby*. Liverpool: University Press, 1988, p. 165
11 John Rae: *The Public School Revolution*. London: Faber, 1981, p. 132
12 ibid., p. 142
13 Edith E. Wright: *The Children of Thy Servants: memories of Highbury and Limpsfield 1850–1937*
14 George Parkin: *Edward Thring*. London: Macmillan, 1898, p. 324
15 John Morris SJ: *The Life of Mother Henrietta Kerr*. London: Burns & Oates, 1886
16 Arthur Marshall: *Giggling in the Shrubberies*. London: Collins, 1985
17 Margaret Fletcher: *O, Call Back Yesterday*. Oxford: Shakespeare Head Press, 1939
18 Sheila MacLeod: *The Art of Starvation*. London: Virago, 1981
19 *Bridlington Chronicle*, 1 January 1915. Quoted by Vera Brittain in *Testament of Friendship*. London: Macmillan, 1940
20 Margaret James: *The Kent College Saga, 1886–1986*, p. 85
21 ibid., p. 86
22 Betty Boyden (ed.): *Call Back Yesterday: a collection of reminiscences to mark the centenary of the Nottingham High School for Girls, 1875–1975*, p. 121
23 Dorothy P. Carew: *Many Years, Many Girls: the history of a school 1862–1942* [Queenwood School, Eastbourne]. Dublin: Browne & Nolan, 1967
24 Susan Hicklin: *Polished Corners, 1878–1978. A hundred years of contemporary life in and out of Francis Holland School, NW1*. 1978
25 ibid.
26 Mary C. Malim and Henrietta C. Escreet (eds): *The Book of the Blackheath High School*. 1927, p. 177
27 Catharine Carr: *The Spinning Wheel: City of Cardiff High School for Girls 1895–1955*, pp. 74, 75
28 A.K. Clarke: *A History of the Cheltenham Ladies' College 1853–1979*. Saxmundham: John Catt, 1979, p. 20
29 Boyden (ed.): op. cit., p. 112
30 Dorothea L. Pullan: *The Record of the Clergy Orphan Corporation School for Girls 1749–1949*

31 Thomas Corbishley SJ: *The Life of Reverend Mother M. Cecilia Marshall IBVM*. London: Hamish Hamilton, 1969, p. 121
32 Elizabeth Hamilton, *A River Full of Stars*. London: Deutsch, 1954, p. 182
33 Winifred I. Candler, Ailsa M. Jaques and B.M.W. Dobbie: *King Edward VI High School for Girls, Birmingham*. London: Benn, 1971
34 Elizabeth Manners (ed.): *Felixstowe College, 1929–1979*. 1980, p. 15
35 Margaret Popham: *Boring – Never!* London: Johnson, 1968, p. 137
36 E.M. Saunders: *A Progress: Channing School 1885–1985*, p. 56
37 Mary Don: 'Some memories and thoughts on a convent education' (letter to author)
38 *Portrait of Benenden, 1924–1974*, p. 93
39 ibid., p. 40
40 Catholic Record Society: *Miscellanea X*. London, 1915
41 'History of the School of Jesus and Mary; early years of the Congregation' (unpublished). 1888
42 Elsie Quarrie: *The School that Refused to Die*. [Francis Holland School, SW1] 1981
43 Logan: op. cit., p. 62

Chapter 14 Envoi

1 Lucy Kinloch: *A World Within a School*. London: Warne, 1937
2 Anne Valery: *The Edge of a Smile*. London: Peter Owen, 1977, p. 21
3 Betty Boyden (ed.): *Call Back Yesterday: a collection of reminiscences to mark the centenary of the Nottingham High School for Girls, 1875–1975*, p. 149
4 Annabel Huth Jackson: *A Victorian Childhood*. London: Methuen, 1932, p. 163
5 Joanna Turner (comp.): *B.M. Sanderson and Badminton School*. 1988, p. 113
6 Reminiscences of Hope Maxwell, Walthamstow Hall archives
7 Kaye Webb: *The St Trinian's Story*. London: Perpetua Books, 1959
8 Diana Hopkinson: *The Incense Tree*. London: Routledge & Kegan Paul, 1968, p. 37
9 Enid Pinto (1910–15), St Paul's Girls' School archives
10 Anne Ridler: *Olive Willis and Downe House*. London: John Murray, 1967, p. 123
11 [Margaret Haig Mackworth] Lady Rhondda: *This Was My World*. London: Macmillan, 1933, p. 79
12 Rosemary Anne Sisson (1936–9), in *Cheltenham Ladies' College Centenary*, 1953
13 *Chronicle* (magazine of the convents of the Sacred Heart), 1963
14 Boyden (ed.): op. cit., p. 130

Bibliography

The bibliography is in six sections: primary sources, secondary sources, fiction, journals and magazines, archives and other unpublished sources, and school histories.

Primary Sources

Angus, Louie: *Blue Skirts into Blue Stockings*. London: Ian Allan, 1981

Arscott, Christine (ed.): *The Headmistress Speaks*. London: Kegan Paul, 1937

Barlow, Amy: *Seventh Child: the autobiography of a schoolmistress*. London: Duckworth, 1969

Beale, Dorothea, *Does Modern Education Ennoble*? London, 1905

—— *On the Education of Women* (paper read to the Social Science Congress, October 1865). London, 1866

Beale, Dorothea, Lucy H.M. Soulsby and Jane Frances Dove: *Work and Play in Girls' Schools*. London: Longmans, 1898

Boyd, Margaret: *Lacrosse Playing and Coaching*. London: Nicholas Kaye, 1959

Brazil, Angela: *My Own Schooldays*. London: Blackie, 1925

Brittain, Vera: *Testament of Youth*. London: Gollancz, 1933

Burstall, Sara A.: *English High Schools for Girls*. London: Longmans, 1907

Burstall, Sara A. and M.A. Douglas (eds): *Public Schools for Girls: a series of papers on their history, aims, and schemes of study*. London: Longmans, 1911

Cannan, May Wedderburn: *Grey Ghosts and Voices*. Kineton: Roundwood Press, 1976

Castle, Egerton (ed.): *The Jerningham Letters*. London: R. Bentley, 1896

Catholic Record Society: *Miscellanea* X. London, 1915

Charlton, Barbara: *The Recollections of a Northumbrian Lady, being the Memoirs of Barbara Charlton*. London: Cape, 1949

Cobbe, Frances Power: *Life*. London: R. Bentley, 1894

Cole, Margaret: *Growing up into Revolution*. London: Longmans, 1949

Coster, Geraldine: *Self-government in Schools*. Oxford: Blackwell, 1923

Defoe, Daniel: *Everybody's Business is Nobody's Business*. London, 1725

Faithfull, Lilian M.: *In the House of My Pilgrimage*. London: Chatto & Windus, 1925

—— *You and I. Saturday talks at Cheltenham*. London: Chatto & Windus, 1927

[Fitzgerald, Percy H.]: *School-days at Saxonhurst*. Edinburgh: A. & C. Black, 1867

Fletcher, Margaret: *O, Call Back Yesterday*. Oxford: Shakespeare Head Press, 1939

Forbush, William Byron: *A Guide Book to Childhood*. London: Hutchinson, 1921
Frankenberg, Charis U.: *Not Old, Madam, Vintage*. Lavenham (privately printed), 1975 (St Paul's Girls' School archives)
Gibberd, Kathleen: *Politics on the Blackboard*. London: Faber, 1954
Ginner, Ruby: *The Revived Greek Dance*. London: Methuen, 1933
Goulter, Mary Catherine: *Schoolday Memories*. London: Burns & Oates, 1922
Graves, Robert: *Goodbye to All That*. London: Cape, 1929
Greene, Graham (ed.): *The Old School*. London: Cape, 1934
Grund, Francis J.: *Aristocracy in America*. [1839] New York: Harper Torchbooks, 1959
Hall, G. Stanley: *Adolescence*. New York: Appleton, 1904
Hamilton, Elizabeth: *A River Full of Stars*. London: André Deutsch, 1954
Harrison, Jane Ellen: *Reminiscences of a Student's Life*. London: L. and V. Woolf, 1925
Hiley, D.F.P.: *Pedagogue Pie*. London: Ivor Nicholson & Watson, 1936
Hopkinson, Diana: *The Incense Tree*. London: Routledge & Kegan Paul, 1968
Howitt, Mary: *An Autobiography*, ed. Margaret Howitt. London: W. Isbister, 1889
Hughes, M. Vivian: *A London Family 1870–1900*. London: Oxford University Press, 1946
Independent Schools Yearbook: Girls' Schools. London: A. & C. Black, 1988
Jackson, Annabel Huth: *A Victorian Childhood*. London: Methuen, 1932
Jones, E.E. Constance: *As I Remember: an autobiographical ramble*. London: A. & C. Black, 1922
[Jones, Elizabeth Wilhelmina]: *Monograph commemorating the thirty-seven years' headship of Harrogate College 1898–1935 of 'M.E.' Jones*
Lear, Winifred: *I Like This Place*. Southport (privately printed), 1980
Locke, John: *Report of the Board of Trade Respecting the Relief of the Poor*. London, 1697
—— *Some Thoughts Concerning Education*. London, 1693
Lumsden, Louisa Innes: *Yellow Leaves: memories of a long life*. Edinburgh: Blackwood, 1933
McCarthy, Mary: *Memories of a Catholic Girlhood*. [1957] London: Penguin, 1963
[Mackworth, Margaret Haig] Lady Rhondda: *This Was My World*. London: Macmillan, 1933
MacLeod, Sheila: *The Art of Starvation*. London: Virago, 1981
Markham, Violet: *Return Passage*. London: Oxford University Press, 1953
Marshall, Arthur (ed.): *Giggling in the Shrubberies*. London: Collins, 1985
Maynard, Constance: *Between College Terms*. London: James Nisbet, 1910
Methods Used to Erecting Charity-Schools. London, 1714
Mitchison, Naomi: *Among You Taking Notes: the wartime diary of Naomi Mitchison 1939–1945*, ed. Dorothy Sheridan. London: Gollancz, 1985
'Lilian Mary Mott', a memoir by her husband, 1956 (Cheltenham Ladies' College archives)
Nevinson, Margaret Wynne: *Life's Fitful Fever*. London: A. & C. Black, 1926
Peck, Winifred: *A Little Learning, or A Victorian childhood*. London: Faber, 1952
Hannah Elizabeth Pipe 1831–1906, In Memoriam (privately printed).
Popham, Margaret E.: *Boring – Never!* London: Johnson, 1968
Pryde, David: *Pleasant Memories of a Busy Life*. Edinburgh: Blackwood, 1893

Schools Inquiry [Taunton] *Commission Report*, 1867–8
Sewell, Elizabeth: *Autobiography*. London: Longmans, 1908
—— *Principles of Education*. London: Longmans, 1865
Shore, Emily: *Journal*. London: Kegan Paul, 1891
Smith, Dodie: *Look Back with Mixed Feelings*. London: W.H. Allen, 1978
Smith, Mary Bentinck: *Ad Vitam: papers of a head mistress*. London: John Murray, 1927
Spain, Nancy: *A Funny Thing Happened on the Way*. London: Hutchinson, 1964
—— *Why I'm not a Millionaire*. London: Hutchinson, 1966
Sperry, Lyman: *Confidential Talks with Young Women*. Philadelphia, 1894
Stall, Sylvanus: *What a Young Boy Ought to Know*. Philadelphia, 1897
Sturge, Elizabeth: *Reminiscences of My Life*. Bristol, 1928
Swanwick, Helena M.: *I Have Been Young*. London: Gollancz, 1935
White, William A.: *The Mental Hygiene of Childhood*. London: Heinemann, 1919
Whitehorn, Katharine: 'Down with skool', *in Only on Sundays*. London: Methuen, 1966
—— 'The playing fields of Roedean', *in Roundabout*. London: Methuen, 1962
Wober, Mallory: *English Girls' Boarding Schools*. London: Allen Lane, 1971
Wood-Allen, Mary and Sylvanus Stall: *What a Young Girl Ought to Know*. Philadelphia, 1897
Yonge, Charlotte M.: *Womankind*. London: Mozley & Smith, 3rd edn 1878

Secondary Sources

Armour, Mary Andrew: *Cornelia*. Society of the Holy Child Jesus, 1979
Bedford, Sybille: *Aldous Huxley*. London: Chatto & Windus, 1974
Binfield, Clyde: *Belmont's Portias: Victorian non-conformists and middle-class education for girls*. London: Friends of Dr Williams's Library, 1981
Borer, Mary C.: *Willingly to School: a history of women's education*. Guildford and London: Lutterworth Press, 1976
Bowerman, Elsie: *Stands There a School: memoirs of Dame Frances Dove, DBE, founder of Wycombe Abbey School*. 1965
Bremner, C.S.: *The Education of Girls and Women in Great Britain*. London: Swan Sonnenschein, 1897
Brittain, Vera: *Testament of Friendship: the story of Winifred Holtby*. London: Macmillan, 1940
Burstall, Sara A.: *Retrospect and Prospect: sixty years of women's education*. London: Longmans, 1933
Cadogan, Mary and Patricia Craig: *You're a Brick, Angela*. London: Gollancz, 1976
Carbery, Mary: *The Farm by Lough Gur*. London: Longmans, 1937
Chambers, Mary Catharine Elizabeth: *The Life of Mary Ward*. London: Burns & Oates, 1882
Corbishley, Thomas, SJ: *The Life of Reverend Mother M. Cecilia Marshall, IBVM*. London: Hamish Hamilton, 1969
Davis, Rachel K.: *Four Miss Pinkertons*. London: Williams & Norgate, 1936
Delamont, Sara: *Knowledgeable Women: structuralism and the reproduction of elites*. London: Routledge & Kegan Paul, 1989

Dockery, John Berchmans, OFM: *They That Build: the life of Mother Clare of Brentwood*. London: Burns & Oates, 1963

Evans, G.E.: *So Hateth She Derknesse: a biography of Edith A. Willey, 1895–1970*. London: Whitefriars Press, 1971

Fletcher, Sheila: *Feminists and Bureaucrats*. Cambridge: University Press, 1980

Gardiner, Dorothy: *English Girlhood at School: a study of women's education through twelve centuries*. London: Oxford University Press, 1929

Gaskell, Elizabeth: *The Life of Charlotte Brontë*. London: Smith Elder, 1857

Gathorne-Hardy, Jonathan: *The Public School Phenomenon*. London: Hodder & Stoughton, 1977

Haddon, Celia: *Great Days and Jolly Days: the story of girls' school songs*. London: Hodder & Stoughton, 1977

Heeney, Brian: *Mission to the Middle Classes: the Woodard schools, 1848–1891*. London: SPCK, 1969

James, Mary E.: *Alice Ottley, First Head-Mistress of the Worcester High School for Girls, 1883–1912*. London: Longmans, 1914

Jones, M.G.: *The Charity School Movement*. Cambridge: University Press, 1938

Kamm, Josephine: *Hope Deferred: girls' education in English history*. London: Methuen, 1965

—— *How Different from Us: a biography of Miss Buss and Miss Beale*. London: Bodley Head, 1958

—— *Indicative Past*. London: Allen & Unwin, 1971

Kelly, Sophia (ed.): *The Life of Mrs Sherwood*. London: Darton, 1857

Kirk, K.E.: *The Story of the Woodard Schools*. London: Hodder & Stoughton, 1937

Lamb, Felicia and Helen Pickthorn: *Locked-up Daughters*. London: Hodder & Stoughton, 1968

Law, Alexander: *Education in Edinburgh in the Eighteenth Century*. London: University of London Press, 1965

May, Jonathan: *Madame Bergman-Österburg*. London: Harrap, 1969

Morris, John, SJ: *The life of Mother Henrietta Kerr*. London: Burns & Oates, 1886

Newsom, John: *The Education of Girls*. London: Faber, 1948

O'Leary, M.: *Education with a Tradition*. London: University of London Press, 1936

Ollard, Richard: *An English Education*. London: Collins, 1982

Ollerenshaw, Kathleen: *Education for Girls*. London: Faber, 1961

Otter, Sir John: *Nathaniel Woodard: a memoir of his life*. London: John Lane, 1925

Parkin, George R.: *Edward Thring*. London: Macmillan, 1898

Percival, Alicia: *The English Miss To-day and Yesterday*. London: Harrap, 1939

Perey, Lucien (ed.): *Memoirs of the Princesse de Ligne*, trans. Laura Ensor. London: R. Bentley, 1887

Phillips, Grace W.: *Smile, Bow, and Pass on: a biography of an avant-garde headmistress, Miss Iris M. Brooks ... Malvern Girls' College 1928–1954*. 1980

Pritchard, F.C.: *Methodist Secondary Education*. London: Epworth Press, 1949

Rae, John: *The Public School Revolution*. London: Faber, 1981

Raikes, Elizabeth: *Dorothea Beale of Cheltenham*. London: Archibald Constable, 1908

Richardson, Mary K.: *Mabel Digby* [Superior-General of the Society of the Sacred Heart 1872–1894]. London: Longmans, 1956

Ridler, Anne: *Olive Willis and Downe House. An adventure in education*. London: John Murray, 1967

Ridley, Annie E.: *Frances Mary Buss and her Work for Education*. London: Longmans, 1895

Sondheimer, Janet and Prunella Bodington: *The Girls' Public Day School Trust 1872–1972: a centenary review*

Steadman, F. Cecily: *In the Days of Miss Beale. A study of her work and influence*. London: E.J. Burrow, 1931

Stewart, W.A. Campbell: *Quakers and Education*. London: Epworth Press, 1953

Stoddart, Anna M.: *Life and Letters of Hannah E. Pipe*. Edinburgh: William Blackwood, 1908

Stuart, Janet Erskine: *The Education of Catholic Girls*. London: Longmans, 1911

Turner, Barry: *Equality for Some: the story of girls' education*. London: Ward Lock, 1974

Vicinus, Martha: *Independent Women*. London: Virago, 1985

Wadham, Juliana: *The Case of Cornelia Connelly*. London: Collins, 1956

Webb, Kaye: *The St Trinian's Story*. London: Perpetua Books, 1959

Zimmern, Alice: *The Renaissance of Girls' Education in England. A record of fifty years' progress*. London: A.D. Innes, 1898

Fiction

Bowen, Elizabeth: *Collected Stories*. London: Cape, 1980

Brazil, Angela: *A Patriotic Schoolgirl*. London: Blackie, 1918

[Bussey, Dorothy Strachey] Olivia: *Olivia*. London: Hogarth Press, 1949

Cannan, Joanna: *The Misty Valley*. London: T. Fisher Unwin, 1922

Elder, Josephine: *Evelyn Finds Herself*. London: Oxford University Press, 1929

Ewing, Juliana Horatia: *Six to Sixteen*. London: Bell, 1875

Kennedy, Margaret: *The Constant Nymph*. London: Heinemann, 1924

[Kilner, Dorothy]: *Anecdotes of a Boarding School*. London: Marshall, 1790

Kinloch, Lucy: *A World Within a School*. London: Warne, 1937

North, Elizabeth: *Dames*. London: Cape, 1981

Oxenham, Elsie J.: *The Abbey Girls Win Through*. London: Collins, 1923

—— *Expelled from School*. London: Collins, 1919

—— *The Girls of the Abbey School*. London: Collins, 1921

—— *The School Without a Name*. Edinburgh: Chambers, 1924

Sharp, Evelyn: *The Making of a Schoolgirl*. London: Marshall & Russell, 1897

—— *Rebel Women*. London: A.C. Fifield, 1910

Shy, Timothy and Ronald Searle: *The Terror of St Trinian's*. London: Max Parrish, 1952

Vaizey, Mrs George du Horne: *A College Girl*. London: Cassell, 1913

—— *Tom and Some Other Girls*. London: Cassell, 1901

Valery, Anne: *The Edge of a Smile*. London: Peter Owen, 1977

Wade, Rosalind: *Children, Be Happy*. London: Gollancz, 1931

White, Antonia: *Frost in May*. [1933] London: Virago, 1978

Willans, Geoffrey and Ronald Searle: *How to be Topp*. London: Max Parrish, 1954

Journals and magazines

Ad Lucem (Oxford High School magazine), centenary number, 1975: Morton N. Cohen: 'Lewis Carroll comes to school'
Barbican (City of London School for Girls magazine), 1969
Bedgebury, 1987
Cheltenham Ladies' College Magazine, 1905
Chronicle (convents of the Sacred Heart magazine), 1963
Fraser's Magazine, June 1874: 'Convent boarding schools for young ladies'
—— October 1874: 'A word for the convent boarding-schools'
Harpers & Queen, July 1980
Heathfield Magazine, January 1942
Holly Club Commemoration Magazine (Lady Eleanor Holles School), 1986
Independent, 16 March 1989: 'Private doubts among the convents'. Sister Mark Orchard, interviewed by Simon Midgley
Machio (Rickmansworth Masonic School magazine) bicentenary number, 1788–1988
Moretonian, 1986–7: 'Further confessions of a house-mistress'
Nineteenth Century, February 1888: Elizabeth Sewell: 'The reign of pedantry in girls' schools'
On the Map (Girls' Schools Association newsletter, autumn 1988): Patricia Lancaster: 'The human predicament'
Paulina, March 1927
Paulina, 1978–9
Paulina, 1904–1979
Prospect (Convent of the Assumption magazine), 1980
Queen, 8 July 1922: 'St Paul's Girls' School'
—— 5 August 1922: 'Wychwood School'
Rye St Antony School Magazine, 1968
St Mary's [Wantage] *School Magazine* (jubilee number), 1923
St Mary's Hall Magazine (centenary number), 1936
School of S. Helen and S. Katharine Magazine, 1969
Shuttle, The (Moira House magazine), January 1925
Stannite (St Anne's School, Windermere, magazine), 1983
Tudorian (Tudor Hall School magazine), 1950, 1985
Victoria Magazine, vol. XXVII, 1876: 'Thoughts on some of the present defects in boarding schools for girls'
West Heath School Magazine, 1969, 1987
Westminster Review, April 1873: Joshua Fitch: 'Charity Schools'
Winchester High School Chronicle, 1899–1900

Archives and other unpublished sources

Bedgebury School archives
Bodleian Library, John Johnson Collection
Cheltenham Ladies' College archives
Moira House archives
New Hall archives

St Catherine's School, Bramley, archives
St Leonards School archives
St Mary's Hall archives
St Paul's Girls' School archives
Walthamstow Hall archives
Anon.: 'Reminiscences of the Ladies' College, Cheltenham'. Cheltenham Ladies' College archives
Diary of Charis Barnett. St Paul's Girls' School archives
'The Book of Bedgebury'. 1920, Bedgebury School archives
Recollections of Emma Catherine Childs (Pollard). Somerville College, Oxford, archives
Diary of Dorothy Christmas, 1963–4
Sister Clare Veronica: 'A century of Catholic education in Richmond, North Yorkshire'. Assumption School, Richmond, 1984

School histories

(Unless otherwise stated, all these were published by the schools in question; they are very often undated. Where there has been a change of name, the present form is used.)

THE ALICE OTTLEY SCHOOL
Valentine Noake: *History of the Alice Ottley School, Worcester*. 1952
E.O. Browne (ed.): *Fifty Years of the Alice Ottley School, Worcester*. 1933
ALL HALLOWS SCHOOL
All Hallows School, Ditchingham, Centenary 1864–1964
BADMINTON SCHOOL
Badminton School, 1858–1958
Jean Storry (ed.): *At Badminton with B.M.B.* 1982
Joanna Turner (comp.): *B.M. Sanderson and Badminton School, 1947–1966*. 1988
THE BAR CONVENT
The History of the Bar Convent. Godalming, n.d.
BEDFORD HIGH SCHOOL
Katharine M. Westaway (ed.): *A History of Bedford High School*. 1932
—— *Seventy-five Years: the story of Bedford High School, 1882–1957*
BENENDEN SCHOOL
Portrait of Benenden, 1924–1974
BERKHAMSTED SCHOOL FOR GIRLS
Berkhamsted School for Girls 1888–1938. 1938
BLACKHEATH HIGH SCHOOL
Mary Charlotte Malim and Henrietta Caroline Escreet (eds): *The Book of the Blackheath High School*. 1927
BRIGHTON AND HOVE HIGH SCHOOL
M.G. Mills: *Brighton and Hove High School 1876–1952*. 1953
BURLINGTON SCHOOL
Marion A. Burgess: *A History of Burlington School* [1938?]
CITY OF CARDIFF HIGH SCHOOL FOR GIRLS
Catharine Carr: *The Spinning Wheel: City of Cardiff High School for Girls 1895–1955*. 1955

CASTERTON SCHOOL

Geoffrey Sale: *The History of Casterton School*. 1983

[Mabel Williams]: *Notes on the Clergy Daughters' School, Casterton*. 1935

CHANNING SCHOOL

E.M. Saunders: *A Progress: Channing School 1885–1985*. 1984

CHELTENHAM LADIES' COLLEGE

Amy K. Clarke: *A History of the Cheltenham Ladies' College 1853–1953*. London: Faber, 1953

—— *A History of the Cheltenham Ladies' College 1853–1979*. Saxmundham: John Catt, 1979

Cheltenham Ladies' College Centenary, 1953

CHRIST'S HOSPITAL

William Lemprière: *A History of Christ's Hospital, London, Hoddesdon and Hertford*. Cambridge: University Press, 1924

Frances M. Page: *Christ's Hospital, Hertford: a history of the school against the background of London and Horsham*. London: Bell, 1953

E.H. Pearce: *Annals of Christ's Hospital*. London: Methuen, 1901

The Christ's Hospital Book. London: Hamish Hamilton, 1953

CLIFTON HIGH SCHOOL

Nonita Glenday and Mary Price: *Clifton High School, 1877–1977*

COBHAM HALL

Mary F. Edmonds (ed.): *Cobham Hall: the founding of a new public school*. 1987

DOWNE HOUSE

Downe House Scrap-Book, 1907–1957

DURHAM HIGH SCHOOL

Joan Trowbridge (ed.): *Durham High School: a centenary celebration 1884–1984* [1984]

EDGBASTON HIGH SCHOOL

Janet Whitcut: *Edgbaston High School, 1876–1976*. 1976

EDGEHILL COLLEGE

Richard Pyke: *Edgehill College, 1884–1957: a triumph of faith*. London: Epworth Press, 1957

A. Mary Shaw (ed.): *When You Were There. Reflections on Edgehill College, 1884–1984*

FARNBOROUGH HILL

Dorothy A. Mostyn: *The Story of a House: Farnborough Hill*. 1980

FELIXSTOWE COLLEGE

Elizabeth Manners (ed.): *Felixstowe College, 1929–1979*. 1980

FRANCIS HOLLAND (CHURCH OF ENGLAND) SCHOOL, REGENT'S PARK

Susan Hicklin: *Polished Corners, 1878–1978. A hundred years of contemporary life in and out of Francis Holland School, NW1*. 1978

FRANCIS HOLLAND (CHURCH OF ENGLAND) SCHOOL, SLOANE SQUARE

Beatrix Dunning (ed.): *Francis Holland Church of England School for Girls. Graham Street Memories*. 1931

Elsie Quarrie: *The School that Refused to Die*. 1981

THE GODOLPHIN SCHOOL

M.A. Douglas and C.R. Ash: *The Godolphin School, 1726–1926*. London: Longmans, 1928

GREENACRE SCHOOL

The Story of Greenacre School. 1987

GREY COAT SCHOOL

[Dorothy F. Chetham Strode]: *History of the Grey Coat Hospital, Westminster, 1698–1959*. 1960

HABERDASHERS' MONMOUTH SCHOOL FOR GIRLS

W.G. Brown and P.M. Nott: *A Brief Outline of the Growth and Development of Monmouth High School, now Monmouth School for Girls* [1947?]

HAYES COURT SCHOOL

Roma Goyder: *Hayseed to Harvest: memories of Katherine Cox and Hayes Court School*. Colchester, 1985

HEMDEAN HOUSE SCHOOL

Molly Casey: *Hemdean House School, Caversham*. 1984

HOWELL'S SCHOOLS

Joan E. McCann: *Thomas Howell and the School at Llandaff*. 1972

HUYTON COLLEGE

Eluned M. Rees: *A History of Huyton College*. 1985

THE SCHOOL OF JESUS AND MARY

'History of the School of Jesus and Mary: early years of the Congregation' (unpublished, 1888)

KENT COLLEGE

Margaret James: *The Kent College Saga, 1886–1986*. 1986

KING EDWARD VI HIGH SCHOOL FOR GIRLS

Winifred I. Candler: *King Edward VI High School for Girls, 1883–1925*. London: Benn, 1928

Winifred I. Candler, Ailsa M. Jaques and B.M.W. Dobbie: *King Edward VI High School for Girls, Birmingham, 1883–1970*. London: Benn, 1971

KING EDWARD'S GRAMMAR SCHOOL FOR GIRLS, HANDSWORTH

King Edward's Grammar School for Girls, Handsworth, 1883–1983

THE LADY ELEANOR HOLLES SCHOOL

Barbara E. Megson: *A History of the Lady Eleanor Holles School*. 1947

LAUREL BANK SCHOOL

Elspeth Mitchell (ed.): *Laurel Bank School, 1903–1953*. Glasgow, 1953

LOUGHBOROUGH HIGH SCHOOL

Alfred White: *A History of Loughborough Endowed Schools*. 1969

MANCHESTER HIGH SCHOOL

Sara A. Burstall: *The Story of the Manchester High School for Girls*. Manchester: University Press, 1911

THE MARY DATCHELOR SCHOOL

The Story of the Mary Datchelor School, 1877–1957. London: Hodder & Stoughton, 1957

THE MARY ERSKINE SCHOOL

Margaret K.B. Sommerville: *The Merchant Maiden Hospital*. 1970

MERCHANT TAYLORS' SCHOOL

Sylvia Harrop: *The Merchant Taylors' School for Girls, Crosby: one hundred years of achievement 1888–1988*. Liverpool: University Press, 1988

MILTON MOUNT COLLEGE

Hilda Harwood: *The History of Milton Mount College* [1871–1946]. 1959

MORETON HALL

Ursula Roberts (ed.): 'Memories of Moreton' (unpublished)

THE MOUNT SCHOOL

H. Winifred Sturge and Theodora Clark: *The Mount School, York, 1785 to 1814, 1831 to 1931*. London, Dent, 1931

NEW HALL

History of the New Hall Community of Canonesses Regular of the Holy Sepulchre. Roehampton, 1899

NORTH LONDON COLLEGIATE SCHOOL

R.M. Scrimgeour (ed.): *The North London Collegiate School, 1850–1950. A hundred years of girls' education*. London: Oxford University Press, 1950

NORWICH HIGH SCHOOL

Prunella R. Bodington (ed.): *Norwich High School 1875–1950*

NOTTINGHAM HIGH SCHOOL

Betty Boyden (ed.): *Call Back Yesterday: a collection of reminiscences to mark the centenary of the Nottingham High School for Girls, 1875–1975*. 1976

NOTTING HILL AND EALING HIGH SCHOOL

Janet E. Sayers: *The Fountain Unsealed: a history of the Notting Hill and Ealing High School*. 1973

OAKDENE SCHOOL

Gwen Farish and Miriam Napier Jones (eds): *Acorn to Oak: some memories of Oakdene School, 1911–1959*

OXFORD HIGH SCHOOL

Violet E. Stack (ed.): *Oxford High School, Girls' Public Day School Trust, 1875–1960*. 1963

THE PARK SCHOOL

Joan Lightwood: *The Park School, Glasgow, 1880–1980* [1980]

THE PERSE SCHOOL FOR GIRLS

M.H. Cattley: *The Perse School for Girls, 1881–1981*. 1981

POLAM HALL

Kathleen Davies: *Polam Hall: the story of a school*. 1981

QUEEN ELIZABETH GIRLS' SCHOOL, BARNET

The Story of Queen Elizabeth Girls' School, 1888–1988

QUEEN'S COLLEGE

Elaine Kaye: *A History of Queen's College, London, 1848–1972*. London: Chatto & Windus, 1972

QUEENSWOOD

H.M. Stafford: *Queenswood, the First Sixty Years 1894–1954*

QUEENWOOD SCHOOL (EASTBOURNE)

Dorothy P. Carew: *Many Years, Many Girls: the history of a school 1862–1942*. Dublin: Browne & Nolan, 1967

REDLAND HIGH SCHOOL

Joan Bungay (ed.): *Redland High School, 1882–1982* [1982]

THE RED MAIDS' SCHOOL

Jean Vanes: *Apparelled in Red: the history of the Red Maids' School*. 1984

RICKMANSWORTH MASONIC SCHOOL

R.M. Handfield-Jones: *The History of the Royal Masonic Institution for Girls, 1788–1974*. 5th edn, 1974

ROEDEAN SCHOOL

The Founders of Roedean. 1935

A History of Roedean School, 1885–1985

Dorothy E. De Zouche: *Roedean School, 1885–1955*

THE ROYAL NAVAL SCHOOL

Philip Unwin: *The Royal Naval School, 1840–1975*. 1976

THE ROYAL SCHOOL FOR DAUGHTERS OF OFFICERS OF THE ARMY

Honor Osborne and Peggy Manisty: *A History of the Royal School for Daughters of Officers of the Army, 1864–1965*. London: Hodder & Stoughton, 1966

ST BRANDON'S SCHOOL

St Brandon's School: 150 years 1831–1981

SCHOOL OF ST CLARE

Peter Laws: *The Centenary Book of the School of Saint Clare, Penzance: 1889–1989*

ST ELPHIN'S SCHOOL

Margaret L. Flood: *The Story of St Elphin's School, 1844–1944*

ST GEORGE'S SCHOOL, EDINBURGH

Nigel Shapley: *Women of Independent Mind: St George's School, Edinburgh, and the campaign for women's education 1888–1988*. 1988

ST HELEN'S SCHOOL FOR GIRLS

Rosalind Onians (ed.): *St Helen's: the first eighty years, 1899–1979*. 1980

ST JAMES'S

Alice Baird (ed.): *I Was There: St James's, West Malvern*. 1956

ST LEONARDS SCHOOL

Julia Grant, Katherine H. McCutcheon and Ethel F. Sanders (eds): *St Leonards School, 1877–1927*. London: Oxford University Press [1928?]

St Leonards School, 1877–1977. 1977

ST LEONARDS–MAYFIELD SCHOOL

Mayfield Centenary 1863–1963

ST MARGARET'S SCHOOL, BUSHEY

Dorothea L. Pullan: *The Record of the Clergy Orphan Corporation School for Girls 1749–1949*

SCHOOL OF S. MARY AND S. ANNE

Violet Mary MacPherson: *The Story of S. Anne's, Abbots Bromley, 1874–1924*

Marcia Alice Rice: *The Story of S. Mary's, Abbots Bromley*. 1947

Anne Wells and Susan Meads (comps): *S. Mary and S. Anne: the second fifty years*. 1974

ST MARY'S SCHOOL, CALNE

Kay Stedmond: *St Mary's School, Calne, 1873–1986*

ST MARY'S SCHOOL, WANTAGE

Sister Phyllis CSMV: *St Mary's School: a personal history*. 1973

ST MICHAEL'S, LIMPSFIELD

Edith E. Wright: *The Children of Thy Servants: memories of Highbury and Limpsfield 1850–1937*

Times Remembered: reminiscences of the Church Missionary Society Home and School and of St Michael's

ST PAUL'S GIRLS' SCHOOL

M.G. Hirschfeld (ed.): *St Paul's Girls' School, 1904–1954*

ST SWITHUN'S SCHOOL

Priscilla Bain: *St Swithun's: a centenary history*. Chichester: Phillimore, 1984

SHERBORNE SCHOOL FOR GIRLS

Sherborne School for Girls, 1899–1949. 1949

TALBOT HEATH

The Jubilee Book: Bournemouth High School – Talbot Heath, 1886–1946

UPPER CHINE

Jocelyn Logan: *Upper Chine*. 1987

URSULINE CONVENT SCHOOL, WESTGATE-ON-SEA

Mary Winefride Sturman: *The Ursulines of Westgate-on-Sea, 1904–1979*

WALTHAMSTOW HALL

Elsie Pike and Constance E. Curryer: *The Story of Walthamstow Hall, 1838–1970*. 1973

WESTONBIRT

M.E. Freeman: *Weston Birt: a short account of the manor and the school*. 1956

WHALLEY RANGE HIGH SCHOOL

Florence A. Field and G.B. Birdsall: *The Coming of Age Souvenir of the Whalley Range High School*. 1912

WROXALL ABBEY

Barbara Bourke (ed.): *The Laurels 1872–1972 Wroxall Abbey*

WYCHWOOD SCHOOL

M.L. Lee: *A Brief History of Wychwood School, Oxford*. n.d.

WYCOMBE ABBEY SCHOOL

Lorna Flint: *Wycombe Abbey School, 1896–1986: a partial history*. 1989.

Index

Many schools have changed their names in the course of their history. They appear in this index under their present nomenclature, except in the case of a few where all the reference in the text has been to their early existence.

Abbaye-aux-bois, 121, 284
Abbots Bromley, *see* S. Mary and S. Anne
accents, as form of class distinction, 2, 15, 124
Adelaide, Queen, 44
Adolescence (Hall), 317
Adult Orphan Institution, *see* Princess Helena College
Alice Ottley School, *see* Worcester High School
All Hallows School, 192
All Saints Comprehensive School, York, 182
Alston Court, 132
Amelia, Princess, 43
American school, 243
Angela Merici, St, 188
Angus, Louie, 31, 279, 283, 289*n*, 318, 340
anorexia, 336
art, 259
Aske, Robert, 40
Aspinal, Mother Ann, 181
Assisted Places, 81, 82, 359
Assumption, Sisters of the, 24, 190
Assumption School, 191, 287
athletics, 275
Augusta, Princess, 43
Badminton School, 84, 86, 88, 105–7, 120, 251, 261, 263; hats, 290; internationalism at, 105, 106; music, 252; religious teaching, 153; 1950s curriculum, 254. *See also* Baker, B.M. and Sanderson, B.M.
Bagnold, Enid, 136
Baird, Alice, 143, 222, 264
Baird, Katrine, 143
Baker, B.M., 105–7, 153, 220
Baldwin, Emily, 46, 288
Barclay, Robert, *Catechism and Confession of Faith*, 160
Bar Convent, 8, 177, 182; in World War II, 350
Barat, St Madeleine Sophie, 187
Barlow, Amy, *Seventh Child*, 231
Barnett, Domenico, 237
barring-out, 284
Bartrum, Dr, (Berkhamsted), 39
Basevi, George, 47
Bath High School, GPDST, 350
Bath, Thomas Henry Thynne, 5th Marquess, 345
Beacon Hill School, 140
Beale, Dorothea, 62, 63, 66, 68, 85, 91–4, 197, 218–20 *passim*; at Casterton School, 50; on educational endowments, 35; religious teaching,

156; interviews erring pupil, 279; Taunton Commission evidence, 3; views on games, 267, 271
Bedford College School (later Bedford College), 56, 62
Bedford High School, 3, 10, 36, 59, 201, 215, 270; early discipline at, 72; religious teaching, 156
Bedford Modern School, 36
Bedford [boys'] School, 36
Bedgebury School, 126, 150, 205, 208, 222, 229, 231, 260
Bedingfield, Mother Frances, 181
Belcher, Marian, 156, 215
Benenden School, 13, 16, 86, 108–10, 123, 129, 205, 212, 238, 253, 274; actor-in residence, 1987, 265; current affairs, 317, 322; domestic staff, 241; hobbies, 261, 263; old girls, 356; school prayer, 124; school services, 153; World War II, 347, 348
Benson, Ada, 36, 64, 216
Benson, E.F., *David Blaize*, 304
Benson, Theodora, 307
Bergman-Osterburg, Sofia Helena, 268, 275
Berkhamsted boys' school, 39
Berkhamsted School for Girls, 39, 65, 66, 260
Bird, K., 106, 107, 153, 238
Blackheath High School, GPDST, 66, 72, 75, 153, 272, 340, 350
Blessed Virgin Mary, Institute of the, 175, 180–2
boarding-school life, 197–213
Board of Education, 359. *See also* inspectors of schools, H.M.
Boord, Mother Angela, 194
Bootham School, 9, 162, 315
Bournemouth High School, *see* Talbot Heath
Bowen, Elizabeth, 103, 104, 206, 320
boys' schools, 5, 26, 85, 247, 323; admission of girls into sixth forms, 16, 330, 331; appropriation of endowments, 34, 37, 38; contact with, 162, 310–5; imitation by girls' schools, 95, 97, 103, 129, 201
Bramston, Anna, 241
Brancker, John Houghton, 91, 327
Brazil, Angela, 119, 200; *Loyal to the School*, 319; *A Patriotic Schoolgirl*, 216
Bremner, C.S., quoted, 8
Brighton and Hove High School, GPDST, 121, 271
Brittain, Vera, 132, 170, 254
Broad, Mary, 6, 71, 222, 285
Brontë, Charlotte, 48
Brontë sisters, 49
Brown, Doris Rowland, 129
Brown, Joyce, 256
Brown, May Rowland, 129, 325
Brown, R.M. Haigh, 214
Bryant, Dr Sophie, 222
Burgess Hill School for Girls, 291, 294
Burlington School, 19, 28, 29, 283, 296
Burnham salary scale, 233
Burton, Decimus, 46
Burton, Thomas, 35
Burton-Brown family (Prior's Field), 136
Busby, T., 241, 349
Buss, Frances Mary, 54, 60, 68, 220; at Queen's College, 62; concern for pupils' health, 87; discipline, 277–9; evidence to Taunton Commission, 55, 267, 277
Butler, Canon William John, 74, 157, 194, 226
Butterstone House, 204

callisthenics, 267
Cambridge, George William Frederick Charles, 2nd duke of, 41, 44, 324
Cambridge local examinations, 55, 224, 230
Cambridge University, 258
Camden School, 3, 58
Campbell, Colin, 28
Capel-y-Ffin School, 140
Cardiff High School for Girls, 235, 272, 280; in World War I, 340, 341
careers, 87, 174, 356; from Merchant Maiden Hospital, 22; mid-Victorian Walthamstow Hall, 53; St Leonards

1880s, 97; Christ's Hospital 1910, 31; St Paul's 1920, 79
Carol of Hollydene School (Wynne), 314
'Carroll, Lewis', *see* Dodgson, Charles Lutwidge
Casterton School, 48–51, 237, 247, 261, 313; early days at Cowan Bridge, 43, 48, 49, 151, diet, 212; fees, 164; low fever, 333; Miss Beale's dislike of, 50; typhus 26; early uniform, 288; visit by Queen Adelaide, 44
Castle Howard, 337, 338
Catholic Advisory Marriage Council, 321
Chamberlain, Beatrice, 65
Channing School, 165, 230, 285, 315, 325; in World War II, 344
Chantry School, 274
Charity, Sisters of, 182
charity hospitals, 18–34 *passim*, 50; curriculum at, 9; definition, 359; health 334; indiscipline 312; religion, 151
charity schools, 34–37; definition, 359
Charters-Ancaster College, GPDST, 82
Chelsea High School, *see* Kensington High School
Cheltenham Ladies College, 12, 63, 84, 90–4, 154, 155, 246, 258, 281; early exams at, 55; financial worries, 327; games, 267; house system at, 117, 118; library, 262; 'lines', 357; Miss Beale's dislike of competitive spirit, 114; Miss Faithfull's addresses to, 119, 286, 307, 314, 315; 'raves', 304, 307; slang, 278; social standing required at, 3; work outside school, 122; in World War II, 343, 347. *See also* Beale, Dorothea
Child Manuela, The (Winsloe), 310
Children, Be Happy (Wade), 301, 310
Children's Friend, 48
cholera, 334
Christian Education, Congregation of, 192, 193
Christ's Hospital, 8, 9, 19–21, 275, 317; Bluecoat dress, 23; charge to leavers, 124; clothes, 288, 289, 295; discipline, 297, 298; financial support for, 30; house system, 118; punishments, 25, 26; religion at, 156; saff, 229, 237, 240; now co-educational, 209
Church Education Corporation, 150
Church Missionaries' Children's Home, *see* St Michael's, Limpsfield
Church Schools Company, 58, 74, 150
City of London School for Girls, 40
Clapham County Secondary School, 214
Clare, Mother (Ursuline Convent, Brentwood), 225, 269, 329
class distinction, part played in girls' education, 1–4, 79, 126, 130; accents, 2, 15, 124; displayed in school uniform, 292; mix in high schools, 57–9, 72, 73; names indicative of, 355; Victorian stratification, 1, 166, 167, 189; at Woodard schools, 168–70
Clergy Daughters' School, Cowan Bridge, *see* Casterton
Clergy Orphan Girls' School, St John's Wood, 33, 41, 264, 297, 332; oral exams at, 56; rules, 86
Clergyman's Daughter, A (Orwell), 126, 134
Clifton High School for Girls, 72, 81; uniform at, 80
Clothworkers' Company, 324
Cobbe, Frances Power, 249, 296
Cobham Hall, 86, 90, 109–11, 147, 208
co-education, 331, 354; at Christ's Hospital, 209
cold baths, 88, 98, 220, 336, 353
Cole, Margaret, 88, 101, 102, 113, 115, 197, 207, 357
Coleridge, Samuel Taylor, 26
College Girl, A (Vaizey), 230, 305
Combe Bank School, 192
confirmation, 157, 158
Congregational schools, 165
Connelly, Cornelia, 174, 176, 184–6, 191
Connelly, Pierce, 184, 185
Constant Nymph, The (Kennedy), 84, 112, 223, 277

constipation, 336
contraception, 321
convent schools, 149, 172–196 *passim*; inflexibility of education before Vatican II, 8; plays, 264; rewards, 299; social segregation at, 2; uniform 287; vicissitudes of, 8, 348–50
conversation, 119
Cooper, Alice Jane, 68, 224
corporal punishment, 27, 297
Coster, Geraldine, 140
Cox, Katherine, 220, 251, 329
Cradle Ship, The (Howes), 319
craft, design, technology, 82, 259
Cranborne Chase School, 266
Creak, Edith, 69, 223, 266, 311
cricket, 115, 116, 138, 261, 274; Alice Ottley's views on, 267
crocodile, 266, 267, 280
croquet, 267
Crossman, Richard, 17
Croudace, Camilla, 63
Croydon High School, GPDST, 67, 350
current affairs, 317, 318, 321
curriculum, 243–260; at charity hospitals, 22, 24, 32, 46; at early GPDSC schools, 68; at Benenden, 109; at convents, 181, 183, 186; at Downe House, 103; at private schools, 127, 139; Quaker, 160, 161

Dalcroze eurhythmics, 139, 269
Dalton Plan, 145, 146
Dames (North), 104, 105, 200, 208
dancing, 269, 270; encouraged at Holy Child schools, 186
Dane, Clemence, *Regiment of Women*, 310
Dancy, John, 330
Dartford College of Physical Training, 268
David Blaize (Benson), 304
Davies, Emily, 11, 54, 55, 245
Day, Elizabeth, 55
Day, Thomas, *History of Sandford and Merton*, 249
day-girls, 52, 73, 194
day schools, 54–82 *passim*
debates, 259, 260
Defoe, Daniel, 23
Delpierre, Eva, 235
Dennett, Christine, 183
Denstone College, 168
deportment, 118; at high schools, 80
Dickens, Charles, *Dombey and Son*, 23
diet, 211–3; at charity hospitals, 26; at Woodard school, 170
diphtheria, 332, 333
direct-grant schools, 15, 76–82 *passim*; Catholic schools choose state system, 196; definition, 359
discipline, 277–287; at charity hospitals, 25–8; at convents, 176–8; at early high schools, 71–72
diseases, 50, 331–5; at charity hospitals, 26
djibbahs, 102, 291
Dodgson, Revd Charles Lutwidge, 68
dogs, 242
Dombey and Son (Dickens), 23
domestic science, 245, 258; lack of at early high schools, 60, 78
domestic staff, 87, 108, 241
Dove, Dame (Jane) Frances, 6, 96–9 *passim* 157, 220, 302; views on games, 115, 274
Downe House, 13, 16, 84, 86, 102–5, 152, 235, 357; discipline, 88, 89; djibbahs, 291; dogs, 242; drama, 264, 265; fictional account of, 104, 200, 208; French at, 250; games at, 115; importance of conversation, 119; Maria Nickel, 241. *See also* Willis, Olive
drainage, 332, 333, 335
drill sergeants, 267, 268
drink, 299, 300
drugs, 299
Duke of Edinburgh's Award, 123, 263
Drapers' Company, 45
Duncan, Canon John, 150
Dunhill, Thomas, 252
Dunottar School, 133, 134
Durham High School, 74–6, 80, 211, 220, 256, 293; uniform, 294

Eastbourne Ladies' College, 247
Edgbaston High School, 65, 72, 76, 223; the Moseley bus, 69; visited by Charles Lutwidge Dodgson, 68; prefects at, 113
Edgehill College, 156, 165, 216; destroyed by fire, 337
Edinburgh Essay Society, 64
Edinburgh Ladies' Educational Association, 64
Edinburgh Merchant Company schools, 21, 27, 30, 32, 33
Education Act, 1870, 21, 268
Education Act, 1902 (Balfour), 76
Education Act, 1916 (Fisher), 283
Education Act, 1944, 80
Edward VI, 20
Elder, Josephine, 305
Elgar, Sir Edward, 252
eleven-plus exam, 81
Eliot, Lady Caroline, 168
Eliot, T.S., 146
Elliot, Revd Henry Venn, 47
Elliott, Phyllis, 147, 148
Eltham College, 50
emotion, 301–10 *passim*
Endowed Schools Act, 1869, 18, 37, 56
Endowed Schools Commission, 10, 18, 30, 31; view on exams, 56
endowed secondary schools, 34–40, 360
English, 246–8 *passim*, 251, grammar, 159, 251
English Ladies, Institute of, 7, 8, 180
epidemics, 50, 381–5
Eric, or, Little by Little (Farrar), 319
Erskine, Mary, 22
esprit de corps, 12, 13, 97, 202, 313
Eton College, 26, 117
etiquette lessons, 121, 178
Eugenie, Empress, 192
eurhythmics, 139, 269
evacuation, in World War II, 341–8
Ewing, Juliana Horatia, *Six to Sixteen*, 130, 237, 261, 333
examinations, 52, 53, 55–7, 245, 253, 258, 259; taken by early high schools, 70; ignored by convents and private schools, 138, 143, 175; Miss Beale's view on local, 3; at Queen's College, 63
expeditions, school, 266

fainting, 98, 220
Faithful Companions of Jesus, 179
Faithfull, Lilian M., 13, addresses to Cheltonians, 119, 286, 307, 314, 315
Farnborough Hill, 192, 288, 325
Farrar, Frederic William, dean of Canterbury, 319
Farringtons, 165
Felixstowe College, 84, 86, 117, 208, 209; fire, 337
finance, 110, 323–9; at charity schools, 29; founding of Perse School, 38; launch of GPDSC, 68; women excluded from discussion of, 34. *See also* fund-raising
finishing schools, 128, 257
fire, 337
first communion, 178
Fitch, Sir Joshua, 19, 30, 68; advice to Royal School, 42; denunciation of charity hospitals, 18, 23, 151; commends Mount School, 161; proposals for reform of Bristol charity schools, 33
Fleming Report, 360
Fletcher, Margaret, 64, 157, 336
football, 271
Fordham, Emily, 217, 223
Franciscan order, 167
Francis Holland School, Regent's Park, 70, 154, 258, 270
Francis Holland School, Sloane Square, 70, 77, 121, 154; fund-raising, 328; health, 335; in World War I, 339, 340; in World War II, 350
Freemasons, 9; support for Royal Masonic Institution, 30
French, 243, 247, 248, 250; compulsory talking of, 131; teachers, 235; Wiseman's doubts concerning, 186
Friends, Society of, 9, 159
friendship, emotional, 303–10
Frost in May (White), 172, 173, 176

fund-raising, 325–8 *passim*; at early charity schools, 29, 43; mid-Victorian, 44; Nathaniel Woodard's methods, 169, 170; nuns' methods, 192

gardens, girls', 265
Gaskell, Elizabeth Cleghorn, 48, 49, 51
Gathorne-Hardy, Jonathan, 301
geography, 246, 248
George V, 44
George VI, 302, 324
George Heriot's Edinburgh, 21
George Watson's College, Edinburgh, 21
George Watson's Ladies' College, Edinburgh, 74
Ghandi, Indira, 106
Gill, Eric, 140, 141
Girls' Public Day School Company, *see* Girls' Public Day School Trust
Girls' Public Day School Trust, 19, 58, 67, 68, 81. *See also* under individual schools
Girls' School Association, 86, 360
Girton College, 10, 19, 115, 245
Godolphin, Charles and Elizabeth, 28, 45
Godolphin, Sir William, 45
Godolphin School, 41, 45, 154, 211, 265, 281, 295; house spirit, 116; school song, 357
Governesses' Benevolent Institution, 62
grammar schools, 360. *See also* high schools
Grant, Julia, 97
Grant, Thomas, bp of Southwark, 186, 192
Graves, Robert, 310
Greek dancing, 269
Greenacre School, 134; in World War II, 345
Grey, Maria, 58, 67
Grey Coat Hospital, Westminster, 9, 19, 24, 25, 27, 28, 31, 312; as Grey Coat School, 32
Guide movement, 263, 264
'guinea-pig' scheme, 14, 15
Gurney, Mary, 67
gymnastics, 116; early gymnasium at Tudor Hall, 145; early costume for, 290, 291
gym tunics, 292

Haberdashers' Company, 39, 40
Haberdashers' Monmouth School for Girls, 122, 154, 242, 252; World War I, 340
Hahn, Kurt, 141
hair, rules regarding, 49, 286, 287
Hall, G. Stanley, *Adolescence*, 317
Harcourt, Janet Vernon, 137, 275, 329, 330
Harpur Trust (Bedford), 35, 36
Harrison, Jane Ellen, 91
Harrison, John, 37
Harrogate Ladies' College, 112, 258, 308, 352
Harrow, 281
Harrow High School, *see* Heathfield School, Pinner
hats, 290
Hawley, Susan, 183
Hayes Court School, 122, 136, 140, 250, 251, 265, 329
headmasters, of girls' schools, 82, 228
headmistresses, 156, 214–229
health, 331–7; Miss Buss's concern for, 87
health certificate, 335
Heather, Lilian, 105
Heathfield School, Ascot, 128, 143, 144, 155, 250; early uniform, 290; curriculum 1980s, 259
Heathfield School, Pinner, GPDST, 82
heating, 26, 98, 111, 336
Helena, Princess, 43
Hemdean House School, 225
high schools, 11–13, 54–82 *passim*, 360; Catholic, 175, 189; class mix at, 4; early curriculum, 60; religious education, 157, 158; Nathaniel Woodard's horror of, 4;
Hill, The (Vachell), 304
Hindle, Anne, 108, 109
history, 248, 317

hobbies, 260, 261
hockey, 271
Holiday House (Sinclair), 244
holidays: at convents, 177, 178; lack of at charity hospitals, 24
Holland, Canon Francis, 70
Holles, Lady Eleanor, 37
Hollington Park, *see* Bedgebury School
Holst, Gustav, 252
Holtby, Winifred, 170, 171, 338
Holy Child, Society of the, 175, 182
Holy Child schools, 184; Duchess of Leeds and, 191
Holy Sepulchre, Canonesses of the, 86, 173, 182, 348
Holy Trinity, Society of the Sisters of, 193
home economics, *see* domestic science
homesickness, 197, 203, 204
Honour of the School, The (Wynne), 314
housemistresses, 238–40
house system, 85, 104, 116, 117; at Roedean, 347
Howell, Thomas, 28, 45
Howell's School, Denbigh, 42, 45, 46
Howell's School, Llandaff, 42, 45–7, 288; early examination system, 56
Howes, Edith, *The Cradle Ship*, 319
How to be Topp (Willans and Searle), 14
Howitt, Mary, 159, 160, 162
Howitt, William, 159
Hughes, M.V., 54, 60, 64, 246, 299
Hugh-Jones, Siriol, 356
Hulme benefaction (Manchester), 35
Hunmanby Hall, 165
Hunt, John, 229
Hurstpierpoint College, 168
Huxley, Julia, 136
Huyton College, 69, 256

Ingham, Charles, 138
influenza epidemic, 1918, 340
Inglis, Nesta, 146, 225, 328
inspectors of schools, H.M., 126, 187; commend Cornelia Connelly, 186; recommendations to Red Maids, 34, and School of St Clare, 326; on Roedean, 101; on Upper Chine School, 135; views on army parents, 43

Jaques-Dalcroze, Emile, 139, 269
James, Margaret, 352, 354
James Allen's Girls' School, 265
Jane Eyre (Charlotte Brontë), 49, 51
Jerningham, Charlotte, 173
Jerningham, Lady, 296
Jersey Ladies' College, 165
Jesus, Society of, 7
Jesus and Mary, Sisters of, 349
Jewish pupils, 58
Joint Oxford and Cambridge Matriculation Boards, 254
Jones, Constance, 132
Jones, Harriet Morant, 224
Jones, William, 40

Kennedy, Margaret, *The Constant Nymph*, 84, 94, 112, 223, 277
Kensington High School, 58, 67, 69, 350
Kent College, 165, 121, 119, 223, 268, 269; Sunday uniform, 288; in World War II, 339
Kerr, Mother Henrietta, 175, 333
Kilvert, Revd Francis, 61
Kilvert, Muriel, 330
King Alfred's School, 140
King Edward VI High School for Girls, Birmingham, 39, 271; and boys' school, 39, 311; domestic science at, 60; early uniform, 80; in World War II, 346
King Edward's Grammar School for Girls, Handsworth, 304, 311
King Edward's [boys'] School, Birmingham, 39
Kinloch, Lucy, *A World Within a School*, 308, 309
Kinnear, Georgina, 65, 73, 224
Knill Court, 337
Knox, Monsignor Ronald, 246
Kyberd, Susan, 274

Laban, Rudolf, 270
Labour party, abolition of direct–grant schools, 15, 17, 81

lacrosse, 274, 275
Ladybarn House School, 274
Lady Eleanor Holles School, 36, 37, 80, 118, 269
Laleham Lodge, 164
Lamb, Charles, 24
Lancing College, 168, 326
Laneton Parsonage (Sewell), 198
Laurels, The, *see* Wroxall Abbey
Laurie, Simon, 33, 111
Lawnswood High School, 63
Lawrence, Elizabeth, 147
Lawrence family (Roedean), 6, 12,
Lawrence, Christabel, 115
Lawrence, Dorothy, 99–101
Lawrence, Millicent, 99–101, 264
Lawrence, Rt Hon. Paul Ogden, 99, 101
Lawrence, Penelope, 99–101, 219, 307; concern for pupils' health, 87; views on games, 273
leadership, 85, 93
Lear, Winifred, 232
Leeds, Louisa Catharine, duchess of, 190
Leeds Girls' Modern School, 121
Leeds Grammar School, 39
Leeds Mechanics Institute, 63
LeRoy, Aimée, 241
lesbianism, 309
Leys, Jemima, 226
libraries, 28, 244, 261, 262
Lightfoot, Joseph Barber, bp of Durham, 74
Lillesden School, *see* Bedgebury School
Lloyd-Williams family (Moreton Hall), 137, 138
Lloyd-Williams, Bronwen, 136
Locke, John, 41; *Some Thoughts Concerning Education*, 212, 336
Longleat, 345, 346
Longman, Thomas, 192
Loreto sisters, 182
Loughborough High School, 35
Louise, Princess, 68, 327
Lowe, Dr Edward Clarke, 169, 170
'low fever', 333
Lowood School, 48, 51
Loyal to the School (Brazil), 319
Lumsden, Louisa, 95, 96, 111
Lyttelton, George William, 4th baron Lyttelton, 30

McCarthy, Mary, 178, 229
MacLeod, Sheila, 206
McDowall, Ada, *see* Benson, Ada
Making of a Schoolgirl, The (Sharp), 303, 313
Malvern Girls' College, 84–86 *passim*, 93, 123, 124, 263; lacrosse at, 274, 275; in World War II, 341
Manchester High School, 10, 55, 65, 66, 157, 254, 261; and Hulme benefaction, 35
Mangnall, Richmal, 61*n*
Mangnall's *Questions*, 61
manners, 118
Mansell, Bee, 106
Marcet, Jane, 61*n*
Markham, Violet, 147
Marlborough College, 16, 330
Marshall, Arthur, 336
Marshall, Mother Cecilia, 175, 182
Martin, Frances, 56
Martyr's Memorial and Church of England Trust, 93, 150
Mary Datchelor School, 13, 55, 79, 268, 269, 324
Mary Erskine School, 356. *See also* Merchant Maiden Hospital
masters, 236, 237
masturbation, 316, 317
mathematics, 248, 255, 257; Elizabeth Sewell's views, 61
matriculation, 77, 253
matrons, 240
Matthews, Marcia, 217, 250
Maurice, Revd Frederick Dennison, 62
Mayfield School, *see* St Leonards-Mayfield
Meade, L.T., 200, 303
Mercers' Company, 40
Merchant Maiden Hospital, Edinburgh, 9, 21–23, 262, 284; health, 334; indiscipline, 312; as Edinburgh Educational Institute for Young

Ladies, 71. *See also* Mary Erskine School
Merchant Taylors' Company, 37
Merchant Taylors' School, Crosby, 37, 38, 217, 330; biology, 320
Merriman, Revd Dr Joseph, 85
Methodist schools, 164, 165
middle schools, 2, 3
midnight feasts, 285
Milton Mount School, *see* Wentworth Milton Mount
Mitchison, Naomi, 107
Moira House School, 14, 128, 138, 139, 274
More House School, 280, 328
Monmouth Grammar School, 40
Moreton Hall, 6, 13, 14, 128, 136–8, 212, 254, 259; dogs, 242; domestic staff, 241; music, 253; Sundays at, 151; uniform, 293
Mount School, York, 9, 159–64, 214, 219, 236, 302, 305, 340; and Bootham School, 162, 315; crocodiles, 266; curriculum, 10; examination day at, 56; playroom, 261; school societies, 259; staff, 234, 241. *See also* Rous, Lydia
Mountbatten of Burma, Louis Francis Albert Victor Nicholas, 1st Earl, 44
Murdoch, Iris, 106, 122
Murray Lindley, 159, 161
music, 259; at Badminton, 107; at Moreton Hall, 137; Quaker attitude to, 162; in Victorian schools, 248, 251, 252

National Union for the Education of Girls, 58
netball, 275
Nevinson, Margaret, 193, 280, 298, 313
New Hall, 86, 175, 177, 178, 183, 187; epidemic, 332; holidays, 264; rewards, 299; early uniform, 288
Neild, Miss (The Mount), 234
Newcastle High School, 231
Nickel, Maria, 241
North, Elizabeth, 105; *Dames*, 104, 200, 208, 321
North Foreland Lodge, 77, 98, 128, 147, 356
North London Collegiate School, 6, 54, 55, 58, 60, 64, 245, 246, 299; callisthenics, 267; discipline at, 277–9; early financial worries, 327; at Canons Park, 75. *See also* Bryant, Dr Sophie; Buss, Frances Mary
Norwich High School, GPDST, 267, 280, 295
Notre Dame schools, 175
Nottingham High School, GPDST, 78, 79, 212, 260; contact with boys' school, 310, 311; discipline, 298; teachers at, 234, 235; in World War II, 344, 346
Notting Hill and Ealing [formerly Bayswater] High School, GPDST, 57, 59, 224, 278

Oakdene, Beaconsfield, 128, 136, 213, 291, 293
old girls, 122, 172, 356
Olivey, Alice, 225
Olivia by Olivia, 301
Orwell, George, *A Clergyman's Daughter*, 126
Ottley, Alice, 74, 156, 221, 225; attitude to sentimental friendship, 306; view of high schools, 4; views on cricket, 267
Oxenham, Elsie J., 200, 269; *Expelled from School*, 303; *The School Without a Name*, 87
Oxford High School, 67, 78, 82; early days at, 58, 59, 64; headmistresses, 214, 216, 234; religious teaching, 157; science 256, 320; uniform, 295; visited by Charles Lutwidge Dodgson, 69
Oxford local examinations, 253
Oxford University, 258

Paddington and Maida Vale High School, GPDSC, 58
Palgrave's *Golden Treasurey*, 248
Park School, Glasgow, 65, 73, 255, 263
Patriotic Schoolgirl, A (Brazil), 216

Peck, Winifred, 246–8; at private school, 111, 112, 298; at Wycombe Abbey, 88, 89, 98, 151, 157, 199, 260; views on prefects, 113
Penrhos College, 164
Penzance High School, *see* St Clare, School of
Perse, Stephen, 38
Perse [boys'] School, 38
Perse School for Girls, 38, 39, 226
Pevsner, Sir Nikolaus, 92
physical education, 266–76
piano, 245, 248, 252
Pipe, Hannah, 164
Polam, Hall, 161
Popham, Margaret, 227, 318, 343, 347
Portsmouth High School, GPDST, 350
Power, Mrs (West Heath), 147
Powys, Revd and Hon. Horace, 47
Poyntz, Mary, 7
prefect system, 13, 113, 114, 202
Princess Helena College, 43; as Adult Orphan Institution, 41, 42, 49, 244; library at, 261
Prior's Field, 128, 241, 272, 281
private schools, 13, 14, 125–48; definition, 360; and exams, 56; treatment of teachers, 231, 232; and university entrance, 15
Procter, Anne, 91, 327
Procter, Jane, 161
public schools, 12, 13, 83–124 *passim*; definition, 360
Pugin Edward, 191
punishment, 277, 296–9; at charity hospitals, 25–7, 312; at Clergy Daughters' School, 49; to be dressed as a charity girl, 23

Quakers, *see* Friends, Society of
Queen Anne's School, Caversham, 32, 272
Queen Ethelburga's School, 117, 170
Queen Margaret's School, 170; in World War I, 338
Queen's College, 62, 63, 237, 265, 295
Queenswood, Hatfield, 165
Queenwood School, Eastbourne, 134, 243

Rae, John, 201, 299, 330
Ramsay, Agnata, 86
Raven, M.M., 93
Raymond, Ernest, 304
Rebel of the School, The (Meade), 303
recognized school, 125, 360
recreation, 211, 260, 261; at charity schools, 24, 46, 47; at convents, 176
Redland High School, 59, 70, 73, 76, 255, school expedition, 1890, 266
Red Maids' School, 9, 26, 29, 32–4, 145, 215, 233; daily routine in 18th c., 25; discipline, 296; dress, 23, 25; health, 234; in World War II, 339
Regiment of Women (Dane), 310
Reid, J. Eadie, 92
religious teaching, 93, 144, 149–171 *passim*; undenominational nature at high schools, 58
Renaissance of Girls' Education (Zimmern), 89
Rhondda, Margaret, Lady, 158, 318
'ribbons', at Sacred Heart schools, 114, 173, 299
Richardson, Prof. A.E., 75
riding, 208, 263
Rickmansworth Masonic School, 9, 29, 32, 288, 295, 324; 'General Rebellion' (1802), 27; holidays 24
Ridler, Anne, 357
Ridley, Nicholas, bp of London, 20
Robertson, E. Arnott, 115, 158
Roedean School, 12, 14, 84, 86, 99–102, 201; as Wimbledon House, 100, 101, 333; discipline, 286, 298; djibbahs, 291; games at, 115; motto, 83; old girls, 356; rules, 87; schwärmerei, 303, 307; technology, 259; in World War II, 347, 350; Margaret Cole at, 207; Katharine Whitehorn at, 236. *See also* Lawrence sisters
Round Square Conference Schools, 141

Rous, Lydia, 10, 161, 214, 221
Royal Masonic Institution, *see* Rickmansworth Masonic School
Royal Naval School, 42, 43, 226, 252, 340; discipline, 296; epidemic, 333
Royal School, 41–3, 158, 215, 252, 270, 324, 340; discipline 296–8 *passim*; fund-raising, 44; health, 332, 335, 336; social rank important at, 2; staff, 233, 236; in World War II, 345, 346, 351
Ruddle, Julia Maria, 269
Rudge, Ruth, 148
rules, 277–300 *passim*; at private school, 112; at public schools, 88, 89
running away, 204
Runton Hill School, 137, 275, 281, 293, 329
Ruspini, Bartholomew, 29
Russell, Bertrand and Dora, 140
Rye St Antony School, 140

Sacred Heart, Order of the, 174, 175, 187, 188; lay sisters, 240
Sacred Heart schools, 173, 317, 346; at Hove, 188; Kilgraston, 188; Roehampton, 172, 187, 188, 333, 347, 350; Tunbridge Wells, 188; discipline, 306; drama, 264; Feast of Immaculate Conception, 172, 316, 358; games, 273; nun's timetable at, 232; ribbons, 299; view of science, 255; Antonia White at, 172. *See also* Woldingham School
Sadler, Prof. Sir Michael, 66, 139, 222
S. Anne, School of, Abbots Bromley, *see* S. Mary and S. Anne
St Anne's, Rewley House, 150, 193
St Anne's School, Windermere, 128, 141, 205; piano-playing, 252
St Augustine, Canonesses of, 328
St Brandon's School, 41, 225
St Catherine's School, Bramley, 83, 85; fire at, 337
St Clare, School of, 3, 266; gas explosion at, 326
St Dunstan's Abbey, 150, 193
St Elphin's School, 47, 324; health, 335
St Felix School, 117, 263
St George's School for Girls, Edinburgh, 74
S. Helen and S. Katharine, School of, 84, 194, 260; discipline, 295, 299
St Helen's School for Girls, Northwood, 129, 325; school crest, 85
St Hilda's College, Oxford, 122
St James's, West Malvern, 6, 118, 125, 128, 142, 143, 235, 241
St Leonards-Mayfield, 185, 192
St Leonards School, St Andrews, 12, 84–6 *passim*, 94–7, 258, 355, 357; careers, 1930s, 120; games, 114–116 *passim*, 270, 274; lack of endowments, 327; house system, 117; library, 262; music, 252, 259; Miss Sandys, 230, 238, 242; science, 255; Seniors, 97, 356; uniform, 290, 291
St Margaret's Convent, Edinburgh, 185
St Margaret's School, Bushey, *see* Clergy Orphan Girls' School
S. Mary and S. Anne, School of, 3, 168–70, 286; diphtheria, 332; discipline, 297
St Mary's Hall, 41, 47, 265, 297, 334; clothing list, 288
St Mary's School, Ascot, 175, 182, 196, 204
St Mary's School, Calne, 150, 217, 250; financial anxiety, 326
St Mary's School, Shaftesbury, 182
St Mary's School, Wantage, 150, 178, 194, 212, 274; discipline, 280, 285, 287, 313; guides, 263
St Mary the Virgin, Community of, 194
St Michael's, Limpsfield, 41, 51, 331, 333
St Michaels Burton Park, 168
St Monica's School, Kingswood, 132
St Paul's [boys'] School, 10
St Paul's Girls' School, 40, 70, 78, 175, 265, 273, 275, 295; class mix at, 57; careers, 1920, 79; condemnation of Angela Brazil, 200; fees, 81; Holst teaches at, 252; Miss Gray's modesty, 316
St Swithun's, 87, 117, 118, 207;

discipline, 284, 298; headmistress, 218. As Winchester High School, 4, 57, 65, 73, 86, 241; games, 272; library, 262; science, 256
St Trinian's, 84, 85, 141, 142
St Trinnean's School, Edinburgh, 141
salaries, 231, 233
Sanderson, B.M., 105–7 *passim*, 153, 218
Sandford and Merton, The History of (Day), 249
Sandys, Miss (St Leonards), 230, 238, 242
scarlet fever, 333, 334
School Favourite, The (Meade), 303
Schools Inquiry Commission (Taunton), 1, 34; on Christ's Hospital, 19, 21; on convent schools, 187; impressed by Mount School, 10; on physical exercise, 267; on private schools, 11, 128, 129; on Scottish education, 21; on teachers, 236; Miss Beale's evidence to, 3; Miss Buss's evidence to, 56, 267, 277
school songs, 83, 100, 357
school stories, 97, 303–6 *passim*, 313
School Without a Name, The (Oxenham), 87
schwärmerei, 102, 199, 304–10
science, 248, 254–6 *passim*; grants for teaching, 76; at Park School, 74; at private schools, 135
Scottish education, 21, 64, 73, 74, 237
Scottish Education, Royal Commission on, 22
Searle, Ronald, 141
self-government, 139, 140, 186
Seventh Child (Barlow), 231
Sewell, Elizabeth, 57, 61, 73, 131, 132, 312; *Laneton Parsonage*, 198
sex, sexuality, 301–15
sex instruction, 318–20
Shackleton, M.H., 227
Sharp, Evelyn, 313; *The Making of a Schoolgirl*, 303
Sheffield High School, GPDST, 82
Sheldon, C., 108, 109, 238
Sherborne School for Girls, 84, 93, 158, 337; drama banned at, 265; games at, 115, 116
Sherwood, Mary Martha, 266
Shirreff, Emily, 67
Shore, Emily, 61
Simpson, Sir John, 83
Sinclair, Catherine, *Holiday House*, 244
Sir William Perkins' School, 36
Six to Sixteen (Ewing), 130, 237, 261
Skeat, Margaret, 147
slang, 278, 285, 286
smoking, 300
social service, 97, 121–3, 144
Society for Promoting Christian Knowledge, 23
Some Thoughts Concerning Education (Locke), 212, 336
Soulsby, Lucy, 234
Spurling, Margaret, 221
Stanley, Henrietta Maria, Lady Stanley of Alderley, 67
state education, upper class view of, 1; Nathaniel Woodard's attitude to, 168
Steadman, Cecily, 238, 290
Stonyhurst College, 187
Streatham Hill and Clapham High School, GPDST, 350
Street, Kate Harding, 226
Strudwick, Ethel, 77, 200
Stuart, Mother Janet Erskine, 174, 250, 257
Sturge, Elizabeth, 210
Summerhill School, 140
Swann, Mona, 139
Swanwick, Helena, 59
Swedish drill, 267
swimming, 269, 275
Sydenham High School, GPDST, 350

Talbot Heath, 6, 71, 323, 328
Taunton Commission, *see* Schools Inquiry Commission
teachers, 229–242; early lack of training, 60, 69; headmistresses' concern for spiritual welfare, 221; male, 236, 237, 311; salaries, 231, 233; training at the Mount, 161;

nuns' training, 175, 185; training college rules, 280; uniform for, 217
team games, 207, 270–6; at convents; 176; at public schools, 13, 85, 111, 114–6
Temple, Frederick, archbp of Canterbury, 132
textbooks, early absence of, 60; F.D. Maurice's comments on, 62
Thomas, Revd Urijah, 73
Thring, Edward, 11, 116, 198, 269
timetable, at early schools, 49, 145; boarding school, 94, 112, 113; convent, 177, 195; for nuns, 232
Tippett, Sir Michael, 252
Todd, Maud, 144
Todd, Revd T.W., 144
Tom and Some Other Girls (Vaizey), 306
Tournély, Léonie de, 188
Trades Maiden Hospital, 21, 22; library at, 28
transport, 69
Tudor Hall School, 14, 64, 117, 145; dogs, 242; at Burnt Norton, 146; buys Wykham Park, 329
Tuke, Esther, 160
typhoid, 332
typhus, 26, 333

uniform, 79, 102, 287–95, 316; at charity schools, 23, 25, 36; convent, 185; at private schools, 127; for teachers, 217
universities, 245, 258; for women in 1912, 174; 1960s expansion of, 15
university classes, at Cheltenham, 91; at Tudor Hall, 145
Unwin, Miss (Walthamstow Hall), 225
Uplands School, *see* Felixstowe College
Upper Chine School, 135, 257, 324; requisitioned in World War II, 351
Uppingham School, 11, 116, 269; typhoid outbreak at, 332
Ursuline Convent, Brentwood, 225, 264, 269, 329, 350
Ursuline Convent School, Westgate-on-Sea, 189
Ursulines, 167, 173, 175, 187–9 *passim*

Vachell, Horace Annesley, *The Hill*, 304
Vaizey, Mrs George du Horne, *A College Girl*, 230; *Tom and Some Other Girls*, 306
Varin, Father Joseph, 187
Vatican II, 195
Voysey, Charles, 136

Wade, Rosalind, *Children, Be Happy*, 310
Walker, Dr Jane, 273
Walthamstow Hall, 41, 52, 53, 120, 154, 205, 225, 241; fund-raising, 44, 325, 327; health, 335, 340
'Wantage Sisters', 194
Ward, Mary, 6–8, 180–2
Ward, William, 40
Watson, Anne, 37
Watts, Louise, 136, 215, 218
Wellington College, 42, 332
Wentworth Milton Mount, 166, 299
Wesley, John, 164
West Heath, Sevenoaks, 128, 147, 260; old girls, 356
Westonbirt, 86, 150, 198, 209, 265, 318
Whalley Range High School, 59
White, Antonia, 306, 358; *Frost in May*, 172, 173, 175, 187
Whitehorn, Katherine, 115, 207, 236, 301
Whitson, John, 28, 29
Willis, Olive, 102–105 *passim*, 219, 221, 251, 285; attitude to silliness, 103, 306; pupil's impression, 89; religious teaching, 152
Wilson, Revd William Carus, 48–51, 151, 334
Wimbledon High School, GPDST, 76, 350
Wimbledon House, *see* Roedean
Winchester College, 117, 246
Winchester High School, *see* St Swithun's

Winsloe, Christa, *The Child Manuela*, 310
Withington High School, 274
Wiseman, Nicholas, archbp of Westminster, 174, 186, 188
Wober, Mallory, 149, 354; quoted, 114 118, 124, 203, 210, 282, 320, 335
Woldingham School, 114, 188, 232. *See also* Sacred Heart, Roehampton
Wolesley-Lewis, Mary, 77, 147
Woodard, Revd Nathaniel, 166, 167, 327; horror of high schools, 4
Woodard Schools, 166–71; social stratification at, 2
Woods, Constance, 132
Woods, Mary Alice, 72
Worcester High School, 74; Alice Ottley's aims for, 75, 76; daily worship at, 157; visited by Charles Lutwidge Dodgson, 68. *See also* Ottley, Alice
World War I, 338–41
World War II, 14, 341–8
World Within a School, A (Kinloch), 308, 309
Wroxall Abbey School, 128, 132, 133, 216, 251; drill sergeant at The Laurels, 267; games at The Laurels, 272, 275
Wyatt, Beatrice, 144
Wychwood School, Oxford, 113, 128, 133, 140, 281, 285
Wycombe Abbey School, 14, 84, 87, 97–9, 124, 246, 260, 265; discipline 310; games at, 115, 274, 291; Winifred Peck at, 88, 89, 98, 151, 157, 199, 260; spirit of, 206; World War II, 342, 343, 351
Wynne, May, 314

Yonge, Charlotte, 57, 61, 72, 75, 92, 167, 168, 198
Young, Georgina Tarleton, 223
Youngest Girl in the School, The (Sharp), 313
Youth Enterprise, 259

Zimmern, Alice, *The Renaissance of Girls' Education*, 89

From a Rule Book

1. While waiting for a lesson to begin, girls are expected to be seated at their desks with their books open in readiness.
2. Girls stand when a member of staff enters the room.
3. At the end of a lesson the blackboard should be cleaned. At the end of a day's lessons, windows and classroom doors should be left shut.
4. No written preparation may be done before Prayers or at Break without permission and all written preparation must be given in before Prayers. Preparation done on Saturday must be given in by 1.00 pm.
5. Every girl should always have a College library book to hand. Only College library books may be read in study periods.
6. Property should be kept tidily in the places allocated. Any litter should be packed up and cleared away.
7. College property must be treated with care.
8. Sacks should be packed and unpacked at the appointed times.
9. When a girl in one classroom wishes to speak to a girl in a different room, permission should first be asked of both class teachers.
10. a. Girls in Lower College should not be in their classrooms at Break, or during the afternoon unless for a lesson.
    b. Girls in Upper College may take their Break in Ground Floor classrooms or the garden, but all milk bottles must be returned to crates, and cartons and biscuit papers discarded in bins.
11. No girl may go to another girl's desk, or a staff desk, without permission. No girl may move another girl's property (for instance in the cloakroom).
12. Girls should use stationery with care and economy.
13. Each piece of written work should be dated in the standard style: e.g. 17.6.86.